Handbook of
Religion and Social Institutions

Handbooks of Sociology and Social Research

Series Editor:
Howard B. Kaplan, *Texas A&M University, College Station, Texas*

HANDBOOK OF DRUG ABUSE PREVENTION
Theory, Science, and Practice
Edited by Zili Sloboda and William J. Bukoski

HANDBOOK OF THE LIFE COURSE
Edited by Jeylan T. Mortimer and Michael J. Shanahan

HANDBOOK OF RELIGION AND SOCIAL INSTITUTIONS
Edited by Helen Rose Ebaugh

HANDBOOK OF SOCIAL PSYCHOLOGY
Edited by John Delamater

HANDBOOK OF SOCIOLOGICAL THEORY
Edited by Jonathan H. Turner

HANDBOOK OF THE SOCIOLOGY OF EDUCATION
Edited by Maureen T. Hallinan

HANDBOOK OF THE SOCIOLOGY OF GENDER
Edited by Janet Saltzman Chafetz

HANDBOOK OF THE SOCIOLOGY OF MENTAL HEALTH
Edited by Carol S. Aneshensel and Jo C. Phelan

HANDBOOK OF THE SOCIOLOGY OF THE MILITARY
Edited by Giuseppe Caforio

A Continuation Order Plan is available for this series. A continuation order will bring delivery of each new volume immediately upon publication. Volumes are billed only upon actual shipment. For further information please contact the publisher.

Handbook of
Religion and Social Institutions

Edited by

Helen Rose Ebaugh

University of Houston
Houston, Texas

 Springer

Helen Rose Ebaugh
Department of Sociology
University of Houston
496 Philip G. Hoffman Hall
Houston, TX 77204-3012

XXX Subject Classification (2000): (Sociology)

Library of Congress Cataloging-in-Publication Data
Handbook of religion and social institutions / edited by Helen Rose Ebaugh
p. cm. – (Handbooks of sociology and social research)
Includes bibliographical references and index.
ISBN 0-387-23788-7
1. Religion and sociology.   I. Ebaugh, Helen Rose Fuchs, 1942–   II. Series.

BL60.H266 2005
306.6—dc22   2004062565

A C.I.P. Catalogue record for this book is available
from the Library of Congress.

ISBN 0-387-23788-7   e-ISBN 0-387-23789-5   Printed on acid-free paper.

Printed in the United States of America.

9 8 7 6 5 4 3 2 1   SPIN 152226

springeronline.com

Preface

The sociology of religion is as old as the discipline of Sociology. Almost without exception, the "founders" focused on the role that religion and religious institutions played during the era of rapid and radical social change in 19th- and early-20th-century Europe. August Comte viewed religious explanations as the most primitive moment in his Law of the Three Stages and argued that Western societies were moving from preoccupation with religious arguments into the third stage, that of scientific reasoning. Durkheim, Weber, and Marx, each in his own way, predicted the demise of religion as rationalization and secularization supplanted the gods and demons that previously were thought to rule the world. As Lemert (1999, p. 241) suggests, "It could well be said that the most unyielding of social scientific puzzles over the last century has been just why religion, which was so firmly the foundation of premodern social order, has lost so *little* of its effective force in post-traditional societies." The chapters in this Handbook are testimony to the fact that religion remains not only "alive and well" in the 21st century but also that throughout sociological specialties scholars are increasingly rediscovering the influence of religious factors.

National surveys (e.g., Greeley and Hout 1999; Gallup and Lindsay 1999) show that the majority (59%) of American adults have a religious affiliation, believe in God (95%) and the afterlife (80%), pray (90%), read the Bible (69%), and say that religion is important in their lives (87%). The importance of socioreligious issues (e.g., abortion, stem cell research, capital punishment, gay marriage) in recent political campaigns demonstrates the centrality of religious interests in the political realm. The "War on Terrorism" that was declared in the aftermath of the 9/11 attacks on the World Trade Center and America's subsequent involvement in Iraq have prompted interfaith dialogue and raised interest in Islam and its sectarian organization. The proliferation of new immigrant religions in the United States within the past 30 years has increased awareness of both non-Christian religions and the many varieties of Christianity which the immigrants practice that are new to the United States. President Bush's Faith-Based and Community Initiative also has called attention to the role that religious institutions play in the social welfare arena. Regardless of which news media one accesses, there is a high probability that some religious story, event, or new study will be reported. In terms of everyday civic life in America, religion is not only an individual force but also a strong presence in the public forum.

Despite the centrality of religion in American life, it has been essentially ignored for the past 70 or so years by the sociological mainstream. Evidence of this is the small number of articles relating to religious topics appearing in the major journals and the fact that only one president of the American Sociological Association (ASA) in the past 99 years could be considered as having a central interest in the study of religion (Milton Yinger, ASA president in 1977). Likewise, it was only in 1994, 40 years after initiating substantive speciality sections, that Sociology of Religion was approved as an ASA section.

There are a number of explanations for why religion was sidelined from mainstream Sociology. As Dillon (2003) maintains, there has been an intellectual bias in social theory against the compatibility of rationality and religion. Sociology, itself a product of the Enlightenment, has a long tradition of skepticism toward religion. Secularization was accepted as a doctrine, rather than a theory, and "the idea of secularization became sacralized" as a taken-for-granted ideology (Hadden, 1989). If religion is obsolete in postindustrial societies, why take it seriously? Dillon (2003, p. 7) calls religion the "forgotten or excluded variable in social scientific studies." She posits that sociologists shy away from incorporating religious variables because the very act of studying religion might be interpreted as legitimating religious belief. The commitment of sociologists to value-free, nonbiased research is sometimes seen as incompatible with the study of religion as a normative, value-laden system. Yet, religion as a system of beliefs, values, norms, and rituals can be and has been studied as "scientifically" and objectively as other social phenomena. Even though the Society for the Scientific Study of Religion has been around for 55 years, its commitment to the nonbiased study of religion has been slow to find its way into mainstream sociology.

The chapters in this volume attest to the fact that religion is reentering the mainstream of the discipline. Increasingly, over the past two decades, sociologists involved in various specialty fields are discovering the influence of religious variables on human behavior. Meso and macro social theories are beginning to include the organizational significance of religious institutions in contemporary society. In a special issue of *Sociological Theory* devoted to a symposium on religion, Calhoun (1999, p. 238) said that "Sociological theory that makes good sense of religion is better sociological theory in general." Increasingly, sociologists are recognizing that explanations of social behavior that neglect religious variables are incomplete and missing what could be a major factor in explaining certain types of behaviors. Alice Rossi (2001) acknowledged this in her study of social responsibility. She found that religion emerged as having a major effect, even though she added a religion variable in her research design as an afterthought.

The organization of the book begins with chapters focusing on the interplay of religion with major social institutions (i.e., politics, economy, education, and social welfare). The impact of religion on family is its own section with three chapters dealing with family in general, adolescence and late life. The next part reviews research relating to religion and inequality, including race/ethnicity, social class, and gender. Part IV turns the spotlight on religion and social control, with chapters on law, crime/delinquency, and adolescent delinquency. Next is discussion of religion and culture, with attention to sports, media, and science/technology. Part VI considers religion *as* a social institution and includes chapters on church membership trends, levels of religious organization, and religious leadership/clergy. The final section considers the transnational and global dimensions of religion in the 21st century.

Rather than writing yet another book about the sociology of religion *for* sociologists of religion (Dillon has done that very aptly in her recent *Handbook of the Sociology of Religion,* 2003), this one is written for sociologists who study a variety of subdisciplines and are interested in recent studies and theoretical approaches that relate religious variables to their particular area of interest. For example, criminologists can read Hoffmann and Bahr's chapter (Chapter 12) on crime/deviance to learn the latest research findings regarding correlations between religious variables and acts of crime/deviance. They could discover, for example, research conducted within the past two years that shows that volunteer work and religious civic participation are associated with lower adult and juvenile homicide rates, even after controlling for the influences of such other social integrative factors as divorce rates, population turnover, and unemployment rates. Likewise, sociologists studying law could discover examples around the world to demonstrate the fact that some religious groups enjoy a position of relative privilege and that the usual legal structures dealing with religious groups are not applied to dominant religious organizations in the same ways they are used with less popular religions (see Chapter 11 by Richardson). Benson and King, in Chapter 6, provide a comprehensive summary of the most recent research concerning the relationships of religion and adolescent development.

Although the 21 chapters in this Handbook cover a vast array of sociological subdisciplines, there are a number of topics that I originally wanted to include but was unable to do so because of my inability to find authors or the lack of a substantial empirical literature on the topic. These include relationships between religion and child development, the military, prisons, and the arts.

It is my sincere hope that sociologists and social scientists, in general, will find this volume helpful as they seek to understand the intersections between religion and their particular area of interest. Perhaps the voluminous citations and findings reported in this Handbook related to the impact of religion on an array of social institutions and research topics will prod social researchers to examine ways in which religious variables impact social life both in the United States and around the world. If that happens, the goal of the volume will have been achieved.

Finally, I would like to thank Howard Kaplan, general editor of the Handbook series, and Teresa Krauss, social science editor for Kluwer/Plenum, for the opportunity to include a Handbook on the Sociology of Religion in their prestigious line-up of volumes. Most particularly, I am grateful to the authors who contributed to the Handbook and were most diligent in following my instructions to present a rich review of research findings on his/her particular topic, to be as inclusive as possible in addressing issues of racial, class, and gender differences, and, finally, to point to new directions of research in exploring relationships between various social institutions and religion.

REFERENCES

Calhoun, C. (1999). Symposium on religion. *Sociological Theory, 17*(3), 237–239.

Dillon, M. (2003). The sociology of religion in late modernity. In M. Dillon (Ed.), *Handbook of the sociology of religion* (Ch. 1). Cambridge, UK: Cambridge University Press.

Dillon, M. (Ed.). (2003). *Handbook of the sociology of religion*. Cambridge, UK: Cambridge University Press.

Gallup, G., Jr., & Lindsay, D. M. (1999). *Surveying the religious landscape: Trends in U.S. beliefs*. Harrisburg, PA: Morehouse.

Greeley, A. M., & Hout, M. (1999). Americans' increasing belief in life after death. *American Sociological Review, 64*, 813–835.

Hadden, J. K. (1989). Toward desacralizing secularization theory. *Social Forces, 65*, 587–611.

Lemert, C. (1999). The might have been and could be of religion and social theory. *Sociological Theory, 17*(3), 240–263.

Rossi, A. S. (Ed.). (2001). *Caring and doing for others: Social responsibility in the domains of family, work, and community*. Chicago: University of Chicago Press.

Contributors

Nancy Ammerman, Boston State University, Boston, Massachusetts 02215

Stephen J. Bahr, Brigham Young University, Provo, Utah, 84602

John Bartkowski, Mississippi State University, Mississippi State, Mississippi, 39762

Peter Benson, President, Search Institute, Minneapolis, Minnesota 55413

Peter Beyer, University of Ottawa, Ottawa, Ontario KIN 6N5

Ram Cnaan, University of Pennsylvania, Philadelphia, Pennsylvania 19104

James D. Davidson, Purdue University, West Lafayette, Indiana 47907

Helen Rose Ebaugh, University of Houston, Houston, Texas 77204

Roger Finke, Pennsylvania State University, University Park, Pennsylvania 16802

Barbara Fisher-Townsend, University of New Brunswick, Fredericton, New Brunswick, Canada E3B 5A3

Jonathan Hill, Notre Dame University, Notre Dame, Indiana 46556

John P. Hoffmann, Brigham Young University, Provo, Utah, 84602

Dean R. Hoge, Catholic University of America, Washington, DC, 20064

Stewart M. Hoover, University of Colorado at Boulder, Boulder, Colorado 80309

Larry Iannoccone, George Mason University, Fairfax, Virginia 22030

Pamela E. King, Fuller Theological Seminary, Pasadena, California 91182

Neal Krause, University of Michigan, Ann Arbor, Michigan 48109

Peggy Levitt, Wellesley College, Wellesley, Massachusetts 02481

James A. Mathisen, Wheaton College, Wheaton, Illinois 60187

Todd Matthews, Mississippi State University, Mississippi State, Mississippi, 39762

Charlene C. McGrew, University of Pennsylvania, Philadelphia, Pennsylvania 19104

Nancy Nason-Clark, University of New Brunswick, Fredericton, New Brunswick, Canada E3B 5A3

Ralph E. Pyle, Michigan State University, East Lansing, Michigan 48824

Mark Regnerus, University of Texas, Austin, Texas 78712

James T. Richardson, University of Nevada, Reno, Nevada 89557

Darren Sherkat, Southern Illinois University, Carbondale, Illinois, 62901

David Sikkink, Notre Dame University, Notre Dame, Indiana 46556

William A. Stahl, University of Regina, Regina, Saskatchewan, Canada S4S 0A2

W. Bradford Wilcox, University of Virginia, Charlottesville, Virginia, 22904

Contents

PART I

RELIGION AND SOCIAL INSTITUTIONS

CHAPTER 1

Politics and Social Movements

Darren E. Sherkat

Religion has been a central topic of study among social movement theorists, even if this often goes unnoticed or unmentioned. Scholars examining deprivation theories looked to new religious movements and sectarian groups for substantive examples (Lofland & Stark, 1965). Resource mobilization theory was forged on Mayer Zald's studies of the YMCA, and Zald has long argued that religious organizations and ideologies are key crucibles for political action (Zald & Ash, 1966; Zald, 1982; Zald & McCarthy, 1987). The burgeoning frame alignment perspective was developed with reference to David Snow's (1993) work on the Nichiren Shoshu Buddhists and Burke Rochford's (1985) examinations of the Hare Krishna. The current turn toward cultural explanations in social movements promises even greater connection between the two subfields (Young 2002; Sherkat 1998).

Religion is best seen as a specific subset of social movements, because, in their contemporary forms, both institutions are defined by the voluntary character of individual participation. My broadened definition of social movements follows Zald's (2000) admonition that normal institutional processes are key to understanding social movement dynamics. By doing so, we will be able to understand collective, political, and religious action in terms of their particular goals. Clear conceptual separation also will help us understand the intersections between religious and political structures—identifying points of resource complementarity and schematic transposition that comprise the intersection of religion and politics (Young, 2002; Sherkat, 1998; Sherkat & Ellison, 1997; Sherkat & Blocker, 1994, 1997).

DEFINING THE TERRAIN: AN ENCOMPASSING VIEW OF SOCIAL MOVEMENTS

In a radical departure from previous definitions of social movements, McCarthy and Zald (1977, p. 1217–1218) defined social movements as preference structures for changing some aspect of the social structure. This definition allowed McCarthy and Zald to distinguish between social movements—potentials for mobilization—-and social movement

---

Darren Sherkat • Southern Illinois University, Carbondale, Illinois, 62901

organizations—mobilization efforts that were successful in generating resources and constitute the institutional bases of voluntary collective action. Given that many movements seek to limit social change, this definition is a bit too narrow. Indeed, a reference to social structures seems unnecessary. Instead, I propose:

> Social movements are constellations of preferences for collective goods—goods that can only be generated using collective resources, and could be enjoyed by all members of a collectivity.

Notably, this definition encompasses all possible collective goods—some of which are cultural and apolitical. A great deal of effort has been unnecessarily expended to try to distinguish social movements from cultural and political movements. These efforts have generally led to the exclusion of religious movements from the realm of social movements, and the confinement of political social movements to those operating outside of the regular processes on institutional politics. Recently, however, scholars working from a variety of perspectives have come to see cultural factors as central to the study of social movements, and the unclear political agendas in some social movements have created a storm of controversy among those studying identity movements (e.g., Duyvendak & Giugni, 1995; Taylor & Whittier, 1992). Is a lesbian feminist reading group a social movement? If a group doesn't engage in collective actions seeking politically generated collective goods can it be a social movement? These have been difficult questions for scholars working on social movements, and my conceptualizations generate clear parameters for identifying the field. Social movement organizations (SMOs) are constellations of voluntarily extracted resources directed at satisfying preferences for collective goods.

Neither the state nor capitalist organizations that deal in private goods are social movements. Both can produce collective goods (and bads); however, they do so using the weight of coercion or the accumulation of capital resources. Neither the state nor capitalist firms rely on the voluntary provision of resources from constituents. Corporate actors may engage in social movement activity by voluntarily giving their resources to try to obtain collective goods, and states create the playing field on which social movements vie for a share of the collective resources forcibly taken by the state through taxation (Tilly 1978, 1985). The Islamic state of Iran is not a religious movement—it is a state that grants easy access to collective resources for certain Islamic groups—and harshly represses other Islamic and non-Islamic groups by raising their costs of mobilization and collective action, and by lowering their rates of return on collective action (Tilly 1978).

Political Movements

Politics is the process of engaging in collective action to seek collective goods from the state—the entity that coercively accumulates collective resources and produces collective goods. Political movements are constellations of preferences for collective goods provided by the state. Attempts at generating collective goods or preventing collective bads that are unmediated by state coercion of collective resources are not political movements. For example, groups of individuals may band together to prevent a flood by filling sandbags and piling them on a levee. Such an effort is a social movement organization, by my definition, as presumably these individuals think of flooding as a collective bad (they prefer not to flood) and they collectively attempt to alleviate the collective bad without appealing to resources from the state. If the group appeals to the government for trucks, shovels, and sandbags, then it is a political movement.

In my definition of political movements, all political movements are social movements, regardless of the relative success of acquiring collective resources from the state through well-developed institutional channels. It matters not that an organized attempt to satisfy preference for collective goods is ingrained in institutional processes for providing collective goods from the state. To say otherwise is to conflate movement success and power—the relative return in collective goods on collective action efforts—with institutional politics, and to marginalize social movement activity to contending groups with limited power and success (Tilly, 1978, 2002; Zald, 2000). "Mainstream politics" is simply the process of mobilization and collective action of successful political movements.

Following Tilly (1978, 2002), in my definition of political movements, there is no room for the common movement narrative, "the personal is political." Personal decisions and cultural affinities are not axiomatically political. Being gay or a religiously conservative Christian, for example, is not political because it does not directly imply a desire for particular state-generated collective goods. Going to a gay bar or to a church is not a political activity (unless such activity is banned by the state, in which case it could be seen as a form of political protest). Frequenting a gay bar is an action seeking primarily private goods. Gay bars generate collective benefits, but these are a result of spillover effects from the consumption of private goods. Because of their focus on excludable private goods, gay bars are not social movements. Churches produce more strictly collective goods, but they have nothing to do with garnering collective benefits from the state. Church participation is social movement participation, but it is not political action. Similarly, many "identity" movements are apolitical. A lesbian feminist reading group is a social movement—it generates some collective benefit and is voluntary in action. However, it is not political—it is not engaged in collective activities that seek a collective good from the state. Identity movements have much in common with religious movements in that regard. The collective benefits that are generated are "in process" goods that are a function of the collective activity itself and the cultural composition of the group.

Religious Movements

Religious movements are social movements seeking collectively generated goods that imbue supernatural rewards and compensators—benefits or promises of future benefits that cannot be evaluated in this world or cannot be attributable to worldly causes (Stark & Bainbridge, 1985, 1987; Stark & Finke, 2000). Religious movements are constellations of preferences for supernatural rewards and compensators, and preferences may not be satisfied by existing religious organizations (a key point of "supply side" theories of religious action). Religious movement organizations are mobilized groups seeking to produce religious goods. This definition of religious movements encompasses established religious firms (denominations in common Christian parlance) as well as more novel religious organizations. Religious goods are collective products because supernatural rewards and compensators are socially constructed explanations that humans might find valuable. The social genesis of these explanations is what provides plausibility to rewards and compensators—implausible explanations are valueless, and plausibility requires that others also hold the explanation to be true. Famously, Peter Berger (1964) once argued that religious plausibility structures would crumble in the presence of diverse explanations. It is interesting that nobody ever argues that about political explanations, where pluralistic preferences for political goods are deemed to be natural and a function of social diversity.

Individuals' religious preferences must be rooted in extant or nascent social structures. Preferences for supernatural rewards and compensators that are not found among existing or developing collective religious resources are not religious—rather, they are clinical evidence of psychosis. Bellah et al.'s (1985) infamous Sheila doesn't have her own religion—Sheila has a psychiatric disorder, which may be mild if she doesn't place much emphasis on her sheilaism. Virtually all of the sociology of religion is encompassed by the study of social movements, perhaps excluding only the sociological study of clergy careers.

Notably, once religious or political movements are mobilized into social movement organizations, they are capable of generating selective incentives for participation, and disincentives for defection (McCarthy and Zald 1977). When SMOs are heavily mobilized (having substantial collective resources and membership), selective incentives can dominate decision making about participation. One may not desire a particular religious or political collective good, but may strongly desire social status, social connections, and tangible incentives that highly mobilized religious and political movements can provide (Ellison & Sherkat, 1995; Sherkat & Cunningham, 1998; Sherkat, 1997, 1998).

RELIGIOUS INFLUENCES ON SOCIAL MOVEMENTS. Religious beliefs and resources are readily transposed into other social movements. The impact of religion is seen in voluntary organizations with minimal political interest, as well as in highly politicized social movements. Religious beliefs are commonly informative of desires for voluntary and political collective goods, and religious organizations command substantial resources that can be used by voluntary organizations and political movements.

RELIGION AND VOLUNTARY ORGANIZATIONS. Religious values and beliefs emanating from all major religious traditions amplify an ethic of social concern—albeit generally limited to fellow co-religionists. Buddhists, Christians, Hindus, Jews, Sikhs, and Muslems are called to sacrifice their own comfort and pleasure for those who are in need. Widows, orphans, the infirmed, refugees from drought and war are singled out in scriptures from each tradition as being worthy of kindness and charity. Indeed, these ethical traditions prescribe adherents to be charitable and merciful. However, there is little research investigating whether or not such values are put into practice more often by religious adherents than by those who deemphasize religious values. Ellison (1993) shows that religious people, more specifically prayerful people, are friendlier toward interviewers, however other measures of conservative Christian religiosity are predictive of hostility toward interviewers (Sherkat & Ellison, 1993). Indeed, experimental research has demonstrated that the effect of religiosity on kindness to strangers is limited to contexts that ensure that voluntary actions will benefit co-religionists (Orbell et al., 1992).

The link between religious organizations and resources, and voluntary and charitable organizations, is more defined. Given religious prescriptions regarding charity, religious institutions have a template for becoming involved in community affairs to alleviate suffering. Religious groups are responsible for substantial resource outlays to fund orphanages, poor houses, hospitals and insane asylums, and victims of natural disasters and war. Indeed, some religious groups have made such causes their primary focus, such as the Red Crescent and the Salvation Army. Religious institutions are well situated to engage in such activities, in part because of a plethora of physical and human capital resources that could be used for such tasks. Religious groups have physical plants, transportation resources, easy access to volunteer labor, and professional activists who might be marshaled in times of need, or to routinely engage in such activities. As a consequence, secular voluntary organizations seek out religious groups for block recruitment of volunteers, and for coopting physical resources such as buildings, buses, kitchens, and the like. Church groups are able to sponsor and staff soup kitchens, homeless shelters, and programs for unwed indigent mothers using their existing buildings, kitchens, and vehicles, and staffed with their normal professional and secretarial help and readily recruited volunteers.

Research demonstrates that individuals who are active in religious organizations are more likely to engage in voluntary activities (Wilson & Janoski, 1995; Janoski & Wilson, 1995) than those who are not religiously active. Activism in religious organizations places people in a web of social affiliations that increases the likelihood of participation. Social ties generated in religious groups lower the cost of participation in voluntary organizations, particularly as these groups often are in concert with religious doctrines. Indeed, even secular groups such as the Lions, Elks, and Shriners will benefit from social ties to religious groups, as these will decrease the burden of individual participation by providing an environment infused with solidary selective incentives. Individuals who are not involved in religious groups are less likely to come into contact with recruiters from voluntary organizations, and will be less likely to know others who are involved in such organizations. This will reduce the likelihood and commitment to volunteer work for those uninvolved in religious groups.

Research has failed to demonstrate a link between religious values and volunteering or participation in voluntary organizations (Cnaan et al., 1993; Wilson & Musick, 1997). However, some denominational differences in volunteering are evident. Although some commentators have claimed that the new niche of "mainline" liberal and moderate denominations is in worldly activism through voluntary organizations (Wuthnow, 1993), empirical research has shown that rates of volunteering are highest among conservative Protestants and Mormons (Wilson & Musick, 1996; Janoski & Wilson, 1995). Still, religiously motivated activism in voluntary organizations is concentrated in organizations supported by religious institutions, and that serve religiously inspired preferences for collective goods. Given this sectarian motivation of religious charity, current enthusiasm for delivering social services using religious institutions—deemed "charitable choice" in the 1996 Welfare Reform Act and by activists favoring state support for religious goals—is untempered by concern that such services would be rendered only to those who subscribe or submit to the influence of religious institutions. Religious institutions provide social services in a religiously inspired manner that many beneficiaries and potential beneficiaries likely find noxious—thus leading to an underutilization of services. The efficiency and effectiveness of state-sponsored religious charity is of growing concern, since a sizeable fraction of the general population and ethnic minorities are nonreligious and non-Christian (Sherkat, 2001, 2002; Sherkat & Alanezi, 2004), and given the persistent need for social services among ethnic minorities and the religiously unaffiliated. What is clear is that social movements militating for state support of religious "charities" crosses the line between religious voluntary action and religious political action. Engaging state resources for delivering social services to the poor or infirmed is political, not charitable.

RELIGION AND POLITICAL SOCIAL MOVEMENTS.   Modern states produce a cornucopia of collective goods and bads, many of which are imbued with religious import. Even seemingly innocuous rights or responsibilities required or proscribed by states can bolster or impede the attainment of religious values. Because of this, religious schemata are readily transposable into the political realm and are critical for evaluating political resources.

Religious schemata are both extensive—having broad appeal across time and space—and intensive—enabling a control over understandings and behaviors (Young, 2002). Because of this, religious schemata are the most powerful ideological elements in any culture. Religious orientations help define collective goods and bads, and also direct the propriety of collective action (Snow et al., 1986). Although classical treatments of religion often assumed that otherworldly religion would hinder political action, contemporary research has shown that religious beliefs, values, and institutions are crucial for supporting contentious tactics (McVeigh & Sikkink, 2001; Sherkat & Ellison, 1991). Religious institutions recognize the power of the state to influence commitments to their own organizations, and to generate favorable or unfavorable environments for their congregants. Furthermore, political movements understand the salience of religious ideological structures and the enormous actual resources commanded by religious institutional infrastructures (Gill, 1996; Billings, 1990; Billings & Scott, 1994). Hence, political actors often seek to coopt religious ideological and actual resources, or to regulate or counteract their operation in the political field.

Classical treatments of political movements evidence a strong "structuralist" bias—assuming that the motivations for political actions come from the relations of production or coercion defined by feudal or capitalist states (e.g., Tilly, 2002). This rendering of history is curious—particularly given the historical and geographic ubiquity of religiously inspired coercive actions engaged in by feudal and modern states, and the omnipresence of religious movements seeking to influence state actions. The formal separation of religious institutions from state institutions in late capitalism only served to alter the dynamics of the process—often resulting in an even more powerful religious influence over politically generated collective goods and bads; as religious elites no longer had to worry about such worldly trivialities as the efficiency, effectiveness, or universal ethics of policies desired by religious zealots (Beyer, 1994). Of course, once religious elites come to control political resources, they are forced to be responsible for other state concerns such as economic development, civil unrest, international relations, and the like (Beyer, 1994). In a stable polity such as the United States, this generally results in cycles of control by religiously inspired movements (Jelen, 1991). In less-developed polities, the imposition of religious domination onto political and economic institutions generates protracted conflict and cyclical revolution, as is evident in occupied Palestine, Pakistan, Iran, India, Malaysia, Nigeria, and elsewhere.

Religious Movements and the Politics of Education and Moral Behavior
Religious values inspire social movements that cut to the core of everyday life and how it is lived. Religiously inspired social movements seek to establish collectively supported or prescribed childrearing activities, patterns of mating and sexual regulation, calendars of work and holiday, and the regulation of product markets deemed threatening to religious salvation (e.g., alcohol, pork, beef, meat, cannabis, clothing, music, literature, film). Religious understandings and institutions are commonly mobilized on issues regarding education, "obscene" depictions in cultural media, and sexual behavior, particularly with contraception/abortion, prostitution, homosexuality, and marriage/divorce. Scholarship on religious influences on moral issues long asserted status motivations—claiming that Protestants were declining in status and sought to protect their status privileges by attacking the symbolic value of Catholic and other alternative lifestyles (Gusfield, 1965). However, conservative Christian moral concern has never been empirically linked to any indicator of status asymmetry or shift (Wood & Hughes, 1985). A more parsimonious explanation is that moral movements are motivated by ethical principles dictated by the gods in the major monolatries (Stark, 2000, 2003a, 2003b).

Religious social movement organizations have been so successful in their control over the regulation of content deemed immoral that such movements scarcely receive scholarly attention—or fade into a mythical "Victorian" or "traditional" value set that is apparently generated from sociological thin air. The power of religious movements to regulate moral life is evident in the widespread destruction of cultural artifacts from pre-Christian and pre-Islamic societies deemed obscene and pagan by Christian and Islamic movement activists. Books, stories, songs, poems, sculptures, paintings, and murals were erased from the historical record by religious activists who viewed such images threatening to salvation (temptations to sin) or examples of idol worship. Indeed, it is remarkably easy to reconstruct a mythical golden era of Christianity and Islam characterized by what contemporary religious activists deem to be "traditional" Christian or Islamic values given the success of these censorship movements. Serious examinations of history conclude that disbelief and nonethical indigenous religious traditions were widespread until quite recently (Stark, 1996, 2002). Importantly, before the rise of the major monolatries, moral issues were substantially less relevant for religious movements—the gods did not require humans to engage in moral behaviors (Stark, 2003a, 2003b).

A key political goal for religious institutions is the establishment of childrearing institutions that indoctrinate young subjects into what they consider to be appropriate moral values and beliefs. Religious control over educational institutions has always been a part of religion-state relations before the differentiation of these institutions in late capitalism (Beyer, 1994; Gill & Keshavarzian, 1999). This arrangement used the force of the state to prevent competition from "alien" or indigenous religious faiths, and to limit the influence of secular ideologies deemed dangerous for the dominant religion. For religious devotees, the training of children is prescribed within the tradition, and any deviations or omissions are considered a collective bad. Secular education is sometimes in conflict with religious interpretations, and this is rightly perceived as a threat to their offspring's religious faith. Research shows a negative impact of secular education on religious belief (Roof & McKinney, 1987; Wuthnow, 1988; Sherkat, 1998), and religious movements on educational issues have thrived in the United States and elsewhere (Darnell & Sherkat, 1997; Sherkat & Darnell, 1999; Deckman, 2004; Page & Clelland, 1978; Rose, 1988; Peschkin, 1986; Milligan, 2001; Tamney, 1994).

Conflicts over education typically involve issues of religious ritual and prayer, and the teaching of materials deemed improper on religious grounds (e.g., biology, evolution, sexual education, social studies), or the employment of nonreligious persons as teachers (e.g., homosexuals, atheists, persons not of the majority faith) (Irvine, 2002; Castillo-Troncoso, 2000; Clark, 2001). Religiously inspired political movements also have been successful in easing school attendance requirements to allow sectarians to "home school" children without credentials, supervision, or evaluation (Apple, 2000; Riegel, 2001; Blacker, 1998), and also are pushing for state funding for religious schools (Layton, 1996).

Alcohol and other drugs also are subject to moral edicts in the major monolatries, and political movements in each tradition have long focused on the regulation of alcohol and other drugs. In the United States, conservative Protestant religious beliefs and organizations were used to militate for the prohibition of alcohol, contrary to the wishes of Catholics and other Protestants who are not proscribed from using alcohol. Indeed, during the period of the prohibition of alcohol, conservative Protestants banded together in the Ku Klux Klan to further limit the influence of other religious groups, and to press for the strict enforcement of prohibition laws (Jenkins, 1988; Wade, 1987). Even in the contemporary United States, religiously inspired regulation of alcohol is evident in "blue laws" that regulate the sale of alcohol on Sunday. Islamic movements have waged similar campaigns in Muslim-dominated countries, as have conservative Hindus in India. Religious communities also have mobilized against other products they consider unwholesome, including beef and pork. Movements against the consumption of other drugs also rely heavily on religious beliefs and resources—and many antidrug campaigns are explicitly Christian in their mission.

Sexual morality is a focus of attention in all of the major religious traditions. In order to satisfy the will of the gods, the faithful must conduct their sexual lives in accordance with religious strictures. Although there is some variance across religious traditions, all major monolatries (Buddhism, Hinduism, Sikhism, Judaism, Mormonism, Islam, Christianity) proscribe nonmarital sexual relations (both pre-marital and extra-marital sex) and homosexuality. Each tradition also directs the faithful to marry, reproduce children, and most directly proscribe divorce, masturbation, contraception, infanticide, and abortion. Interpretations of these religious prescriptions and proscriptions vary considerably within each religious tradition. Indeed, on most issues of sexual morality there are religiously based social movement organizations working on BOTH sides of the moral issue. The issue of the legalization of divorce has prompted substantial religiously inspired social movements, primarily but not exclusively opposing the legalization of divorce in Catholic strongholds of Spain, Italy, and Ireland (Alberoni, 1979; Dillon, 1995, 1996). The legalization of contraception also spurred substantial social movements, with most oppositional movements rooted in religious beliefs and institutions. Indeed, religious social movements opposed to contraception have hindered social policy regarding the spread of AIDS in Africa—although these social movements in Africa are largely undocumented.

Religious movements on the legality of abortion are well studied, particularly in the United States. Conservative Protestants and Catholics are both staunchly opposed to legalized abortion (Hoffman & Miller, 1997, 1998; Hughes & Hertel, 1986; Petersen, 1998), and Catholic and conservative Protestant religious groups have forged substantial (though largely separate) social movement organizations seeking to combat legalized abortion (Blanchard, 1994). Importantly, religious activists have long crusaded on the other side of the fence—supporting legalized abortion—and most religious bodies have active social movements on both sides of the issue (Dillon, 1995; Luker, 1984; Staggenborg, 1991). Indeed, religious coalitions were substantially involved in the process that legalized abortion in the United States—and the liberal leadership of the Southern Baptist Convention (along with most liberal and moderate Protestant groups) helped forge a friend of the court brief in support of legalization.

Religious movements also have been consequential as oppositional SMOs against civil rights for homosexuals. Religious conservatives hold significantly more negative appraisals of homosexuality and homosexual civil rights (Peterson & Donnerworth, 1998), and these values and beliefs are put into action through organized social movements. Many of these movements target a variety of moral issues—often called family concerns—but homosexuality is one of the most salient targets of collective action for groups such as the American Family Association and Focus on Family. Generally, these movements have suffered losses in collective good over the last decades—with homosexuals being granted basic civil rights in most cases, and seem poised to be granted the right to marriage or civil union in some states in the United States. However, these victories are likely to spur substantial mobilization efforts among religious conservatives (Meyer & Staggenborg, 1996). Religious movements opposing civil rights for homosexuals have successfully passed ordinances restricting homosexual rights and defeated ordinances that would have granted equal protections (Bernstein, 1997). With homosexuality (and abortion), social movements move quickly from issues of morality—the regulation of behavior—to rights—the treatment of people by the state. The issue of human rights opens up new directions, which I will deal with below.

Literature and pictorial images of sexuality have also been targets of moral movements (Zurcher et al., 1980; Wood & Hughes, 1984; Swatos, 1986). Religious values and beliefs about the propriety of sexual imagery and the potential consequences of reading or viewing such materials are transposed into a desire to move the state to regulate the production and distribution of materials deemed sexually explicit, pornographic, or profane (Sherkat & Ellison, 1997; Wood & Hughes, 1984). Many religious social movement organizations address these issues at the local level—attempting to shut down adult bookstores, have books removed from libraries, purge museums of art that is deemed lewd or blasphemous, or ban nude dancing. Importantly, for anti-pornography movements there is little vigorous opposition, and in this one realm of morality, there are no substantial religiously inspired countermovements (in contrast to the issues of homosexuality, abortion, divorce, and contraception). Indeed, the issue of pornography regulation is one that largely unites religious liberals and religious conservatives.

Most modern movements regarding state regulation of morality cut across specific substantive issues, and in modern representative democracies their goals are best met through the electoral process, through lobbying, campaign financing, public petition, and mobilizing voters (Bruce, 1988; Rothenberg & Newport, 1984; Jelen, 1991,1998; Leege & Kellstedt, 1993; Green et al., 2003; Layman, 1997, 2001). For the last three decades, sociologists and political scientists have devoted considerable attention to the political beliefs and behaviors of conservative Christians, and their formation of interdenominational social movement organizations such as the Moral Majority, Focus on Family, American Family Association, and Christian Coalition. Notably, this body of research has found that conservative Christians are conservative only on moral issues (Hoffman & Miller, 1997, 1998). Despite high profile attempts by social movement cadre workers such as Pat Robertson to link conservative capitalism with Christian edicts, members of conservative sects are not significantly different from other Americans on environmental policy, redistributional/welfare issues, or labor-business relations (Iannaccone, 1993; Sherkat & Ellison, 2004). Along with other factors, this inconsistency in the political conservatism of sectarian Christians makes long-term coalitions unstable (Jelen, 1991)—and leads to trepidation among economic conservatives about forming alliances with religious conservatives.

Studies of political behavior and voting in the United States have yielded mixed results. Although many observers claimed and expected to find political hyperactivity among religious conservatives, and shifts in their political behavior over time (cf. Liebman & Wuthnow, 1983; Moen, 1992), analyses of individual level data do not reveal heightened political activism in terms of mainstream political behaviors (voting, working for candidates, donating money to candidates) when compared to other citizens—although there is a modest positive association between church attendance and these behaviors (Rothenberg & Newport, 1984). Ties to conservative religious organizations and beliefs are increasingly associated with Republican Party affiliation and voting, attributable to the shift in this party to the right on moral issues over the last three decades (Rothenberg & Newport, 1984; Layman, 1997, 2001). However, many studies of voting behavior claim to find no influence of religious factors, or declining influence (Manza & Brooks, 1997; Brooks & Manza, 1997a, 1997b). These studies are flawed in that they only focus on presidential voting—which can be confusing for religiously inspired voters. Who was the Christian candidate in 1980, Reagan or Carter? Jimmy Carter was a dyed-in-the-wool Southern Baptist, and equally conservative on most social issues. Reagan embraced conservative Christian causes, but he was not an active church member, did not affiliate with a conservative Protestant denomination, he drank, and was divorced. A similar problem is evident in 1988 and 1992, when the elder and less religious Bush was the Republican candidate. Indeed, the Christian Right openly challenged the elder Bush for his Republican nomination for president. The problem is not lost on conservative Christian social movement organizations such as the Moral Majority and Christian Coalition, each of which have published and distributed millions of elaborate and geographically specific voter guides for their adherents and constituents. These guides have been shown to be widely used and followed by conservative Christians going to the polls (Regnerus et al., 1999).

Religious Movements for Political Inclusion and Exclusion and Human Rights

Religious movements are often deeply involved in the politics of human rights—the privileges and sufferings produced by modern states. Modern nation-states control the means of coercion, and can forcibly extract resources from the populous under their control. This force includes the ability to tax economic resources, as well as the ability to coerce citizens to work for the state, usually in a military capacity. Issues of representation and voice in states' policies have been paramount concerns of political movements in the last four centuries. Forced taxation means that resources are taken from the faithful and put to use in ways deemed appropriate by the state, and forced conscription enables states to potentially sacrifice the lives of subjects for the good of the state. Given that the collective goods produced by modern states are incredibly diverse, it is a virtual certainty that some of these "goods" are considered collective bads by some plurality of the population—and religious devotees may be particularly likely to object to certain uses of collective resources. This is especially true because state resources are often used to maintain a monopoly for privileged religious institutions (Iannaccone, 1991; Gill, 1996). Religious beliefs and institutions are also interested in more penetrating issues, including the propriety of state domination, and the duty of states to serve the needs of their subjects. As noted earlier, all major monolatries amplify the value of charity, and this ideological element is easily transposed from a requirement for godly individuals, to an ethical directive for states that command even more considerable resources. Religious legitimation of states has a rationale based on religious prescriptions and proscriptions, with ethical demands on individuals applied in a more general way to collectivities and the state.

Throughout human history, and continuing into the present, the collective goods generated by states have benefited a small proportion of the population, at the expense of the majority of the population. This characteristic of human social organization is not lost on religious institutions, all of which address issues of state domination in their sacred texts. Should good religious people pay taxes to an unholy ruler? Must the faithful serve in the military of an infidel king? If one kills in the service of a secular state, is that a sin? Is disobedience to an ungodly state a sin, or a requirement for salvation? Obviously the answers to these questions vary radically across and within religious groups, and over time and space. Religious prescriptions and proscriptions have been used to justify political quiescence, as well as to amplify the necessity of radical political action (Zald, 1980; Zald & McCarthy, 1987; Billings, 1990). Furthermore, religious ethical demands place responsibilities on wealthy societies to care for the sick, orphaned, indigent, and elderly—often ignoring the boundaries of nations. This characteristic of religious ethical movements has made them important for shaping foreign policies, and has forged substantial cross-national movements.

Religion, Political Inclusion, and Human Rights

Religious values and institutions helped spur movements for the abolition of slavery in the United States and Britain (Stark, 2003b; Young, 2002). Critical for these movements was the religious foundations of morality that were interpreted as proscribing good Christians and Christian nations from holding slaves (Stark, 2000, 2003b). The interpretation of Christianity that developed in early capitalism was one that embraced the divine sanctity of the individual, and accorded individuals both human and political rights. This interpretation of Christianity is incompatible with authoritarian dictatorship, because it views human rights as accorded by the gods, and not by humans. Similar movements are evident across religious traditions, and are the ideological foundation of religiously inspired political revolution. Unfortunately, most studies of revolutionary movements go to great lengths to omit or downplay religious bases in beliefs and institutions. Even scholarship on the Islamic revolution in Iran has almost uniformly pointed to mythical social class bases of protest, and ignored transformations in Shiite Islamic thought that enabled political mobilization (Ayubi, 1994). In Christianity, the abolitionist movement also helped spark movements to provide for basic human needs. If God grants the right to live, humans are failing if they construct social systems that result in infant mortality, disease, and poverty. Indeed, this "social gospel" movement went further to argue that in absence of basic human needs, people become animalistic and incapable of moral judgment that can lead to religious salvation. Hence, in order to save souls, religiously inspired SMOs sought to first combat poverty, hunger, and disease. Although some of these movements were apolitical (as defined earlier), many others engaged the political system directly by seeking resources from the state to combat social problems.

Most impressively, religious beliefs and institutions were marshaled in support of the movement for civil rights for African Americans (Morris, 1984; Robnett, 1996, 1998). African-American churches provided both the ideological foundation for justifying collective action and overcoming oppression, as well as the tangible support of leadership, physical plants, mail, literature, and other important tools for collective action (Morris, 1984). Furthermore, liberal white religious groups provided substantial resources for the civil rights movement, particularly through such movement "halfway houses" as the Fellowship on Reconciliation (Morris, 1984). The Christian character of this movement was an important symbolic resource in and of itself—because it helped to limit violent repression, and to establish some ideological common ground between supporters of civil rights and the largely conservative Christian plurality that opposed the extension of human rights to African Americans. Indeed, many white conservative Christians view the civil rights period as their greatest spiritual failure—and the Southern Baptist Convention even issued a formal apology for opposing the Civil Rights movement. Some religious activists see conservative Christian movements such as the Promise Keepers and racially inclusive megachurches as the most promising avenues for reducing racism and prejudice (Bartkowski, 2004).

Liberal Christian religious organizations became deeply concerned with human rights issues in less-developed nations—in tandem with their decreased emphasis in spiritual missions seeking conversion (Finke & Stark, 1992; Stark & Finke, 2000). These movements have pointed to the political abuse of power in a variety of nations, and have documented and attempted to counter human rights abuses under Soviet and Chinese Communism, and in African, Asian, and South American dictatorships. Some scholarship has systematically examined a few movements of this type, most notably the largely Catholic and liberal Protestant movements that sought to reduce United States support for brutal dictatorships in Latin American (Gill, 1996; Smith, 1996).

Religion and Political Exclusion

Religious beliefs and institutions are commonly used to justify the political exclusion and even the extermination of nonbelievers. Indeed, religiously inspired themes regarding racial purity and the superiority of Christians, Jews, Hindus, Buddhists, and Muslims abound, and movement organizations in each tradition actively militate against the political enfranchisement of others. Successful movements of this sort have engaged in widespread genocide and forced removal of nonbelievers, less radical solutions generally focus on maintaining a political and economic caste system through disenfranchisement and legal discrimination.

In the United States, Christian religious beliefs and organizational resources helped justify the slave system and provide a countermovement to the abolitionist movement. Notably, because of their support of slavery, the Southern branches of the Methodist and Baptist churches split from their northern counterparts. White Christian religious organizations contributed deeply to the anti–Civil Rights movement, beginning with mobilizations following the American Civil War that helped reestablish white political supremacy and successfully disenfranchised former slaves. Research on these movements is quite limited. Although there are some works on the Ku Klux Klan, most of the best works focus on the 1920s-era Klan, which mobilized largely against Catholics and their cultural influence. Research is lacking on the more powerful and ubiquitous White Citizens Councils and their relationships to religious organizations, and use of religious beliefs to bolster support. Barkun (1994) provides a fascinating history of the theological beliefs undergirding racist Christian movements in the United States. Aho (1990) has shown important connections between Christian religious beliefs and affiliations and participation in right-wing hate groups. Aho's research demonstrates Mormon proclivities for "Christian constitutionalism"—a sacralization of the United States constitution and the interpretations made of it in these communities. Aho finds that conservative Protestants have an affinity for identity Christianity, which claims that only European whites can be true Christians and all other races are children of Satan.

In Apartheid-era South Africa, Kuyperian variants of Dutch Calvinism provided a religious legitimation for the racial caste system and the political exclusion of nonwhites (Tiryakian, 1957; Du Toit, 1985). Contemporary Zionist movements argue that Palestine was territory given by God to the Jews, and that only faithful Jews should reside or have political rights in Palestine. Hindu nationalism is increasingly militant in its emphasis on Hindu superiority, and the expulsion of Muslims and other non-Hindus from the Indian subcontinent. Islamic nations use religious ideologies to justify the continuation of tribal monarchies (contrary to democratic values), and the exclusion of non-Moslems from the political process. Sri Lankan Hindu and Buddhist activists each demand "home rule" that essentially would require the forced removal or political exclusion of minorities in the respective zones of control (Ellison, 1987). Similar controversies undergird protracted conflicts between Protestants and Catholics in Northern Ireland (White, 1989). Unfortunately, social scientific exclusion of religious explanations over the last century has left this area of research largely unexplored—particularly in non-Western settings where religious violence is generally heaped into "ethnic violence" (Hadden, 1987)—a scientifically unjustifiable assessment that seems to suggest that "ethnic" political mobilizations are the result of irrational races fighting with one another.

FUTURE DIRECTIONS. The systematic study of religion and social movements is scarcely two decades old, and a tremendous amount of substantive and theoretical work remains. Most glaring is the general lack of studies examining polities and religious commitments outside of the United States. Indeed, there have been few studies of connections between religion and politics that have been applied to Europe. Even the ongoing Protestant-Catholic conflict in Northern Ireland is discussed as if religion has nothing to do with it. The rise of religiously motivated right-wing nationalist parties throughout Europe dismays European political scientists and sociologists who are uncomfortable dealing with cultural influences on political and economic resources. What little research has addressed Islamic and Zionist movements comes from an "international relations" perspective that is devoid of data and theory, and is more political commentary than social science. Beyond the Middle East, social scientific analyses of religion and politics in Asia and Africa are almost nonexistent.

Studies of religion and politics are also lacking in their connection to novel developments in sociological theory. Social movement theorists have pointed to the importance of identities for motivating participation—but even these treatments lack nuance or a connection to broader theories of individual and collective identities in social psychological theory (Zajonc, 1980,1984). Similarly, discussion of movement narratives as meaning construction exercises have not been examined by scholars studying religion and politics, despite the ubiquity of religious narratives for political movements. With a few exceptions (Williams, 1995; Williams & Blackburn, 1996), sociologists of religion have been slow to embrace frame analytic (Snow et al., 1986; Benford, 1993, 1997; Benford & Snow, 1992) and structuration perspectives to help make sense of the connections between ideas and the negotiation of commitments between members and movements.

This chapter has attempted to clarify the conceptual discourse regarding religious movements, social movements, and political movements. With a more standard and scientifically defined conceptual apparatus, analyses of religious influences on social movements and politics will be less subject to the interpretive whims of religious and political activists or to the fickle fancy of humanist scholars. Religion plays a dominant role in the production of collective goods. Religious values influence what people and communities believe are worthy public goods and noxious collective bads. Religious institutions provide resources for both the collective production of secular and religious collective goods, and also for political mobilizations to influence the production of collective goods by the state. Importantly, religious diversity makes it axiomatic that politically generated collective goods for one religious group are likely collective bads for another religious group or for those who do not desire religion. Much work remains, and future theoretical efforts should focus on the nature of intra- and interinstitutional ties, their measurement, and consequences. Scholars undertaking such contributions will need to define and theorize about network structures within and between religious institutions, social movements, and political movements.

REFERENCES

Aho, J. (1990). *The politics of righteousness: Idaho Christian patriotism.* Seattle, US: University of Washington Press.

Alberoni, F. (1979). Social movements and Italian society. *Rassegna Italiana de Sociologia, 20,* 359–388.

Apple, M. W. (2000). Away with all teachers: The cultural politics of home schooling. *International Studies in Sociology of Education, 10,* 61–80.

Ayubi, N. (1994). *Political Islam: Religion and politics in the Arab world.* New York: Routledge.

Barkun, M. (1997). *Religion and the racist right.* Chapel Hill: UNC Press.

Bartkowski, J. P. (2004). *The Promise Keepers.* Rutgers: New Brunswick, NJ.

Bellah, R. N., Madsen, R., Sullivan, W. M., Swidler, A., & Tipton, S. M. (1995). *Habits of the heart: Individualism and commitment in American life.* Berkeley: Univ. of California Press.

Berger, P. (1964). *The sacred canopy.* Anchor Books.

Benford, R. D. (1993). Frame disputes within the nuclear disarmament movement. *Social Forces, 71,* 677–701.

Benford, R. D. (1997). An insider's critique of the social movement framing perspective. *Sociological Inquiry, 4,* 409–430.

Bernstein, M. (1997). Celebration and suppression: The strategic uses of identity by the lesbian and gay movement. *American Journal of Sociology, 103,* 531–565.

Beyer, P. (1994). *Religion and globalization.* London: Sage.

Billings, D. (1990). Religion as opposition: A Gramscian perspective. *American Journal of Sociology, 96,* 1–31.

Billings, D. B., & Scott, S. L. (1994). Religion and political legitimation. *Annual Review of Sociology, 20,* 173–202.

Blanchard, D. (1994). *The anti-abortion movement and the rise of the religious right.* New York:: Twayne.

Blacker, D. (1998). Fanaticism and schooling in the democratic state. *American Journal of Education, 106,* 241–272

Brooks, C., & Manza, J. (1997a). Class politics and political change in the United States 1952–1992. *Social Forces, 76,* 379–408.

Brooks, C., & Manza, J. (1997b). The social and ideological bases of middle class political realignment in the United States 1972–1992. *American Sociological Review, 62,* 191–208.

Bruce, S. (1988). *The rise and fall of the new Christian right.* Oxford: Clarendon.

Castillo Troncoso, A. D. (2000). La polemica en torno a la educacion sexual en la ciudad de Mexico durante la decada de los anos treinta: Conceptos y representaciones de la infancia. *Estudios Sociologicos, 18,* 203–226.

Clark, J. A. (2001). Sex education in the New Zealand primary school: A tangled skein of morality, religion, politics and the law. *Sex Education, 1,* 23–30.

Cnaan, R. A., Kasternakis, A., & Wineburg, R. J. (1993). Religious people, religious congregations, and volunteerism in human services: Is there a link? *Non-Profit and Volunteer Sector Quarterly, 22,* 33–51.

Darnell, A., & Sherkat, D. E. (1997). The impact of Protestant fundamentalism on educational attainment. *American Sociological Review, 62,* 306–316.

Deckman, M. (2004). *School board battles: The Christian right and local politics.* Washington, DC: Georgetown University Press.

Dillon, M. (1996). Cultural differences in the abortion discourse of the Catholic Church: Evidence from four countries. *Sociology of Religion, 57,* 25–36.

Dillon, M. (1995). Institutional legitimation and abortion: Monitoring the Catholic Church's discourse. *Journal for the Scientific Study of Religion, 34,* 141–151.

Du Toit, A. (1985). Puritans in Africa? Afrikaner "Calvinism" and Kuyperian Neo-Calvinism in late nineteenth-century South Africa. *Comparative Studies in Society and History, 27,* 209–240.

Duyvendak, J. W., & Giugni, M. G. (1995). Social movement types and policy domains. In *New Social movements in Western Europe: A comparative analysis* (pp. 82–110). Minneapolis: University of Minnesota Press.

Ellison, C. G. (1987). Elites, competition, and ethnic mobilization: Tamil politics in Sri Lanka, 1947–1977. *Journal of Political and Military Sociology, 15,* 213–228.

Ellison, C. G. (1993). Are religious people nice people? Evidence from the National Survey of Black Americans. *Social Forces, 71,* 411–430.

Fendrich, J. M. (1993). *Ideal citizens: The legacy of the civil rights movement.* Albany: State University of New York Press.

Finke, Roger, & Stark, R. (1992). *The churching of America, 1776–1990: Winners and losers in our religious economy.* New Brunswick, NJ: Rutgers University Press.

Gill, A. (1996). *Rendering unto Caesar: The Catholic Church and the state in Latin America.* Chicago: University of Chicago Press.

Gill, A., & Keshavarzian, A. (1999). State building and religious resources: An institutional theory of church-state relations in Iran and Mexico. *Politics and Society, 17,* 431–465.

Green, J., Rozell, M. J., & Wilcox, C. (2003). *The Christian right in American Politics.* Washington, DC: Georgetown University Press.

Gusfield, J. (1965). *The symbolic crusade.* Champaign: University of Illinois Press.

Hadden, J. (1987). Toward desacralizing secularization theory. *Social Forces, 65,* 587–611.

Hertel, B. R., & Hughes, M. (1987). Religious affiliation, attendance, and support for "pro-family" issues in the United States. *Social Forces, 65,* 858–882.

Hoffmann, J. P., & Miller, A. S. (1997). Social and political attitudes among religious groups: Convergence and divergence over time. *Journal for the Scientific Study of Religion, 36*, 52–70.

Hoffmann, J. P., & Miller, A. S. (1998). Denominational influences on socially divisive issues: Polarization or continuity? *Journal for the Scientific Study of Religion, 37,* 528–546.

Hunt, S. A., Benford, R. D., & Snow, D. A. (1994). Identity fields: Framing processes and the social construction of movement identities. In E. Larana, H. Johnston, and J. R. Gusfield (Eds.), *New social movements: From ideology to identity* (185–208). Philadelphia: Temple University Press.

Iannaccone, L. (1991). The consequences of religious market structure: Adam Smith and the economics of religion. *Rationality and Society, 3,* 156–177.

Iannaccone, L. (1993). Heirs to the Protestant ethic? The economics of American fundamentalists. Chicago: University of Chicago Press.

Irvine, J. M. (2002). *Talk about sex: The battles over sex education in the United States.* Berkeley: University of California Press.

Janoski, T., & Wilson, J. (1995). Pathways to volutarism: Family socialization and status transmission models. *Social Forces, 74*(1), 271–292.

Jelen, T. G. (1998). Research in religion and mass political behavior in the United States. *American Politics Quarterly, 26,* 110–134.

Jelen, T. G. (1991). *The political mobilization of religious beliefs.* New York: Praeger.

Jenkins, W. D. (1990). *Steel Valley Klan.* Kent, OH: Kent State University Press.

Layman, G. C. (1997). Religion and political behavior in the US: The impact of beliefs, affiliations, and commitment from 1980–1994. *Public Opinion Quarterly, 61,* 288–316.

Layman, G. C. (2001). *The great divide: Religious and cultural conflict in American party politics.* New York: Columbia University Press.

Layton, D. H. (1996). Religion and the politics of education: An introduction. *Education and Urban Society, 28,* 275–278.

Leege, D. C., & Kellstedt, L. A. (1993). *Rediscovering the religious factor in American politics.* Armonk, NY: M. E. Sharpe.

Liebman, R. C., & Wuthnow, R. (1983). *The new Christian right: Mobilization and legitimation.* Hawthorne, NY: Aldine.

Lofland, J. (1993). Theory bashing and answer improving in the study of social movements. *American Sociologist,* 37–58.

Lofland, J., & Stark, R. (1965). Becoming a world saver: A theory of conversion to a deviant perspective. *American Sociological Review, 30,* 862–875.

Luker, K. (1984). *Abortion and the politics of motherhood.* Berkeley: University of California Press.

Manza, J., & Brooks, C. (1997). The religious factors in US presidential elections 1960–1992. *American Journal of Sociology, 103,* 38–81.

McCarthy, J. D., & Zald, M. N. (1977). Resource mobilization and social movements: A partial theory. *American Journal of Sociology, 82,* 1212–1239.

McVeigh, R., & Sikkink, D. (2001). God, politics, and protest: Religious beliefs and the legitimation of contentious tactics. *Social Forces, 79,* 1425–1458.

Meyer, D., & Staggenborg, S. (1996). Movements, countermovements, and the structure of political opportunity. *American Journal of Sociology, 101,* 1628–1660.

Milligan, J. A. (2001). Religious identity, political autonomy and national integrity: Implications for educational policy from Muslim-Christian conflict in the Southern Philippines. *Islam & Christian-Muslim Relations, 12,* 435–448.

Moen, M. (1992). *The transformation of the Christian right.* Tuscaloosa: University of Alabama Press.

Morris, A. (1984). *The origins of the civil rights movement.* New York: Free Press.

Orbell, J., Goldman, M., Mulford, M., & Dawes, R. (1992). Religion, context, and constraint toward strangers. *Rationality and Society, 4,* 291–307.

Page, A., & Clelland, D. (1978). The Kanawha County textbook controversy: A study in alienation and lifestyle concern. *Social Forces, 57,* 265–281.

Peshkin, A (1986). *God's choice: The total world of a fundamentalist school.* Chicago: University of Chicago Press.

Petersen, L. R., & Donnenwerth, G. V. (1998). Religion and declining support for traditional beliefs about gender roles and homosexual rights. *Sociology of Religion, 59,* 353–371.

Regnerus, M., Sikkink, D., & Smith, C. (1999). Voting with the Christian right: Contextual and individual patterns of electoral influence. *Social Forces, 77,* 1375–1401.

Riegel, S. (2001). The home schooling movement and the struggle for democratic education. *Studies in Political Economy, 65,* 91–116.

Robnett, B. (1996). African American women in the Civil Rights movement 1954–1965: Gender, leadership, and micromobilization. *American Journal of Sociology, 101,* 1661–1693.

Robnett, B. (1998). *How long? How long? African American women in the struggle for civil rights.* Oxford: Oxford University Press.

Rochford, E. B. (1985). *Hare Krishna in America.* New Brunswick, NJ: Rutgers University Press.

Roof, W. C., & McKinney, W. (1987). *American mainline religion.* New Brunswick, NJ: Rutgers University Press.

Rose, S. D. (1988). *Keeping them out of the hands of Satan: Evangelical schooling in America.* New York: Routledge, Chapman, Hall.

Rothenberg, S., & Newport, F. (1984). *The evangelical voter: Religion and politics in America.* Washington, DC: Institute for Government and Politics.

Sewell, W. H., Jr. (1992). A theory of structure: Duality, agency, and transformation. *American Journal of Sociology, 98,* 1–29.

Sherkat, D. E. (1991). Leaving the faith: Testing theories of religious switching using survival models. *Social Science Research, 20,* 171–187.

Sherkat, D. E. (1997). Embedding religious choices: Integrating preferences and social constraints into rational choice theories of religious behavior. In L. A. Young (Ed.), *Rational choice theory and religion: Summary and assessment* (pp. 65–86). New York: Routledge.

Sherkat, D. E. (1998). Counterculture or continuity? Competing influences on baby boomers? Religious orientations and participation. *Social Forces, 76,* 1087–1115.

Sherkat, D. E. (2001). Tracking the restructuring of American religion: Religious affiliation and patterns of mobility, 1973–1998. *Social Forces, 79,* 1459–1492.

Sherkat, D. E. (2002). African American religious affiliation in the late 20th century: Trends, cohort variations, and patterns of switching, 1973–1998. *Journal for the Scientific Study of Religion, 41,* 485–494.

Sherkat, D. E., & Alanezi, F. (2004). *The religious participation of U.S. immigrants: Integrating explanations from ethnic community and rational actor theories.* Paper presented at the annual meeting of the American Sociological Association, San Francisco, CA, August 2004.

Sherkat, D. E., & Blocker, T. J. (1994). The political development of sixties activists: Identifying the impact of class, gender, and socialization on protest participation. *Social Forces, 72,* 821–842.

Sherkat, D. E., & Blocker, T. J. (1997). Explaining the political and personal consequences of protest. *Social Forces, 75,* 1049–1076.

Sherkat, D. E., & Cunningham, S. A. (1998). Extending the semi-involuntary institution: Regional differences and social constraints on private religious consumption among African Americans. *Journal for the Scientific Study of Religion, 37,* 383–396.

Sherkat, D. E., & Darnell, A. (1999). The effect of parents' fundamentalism on children's educational attainment: Examining differences by gender and children's fundamentalism. *Journal for the Scientific Study of Religion, 38,* 23–35.

Sherkat, D. E., & Ellison, C. G. (2004). *Religion and environmental attitudes and activism.* Unpublished manuscript.

Sherkat, D. E., & Ellison, C. G. (1997). The cognitive structure of a moral crusade: Conservative protestantism and opposition to pornography. *Social Forces, 75,* 957–982.

Sherkat, D. E., & Ellison, C. G. (1993). Are religious people really nice people? Paper presented at the Southern Sociological Society, New Orleans, LA, March 1993.

Sherkat, D. E., & Ellison, C. G. (1991). The politics of black religious change: Disaffiliation from black mainline denominations. *Social Forces, 70,* 431–454.

Sherkat, D. E., & Wilson, J. (1995). Preferences, constraints, and choices in religious markets: An examination of religious switching and apostasy. *Social Forces, 73,* 993–1026.

Smith, C. (1996). *Resisting Reagan: The U.S. Central American peace movement.* Chicago: University of Chicago Press.

Smith, C. (Ed.). (1996). *Disruptive religion.* New York: Routledge.

Snow, D. A. (1993). *Shakubuku: A study of the Nichiren Shoshu Buddhist movement in America, 1960–1975.* New York: Garland Press.

Snow, D. A., & Benford, R. D. (1992). Master frames and cycles of protest. In A. Morris & C. McC. Mueller (Eds.), *Frontiers in social movement theory.* New Haven, CT: Yale University Press.

Snow, D. A., & Benford, R. D. (1988). Ideology, frame resonance, and participant mobilization. *Research in Social Movements, Conflict, and Change, 1,* 197–217.

Snow, D. A., Rochford, E. B., Worden, S. K., & Benford, R. D. (1986). Frame alignment processes, micromobilization, and movement participation. *American Sociological Review, 51,* 464–481.

Staggenborg, S. (1991). *The pro-choice movement.* Oxford: Oxford University Press.

Stark, R. (1996). *The rise of Christianity.* Princeton, NJ: Princeton University Press.

Stark, R. (2000). Religious effects: In praise of idealistic humbug. *Review of Religious Research, 41,* 289–310.

Stark, R. (2003a). *One true God: The historical consequences of monotheism.* Princeton, NJ: Princeton University Press.

Stark, R. (2003b). *For the glory of God: How monotheism led to reformations, science, witch-hunts, and the end of slavery.* Princeton, NJ: Princeton University Press.

Stark, R., & Bainbridge, W. S. (1987). *A theory of religion.* New York: Peter Lang.

Stark, R., & Bainbridge, W. S. (1985). *The future of religion: Secularization, revival, and cult formation.* Berkeley: University of California Press.

Stark, R., & Finke, R. (2000). *Acts of faith: Explaining the human side of religion.* Berkeley: University of California Press.

Swatos, W. H., Jr. (1988). Picketing Satan enfleshed at 7-Eleven: A research note. *Review of Religious Research, 30,* 73–82.

Tamney, J. B. (1994). Conservative government and support for religious institution: Religious education in English schools. *British Journal of Sociology, 45,* 195–210.

Taylor, V., & Whittier, N. E. (1992). Collective identity in social movement communities: Lesbian feminist mobilization. In A. Morris & C. McC. Mueller (Eds.), *Frontiers in social movement theory* (pp. 104–129). New Haven, CT:. Yale University Press.

Tilly, C. (1978). *From mobilization to revolution.* New York: Random House.

Tilly, C. (1985). War making and state making as organized crime. In P. Evans, D. Reuschemeyer, & T. Skocpol (Eds.), *Bringing the state back in* (169–191). Cambridge: Cambridge University Press.

Tilly, C. (2002). Comment on Young: Buried gold. *American Sociological Review, 67,* 689–692.

Tiryakian, E. (1957). Apartheid and religion. *Theology Today, 17,* 385–400.

Wade, W. C. (1987). *The fiery cross.* New York: Simon & Schuster.

White, R. W. (1989). From peaceful protest to guerrilla war: Micromobilization of the Provisional Irish Republican Army. *American Journal of Sociology, 94,* 1277–1302.

Williams, R. H. (1995). Constructing the public good: Social movements and cultural resources. *Social Problems, 42,* 124–144.

Williams, R. H., & Blackburn, J. (1996). Many are called but few obey: Ideological commitment and activism in Operation Rescue. In C. Smith (Ed.), *Disruptive religion: The force of faith in social movement activism* (pp. 167–188). New York: Routledge.

Wilson, J., & Janoski, T. (1995). The contribution of religion to volunteer work. *Sociology of Religion, 56,* 137–152.

Wilson, J., & Musick, M. (1997). Who cares? Toward an integrated theory of volunteer work. *American Sociological Review, 62,* 694–713.

Wood, M., & Hughes, M. (1984). The moral basis of moral reform: Status discontent versus culture and socialization as explanations of the anti-pornography social movement. *American Sociological Review, 49,* 86–99.

Wuthnow, R. (1988). *The restructuring of American religion.* Princeton, NJ: Princeton University Press.

Wuthnow, R. (1993). *The future of Christianity.* Princeton, NJ: Princeton University Press.

Young, M. P. (2002). Confessional protest: The religious birth of U.S. national social movements. *American Sociological Review, 67,* 660–688.

Zald, M. N. (2000). Ideologically structured action: An enlarged agenda for social movement research. *Mobilization, 5,* 1–16.

Zald, M. N. (1982). Theological crucibles: Social movements in and of religion. *Review of Religious Research, 23,* 317–331.

Zald, M. N., & Ash, R. (1966). Social movement organizations: Growth, decay and change. *Social Forces, 44,* 327–341.

Zald, M. N., & McCarthy, J. D. (1987). *Social movements in an organizational society.* New Brunswick, NJ: Transaction.

Zajonc, R. (1980). Feeling and thinking: Preferences need no inferences. *American Psychologist, 35,* 151–175.

Zajonc, R. (1984). On the primacy of affect. *American Psychologist, 39,* 117–123.

Zurcher, L. A., & Kirkpatrick, G. (1976). *Citizens for decency: Antipornography crusades as status defense.* Austin: University of Texas Press.

CHAPTER 2

Economy

LARRY IANNACCONE

To the horror of some and the surprise of nearly everyone, a new body of religious research roams our journals and conventions. Born of neglected data and rejected theory, the body is variously known as economics of religion, the rational choice approach, the religious economies model, and "the new paradigm." By any name, however, it has animated research on secularization, pluralism, church growth, religious extremism, rational choice, and more. And by any measure, it continues to grow and gain attention. A field that scarcely existed before 1990 can now claim hundreds of papers, scores of contributors, centers at major universities, a yearly conference, a new association, a major grant initiative, and an official AEA subject code.[1] The field also can claim a host of critics, the most strident of whom decry rational choice as the "the malign influence of a small clique" and a theory in need of a "stake through the vampire's chest."[2] Faced with diverse applications and divergent assessments, our challenge is to scan the whole while not getting lost among the parts.

Contemporary research on religion and economics can be sorted into three major lines of inquiry. The first explores economic *theories* of religion. The second studies the economic *consequences* of religion. Adam Smith's critique of state-supported religion exemplifies the former; Max Weber's protestant ethic thesis, the latter. Together these two lines constitute *the economics of religion*. This essay focuses on economic theories of religion—in part because it is what I know best, but also because the literature on religion's economic consequences is so vast.

Religious economics forms a third line of inquiry. Despite its size and scope, this literature is too far removed from mainstream sociology or economics to warrant inclusion in this essay. Religious economics seeks to evaluate economic action in the light of sacred precepts. The subject is as old as religion itself, for one can preach little of consequence while ignoring property, production, and exchange. The main monotheistic faiths have inspired especially large bodies of economic doctrine and debate. With the help of economists and philosophers, contemporary clerics keep this topic alive, debating the merits of private property, income inequality, tax laws, deficit spending, monetary policy, income redistribution, workers rights, interest rates, banking laws, entrepreneurship, government regulation, international trade, debt relief, unionization, entitlement programs, and much more. Among

LARRY IANNACCONE • George Mason University, Fairfax, Virginia 22030 the many fine introductions to this literature are books by Oslington (2004) and Gay (1991), review articles by Siddiqi (1981) and Waterman (1987), and essays in the journal of *Markets and Morality* (http://www.acton.org).

This essay is a work of informed opinion. Although seeking to avoid bias, I do not claim disinterest or neutrality when it comes to the economics of religion. My "revealed preference" for formal models and rational choice theory is a matter of record. Nor is this my first attempt to grapple with the field as a whole. Given the ease with which readers can access my past work via on-line sources such as ATLA, JSTOR, and EconomicsofReligion.com, I shall neglect many contributions that predate my 1998 *Introduction to the Economics of Religion* (Iannaccone, 1998). I shall likewise skim the criticisms addressed in Iannaccone (1995b) and gloss the assumptions and applications described in Iannaccone (1997). The present goal is to extend, rather than merely update, these earlier works. Faced with a sprawling field that no longer admits a chapter-sized review, I have economized—focusing on topics that strike me as "best bets" for current and future research, while relegating the broader literature to an on-line appendix (accessible through EconomicsofReligion.com).

ECONOMIC THEORIES OF RELIGION

Despite the extraordinary foundation laid by Adam Smith in 1776, economic theories of religion languished from the 1770s through the 1970s. In *The Wealth of Nations,* Smith (1981 [1776], pp. 788–814) had argued that self-interest motivates clergy just as it does secular producers; that market forces constrain churches just as they constrain secular firms; and that the benefits of competition, the burdens of monopoly, and the hazards of government regulation are as real for religion as for any other sector of the economy. Along the way, he also developed a theory of sectarianism, a theory of religious violence and civility, and a general theory of church and state.

In 1950 and again in 1968, the great economist Kenneth Boulding (1970, p. 188) noted the "curious" fact that "no economist since Adam Smith seems to have dealt at any length with the economics of religion." For two centuries, Smith's observations represented "almost everything that economists, *qua* economists, . . . said on this subject." As Boulding recognized, this neglect hurt the social sciences twice over.[3] Economists lost a provocative "nonmarket" application that broadens the field and encourages cross-disciplinary research. And religious scholars lost a paradigm that complements, and sometimes contradicts, the alternative perspectives of sociology, psychology, history, theology, and anthropology.

Economists finally returned to the study of religion in the 1970s, inspired by Gary Becker's pathbreaking work on the family. The first papers modeled church attendance and contributions as a special form of household production—one that involved tradeoffs between time and money inputs, secular versus religious outputs, and present versus afterlife utility (Azzi & Ehrenberg, 1975; Ehrenberg, 1977). Extensions to this model soon added preference formation and human capital, thereby broadening its application to childhood socialization, age effects, conversion, intermarriage, and family interactions (Iannaccone, 1984; Neuman, 1986; Iannaccone, 1990; Lehrer & Chiswick, 1993). Around the same time, several sociologists of religion began mining old data sources with new theories of rational exchange and market competition (Stark & Bainbridge, 1980, 1985, 1987; Finke & Stark, 1988, 1992). By the 1990s, these economic and sociological streams of scholarship together included studies of sectarianism, denominational vitality, religious extremism, doctrinal innovation, church and state, religious markets, non-Western faiths, religious history, and more.

In the mid-1990s, it was easy to classify contributions to this literature based on their primary level of analysis—individual, group, or population. The classification system worked well because each level tended to emphasize a distinct set of economic concepts. At the individual level, theories of household production and human capital helped explain demographic determinants of religiosity and typical patterns of attendance, contributions, intermarriage, and conversion. At the group level, the neoclassical theory of firm (and the theory of economic "clubs") helped explain the contrasting features of exclusive sects and mainstream churches. And at the level of populations, theories of competition versus monopoly challenged traditional models of secularization, while emphasizing the benefits of free and competitive religious markets.

Although the three-level scheme retains some value, many recent contributions defy simple classification. I shall therefore focus on ideas and issues rather than levels of aggregation.

Choice and Rationality

Nearly all economic theories employ the twin assumptions of *rational choice* and *stable preferences*. Within such theories, each individual is assumed to evaluate the costs and benefits of all potential activities and then act so as to maximize net benefits relative to his or her ultimate preferences. In the realm of religion, this means choosing which religion, if any, to accept and how extensively to participate in it. These optimal choices need not be permanent. Indeed, the theory is well suited for explaining differences in the level or content of religious activity—both over time and across individuals. The stable preference assumption means, however, that explanations rarely rely on varied tastes, norms, or beliefs. A good economic story explains behavior in terms of optimal responses to varying circumstances—such as prices, incomes, skills, experiences, technologies, or resource constraints.

I speak of economic *stories* to underscore the importance of intuition, judgment, and aesthetic criteria in economic scholarship—a fact amply documented by McCloskey (1994, 1998). After decades of mathematical modeling and empirical estimation we have good reason to doubt that economic science will ever succeed by the standards of physics. David Friedman (1996, p. xi) thus describes "good" economics as "a blend of theory, intuition, real world puzzles, and ingenious, if sometimes bizarre, solutions." (And David should know, for he is the son of Nobel Laureate Milton Friedman, a great economist in his own right, and a Ph.D. physicist to boot!) Economists of religion must be especially sensitive to the limitations of formal theory and statistical computation, lest they crank out claims that are irrelevant or absurd.

For sociologists of religion the challenge is essentially the reverse. Sociological training not only emphasizes the limitations described earlier, it also instills distaste for formal theory and economic reasoning—partly because the founders of sociology defined their domain and methods as correctives to the omissions of economics and partly because economists continue to threaten sociology's academic turf and resources (Wrong, 1961, p. 190; Swedberg, 1990, p. 8–18).[4] Toss in the influence of Max Weber (1963), who made "rationality" central to his work but applied it in ways foreign to most contemporary economists, and you have a recipe for miscommunication.

As I see it, scholars have pursued the debate over rationality far past the point of diminishing returns. For my own part, I have chosen (rationally, I hope) to emphasize rationality's "status as a simplifying *assumption*" (Iannaccone, 1997, p. 26). I can (and do) assert its usefulness without for a moment believing that people always act logically, efficiently, or in accordance with their own self-interest. For those wishing to read the full debate over rational choice theories of religion, I recommend Bruce (1993), Chaves (1995), Demerath (1995), Ellison (1995), Iannaccone (1995b, 1995c), and Young (1997). But I also recommend devoting one's *own* scholarly energies elsewhere. The twin assumptions of rationality and preference stability are false but useful. Not much else matters.

Production and Substitution

The simplest models of religious behavior (such as those of Azzi and Ehrenberg 1975; Iannaccone 1990) ignore interpersonal interactions and market equilibrium, focusing instead on the behavior of individuals. These models view religion as just one of the many commodities available to consumers, and they thereby explain patterns of religious participation as the result of commodity choice and production. Of course, most religious commodities are neither tangible goods like cars and computers nor commercial services like haircuts and banking. Rather, they are "household commodities" as defined by Becker (1976)—valued goods and services that families and individuals produce for their own consumption. Household commodities may be as concrete as meals and laundry or as abstract as relaxation and love.

Although we cannot directly observe most religious commodities, we can observe the inputs used to produce them. The principal time and money inputs—attendance and contributions—are routinely measured by sociological researchers. More specialized studies provide detailed information on time (such as time devoted to religious services, private prayer and worship, religious charity, and many other religious activities) and money (such as expenditures for special attire, transportation, religious books and paraphernalia, sacrificial offerings, and contributions used to finance staff, services, and charitable activities of religious organizations).

Attention to input *substitution,* as opposed to mere inputs, distinguishes the household production models from their sociological counterparts.[5] Virtually all productive activities, whether household or commercial, concrete or abstract, require both time and money inputs. But the ratio of these inputs can often be varied. Meals can be cooked at home or purchased in restaurants; lawns can be watered by hand or by automated sprinklers; trips can be taken by car or by plane; and children can be cared for by parents or preschools. In every case, people with higher values of time will tend to substitute time-saving, money-intensive forms of production for money-saving, time-intensive forms. Hence, high-wage households are more likely to dine out, install sprinklers, travel by air, and send their children to preschools.

People with high monetary values of time will tend to engage in time-saving, money-intensive forms of religion. Their *ratio* of contributions to attendance will be relatively high. People with low monetary values of time will adopt more time-intensive practices and contribute relatively less money. These predictions have no precedent within traditional, noneconomic models of religious but are strongly confirmed both by survey statistics and case studies. Early studies of substitution between contributions and attendance include Ehrenberg (1977), Sullivan (1985), and Iannaccone (1990). Recent work by Hungerman

(2003) and Gruber (2004) give more attention to statistical problems of endogeneity, but all studies confirm the tendency to substitute between money and time.

Although surveys fail to show *how* people substitute money for time, direct observation indicates that richer congregations opt for a variety of time-saving, money-intensive practices. These include shorter services, more reliance on professional staff, more elaborate and costly facilities, fewer volunteer workers, and more purchased goods, such as catered meals in place of potlucks.

Both in theory and in fact, substitution encourages different denominations to adopt different in methods of organization and worship. Relatively rich members can be quite stingy about spending time on religion. Hence, even a very well-endowed Episcopalian or Presbyterian congregation with plenty of (bequeathed) money to cover its salaries and operating expenses may find itself hard-pressed to recruit volunteers for its choir, youth programs, committees, and many other traditional programs. For the so-called Protestant "mainline," prosperity has proved a mixed blessing.

Other economic trends have forced adaptation in all denominations, and none more so than the growth of women's wages and workforce participation. As women have moved into the labor force and overall family earnings have grown, congregations have had to purchase many services formerly supplied by volunteers. The pattern is illustrated by Luidens and Nemeth's (1994) study of expenditure trends in Presbyterian and Reform denominations. Although real per-capita giving increased dramatically in both denominations (from around $200 per person in the 1940s to nearly $800 in the 1990s), nearly all the added money went to fund local congregational expenses. According to Luidens and Nemeth (1994, p. 119), "heightened demand for specialized services and professionally-staffed programs" has squeezed out increased funding at all other denominational levels. Substitution strikes again.

In studies too numerous to list, scholars have explored other implications of production and substitution. (For an especially striking example, see Carmel Chiswick's [1995] work on American Jewish adaptations to economic success, which range from reduced rates of individual observance to the establishment of an entirely new branch of Judaism—Reform—designed to minimize the cost of religious observance in a prosperous and pluralistic environment.) Suffice to say, substitution and production remain good candidates for great research, especially where economic conditions have changed rapidly.

Religious Capital

Sociologists have often criticized economic models for their "undersocialized" view of human action. James Coleman (1988, p. 97) introduced the concept of "social capital" to rescue rational choice theory from this deficiency. Around the same time, I introduced the concept of "religious capital" to rescue religious production from the same shortcomings (Iannaccone, 1984, 1990). Each concept took its inspiration from the economic theory of human capital (Schultz, 1961; Becker, 1964), but each extended the standard theory by emphasizing *relationships and social networks* rather than purely individual capacities.

As I have used the term, "religious capital" denotes the accumulated stock of skills, sensitivities, and relationships that alter a person's (real or perceived) benefits from subsequent religious activity. The concept can readily subsume a variety of other terms, including habits, preferences, spiritual capital, social capital, and social networks. Sometimes it helps to distinguish between different types of religious capital, such as that which is specific to a particular religious tradition or embedded in relationships. (see, for example, Stark & Finke, 2000). But most capital-oriented distinctions prove largely semantic and unproductive. (In that list, I would definitely include debates contrasting "religious" versus "spiritual" capital, or "preference change" versus "capital formation.") Whatever the terminology, capital has several key features. The first is that past experience alters the value of current religious activities, and thereby affects rates of religious participation. The second is that most religious experience is "context specific"—relevant only to a specific relationship, congregation, location, denomination, or religious tradition. This means that capital also shapes patterns of religious affiliation.[6] Yet another feature of capital is its tendency to depreciate, and to initially rise but eventually fall over the life cycle.

Capital models yield numerous predictions concerning denominational mobility, religious intermarriage, the timing of conversions, the influence of religious upbringing, the impact of mixed-faith marriage, the age-profile of religiosity, and much more (Iannaccone, 1990). For example, insofar as people accumulate religious capital over time, increased age will lead to increased religious participation. The similarities between religious capital and professional capital lead us to predict that most conversions and religious mobility will, like career choices and job mobility, occur at relatively young ages. Rates of inter-generational mobility are especially low within distinctive religious traditions, as most children accumulate their religious capital in a (home and church) context determined by their parents. Switching will be most prevalent between relatively similar denominations (which allow the switchers to conserve on the value of their previous religious investments). Similar patterns will characterize religious intermarriage. Moreover, the complementarities inherent in shared-faith marriages will lead to higher rates of religious participation, lower rates of divorce, higher fertility, and many other outcomes associated with greater marital compatibility (Lehrer & Chiswick, 1993; Lehrer, 1999; Waite & Lehrer, 2003).

The great strength of religious capital is its capacity to integrate existing generalizations and observations while also suggesting new generalizations and new avenues for research. Survey data and case studies provide strong support for most capital-based predictions. Iannaccone (1990) remains a good introduction to religious capital theory, predictions, and data. The empirical studies of Sherkat and his associates provide further confirmation, and illustrate the manner in which religious capital may be reconceived as preferences, habits, and social constraints (Ellison and Sherkat 1995; Sherkat and Wilson 1995; Sherkat 1997).

Social Capital

It is but a small step from human capital to social capital. So small, in fact, that both theorists and empiricists have trouble distinguishing the two. By any definition, however, religion plays a major role in the formation and maintenance of relationships, social networks, and shared norms. Empirical studies find that nearly half of all associational memberships, personal philanthropy, and volunteering in the United States are church-related, leading Robert Putnam (2000) to conclude that "[f]aith communities ... are arguably the single most important repository of social capital in America."

Religion is, however, all but ignored in the immense contemporary literature on social capital. See, for example, the literature reviews by Dasgupta (1999) Portes (1998) and Sobel (2002). One can scarcely imagine a better "market opportunity" for high-impact research (made all the more timely and marketable thanks to the Templeton Foundation's recent

"Spiritual Capital" research initiative). The opportunities are further magnified by the links from social capital to other lively areas of economic and sociological research on "social multipliers," "threshold effects," and "social networks." See Becker (2000), Granovetter (1978), and Kuran (1995) for ideas and applications that deserve more attention in the study of religion.

Belief and Uncertainty

Capital also helps us study religious beliefs. Modeling beliefs as a combination of personal and social capital is straightforward, and it conveniently captures the fact that people tend to believe what they have been taught, what they have previously espoused, and what those around them believe. As with other forms of capital, belief-related capital and belief-related actions are closely related: beliefs shape actions by altering their perceived costs and benefits, and current actions shape *future* beliefs. Studies along these lines are few, but I would expect many more as researchers adapt insights from the relatively new economic literature on preference formation and "rational addiction" (Becker, 1996). The models become more complex, but also more rich and interesting, when we add social effects (Schelling, 1978; Kuran, 1995).

How do we explain the *content* of religious beliefs? Existing economic models provide very little guidance at this point, nor does contemporary sociology. Sociologists of religion still cite the grand theories of Marx, Weber, Durkheim, and other 19th-century luminaries, but when accounting for specific beliefs they almost fall back on individual rationality ("Person X embraces belief Y in order to feel better") or collective rationality ("Society X embraces belief Y in order to function better").

Some will argue that the answer lies in psychology. With titles such as *Religion Explained* and *Darwin's Cathedral,* one gets the impression that evolutionary psychologists Pascal Boyer (2001) and David Wilson (2002) have all but wrapped up the search for God. But I expect most sociologists will come away disappointed, convinced that little has been explained and no great edifice raised. Current work in cognitive, behavioral, and experimental psychology strike me as equally limited. Despite some valuable ideas, none yields anything approaching a general theory of religious belief.

Rational choice offers another approach, one that harkens back to the much maligned "rationalistic positivism" of Edward Tylor, Herbert Spencer, and James Frazer. These and other 19th-century scholars viewed religion as a product of the flawed but basically rational attempts of "primitive" peoples to understand the world and their place in it. *A Theory of Religion,* by Rodney Stark and William Bainbridge (1987) shows that this approach remains powerful, particularly when married to 20th-century field studies, historical findings, and survey research. (As became apparent from the moment anthropologists began doing serious field work early in the 20th century, the source material used by Tyler and others was shot full of factual errors concerning "primitive" societies.) Stark and Finke (2000, chapter 4) offer a similar but streamlined theory in *Acts of Faith.* My own more economic approach is outlined in Iannaccone (1999) and detailed in a forthcoming book.[7]

All three contemporary theories of rational religious belief share some compelling features. They begin with just a few assumptions about human nature and the human condition—in essence scarcity, rationality, and the capacity to conceive of supernatural beings or forces. From these, they derive a universal demand for supernaturalism and a universal distinction between magic and religion. (By definition, "magic" emphasizes the control of supernatural forces, whereas "religion" emphasizes interactions with supernatural beings.) Specialized suppliers arise naturally in both realms, and the theory predicts that markets for magic operate quite differently from markets for religion. In particular, only the latter can sustain long-term relationships, high levels of commitment, and moral communities. The theories thus derive Durkheim's famous dictum that "there is no church of magic."

The theories, however, do not end with Durkheim. They also explain why "moral communities" are so difficult to maintain, even for religions, and why they typically demand exclusivity and sacrifice. Absent these costly constraints, rational consumers will patronize many different suppliers, investing so to speak in diversified *portfolios* of supernatural commodities. This last observation is strongly affirmed by historical and cross-cultural evidence, but it is far from obvious for people raised in the exclusive religious traditions of the monotheistic West. The demand for diversified religion is natural, however, given the tremendous uncertainty that surrounds most religious claims. Even a child can appreciate the wisdom of not putting all your eggs in one basket.

Uncertainty offers yet another "market opportunity" for contemporary research. Not since Peter Berger's (1969) work on "plausibility structures" have sociologists of religion given much attention to this central feature of faith. As I sought to demonstrate in "Risk, Rationality, and Religious Portfolios" (Iannaccone, 1995a), uncertainty is not just understudied, it is also a theme well suited to rational choice theory.

Churches as "Clubs"

If people are both rational and risk-averse, how can exclusive religions survive? Why does not every worshipper assemble a "portfolio" of beliefs, practices, and churches? The modern theory of church and sect provides offers an answer. Congregations are sustained by collective production.[8] Except for a few full-time religious professionals and a handful of benchwarmers, most members contribute both to production and consumption of these religious commodities. Highly effective congregations require highly committed members, not mere customers. In this respect, effective congregations are more like families than firms.

The problem is that "shirking," "defection," and "free-riding" tend to overwhelm collective action in large groups, and sometimes even in small families. Paying people to do their job well fails to solve the problem, because members' "jobs" can neither be defined nor observed with precision, and because payments reward motivations that are the opposite commitment. But free-rider problems *can* be mitigated by seemingly gratuitous costs—the sacrifice and stigma characteristic of deviant religious group. Examples of such costs include: distinctive diet, dress, or sexual conduct; physical separation from mainstream society; painful or costly rites; rules that limit social contact with nonmembers; and prohibitions restricting normal economic or recreational activities. Sacrifice and stigmas drive away people who lack commitment while also boosting levels of involvement among those who remain (for what else is there to do?). The net effect is a "good deal" for committed members. Moreover, the resulting congregations manifest a long series of distinctive characteristics that empirical researchers have long associated with "sectarian" religious groups. For more on the modern theory of church and sect, see Iannaccone (1988, 1992).

We have thus solved the problem of risk, rationality, and religious portfolios in an unexpected but highly informative way. The demand for diversification does not undermine every call for sacrifice, commitment, or community. People can be induced to commit themselves to a single church, but only if that church can offer rewards that more than make up the increased risk and inconvenience associated with exclusivity. The strategy depends entirely on the collective character of religious rewards. Analogous strategies do not work in standard markets, because exclusivity does not enhance the production of standard (noncollective) goods and services.

The sacrifice and stigma model has received wide acceptance, in part because it fits so much survey data and so many case studies. Despite some lingering debate over the extent of free rider problems in mainline churches or the actual level of costs imposed by contemporary conservative churches, the basic model remains the natural starting point for studies of high cost groups. It works well not only with the religious groups routinely called sects, cults, and fundamentalisms but also with communes, gangs, radical militias, and even many terrorist organizations. See for example, Berman (2000, 2003) and Iannaccone (2005).

Churches as Firms

Whereas "club" models focus attention on the collective side of religious production, firm models draw attention to the differing roles of clergy and laypeople. Never mind that most churches are membership organizations, hence more like clubs than firms. The theory of the firm is too well developed and too useful to ignore. Like Weber's "ideal types," religious firms would be worth analyzing even if none actually existed. Both neoclassical theory and new institutional economics provide fresh insight into the doctrine, structure, and practices of the idealized religious "firm."

Note also that many religious organizations do operate as legal firms, and many more look surprisingly firmlike. This should come as no surprise because even the highly abstract theories of religion described above predict the existence of different market segments. The segments include: exclusive "sects" that operate like clubs; inclusive "churches" sustained by a core of professionals; and markets for "magic" organized around simple exchanges between practitioners and clients.

Rodney Stark and William Bainbridge (1985, pp. 171–188) have thus emphasized the role individual entrepreneurship plays in the formation of new religions. Miller (2002) applies insights from strategic management to analyze political strategies and alliances among denominations. Finke and Stark (1992) trace the explosive growth of Methodist and Baptist churches in 19th-century America to superior marketing, organization, and clergy incentives. And Schmidtchen and Mayer (1997), Zech (2002), and Terkun (2004) are among the many scholars to apply franchise models to the study of churches and denominations.

To date, the most ambitious work analyzing churches as firms is Robert Ekelund et al.'s (1996) book on the political economy of the medieval Catholic church. Following Adam Smith's (1981 [1776], p. 797) classic observation that "the clergy of every established church constitute a great incorporation," Ekelund et al. explain numerous features of medieval Catholicism in terms of its monopoly status. They view the Church as a monopolistic "multidivisional" firm characterized by a central office that controls overall financial allocations and conducts strategic, long-range planning, but allows its (usually regional) divisions a high degree of autonomy in day-to-day operations. Drawing on standard theories of monopoly, rent-seeking, and transaction costs, they offer economic explanations for interest rate restrictions, marriage laws, the crusades, the organization of monasteries, indulgences, and the doctrines of heaven, hell, and purgatory.

Work on churches as firms continues to grow rapidly, in part because firms are easier to model than clubs, but also because the theory of the firm is so rich in predictions and data.

Markets and Monopoly

If individual denominations function as religious firms, then they collectively constitute a *religious market*. Recognizing this, Adam Smith (1981 [1776], p. 788–814) argued that established religions face the same incentive problems that plague other state-sponsored monopolies.[9] No other economic insight has generated as much discussion and debate within the sociology of religion. Sadly, however, the discussion and debate have tended to collapse down to a single issue: the consequences of American-style religious pluralism. When today's sociologist speak of "religious economies" or "the market model" they almost always mean claims concerning pluralism's capacity to reverse religious decline. This is unfortunate, for it submerges numerous insights and avenues for research beneath simplistic slogans and flawed methods. It also misrepresents what economics really teaches about market structure.

Before turning to these problems, note that the core elements of religious market theory have utterly won the day. Almost everyone now accepts the notion that religion in America constitutes a vast competitive market, overflowing with "products" that range from New Age paraphernalia to orthodox liturgies. Scholars likewise accept that market success requires entrepreneurship, innovation, and sensitivity to the demands of consumers. As a result, themes that rarely surfaced prior to Finke and Stark's *Churching of America* (1992) now parade as common sense in books and articles with titles such as "Selling God" (Moore, 1994), "Shopping for Faith" (Cimino, 1998), and "Healing in the Spiritual Marketplace" (Bowman, 1999).[10] Even the harshest critics of rational choice theory (such as Bruce, 1999), emphasize the centrality of religious choice in today's world.

The market model is certain to remain popular for years to come for the simple reason that it works. The most informative studies, however, will remain those that closely study how markets actually work. Successful "business strategies" vary across time, place, and people. Hence, good market-oriented research must carefully address numerous issues, including product attributes, marketing strategies, incentive structures, exchange relationships, consumer characteristics, and so forth. Andrew Chestnut's (2003) study of "pneuma-centric" religion in Latin America illustrates this point by showing how specific religions offer distinctive products that directly address the health and family oriented concerns of poor and middle-class women. In a similar manner, Anthony Gill (1998) compares Catholicism across Latin America and finds that the Church is much more likely to side with the poor (as opposed to the rich and politically powerful) in countries where Protestant growth threatens the Church's historic monopoly.

I take a much less positive view of the literature on "pluralistic" versus "monopolistic" markets. A tremendous amount of effort has been expended (and mostly wasted) running regressions that relate measures of pluralism to measures of religious vitality. Voas, Olson, and Crockette (2002) have correctly emphasized that major statistical problems plague these studies. The main problem, however, runs far deeper. There has never been much reason to infer monopoly power from absence of pluralism in 20th-century America—no matter how one measures religious pluralism—because barriers to entry have always been low. Good economists know not to confuse market concentration with monopoly power, and they also know not to equate monopoly power with inefficiency.

Share-based measures of market concentration (including the standard diversity index favored by the religious researchers) provide no direct information about barriers to entry.[11] Barrier size depends on technological, legal, and regulatory factors. Market concentration is at best a weak and indirect indicator of these. The relevant market is also difficult to define, as illustrated by the debate over whether religious market concentration is best measured at the level of communities, regions, or nations. The modern theory of industrial organization thus emphases market *power* rather than market *share,* especially in the case of so-called contestable markets (which by definition lack major barriers to entry).[12]

The notion of "lazy monopolists" is likewise problematic, and not just because a firm must often work quite hard to acquire and maintain monopoly status. The classic monopoly firm gains super-normal profits by charging relatively *high prices* and selling relatively *low quantities,* but it sacrifices profits if it operates inefficiently, reduces product quality, or ignores consumer preferences. It is not monopoly but, rather, *government regulation* that routinely gives rise to inefficiency. This was precisely Adam Smith's point when he critiqued the "established" churches of his day. A church that derives special status from law and government has little reason to "waste" resources on the captive customers is supposedly serves, but it has every reason to lavish attention on its legal and political constituencies. So it was that Smith (1981 [1776], p. 789–790) condemned the established (Protestant) churches of Northern Europe for "having given themselves up to indolence," while simultaneously claiming that "in the church of Rome, the industry and zeal of the inferior [i.e., lower rank] clergy is kept more alive by the powerful motive of self-interest, than perhaps in any established Protestant church."

As I see it, statistical studies of pluralism versus vitality long ago passed the point of diminishing returns, and not even mathematically heroic efforts along the lines of Montgomery (2003) are likely to reenergize them. Modern economic theory strongly suggests a higher payoff to research that more directly observes market power, competition, effort, innovation, efficiency, and so forth. Barriers to entry deserve emphasis, and case studies may prove especially enlightening. A decade of statistical debate has obscured the fact that the religious economies model has always drawn its sharpest insights from historical work—whether that of Adam Smith or that of Finke and Stark (1992).

Pluralism and Secularization

Beneath the frequently spurious statistics on pluralism and religiosity lie fundamental questions about religious change. Most arguments about "rational choice" or "religious economies" are veiled battles over secularization. The proxy war arose in part because contemporary secularization theorists (especially Berger, 1969) saw pluralism as a major factor undermining religious plausibility in the modern world.[13] In contrast, economically oriented scholars stressed pluralism's link to competition, which promotes market vitality.

The competing claims are, however, less contradictory than they initially appear. The former emphasizes trends—the presumed tendency for pluralism to corrode religious plausibility *over* time. The latter emphasizes levels—the tendency for (pluralistic) competition to increase religious participation at any *given* time. In principle both could be true or both false. Pluralism could raise equilibrium levels of religiosity in any given period yet still promote long-run decline. One might even invoke rational choice and social capital to model the process whereby pluralism eventually undercuts religious plausibility. In short, although religiosity may indeed be higher in a competitive market than in an otherwise identical state-regulated market, that differential tells us relatively little about long-run trends in *either* market.

By contrast, this ambiguity does little to reinstate secularization. The secularization thesis has never been a simple statement about trends but rather a theory of modernization—and in particular a theory about why modernization inevitably and irreversibly undercuts religion. As Berger and Luckmann (1995, p. 36–37) have themselves emphasized, this thesis receives very little support outside of Western Europe.[14]

Trends—Past and Future

Although numerous mistakes and misunderstandings have marred debates over secularization and pluralism, religious trends deserve continued study. Quite apart from their intrinsic interest and their relevance for the future, we need more and better trend research to determine how religion relates to other social and economic factors. This relationship lies at the heart of debates over the economic *consequences* of religion.

Studies of religious trends suffer from disproportionate attention to a small body of data—namely, survey studies of American church attendance from the 1950s through the present. Here again, the marginal product of additional studies is low—whether they extend the time series to the latest General Social Survey or subject the data to the latest time series technique. The prospects look better for comparative studies, especially if tied with less standard forms of data collection, such as the analysis of retrospective data (Iannaccone, 2002) or detailed collections of comparative-historical data Woodberry (2004). To speak meaningfully of trends, we especially need data on the character, as opposed to mere quantity, of religious observance over time—a subject not readily assessed by standard surveys, but potentially measurable through numerous forms of content analysis.

The Economic Consequences of Religion

Although not the first study of religion's economic consequences, Max Weber's (2002) *Protestant Ethic* certainly remains the most influential. And thanks to Weber this literature is too large—and its core ideas too well known by sociologists—to permit any meaningful review.[15] In the spirit of *The One Minute Manager* (Blanchard and Johnson 1982), I shall therefore limit myself to a few observations. For more on the economic consequences of religion, see the online appendix to this chapter and Iannaccone (1998).

The economic and social impact of religion is a subject both endlessly fascinating and genuinely important. Despite the volume of past and current work, however, there is nothing approaching consensus concerning the impact of Protestantism, Christianity, monotheism, or religion in general. After leaving the field to sociologists and political scientists, economists have reentered (e.g. Guiso 2002; Barro and McCleary 2003; Kuran 2004) and there is much more to come. One hopes that researchers can resist the temptation simply to add religiosity variables to standard (and already problematic) statistical models of economic growth. As development economists have learned, such methods yield many publications but few real advances in understanding. By contrast, attention to religion is both welcome and overdue. Attempts to promote development in poor and postcommunist countries strongly affirm the importance of norms and moral precepts—and religion appears to be source and sustainer of many such "cultural" factors.[16] Communism is the most striking example of an economically and socially destructive religion, albeit a religion without deities. In this sense, the most compelling evidence for Weber-like theories may be negative—some widely embraced systems of belief *do* halt progress and destroy civilization.

Evidence of religion's social and economic impact is stronger at the level of individuals, families, and communities. Numerous empirical studies suggest that religious belief and participation do influence numerous outcomes: mental health, physical health, sexual conduct, substance use, crime, education, work, political orientation, family behavior, fertility, rates of marriage, divorce, and cohabitation, and much more. (Interestingly, economic attitudes are one of the few outcomes often *not* related to religion.) Keep in mind, however, that problems of spurious correlation remain, despite careful attempts to eliminate them, and that nearly all the data are contemporary and American. We need *much* more information about different religions in different settings, and we cannot possible obtain it from American-based estimates of socioeconomic status (SES) and denominational effects. To illustrate how great the need may be, consider that nearly all religions advocate specific rules of sexual conduct, although by no means the same rules nor with equal success. Whether some religions persuade more people to avoid sexual promiscuity, let alone other forms of opportunistic behavior, is literally a matter of life and death. AIDS alone causes millions of deaths each year, continues to spread rapidly, and threatens to radically reduce health, longevity, and economic well-being of poor people and poor nations throughout the world.

CONCLUDING REMARKS

The economics of religion has animated research on secularization, pluralism, church growth, religious extremism, rational choice, the social consequences of religion, and more. For the social-scientific study of religion—a field long on data but short on theory—these recent contributions are no small thing. In the late 1980s, Wuthnow (1988: 500) lamented that sociology of religion "has grown more rapidly in inductive empirical research and in subspecializations than it has in attempts to identify theoretically integrative concepts.... The problem is not one of lively disagreement over serious intellectual disputes but an absence of unifying constructs." Around the same time, Stark and Bainbridge (1987, p. 11) complained that "there has been little theorizing about religion since the turn of the century" despite "an amazing variety of new and well-tested facts."

If nothing else, the economic invasion has shaken things up. Rational choice is a unifying construct *par excellence.* Proponents invoke the economic paradigm to explain empirical regularities, resolve old questions, and integrate previously distinct predictions. Other researchers remain unconvinced, and so much so that critiquing rational-choice has become its own little industry. "Lively disagreements over serious intellectual disputes" have thus been standard fare since the early 1990s. The debates have generated some light and much heat—welcome developments given the tendency for social science to leave religion out in the cold.

As economic theory has entered the study of religion so also have economic researchers. This, too, is a welcome development, especially if it promotes cross-disciplinary exchange.

Economists may be the world's most forceful advocates of free and open trade, but they rarely sample and almost never buy the output of other social sciences. Without the data, case studies, and generalizations that lie beyond the shores of economics, rational choice theory easily can drift toward emptiness or absurdity.

We need more intellectual exchange, but perhaps less work on a few tired topics. Regression studies of religious pluralism versus religious vitality may have passed the point of diminishing returns, as has the standard debate over secularization. The rate of return is equally low for most statistical studies of widely available survey data. The standard research questions remain important, but many standard techniques have ceased to inform. Just as economic approaches have enriched our stock of theories, so we need to augment our stocks of data and methods.

With one foot in economic history and one in sociology, Max Weber sought to answer great questions about religion more than a century ago. Subsequent generations of sociologist aimed lower, and economists aimed not at all. Perhaps the 21st century will at last find answers to some of those great questions thanks to a fruitful fusion of both fields.

NOTES

1. For a fairly complete list of papers and contributors, see http://www.EconomicsofReligion.com. The same Web site describes the Association for the Study of Religion, Economics, and Culture and includes past programs for the association's annual conference. The new university centers include Harvard's Center for the Study of Religion, Political Economy, and Society; George Mason University's Consortium for the Economic Study of Religion; and the Economics and Religion Research Group in Australia. The major research initiative was launched by the Templeton Foundation, and the American Economic Association subject code for research on religion is Z12.

2. These statements come from the introduction to Steve Bruce's (1999) *Choice and Religion: A Critique of Rational Choice Theory*. For similar sentiments and rhetoric, see Yamne (1997) and Hadaway and Marler (1996). Other critiques include Robertson (1992), Demerath (1995), Marwell (1996), Chaves (1995), and Neitz and Mueser (1997).

3. It does, however, seem likely that Smith's theory of sects influenced Weber, especially the notion that sect membership enhanced a person's reputation and business prospects. Although *The Protestant Sects* and the *Spirit of Capitalism* fails to cite Smith, *The Wealth of Nations* was required reading for all 19th-century students of economics, and Weber held a chair in economics at the University of Heidelberg. Weber's longer treatise on *The Protestant Ethic* and the *Spirit of Capitalism* (2002, p. 40, 107, 184) cites several passages from *The Wealth of Nations*, and describes them as "familiar" and "well-known."

4. According to Dennis Wrong (1961: 190), modern sociology "originated as a protest against the partial views of man contained in such doctrines as utilitarianism, classical economics, social Darwinism, and vulgar Marxism. All the great nineteenth and early twentieth century sociologists saw it as one of their major tasks to expose the unreality of such abstractions as economic man, the gain-seeker of the classical economists."

5. Household production also strengthens the theoretical justification for empirical studies that sift survey data for correlates of attendance and contributions. Statistically "significant" predictors—such as income, education, age, race, region, marital status, and gender—can be interpreted as determinants of the demand for religious participation. In practice, however, the results differ little from those previously documented in sociological studies.

6. Although most applications of the capital concept emphasize its tendency to *increase* religious activity, the opposite occurs when the capital is specific to an institution or environment that becomes less accessible or appealing. Voas's (2003) recent study of Scottish religion may illustrate this point. The theoretical result is analogous to sustained unemployment among older workers who lose long-held jobs.

7. The relevant draft chapters are available on request.

8. The skeptical reader will wonder why congregations cannot operate like commercial firms, hiring their labor and selling their products. The simple answer is that the typical congregation operates as mutual benefit organizations dedicated to the collective production of worship services, religious instruction, social

activities, and other quasi-public "club goods" (Sandler & Tschirhart, 1980). Of course, this begs the question *why* standard firms cannot offer the same goods and services. The answer seems to lie in the distinctive, faith-based character of religious "products." Most religious "firms" require *networks* of faith as opposed to mere *pools* of labor.

9. Smith's insight is too important not to quote: "The teachers of [religion]..., in the same manner as other teachers, may either depend altogether for their subsistence upon the voluntary contributions of their hearers; or they may derive it from some other fund to which the law of their country many entitle them.... Their exertion, their zeal and industry, are likely to be much greater in the former situation than the latter. In this respect the teachers of new religions have always had a considerable advantage in attacking those ancient and established systems of which the clergy, reposing themselves upon their benefices, had neglected to keep up the fervour of the faith and devotion in the great body of the people."

10. The brilliant and iconoclastic economist Kenneth Boulding deserves credit for discussing economic features of religion long before Berger (1970), Stark (1972), and others did so. Unfortunately, his insights about religion appear to have had no impact on economists or sociologists. Boulding's 1950, 1952, and 1957 essays on religion and economics appear in *Beyond Economics* (Boulding, 1970).

11. To calculate the diversity index for any given market, square the market share of each firm currently operating in the market. (In the case of religion, we typically interpret each denomination's "market share" as the fraction of the population affiliated with it.) Then sum these squared-shares to obtain the "Herfindahl" index of market concentration. The indices of diversity and concentration are complementary, so $D = 1 - H$, and D measures that probability that any two people, chosen at random, are affiliated with different denominations. For more on these indices, see Iannaccone (1991, p. 164–167).

12. In so-called *contestable markets* (where firms can easily entry or exit markets) latent competition takes the place of actual competition. A single firm may account for all current sales in such a market but still lack monopoly power, because it will immediately be displaced by new entrants unless its prices and quality remain near competitive levels.

13. In fact, Berger and Luckman (1995) later concluded that pluralism was a much more powerful secularizing force than modernity itself.

14. Proponents of secularization theory apply the term "modernization" to the combined forces of urbanization, education, rationalization, and increased pluralism. See Roberts (Roberts 1990: 303–323) for an extended summary of variants on the secularization thesis promoted by Peter Berger and Thomas Luckman, Thomas O'Dea, Talcott Parsons, Robert Bellah, and others. For a historical overview of the secularization thesis and debate, see Swatos and Christiano (1999).

15. Delacroix and Nielsen note that despite numerous studies challenging the empirical validity of Weber's argument, the Protestant Ethic thesis lives "as an article of faith in sociology primers, international business textbooks of all stripes, [and] the middlebrow press" (cf. Eisenstadt, 1968; Samuelsson, 1993; Tawney, 1998; Delacroix & Nielsen, 2001).

16. For a brilliant analysis along these lines, see Hayek (1988), especially the chapter entitled "Religion and the Guardians of Tradition."

REFERENCES

Azzi, C., & Ehrenberg, R. (1975). Household allocation of time and church attendance. *Journal of Political Economy, 84*, 27–56.

Barro, R. J., & McCleary, R. M. (2003). Religion and economic growth across countries. *American Sociological Review, 68*(5), 760.

Becker, G. S. (1964). *Human capital: A theoretical and empirical analysis.* New York: Columbia University Press for the National Bureau of Economic Research.

Becker, G. S. (1976). *The economic approach to human behavior.* Chicago: University of Chicago Press.

Becker, G. S. (1996). *Accounting for tastes.* Cambridge, MA: Harvard University Press.

Becker, G. S., & Murphy, K. M. (2000). *Social economics: Market behavior in a social environment.* Cambridge, MA: Belknap Press of Harvard University Press.

Berger, P. L. (1969). *The sacred canopy: Elements of a sociological theory of religion.* New York: Anchor Books.

Berger, P. L. (1970). A market model for the analysis of ecumenicity. *American mosaic: Social patterns of religion in the United States* (pp. 177–190). In: P. E. Hammond & B. Johnson (eds.), New York: Random House.

Berger, P. L., & Luckmann, T. (1995). *Modernity, pluralism, and the crisis of meaning: The orientation of modern man*. Gutersloh: Bertelsmann Foundation Publishers.

Berman, E. (2000). *Sect, subsidy, and sacrifice: An economist's view of Ultra-Orthodox Jews. Quarterly Journal of Economics, 115*(3): 905–953.

Berman, E. (2003). *Hamas, Taliban and the Jewish Underground: An economist's view of radical religious militias.* (NBER Working Paper no. w10004).

Blanchard, K. H., & Johnson, S. (1982). *The one minute manager*. New York: Morrow.

Boulding, K. E. (1970). *Beyond economics: Essays on society, religion, and economics*. Ann Arbor, MI: Ann Arbor Paperbacks.

Bowman, M. (1999). Healing in the spiritual marketplace: Consumers, courses and credentialism. *Social Compass, 46*(2), 181–189.

Boyer, P. (2001). *Religion explained: The evolutionary origins of religious thought*. New York: Basic Books.

Bruce, S. (1993). Religion and rational choice: A critique of economic explanations of religious behavior. *Sociology of Religion, 54*(2), 193–205.

Bruce, S. (1999). *Choice and religion: A critique of rational choice theory*. Oxford and New York: Oxford University Press.

Chaves, M. (1995). On the rational choice approach to religion. *Journal for the Scientific Study of Religion, 34*(1), 98–104.

Chesnut, R. A. (2003). Pragmatic consumers and practical products: The success of pneumacentric religion among women in Latin America's new religious economy. *Review of Religious Research, 45*(1), 20–31.

Chiswick, C. U. (1995). The economics of American Judiasm. *Shofar, 13*(4), 1–19.

Cimino, R. P. (1998). *Shopping for faith: American religion in the new millennium*. San Francisco: Jossey-Bass.

Coleman, J. S. (1988). Social capital in the creation of human capital. *American Journal of Sociology, 94*(Supplement), S95–S120.

Dasgupta, P., & Serageldin, I. (Eds.). (1999). *Social capital: A multifaceted perspective*. Washington, DC: World Bank.

Delacroix, J., & Nielsen, G.F. (2001). The beloved myth: Protestantism and the rise of industrial capitalism in nineteenth-century Europe. *Social Forces, 80*(2), 509–553.

Demerath, N. J. (1995). Rational paradigms, A-rational religion, and the debate over secularization. *Journal for the Scientific Study of Religion, 34*(1), 105–112.

Ehrenberg, R. G. (1977). Household allocation of time and religiosity: Replication and extension. *Journal of Political Economy, 85*(2), 415–423.

Eisenstadt, S. N. (1968). *The Protestant ethic and modernization: A comparative view*. New York: Basic Books.

Ekelund, R. B., Jr. et al. (1996). *Sacred trust: The medieval church as an economic firm*. New York and Oxford: Oxford University Press.

Ellison, C. G. (1995). Rational choice explanations of individual religious behavior: Notes on the problem of Social Embeddedness. *Journal for the Scientific Study of Religion, 34*(1), 89–97.

Ellison, C. G., & D. E. Sherkat (1995). The "semi-involuntary institution" revisited: Regional variations in church participation among Black Americans. *Social Forces, 73*(4), 1415–1437.

Finke, R., & R. Stark (1988). Religious economies and sacred canopies: Religious mobilization in American cities, 1906. *American Sociological Review, 53*(1), 41–49.

Finke, R., & Stark, R. (1992). *The churching of America, 1776–1990: Winners and losers in our religious economy*. New Brunswick, NJ: Rutgers University Press.

Friedman, D. D. (1996). *Hidden order: The economics of everyday life*. New York: HarperBusiness.

Gay, C. M. (1991). *With liberty and justice for whom? The recent evangelical debate over capitalism*. Grand Rapids, MI: Eerdmans.

Gill, A. (1998). *Rendering unto Caesar: The Catholic church and the state in Latin America*. Chicago: University of Chicago Press.

Granovetter, M. (1978). Threshold models of collective behavior. *American Journal of Sociology, 83*(6), 1420–1443.

Gruber, J. (2004). *Pay or pray? The impact of charitable subsidies on religiosity*. (NBER Working Paper no. w10374).

Guiso, L., Sapienza, Paola,, & Zingales, Luigi (2002). *People's opium? Religion and economic attitudes*. Working Paper 9237, University of Chicago, School of Business.

Hadaway, C. K., & P. L. Marler (1996). Response to Iannaccone: Is there a method to this madness? *Journal for the Scientific Study of Religion, 35*(3), 217–222.

Hayek, F. A. (1988). *The fatal conceit: The errors of Socialism*. Chicago: University of Chicago Press.

Hungerman, D. (2003). *Are church and state substitutes? Evidence from the 1996 welfare reform*. Working Paper, Duke University, Department of Economics.

Iannaccone, L. (in press). The market for martyrs. In E. Meyersson- Milgrom (ed.), *The market for martyrs: A multi-disciplinary inquiry into suicide bombing*. Princeton, NJ: Princeton University Press.

Iannaccone, L. R. (1984). *Consumption capital and habit formation with an application to religious participation*. Unpublished doctoral dissertation, University of Chicago.

Iannaccone, L. R. (1988). A formal model of church and sect. *American Journal of Sociology, 9*(Supplement), s241–s268.

Iannaccone, L. R. (1990). Religious participation: A human capital approach. *Journal for the Scientific Study of Religion, 29*(3), 297–314.

Iannaccone, L. R. (1991). The consequences of religious market structures: Adam Smith and the economics of religion. *Rationality and Society* (April), 156–177.

Iannaccone, L. R. (1992). Sacrifice and stigma: Reducing free-riding in cults, communes, and other collectives. *Journal of Political Economy, 100*(2), 271– 292.

Iannaccone, L. R. (1995a). Risk, rationality, and religious portfolios. *Economic Inquiry, 38*(2), 285–295.

Iannaccone, L. R. (1995b). Second thoughts: A response to Chaves, Demerath, and Ellison. *Journal for the Scientific Study of Religion, 34*, 113–120.

Iannaccone, L. R. (1995c). Voodoo economics? Defending the rational approach to religion. *Journal for the Scientific Study of Religion, 34*, 76–88.

Iannaccone, L. R. (1997). Rational choice: Framework for the social scientific study of religion. In L. Young (ed.), *Rational Choice Theories of Religion* (pp. 25–45). New York: Routledge.

Iannaccone, L. R. (1998). An introduction to the economics of religion. *Journal of Economic Literature*.

Iannaccone, L. R. (1999). Religious extremism: Origins and consequences. *Contemporary Jewry, 20*, 8–29.

Iannaccone, L. R. (2002). *Looking backward: Estimating long-run church attendance trends in eighteen countries*. (Working Paper, George Mason University).

Kuran, T. (1995). *Private truths, public lies: The social consequences of preference falsification*. Cambridge, MA: Harvard University Press.

Kuran, T. (2004). *Islam and Mammon: The economic predicaments of Islamism*. Princeton, NJ: Princeton University Press.

Lehrer, E. L. (1999). Religious intermarriage in the United States: Determinants and trends. *Social Science Research, 27*(3), 245–263.

Lehrer, E. L., & C. U. Chiswick (1993). Religion as a determinant of marital stability. *Demography, 30*(3), 385–404.

Luidens, D., & R. Nemeth (1994). Congregational vs. denominational giving: An analysis of giving patterns in the Presbyterian church in the United States and the reformed church in America. *Review of Religious Research, 36*(2), 111–122.

Marwell, G. (1996). We still don't know if strict churches are strong, much less why: Comment on Iannaccone. *American Journal of Sociology, 101*(4), 1097–1108.

McCloskey, D. N. (1994). *Knowledge and persuasion in economics*. Cambridge: Cambridge University Press.

McCloskey, D. N. (1998). *The rhetoric of economics*. Madison: University of Wisconsin Press.

Miller, K. D. (2002). Competitive strategies of religious organizations. *Strategic Management Journal, 23*, 435–456.

Montgomery, J. D. (2003). A formalization and test of the religious economies model. *American Sociological Review, 68*(5), 782.

Moore, R. L. (1994). *Selling God: American religion in the marketplace of culture*. New York: Oxford University Press.

Neitz, M. J., & P. R. Mueser (1997). Economic man and the sociology of religion. In L. A. Young (ed.), *Rational Choice Theory and Religion* (pp. 107–118). New York: Routledge.

Neuman, S. (1986). Religious observance within a human capital framework: Theory and application. *Applied Economics, 18*(11), 1193–1202.

Oslington, P. (Ed.). (2004). *Economics and religion*. Edward Elgar.

Portes, A. (1998). Social capital: Its origins and applications in modern sociology. In J. Hagan & K. S. Cook (eds.), *Annual Review of Sociology* (Vol. 24, pp. 1–24). Palo Alto, CA: Annual Reviews.

Putnam, R. D. (2000). *Bowling alone: The collapse and revival of American community*. New York: Simon and Schuster.

Roberts, K. A. (1990). *Religion in sociological perspective*. Belmont, CA: Wadsworth.

Robertson, R. (1992). The economization of religion? Reflections on the promise and limitations of the economic approach. *Social Compass, 39*(1), 147–157.

Samuelsson, K. (1993). *Religion and economic action: The Protestant ethic, the rise of capitalism, and the abuses of scholarship*. Toronto: University of Toronto Press.

Sandler, T., & J. T. Tschirhart (1980). The economic theory of clubs: An evaluative survey. *Journal of Economic Literature, 18*(Dec), 1481–1521.

Schelling, T. C. (1978). *Micromotives and macrobehavior*. New York: W. W. Norton Company.

Schmidtchen, D., & A. Mayer (1997). Established clergy, friars and the pope: Some institutional economics of the medieval church. *Journal of Institutional and Theoretical Economics, 153*(1), 122–149.

Schultz, T. W. (1961). Investment in human capital. *American Economic Review* (March), 1–17.

Sherkat, D. E. (1997). Embedding religious choices: Integrating preferences and social constraints into rational choice theories of religious behavior. In L. A. Young (Ed.), *Rational Choice Theory and Religion: Summary and Assessment*. Routledge.

Sherkat, D. E., & J. Wilson (1995). Preferences, constraints, and choices in religious markets: An examination of religious switching and apostasy. *Social Forces, 73*, 993–1026.

Siddiqi, M. N. (1981). *Muslim economic thinking: A survey of contemporary literature*. Leicester: Islamic Foundation.

Smith, A. (1981 [1776]). *An inquiry into the nature and causes of the wealth of nations*. Indianapolis: Liberty Classics.

Sobel, J. (2002). Can we trust social capital? *Journal of Economic Literature, 40*(1), 139–154.

Stark, R. (1972). The economics of piety: Religious commitment and social class. In G. W. Theilbar & S. D. Feldman (Eds.), *Issues in Social Inequality* (pp. 483–503). Boston: Little, Brown.

Stark, R., & W. S. Bainbridge (1980). Towards a theory of religion: Religious commitment. *Journal for the Scientific Study of Religion, 19*(2), 114–128.

Stark, R., & W. S. Bainbridge (1985). *The future of religion*. Berkeley: University of California Press.

Stark, R., & W. S. Bainbridge (1987). *A theory of religion*. Bern: Peter Lang Publishing.

Stark, R., & R. Finke (2000). *Acts of faith: Explaining the human side of religion*. Berkeley: University of California Press.

Sullivan, D. H. (1985). Simultaneous determination of church contributions and church attendance. *Economic Inquiry, 23*(2), 309–20.

Swatos, W. H., & K. J. Christiano (1999). Secularization theory: The course of a concept. *Sociology of Religion, 60*(3), 209–228.

Swedberg, R. (1990). *Economics and sociology. Redefining their boundaries: Conversations with economists and sociologists*. Princeton, NJ: Princeton University Press.

Tawney, R. H. (1998). *Religion and the rise of capitalism*. Reprint edition. New intro. A. B. Seligman. New Brunswick, NJ: Transaction.

Terkun, K. (2004). *Franchise conflict: The tide of antipopes in the aftermath of the Eastern schism*. Working Paper, Clemson University, Department of Economics.

Voas, D. (2003). *They'd rather quit than switch: The Scots and religion*. Norfolk, VA: Society for the Scientific Study of Religion.

Voas, D., Olson, D. V. A., et al. (2002). Religious pluralism and participation: Why previous research is wrong. *American Sociological Review, 67*, 212–230.

Waite, L. J., & Lehrer, E. L. (2003). The benefits from marriage and religion in the United States: A comparative analysis. *Population and Development Review, 29*(2), 255–75.

Waterman, A. M. C. (1987). Economists on the relation between political economy and Christian theology: A preliminary survey. *International Review of Economics and Ethics, 2*(2), 46–68.

Weber, M. (1963). *The sociology of religion*. Boston, Beacon Press.

Weber, M. (2002). *The Protestant ethic and the spirit of capitalism*. Los Angeles, CA: Roxbury Publishing.

Wilson, D. S. (2002). *Darwin's cathedral: Evolution, religion, and the nature of society*. Chicago: University of Chicago Press.

Woodberry, R. D. (2004). *The shadow of empire: Church state relations, colonial policy and democracy in post-colonial societies*. Chapel Hill: University of North Carolina.

Wrong, D. H. (1961). The oversocialized conception of man in modern sociology. *American Sociological Review,* *26*(2), 183–193.

Yamne, D. (1997). Secularization on trial: In defense of a neosecularization paradigm. *Journal for the Scientific Study of Religion, 36*(1), 109–122.

Young, L. A. (1997). *Rational choice theory and religion: Summary and assessment.* New York: Routledge.

Zech, C. (2002). *Regulation versus resourcing in denominational structures: Churches as franchise organizations.* Working Paper, Villanova University, Department of Economics.

CHAPTER 3

Education

DAVID SIKKINK AND JONATHAN HILL

The relationship between religion and education has been at the heart of numerous cultural conflicts in the United States. Struggles over educational institutions have in many ways defined the relation of religious groups to U.S. public life. The orientation of Mainline Protestantism to public life in the early to mid-20th century was reflected in their active support for a general Protestant ethos within the public schools (Handy, 1967). Many conservative Protestants define the boundary between themselves and dominant trends in U.S. culture through their interpretation of cultural conflict in the public schools (Sikkink & Smith, 2000). In his well-known work on "culture wars," James Hunter (1991) argued that education was a crucial front in the battle of orthodox and progressive ways of knowing. Progressive views of truth, which see morality as unfolding rather than fixed, lie behind an emphasis in secular educational institutions on child-centered education, and this perspective is at war with traditional views of absolute morality (Hunter, 2000; Nolan, 1998). This shift increases the tendency of conservative religious groups to frame their relation to dominant American culture in terms of a cultural conflict over schooling institutions.

Historians of education have employed the cultural conflict frame to shed light on the education and religion nexus. Diane Ravitch (1974) uncovered the central role of Catholic and Protestant conflict in the emergence of the public school sector as the sole government-funded educational institution on the primary and secondary level. The conflict shaped the relationship of Catholicism to dominant forms of American culture, contributing to 19th- and 20th-century discrimination against Catholicism in public life. Jorgenson (1987) sees this in more stark terms, interpreting the establishment of the U.S. public school system as the imposition of Protestant cultural hegemony. Fearing immigrant pluralism and the influence of the Vatican, Protestant public schools were designed to marginalize Catholic voices in American public life (Jorgenson 1987). That public schools would be a key site of cultural struggle linked to religious groups and ideologies was cemented in the expansion of public schools in the late 19th century, which was intimately related in the West and North to the organizational and cultural resources of evangelical Protestantism. John Meyer and

DAVID SIKKINK • Notre Dame University, Notre Dame, Indiana 46556
JONATHAN HILL • Notre Dame University, Notre Dame, Indiana 46556

colleagues found evidence that the expansion of public schools depended in large part on a millennial theology of evangelical Protestantism, which included an emphasis on freedom of the individual from constraining forces of ignorance and the importance of education for achieving the good life (Meyer et al., 1979).

Ironically, cultural conflict within educational institutions was also closely connected with secularization in the United States through the 20th century (Smith, 2003b). The differentiation of religious and educational institutions in the United States not only was one of the most important changes in creating a more secular public sphere but also played a central role in realigning the religious field toward a conservatives-liberal divide (Wuthnow, 1988). It also shaped the character and size of the religious school and college sectors in the United States. Controversies over creation and evolution in public school science classes was driven in part by the development of a monopoly of scientific knowledge that placed religion and science in separate spheres (Gieryn, Bevins, & Zehr, 1985). A further secularizing impetus was the shift in public schools from a Protestant ethos, which intimately linked moral development and the educational task, to a managerial organizational culture focused on efficiency and professionalism (Tyack, 1974). This was no more evident than in the changes in the organization and culture of the National Education Association, which moved from strong support for public schools as nurturing moral character with the assistance of a general Protestant morality to vigorous defense of the neutral and professional character of public schools (Beyerlein, 2003). Influenced by the Progressive movement, teaching practices reacted against the influence of general Protestantism (Thomas, Peck, & De Haan, 2003) and toward a therapeutic ethos dominated by frameworks from psychology (Hunter, 2000).

Cultural battles within higher education that contributed to secularization in the college sector have been well charted (Burtchaell, 1998; Reuben, 1996). George Marsden (1994) explains the movement from colleges that explicitly integrated the ethos and theology of a particular denomination to colleges and universities that embedded a general Protestant ethos, which later became superfluous to the practice of the university and was set aside in the middle of the 20th century. In this process of differentiation between religious and higher education institutions, capitalist elites played a crucial role in providing the finances that severed the ties between sponsoring denominations and colleges and universities (Marsden, 1994; Burtchaell, 1998). This differentiation set the stage for institution building efforts of fundamentalists and later evangelicals to develop conservative Protestant or "Christian" colleges (Carpenter, 1997).

Recent sociological work has asked whether fundamentalist and evangelical Protestant colleges would remain religiously distinctive in the face of secular models of institutions of higher education (Hunter, 1987). This research provides some evidence that secularization is not an inevitable process (Smith et al., 1998). Schmalzbauer and Wheeler (1996) analyze 30 years of campus newspapers articles and other materials from six evangelical colleges to look at the changing role of campus rules at these institutions. They argue that the weakening of campus rules does not necessarily lead to secularization. Although the discourse resembled secular "in loco parentis" debates in some ways, the majority of the evidence revealed the use of religious arguments that were "grounded in the central doctrines of Reformation Protestant orthodoxy." Both secularizing and sacralizing dynamics were at work in evangelical Christian colleges in the late 20th century, although there is need for more thorough evidence on this score.

RELIGION AND THE POLITICS OF EDUCATION

Nineteenth- and early-20th-century conflicts over elementary and secondary schooling were shaped by religious divisions, most notably the effort of social-gospel Protestants to remake immigrants in their own image (Glenn, 1988; Reese, 1982; Rippa, 1988). Morality and values in public schools remains an important part of the politics of education, and religion plays an important role in shaping this conflict (Gaddy, Hall, & Marzano, 1996; McCarthy, 1996; Nord, 1995; Page & Clelland, 1978; Sargeant & West, 1996). Conservative Protestant opposition to a "secular" public school system is believed to lie behind the growth of nonpublic schooling, such as Christian schools and home schooling (Apple, 2000; Lines, 1996).

Some have emphasized the role of conservative Protestantism in fomenting a culture war over the legitimacy of the public and secular role of public schools in our democracy (Apple, 1996; Cookson, 1994; Diamond, 1998; Provenzo, 1990; Spring, 1998). The culture wars framework has been challenged (Davis & Robinson, 1996; DiMaggio, Evans, & Bryson, 1996; Evans, 1997; Jelen & Wilcox, 1997; Williams, 1997), although some conflicts over public schools may fit this framework, such as sex education (Davis & Robinson, 1996). But in most of these political struggles over public schools, it is important to take a careful look at the relationship between specific religious traditions and public educational institutions to understand how religion shapes the politics of education.

For better and worse, mainline Protestantism has been closely identified with the establishment of public schooling in its current form. Common notions of the public school mission, melding diversity into an American whole and preparing citizens for democracy, owes much to the mainline Protestant understanding of public life and the relation of religion to it. The quiet approach to religion in public life of the mainline (Sikkink, 1998a; Wuthnow & Evans, 2002) is expressed in support for a school system in which schools are designed to be an expression of the collective identity of the community. Mainline religious identities avoid creating tension with the surrounding culture (Hoge, Johnson, & Luidens, 1994; Smith, Emerson, Gallagher, Kennedy, & Sikkink, 1998; Stark & Bainbridge, 1985), and are more likely to be comfortable with the value-neutrality and professionalism of today's public schools. Catholics who attend regularly also see no reason to construct a symbolic boundary between themselves and public schools. Estrangement of Catholics from the Protestant-dominated public schools of the past seems to have disappeared among most Catholics today (Sikkink, 1999), perhaps because Vatican II and Catholic social and educational mobility has changed the relationship between Catholics and American culture (Gleason, 1995; Greeley, 1977).

Some religious conservatives juxtapose family and church to the professionalized and "non-normative" culture that increasingly characterizes the public school system (Arons, 1983; Meyer et al., 1994). Conservative religious traditions that construct strong symbolic boundaries with the professional and bureaucratic organization of public schools are more likely to see public schools as hostile to their moral and spiritual values (Sikkink, 1999). Orientations to public schools, however, differ within the family of conservative Protestant religious traditions.

The fundamentalist Protestant religious movement arose during anti-modernist battles with liberal Protestants in the early 20th century (Marsden, 1980), which ended with fundamentalists setting up alternative institutions outside the "mainstream" (Carpenter, 1997). This separatist history and the development of countercultural institutions leads to strong alienation from public schools and greater support for alternative schooling over public schooling among fundamentalists. Beginning in the 1940s, evangelical traditions opposed the separatist strategy of fundamentalists, and attempted to move conservative traditions into contact with the surrounding culture and society (Marsden, 1987; Marsden, 1991). Moreover, the post–World War II formative period for evangelical traditions was marked by a strong cultural link between nation, community, and school. With this genealogy, evangelical thought and practice emphasizes the importance of religious presence in public institutions (Glenn, 1987). The evangelical sense of a custodial relationship of religion in relation to public life (Wacker, 1984) creates a greater sense of obligation to public schools, despite a high degree of alienation from public schools (Sikkink, 2003). Evangelicals, and especially evangelical women, tend to support public schooling over the religious alternatives (Sikkink, 1999).

The charismatic movement grew in the 1960s and 1970s, emphasizing a strongly countercultural spiritual community of worship (Miller, 1997; Neitz, 1987). The movement was affected by the growing disillusionment with dominant institutions of American life, which was part of a long process that would weaken the historically tight link between community, nation, and public schools. Pentecostalism emerged during the first two decades of the 20th century, in opposition to the rationalistic tendencies of conservative Protestant groups (Riesebrodt, 1993). The lower-class, pietist origins of the pentecostal movement (Anderson, 1979), as well as their emphasis on special spiritual experience, includes a strong sense of outsider status vis-à-vis the surrounding society and culture (Wacker, 2001). The pentecostal and charismatic movements do not emphasize the evangelical custodial relationship between religion and public life. These traditions are less focused on a public presence for religion than on creating spiritual separation between family, individual faith, and religious community; and the outside world. Sharing a similar countercultural bent, charismatics and pentecostals are highly alienated from and willing to abandon public schools (Sikkink, 1999). These differences among conservative Protestants tend to mitigate the extent that conservative Protestantism poses a united front in challenging public schools.

Public school legitimacy, built on the school role as an expression of a geographic community, has been undermined by conditions of modernity, such as geographic mobility, differentiation, and pluralism. An additional challenge is the global resurgence of religion in the public square (Casanova, 1994). Religion has not remained sequestered in the private, subjective experiences of individuals (Luckmann, 1967). Clifford Geertz argues that religion is being driven "outward toward . . . the polity, the state, and that complex argument we call culture," creating a "religious refiguration of power politics" (Geertz, 1998). This calls for empirical study of religious collective identities that unite religious experience and identity directly with engagement in the "mundane" affairs of politics, economics, and schooling.

In the United States, local and state-level public school conflicts over sex education, science curriculum, and so on are shaped by religious collective identities, and challenge the secular, professional, and bureaucratic basis of public school legitimacy (Apple & Oliver, 1996; Bates, 1993). In some cases, these challenges are instances of the "deprivatization" of religion (Casanova, 1994). These challenges from conservative religion are believed by some scholars to threaten the differentiation of religion, morality, and values in the public schools (Apple, 2001; McCarthy, 1996), and developments in the politics of education, such as the school choice, may alter the relation of religious groups and public life.

Among the early defining issues in the role of religion in the politics of education were school prayer, the teaching of evolution in the classroom, and textbook controversies.

Conflict over school textbooks by religious groups has been interpreted as an instance of the "politics of lifestyle concern" (Clelland & Page, 1980; Page & Clelland, 1978). Similar to Hunter's culture wars, Page and Clelland rooted the conflict in differences in the normative ways of life of the traditionalist and modernist orientations. Other interpretations attempt to show the relation of religion to class conflict (Billings & Goldman, 1979; Billings, 1990). Sources of support for school prayer also have been linked to deeper cultural conflicts over lifestyles, rather than to conservative religious beliefs in the benefit of prayer or in a particular view of child socialization. The politics of school prayer represented a deeper conflict in which cultural fundamentalists sought to dramatize the need for a return to traditional values (Moen, 1984). Later evidence showed that Americans were diverging on this issue, with conservative Protestant providing the main source of support for school prayer (Hoffmann & Miller, 1997).

Evidence has shown that support for teaching creationism in the science classroom was strongly linked to biblical literalism, even while school prayer drew support from a variety of sources (Woodrum & Hoban, 1992). Some have interpreted support for creationism as an expression of fundamentalist religious identities, which seeks through political action to "bring the world to God" (Apple, 2001). The politics of school prayer and creationism represents in this view the politics of authoritarian populism (Apple, 1996; Provenzo, 1990). Although collective religious identities are important to the politics of education, these interpretations seem overly general, describing some fundamentalist leaders and groups at a particular time but not the whole of conservative Protestantism. It is not likely that school prayer or creationism provides the glue that holds together a tight-knit conservative Protestant political lobby, as only on issues of sexual morality do conservative Protestants show attitude constraint (Jelen, 1990).

One of the important current issues in the politics of education is school choice, and religious tradition plays a defining role in this debate (Cookson, 1994; Hanus & Cookson, 1996). Over time, school choice advocates attempting to include religious schools in choice plans have attempted to shift the argument for school choice away from arguments about the importance of religion and morality to educational practice and toward multiculturalism and family choice as the justification for school choice (Davies, 1999). Although more palatable in the current political culture, this reframing has the ironic effect of furthering the trend toward recognizing religious claims in the public sphere only under the banner of individual rights.

At the individual level, religion has continued to shape commitment to the public school system in the United States and support for school choice. School board candidates that support school prayer, creationism in the classroom, and school vouchers are much more likely to be conservative Protestant, although this research shows the difficulty of sorting out religious from political conservatism, which is the strongest predictor of support for vouchers (Deckman, 2002). Other research at the individual level shows that mainline Protestants remain among its strongest opponents, whereas conservative Protestants are strongly in favor.

Conservative Protestants do not always operate as a monolithic bloc opposed to public school innovation. In the case of multiculturalism in the classroom, conservative Protestants are not more likely to oppose the teaching of respect for diverse races, religions, and cultures than are mainline Protestants, and charismatics are more supportive of diversity education than mainline Protestants. And those who see religious authority as a matter of the heart rather than as an external authority, such as the Bible or the church, support multiculturalism as a top priority for the education of children. Seeing one's faith as an expression of an authentic self (Bellah, 1985; Taylor, 1991) creates support by analogy for multiculturalism in schools as a way in which diverse self-expressions are recognized and understood (Sikkink & Mihut, 2000).

At the organizational level, Catholic schools and leaders have played a strong role in the school choice lobby. The commitment of Catholic schools to remain in the inner city, despite the financial difficulties and the change to a primarily non-Catholic clientele, has added a new dimension to the historic Catholic commitment to government funding of religious schools. In the Cleveland legal case in which the Supreme Court approved inclusion of religious schools, 90% of students using the city voucher to attend the school of their choice were served by Catholic schools. Based on data from the 2000 National Election Study, Catholics who regularly attend services are strongly supportive of school vouchers, although this support is tempered somewhat by the traditional Catholic concern that government play an important role in achieving social equality—in this case, through the public schools. The strong defense that Catholics make for achieving public purposes through government support of faith-based institutions appears to lie behind their support for school vouchers. High attending conservative Protestants are strongly supportive of school vouchers, although evidence shows that their support is more strongly influenced by their view that morals have declined in the last 5 years (Sikkink, 2002).

How does religion affect actual schooling choices for children? What are the religious characteristics of those who have their children in some form of alternative schooling, such as private school or homeschool? Alternative schooling is higher among the more highly religious, who seek value communities that are not found in many public schools. Both church-related schooling and home schooling are strongly associated with higher church attendance, according to data from the 1996 National Household Education Survey (Sikkink, 1998b).

An analysis of the types of religious identities associated with alternative schooling offers a more nuanced picture of the religious motives that drive alternative schooling. An analysis of churchgoing Protestants reveals that the most likely candidates for alternative schooling are those identified with religious traditions that are most likely to be withdrawing into separate religious worlds, the fundamentalists and charismatics. Fundamentalists, who tend to be rooted in strong religious networks, are positively associated with alternative schooling. It appears that the establishment of value communities and some form of closure of social networks would explain fundamentalists movement into alternative schooling. Charismatic skepticism about public institutions is apparent in their support for opting out of public schools. One additional factor explains the charismatic move into alternative schooling: the religious practice of charismatics is strongly countercultural, and charismatic identity is built through juxtaposing the rational expert with the emotional, spiritual authority within charismatic circles (Sikkink, 1998b). The religious groups that are moving into alternative schooling, however, do not provide support for claims that the meaning of alternative schooling is to gain greater control over society through control of the socialization of children (Rose, 1993). Many of the misunderstandings of the alternative school movement result from inattention to the differences between conservative Protestant religious traditions. Over the long run, the fundamentalists and charismatics are not likely to have a sustained interest in political power. And evangelicals, enveloped in a religious movement most interested in a public role for religion (Regnerus & Smith, 1998), are deeply divided on schooling choices for children. According to the 1996 Religious Identity and Influence Survey, evangelical religious identity is not significantly related to the choice of nonpublic schooling for children, as evangelicals favor a public school strategy that is consistent with their tradition of "engaged orthodoxy," or a "witness" through presence in public schools (Sikkink, 2003).

RELIGIOUS SCHOOLS

The growth of the conservative Protestant schools in the 1970s and 1980s contributed to the rise of the Christian Right in U.S. politics (see Guth, Liebman, & Wuthnow, 1983). Cultural conflict involving religion and education has played a major role in the expansion of conservative religious primary and secondary schools in the United States in the 1970s and 1980s. The growth of conservative Christian schools coincided with the racial integration of public schools, leading many to claim that "segregationist academies" predominated in the early years of conservative Christian schooling (Nevin & Bills, 1976). No doubt racial integration in public schools played a large role in spawning many Christian schools in the past. But the larger issue for most of today's Christian schools is the cultural shifts of the 1960s and 1970s, which were symbolized so vividly for conservative Christians in the Supreme Court decisions banning school prayer and Bible reading in the public schools. In general, what has come to be known as the "Christian school" movement[1] of the 1970s and 1980s responded to the events and trends of the turbulent 1960s: the consolidation of a secular science curriculum after the Soviet Union raced ahead in space exploration, the counterculture and urban riots, and Supreme Court decisions on school prayer and Bible reading in public schools. These changes contributed to the sense that the traditional family that conservative Protestants had championed in the 1950s and 1960s was under siege (Bendroth, 1999).

In this context, Conservative Protestant religious organizations were well positioned—both in organizational and ideological strength—to respond with a bricks-and-mortar campaign. The new breed of Christian schools grew from roughly 2,500 in 1972 to about 9,000 today, and now comprise about 25% of all private schools in the United States. The most recent available data from the National Center of Education Statistics is the Private School Survey for the 1999–2000 school year. This survey attempts to capture the population of private schools in the United States. Private school enrollment is estimated at 5.1 million, which is about 10% of total school enrollment in the United States. About half of the private school students attend a Catholic school, whereas 36% attend some other type of religious school, and 16% attend a nonreligious private school. Of the approximately 27,000 private schools in the United States, many of the non-Catholic religious schools in existence in the fall of 1993 were founded between 1974 and (1983). About 60% of conservative Christian schools existing in 1993 were founded between 1974 and (1983). In contrast, only 2% of Catholic schools were founded between 1974 and 1983 (Bianchi, 1982; McLaughlin & Broughman, 1997).

The Christian school landscape reflects some of the differences between fundamentalists, evangelicals, charismatics, and Pentecostals. And, in a few cases, the diversity of Christian schools springs from denominations. The Lutheran Church–Missouri Synod (LCMS), a conservative branch of the Lutheran church, has a tradition of Christian schools that reaches back to the 19th century. Schools affiliated with the LCMS, which, for a single denomination, boasts the largest number of schools (over 1,000) outside of the Catholic Church, have their origins in the German ethnic communities in the Midwest. Another important denominational source of Christian school organizations—especially considering the small size of the denomination—is the Christian Reformed denomination, which traces its theological heritage not to Luther but to John Calvin. Largely based in Michigan and Iowa, Christian Reformed churches developed schools in keeping with their Dutch ethnic heritage and their religiously grounded belief that education is inherently value-laden, and therefore Christians must attempt to integrate a Christian perspective on knowledge into education (Sikkink 2001).

How Conservative Religious Schools Work

One of the most widely cited works on Christian schools by Alan Peshkin (1986) claims that this fundamentalist school fits the model of "total institution" (Goffman, 1961). The school is founded and structured on the absolutist claim to ultimate truth, and places rigid control on student's lives. Although lauding the discipline and caring relationships he found between students and teachers, Peshkin expressed concern about the tension between the school culture and practices and broader values of a liberal democracy. Peshkin's ethnography is compelling, but questions remain about whether his findings can be generalized to most conservative Protestant schools. Nancy Ammerman (1987) investigates a Baptist school, finding that religious influence permeates the school through very strict rules, including clothing and grooming restrictions, and student expectations for positive attitudes and courteous and respectful behavior toward authority. Ammerman concludes that the students have little opportunity to try on different roles and identities during their adolescent years. Unlike Peshkin, Ammerman is clear that the fundamentalist school that she studied would not be representative of all conservative Protestant schools.

But other studies show marked differences between evangelical and fundamentalist schools. Susan Rose (Rose, 1988) found that the pedagogy of fundamentalist schools often leaves little room for teacher-student interaction and the exploration of ideas. By contrast, evangelicals tend to shape Christian schools toward less tension with the outside world, greater emphasis on academic excellence, less rigid social control of students and greater room for individual creativity and expression (Sikkink, 2001). Some have seen these differences as at least partially rooted in class (Rose, 1988).

The most important qualitative book on conservative Protestant schools adds nuance to interpretations of conservative religious schools that overemphasize class and social control. Melinda Bollnar Wagner (Wagner, 1990) frames conservative Protestant schools not as "total institutions" but as sites that meld dominant streams of American culture with elements from their conservative Protestant worldview. Wagner points out that many conservative Protestant schoolteachers rely heavily on secular pedagogical techniques and materials, and students are hardly oblivious or dismissive of "worldly" teenage lifestyles. Wagner concludes that these compromises are all part of a long process of adaptation that, in the face of market pressures to maintain adequate enrollments, ensures the continued existence of these schools. Even further, Wagner argues that conservative Protestant schools generate a "generic" panconservative Christianity that tends to ignore historic doctrinal differences within conservative Protestantism (Wagner, 1997). Under the influence of market pressures, conservative Protestant schools tend to broaden their theological umbrella in order to appeal to religious conservatives within several religious traditions, including Catholicism.

Religious Schools, Network Closure, and Educational Achievement

Although many of the studies of religion and education in the United States fit within the framework of cultural conflict, a surprising source of interest in religion and education emerged from developments in sociology of education toward understanding the corre-lates of effective schools. The first national study of school effectiveness (Coleman, 1966) generated a great deal of research on religion and education at the organizational level. In particular, interest in school effectiveness turned the literature toward the question of whether and how religious schools shape educational outcomes. Commonly referred to as the "Coleman Report," this study concludes that family background characteristics con-tribute far more to academic outcomes than characteristics of schools. That these studies focused on public and private school differences ensured that religion at the school level would be one point of contention, as well over half of private schools are religious schools (Baker, Han, & Broughman, 1996).

The work of Andrew Greeley, James Coleman, and colleagues on the 1980 High School and Beyond dataset argued that, on average and after controlling for family background, Catholic schools are more academically effective than public schools. And Catholic schools have a larger effect for those who are more disadvantaged (dubbed the "common school" effect). In Catholic schools, academic achievement does not depend as strongly on family background characteristics as it does in the public sector. But the sources of the Catholic school advantage are not easily located in religion. This research claims that Catholic schools produce higher-achieving students because they place more students in academic programs, require more semesters of academic coursework, and assign more homework. Catholic schools are far less "vocational" and far more "academic" in orientation (Coleman, Hoffer, & Kilgore 1981a, 1982a, 1982b; Coleman, Kilgore, & Hoffer, 1982; Greeley, 1982).

Does religion play a role here? Most research has pointed to more general charac-teristics of religious schools. Greeley focused on black and Hispanic students' academic achievement, showing that higher academic and disciplinary emphasis of Catholic schools contributes to the Catholic school effect. The Catholic school advantage was attributed to higher levels of discipline and academic demands. But public schools that have similar levels of discipline and academic demands as Catholic schools produce similar levels of achievement.

Other research argues that religion plays an important role in academic effectiveness. A study of inner-city private and primarily Catholic elementary schools found that the effec-tiveness of these schools derived from the strong leadership, shared values of teachers and staff, orderly and disciplined environment, and a clear school mission (Cibulka, O'Brien, & Zewe, 1982). At the organizational level, according to this research, religion shapes school effectiveness through shared values and mission, and social order.

Coleman and Hoffer (1987) offer a more complete theoretical model of the Catholic school effect. Catholic schools, according to this model, benefit from the more cohesive community that they serve. Catholic schools offer nonmonetary resources in the form of social capital that the public schools do not. Parents of Catholic school students are more likely to know one another, which is likely to create intergenerational closure and facilitate information exchange and social control. Therefore, students with low human capital (minority and other disadvantaged students) benefit from the higher social capital of the community that is served by Catholic schools. In this work, the effect of religion on school effectiveness is primarily through its effect on social capital.

The role of religion in explaining the Catholic school effect is most prominent in the seminal work by Anthony Bryk and colleagues (Bryk, Lee, & Holland, 1993). This work argued that the organizational makeup of Catholic schools engenders a "common school" ideal. Catholic schools create a communal organization, which is built on a high degree of shared values among teachers and students as well as shared activities. Religion provides an inspirational ideology that animates the school mission and common symbols and assumptions that bind the school community. Religious commitments of school personnel also infuse relationships in the schools with an ethic of caring. The authors explain much of the Catholic school effect as the result of the influence of religion on academic organization and communal organization. For academic organization, they find that the number of academic courses required for all students and the breadth of curricular offered impacts differential student learning opportunities. The constrained academic structure of Catholic schools minimizes initial student differences, whereas the comprehensive and highly differentiated public schools accentuate them. The commitment to a common curriculum, according to Bryk and colleagues, is rooted in religious conceptions of persons as created in the image of God.

The work on Catholic schools inspired by Coleman and Greeley was not without its critics. The positive effect of religion in Catholic schools has been challenged—at least in the assumed positive effect of religion that is mediated through social capital. Morgan and Sorensen (1999) addressed the extent that the Catholic school effect is explained by variation in intergenerational network closure. Coleman held that Catholic schools were endowed with nonmonetary resources in the form of social capital. One of the primary resources of this social capital was intergenerational social closure, which putatively explained the slight academic advantage of Catholic schools. Morgan and Sorensen distinguish between Coleman's "norm-enforcing" school and what they call a "horizon-expanding" school, which is characterized by tight bonds between students and teachers, but not between parents and school. This network structure, according to Morgan and Sorenson, contrasts with a norm-reinforcing school, with its high levels of intergenerational closure, in that horizon expanding social capital does not constrain creativity and learning by the limited information and norms available in the family. Morgan and Sorenson find that intergenerational closure is *negatively* associated with mathematics test scores in the public sector, which provides evidence that horizon expanding schools are best for student learning. The authors conclude, then, that the Catholic school effect cannot be explained by parental social closure. The implication is that in many religious schools the norm-reinforcing character of social bonds hinders academic success of students. If correct, religion is likely to hinder academic success in some private schools because it does not allow students to bridge beyond their religious enclave, in which norms and limited information hinder the educational task.

Important work on immigrants also points away from intergenerational closure but toward the importance of religious organizations for educational achievement. Bankston and Zhou (2002) argue that family network closure does not explain variation in school achievement of children in immigrant families. But participation in immigrant religious institutions does improve school performance of children. Using data from the National Longitudinal Study of Adolescent Health, they find that the average grades of immigrant children are not affected by parental involvement in social networks. Bankston and Zhou argue that participation in an ethnic church helps immigrants recover some of the social capital lost by migration (see also Bankston & Zhou, 1995; Bankston & Zhou, 1996). These results appear to be consistent with the Morgan and Sorenson argument that family social capital can be norm-reinforcing, and may hinder educational success. However, in the case of immigrant students, participation in religious organizations, which Morgan and Sorenson may see as sources of norm-reinforcing social capital, actually improves educational achievement.

In sum, the literature on school effectiveness has led to the claim that religion at the school level may have some impact on the nature of relationships in the school, and has provided stronger evidence that religion provides a moral order and common mission that affects educational outcomes. Religion also shapes social networks within the school, but the evidence does not confirm whether the overall effect is positive or negative on educational outcomes.

Religious Schools and Deviance

Although the effects of religious schools on educational achievement are mixed, one would expect that the social capital and normative environment of religious schools would affect student deviance. Existing studies use careful controls to deal with possible selection effects, and often use the more conservative strategy of determining whether religious schools affect *change* in deviance over time. Although these studies are conservative tests, it is still surprising that the results are mixed at best. One study, using the National Education Longitudinal Survey (NELS), found that attending private religious school decreases the likelihood of involvement in sexual activity, arrests, and the use of hard drugs, but does not affect alcohol, tobacco, or marijuana use. The positive effects are particularly strong for students in suburban, two-parent households (Figlio & Ludwig, 1999; see also Sander, 2001). Other work on Add Health data, however, did not find that the protective effect of religious schools applies to Catholic schools. After including a rich set of controls, including risk aversion of the student and parental supervision, Catholic schools do not affect selling drugs, committing theft, robbery and burglary, having sex, engaging in gang-related fights, attempting suicide, and running away from home (Mocan, Scafidi, & Tekin, 2002). The effect of religious schools on deviance appears to be limited to non-Catholic religious schools, and to more extreme forms of teenage deviance. Another recent study found no protective effect of private schools on the incidence of teenage suicide (Watt, 2003), but it should be pointed out that selection effects, the bane of school sector studies, may operate in reverse in this case. Because suicide is relatively rare, the lack of a positive effect of private school could be affected by a small number of parents who move their troubled child to private schools in hopes that a school change would help. Nor does this study evaluate religious schools separately from other private schools.

Religious Schools and Democratic Citizenship

Recent research on private schools has revived old questions about the relationship between private education and the public good. Much of the debate on school vouchers has used the assumption that private schools—specifically fundamentalist and evangelical private schools—are not fit to educate children for participation in a democratic society (Blacker, 1998). Generally this research shows important contributions of religious schools to democratic education, but there are some mixed results for conservative Protestant schools.

For example, Godwin, Ausbrooks, and Martinez (2001) use a sample of 2,184 students from 7 public and 24 private schools in New York City and Fort Worth, Texas. They find that students enrolled in evangelical schools are far more likely to identify groups that are vying for political equality as their least-liked groups as compared with public school students. In addition, evangelical school students are far less likely to choose racist groups as their least-liked group compared to public school students. However, once controls are added for selection into school sectors, the family effects were able to account for these differences in tolerance. The findings show that *non*evangelical private school students have greater support for democratic norms than public school students, that there is no difference between private and public schoolers on levels of political tolerance, and that there is no difference between public and private schoolers on perceived threat from their least-liked group. Private school students also report a higher incidence of interethnic friendship than public schoolers. In sum, this research found no evidence that evangelical schooling necessarily leads to decreased levels of tolerance. Concerns about democratic skills generated by religious schools receive mixed support in other research. Non-Catholic religious schools (primarily conservative Protestant schools) score higher in civic confidence but lower in political tolerance (Campbell, 2001). On the other three measures, community service, civic skills, and political knowledge, non-Catholic religious schools are no different than students in public school.

As early as the 1960s, Greeley and Rossi (1966) found some evidence that Catholic school students were no worse than public school students on measures of community involvement, interaction with non-Catholics, concerns about "worldly problems," and attitudes toward other non-Catholic groups, such as Jews, blacks, and Protestants. The strongest association between Catholic education and socially tolerant attitudes was found with those respondents that attended a Catholic college. These students are more "liberal" than Catholics who did not attend Catholic college, and they are more "liberal" than college-educated Protestants (Greeley & Rossi, 1966). Wolf, Greene, Kleitz, and Thalhammer (2001) use a sample of college students in introductory courses on American government to examine political tolerance. They conclude that private school students (both religious and secular) score higher on their measures of political tolerance. The effect is even greater for those that spent most or all of their previous education in private schools.

Recent data from NELS has been used by Greene (1998) to argue that private schools are better racially integrated within the classroom, have more racially tolerant attitudes, and encourage more volunteering. Private schools are more likely to promote friendship across racial and ethnic lines and less likely to have fighting in the school among racial or ethnic groups. However, Gill et al. (2001) warn that Greene's controls may not be sufficient to counter selection into the private sector, nor does he adjust for unobserved prior differences in values and attitudes. Campbell (2001) provides a better set of controls that perhaps overcomes the selection problem. His results indicated that students in Catholic schools do better in all five domains he tests: community service, civic skills, civic confidence, political knowledge, and political tolerance. Overall, the extant literature on Catholic schools confirms Bryk's (1994) claims that this religious school sector makes an important contribution to the common good. Other analyses on the 1996 National Household Education Survey show that parent civic participation is enhanced through involvement in Catholic schools, but not through active participation in non-Catholic religious schools (Sikkink, 2003).

RELIGION AND EDUCATIONAL ACHIEVEMENT

How does religion at the individual level affect educational success? Historically, religion has provided a crucial impetus to educational endeavors (Meyer et al., 1979). Yet an important article on religion and education in *American Sociological Review* places John Calvin in the anti-intellectualist camp (Darnell & Sherkat, 1997),[2] which would have surprised Calvin's contemporaries. The important emphasis on integrating religion and educational pursuits—and the obligation to pursue excellence in education—remains in Calvinist movements today, such as the Christian Reformed denomination. Similarly, post Vatican II Catholicism provides a religious impetus for educational pursuits.

There have been religious movements that discouraged education as a worldly pursuit. The Amish provide the most well-known example today. And the fundamentalist movement in 20th-century U.S. Protestantism certainly was suspicious of "modern" learning, such as evolution and higher criticism of the Bible (Marsden, 1980). Some have claimed that fundamentalists are an important carrier of persistent cultural trends toward anti-intellectualism (Hofstadter, 1963). But even here it is difficult to sort out the extent that the fundamentalist emphasis was because of opposition to education per se or to the content of an increasingly secular education and the differentiation of religion from educational institutions. The effort that fundamentalist religious groups put into building religious colleges (Carpenter, 1997; Marsden, 1987) should not only be seen as an attempt to shield their children from the world but also as a partial acknowledgment of the value of education.

Other important movements within conservative Protestantism today may place a damper on educational aspirations and achievement. The Pentecostal and to some extent the charismatic movement emphasis on religious experience embeds an anti-intellectual bent that may lead to less emphasis on education (Wacker, 2001). But one of the dominant players in the conservative Protestant camp, the evangelical movement that emerged in the 1940s, has been largely supportive of the importance of education.

Do empirical studies show any effect of religion on individual educational achievement? We do not have an overabundance of studies in this area, but there are important exceptions. Lenski (1961) pioneered work on religion and educational outcomes, showing that Catholics do poorly on educational outcomes. Lenski attributed this difference to Roman Catholic authoritarianism and anti-intellectualism, whereas Protestants were educationally advantaged by a religious emphasis on individualism. The post–Vatican II era, according to most research, has erased the Protestant-Catholic educational gap. Mueller (1980) uses birth cohort data from the General Social Survey (GSS) (1973–1978) to analyze the relationship between religious background and educational attainment. He finds no clear advantage for Protestants or Catholics over time, and notes that the net influence of religious background on educational attainment has never been very large.

The world of Protestant-Catholic-Jew (Herberg, 1960) has largely disappeared, but more careful measurement of religious differences have found that religion matters for educational success. Darnell and Sherkat (1997) use the Youth Parent Socialization Panel Study (1965–1982) to investigate the effect of religion on educational outcomes. They find that youth who affiliated with conservative Protestant denominations and youth who held the view that the Bible is without errors had lower educational aspirations. These religious conservative groups also were less likely to take college prep courses in high school. Having parents who believed that the Bible was without errors also predicted less enthusiasm for taking college prep courses in high school. Darnell and Sherkat attribute these findings to the fact that, in contrast to most Americans, conservative Protestants are likely to view the good life in terms that discount education relative to higher religious callings. Sherkat and Darnell (1999), using the same data, find that parents with conservative views of the Bible are more supportive of their sons' educational advancement but have a greater negative impact on a daughter's likelihood of taking college prep courses when the daughter disagrees with the parents' conservative religious beliefs.

Lehrer (1999) looks at the influence of religious identity—again measured by denominational affiliation—on years of schooling using the 1987–1988 National Survey of

Families and Households. When family background is held constant, religious differences are still evident. Jews have the highest educational attainment and conservative Protestants have the lowest. Catholics and mainline Protestants are in the middle and appear to be very similar. However, other analyses of the National Survey of Families and Households showed some lingering negative effects of being raised in a Catholic family (Sikkink & Fischer, 2004). According to Lehrer, the importance of human capital investment to Jewish families explains their higher levels of educational achievement, whereas the fundamentalist suspicion of the critical search for knowledge implied in the scientific method and the high cost and limited supply of acceptable religious educational institutions explains the lower levels of educational attainment within this group.

We note that these studies of educational attainment often lack accurate measures of conservative Protestants. Reliance on literal views of the Bible as the indicator of conservative Protestants tends to capture the more fundamentalist, Pentecostal, and less educated adherents of conservative Protestantism, which may account for some of the religion and educational achievement findings. Beyerlein (2004) shows how results can differ depending on how conservative Protestants are measured. Using data from the 2000 GSS, he finds that self-identified evangelicals and fundamentalists do not differ from average Americans in emphasizing the importance of going to college. The source of lower educational aspirations among adult conservative Protestants, according to Beyerlein, is limited to Pentecostals.[3] The discrepant findings point to the importance of avoiding the use of views of the Bible as the sole measure of religious difference in studies of educational aspirations and achievement.

Several other studies have discounted the effect of religious tradition on educational outcomes and focused on the general effect of religious participation. In an important study, Muller and Ellison (2001) use the second and third wave of the National Educational Longitudinal Survey (NELS) to assess religious involvement and access to social capital within families; and the association of religious involvement and academic progress, including locus of control, educational expectations, effort, opportunities and demands, and rewards. They then attempt to answer the question of whether the connection between religious involvement and academic progress is due to access to social capital. They find that religious participation is associated with higher levels of social capital in the family and community. Religious students report greater educational expectations from parents, more parent-child interaction, greater intergenerational closure, and stronger relations with academically oriented peers. They also find that religious involvement enhances academic effort and reward, and is slightly positively associated with self-concept and educational expectations. The effect of religious involvement on educational outcomes is largely but not entirely explained by family and community social capital. And the religion effect appears to be greatest for the most able students and for those most at risk for failing.

Why would religious involvement have these positive effects? Muller and Ellison suggest several possible explanations: First, religious involvement exposes adolescents to nonrelated adults who act as role models and provide guidance for the teenager. Second, the religiously active are more likely to take to heart messages from the religious community about respect for authority, and the importance of good character and virtue. Third, time spent in religious institutions may simply crowd out time that could be spent in less productive pursuits that hinder a focus on education, such as drug use and other teenager deviance. Jordan and Nettles (2000) find some support for this argument using two waves of the NELS data. They find that for 12th graders spending time in religious activities results in modest increases in school engagement, academic achievement, and perception of life chances, net of control variables. The authors argue that religious involvement provides structured out-of-school activity that mitigates the extent of "unstructured" activity, such as hanging out with friends, which does little for educational achievement.

Loury (2004) confirms the importance of religious involvement for educational attainment by using data from the National Longitudinal Study of Youth. Loury claims that past efforts at studying this link have been hindered by a large possibility of omitted-variable bias when models fail to take into account important family, community, and individual characteristics. Loury's study corrects for these problems by including the number of older siblings who attended college and the number who dropped out of high school (this controls for unobservables that are common among siblings). The study also controls for ability test scores and student educational aspirations to account for unobservable individual characteristics. It finds that church attendance significantly increases the years of schooling completed. Attending church weekly compared to not attending at all improves educational attainment by least 3 years of schooling.

Regnerus (2000) uses the High School Effectiveness Study with matched Common Core of Data and Census information to estimate the effect of religious involvement on academic achievement and attainment. He hypothesizes that religious socialization involves building relationships and routinizing practices that contribute to educational outcomes regardless of religious affiliation. He finds a modest positive relationship between religious involvement and academic outcomes, even after controlling for extracurricular activities and intact two-parent families.

The literature on religion and success in college is more limited. With a limited sample from one Northeastern university, Zern (1989) found that past or present religiosity was unrelated to GPA in college. However, those students who were more religious than the atmosphere in which they grew up had significantly higher GPAs.

Keysar and Kosmin (1995) addressed the question of gender, religion, and educational attainment through an analysis of the CUNY Graduate Center's National Survey of Religious Identification. After placing respondents on a continuum from religious conservative to liberal, they find that among younger women (aged 18–24), religious traditionalism was more strongly associated with getting married younger and having children, which indirectly reduces educational attainment. Among older women (aged 25–44), they found a stronger direct effect of religious traditionalism on educational attainment. They explain this finding by suggesting that religious identification for older women is more likely to reflect actual religious beliefs, whereas it may reflect more religious background and household of origin for younger women.

In sum, there is evidence that conservative Protestants have lower levels of educational attainment, whereas children from Jewish families tend to attain higher levels of education. Studies of educational attainment, family size, and religion illuminate the mechanisms through which religious tradition affects educational achievement. Research on family size suggests that the number of siblings in a family is negatively related to educational performance because parental resources are finite. Each additional child in a family dilutes the quantity of parental resources any one child receives (Downey, 1995; Downey & Neubauer, 2001; Steelman et al., 2002). In particular, parent's time, money, and energy are diluted as family size increases (Powell & Steelman, 1993; Teachman, 1987). A handful of studies find that religious traditions may affect the relationship between family size and educational attainment. Religious communities, as found in Mormonism, for example, appear to moderate the effect of sibship size on educational attainment of children (Downey & Neubauer, 2001; Shavit & Pierce, 1991). Another study, using the National Survey of Families and

Households, shows that conservative Protestant families tend to lessen the negative impact of number of siblings on educational attainment, whereas family size is even more detrimental for educational attainment in Jewish families (Sikkink & Fischer, 2004). This study also showed that the negative relationship between Catholic upbringing and educational attainment is entirely explained by the larger size of Catholic families.

One explanation for these findings focuses on social capital differences across religious groups. Although evangelical Protestant groups emphasis bonding social capital, and tight networks that generate a strong sense of collective identity, mainline, Catholic, and Jewish congregation social organization are much more likely to build bridging social capital (Putnam, 2000; Wuthnow, 1999), which is less tightly bound internally and connects participants to those outside the group. Some have argued that this strong bonding social capital is effectively norm-reinforcing, reducing educational achievement for those in religious schools (Morgan & Sorensen, 1999). But the strong bonding social capital of conservative religious groups helps to overcome the dilution of parent time and energy that negatively affects educational attainment. Although strong ties in conservative religious communities may be detrimental for civic participation and other social goods (Fiorina, 1999; Wuthnow, 1999), this social organization is helpful when it comes to providing the resources for children from large families to achieve high levels of education. Conservative Protestant organizations create for youth significant and trusted connections to adults outside the family. In particular, these conservative religious organizations are likely to embed youth in activities such as Sunday School and youth group that provide connections to adults and normative guidance for youth (Smith, 2003a). Conservative religious youth groups may provide additional social capital that provides support for youth.

Another mechanism through which religion may alter the effect of family size on education is the relative emphasis placed on family and children within different religious traditions. Religious groups that foster and promote close family relationships may lessen the negative effects of sibship size. Theologically conservative parents tend to use more positive emotional work when relating with children (Wilcox, 1998), and conservative Protestant fathers are more committed to and involved in their families (Wilcox, 2004). The emphasis on family within this religious tradition may extend to heightened concern for spending time with each child. Parental involvement in families, in turn, is important for educational success.

HOW EDUCATION SHAPES RELIGION

In much of the education and religion literature, the focus is on the influence of religion on education. But important research also has reversed the causal direction, pointing to the important role that education plays in shaping religion. Robert Wuthnow (1988) has pointed out the central importance of rising levels of education for dividing the religious field into liberal and conservative camps. Through the 1960s and 1970s, rising education levels led to differentiation within denominations over religious issues, such as the view of the Bible and Jesus Christ.

At the individual level, education has long been thought to influence religious commitment and belief. The differentiation of denominations and institutions of higher education was expressed in the level of religiosity of faculty. As early as 1916, Leuba showed that professors and scientists were less religious than the public. A large national study of faculty in 1969 showed that 20% of academics reported no religious ties whatsoever, whereas only

4% of other Americans were had no ties to religion (Steinberg and Carnegie Commission on Higher Education 1974). Using the 1969 Carnegie-Ace faculty survey, Stark and Finke (2000) point out the general irreligiousness of the social sciences compared to the natural sciences. Wuthnow (1989) provides a macro-cultural explanation for this variation. The less "codified" disciplines, such as the social sciences and humanities, have a weaker claim to the status of being a well developed science. To make up for this perceived cultural status deficit, these disciplines erect external boundaries with the (primarily religious) public in order to maintain the plausibility of their scientific orientations (Wuthnow, 1989, p. 153). This boundary maintenance in response to the position of the discipline in the scientific field results in corresponding lifestyles, values, and attitudes of the faculty, which are decidedly secular. Thus, the conflict of religion and science in this framework is less rooted in irreconcilable epistemological differences than in the cultural necessity for disciplines to struggle for legitimacy in the scientific field.

Similar studies have focused on graduate students. In 1963, Rodney Stark. used one of the earliest NORC surveys of arts and science graduate students and found that graduate students as a whole are much less religious than the general population. Stark tentatively argued that this finding was because of selection effects, but Greeley (1963) suggests that educational experiences tend to lead to lower levels of religiosity. The 1958 NORC study also shows that religious apostasy (being raised in a religious tradition but no longer identifying with it) among college students was higher for those who attended elite colleges. Zelan (1968) argued that elite college students are socialized more completely into an identity that serves as a functional alternative to religion. In Greeley's study, Catholic students are more successful than other religious groups in maintaining their religiosity regardless of higher education, whereas the experience of education has the greatest secularizing effect on those from Jewish families. This early work suggests, according to Greeley, that there is some value incompatibility between religion and science. Other early studies confirmed Stark's findings, though Campbell and Magill (1968) pointed to important differences depending on the denominational affiliation of Protestants.

The negative effect of experiences in educational institutions on religiosity is far from conclusive. Hunsberger (1978), using a cross-sectional study of 457 students at the University of Manitoba and a 2.5-year longitudinal study of 212 Wilfrid Laurier University students, found little support for the theory that college liberalizes religious views, such as belief in God and Jesus Christ and frequency of prayer, although the extent of church attendance was negatively affected by college attendance. The effect of educational experiences on individual religious commitment and belief may depend on the educational context in surprising ways. Hammond and Hunter (1984), comparing undergraduates at distinctly evangelical universities and colleges to undergraduates at University of California, Santa Barbara, found that evangelicals on secular campuses were able to thrive and strengthen their Christian worldview, whereas evangelicals on insular Christian campuses do not. Those who measured "high" on their evangelicalism index (measured theologically) increased in religiousness from their freshman to senior year in the secular campus while they decreased or stayed the same on the evangelical campuses. The external threat to the plausibility structure of evangelicalism encourages Christians to join evangelical "ghettos," usually through some parachurch organization such as Campus Crusade for Christ or InterVarsity Christian Fellowship. In contrast, evangelicals on Christian college campuses relax their "defensive posture" and take their religious worldviews for granted. The data is cross-sectional, not longitudinal, so conclusions about change over time are tentative at best.

Moreover, methodological questions plague existing research on the effect of education on religion at the individual level. Johnson (1997), for example, suggests that existing regression models, showing a slight negative effect of increased education on maintaining religious beliefs, are inadequate. The regression techniques focus on changes in means, and therefore are not able to reveal whether education erodes religious belief for most people, or if it creates a "fissure" by pushing people to either end of the religious-secular spectrum. Using a categorical method on data from the GSS, he finds that a combination of erosion and polarization makes the most sense of the data.

Other studies show that the education-religiosity relationship is not uniform across time and space. How education affects religion requires careful attention to historical and educational context. Hunter (1987) pointed to the secularizing effect of education on evangelical college students, but this has been countered by more recent evidence (Penning & Smidt, 2002). Moberg and Hoge (1986), studying Catholic students across time, found that between 1961 and 1971 students became much more individualistic concerning religion and morals, doubts increased, and mass attendance dropped drastically (see also Moberg & McEnery, 1976). Between 1971 and 1982 there continued a trend away from traditional sexual morality, but the demand for intellectual autonomy was not as great and there was evidence of a move toward more traditional religious positions, such as regular reception of Communion and membership in Catholic organizations. They suggest that the 1960s provided a shock to Catholics with the combination of Vatican II, Humanae Vitae, and the Kennedy presidency. The 1970s was far quieter and the changes occurring among Catholic students were very similar to the changes occurring among secular students nationwide.

A similar study of undergraduate men at Dartmouth College and the University of Michigan found that major trends in values from the 1950s to the 1970s had reversed themselves by 1984 (Hoge, Hoge, & Wittenberg, 1987). The percent with no religious preference was highest in 1974 and then dropped sharply. The percent expressing belief in a Divine God began to rise in 1979 and (1984). Traditional religion as a whole began increasing in 1979 and strengthened even more in 1984 (see also Hoge, 1974; Hoge, Luna, & Miller, 1981).

Then there is the interesting question of *religious* educational institutions affect on individual religious commitment and orientation. Would educational effects on religiosity also apply to religious schools, which often follow secular cultural models of education (Scott, Meyer, and National Institute of Education [U.S.] 1984)? Most of the work in this area focuses on Catholic schools. In the 1960s, some evidence showed that exclusive attendance at Catholic schools led to moderate positive effects on religious orthodoxy, participation in sacraments, and knowledge of church doctrine. However, these effects seemed to boost those who entered from a fervent Catholic family, and do not affect other students (Greeley & Rossi, 1966). Research after Vatican II seemed to show an increase in the Catholic school effect on religiosity. Although Catholics on average decreased levels of religious practice post–Vatican II, the drop was not nearly as severe among those who had attended Catholic school. "Catholic education [was] second only to religiousness of spouse in predicting religious behavior" (Greeley, McCready, & McCourt, 1976, p. 306). Catholic schooling seemed to affect the level of institutional support of the Catholic Church, especially in shaping positive attitudes toward the clergy (Greeley, McCready, & McCourt, 1976).

More recent findings have been more mixed. One study, which compared those with a Catholic school education to other Catholics, found that Catholic school effects were limited to those with 12 or more years in Catholic education. Catholic school experience increased the likelihood that Catholics hold traditional beliefs and practices, agree with the church on social teachings and sexual ethics, and decreased the likelihood that Catholics supported heterodox ideas, such as the ordination of women. Interestingly, Catholic education seems to result in greater knowledge and awareness of Vatican II, which is related to the likelihood that Catholics take up Vatican II emphases, such as the importance of service to humanity and working toward social justice (Davidson, 1997). Significant years of Catholic education (9–12 years) also has been linked to stronger Catholic identity, belief in life after death, and increased giving to the Church, but is not related to church attendance (Sander, 2001).

Recent findings on post–Vatican II Catholics again show moderate to strong effects on religiosity for those who attend significant years of Catholic education, and are stronger for those who also attended a Catholic college (D'Antonio, 1995). What is particularly interesting in this research are the findings that show evidence of both religious school and general education effects. The findings suggest that those with all Catholic schooling have very high levels of commitment to the church, but nontraditional views on church authority. Although Catholic schoolers have great confidence in church authority, they also are more likely than other Catholics to favor a democratic system within the church with greater authority given to the individual conscience. They were the most likely to stress lay participation in decisions concerning divorce, birth control, and the ordination of women. However, they were less inclined than other young Catholics to give authority to the individual on the abortion issue (D'Antonio, 1996). Rather than the "total institutions" of Peshkin's fundamentalist school, the Catholic schools seem to have moderate liberalizing effects on young Catholics, while committing Catholic school students to the reforms of Vatican II (Ebaugh, 1991).

RELIGION AND EDUCATION IN THE EARLY 21ST CENTURY

It would be surprising if cultural conflict linked to religion does not continue to be expressed in political struggle over public educational institutions. The increasing diversity and extent of school choice will ensure that religion plays a large role in the politics of education. But this does not ensure a movement toward full school vouchers. Besides disagreement within conservative Protestantism and opposition from mainline Protestantism, voucher support among conservative Catholics and evangelical Protestants is often used effectively to cast doubt on the motives of voucher supporters. But there also is evidence that the social conditions that gave legitimacy to the civic purposes of public schools are giving way to notions of education as a private choice. The strength of the cultural frames of individualism and autonomous, private choice, particularly in a consumer capitalist society, are likely to play a much larger role in creating an increasingly strong public voice in support of school vouchers. How mainline Protestantism will respond to this shift provides an important topic for research in the politics of education.

Understanding the direction of religion and the politics of education depends on an account of religious differences within conservative Protestantism. The balance of power in the religious field between the pentecostal, charismatic, and evangelical movements will have some impact on conflicts over public schools and the relationship of religion and public institutions. Although the pentecostal and charismatic movements are growing rapidly, the evangelical movement seems the dominant player in the conservative religious field. It is clear that religious conservatives are deeply divided on schooling issues; it is less clear how that division will affect schooling issues in the future. The strength of pentecostal and charismatic support for alternative schooling, which contrasts with evangelicals support for public schooling, is an important part of this division within the Protestant house. But note that the alternative schooling movement within evangelicalism itself is much younger than the traditional evangelical position of engagement as individuals in "secular" public institutions as "witnesses" to the world. The evangelical tradition of a custodial relation to public institutions—a tradition that lends legitimacy to many of the cultural and structural divides between "sacred" and "secular" within public schools (Sikkink & Smith, 2000)—faces the challenge that the alternative schooling movement, although small, is gaining more legitimacy among evangelicals. Combined with challenges from the charismatic movement, older expectations about the relationship of evangelical religion and public schooling may give way.

A dynamic area of research that is now being charted in education and religion involves central issues of sociology of education. Better measures of religion in existing longitudinal datasets will allow more careful understanding of the mechanisms through which religion shapes educational aspirations and achievement at the individual level. Several mechanisms have been suggested, such as adult role models, discipline, time substitution, and religious traditions, but the evidence is not conclusive. In particular, closer attention to the concept of social capital, and its relation to religion and educational success are necessary to understand the relation of religion and educational success.

Secularization through the effect of experiences in educational institutions seems less likely. Conservative religious groups are more experienced and organized in their quest to keep their children in the fold (Smith & Sikkink, 2003), and Catholic and mainline institutions are in some cases reasserting religious distinction. It appears that secularization at the organizational level will compete with sacralization. Still, much remains to be done to understand how religion and education interact within individuals and organizations. Longitudinal studies at the individual level are necessary to understand the effect of education on religion in an age when scientific certainty is less compelling and parachurch organizations within the universities are more mature.

NOTES

1. Forty years ago, mainline Methodist and Episcopal schools, and perhaps even Catholic schools, would be numbered among the country's "Christian schools." The dramatic growth in the 1970s of schools within conservative Protestant religious movements (which emphasized individual salvation through a personal relationship with Jesus Christ, the authority of the Bible, missionary outreach, and close ties between individual faith and everyday life) led to a narrower definition: a "Christian school" is one that is affiliated with Conservative Protestant denominations, such as the Southern Baptist and Lutheran Church–Missouri Synod, and, in general, with the dominant streams within Conservative Protestantism in the second half of the 20th century, the evangelical, charismatic, fundamentalist, and pentecostal religious movements.
2. According to personal communication with Darren Sherkat, this was the result of an editorial decision.
3. Beylerlein also shows that his findings match Darnell and Sherkat (1997) when he replicates their less precise measuring scheme.

REFERENCES

Ammerman, N. T. (1987). *Bible believers: Fundamentalists in the modern world*. New Brunswick, NJ: Rutgers University Press.

Anderson, R. M. (1979). *Vision of the disinherited: The making of American Pentecostalism*. New York: Oxford University Press.

Apple, M. W. (1996). *Cultural politics and education.* New York: Teachers College Press.

Apple, M. W. (2000). Away with all teachers: The cultural politics of home schooling. *International Studies in Sociology of Education, 10*(1), 61–80.

Apple, M. W. (2001). Bringing the world to God: Education and the politics of authoritarian religious populism. *Discourse, 22*(2), 149–172.

Apple, M., & Oliver, A. (1996). Becoming right: Education and the formation of conservative movements. In M. Apple (Ed.), *Cultural politics and education* (pp. 42–67). New York: Teachers College Press.

Arons, S. (1983). *Compelling belief: The culture of American schooling.* New York: McGraw-Hill.

Baker, D., Han, M., & Broughman, S. (1996). How different, how similar? Comparing key organizational qualities of American public and private secondary schools. *NCES 96–322* (i–88). Washington, DC: U.S. Department of Education.

Bankston, C. L., & Zhou, M. (1995). Religious participation, ethnic identification, and adaptation of Vietnamese adolescents in an immigrant community. *The Sociological Quarterly, 36*(3), 523–534.

Bankston, C. L., & Zhou, M (1996). The ethnic church, ethnic identification, and the social adjustment of Vietnamese adolescents. *Review of Religious Research, 38*(1), 18–37.

Bankston, C. L., & Zhou, M. (2002). Social capital and immigrant children's achievement. *Research in Sociology of Education, 13*(13–39), –39.

Bates, S. (1993). *Battleground: One mother's crusade, the religious right, and the struggle for control of our classrooms.* New York: Poseidon Press.

Bellah, R. N. (1985). *Habits of the heart: Individualism and commitment in American life.* Berkeley: University of California Press.

Bendroth, M. L. (1999). Fundamentalism and the family: Gender, culture, and the American pro-family movement. *Journal of Women's History, 10*(4), 35–54.

Beyerlein, K. (2003). Educational elites and the movement to secularize public education: The case of the National Education Association. In C. Smith (Ed.), *The secular revolution: Power and conflict in the secularization of America* (pp. 160–196). Berkeley: University of California Press.

Beyerlein, K. (2004). Specifying the impact of conservative protestantism on educational attainment. *Journal for the Scientific Study of Religion, 43.*

Bianchi, S. M. (1982). Private school enrollment: Trends and debates. *Research in Sociology of Education and Socialization, 3*(233–258).

Billings, D. B. (1990). Religion as opposition: A Gramscian analysis. *American Journal of Sociology, 96*(1), 1–31.

Billings, D., & Goldman, R. (1979). Comment on "The Kanawha Textbook Controversy." *Social Forces, 57*(4), 1393–1398.

Blacker, D. (1998). Fanaticism and schooling in the democratic state. *American Journal of Education, 106*(2), 241–272.

Bryk, A. S., Lee, V. E., & Holland, P. B. (1993). *Catholic schools and the common good.* Cambridge, MA: Harvard University Press.

Burtchaell, J. T. (1998). *The dying of the light: The disengagement of colleges and universities from their Christian churches.* Grand Rapids, MI: Eerdmans.

Campbell, D. E. (2001). Making democratic education work. In P. E. Peterson & D. E. Campbell (Eds.), *Charters, vouchers, and public education.* Washington, DC: Brookings Institution Press.

Campbell, D., & Magill, D. (1968). Religious involvement and intellectuality among university students. *Sociological Analysis, 29*(2), 79–93.

Carpenter, J. A. (1997). *Revive us again: The reawakening of American Fundamentalism.* New York: Oxford University Press.

Casanova, J. (1994). *Public religions in the modern world.* Chicago: University of Chicago Press.

Cibulka, J. G., O'Brien, T. J., & Zewe, D. (1982). *Inner-city private elementary schools: A study.* Milwaukee, WI: Marquette University Press.

Clelland, D. A., & Page, A. L. (1980). Kanawha County revisited: Reply to Billings and Goldman. *Social Forces, 59*(1), 281–284.

Coleman, J. S. (1966). *Equality of educational opportunity.* Washington, DC: U.S. Dept. of Health, Education, and Welfare, Office of Education.

Coleman, J. S., & Hoffer, T. (1983). Response to Taueber-James, Cain-Goldberger and Morgan. *Sociology of Education, 56,* 219–234.

Coleman, J. S., & Hoffer, T. (1987). *Public and private high schools: The impact of communities.* New York: Basic Books.

Coleman, J. S., Hoffer, T., & Kilgore, S. (1981a). *Public and private schools.* Chicago: National Opinion Research Center.

Coleman, J. S., Hoffer, T., & Kilgore, S. (1981b). High school achievement: Public, catholic, and other private schools compared. *Harvard Educational Review, 51,* 526–545.

Coleman, J. S., Hoffer, T., & Kilgore, S. (1982a). *High school achievement: Public, catholic, and private schools compared.* New York: Basic Books.

Coleman, J. S., Hoffer, T., & Kilgore, S. (1982b). Cognitive outcomes in public and private schools. *Sociology of Education, 55,* 65–76.

Cookson, Peter W. (1994). *School choice: The struggle for the soul of American education.* New Haven, CT: Yale University Press.

D'Antonio, W. V. (1995). *Laity American and Catholic: Transforming the church.* Kansas City, MO: Sheed & Ward.

Darnell, A., & Sherkat, D. E. (1997). The impact of Protestant fundamentalism on educational attainment. *American Sociological Review, 62*(2), 306–315.

Davidson, J. D. (1997). *The search for common ground: What unites and divides Catholic Americans.* Huntington, IN: Our Sunday Visitor Publishing Division.

Davies, S. (1999). From moral duty to cultural rights: A case study of political framing in education. *Sociology of Education, 72*(1), 1–21.

Davis, N. J., & Robinson, R. V. (1996). Are the rumors of war exaggerated? Religious orthodoxy and moral progressivism in America. *American Journal of Sociology 102*(3), 756–787.

Deckman, M. (2002). Holy ABCs! The impact of religion on attitudes about education policies. *Social Science Quarterly, 83*(2), 472–487.

Diamond, S. (1998). *Not by politics alone: The enduring influence of the Christian Right.* New York: Guilford Press.

DiMaggio, P., Evans, J., & Bryson, B. (1996). Have Americans' social attitudes become more polarized? *American Journal of Sociology, 102*(3), 690–755.

Downey, D. B. (1995). When bigger is not better: Family size, parental resources, and children's educational performance. *American Sociological Review, 60*(5), 746–761.

Downey, D. B., & Neubauer, S. (2001). Is resource dilution inevitable? The association between number of siblings and educational outcomes across subgroups.

Ebaugh, H. R. (1991). The revitalization movement in the Catholic Church: The institutional dilemma of power. *Sociological Analysis, 52*(1), 1–12.

Evans, J. H. (1997). Worldviews or social groups as the source of moral value attitudes: Implications for the culture wars thesis. *Sociological Forum, 12*(3), 371–404.

Figlio, D., & Ludwig, J. (1999). Sex, drugs, and Catholic schools: Private schooling and non-market adolescent behaviors. Cambridge, MA: National Bureau of Economic Research.

Fiorina, M. P. (1999). Extreme voices: The dark side of civic engagement. In T. Skocpol & M. P. Fiorina (Eds.), *Civic engagement in American democracy* (pp. 395–426). Washington, DC: Brookings Institution Press.

Gaddy, B. B., Hall, T. W., & Marzano, R. J. (1996). *School wars: Resolving our conflicts over religion and values.* San Francisco: Jossey-Bass Publishers.

Geertz, C. (1998). The William James lecture. *Religion and Values in Public Life, 6*(4), 9–12.

Gieryn, T. F., Bevins, G. M., & Zehr, S. C. (1985). Professionalization of American scientists: Public science in the creation/evolution trials. *American Sociological Review, 50*(3), 392–409.

Gill, B. P. (2001). *Rhetoric versus reality: What we know and what we need to know about vouchers and charter schools.* Santa Monica, CA: Rand Education.

Gleason, P. (1995). *Contending with modernity: Catholic higher education in the twentieth century.* New York: Oxford University Press.

Glenn, C. (1987). Religion, textbooks, and the common school. *Public Interest, 88,* 28–47.

Glenn, C. L. (1988). *The myth of the common school.* Amherst: University of Massachusetts Press.

Godwin, K., Ausbrooks, C., & Martinez, V. (2001). Teaching Tolerance in public and private schools. *Phi Delta Kappan, 82,* 542–546.

Goffman, E. (1961). *Asylums: Essays on the social situation of mental patients and other inmates.* Garden City, NY: Doubleday.

Greeley, A. M. (1982). *Catholic high schools and minority students.* New Brunswick, NJ: Transaction Books.

Greeley, A. M. (1977). *The American Catholic: A social portrait.* New York: Basic Books.

Greeley, A. M. (1963). Comment on Stark's "On the Incompatibility of Religion and Science." *Journal for the Scientific Study of Religion, 3,* 239.

Greeley, A. M., McCready, W. C., & McCourt, K. (1976). *Catholic schools in a declining church.* Kansas City, MO: Sheed and Ward.

Greeley, A. M., & Rossi, P. H. (1966). *The education of Catholic Americans.* Chicago: Aldine Publishing Co.

Greene, J. (1998). Civic values in public and private schools. In P. E. Peterson & B. C. Hassel (Eds.), *Learning from school choice.* Washington, DC: Brookings Institution.

Guth, J. L., Liebman, R. C., & Wuthnow, R. (1983). *The new Christian right: mobilization and legitimation.* Hawthorne, NY: Aldine Publishing Co.

Hammond, P. E., & Hunter, J. D. (1984). On maintaining plausibility: The worldview of evangelical college students. *Journal for the Scientific Study of Religion, 23*(3), 221–238.

Handy, R. T. (1967). *The Protestant quest for a Christian America, 1830–1930.* Philadelphia: Fortress Press.

Hanus, J. J., & Cookson, P. W. (1996). *Choosing schools: Vouchers and American education.* Washington, DC: American University Press.

Herberg, W. (1960). *Protestant, Catholic, Jew: An essay in American religious sociology.* Garden City, NY: Anchor Books.

Hoffmann, J. P., & Miller, A. S. (1997). Social and political attitudes among religious groups: Convergence and divergence over time. *Journal for the Scientific Study of Religion, 36*(1), 52–70.

Hofstadter, R. (1963). *Anti-intellectualism in American life.* New York: Knopf.

Hoge, D. R. (1974). *Commitment on campus: Changes in religion and values over five decades.* Philadelphia: Westminster Press.

Hoge, D. R., Hoge, J. L., & Wittenberg, J. (1987). The return of the fifties: Trends in college students' values between 1952 and 1984. *Sociological Forum, 2*(3), 500–519.

Hoge, D. R., Johnson, B., & Luidens, D. A. (1994). *Vanishing boundaries: The religion of mainline Protestant baby boomers.* Louisville, KY: Westminster/John Knox Press.

Hoge, D. R., Luna, C. L., & Miller, D. K. (1981). Trends in college students' values between 1952 and 1979: A return of the fifties? *Sociology of Education, 54*(4), 263–274.

Hunsberger, B. (1978). The religiosity of college students: Stability and change over years at university. *Journal for the Scientific Study of Religion, 17*(2), 159–164.

Hunter, J. D. (1987). *Evangelicalism: The coming generation.* Chicago: University of Chicago Press.

Hunter, J. D. (1991). *Culture wars: The struggle to define America.* New York: Basic Books.

Hunter, J. D. (2000). *The death of character: Moral education in an age without good or evil.* New York: Basic Books.

Iannaccone, L. R. (1994). Why strict churches are strong. *American Journal of Sociology, 99*(5), 1180–1211.

Jelen, T. G. (1990). Religious belief and attitude constraint. *Journal for the Scientific Study of Religion, 29*(1), 118–125.

Jelen, T. G., & Wilcox, C. (1997). Conscientious objectors in the culture war? A typology of attitudes toward church-state relations. *Sociology of Religion, 58*(3), 277–287.

Johnson, D. C. (1997). Formal education vs. religious belief: Soliciting new evidence with multinomial logit modeling. *Journal for the Scientific Study of Religion, 36*(2), 231–246.

Jordan, W. J., & Nettles, S. (2000). How students invest their time outside of school: Effects on school-related outcomes. *Social Psychology of Education, 3*, 217–243.

Jorgenson, L. P. (1987). *The state and the non-public school, 1825–1925.* Columbia: University of Missouri Press.

Keysar, A., & Kosmin, B. A. (1995). The impact of religious identification on differences in educational attainment among American women in 1990. *Journal for the Scientific Study of Religion, 34*(1), 49–62.

Lehrer, E. L. (1999). Religion as a determinant of educational attainment: An economic perspective. *Social Science Research, 28*(4), 358–379.

Lenski, G. E. (1961). *The religious factor: A sociological study of religion's impact on politics, economics, and family life.* Garden City, NY: Doubleday.

Lines, P. M. (1996). *Homeschooling.* Washington, DC: U.S. Dept. of Education Office of Educational Research and Improvement.

Loury, L. D. (2004). Does church attendance really increase schooling? *Journal for the Scientific Study of Religion, 43*(1), 119–127.

Luckmann, T. (1967). *The invisible religion: The problem of religion in modern society.* New York: Macmillan.

Marsden, G. M. (1980). *Fundamentalism and American culture: The shaping of twentieth century evangelicalism, 1870–1925.* New York: Oxford University Press.

Marsden, G. M. (1987). *Reforming fundamentalism: Fuller Seminary and the new evangelicalism.* Grand Rapids, MI.: W.B. Eerdmans.

Marsden, G. M. (1991). *Understanding fundamentalism and evangelicalism*. Grand Rapids, MI.: W.B. Eerdmans.

Marsden, G. M. (1994). *The soul of the American university: From Protestant establishment to established non-belief*. New York: Oxford University Press.

McCarthy, M. M. (1996). People of faith as political activists in public schools. *Education and Urban Society, 28*(3), 308–326.

McLaughlin, D., & Broughman, S. (1997). Private schools in the United States: A statistical profile, 1993–94. *NCES 97–459* (1–245). Washington, DC: U.S. Department of Education.

Meyer, J. W., Scott, W. R., Strang, D., & Creighton, A. (1994). Bureaucratization without centralization: Changes in the organizational system of U.S. public education, 1940–80. In W. R. Scott, J. W. Meyer, & J. Boli (eds.), *Institutional environments and organizations: Structural complexity and individualism* (pp. 179–206). Thousand Oaks, CA: Sage Publications.

Meyer, J. W., Tyack, D., Nagel, J., & Gordon, A. (1979). Public education as nation-building in America: Enrollments and bureaucratization in the American states, 1870–1930. *American Journal of Sociology, 85*(3), 591–613.

Miller, D. E. (1997). *Reinventing American Protestantism: Christianity in the new millennium*. Berkeley: University of California Press.

Moberg, D. O., & Hoge, D. R. (1986). Catholic college students' religious and moral attitudes, 1961 to 1982: Effects of the sixties and the seventies. *Review of Religious Research, 28*(2), 104–117.

Moberg, D. O., & McEnery, J. N. (1976). Changes in church-related behavior and attitudes of Catholic students, (1961–1971). *Sociological Analysis, 37*(1), 53–62.

Mocan, N., Scafidi, B., & Tekin, E. (2002), Catholic schools and bad behavior. Cambridge, MA: National Bureau of Economic Research.

Moen, M. C. (1984). School prayer and the politics of life-style concern. *Social Science Quarterly, 65*(4), 1065–1071.

Morgan, S. L., & Sorensen, A. B (1999). Parental networks, social closure, and mathematics learning: A test of Coleman's social capital explanation of school effects. *American Sociological Review, 64*(5), 661–681.

Mueller, C. W. (1980). Evidence on the relationship between religion and educational attainment. *Sociology of Education, 53*(3), 140–152.

Muller, C., & Ellison, C. G. (2001). Religious involvement, social capital, and adolescents' academic progress: Evidence from the National Education Longitudinal Study of 1988. *Sociological Focus, 34*(2), 155–183.

Neitz, M. J. (1987). *Charisma and community: A study of religious commitment within the charismatic renewal*. New Brunswick, NJ: Transaction Books.

Nevin, D., & Bills, R. E. (1976). *The schools that fear built: Segregationist academies in the South*. Washington, DC: Acropolis Books.

Nolan, J. L. (1998). *The therapeutic state: Justifying government at century's end*. New York: New York University Press.

Nord, W. A. (1995). *Religion & American education: Rethinking a national dilemma*. Chapel Hill: University of North Carolina Press.

Page, A. L., & Clelland, D. A. (1978). The Kanawha County textbook controversy: A study of the politics of life style concern. *Social Forces, 57*(1), 265–281.

Penning, J. M., & Smidt, C. E. (2002). *Evangelicalism: The next generation*. Grand Rapids, MI: Baker Academic.

Peshkin, A. (1986). *God's choice: The total world of a fundamentalist Christian school*. Chicago: University of Chicago Press.

Powell, B., & Steelman, L. C. (1993). The educational benefits of being spaced out: Sibship density and educational progress. *American Sociological Review, 58*(3), 367–381.

Provenzo, E. F. (1990). *Religious fundamentalism and American education: The battle for the public schools*. Albany: State University of New York Press.

Putnam, R. D. (2000). *Bowling alone: The collapse and revival of American community*. New York: Simon & Schuster.

Ravitch, D. (1974). *The great school wars, New York City, 1805–1973: A history of the public schools as battlefield of social change*. New York: Basic Books.

Reese, W. J. (1982). Public schools and the great gates of Hell. *Educational Theory, 32,* 9–17.

Regnerus, M. D. (2000). Shaping schooling success: Religious socialization and educational outcomes in metropolitan public schools. *Journal for the Scientific Study of Religion, 39*(3), 363–370.

Regnerus, M. D., & Smith, C. (1998). Selective deprivatization among American religious traditions: The reversal of the great reversal. *Social Forces, 76*(4), 1347–1372.

Reuben, J. A. (1996). *The making of the modern university: Intellectual transformation and the marginalization of morality.* Chicago: University of Chicago Press.

Riesebrodt, M. (1993). *Pious passion: The emergence of modern fundamentalism in the United States and Iran.* Berkeley: University of California Press.

Rippa, S. A. (1988). *Education in a free society: An American history.* New York: Longman.

Rose, S. (1993). Fundamentalism and education in the United States. In M. E. Marty & S. Appleby (Eds.), (452–489). Chicago: University of Chicago Press.

Rose, S. D. (1988). *Keeping them out of the hands of Satan: Evangelical schooling in America.* New York: Routledge.

Sander, W. (2001). *Catholic schools: Private and social effects.* Boston: Kluwer Academic Publishers.

Sargeant, K., & West, E. (1996). Teachers and preachers: The battle over public school reform in Gaston County, North Carolina. In J. L. Nolan (ed.), *The American culture wars: current contests and future prospects* (35–60). Charlottesville: University Press of Virginia.

Schmalzbauer, J. A., & Wheeler, C. G. (1996). Between fundamentalism and secularization: Secularizing and sacralizing currents in the evangelical debate on campus lifestyle codes. *Sociology of Religion, 57*(3), 241–257.

Scott, W. R., Meyer, J. W., & U.S. National Institute of Education. (1984). *Environmental linkages and organizational complexity: Public and private schools.* Palo Alto, CA: Dept. of Sociology, Institute for Research on Educational Finance and Governance, Stanford University.

Shavit, Y., & Pierce, J. L. (1991). Sibship size and educational attainment in nuclear and extended families: Arabs and Jews in Israel. *American Sociological Review, 56*(3), 321–330.

Sherkat, D. E., & Darnell, A. (1999). The effect of parents' fundamentalism on children's educational attainment: Examining differences by gender and children's fundamentalism. *Journal for the Scientific Study of Religion, 38*(1), 23–35.

Sikkink, D. (1998a.) "I just say I'm a Christian": Symbolic boundaries and identity formation among church-going Protestants. In D. Jacobsen & W. V. Trollinger (eds.), *Re-forming the center: American Protestantism, 1900 to the present.* Grand Rapids, MI: Eerdmans.

Sikkink, D. (1998b). Public schooling and its discontents: Religious identities, schooling choices for children, and civic participation. Unpublished doctoral dissertation, University of North Carolina, Chapel Hill.

Sikkink, D. (1999). The social sources of alienation from public schools. *Social Forces, 78*(1), 51–86.

Sikkink, D. (2001). Speaking in many tongues: Diversity among Christian schools. *Education Matters, 1*(2), 36–45.

Sikkink, D. (2002). *The religious sources of support for school vouchers.* 2004, at American Educational Research Association.

Sikkink, D. (2003). The loyal opposition: Evangelicals, civic engagement, and schooling for children. In *A public faith: Evangelicals and civic engagement.* New York: Rowman and Littlefield.

Sikkink, D., & Fischer, B. (2004). Religious tradition, family size, and educational attainment.

Sikkink, D., & Mihut, A. (2000). Religion and the politics of multicultualism. *Religion and Education, 27*(2), 30–46.

Sikkink, D., & Smith, C. (2000). Evangelicals on education. In C. Smith (Ed.), *Christian America?: What evangelicals really want.* Berkeley: University of California Press.

Smith, C. (2003a). Religious participation and network closure among American adolescents. *Journal for the Scientific Study of Religion, 42*(2), 259–267.

Smith, C. (2003b). *The secular revolution: Power, interests, and conflict in the secularization of American public life.* Berkeley: University of California Press.

Smith, C., Emerson, M., Gallagher, M., Kennedy, P., & Sikkink, D. (1998). *American evangelicalism: Embattled and thriving.* Chicago: University of Chicago Press.

Smith, C., & Sikkink, D. (2003). Social predictors of retention in and switching from the religious faith of family of origin: Another look using religious tradition self-identification. *Review of Religious Research, 45*(2), 188–206.

Spring, J. H. (1998). *Conflict of interests: The politics of American education.* Boston: McGraw-Hill.

Stark, R. (1963). On the incompatibility of religion and science: A survey of American graduate students. *Journal for the Scientific Study of Religion, 3*, 3–20.

Stark, R., & Bainbridge, W. S. (1985). *The future of religion: Secularization, revival, and cult formation.* Berkeley: University of California Press.

Stark, R., & Finke, R. (2000). *Acts of faith: Explaining the human side of religion.* Berkeley: University of California Press.

Steelman, L. C., Powell, B., Werum, R., & Carter, S. (2002). Reconsidering the effects of sibling configuration: Recent advances and challenges. *Annual Review of Sociology, 28,* 243–269.

Steinberg, S., & Carnegie Commission on Higher Education. (1974). *The academic melting pot: Catholics and Jews in American higher education.* New York: McGraw-Hill.

Taylor, C. (1991). *The ethics of authenticity.* Cambridge, MA: Harvard University Press.

Teachman, J. D. (1987). Family background, educational resources, and educational attainment. *American Sociological Review, 52*(4), 548–557.

Thomas, G. M., Peck, L. R., & De Haan, C. G. (2003). Reforming education, transforming religion, 1876–1931. In C. Smith (Ed.), *The secular revolution: Power, interests, and conflict in the secularization of American public life* (355–394). Berkeley: University of California Press.

Tyack, D. B. (1974). *The one best system: A history of American urban education.* Cambridge, MA: Harvard University Press.

Wacker, G. (1984). Uneasy in Zion. In G. M. Marsden (Ed.), *Evangelicalism and modern America* (16–28). Grand Rapids, MI: Eerdmans.

Wacker, G. (2001). *Heaven below: Early Pentecostals and American culture.* Cambridge, MA: Harvard University Press.

Wagner, M. B. (1997). Generic conservative Christianity: The demise of denominationalism in Christian schools. *Journal for the Scientific Study of Religion, 36*(1), 13–24.

Wagner, M. B. (1990). *God's schools: Choice and compromise in American society.* New Brunswick, NJ: Rutgers University Press.

Watt, T. T. (2003). Are small schools and private schools better for adolescents' emotional adjustment? *Sociology of Education, 76*(4), 344–367.

Wilcox, W. B. (1998). Conservative protestant childrearing: Authoritarian or authoritative? *American Sociological Review, 63*(6), 796–809.

Wilcox, W. B. (2004). *Soft patriarchs, new men: How Christianity shapes fathers and husbands.* Chicago: University of Chicago Press.

Williams, R. H. (1997). *Cultural wars in American politics: Critical reviews of a popular myth.* New York: Aldine de Gruyter.

Wolf, P., Greene, J., Kleitz, B., & Thalhammer, K. (2001). Private schooling and political tolerance. In P. E. Peterson & D. E. Campbell (Eds.), *Charters, vouchers, and public education.* Washington, DC: Brookings Institution Press.

Woodrum, E., & Hoban, T. (1992). Support for prayer in school and creationism. *Sociological Analysis, 53*(3), 309–321.

Wuthnow, R. (1999). Mobilizing civic engagement: The changing impact of religious involvement. In T. Skocpol & M. P. Fiorina (Eds.), *Civic engagement in American democracy* (331–366). Washington, DC: Brookings Institution Press.

Wuthnow, R. (1988). *The restructuring of American religion: Society and faith since World War II.* Princeton, NJ: Princeton University Press.

Wuthnow, R. (1989). *The struggle for America's soul: Evangelicals, liberals, and secularism.* Grand Rapids, MI: Eerdmans.

Wuthnow, R., & Evans, J. H. (2002). *The quiet hand of God: Faith-based activism and the public role of mainline Protestantism.* Berkeley: University of California Press.

Zelan, J. (1968). Religious apostasy, higher education and occupational choice. *Sociology of Education, 41*(4), 370–379.

Zern, D. S. (1989). Some connections between increasing religiousness and academic accomplishment in a college population. *Adolescence, 24*(93), 141–154.

CHAPTER 4

Social Welfare

RAM A. CNAAN AND CHARLENE C. MCGREW

INTRODUCTION

Although it is commonly agreed that social welfare ideas and philosophies emanate from many faith traditions, the complex link between religion and social welfare merits careful examination. Prowelfare values only set the overall social expectations; they do not create formal social welfare programs. Helping the needy can range from a one-time help for a known neighbor to the establishment of a national welfare state program.

In light of this complexity, this chapter commences with a short discussion of the conceptual relationship between religion and welfare and moves on to discuss the history of this relationship in the United States. After reviewing the link between religion and the foundations of welfare in America, we will discuss the various forms in which religious people and organizations provide welfare. We will discuss the question, what is a religious-related social service? And we will provide a typology of the various religious welfare providers.

Recently, public policy makers, politicians, and the media have been paying homage to the role of the faith-based community in social services provision. In particular, the 1996 Charitable Choice initiative brought public attention to the nexus between religion and welfare. In order to understand this phenomenon, we review the advantages that faith-based organizations can offer in the social welfare arena, and then we discuss their potential drawbacks. We then explicate the Charitable Choice legislation as a means to examine current developments in the field. Next, we attempt the difficult task of assessing the contribution of the faith-based community to social welfare provision. Finally, we consider how current trends in religion and social welfare are likely to shape the coming decades in the United States.

The Religious Imperative to Help the Needy

The doctrine of helping others in need is not biologically determined but, rather, a norm that one acquires through socialization and observation (Keith-Lucas, 1972). The act of

RAM A. CNAAN • University of Pennsylvania, Philadelphia, Pennsylvania 19104
CHARLENE C. MCGREW • University of Pennsylvania, Philadelphia, Pennsylvania 19104

helping another person, in many cases, provides no apparent benefit to the helper, and often seems contrary to his or her best interests. Although helping one's family and neighbors may be explained as an investment, this is not the case in helping a stranger. To develop altruism as a social norm, the value of helping strangers and anonymous giving must be inculcated in people and transmitted through generations. Perhaps partly to this end, all major religions include in their theology and moral code mechanisms to help others in need (Cnaan, Wineburg, & Boddie, 1999).

Sociologically speaking, most religious teachings facilitate social order and cohesion among their followers. By including all members of society and showing concern for the poor, desertion from the faith is minimized, and belief in the rightness of the faith tradition is preserved. Socially conscious religious teachings unify core believers and perpetuate mutual responsibility. It is true that many—even most—nominal members of faith communities do not adhere to such teachings. However, they still serve to show the groups' value of moral standards and care for humanity. Regardless of the function of the teaching and its various interpretations, religious teachings are where we find the earliest clear examples of human values that call on us to care for the needy among us. Religious social teachings have a powerful and lasting effect on people's attitudes and behaviors even in secular societies. We briefly review the social teachings of a few of the major religions to show that all world religions exhort serving the needy. The *Jewish tradition* distinguishes between values and rules that define relationships with the Deity and those that define individual and communal relationships with others. It is the latter tradition that has given rise to the concepts of *Tzedakah* and *Hessed*, which mean justice or charity and deeds of love and kindness, including mercy. The concept of *Tikkun Olam* stands for social justice and integrity. These principles call upon the believer to feed the hungry, to leave part of the food production for the local poor to gather, to care for orphans and widows, respect and care for older parents, and to treat everyone with dignity (Sarna & Dalin, 1997).

Christianity's mandate to help others is best illustrated in the parable of the "Good Samaritan." In brief, the parable tells of a man traveling to Jericho who was attacked by thieves, stripped, robbed, wounded, and left for dead. A nobleman, a priest, and a Samaritan passed by, but only the Samaritan stopped to help. Jesus then said that he who showed mercy was the true neighbor and commanded his followers to do likewise. Wuthnow (1991) has found that most Christians who are engaged in helping others know this parable.

The New Testament, like the Old Testament, has many references to helping the less fortunate. Jesus tells his disciples that those who fed him when he was hungry and clothed him when he was naked will be rewarded on Judgment Day. When challenged by his disciples to reveal when anyone saw him hungry or naked, he responded: "When you did it to one of these [the poor and dispossessed of his time], the least of my brothers, you did it to me" (Matthew 25:31–46). Here, the Christian text explicitly informs the reader that identification with Jesus involves the obligation to care for the poor.

One concept used often in Christian teaching is *agape. Agape* love is the valuing, respect, willingness to assist, and commitment to the well-being of another person. *Agape* love originated from the understanding of the nature of God as merciful and unconditional care provider (Keith-Lucas, 1989).

Islam, like Judaism and Christianity, places a high value on charitable acts and giving. The *Qur'an* emphasizes the importance of *Zakat*, which literally means "to thrive or to be wholesome." In practice, *Zakat* is a contribution or tax on property that is earmarked for the poor, the needy, those in captivity, debtors, travelers in need, and those who serve Islam (Zayas, 1960). The *Qur'an* also calls for the practice of *sadaqah* which is voluntary giving to those in need. As in Judaism and Christianity, charity and social responsibility in Islam are moral obligations rooted in the belief that the world belongs to God and not to people. As such, giving is a statement about one's belief in God.

Giving alms to the needy is one of the five pillars of the Islamic faith, and the *Qur'an* states that divine punishment and reward are determined by the extent to which the faithful fulfill these five principles. The other principles include: belief in one God and in Muhammad as his prophet, the saying of prayers five times daily, fasting during the month of Ramadan, and a pilgrimage to Mecca.

Nonmonotheistic religions also focus on helping others as a key religious tenet. *Buddhism* is predicated on sympathy to poor people and the virtue of poverty. Many Buddhists undertook to become—rather than support—beggars, as begging was considered the breeding ground for virtues such as modesty and appreciation of simplicity. These virtues enabled a life of contemplation, which was considered the only justification of human existence. Others, who did not choose the life of a beggar, were expected never to pass a beggar without giving alms and never to refuse a request for supporting a philanthropic cause (Conze, 1959).

In Buddhism, the one who practices charity and compassion is born to a state that moves him or her closer to Nirvana. It is believed that positive acts radiate positive karma, whereas negative acts radiate negative karma. Thus, all life is interdependent, and reciprocity is a central tenet of Buddhist philosophy. However, there remains the deterministic belief that only a few will succeed in life, and the poor provide an opportunity for others to give in order to improve their karma.

In *Hinduism*, the concept of nonviolence (Ashima) has been central to most of India's religious and philosophical traditions since the Vedic period (1500–900 B.C.) and is clearly demonstrated in the classical Hindu text of the Upanishads (Chekki, 1993). The Upanishads also make clear references to almsgiving and support of people in need. We are told that "the eighty verses (of the hymn) are like food with reference to the gods as well as with references to men. For all those beings breathe and live by means of food indeed. By food (given in alms, etc.) he conquers this world, by food (given in sacrifice) he conquers the other" (Aitareya-Aranyaka, 2nd Aranyaka, 1st Adhyaya, 2nd Khanda: 13). Like the monotheistic religions, the Upanishads teach that the one who is generous to others will benefit while others will suffer.

The Hindu religious community is most identified with the inequalities of the caste system, belief in reincarnation, and the belief that poverty is inevitable. The Hindu faith tradition teaches social harmony and social order that is best reflected in collective responsibility among families, clans, and castes. Although the Hindu views poverty as a personal condition and the result of karma, the community remains responsible to care for the poor. Individual responsibility to perform actions that will gain merit in the next life and responsibility for the collective has created the motivation for giving to those in need. In the Hindu tradition, gift-giving not only became a religious ritual and means to distribute wealth among members of a clan but also a means to gain status for the donor and recipient of the gift. *Dana*, the act of giving, and *daks'ina*, gifts displaying purity and respect, were made to priests as sacrificial gifts or exchanges and redistribution of wealth among clan members.

In sum, the tenets of all faith traditions have helped shape both the social values and the institutions that are the foundation of modern social service provision in the secular and religious arenas. Provision of services to the poor, orphans and widows, sick and disabled, prisoners and captives, travelers, and neighbors in times of calamities were both emphasized and fostered in the sacred texts, and this spirit of faith-based service remains strong among modern-day followers of these faith traditions.

Social Welfare and Religon in the United States: A Brief History

Leiby (1978) wrote that "religious ideas were the most important intellectual influence on American welfare institutions in the nineteenth century." To understand the significant role that religion has played in forming our current social service system, it is necessary to consider America's historic religious tradition from its earliest days (1620) to modern times (1935).

THE COLONIAL ERA (1620–1775). The church of the 17th and 18th centuries played only a minor role in social service provision, although it was an important social institution in all of the colonies. Most civic leaders were church members, and the best educated people in the community were usually the local pastors (Morgan, 1966). The American church of colonial times, however, was not a benevolent institution per se. These societies began to focus more on the welfare of people in the community only with the legal separation of church and state: a slow process that began with the First Amendment and was not complete until 1833, when Massachusetts forswore Congregationalism as the state church.

The state churches in Colonial America were supported by taxes imposed on believers and unbelievers alike (Hammack, 1998). With their salaries secured and competing religions banned or dispreferred by the state, clergy members had little incentive to develop social ministries, as these efforts are difficult to organize and unnecessary to establish the credibility and importance of the church in the community. In the United States, before the Revolution and independence, religious affiliation declined to a very low rate (Finke & Stark, 1992). Even in colonies where church attendance was considered an obligation for citizenship, religious apathy and lack of church attendance were the norm.

However, some of the nonestablished denominations did attempt to develop social services in the colonial era. In Philadelphia during the early 1700s, the Quakers included help for the poor (usually in the form of food, clothing, shelter, and coal) on the agenda of their monthly meetings. In 1713 they established the Friends Almshouse to provide relief to the poor (Compton, 1980). In 1724, the Episcopalians established the Boston Episcopal Society to provide help to members in need (Axinn & Stern, 2001). As early as 1729 in New Orleans, the Ursuline Sisters established the first home for children and women who were the victims of the Indian Massacres. Such religious-based social service providers encouraged acts of charity.

FROM INDEPENDENCE TO THE INDUSTRIAL AGE (1776–1896). In 1826, Joseph Tuckerman, a Unitarian clergyman from Boston, initiated "ministry-at-large" in response to the devastating economic depression of 1819. He proposed that the church help needy families regardless of religious affiliation, a revolutionary idea at the time. Initially interested in spiritual needs of the poor, Tuckerman became engrossed in such issues as housing conditions, wages, public education, delinquency, and public relief. In 1832 he organized a company of visitors to the poor and in 1833 began an interdenominational union of ministers to provide mutual help and consultation. These initiatives paved the way for the Association of Delegates from the Benevolent Societies of Boston in 1834 (Watson, 1922). Whereas

Tuckerman was active in Boston, the New York Mission and Tract Society was ministering to the poor and imprisoned as well as to new immigrants by providing temporary assistance to poor families and helping the unemployed find jobs.

The 18th and 19th centuries saw the emergence of many voluntary societies. These independent bodies were formed for particular social, missionary, or benevolent endeavors. For example, the Hartford Asylum for the Education and Instruction of the Deaf and Dumb was established under the leadership of Reverend Thomas Gallaudet, and the Hartford Retreat for the Insane was founded in 1822–1824 (Ahlstrom, 1972). In 1797, Philadelphia Catholic parishioners met to organize an orphanage for children whose parents had died following an outbreak of yellow fever (Oates, 1997). By 1806, they had established the Roman Catholic Society of St. Joseph for the Maintenance and Education of Orphans. In New York, in the 1830s, Bishop John Dubois ordered that all church collections on Christmas and Easter go to the care of orphans. These collections were the forerunner of the Campaign for Human Development which annually distributes some $50 million dollars to community-based social services.

The 1870s saw the rise of regional and national conferences devoted to welfare. In 1872, the first meeting of charities and correction people from three Midwest states (Michigan, Wisconsin, and Illinois) took place at the Sherman House. This was the modest beginning of the National Conference of Charities and Corrections. Two years later, in New York, a conference was held under the auspices of the American Social Science Association. The proceedings of that meeting indicate that key issues were care for the insane, residency rules and practices, and building a questionnaire to study juvenile delinquency. Almost two thirds of the participants were church officials.

Another key figure in the mid-19th-century social service arena was Charles Loring Brace. Brace studied for the ministry and worked as a missionary with prisoners on Blackwell's Island just outside New York City. He left this ministry to establish the Children's Aid Society in 1853, and remained its executive officer for almost 40 years. Some of Brace's solutions for the city's growing social problems were to find foster families for children-at-risk, teach religion to New York's many street children, provide children with some form of education, and employ doctors and nurses to provide care for sick children. The Children's Aid Society is still active today in many child welfare projects (Bremner, 1972).

THE SOCIAL GOSPEL MOVEMENT AND CHARITY ORGANIZATION SOCIETY (1890–1920). The social gospel movement was another powerful influence in the social service arena of the day. The social gospel represented an attempt to respond to serious social problems of the times such as slums, labor unrest, urban blight, and exploitation of the poor. It was also a reaction to the evolving social Darwinism approach that called on the wealthy to share with the poor. Proponents of the social gospel believed that the material blessings of the few would, with proper stewardship, "trickle down" to the impoverished many. The Social Gospel Movement sought to improve the lives of the masses by introducing the Christian values of just and harmonious living in society (Curtis, 1991).

In response to the Social Gospel movement, thousands of individual Christians and churches became actively involved in the resolution of the social problems ranging from helping a neighbor to challenging the social order. Hopkins (1940) noted that the social gospel spawned a variety of social action initiatives such as "workingmen's clubs." These religious-based clubs practiced cooperative buying and some owned their own libraries and meeting places similar to the co-op movement of the 1960s, which was secular at best and smacked of being antireligious. Social gospel participants also were involved in helping the poor, improving education, combating prostitution, opposing alcohol abuse, and helping immigrants assimilate into the American society. The power of the social gospel was in its wide reach and the fact that a social theology managed to move so many people into being involved in social service provision and social change.

The Christian Women's Temperance Union (CWTU) represents an early advocacy effort of Christian women in America (Axinn & Stern, 2001). This national organization summoned women to protest the damaging effects of alcohol on the family and to contain the manufacture and sale of alcoholic beverages. This organization formed in 1874 and quickly grew in influence and numbers, gradually exceeding 200,000 members.

One group that was highly influential in the Social Gospel movement was the Salvation Army. In 1890, General Booth published *In Darkest England* in which he called for members of the Army to reach out to the poorest people in society. He argued that the moral improvement of the poor was dependent on the amelioration of their material conditions and well-being. The overt presence of the Army's religious and social soldiers made their campaign visible and popularized the responsibility of religious people to help others in need. The phrase, "No place was forsaken for the Army, no man or woman sunk so low as to be excluded from God's bounty," best represents this denomination's social perspective. Because all are God's creatures, the Salvation Army made no distinction between the worthy and the unworthy poor.

Only at the end of the 19th century did religious-based social services in America begin to give way to secular forms of help. Reverend Samuel H. Gurteen paved the way by establishing the Buffalo Charity Organization Society (COS) in 1877 (Gurteen, 1881). Gurteen based his society on the London and Glasgow COSs (Leiby, 1984). The British model's principle was a simple one: members of the congregation, together with the wealthy members of the community, were obliged to meet the needs of the poor. Church deacons visited the poor, counseled them, and supervised their use of charitable alms. Under Gurteen's leadership, the COS movement substituted "friendly visitors" for deacons, a major feature of what was to become the new benevolent gospel and a continuation of the tradition started in AICP. The COSs continued to change the face of American services. Through their efforts, social services eventually left their community-religious base for one that was city-wide, temporal, and professional (Magnuson, 1977; Tice, 1992), and the delivery of social services became less arbitrary and more systematic. Gurteen's work laid the foundation for scientific charity, and his claim to fame was that the work of the Buffalo COS saved the city $50,000 annually. In Gurteen's words: "... the Organization plan keeps taxation down to the lowest possible figure, and this without any unkindness to the poor; since in every case where either a person is cut off from receiving official aid, or is prevented from applying to it, *work* is invariably produced by the Society in order to make up for the degrading official dole which has been withheld or withdrawn" (Gurteen, 1881, p. 7).

The use of churches became problematic because churches were often given responsibility for districts where many residents were not of their faith. Thus, the churches' friendly visitors did not visit as frequently as required; reports to the COS headquarters were sporadic, and the churches were often unwilling to help. When the local COS worked directly with the friendly visitors, the results improved, so the COS gave up working through local churches. This movement of service delivery away from the churches presaged an even greater change that was to occur in the 20th century: the secularization of social welfare, due in part, to the contributions of Mary Richmond and the philosophy of the Charity Organization Societies (COSs).

TWENTIETH CENTURY. Johnson (1930) enumerated the elements of church work that were socially oriented and not faith-required and that overlapped with the newly evolving profession of social work. These included: (1) social evangelism; (2) miscellaneous services such as employment services and hospital visitation; (3) cooperation / joint action with other agencies (e.g., provision of probation workers or hospital workers for those with religious affiliation or requesting Christian care); (4) church advocacy for moral and social issues by supporting legislation and urging members to vote (e.g., prohibition law); (5) development of social attitudes on industrial relations, international issues, and race relations; (6) social education (training for volunteer service, industrial and racial situations, social hygiene) and research such as study of crime in Pittsburgh or social conditions in Baltimore; (7) social service experiments (e.g., coffee clubs as a social substitute for saloons, scholarships to provide juvenile delinquents with shelter, schooling, and employment placement); and (8) cooperation with agencies (e.g., Minneapolis Church Federation in 1928 conference for ministers and social workers). Johnson acknowledged that some religious organizations had not sought the aid of community organizations because "it would not be worth the resulting complications, public scrutiny necessary for endorsement, or compromise in their service" (p. 101). He concluded that "the role of religion as a vital factor in the social rehabilitation of failures and misfits has been increasingly recognized in recent years."

The growth of faith-based social services was severely curtailed through the Great Depression and after the passage of the Social Security Act in 1935. The Great Depression proved to that generation that private welfare was incapable of meeting human needs and that massive public intervention was required. Indeed, from 1935 until the Reagan administration, public social services surpassed those of the voluntary community. These public services reached a peak with the Johnson administration and the Great Society. In a span of 60 years, religious social services were pushed from center stage and became ancillary to public social responsibility. However, since the Reagan administration, the public commitment to welfare has been waning, and fiscal allocations and actual public services are diminishing. When the public sector withdrew from providing social services, religious groups slowly moved in. This crowding-out process culminated with the passage of the 1996 welfare reform, which included Charitable Choice (Cnaan & Boddie, 2002; Skocpol, 2000).

Charitable Choice and Faith-Based Initiatives

The key sociopolitical issue is why religious organizations are called on to provide social services. In all modern advanced democracies welfare is the role of the government, and religious organizations are rarely tapped to provide welfare. The enhanced role of religious organizations in welfare provision has its roots in two related trends in U.S. policy. First, recent years have seen a marked shift toward the federal government shedding public responsibilities. At the same time, the government has moved toward contracting out activities that formerly were the exclusive purview of government agencies.

The first trend is a key part of the "new federalism" approach that has characterized the new right since the Reagan administration. Under this approach, the federal government devolves responsibility for social welfare onto state, city, and local communities. The government succeeded in shrinking the American welfare system to a minimum, but the needs did not vanish. Often they were simply left unattended. When the burden landed in local communities, often it was local congregations who picked it up. Motivated both by creed and the need to solidify the ranks by doing worthy projects, organized religion started to play a major role in the welfare arena. This is a role that had emerged in the mid-19th century, diminished after 1935 (passage of the Social Security Bill), and reemerged since 1980 when public welfare was curtailed (Cnaan, Wineburg, & Boddie, 1999).

The second trend relates to all levels of government preferring to hire outside private providers rather than provide services themselves. The contracting-out trend extends across the whole range of government responsibilities—everything from welfare right up to warfare (Smith & Lipsky 1995; Singer, 2003). Contracting lets for-profit and nonprofit organizations compete for government funds to deliver government services. Religious organizations' existent proclivity to help people in need made them favored partners in the emergent field of contract welfare provision (Conlan, 1998). The major breakthrough in this respect and the culmination of this development, however, was the passage of Charitable Choice in 1996, which will be outlined in this section.

As the U.S. social welfare system continues to undergo radical transformation under-scored by the Personal Responsibility and Work Opportunity Reconciliation Act of 1996 (P.L. 104–193), limited attention has been given to an important component of the welfare reform law, section 104 also referred to as "Charitable Choice." This provision significantly changed the historic relationship of the religious community and the public sector by open-ing the door for mixing religion and publicly supported social services. Section 104 outlines the primary feature of this provision as follows:

> The purpose of this section is to allow States to contract with religious organizations, or to allow religious organizations to accept certificates, vouchers, or other forms of disbursement . . . on the same basis as any other non-governmental provider without impairing the religious character of such organizations, and without diminishing the religious freedom of beneficiaries of assistance funded under such program.

The objectives of Charitable Choice are to: (1) encourage states and counties to increase the participation of nonprofit organizations in the provision of federally funded welfare pro-grams, with specific mention of religious-based organizations; (2) establish eligibility for religious-based organizations as contractors for service on the same basis as other organiza-tions; (3) protect the religious character and employment exemption status of participating religious-based organizations; and (4) safeguard the religious freedom of participants.

Charitable Choice applies to services under the Temporary Assistance for Needy Fam-ilies (TANF) program that replaced AFDC. Charitable Choice also applies to food stamps, Medicaid, Supplemental Security Income (SSI), and a wide array of services that will assist recipients of TANF to become self-sufficient. The range of services that religious-based organizations can contract with states or counties to provide includes the following areas: food (such as subsidized meals, food pantry, nutrition education, food budgeting counseling, or soup kitchen); work (such as job search, job-skills training, job readiness training, vocational education, GED preparation, and ESL programs); community service positions; domestic violence counseling; medical and health services (such as abstinence education, drug-and-alcohol treatment centers, health clinics, wellness centers, and immu-nization programs), and maternity homes (such as residential care, second-chance homes, and supervised community housing). By law, religious-based organizations may not only provide such services but also are encouraged to play a larger role in the provision of these services (Cnaan & Boddie, 2002).

In 1998, the scope of Charitable Choice was further expanded to include Community Services Block Grants to establish individual development account (IDA) demonstration projects for individuals and families with limited means to accumulate assets through a savings program. Other bills pending in the U.S. Congress may expand Charitable Choice to include programs such as mental health, literacy, adoption, and juvenile delinquency services. In fact, a Senate bill—the Charitable Choice Expansion Bill—if passed will expand coverage of Charitable Choice to all federally funded social, health, and community development programs. Charitable Choice is also being broadly used by some states to include any collaboration between the government and religious-based organizations (Sherman, 2000).

In January 2001, President George W. Bush made faith-based help for the poor his key domestic policy. By establishing the White House Office of Faith Based and Community Initiatives (OFBCI) the president demonstrated that care for the neediest members of our society will be encouraged to come from the local faith-based organizations and mainly from congregations. The office, with branches in 10 government departments, is now in charge of "leveling the playing field" and making sure that when granting public service contracts, faith based groups are not discriminated against.

What Is Charitable Choice and the Faith-Based Initiative?

What is so unique about the Charitable Choice provision? To answer this question, we must explain what the normative relationship between church and state was. Consider the case of a religious organization (such as a congregation or a faith-based nonprofit organization) that wishes to provide a publicly funded social program. Until 1996, the prevailing conditions for contracting with the government meant that a religious-based organization had to remove all religious symbols from the room where service was provided; forego any religious ceremonies (such as prayers at meals); accept all clients, even those opposed to the beliefs of the providers; hire qualified staff that reflected society at large and not the organization's spirit and belief system; adhere to government contract regulations; and incorporate separately as a 501(c)(3) designated nonprofit organization. No religious entity could apply for public funds unless incorporated as a nonprofit. As 501(c)(3) designated nonprofits, religious-based organizations were liable to public scrutiny and the same laws governing secular nonprofit organizations. Qualifying religious-based organizations such as Catholic Charities or the Salvation Army have a history of receiving public funding and maintaining their religious character, whereas other organizations that receive public funding have become more secular in their service practices.

Given that in the past religious organizations and congregations were heavily involved in social service provision, voluntarily or with public funds, why does the Charitable Choice provision represent a dramatic shift in the relationship between religious organizations and public sector social services? One important feature of this legislation is that religious-based service providers retain their religious autonomy. The law specifically states:

> A religious organization with a contract described in subsection (a)(1)(A), or which accepts certificates, vouchers, or other forms of disbursement under subsection (a)(1)(B), shall retain its independence from Federal, State, and local governments, including such organization's control over the definition, development, practice, and expression of its religious beliefs [subsection (d)(1)].

Additionally, under this law, the government cannot curtail the religious expression or practice of a religious-based service provider by requiring them to change their internal governance or remove from their property any "religious art, icons, scripture, or other symbols" [subsection (d)(2)].

The exemption from compliance with employment policies mandated by section 702 of the Civil Rights Act of 1964 has also been preserved for congregations and religious organizations providing services under this provision [subsection (a)(2)]. This allows religious-based organizations to have discretion in hiring only those people that share their religious beliefs or tradition and to terminate employees that do not exhibit behavior consistent with the religious practices of the organization. Such an arrangement should safeguard religious-based providers from acting as mere arms of the government.

Religious-based organizations contracting with the government to provide services are no longer required to establish a separate, secular 501(c)(3) nonprofit organization. Although creating a separate 501(c)(3) may be prudent to protect the primary religious-based organization from legal and financial liabilities, it is now acceptable for service providers to simply maintain a separate accounting system for the contracted services. Religious-based organizations are fiscally accountable to use government funds for the intended social service purpose and not for religious worship, instruction, or proselytization [subsection (h)(1–2); subsection (j)]. Religious-based organizations that offer religious activities with social services must cover the cost of these activities from nongovernmental funding. By mandating that the funds are used solely for contracted social services, this law seeks to maintain the separation of church and state.

The Charitable Choice provision also protects the religious freedom of the beneficiaries of the services. Under the law, religious-based service providers cannot discriminate against participants in their programs on the basis of religion, a particular religious belief, or refusal to participate in a religious activity [subsection (2)(g)]. Participants in welfare programs are free to choose their provider. It is the burden of the state or county to offer a comparable service for participants that object to receiving services from a religious-based provider. Therefore, participants are protected from pressure or coercion to join a religious community or participate in religious activities.

Finally, under the welfare reform law states receive block grants from the federal government and have the discretion to disburse funding through cost reimbursement contracts, performance-based contracts, and vouchers (Sherman, 2000; Etindi, 1999). In cases of direct financial collaboration religious-based organizations provide services such as job training and mentoring under traditional cost reimbursement contracts or performance-based contracts that are contingent on achieving certain benchmarks related to the participant's transition to work such as program enrollment, program completion, employment placement, or employment retention. Performance-based contracts and the voucher system present financial challenges to organizations that may not have the capital to invest in a program for an extended period without government payment and a guaranteed number of participants. In cases of indirect financial collaborations, congregations provide mentoring, administer government funds to participants for initial employment expenses, or subcontract with for-profit companies.

A notable difference under the Charitable Choice provision is the willingness that government agencies demonstrate to include religious-based social service providers in welfare-to-work initiatives. A few states (for example, Arizona, Texas, and Wisconsin) amended their laws on social services contracting to include the language of Charitable Choice. Other states, for example, Colorado, have established policies under the auspices of the social service departments to protect the religious freedom of beneficiaries (Owens, 2000). In the spirit of Charitable Choice, many states have appointed a staff person to link congregations to participants in welfare programs or provide technical assistance for the contracting process (Sherman, 2000).

Charitable Choice did not open the door to traditional religious organizations such as Catholic Charities or Jewish Children and Families Services. These organizations were welcome before to apply for public funds and were quite successful at obtaining such funds. The new actors are congregations that are not required to incorporate and fundamental religious groups that are incorporated but refused public funds and influence as it entailed "going secular." The traditional religious service providers, however, could now reemphasize religious doctrine and incorporate more religious content in service delivery if so desired. Experts expect that Charitable Choice will test the church-state separation to an extent that its constitutionality will be challenged before the Supreme Court (a good review of its chances to withstand constitutional challenge in the Supreme Court is offered by Kuzma, 2000).

Although the debate on Charitable Choice captures the political scene and will mark the terrain of church-state relationships, in fact, there is no new money for faith-based welfare programs. Religious providers are encouraged to compete with traditional secular providers for the same limited public funds. In the words of the Bush administration, the aim of Charitable Choice is to "level the playing field" rather than add new resources. The aim is to make sure the federal departments, states, and local authorities will allow and even encourage religious providers to apply for public service contracts which these providers will hopefully carry out cheaper and better.

The history of the link between welfare and religion culminated in Charitable Choice and the establishment of the White House Office of Community and Faith-Based Initiatives in 2001; however, one crucial issue still remains. As the next section will show, it remains unclear precisely what a religious social agency is. In dealing with religious social services, it is important to remember the fluidity of the religious content of the serving agency.

What Is a Religious-Related Social Service?

Whether the soup kitchen is provided by the public sector or a religious congregation, the food will be the same and may often be provided by the same volunteers. Can we define an organization that uses a religious congregation's property as religious just because it is housed in a sacred place? Can we define an organization that began as a social ministry of a church and ultimately became independent as a religious organization? The line is blurred, so we intend to clarify what types of organizations will be included in this chapter as religious-based social service organizations (Ebaugh, Pipes, Chafetz, & Daniels, 2003; Jeavons, 1994).

Smith and Sosin (2001) were among the first to study empirically religion and the role of religion in various faith-based social service agencies. They found that the level that religion plays in the organization varies between organizations. In fact, they found that these organizations are constrained in the way faith plays in their activities. What is religious in an organization is mostly the sense of dignity and rights. They strive to provide services with low levels of stigma. Finally, they are not rigid with their ties to religion and change their level of religiosity as time goes by.

If we stipulate that the religious tenets of an organization and its staff inform its social service mission, then the religiosity of this organization is clearly of great importance to our analysis. There is a broad continuum of "religious" social service agencies in the United States, from those who consider themselves very religious to those who may have been established for religious purposes, or by a religious person, but that have since become indistinguishable from secular service agencies. For example, the Young Men's Christian Association (YMCA) no longer sponsors religious activities and is open to people of all faiths.

The analysis allowing this arrangement of religious organizations along a scale derives from the work of Sider, Olson, and Unruh (2002), Monsma and Mounts (2002), Schneider (2002), and Jeavons (1994). These authors notably lay the groundwork for principles to use when determining the religious identity of an organization. They observe the presence of religious elements in social service activities of organizations, including actually giving of services and hiring of staff.

Jeavons (1994) was the first to study this complex issue. To determine the religiosity of an organization, he suggests a form of organizational analysis. Organizations may be observed for their traditional organizational characteristics, but specifically for the religiousness of those facets. These include the organization's self-identity, participants, material resources and sources, goals, products or services, decision-making process, definition and distribution of power, and fields in which it interacts. However, what qualifies as "religious" remains to be more clearly defined. More recently, Schneider (2002) considers the influence of religious beliefs and traditions on operational dimensions of para-church organizations. These organizations, as will be discussed below are not officially affiliated with any religion or denomination, yet they are based on religious principles and have strong theological undertones in their mission statements.

Sider and Unruh (2004) distinguish between organizational religious characteristics (mission statement, founding, affiliation, controlling board, senior management, other staff, support, and personnel religious practices) and program religious characteristics (religious environment, program content, integration of religious components, and expected connection between religious content and desired outcome). Based on these characteristics they propose a five-category typology of religious organizations. In *faith-permeated* organizations faith is evident at all levels of mission, staffing, governance, and support. Faith permeated programs extensively integrate explicitly religious content. *Faith-centered* organizations are those that remain strongly connected with the religious community through funding sources and affiliation, and require the governing board and most staff to share their faith commitments. Although programs are religious in nature, clients can readily opt out of these activities and still expect the benefits of the program's services. *Faith-affiliated* organizations retain some of the influence of their religious founders but do not require staff to affirm religious beliefs or practices. Although they incorporate little or no explicitly religious content, they may be spiritual in nature. *Faith-background* organizations tend to look and act secular, although they may have a historical tie to a faith tradition. A *faith-secular partnership* is a secular (or faith-background) entity that joins with one or more congregations or other explicitly religious organizations. *Secular* organizations have no reference to religion in their mission or founding history, and they regard it as improper to consider religious commitments as a factor in hiring and governance. Secular programs include no religious content.

In determining the "religiosity" of an organization, evaluators may observe declarations of faith. For example, the mission statements of an agency, or more informal declarations of being a follower of a certain religious figure, may provide "proof" that an organization is in fact religious. However, the actual operations of organizations may not reflect the tenets and beliefs reflected in such creeds. As a result, some scholars have suggested observing the actual practices of an organization for "religious" character of those activities. The methodology given by Monsma (2004) is twofold. Monsma distinguished between faith-based/segmented and faith-based integrated. This distinction is based on the faith-based programs' responses to a list of 11 potential religiously rooted practices. A scale was developed depending on the number and the nature of the religiously rooted practices in which the programs reported engaging. Those practices that had a more integrative nature—such as "using religious values or motivations to encourage clients to change attitudes or values" and "hiring only staff in agreement with your religious orientation"—were weighed more heavily than less integrative practices—such as "placing religious symbols or pictures in the facility where your program is held" and "using religious values as a guiding motivation for staff in delivering services." The answers are tallied and those organizations with high positive scores are "integrated" and the others are "segmented."

Practitioners may observe programs or organizations in a more cursory fashion to place them in one of four categories. Determining where an organization falls involves observing the extent to which religious elements are integrated in welfare-related services. Non-faith-based groups offer no religious activities. If religious elements or activities are largely separate from services provided in an organization, it is defined as faith-based/segmented. If those elements or activities are combined with elements or activities of the welfare program of an organization, it is faith-based/integrated. These scholars have categorized organizations rather then leaving them on a continuum. Employing a continuum is also possible, as it may be difficult to draw a sharp line between a faith-based/integrated and a faith-based segmented organization.

The bipartisan think tank, Search for Common Ground (2003) defined a faith-based organization as any entity that is self-identified as motivated by or founded on religious conviction. As such they resorted to the organization's self proclamation in the same way that Kearns (2003) used to study such organizations in Allegheny County, Pennsylvania.

The second prong of the method is to record whether a social service organization undertakes certain religious activities or displays certain religious symbols. The "laundry list" of religious elements includes the use of religious values to encourage clients to change attitudes, the use of religious values in motivating staff, and the opening or closing of activities with prayer. When Monsma and Mounts (2002) studied 1,559 welfare-to-work programs in four cities, they showed that faith-based organizations that were integrated exhibited more elements from the "laundry list" than faith-based organizations that were less integrated/segmented. For example, the element of "using religious values to encourage clients to change attitudes" was present in 95.8% of the faith-based/integrated programs or organizations in the study pool, whereas it was present in 37.5% of the faith-based/segmented programs or organizations. Another example is that 79.2% of the former organizational type opened or closed sessions with prayer, whereas 16.7% of the latter type did so.

The importance of this line of work is that it helps discriminate between different kinds of religious organizations, based on some objective measures of how religious their current practice is. Although it is essential to distinguish between faith-based social service providers by the level of their religiosity, it also is important to distinguish between them based on their key organizational structures. After all, the capacity of a small local church is very different than that of a national social service organization such as the Salvation Army or Catholic Charities.

Types of Religious Welfare Providers

The complexity of *religious-(or faith-)based social service* is because of variation not only in organizations' level of religiosity but also on variation in the size of organizations and the geographic areas they cover. Quite a number of attempts have been made to solve this problem and systematize the field of study. For example, Search for Common Ground (2003) identified five categories of faith-based organizations: faith-permeated, faith-centered, faith-affiliated, faith-background, and faith-secular partnership. They also acknowledged that within the same organization, different projects may have different levels of faith adherence. Yet, they advocate for scholars to see the organization as a whole. To assess religiosity of an organization, one needs to look at its mission statement, founding history, affiliation with external agencies, controlling board, senior and other staff selection, and financial and nonfinancial support. To assess religiosity of a program, one needs to consider its religious environment, religious program content, integration of religious content with other program components, and expected connection between religious content and desired outcomes.

Based on McCarthy and Castelli's (1997) work, John Orr and colleagues (2000) propose another typology closer to the one we discuss below. Their five category typology includes: congregations, denominations, faith-based national networks, freestanding public nonprofit corporations, and faith-based for-profit corporations. As for the latter one, although it is rarely studied in welfare to work programs, Bielefield (2001) found that they are quite active and relevant.

Hence, our definition includes five types of religious service organizations. These five types are: (1) local congregations; (2) interfaith agencies and ecumenical coalitions; (3) city- or regionwide sectarian agencies; (4) para-denominational advocacy and relief organizations; and (5) religious-affiliated international organizations. We have chosen to use a typology that is based on the geographical locus of service and, by default, the organizational complexity.

LOCAL CONGREGATIONS.   Congregations are groups of persons who voluntarily band together for religious purposes, and who share an identity with one another. These groups of people usually own a property where they periodically meet, and they observe a theological doctrine that to some extent governs their governance and worship practices. Based on the work of Wind and Lewis (1994), we propose that a congregation is a group that: (1) has a shared identity as a religious congregation; (2) meets regularly on an ongoing basis; (3) convenes primarily for religious worship or the spiritual practice of accepted religious teachings or rituals (as opposed to people in prison, workplaces that allow prayers or people who happen meet in airports or other places where people in transit may pray together); (4) meets and engages in their religious/spiritual practices at a designated place; (5) has voluntary membership and no requirement of working or living together (family devotions are excluded by this criterion, as are convents and monasteries); (6) has an identifiable leader or group of leaders; and (7) has an official name and a formal structure that conveys its religious/spiritual purpose and identity.

Many of these congregations carry out numerous social programs to improve the quality of life of their communities. The terms applied to these efforts include social ministry, social outreach, mission stance, and social action. Programs underwritten by the congregation are often the means by which the members express their faith. Programs offered by congregations range from the small and informal (church-based service) to incorporated organizations which have their own boards and tax-exempt status (Jeavons & Cnaan, 1997). Examples of such programs include food pantries, provision of space for Alcoholics Anonymous (AA) meetings, clothing closets, volunteer visitors, day care for children or the elderly, free transportation, soup kitchens, in-home assistance, and support for agency efforts with volunteers or money.

INTERFAITH AGENCIES AND ECUMENICAL COALITIONS. The second type of religious service organization includes interfaith agencies such as ecumenical coalitions (Johnson & Dubberly, 1992; Pipes & Ebaugh, 2002). In these coalitions, organizations and local congregations join together for purposes of community solidarity, social action, or providing large-scale services that are beyond the scope of a single congregation. In some cases, the coalition is based on one religion (such as all Christian denominations of a certain area or a local evangelical alliance). In others, the coalition may include congregations of all religions.

CITY/REGIONWIDE SECTARIAN AGENCIES. The third type of religious service organization and the one most often identified with religious-based social service delivery is the city-/regionwide sectarian agency. Sectarian agencies can be further differentiated based on their governance, affiliation with a religious body, and funding sources. For example, agencies such as the Salvation Army are church organizations that provide social programs and receive government contracts and funding. Catholic Charities, Lutheran Youth Services, Episcopal adoption agencies, Habitat for Humanity, the YMCA, and the YWCA are religious-based organizations that maintain affiliation with the originating religious body while developing services and programs that are provided primarily by professional staff and significantly funded by government revenue. Their boards of trustees consist of clergy or lay leaders from the relevant denomination. They may receive some financial support from the religious parent body, either directly from an area-wide headquarters (such as a diocese) or through local congregational fund-raising, and were established by members of the religious order. Jewish Family and Children's Services, in many cities, is essentially a secular organization that maintains a Jewish identity and commitment to the Jewish community, both secular and religious. The organization is often partially or fully funded by the local Jewish Federation.

Sectarian agencies often employ social workers as service providers and managers and serve as placement sites for social work students. The organization of many sectarian agencies is similar to that of secular social service agencies because, as recipients of public funds, they are required to employ qualified professionals and cannot discriminate on the basis of gender, race, religion, disability, or sexual orientation.

PARA-DENOMINATIONAL ADVOCACY AND RELIEF ORGANIZATIONS. The fourth type of religious service organization is the para-denominational advocacy and relief organization. These organizations serve or advocate for people in need or are concerned with improving educational opportunities for people. What is unique about these organizations is that, although they are not officially affiliated with any religion or denomination, they are based on religious principles and have strong theological undertones in their mission statements. The goal of these organizations is to improve social conditions by applying religious principles to a secular world. Often a group of concerned citizens who are members of a particular denomination or religion form an organization for the purpose of helping others. These organizations freely acknowledge that their activities are influenced by the denominational or religious doctrines but in a way that makes them independent of any religious body. Their members prefer not to be affiliated with any specific denomination so that their activities will attract a wider range of support and clients.

Examples of such organizations include Bread for the World, founded by the Lutheran Church to foster education and research on hunger, Friends in Service Here (FISH), Pioneer

Clubs, Promise Keepers, and Pax Christi USA, a Catholic peace education and activist or-ganization. Organizations such as these are not agents of any church or denomination, but they do provide service and advocate according to religious tradition. Some organizations have local branches (Coleman, 1996). A subtype is the local para-denominational service organization. For example, Hope House in Nampa, Idaho is a residential facility for 51 abandoned and severely abused children. The 12 full-time staff members work without pay as an expression of their religious beliefs (Shapiro & Wright, 1996). In this case, the people who established the residential facility based on their religious ideology came into conflict with the authorities not because of payment for services but, rather, whether or not they have the credentials and qualifications to provide the services they are offering.

RELIGIOUSLY AFFILIATED INTERNATIONAL ORGANIZATIONS. Religiously affiliated international organizations that focus on helping people in other countries are either directly related to or influenced by a certain denomination or religion. Many of these organizations originated in the missionary movement, the aim of which was to convert people in undeveloped countries to Christianity. Although missionary work acquired a questionable reputation in many countries in previous centuries, today most religiously affiliated international organizations emphasize bringing relief and aid to underserved peoples of the world's poorest nations. In many countries in which these organizations are active, they are defined and operate as Non-Governmental Organizations (NGOs), whereas in other countries they assume the form of missionary agencies. It is often assumed that religious-based international NGOs have greater clout that enables them to serve people who otherwise may not be served, such as the "untouchables" in India. Some such groups collect donations from the public at large, while others restrict their collection to members of the faith.

Examples of religiously affiliated international organizations include The American-Jewish Joint Distribution Committee (AJJDC or "The Joint"), the Catholic Relief Committee (Caritas); and the International Friends Service Committee, which provided assistance in the Rwandan and Somalian famines. As Kniss and Campbell, (1997) show, all American religious denominations and many ecumenical groups are engaged in international relief. The difference between them is not in whether they help but in how they ideologically justify their international mission.

Advantages of Social Services Provision by Religious Organizations

Why have religious organizations recently become the focus of attention regarding social welfare? In most advanced democracies, the social welfare domain is primarily occupied by the government. In order to understand the American fascination with faith-based social welfare, we need to discuss its advantages.

INTERMEDIARY FUNCTION. In a world in which large institutions dominate the life of individuals, there is a need for intermediary organizations. Such organizations curtail the power of corporations and large public bureaucracies and represent the needs of regular people (Berger & Neuhaus, 1977). In many countries, this role is played by labor unions, by neighborhood representing organizations, and by civic groups. In America, organized religion (from local congregations to national denominations) often fills the role of intermediary group. This is an important concept because it speaks directly to the question of what holds civil society and community together. One important component of the American answer has been the same from Tocqueville to the present day: voluntary associations and religious institutions. Compared to the other major democracies, a vast number of Americans participate in religious life in myriad religious organizations. These organizations work to buffer the power of cold anonymous big structures.

GEOGRAPHICAL DISTRIBUTION.   With the disappearance of many factories to the suburbs and to developing countries and the decline of fraternity organizations such as Rotary Clubs and the Lions, secular community institutions are disappearing from America (Wuthnow, 1998). Among the remaining vibrant social organizations in American inner cities—and thus the main trustees of the hope for revitalization—are the congregations. Although it is easy to lament what is missing, Kretzmann and McKnight (1993) remind us that we ought to focus on the existing local organizations as a means to rebuild communities in trouble. Their "mobilizing community's assets" approach involves harnessing existing prosocial powers into action for the local community. There is no existing social institution so well placed for such action as the local congregation. In Philadelphia, with a total of about 133 square miles, we found 2,120 congregations. This reported square mileage includes the large Fairmount Park, the train station, industrial parks, and two airports. That is, the inhabited area is considerably less than 133 square miles. But even if we figure 133 square miles, there are about 16 congregations per square mile (Cnaan & Boddie, 2001). As integral parts of every community, religious groups can assess real and changing needs in that community and can reach people where they live. Not surprisingly, Kennedy (2003) found that strongly religious organizations tend to serve more people from the neighborhood when providing welfare-to-work services compared with secular or moderately religious organizations.

NORMS OF HELP.   As outlined above, all major faith traditions emphasize helping the needy. This teaching is translated into daily activates and norms that call on religious groups to provide help to those in need. Ammerman (1997) summarized the spirit she found among congregants in her study in the following manner:

> Our culture sees helping the needy as a religious virtue and expects religious organizations to be engaged in service activities. The people in the congregations we studied were no exception. Eighty-eight percent said that helping the needy is very important or essential to living the Christian life, and 92 percent said that the service to the needy is very important or essential to the ministry of their congregation. Part of the cultural definition that surrounds religious institutions is that they will provide direct services to people who need their help. That same cultural definition makes it likely that people in need will seek out congregations as sources of help. (pp. 366–367)

VOLUNTEERS.   Religious organizations are usually composed of many volunteers who are motivated by faith and by their co-religionists. Having a pool of potential volunteers makes the provision of social services less costly and often more personal (Ebaugh et al., 2003). Furthermore, having volunteers also provides space for the volunteer members to grow in their faith, build personal relationships with co-religionists, and bond together (Baggett, 2000).

Kearns (2003) reported from a study of faith-based and secular human service corporations in Pittsburgh that faith-based organizations attracted more volunteers and ones more committed (allocated more hours) than their secular counterparts. Furthermore, faith-based organizations did not lose volunteer commitment in the presence of paid professional staff; while in secular organizations staff tended to replace volunteers. Similar findings were found in New York City by Wolpert and Seley (2004) and Kennedy (2003) in her three-state study.

PROPERTY.   Most religious organizations own at least one property that they use for religious purposes a few times a week. Most congregations, for example, own a worship hall that is used on the weekend and perhaps one evening during the week. Most can therefore allocate space for social causes. Instead of allowing the sacred properties to stand empty, many religious organization open their doors to various social causes, most notably 12-step groups (AA and NA are the most common users), scouts troops, day care centers, ESL classes, and youth groups. These properties also allow the faith communities to offer their own services or to contract for publicly funded service delivery at a lower cost while using the space that otherwise is unused.

ADMINISTRATIVE FLEXIBILITY.   One of the key criticisms of public services is their inability to bend the rules and eligibility criteria to meet unique personal needs. Once a public program has been authorized and set in motion, no personal adjustments are to be made. The authorization process is a long one that includes hearing and public debates, and changes require a similarly lengthy process. Furthermore, a new public allocation takes time to plan and authorize, so emerging needs are often not met for quite a time. Many faith-based organizations, however, are less bureaucratic and can adjust their services to meet changing needs. It is common for faith-based groups to change their programs to meet new needs and to be relevant to their members. Furthermore, as they use some of their resources they can adjust eligibility criteria to help clients with special needs that are not "by the book." Religious organizations thus serve as a barometer for changing needs and as service providers for what political scientists call "people with discriminate taste" or those "outside the median voter zone." Cnaan and Boddie (2001) found that on average congregational programs are less than 12 years old, and more than half of them had started in the past 6 years.

SEGREGATION AS AN OUTREACH TOOL.   The segregated nature of congregations is quite universal in the United States. Most congregations are attractive to certain subgroups of ethnic, country of origin, educational, or income. Members choose to which congregation to belong and they gravitate toward congregations that are full of other people like themselves (McRoberts, 2003; Emerson & Smith, 2000). As Emerson and Smith (2000) found, even among white evangelical Christian the congregations are divided by theology and socioeconomic factors. In a country with some 350,000 places of worship it is naïve to expect them all to be alike. This diversity is both an asset and a limitation. It generates trust and willingness among insiders and fosters a sense of community, mutual support, and joint ownership of congregational projects. Although many of these congregations and other religious organizations may be segregated and somewhat exclusive, there are enough of them to reach every subgroup in our society and provide them with sensitive and relevant services. Just as not all nonprofit organizations care for the plight of the needy, as some are concerned with music, arts, or education, so do religious groups care for various causes and needs those that are dear to their hearts. As such, the tapestry of social care providers is significantly enriched in numbers and in variety.

FINANCIAL SUPPORT FROM NONPUBLIC SOURCES.   A few scholars who compared faith-based and secular nonprofit organizations found that although secular organizations tend to get a large share of their budget from public contracts faith-based organizations get more money from individuals, congregations, and denominations (Ebaugh et al., 2003; Kearns, 2003; Monsma & Mounts, 2002; Wolpert & Seley, 2004). Relying on private money enables faith-based organizations to be flexible in services and to give individual care when deemed relevant. Furthermore, many of these organizations refuse public funds and maintain their own private welfare system that complements the public system.

The Drawbacks for Religious Organizations as Social Service Providers

The criticism against the use of faith-based groups as social services providers comes from two directions. One camp of opponents is worried about the erosion in the church-state separation. The other camp is concerned with congregational and other faith-based organizations' capacity to provide quality services.

CHURCH-STATE SEPARATION ISSUES.   Ever since disestablishment became the law of the land and the American way of life, the separation of church and state has been a hotly contested issue. Although almost everyone applauds the services voluntarily provided by religious organizations, many are concerned with the role religious organizations can play as social welfare providers through public funding. In particular, many liberals groups see the passage of Charitable Choice (see later) and the formation of the White House Office of Faith-Based and Community Initiatives as a threatening trend. Their criticism is not centered on the ability of religious organization to ameliorate social ills but on the fact that the government finances faith-related activities. Critics further worry that vulnerable welfare recipients may be coerced or enticed to join religious activities while being helped.

CAPACITY ISSUES.   Another criticism regarding the role of religious organizations in social welfare is predicated on the assumption that these organizations are of low capacity and cannot really rise up to the challenge of caring for the needy. The most vocal opponents of religious based social services on these grounds are Mark Chaves, Arthur Farnsley, and Robert Wineburg. In a series of publications (Chaves, Konieczny, Beyerlein, & Barman, 1999; Chaves & Tsitsos 2001), Chaves asserts, based on a national study of over a thousand congregations, that most religious congregations are too small and lack the sophistication required for social welfare programs (some of these findings are presented below). He argues that because most congregations have less than 100 adult members and can raise few resources, many of the advantages listed above do not obtain.

Similarly, Farnsley (2003), based on a thorough study of congregations in Indianapolis, Indiana, suggests that some of the "accepted" advantages of faith-based organizations are incorrect. Specifically, he contends that (1) many congregations do not possess important local knowledge, and they are ignorant about the communities in which they worship; (2) congregations cannot provide services with the least amount of bureaucratic or regulatory interference, as they are also bureaucratically complex; and (3) when congregations bring moral teaching to bear they also force their ideology and theology on clients. The latter point is similar to that of those concerned with the church-state separation discussed earlier. Farnsley, however, tempers his criticism by stating that "Anyone who does not realize how much congregations do both for their members and for the broader community is just not paying attention. Congregations will continue to do great good, but it is not clear which ones will take on the added role of partnering with public institutions in the interest of strengthening civil society" (p. 13).

It should be noted that both Chaves and Farnsley focused their works on congregations and did not study other forms of religious organizations. As Wineburg (2000) argues, "The congregations and faith organizations that the policymakers want so desperately to be the elixirs to our problems simply don't have the skills or capacity to handle the complex problems they are being forced to address. If there were huge increases in funds for training programs, planning activities, and the like, I'd say there might be a chance for church based services to make a difference" (p. 9).

Other scholars who compared noncongregational faith-based organizations found them comparable to the nonprofit organizations. Kearns (2003) surveyed all 501(c)(3) organizations in the Pittsburgh area in an attempt to compare faith-based and secular organizations. He noted that the faith-based organizations were comparable to secular nonprofits in many respects such as size, funding, self-reported organizational capacity, and management sophistication. Similar findings also were reported by Seley and Wolpert (2004) regarding nonprofits in New York. These authors found that religious and secular charities spend equally on programs (a sign of efficiency). Monsma and Mounts (2002) studied welfare-to-work programs in four cities covering a range of secular and religious providers. Although they found various differences in how these organizations provide service, overall, the religious organizations were quite similar to the secular ones in capacity and organizational sophistication.

Two studies with small sample sizes (30 and 15 organizations, respectively) found that faith-based nonprofit organizations had greater difficulties in managing contracts and attracting clients when managing public welfare contracts. In both studies, this difference, however, was compounded by the age and size of the organization. The longer it had been involved in contracting with the government, the more efficient it was in achieving these tasks. Faith-based nonprofits, however, were more efficient in meeting internal goals such as communication, fostering a good work environment, obtaining funding, and using information technology (Bielefield, 2001; Poole, Ferguson, DiNitto, & Schwab, 2002).

Assessing the Effectiveness of Faith-Based Organizations and Secular Providers

One of the most difficult tasks is to assess the involvement and contribution of religious organizations in the welfare arena. In order to assess this issue, researchers have begun to document their involvement in social welfare. The first group of studies focused on congregations and their social service involvement. One study by Mark Chaves found that only 59% of U.S. congregations are involved in any social service programs, and that these are often very modest, small-scale, temporary programs. His study is based on the National Congregations Study (NCS) and was conducted in conjunction with the 1998 General Social Survey (GSS). GSS respondents who said they attend religious services were asked to name their congregation and provide contact information. This procedure generated a nationally representative sample of 1,456 congregations. The NCS gathered data via a 60-minute interview with one key informant—a minister, priest, rabbi, or other leader—from 1,236 of the nominated congregations, a cooperation rate of 85%. The advantage of this method is that even nonlisted congregations can be accessed via their members. However, the way the social services questions were asked and measured was susceptible to underreporting.

With the exception of Chaves's research, all studies found that 9 out of 10 congregations provide at least one social service program that benefits people in the community who are often not members of the congregation (Cnaan & Boddie, 2001; Grettenberger & Hovmand, 1997; Hill, 1998; Hodgkinson et al., 1993; Jackson, Schweitzer, Cato, & Blake, 1997; Kinney, 2003; Printz, 1998; Silverman, 2000).

For example, Nancy Kinney (2003) reported findings from a study of 631 religious congregations across the 12-county St. Louis MO-IL Metropolitan Statistical Area. She noted that almost all congregations (97.9%) reported providing at least one social program. A small group (15.5%) reported only one program and the rest reported anywhere from 2 to 18 programs. Programs for youth were most frequently cited (59.9%), followed by another youth program, summer camps (37.9%). Food pantries were reported by 31.1% and senior programs by 28.2%.

Cnaan and Boddie (2001) carried out a census of congregations in Philadelphia. They covered the city block-by-block and recorded all existing congregations. From a list of 2,120 congregations, they conducted face-to-face interviews with the senior clergy or his/her representative for 3 hours in 1,393 congregations (66%). These authors found that 9 out of 10 congregations provide at least one social program that benefits people in the community. On average, each congregation provides 2.41 programs and serves 102 people per month; two thirds of them are not members of the congregation. The primary beneficiaries are children (served by 49.2% of all programs) followed by youth (43.6%) and the community at large (48.6%).

Cnaan and Boddie also studied the replacement value of congregational social welfare programs. By replacement value they do not mean how much it costs the congregations to run their programs in dollar terms. What they mean is how much it would cost others to provide the same services or programs at the same level without depending on availability of congregational property and member volunteers. The fact that a congregation pays a mortgage for a building in which a social program is offered means that the value of the space is a congregational contribution which has financial value. Similarly, if the clergy member invests time in a social program, some percentage of his or her salary should be reckoned as part of the congregation's financial commitment to providing community-oriented services. The replacement value takes into account seven costs associated with social programs provided by local religious congregations: (1) cash support; (2) the value of in-kind support (such as transportation, food, clothing, printing, and telephone); (3) the value of the building utilities (such as heating, cooling, lighting, and cleaning); (4) the estimated value of renting an equivalent space; (5) the number of hours clergy members invest in the programs; (6) the number of hours that staff members invest in the program; and (7) the number of hours invested by volunteers in carrying out the programs.

The study revealed that for Philadelphia, a city of about 1.5 million residents, the total replacement value for social services offered by congregations is about $250 million annually. This valuation of congregational contribution, however, does not include the many religious nonprofit organizations. If one assumes that Philadelphia is representative of the country as a whole, then this estimate for a country of about 293 million residents has to be multiplied by 195—roughly $50 billion.

Although these studies document substantial involvement by religious congregations, it is much more difficult to assess the impact and value of other faith-based welfare providers. It is well established that Catholic Charities, the Salvation Army, Jewish Family and Children

Services, Lutheran Homes, Episcopalian Youth Services, and many other smaller organizations annually contract with the government for billions of dollars. As a means of giving a picture of their involvement in welfare provision, we use the following somewhat outdated statistics. In 1993, Catholic Charities took in more than $1.25 billion in federal, state, and local funds. Public money accounted for 65% of its total revenue for that year. In 1996, based on responses from 1,400 agencies and residential facilities, it was estimated that out of a combined budget of $2.1 billion, 64% came from federal, state, and local funds (Flynn, 1997). The same study assessed that Catholic Charities assisted 12.8 million people throughout the country.

Another way of assessing the impact of religious organizations in welfare provision is offered by Wolpert and Seley (2004). These authors mapped all the nonprofit organizations in New York (8,034) and studied the "operating charities." They found that of 2,797 charities more than a third (37%) can be defined as religious organizations.

Only a few studies that attempted to assess the relative effectiveness of faith-based social service providers suffer from key methodological issues. Yet, some interesting findings emerge. Monsma and Sofer (2003) in a study of welfare to work programs in Los Angeles found that although faith-based organizations were most liked and respected by clients, for-profit organizations were the most effective in helping women escape unemployment and retain employment. Kennedy (2003), in an interim report of welfare-to-work programs in three states (Indiana, North Carolina, and Massachusetts) found that faith-based organizations are somewhat less successful when compared with secular nonprofit organizations. Her interim findings show that faith-based organizations working with welfare recipients place their clients into jobs at similar rates and wage levels as secular providers, but that the clients of these organizations work substantially fewer hours per week and are less likely to be offered health insurance. Kennedy also found that very few faith-based organizations had opted to collaborate with the government and her findings are limited to a few who ventured to do so. Her findings suggest that even those religious organizations that provide social services retain a considerable reluctance to partnering with government. Both Monsma and Kennedy acknowledged that their findings are very preliminary and that they reflect one industry (welfare-to-work), in a few locations, and with organizations that used to contract with the public sector prior to the 1996 Charitable Choice provision.

Assessing these numbers and findings together suggests that although it is impossible to assess the exact role of religious groups in welfare provision, it is clear that it is quite large. Second to the public sector, religious organizations provide from their own resources and through contract with the government a great deal of social services. In fact, in the United States most "safety net" services such as food for the hungry, clothing for the poor, and shelter for the homeless are provided by or through religious services (Cnaan et al., 2002). As to their relative effectiveness, much studying is needed before the picture will become clear. Yet, preliminary findings suggest that they do not offer any visible advantage, nor do they seem to be visibly inferior to other providers.

Implications for the Future

The trend represented by the Charitable Choice provision is unmistakable. The Congress, the President of the United States, local policy makers, and the public at large are seeking greater involvement of the religious community in the provision of welfare services and now even publicly-funded social services. As early as the Reagan years, the religious community has been voluntarily increasing its involvement in social service delivery (Cnaan, Wineburg, & Boddie, 1999).

It is likely that with access to government funding that no longer regards the religious character of the service provider as a threat to the separation of church and state, many more congregations and religiously fundamental nonprofit organizations may engage in partnerships with the public sector. This represents a significant change and one that may have a major influence on social service delivery as we have known it. For example, it may increase the number of social workers working in or with religious-based organizations. But it is also likely to foster deprofessionalization of social services. One key trend in transferring social services to faith-based group is a possible waiver not to employ fully qualified professionals (graduates of relevant academic programs) and allow less qualified people (people with high school diplomas) to provide the service. Many religious groups claim that in cases of day-care centers, drug rehabilitation programs, welfare to work projects and so forth, good spirit and personal commitment are more important than a professional education, and they ask and often receive a waiver not to employ such professionals. This trend may simultaneously reduce the cost of services and, in the long run, the quality of service. Secular services, with higher personnel and overhead costs than corresponding congregational services, may have trouble competing.

Somewhat against the trend, it is worth noting that many religious-based organizations that are interested in greater involvement in social service provision are still unlikely to invoke Charitable Choice and compete for public funding. They refuse to contract with government because they fear losing their religious character and independence. They fear government intrusion and prefer to work within their own means. Charitable Choice would allow them to provide government-funded service and maintain their religious environment, but they would not be allowed to proselytize. Many religious groups still see it as too restrictive of their mission. They almost always proselytize openly and do not want to accept the public restrictions that come with accepting public money. Their philosophy is that they can choose which clients to admit based on their willingness to accept the religious credo and which employees to hire based on their commitment to their faith. There are too few studies on these groups and their contribution to the American welfare. Some examples include Teen Challenge (Bicknese, 1999), the Union Gospel Mission (Jeavons, 1994), and the Lutheran Mission Society of Maryland (Cnaan, Wineburg, & Boddie, 1999).

Although Charitable Choice and the increased reliance on religious organization to engage in welfare delivery may change the nature and appearance of social services in the United States, many questions are yet unresolved. Although clients are to be offered a secular alternative of equal quality, it is quite feasible that some clients will feel pressured to participate in religious activities within and outside the service delivery sphere. In particular, overt or covert pressure to pray or to attend worship when receiving service may be a source of future legal challenges. Similarly, the practice of hiring, promoting, and firing staff based on religious adherence rather than professional merit also may be a cause for future legal challenges. The law is still vague in several areas. For example, the law says a state may contract solely with a religious organization, but it also must provide for participants who prefer nonsectarian services. Such services must be of equal quality and in close proximity to the participant, but these are terms that are difficult to define concretely. How will this be accomplished? The law also allows religious-based service providers to use principles based on their religious tradition to foster responsibility and a strong work ethic. How much religious beliefs can be integrated in the delivery of social services, and how much influence religious providers can have over services, are yet to be determined. The law protects participants from religious coercion. However, what is pressure? Where does instilling foundational virtues of responsibility that emanate from religious teaching end and proselytism start? For example, a participant may feel compelled to please his or her social worker by attending Sunday religious services. The participant does not attend the worship service due to an overt pressure or explicit request but due to an assumption that he or she will receive better services by exhibiting a desire for religious beliefs that reflect the social worker's religious framework. Is this coercion? Religious tenets call on religious adherents to assist the needy. Government retrenchment of welfare services made this field especially attracting to religious groups. Now, we face a new reality in which welfare is more and more the domain of religious groups and our society is gradually adapting to it. For as long as Americans refuse to pay higher taxes, for as long as government sheds its welfare responsibility, and for as long as Americans remain connected to organized religion, religious organizations will remain a crucial and complicated component of social welfare provision.

REFERENCES

Ahlstrom, S. E. (1972). *A religious history of the American people.* New Haven, CT: Yale University Press.

Ammerman, N. T. (1997). *Congregation & community.* New Brunswick, NJ: Rutgers University Press.

Axinn, J., & Stern, M. J. (2001). *Social welfare: A history of the American response to need* (5th ed.). Boston: Allyn & Bacon.

Baggett, J. P. (2000). *Habitat for Humanity building private homes, building public religion.* Philadelphia: Temple University Press.

Berger, P., & Neuhaus, R. (1977). *To empower people.* Washington, DC: American Enterprise Institute for Public Policy Research.

Bielefield, W. (2001, November). *IMPACT in Indiana: Preliminary comparison of faith-based and non-faith-based providers.* Paper presented at the annual meeting of the Association for Research on Nonprofit Organizations and Voluntary Action, Miami, FL.

Bicknese, A. T. (1999). *The teen challenge drug treatment program in comparative perspective.* Unpublished doctoral dissertation. Northwestern University, Political Science Department.

Bremner, R. H. (1972). *From the depths: The discovery of poverty in the United States.* New York: New York University Press.

Chaves, M., Konieczny, M. E., Beyerlein, K., & Barman, E., (1999). The National Congregations Study: Background, methods, and selected results. *Journal for the Scientific Study of Religion, 38,* 458–476.

Chaves, M., & Tsitsos, W. (2001). Congregations and social services: What they do, how they do it, and with whom. *Nonprofit & Voluntary Sector Quarterly, 30,* 660–683.

Cnaan, R. A., & Boddie, S. C. (2001). Philadelphia census of congregations and their involvement in social service delivery. *Social Service Review, 75,* 559–580.

Cnaan, R. A., & Boddie, S. C. (2002). Charitable choice and faith-based welfare: A call for social work. *Social Work, 47,* 247–235.

Cnaan, R. A., Boddie, S. C., & Wineburg, R. J. (1999). *The newer deal: Social work and religion in partnership.* New York: Columbia University Press.

Cnaan, R. A., Boddie, S. C., Handy, F., Yancey, G., & Schneider, R. (2002). *The invisible caring hand: American congregations and the provision of welfare.* New York: New York University Press.

Chekki, D. A. (1993). Some traditions of nonviolence and peace. *International Journal on World Peace, 10*(3), 47–54.

Coleman, J. A. (1996, May 11). Under the cross and the flag: Reflections on discipleship and citizenship in America. *America, 174*(16), 6–14.

Compton, B. R. (1980). *Introduction to social welfare and social work: structure, function, and process.* Homewood, IL: Dorsey.

Conlan, T. (1998). *From new federalism to devolution: Twenty-five years of intergovernmental reform.* Washington, DC: Brookings Institution Press.

Conze, E. (1959). *Buddhism: Its essence and development.* New York: Harper & Row.

Curtis, S. A. (1991). *A consuming faith: The social gospel and American culture.* Baltimore, MD: Johns Hopkins University Press.

Ebaugh, H. R., Pipes, P. F., Chafetz, J. S., & Daniels, M. (2003). Where's the religion: Distinguishing faith-based from secular social service agencies. *Journal for the Scientific Study of Religion, 42,* 411–426.

Emerson, M. O., & Smith, C. (2000). *Divided by faith: Evangelical religion and the problem of race in America.* New York: Oxford University Press.

Etindi, D. (Winter, 1999). Charitable choice and its implications for faith-based organizations. *The Welfare Reformer, 1*(1), 6–11.

Farnsley, II, A. E. (2003). *Rising expectations: Urban congregations, welfare reform, and civic life.* Bloomington: Indiana University Press.

Finke, R., & Stark, R. (1992). *The churching of America 1776–1990: Winners and losers in our religious economy.* New Brunswick, NJ: Rutgers University Press.

Flynn, P. (1997). *Catholic Charities USA: 1996 annual survey findings.* Harpers Ferry, WV: Flynn Research.

Grettenberger, S., & Hovmand, P. (1997, December). *The role of churches in human services: United Methodist Churches in Michigan.* Paper presented at the 26th annual meeting of the Association for Research on Nonprofit Organizations and Voluntary Action, Indianapolis, IN.

Gurteen, S. H. (1881). *What is charity organization?* Buffalo, NY: Courier Company Printers.

Hammack, D. C. (1998). *Making the nonprofit sector in the United States: A reader.* Bloomington: Indiana University Press.

Hill, R. B. (1998). *Report on study of church-based human services.* Baltimore, MD: Associated Black Charities.

Hodgkinson, V. A., & Weitzman, M. S. with Kirsch, A. D., Noga, S. M., & Gorski, H. A. (1993). *From belief to commitment: The community service activities and finances of religious congregations in the United States.* Washington, DC: Associated Black Charities.

Hopkins, C. H. (1940). *The rise of the social gospel in American Protestantism, 1865–1915.* New Haven, CT: Yale University Press.

Jackson, M. C. Jr., Schweitzer, J. H., Blake, R. N. Jr., and Cato, M. T. (1997). *Faith-based institutions: Community and economic development programs serving Black communities in Michigan.* Kalamazoo: Michigan State University.

Jeavons, T. J. (1994). *When the bottom line is faithfulness: Management of Christian service organizations.* Bloomington: Indiana University Press.

Jeavons, T. H., & Cnaan, R. A. (1997). The formation, transitions, and evolution of small religious organizations. *Nonprofit and Voluntary Sector Quarterly, 26,* s62–s84.

Johnson, D. P., & Dubberly, K. (1992, October). *Local interchurch cooperation in downtown redevelopment.* Paper presented at the 1992 meeting of the Religious Research Association, Washington, DC.

Johnson, F. E. (1930). *Social work of the churches: A handbook of information.* New York: Department of Research and Education of the Federal Council of the Churches of Christ in America.

Kearns, K. P. (2003). *Comparing faith based and secular human service corporations in Pittsburgh.* Paper presented at the annual meeting of the Association for Research on Nonprofit Organizations and Voluntary Action, Denver, CO.

Keith-Lucas, A. (1972). *Giving and taking help.* Chapel Hill: University of North Carolina Press.

Kennedy, S. S. (2003). *Charitable choice: First results from three states.* Indianapolis: Center for Urban Policy and the Environment, School of Public and Environmental Affairs, Indiana University–Purdue University.

Kinney, N. T. (2003, November). *Potential to match the promise? Findings from a regional dataset about the community service activities of religious congregations.* Paper presented at the annual meeting of the Association for Research on Nonprofit Organizations and Voluntary Action, Denver, CO.

Kniss, F., & Campbell, D. T. (1997). The effect of religious orientation on international relief and development organizations. *Journal for the Scientific Study of Religion, 36,* 93–103.

Kretzmann, J. P., & McKnight, J. L. (1993). *Building communities from the inside out: A path toward finding and mobilizing a community's assets.* Chicago: Institute for Policy Research, Northwestern University.

Kuzma, A. L. (2000). Faith-based providers partnering with government: Opportunity and temptation. *Journal of Church and State, 4,* 1–37.

Leiby, J. (1978). *A history of social welfare and social work in the United States.* New York: Columbia University Press.

Magnuson, N. A. (1977). *Salvation in the slums: Evangelical social work, 1865–1920.* Metuchen, NJ: Scarecrow Press.

McCarthy, J. & Castelli, J. (1997). *Religion-sponsored social service providers: The not-so-independent sector.* Washington, DC: Nonprofit Sector Research Fund, The Aspen Institute.

McRoberts, O. M. (2003). *Streets of glory: Church and community in a Black urban neighborhood.* Chicago: University of Chicago Press.

Monsma, S. V. (2004). *Serving those in need: Public-private welfare-to-work partnerships.* Ann Arbor: University of Michigan Press.

Monsma, S. V., & Mounts, C. M. (2002). *Working faith: How religious organizations provide welfare-to-work services.* Philadelphia: Center for Research on Religion an Urban Civil Society.

Monsma, S. V., & Sofer, J. C. (2003, November). *The comparative effectiveness of welfare-to-work programs in Los Angeles.* Paper presented at the annual meeting of the Association for Research on Nonprofit Organizations and Voluntary Action, Denver, CO.

Morgan, E. S. (1966). *The Puritan family, religion & domestic relations in seventeenth-century New England.* New York: Harper & Row.

Oates, M. J. (1995). *The Catholic philanthropic tradition in America.* Indianapolis: Indiana University Press.

Orr, J., Spoto, P., Mounts, C., Cox, L., Lanausse, Y., & Ricks, B. (2000). *Faith-based organizations and welfare reform: California religious community capacity study, qualitative findings and conclusions.* Los Angeles: Center for Religion and Civic Culture, University of Southern California.

Owens, M. L. (2000). *Sectarian institutions in state reforms: An analysis of charitable choice.* Albany: The Nelson A. Rockefeller Institute of Government, State University of New York.

Pipes, P. F., & Ebaugh, H. R. (2002). Faith-based coalitions, social services and government funding. *Sociology of Religion, 63,* 49–68.

Poole, D. L., Ferguson, M., DiNitto, D., & Schwab, A. J. (2002). The capacity of community- based organizations to lead innovations in welfare reform: Early findings from Texas. *Nonprofit Management and Leadership, 12,* 261–276.

Printz, T. J. (1998). *Faith-Based Service Providers in the Nation's Capital: Can They Do More?,* Policy Brief No. 2 in Charting Civil Society, Center on Nonprofits and Philanthropy. Washington, DC: The Urban Institute.

Sarna, J., & Dalin, D. G. (1997). *Religion and state in the American Jewish experience.* Notre Dame, IN: University of Notre Dame Press.

Schneider, J. A. (2002, October). *Serving many masters: Lessons on keeping the faith in faith based initiatives from the refugee resettlement program.* Paper presented at the Annual Meeting of the Association for Research on Nonprofit Organizations and Voluntary Action (ARNOVA). Montreal, Canada.

Skocpol, T. (2000). Religion, civil society, and welfare provision in the United States. In: M. J. Bane, B. Coffin, & R. Theimann (Eds.). Who will provide? The changing role of religion in American social welfare. Boulder, CO: Westview.

Search for Common Ground. (2003). *Harnessing civic and faith based power to fight poverty.* Retrieved on March 26, 2004, from http://www.working-group.org/Documents/SFCGbook2003Final.pdf

Shapiro, J. P., & Wright, A. R. (1996, September 9). Can churches save America? *U.S. News and World Report, 121*(10), 46–53.

Sherman, A. (2000). *The growing impact of charitable choice.* Washington, DC: Center for Public Justice.

Sider, R. J., & Unruh, H. R. (2004). Theology of religious characteristics of social service and educational organizations and programs. *Nonprofit and Voluntary Sector Quarterly, 33,* 109–134.

Sider, R. J., Olson, P. N., Unruh, H. R. (2002). *Churches that make a difference.* Grand Rapids, MI: Baker Books.

Silverman, C. (2000). *Faith-Based Communities and Welfare Reform: California Religious Community Capacity Study.* San Francisco: Institute for Nonprofit Organization Management, University of San Francisco.

Singer, P. W. (2003). *Corporate warriors: The rise of the privatized military industry.* Ithaca, NY: Cornell University Press.

Smith, S. R., & Lipsky, M. (1995). *Nonprofits for hire: The welfare state in the age of contracting.* Cambridge, MA: Harvard University Press.

Smith, S. R., & Sosin, M. R. (2001). The varieties of faith-related agencies. *Public Administration Review, 61,* 651–669.

Tice, C. (1992). The battle for benevolence: Scientific disciplinary control vs. indiscriminate relief: A case study of the Lexington Associated Charities vs. the Salvation Army. *Journal of Sociology and Social Welfare, 21*(2), 59–77.

Watson, F. D. (1922). *The charity organization movement in the United States.* New York: Macmillan.

Wind, J. P., & Lewis. J. W. (1994). *American congregations: Volume 2—New perspectives in the study of congregations.* Chicago: University of Chicago Press.

Wineburg, R. J. (2000b). *The spirit of charitable choice.* Unpublished manuscript, University of North Carolina at Greensboro Department of Social Work, Greensboro.

Wolpert, J., & Seley, J. E. (2004). *Nonprofit services in New York City's neighborhoods: An analysis of access, responsiveness, and coverage.* New York: The New York City Nonprofits Project.

Wuthnow, R. (1991). *Acts of compassion: Caring for others and helping ourselves.* Princeton, NJ: Princeton University Press.

Wuthnow, R. (1998). *Loose connections: Joining together in America's fragmented community.* Cambridge, MA: Harvard University Press.

Zayas, F. G. De. (1960). *The law and philosophy of Zakat.* Damascus, Syria: Al-Jadiah Printing Press.

PART II

FAMILY AND LIFE CYCLE

CHAPTER 5

Family

W. BRADFORD WILCOX

In the last four decades, the United States has witnessed revolutionary changes in the organization of family life and gender relations. A large number of sociological observers of American religion in recent years have argued that religious institutions in the United States must accommodate themselves to the "changing family" by reaching out to and symbolically affirming persons in a range of nontraditional families: unmarried singles, stepfamilies, single mothers, dual-career families, and gays and lesbians (D'Antonio & Aldous, 1983; Edgell, 2005; Marler, 1995; Roof & Gesch, 1995). Pointing to marked changes in the organization of family and work, from rising rates of female labor force participation to the increasingly pluralistic character of American family life, these scholars argue that religious institutions must change their family-related discourse and practice to accommodate the family and gender revolutions of the last four decades if they seek to flourish in the 21st century. For instance, Penny Long Marler, writing about the absence of nontraditional families from mainline Protestant churches, observes (1995, p. 52):

> Unfortunately, the "missing families"—mostly nontraditional—continue to "take their business elsewhere." Clearly, while bowing to the critical contributions of traditional families, past and present, congregations must cast their nets farther and more conscientiously. Otherwise, contemporary white Protestantism may be forever "lost in the fifties." Given the realities of an aging population and a shrinking traditional family base, it is clear that a future mired in the past is really no future at all.

This accommodationist perspective raises important religious and moral questions, but it also begs fundamental sociological questions: Does the institutional vitality of religion depend upon the institutional vitality of the family? Or, as this scholarship would suggest, can religious institutions capitalize on recent declines in the institutional vitality of the family?

Ironically, many sociological observers of the American family take a more pessimistic view of the implications of recent family changes for religious institutions. They argue that family changes in the developed world are consigning and will continue to consign religion to a marginal position as a cultural and practical influence over the family (Bumpass, 1990, 2001; Coltrane, 2001; Coontz, 1992; Goode, 1993). This view, which I call the

---

W. BRAD WILCOX • University of Virginia, Charlottesville, Virginia, 22904

family modernization perspective, argues that macro-level changes in the economy, the culture, and the state—from the growth of individualism to the rise of the postindustrial economy—are ineluctably stripping the family of its functions, salience, and authority (Wilcox, 2004). Proponents of the family modernization perspective further argue that religious institutions, tied as they are to more traditional forms of family life, are becoming increasingly marginalized by these trends, and are powerless to slow or reverse them. For instance, Scott Coltrane argues that the "recent trend toward diversity in family forms is inevitable," an irreversible consequence of changes in the economic and cultural realms. He further contends that religious efforts to "promote idealized father-headed families will have little influence on marriage rates or fathering practices" (Coltrane, 2001, p. 391). This perspective also raises important sociological questions: Do religious institutions shape family life in the United States, particularly in the direction of strengthening the family as an institution? Or, are religious institutions, as this scholarship would suggest, incapable of reversing central manifestations of family decline, such as marriage rates and fatherlessness?

This chapter addresses these questions by reviewing recent scholarship focusing on the reciprocal relationship between religion and the family, and by offering a number of propositions to guide future research on the subject. The focus of this chapter is largely on research in the United States—especially research focusing on marriage, parenthood, and religious responses to the family revolution of the last four decades—but the arguments articulated in this chapter should apply to the developed world.

In general terms, I argue that religious institutions and families are linked together by "relationships of dependency and control" (Edgell, 2003: 164) that make the vitality of the family and religious institutions dependent, to a large degree, on one another. Religious institutions depend on stable, happy, and fertile families to successfully socialize children into religious institutions and to orient adults to the social, moral, and religious family-related goods that religious institutions have to offer (Christiano, 2000; Edgell, 2003; Hout, Greeley, & Wilde, 2001; Sherkat, 2003; Stolzenberg, Blair-Loy, & Waite, 1995; Wilcox, 2002a). Families depend on religious institutions to provide religious and moral guidance, as well as social support and control, on behalf of marriage, parenting, and reproduction (Berger, 1967; Christiano, 2000; Edgell, 2003; Thornton, 1985; Wilcox, 2002a; Wilcox, 2003). Consequently, the family modernization perspective is correct to argue that declines in the institutional vitality of the family will be associated, other things being equal, with declines in religious vitality—measured by individual religious participation, belief, and affiliation—at the societal level.

But this analysis departs from the family modernization perspective by suggesting three ways that the generic relationship between religious institutions and the family does not always hold. First, I argue that sectarian religious institutions can thrive amidst family decline in the larger society. They do so in part by capitalizing on the cultural and practical discontents of family modernization, such as the sense of anomie that children often experience in the wake of a parental divorce (Wilcox, 2004). Second, I argue that these family trends, and their religious correlates, are not ineluctable, especially in societies where religious institutions remain vital (Pankhurst & Houseknecht, 2000; Wilcox, 2004). In such societies, such as the United States, religiously based family movements can successfully resist family decline by devising strategies that invest the family with new meaning, functions, and authority (Pankhurst & Houseknecht, 2000; Wilcox, 2004). Third, this chapter suggests a number of ways in which religion in the United States remains an influential force in family life.

This chapter also suggests the accommodationist perspective is correct, on two counts, to recognize that religious institutions must adapt to the changing institutional contexts of family life. First, religious institutions need to accommodate some elements of the larger social environment—in the contemporary case, new work-family patterns and expectations for male familial involvement—if they wish to thrive in a changing social milieu. Second, in times of dramatic family transformation, religious institutions will only thrive if they respond with pastoral sensitivity to families and individuals who depart from traditional family forms by accentuating the "lov[ing] and caring features of religious teachings" (D'Antonio & Aldous, 1983, p. 106).

Nevertheless, this chapter departs from the accommodationist perspective in arguing that religious institutions need to lend normative and pastoral commitments to the sanctity of marriage, the value of childbearing, and the importance of the parental vocation if they wish to thrive in the midst of rapid social change. Finally, this chapter argues that sectarian religious organizations, rather than churchly religious organizations, will be more successful in managing the difficult tasks of responding to family change in an innovative and pastorally sensitive, yet familistic, fashion. Sectarian organizations are better suited than more mainstream religious institutions to respond to social change with a form of innovative familism because they enjoy strong internal solidarity, high levels of religious commitment and belief, and strong boundaries against the wider society (Smith, 1998; Sherkat & Ellison, 1999; Stark & Finke, 2000).

FAMILIAL LINKS TO RELIGIOUS INSTITUTIONS

Religiosity, defined here at the individual level by religious participation, religious belief, and personal religious devotion, is influenced by a host of cultural, social, and political factors external and internal to the religious sphere—from the state's regulation of the religious sphere to the degree of religioethnic conflict found in a society (Casanova, 1994; Houseknecht & Pankhurst, 2000; Smith, 1998; Stark & Finke, 2000; Warner, 1993). One of the most important factors influencing the vitality of individual religiosity in the developed world is the institutional vitality of the family (Christiano, 2000; Houseknecht & Pankhurst, 2000). The array of practical and cultural tasks and products associated with the family—from the meaning afforded life by parenthood to the economic challenges of supporting a household—often orient individuals to the social, religious, and moral goods produced by religious institutions (Dollahite, Marks, & Goodman, 2004; Wilcox, 1998).

The dependency of religion on the family is particularly strong in the developed world, where both religion and family life have, for the most part, been privatized (Christiano, 2000; Houseknecht & Pankhurst, 2000). As the family and religious institutions have come to exercise a smaller role in the public sphere—for example, in influencing economic production, social welfare, and the law—they have focused more attention on the domestic world, particularly the expressive and moral dimensions of family and community. Likewise, other sources of religious strength—such as religiously-sanctioned economic relations or nationalism—have become less important in fostering individual religiosity. Consequently, religious institutions are even more dependent on the institutional strength and success of the family than they are in less developed societies, or societies from the past, where religion drew on a range of interinstitutional ties, and sources of collective identity, to derive its vitality. As Peter Berger (1967a, p. 373) observes, "religion has found itself in a state of social 'proximity' to the family in the private sphere. The family is the institutional arena in which traditional religious symbols continue to have the most relevance in actual everyday living."

Mechanisms Linking Children to Religious Institutions

What are the specific mechanisms whereby the family influences the vitality of religious institutions? This chapter focuses on five important mechanisms: socialization, solidarity, religious unity, procreation, and familism. The first four mechanisms—socialization, solidarity, religious unity, and procreation—play a particularly central role in fostering religiosity at the beginning of the life course, that is, as individuals move from infancy to young adulthood.

The parental socialization of the child plays a crucial role in fostering the child's religiosity. Children are more likely to develop a strong religious identity if their parents engage in religious education and practices in the home, devote a large amount of time to parenting, and take a strict but not authoritarian approach to discipline. Research on religion over the life course indicates that individuals are disposed most favorably toward the religious beliefs and practices with which they have been raised—that is, toward the religiously familiar—and that their religious dispositions are strongest and most stable if individuals have been raised in a highly religious home. Specifically, children who have been socialized by parents who regularly display religious faith and teach their children their faith are more likely themselves to practice and identify with the religious tradition of their parents as adults (Myers, 1996; Sherkat, 2003). There is also some evidence that grandparents can play a role in fostering religiosity in their grandchildren if they take an active role in the lives of their grandchildren (Elder & Conger, 2000).

With respect to socialization, the style of parenting also matters. Parents who take an authoritative approach to parenting—characterized by high levels of parental involvement and moderately high levels of parental strictness (Baumrind, 1971)—also have children who are more likely to be religious as adults (Myers, 1996; Roof, 1993). As Wade Clark Roof (1993, p. 163) observes, "Those [Baby Boomers] brought up in a permissive child-rearing environment dropped out in far greater numbers and are less likely to return to church or synagogue. . . . A disciplined approach to bringing up children appears to instill religious values and the habits of religious observance." However, there is evidence that excessive discipline is counterproductive. Parents who take an authoritarian approach to discipline marked by excessively controlling behavior and emotional outbursts unwittingly encourage their children to leave the faith as adults (Baumrind, 1971; Myers, 1996). The larger point here is that children who receive the requisite support and structure from their parents are more likely to gravitate toward religious practice as adults.

Solidarity—both in the marital relationship and in intergenerational family relationships—also plays a central role in religious transmission. Both structural and emotional solidarity in the family matter for children. Children who grow up in an intact, married family are more likely to pray, to attend religious services, and to affiliate with a religious tradition than children who grow up in a stepfamily or single-parent family (Lawton & Bures, 2001; Marquardt, 2004; Myers, 1996; Wallace, Forman, Caldwell, & Willis, 2003). For instance, research on religion and divorce indicates that some of the negative association between a childhood divorce and religiosity appears to be an artifact of lower levels of parental religiosity, along with parental conflict, before the divorce (Marquardt, 2004). But divorce also seems to undermine the symbolic and social support that parents can otherwise provide to religion. Children of divorce are more likely to doubt the sincerity of their parents' faith, to have difficulty accepting religious teachings about God as father, and to discount religiously based familistic values, in large part because they are more likely than other children to feel abandoned by a nonresidential parent or let down by their parents (Marquardt, 2004; Wallace, Forman, Caldwell, & Willis, 2003). Children of divorce are also more likely to have difficulty attending worship services on weekends as they shuttle back and forth between the households of their mother and father, which further distance them from religious practice and belief (Marquardt, 2004). Consequently, in the wake of divorce, adolescents are also more likely to pray less often and report lower levels of religious commitment (Wallace, Forman, Caldwell, & Willis, 2003). Thus, research suggests that growing up in an intact, married family provides children with social and symbolic support for religious belief, practice, and affiliation.

Emotional solidarity within and between generations—for example, husband and wife, parents and children—also plays a crucial role in fostering religiosity over the life course. Children who grow up in homes in which husband and wife are happily married are significantly more likely to be religious as adults (Amato & Booth, 1997; Myers, 1996). Likewise, children who receive high levels of affection and positive reinforcement from their parents are more likely to identify with the religious tradition of their parents, and to return to the fold if they drop out in adolescence or young adulthood (Myers, 1996; Roof, 1993). This research suggests that when a high level of emotional solidarity is found in the family that the religious participation of adult children is motivated both by an extrinsic desire to maintain social solidarity with their parents and by an intrinsic desire to identify with a religious belief-system that they link cognitively to a happy family life (Sherkat, 2003). In sum, the literature indicates that high levels of investments in marriage and parenting, along with marital stability, foster religious belief, practice, and affiliation in the next generation.

Religious unity in the family of origin also plays an important role in fostering the religiosity among individuals over the life course. Children who grow up in a family where their parents share the same religious belief are more likely to experience a greater number of reinforcing religious cues—both in word and deed—from their parents than children who grow up in families marked by religious heterogeneity. They are also more likely to live with parents who share a higher level of religious practice and commitment (Sherkat, 2003). By contrast, parents who hold different faiths are more likely to minimize the importance of faith or send conflicting messages about religious faith to their children. Not surprisingly, research indicates that parents who share the same religious faith are more likely to have children who come to internalize those beliefs and to put those beliefs into practice (Myers, 1996). Studies (Sherkat, 2003) also indicate that children are more likely to apostatize later in life from their childhood religious faith if their parents were affiliated with different religious traditions while they were growing up.

Finally, procreation is tied in obvious ways to religiosity. Specifically, fertility rates appear to be particularly important engines of religious growth for specific religious traditions. Religious institutions depend largely on procreation as their primary vehicle for new members, because conversions tend to be markedly less common as a vehicle for new members than procreation (Hout, Greeley, & Wilde, 2001; Stark, 1996). Consequently, the survival or growth of particular religious traditions is tied to the success they have in fostering high levels of procreation among their members and then in successfully socializing the children born into their religious tradition (Hout, Greeley, & Wilde, 2001; Stark, 1996). Obviously, religious groups who have higher fertility rates and higher retention rates than other religious groups will, other things being equal, grow at a higher rate than groups with lower fertility and retention rates.

Mechanisms Linking Adults to Religious Institutions

When it comes to understanding the religious practice, beliefs, and affiliations of adults, four family-related mechanisms are particularly important in understanding religiosity: solidarity, religious unity, familism, and procreation. First, regarding solidarity, the presence, quality and stability of the marital bond plays an important role in fostering religiosity. Because marriage is a status that is associated with a range of conventional normative behavior—especially religious participation—for adults, and because religious institutions typically offer religious, normative and social support for married couples, men and women who marry attend at higher levels than those who do not; the effect of marriage on religious participation is particularly strong for men, who have fewer nonfamilial reasons to be religious than women (Becker & Hofmeister, 2001; Hertel, 1995; Miller & Stark, 2002; Nock, 1998; Stolzenberg, Blair-Loy, & Waite, 1995; Thornton, Axinn, & Hill, 1992; Tilley, 2003). The quality of the marital relationship is also an important predictor of religious practice and salience. Couples who are happily married attend religious services more often and are more likely to report that religion influences their daily life than couples who are not happily married (Booth, Johnson, Branaman, & Sica, 1995). In all likelihood, the marriage-friendly environment found in most congregations is particularly attractive to happily married couples as opposed to couples facing marital difficulties. Men who divorce are less likely to be church members and to attend religious services than men who are married but there is some evidence that women actually increase religious participation in the wake of a divorce (Nock, 1998; Stolzenberg, Blair-Loy, & Waite, 1995). This finding is but another indication that men's religious attendance is more dependent on family status than is women's religiosity. Overall, however, structural and emotional solidarity in marriage is associated with higher religiosity among adults.

Religious unity for married couples is also an important predictor of religiosity. Couples who share the same religious faith are able to lend cognitive and social support to one another's faith; they are also more likely to agree on key religious and moral questions that shape religiosity. This religious unity can be particularly valuable when one spouse converts to his or her spouse's religious tradition (Sherkat, 2003; Stark & Finke, 2000). Such a move can help cement their marital bond and deepen their commitment to a religious tradition that has become a defining part of their identity as a couple. In any case, married couples who share the same religious faith are more religious than couples who have a religiously heterogamous marriage (Heaton, 1984; Shehan, Bock, & Lee, 1990).

Familism is another factor linking the family to religious institutions. Familism is an ideology that accords the family, the obligations attendant to social relations in the family, the emotional life of the family, and the civic functions of the family paramount value (Christiano, 2000; Wilcox, 2004). Adults who accord marriage high value, and who also report that they think it is important to live close to parents and relatives, are more likely to be members of a religious congregation and to participate in religious services and activities (Stolzenberg, Blair-Loy, & Waite, 1995). Here again, the normative and social support that religious institutions afford marriage and family life makes religious involvement more attractive to familistic men and women. Moreover, adults who think it is best for family members to "attend church/synagogue as a family" report higher levels of religious belief and practice than parents who think family members should make "individual choices about religion" (Roof & Gesch, 1995, p. 64). It would seem that the association between familism and religiosity is particularly powerful when familism is associated with religious unity in the family.

Perhaps the strongest family-related factor that fosters religious participation, belief and affiliation among men and women is procreation (and the attendant opportunities and challenges of childrearing). The arrival of a child often imbues life with new meaning and fosters a heightened level of concern with the common good. These developments often prompt parents to reexamine or return to the religious beliefs of their childhood, to consider a religious worldview for the first time, and to begin or increase their level of religious practice (Dollahite, 2003; Palkovitz, 2002; Roof & Gesch, 1995). Similarly, as children move into their school-age years, parents often begin attending or increase their attendance at religious services to supply their children with religious and moral formation (Becker & Hofmeister, 2001; Ammerman, 1997a; Marler, 1995; Nock, 1998; Roof, 1993; Stolzenberg, Blair-Loy, & Waite, 1995). In the words of Wade Clark Roof (1993, p. 157): "The presence of young, school-age children and feelings of parental responsibility for them drives boomers back to church and to enroll their children in religious education classes." This attendance, in turn, can deepen their social and religious ties to a particular religious tradition or congregation, insofar as attendance provides them with opportunities to be exposed to a range of religious beliefs and practices and to be integrated into religious networks.

The effects of procreation and childrearing appear to be strongest for parents who have and rear their children in a conventional manner—that is, both in terms of timing and family structure. Parents who have children about when most of their peers are having children attend at higher rates than parents who have their children markedly earlier or later than most adults (Argue, Johnson, & White, 1999; Stolzenberg, Blair-Loy, & Waite, 1995). This may be because parents and other adults in congregations are most likely to extend social and normative support to conventionally timed childbearing.

Research also indicates that fathers who live apart from their biological children, or who live only with stepchildren, attend religious services at significantly lower rates than fathers who live in an intact, married household with their biological children (Eggebeen & Knoester, 2001; Stolzenberg, Blair-Loy, & Waite, 1995). This association is probably rooted in two social processes. First, fathers who live apart from their biological children or who live with stepchildren tend to have weaker ties to those children (Furstenberg, 1988; Hofferth, 2003); consequently, they may have weaker family-related motivation to be religiously involved. Second, religious congregations may be, on average, less welcoming to fathers in nontraditional families. In any case, the association between family formation and adult religiosity appears to be strongest for adults who have children in a conventional manner: that is, in the context of marriage and about the same time as their peers.

Linking Family Vitality to Religiosity

This review has identified five mechanisms where the vitality of the family as an institution—measured by the quality, stability, and religious character of family ties, as well as adults' normative commitment to familism—influences individual religiosity. Thus, it provides support at the micro level for the thesis that the vitality of the family is strongly associated with the vitality of religious institutions in a society. A number of studies at the macro level provide further confirmation for this linkage. Studies of religious participation at the national level and the community level indicate that religious participation is strongly associated with the number of nuclear families (married couples with children) in a given community or society (Ammerman, 1997b; Chaves, 1991; Wilcox, 2002a). Research focusing on trends over the last half-century indicates that declines in religious attendance after the 1960s are closely connected to changes in patterns of procreation: namely, lower rates of childbearing and delayed childbearing (Wuthnow, 1998; Wilcox, 2002a). Recent research on religious affiliation in the United States indicates that religious traditions with high fertility levels and intensive religious socialization have grown at a significantly larger pace than traditions with lower fertility levels and less intensive patterns of religious socialization (Hout, Greeley, & Wilde, 2001). Given the strong ties between family strength and religious vitality, I propose the following hypothesis:

> *Hypothesis 1*: Societies (and communities) where the family is strong—that is, where marriages are stable and happy, and where adults are deeply invested in the parenting enterprise—will witness higher levels of religious attendance, belief, and affiliation than societies where the family is weak.

Strong families produce more children and socialize them into religious traditions more effectively than families characterized by instability, unhappiness, and religious heterogamy. Furthermore, strong families also foster adult religiosity, especially among men, by turning the attention of adults toward children and by linking adults to family networks guided by familistic values and norms—all of which tend to be reinforced and legitimated by religious institutions.

A number of scholars have argued that the dependence of religious institutions on strong families is more vestigial than real (D'Antonio & Aldous, 1983; Marler, 1995; Roof & Gesch, 1995). They argue that religious institutions would thrive if they did more to accommodate changes in the larger social world—particularly as they relate to recent shifts in the organization of work and family. They are correct to argue that religious institutions must adapt to some aspects of their larger social environment if they wish to survive. In the contemporary era, for instance, religious congregations must accommodate, both pastorally and discursively, changes in the organization of work—for example, by offering a Bible study for working mothers in the evening—if they seek to continue to attract and incorporate families into the life of their communities (Edgell, 2003).

These scholars also argue that religious institutions need to accommodate family pluralism. In their view, the dependence of religious institutions on intact, married families with children is largely an artifact of the fact that most congregations have historically adopted organizational practices that focus—at least at the pastoral level—on conventional families (Edgell, 2003; Marler, 1995). If congregations would only adapt inclusive pastoral practices and rhetoric about family pluralism, the argument goes, they would successfully attract singles, cohabiting couples, childless married couples, and gays and lesbians (D'Antonio & Aldous, 1983; Edgell, 2003; Marler, 1995; Roof & Gesch, 1995). For instance, Roof and Gesch (1995, p. 77) argue that religious congregations need to stop holding up the "old normative model of the family" and instead adapt a supportive posture to a "variety of family forms, and relat[e] to each of them in helpful and sustaining ways."

But this line of argument is largely untenable. Although it is true that a few congregations may thrive by catering in rhetoric and practice to adults who live in nontraditional families, as a whole, religious institutions will not thrive if they do not lend discursive and practical support to a familistic way of life that fosters strong families united by a common religious faith. After all, as this analysis suggests, stable and happy marriages, high fertility rates, devoted parents, and familial religious unity are all important ingredients of religious vitality. Because they will not enjoy the social and cultural mechanisms linking these dimensions of family life to religious belief and practice, religious institutions that do not promote a family-centered way of life are going to have difficulty attracting, keeping, and socializing members; they are also going to have a difficult time generating high levels of commitment among the members that they do attract. That is, absent children and a religiously-unified marriage that reinforces their faith, not to mention a familistic worldview that prioritizes the good of others before the self, adults—especially men—will have fewer reasons to consider, continue with, or commit to religious belief and practice.

Variations by Church/Sect Status

An important caveat here is that the above dynamic will be most pronounced for churches as compared with sects. Assuming that religious institutions can be categorized on a continuum from church to sect (Niebuhr, 1929; Stark & Finke, 2000), religious institutions that take a more accommodating stance toward the wider society, enjoy lower levels of individual religiosity, and have less internal solidarity may be categorized as churches (e.g., the Episcopal Church, Reform Judaism). By contrast, religious institutions that operate in tension with the wider society, enjoy higher levels of individual religiosity, and have high levels of internal solidarity may be categorized as sects (e.g., the Latter-Day Saints, Hassidic Judaism).

Churches will be most affected by the vitality of the family as an institution because they offer fewer religious and social goods to current, potential, and future adherents than do sects. For instance, in comparison with sects, they do not offer their adherents a strong supernatural worldview, nor do they offer them high levels of social support. Consequently, in societies and communities where the family is comparatively weak, individuals who might be attracted to a church for primarily family-related reasons but are unmarried or childless will be less likely to attend religious services and, as a consequence of their weaker ties to congregation life, of developing a strong and salient religious faith. Thus, churchly religious institutions in societies where the family is weak should experience particularly low levels of religious attendance, belief, and affiliation.

Indeed, the experience of countries as disparate as Sweden, Iran, and Japan suggests that declines in family vitality—measured, for instance, by decreases in fertility, marriage formation, or popular commitment to familism—are particularly consequential for churches, mosques, and temples that are organized along more churchly lines (Abbasi-Shavazi, 2001; Trost & Palm, 2000; Sciolino, 2001; S. Smith, 2000). In the United States, declines in the vitality of the family since the 1960s have had particularly dramatic consequences for mainline Protestantism, where a primary motivation for religious attendance among adults is the religious and moral socialization of children (Ammerman, 1997a). Specifically, a large body of research links fertility declines, increases in age at first marriage and childbearing, and less public support for familism since the 1960s to declines in the vitality of mainline Protestantism (Chaves, 1991; Hout, Greeley, & Wilde, 2001; Wuthnow, 1998; Wilcox, 2002a; Wilcox, 2004). As Mark Chaves (1991, p. 512) has observed, "As the fortunes of that family/household type [two parents with children] rise and fall, so will the fortunes of mainstream organized Protestantism." Thus, I propose the following hypothesis:

> *Hypothesis 2*: Religious vitality—measured by individual religious attendance, belief, and affiliation—will be particularly low for churches in societies and communities where the family is weak, compared to churches in societies and communities where the family is strong.

By contrast, family decline need not necessarily lead to reductions in religious vitality for sects. Because they tend to offer a strong sense of collective identity, a distinctly supernatural worldview, and a high measure of internal solidarity to current, potential, and future members, sectarian religious institutions depend less on family-related factors to attract and keep adherents. In other words, the range of nonfamilial religious and social goods they offer members enable them to attract and maintain adherents who are not motivated by familistic concerns. Consequently, they are affected less by declines in the vitality of the family.

Furthermore, sects can often rely on the boundaries they assert against the wider society, along with the significant level of institutional resources they control, to maintain high levels of family strength among their active members even if the family in the broader society is weak (Smith, 1998; Smith, 2000; Wilcox, 2002a; Wilcox, 2004). Mormonism, for instance, continues to enjoy high marriage and fertility rates even though marriage and fertility rates have declined dramatically in the United States as a whole (Heaton, 1986). Similarly, religiously active evangelical parents—including evangelical fathers—devote significantly more time and emotional effort to parenting than do most American parents, in part because evangelical institutions teach that the family is the most important instrument for the religious socialization of the young (Wilcox, 1998; Wilcox, 2004). Thus, because sects depend less on family-related factors to maintain their institutional strength and because they often maintain strong families in the face of broader declines in family strength in the society at large, sects are less likely to experience declines in their religious vitality even if the family is weak in the community or the society within which they find themselves.

Indeed, sects can actually capitalize on family decline in the wider society (Riesbrodt, 1993; Wilcox, 2004). The correlates of family weakness—for example, higher divorce rates, more single-parent families, and more adults living on their own—create their own discontents among some children and adults affected by recent family trends in the developed world: loneliness, depression, role overload, and so on (Amato & Booth, 1997; McLanahan & Sandefur, 1994; Waite & Gallagher, 2000). To the extent that children and adults respond to the family discontents of late modernity by turning to religion, the evidence suggests that they may turn to sectarian religious institutions that offer them a religious worldview and a high level of social solidarity, both factors that can compensate for the weakness of their own families. For instance, children of divorce in the United States are more likely to join an evangelical church than they are to join a mainline Protestant church (Lawton & Bures, 2001; Sherkat, 1991).

Sects that combine strong pro-family rhetoric with a compassionate pastoral ethic towards individuals who fall short of their family ideals may be most effective in attracting children and adults who have been negatively affected by family dysfunction. In the United States, there is growing evidence that evangelical churches—especially large churches in urban and suburban communities—are able to combine normative support for familism, and ministries for married couples with children, with a compassionate message for adults and children in nontraditional families, and ministries that help adults and children struggling in the wake of some family misfortune (Browning, Miller-McLemore, Couture, Lyon, & Franklin, 1997; Edgell, 2003; Wilcox, 2004).

One of the reasons that evangelical churches seem to be more inclined than mainline Protestant churches to offer pastoral support to adults and children in nontraditional families is that they are more likely to frame divorce, single-parenthood, and stepfamilies as problematic departures from a family ideal, whereas mainline Protestant churches are more likely to define life in nontraditional families as functionally and morally equivalent to life in an intact, married family. Consequently, evangelical churches offer ministries specifically targeted to individuals suffering from family "brokenness" and mainline churches shy away from offering ministries targeted to individuals living in families that they view as just as functional as intact, married households (Wilcox, 2002a, 2004). Perhaps as a consequence, evangelical Protestant churches have higher numbers—both proportionally and in real terms—of active members who are single parents or childless adults, compared to mainline Protestant churches (Wilcox, 2002a). Moreover, in the midst of dramatic declines in family strength over the last 30 years, the percentage of active churchgoing conservative Protestants in the U.S. population has grown even as the percentage of active churchgoing mainline Protestants has fallen (Wilcox, 2002a). Indeed, since the early 1980s, the number of people in evangelical churches on any given Sunday has consistently surpassed the number of people in mainline Protestant churches (Wilcox, 2002a). In the United States, at least, there appears to be some evidence that the fortunes of churchly religious institutions rise and fall with the fortunes of the nuclear family, while the fortunes of sectarian religious institutions rise with the falling fortunes of the nuclear family. The forgoing analysis suggests the following hypotheses:

> *Hypothesis 3*: The religious vitality—measured by individual religious attendance, belief, and affiliation—of sects will not be lower for sects in societies and communities where the family is weak, compared to sects in societies and communities where the family is strong. Indeed, sects in societies where the family is weak may be able to capitalize on the discontents associated with weak families, especially if they offer pastorally sensitive messages and ministries to adults and children affected by family dysfunction.

> *Hypothesis 4*: In periods of family decline, sects capture a larger share of the religiously observant population than do churches.

RELIGION AS AN INSTITUTIONAL BULWARK OF THE FAMILY

Most religious traditions around the world combine a familistic ideology with a family-centered logic of practice (Kurtz, 1992; Houseknecht & Pankhurst, 2000; Wilcox, 2002b). In the developed world, and especially in the Abrahamic religions, the ideological and practical focus of religious institutions centers in large part on marriage and parenting. The forgoing analysis suggests that this focus is not accidental. Insofar as religious institutions depend to a large degree on the health of the family, it should not be surprising that the world's largest religious traditions devote so much effort to legitimate and inculcate norms and practices conducive to marriage, procreation, and parenthood among their members. This section focuses on the myriad ways in which the health of the family depends in part on the religious vitality of the society or community in which families find themselves. Thus, there is an elective affinity between religion and the family, such that numerous cultural and social-structural features of both these institutions bind them together. But how, specifically, does religion shape the family?

This analysis of the reciprocal relationship between religion and the family takes place against the backdrop of a larger theoretical debate about the influence of religion on the family. Much of the recent work on religion and the family have argued that generic religiosity is the most salient determinant of family behavior, and that the distinctive religious and family culture associated with particular religious traditions no longer plays a key role in influencing such behavior—at least in the United States (Alwin, 1986; Clydesdale, 1997;

Pearce & Axinn, 1998). However, other new research focusing on evangelical Protestantism suggests that the distinctive religious and family ideologies produced in this subculture can and do have significant, independent effects on parenting and marriage behavior, apart from the effects of generic religiosity (Ellison, Bartkowski, & Segal, 1996; Sherkat & Ellison, 1999; Wilcox, 1998, 2004). This work suggests that sectarian religion may have distinctive effects on the family. Hence, in this section, I review the central claims made by both perspectives to develop a theoretical framework that integrates the contributions of both perspectives and then go on to discuss some of the ways in which religion influences marriage, parenthood, and men in families.

Ties between Religiosity and Family Behavior

Why might generic religiosity—defined as any form of religious participation, individual religious devotion, or religious belief—have fairly uniform effects on family life? Emile Durkheim (1951, p. 170) argued that religion fosters the collective good by inculcating "a certain number of beliefs and practices common to all the faithful, traditional and thus obligatory. . . . The details of dogmas and rites are secondary. The essential thing is that they be capable of supporting a sufficiently intense collective life." In other words, the cultural content of particular religious activities, beliefs, and practices is not overly important in promoting prosocial behavior; what is important is that religious institutions promote beliefs and practices that bind individuals to a common way of life that affords them a sense of purpose, solidarity, and self-control and that makes them embrace the duties attendant to social institutions such as the family. Thus, religion's primary function is to integrate persons into the social and normative structure of society's many institutions, including the family.

A number of mechanisms may account for generic associations between religion and family life. First, most major religious institutions—from Roman Catholicism to Hinduism—foster religious and moral beliefs that have direct and indirect effects on family life. These institutions endow family relations, including conjugal and parental relations, with a measure of transcendent significance (Pearce & Axinn, 1998; Wilcox, 2002b). They also encourage specific moral norms about marriage, parenting, and a range of other-family related behaviors, and legitimate them with theological claims (Thornton, 1985). Religious institutions also support generic moral norms, such as the Golden Rule, that foster ethical behavior in a wide range of social domains, including the family (Ammerman, 1997a). Finally, religious beliefs often help persons cope with stressful events, such as unemployment or the death of a loved one, that would otherwise cause them to withdraw from family life or to adopt a harsh and punitive pattern of relating to their family members (Dollahite, 2003; Mahoney, Pargament, Tarakeshwar, & Swank, 2001; Pargament, 1997) Consequently, as a number of studies suggest (Christiano, 2000; Dollahite, 2003; Mahoney, Pargament, Tarakeshwar, & Swank, 2001; Sherkat & Ellison, 1999), men and women who have strong religious beliefs bring the sacred into their secular spousal and parental roles by investing more time and emotional effort in these roles.

The second set of mechanisms involves the family-centered rituals and ethos associated with religious institutions. Religious institutions offer rituals—from bar mitzvahs to baptisms—that mark important stages in the life course and imbue family roles with religious significance. Through worship services, religious institutions also provide families with regular opportunities to spend time together. Religious institutions also provide family programming—couple retreats, youth groups, and family camps—that provide spouses and parents with opportunities to deepen their relationships with family members (Pearce & Axinn, 1998). More generally, religious institutions tend to foster a family-centered ethos characterized by a range of explicit and implicit norms and rituals that reinforce a family-centered lifestyle. For all these reasons, individuals who are exposed regularly to family-centered rituals and ethos through regular religious participation are more likely to have strong, positive relationships with family members, compared to individuals who do not participate in the life of a religious institution (Wilcox, 2004).

The family-centered character and functions of the social ties found in religious institutions is the third set of mechanisms accounting for generic associations between religion and family behavior. Observers of the contemporary American religious scene, such as Penny Edgell (2003), note that religious institutions—regardless of their ideological stripe—often embrace familism at the level of practice, even when their denominational elites and clergy explicitly endorse a liberal, inclusive family ideology (Roof, 1999; Wilcox, 2002a). This means—at least at the congregational level—that most religious institutions continue to offer rituals, generic moral messages, and, to some extent, family-specific messages that appeal to nuclear families composed of married couples with children. Consequently, religious institutions in the United States attract a disproportionate share of their active adult members from the ranks of nuclear families who seek out religious participation in part because of the religious and moral significance they attach to family life (Marler, 1995; Hertel, 1995; Stolzenberg, Blair-Loy, & Waite, 1995; Wilcox, 2002a).

Accordingly, the social networks found in religious institutions tend to offer more family-related social support and social control than that found in other institutions (besides the extended family). Adults can seek family support from their religious congregations and fellow congregants in the form of advice, free childcare, and emotional and financial support in times of crisis. The family-centered character of these social networks exposes them to implicit and explicit norms that prioritize family life. More generally, these networks legitimate a family-centered lifestyle in a society that often emphasizes work, leisure, and consumption in ways that compete with family life (Wilcox, 2004). Finally, these social networks can also exercise social control over adults who depart from community family norms in one way or another. Actions that threaten family life—such as physical abuse, child neglect, excessive time devoted to work, and extramarital sexual activity—can lead to formal and informal sanctions from the religious community. For all these reasons, the social ties found in religious institutions can reinforce, affirm, and deepen congregants' commitment to family life. There are thus three sets of mechanisms—associated with the normative, practical, and social character of most religious institutions—that would lead us to expect that individual religiosity is generically associated with higher levels of familial involvement and expressive behavior.

There are two important caveats to the expectation that religiosity has generic effects on family behavior. First, norms and behaviors regarding parenting, marriage, and other family relations are more likely to be universally cultivated, both explicitly and implicitly, by religious institutions if they are held throughout much of the society. That is, given the ideological and religious diversity characteristic of religious institutions, religious institutions are more likely to embrace family norms and practices on a nearly universal basis if those norms and practices command widespread support in the society (Wilcox, 2004).

Second, as Durkheim's work suggests, religious institutions must have a minimum level of collective vitality to influence the beliefs and behaviors of their members. Specifically, only those religious institutions that have a "sufficiently intense collective life" are likely to provide the level of social integration associated with prosocial behavior, including higher levels of practical and emotional investment in family life. Accordingly, religious institutions that do not enjoy sufficiently high levels of religious vitality should be less likely to foster family-related beliefs, practices, and networks (Wilcox, 2004).

Ties between Sectarian Religiosity and Family Behavior

Indeed, these caveats are suggestive of the ways in which sectarian religious institutions may have distinctive effects on family behavior. Three sets of mechanisms explain why sects may exert a unique influence on family life. First, because sects enjoy particularly high levels of religious vitality, they are better able to cultivate an "intense collective life" that secures high levels of social integration (Durkheim, 1953, p. 170; Smith, 1998; Stark & Finke, 2000). Such institutions tend to cultivate strong ideological assent, exert a large measure of social control, and generate high levels of solidarity among their members.

This high level of integration, in turn, makes their members particularly resistant to succumbing to the anomic pressures of contemporary life, to life stresses such as unemployment, poverty, and illness, and to despair in the face of the challenges associated with family life. Thus, adults in sectarian religious communities should be better parents and partners because they are more resilient than other adults to stresses that can harm family life (Ellison, 1994). The high level of social integration promoted in strong religious institutions also means that individuals are exposed to higher levels of family-related social support and control, as well as the family-related and generic moral norms typically promoted in religious institutions (Wilcox, 2004). For all these reasons, individuals whose religiosity is tied to a religious institution characterized by high levels of religious vitality usually invest more time and emotional energy in family life.

The second and third sets of mechanisms that account for distinctive sectarian effects on family behavior are cultural: specifically, insofar as sectarian religious institutions promote a distinctive symbol-laden "logic of practice" and a distinctive normative-ideological outlook, these institutions also may have distinctive effects on family behavior—for good or ill. In terms of the "logic of practice," to use Bourdieu's (1990) formulation, the type of rituals and the broader ethos found in religious institutions may have implications for family life. Different types of rituals can serve to clarify, communicate, and reinforce particular types of family behaviors and norms, both for those who directly participate in these rituals and for those who witness them. Religious traditions that rely on a particularly solemn wedding ceremony, for instance, may reinforce the sense of sanctity with which newlyweds view their marriage; they also may revive the marital commitment of onlookers at the ceremony.

Third, and perhaps most important, sectarian religious institutions can produce distinctive family-related ideologies—and attendant norms—that influence family behavior in unique ways. Particularly in "unsettled times" when family ideals and norms have lost their taken-for-granted character, religiously-inspired ideologies and norms can guide family behavior (Swidler, 1986; Wilcox, 2004). Sects are most likely to produce ideologies that dramatize the moral obligations and ends associated with family life by situating them within a coherent and compelling worldview. These ideologies can then motivate individuals to imbue their family roles with heightened significance. The emphasis that religiously rooted familism places on the mother-child bond, for instance, may lead a new mother to accord her maternal role great social and religious significance.

Sects can also promote distinctive family-related norms, especially when these norms are associated with central features of their religious tradition. Thus, the Mormon theological belief that "parents have a sacred duty to rear their children in love and righteousness [and that they] will be held accountable before God" for their parenting is associated with a Family Home Evening held weekly on Mondays, where the family gathers to worship and discuss the teaching of the Church of Jesus Christ of Latter-Day Saints (Marks & Dollahite, 2001, pp. 628–629). The effect that religiously produced family-related ideologies and norms have on behavior should be particularly strong for individuals who identify with these ideologies and norms and who are integrated into the life of their sect through regular religious practice.

The point here is that the cultural content of particular religious activities, beliefs, and practices can matter for family behavior. Variations in religious strength, the religious logic of practice, and family-related ideologies and norms across religious traditions may be associated with distinctive levels of familial involvement and patterns of familial interaction. Religious institutions that have a substantial measure of religious vitality, a distinctive style of religious worship and expression, and a family worldview that is—in important respects—countercultural are especially likely to have a distinctive effect on the family life of their members. In turn, individuals who identify with the religious and family-related ideologies produced by their sectarian religious institutions, or who are integrated into the life of a religious institution, will probably be more influenced in their family behavior by the cultural content of their religion.

In sum, I offer the following two hypotheses for understanding the influence of religion on the vitality of the family:

> *Hypothesis 5*: In general, religion will have a generic prosocial effect on family behavior insofar as most religious institutions enjoy a modicum of religious vitality that promotes social integration and fosters rituals and norms that foster heightened investments in family life.

> *Hypothesis 6*: But we can also expect sectarian religious institutions to have a distinctive effect on family life, where they are able to rely on their religious vitality, their religious ethos, and the family-related ideologies and norms they promote to foster particularly high investments in family life.

I turn now to a brief consideration of the generic and distinctive effects of religiosity on parenting, marriage, and male familial involvement.

RELIGION AND PARENTING

Contrary to assertions made by proponents of the family modernization perspective (e.g. Coltrane, 2001), a growing body of research suggests numerous ways in which religious institutions in the United States continue to influence family life and, in some important respects, actually strengthen the family. Turning first to parenting, the literature indicates that religiosity is associated with higher levels of parental involvement and emotion work (e.g., praising and hugging one's children). Parents who attend religious services on a weekly basis spend more time with their children in one-on-one activities, they have dinner with their children more often, and they spend more time in youth-related activities such as the Boy Scouts and youth soccer, compared to parents who attend services infrequently or not at all (Smith & Kim, 2003; Wilcox, 2002d). The association between parental involvement and religiosity is particularly strong for parents who report doing religious activities together as a family (e.g., reading the Bible, saying the rosary, observing Shabbat) more than once a week (Smith & Kim, 2003). Parents who attend religious services weekly or more are also more likely to engage in positive emotion work with their children: that is, they are more likely to praise and hug their children than less religious parents (Smith & Kim, 2003; Wilcox, 1998).

Consistent with Hypothesis 6, parents who report an evangelical Protestant, traditional Catholic, or Orthodox Jewish religious identity tend to be particularly involved in the lives of their children (Wilcox, 2002d). For instance, one study found that evangelical Protestant, traditional Catholic, and orthodox Jewish parents were 50% more likely than unaffiliated parents to score in the top third of parental involvement (Wilcox, 2002d). Another study found that theologically conservative Protestant parents are 147% more likely to praise and hug their preschool children very often, compared to parents who are theologically liberal (Wilcox, 1998). This research suggests that parents associated with sectarian religious movements are more invested in the parenting enterprise than other parents.

Parents who attend religious services regularly are also stricter than other parents. They are more likely to expect obedience from their children, more likely to monitor their children's activities outside the home, and more likely to set high expectations for prosocial behavior for their children (Alwin, 1986; Ellison & Sherkat, 1993b; Smith, 2003). They are also more likely to endorse and resort to corporal punishment (Ellison & Sherkat, 1993a; Ellison, Bartkowski, & Segal, 1996).

Discipline appears to be a particularly salient issue among parents hailing from a sectarian religious tradition. In the United States, evangelical Protestant parents are particularly strict, as measured by their support for and use of corporal punishment (Ellison & Sherkat, 1993a; Ellison, Bartkowski, & Segal, 1996). They also devote more time and attention to monitoring the activities of their adolescent children (Wilcox, 2004). Some scholars have speculated that this focus on discipline results in an authoritarian parenting style characterized by needlessly harsh and punitive approach to parenting (Gottman, 1998; Strauss, 1994). But other research indicates that evangelical parents are less likely to yell at their children than are other parents (Bartkowski & Wilcox, 2000). This suggests evangelical parents may take a uniquely neotraditional approach to parenting that combines a strict but self-controlled approach to discipline, along with high levels of involvement and affection (Wilcox, 1998, 2004). This approach probably falls closer to the authoritative style than the authoritarian style of parenting and does not appear to have negative outcomes for children (Wilcox, 1998; Sherkat & Ellison, 1999).

If the U.S. experience is any indication, research on religion and parenting suggests the following hypotheses:

> *Hypothesis 7*: Religiosity is associated with more parental time invested in childrearing, with more displays of affection, and with a stricter approach to discipline.

> *Hypothesis 8*: In part because they are highly motivated to shape the religious and moral climate their children encounter, members of sectarian religious institutions spend particularly high amounts of time with their children and are especially attentive to the discipline of their children.

RELIGION AND MARRIAGE

Similar trends can be seen in the research on religion and marriage in the United States. In general, religiosity is associated with higher rates of marriage, higher marital quality, and marital stability. Women who attend religious services several times a month or more are less likely to bear a child outside of wedlock; they are also about 50% less likely to cohabit compared to women who never attend religious services (Bumpass & Sweet, 1995; Wilcox & Wolfinger, 2004). Marital commitment is higher, and marital conflict is lower, among religious couples (Dollahite, Marks, & Goodman, 2004; Sherkat & Ellison, 1999). Religious couples also report more emotional and physical pleasure in the sexual domain of their marriages (Waite & Lehrer, 2003). Consequently, reports of marital happiness are higher among couples who attend religious services weekly or more—especially when they attend together (Christiano, 2000; Heaton & Pratt, 1990; but see Booth, 1995). Furthermore, divorce rates are between 35 and 50% lower among couples who attend religious services together several times a month or more compared to couples where neither spouse attends religious services regularly (Call & Heaton, 1997; Laumann, Gagnon, Michael, & Michaels, 1994; Mahoney, Pargament, Tarakeshwar, & Swank, 2001; Wilcox, 2005). Thus, generic religiosity is associated with stronger marriages—measured by prevalence, quality, and stability—in the United States.

There is also some evidence that sectarian religious institutions promote stronger marriages, although the evidence here is less conclusive. Research suggests that Mormons and evangelical Protestants are less likely to have children outside of wedlock and are more likely to marry earlier than other Americans (Lehrer, 2000; Wilcox & Wolfinger, 2004). Thus, in these communities, the normative and practical link between marriage and childbearing remains strong. Evangelical Protestant men and women also are more likely to report higher levels of marital satisfaction than other married couples (Wilcox & Bartkowski, 1999; Smith, 2000).

Nevertheless, the association between sectarian religiosity and divorce is more ambiguous. Divorce rates are not lower among evangelical Protestants (Mahoney, Pargament, Tarakeshwar, & Swank, 2001; Wilcox, 2005); however, there is evidence that Mormon couples have lower divorce rates (Mahoney, Pargament, Tarakeshwar, & Swank, 2001). One of the reasons that the relationship between sectarian religiosity and divorce may be ambiguous is that sectarian couples marry at a young age, in part to avoid premarital sex, and early marriage is a risk factor for divorce (Wilcox, 2003). A similarly ambivalent relationship between sectarian religiosity and divorce also has been observed in some Islamic societies, in which early marriage is linked to higher divorce rates (Cammack, Young, & Heaton, 1997). Accordingly, the forgoing analysis leads to the following propositions:

> *Hypothesis 9*: Religiosity is associated with stronger marriages—measured by childbearing in marriage, marital quality, and marital stability.

> *Hypothesis 10*: Sectarian religiosity is associated with somewhat stronger marriages, as reflected by childbearing patterns and marital quality, but not necessarily marital stability.

RELIGION AND THE DOMESTICATION OF MEN

Traditionally, men have devoted less time and attention to the family than women—at least measured in terms of practical and emotional work associated with parenting, housework, and marriage (Pleck, 2004; Thompson & Walker, 1989). With important variations, this pattern continues up to the present, especially with rising rates of fatherless families where men spend little time with the children they beget and even less time with the mothers of these children (Furstenberg, 1988; Popenoe, 1996). This pattern of male distance from family life has been described as the "male problematic" by the theologian Don Browning (2003), who argues that biological and cultural factors put men at risk of being less invested in the children they help bring into the world.

Consequently, one of the central tasks that religious institutions take on in relation to the family is the domestication of men (Browning, 2003; Wilcox, 2004). Religious institutions seek to domesticate men by according status to family-focused men in their communities status, by linking male members to family-focused men in their congregations, and by reserving unique roles—often centered on the performance of particular religious tasks or family leadership—to men in the family (Davidman, 1991; Gill, 1990; Wilcox, 2004). Research on male familial involvement in the United States suggests that men who attend religious services regularly are more attentive to the familial ideals and aspirations of their wife and children. Churchgoing men devote more time and emotional energy to parenting; they also spend more time with their wives, and they are more likely to be described as affectionate by their wives (Wilcox, 2004). Their wives also report fewer incidents of domestic violence than wives who are married to men who do not attend religious services on a regular basis (Ellison, Bartkowski, & Anderson, 1999; Wilcox, 2004; but see Nason-Clark, 1997). But there is no evidence that religious participation is associated with higher levels of housework (Wilcox, 2004). Thus, religiosity does appear to foster a family focus among men.

There is also some evidence that sectarian religious organizations are particularly successful in fostering a family orientation among men (Dollahite, 2003; Wilcox, 2004). In the United States, evangelical institutions devote more rhetorical and pastoral attention to men's family responsibilities than do Catholic and mainline Protestant institutions (Bartkowski, 2001; Edgell, 2003; Wilcox, 2004). Churchgoing evangelical men tend to devote more time and emotional energy to parenting and their marriages than churchgoing men from other religious traditions, though the differences are not always statistically significant (Wilcox, 2004). Churchgoing evangelical men also have the lowest rates of domestic violence of any major religious tradition in the United States (Wilcox, 2004). Here, however, religious homogamy is important. Evangelical men who are married to women who are theologically liberal have higher rates of domestic violence than other men (Ellison, Bartkowski, & Anderson, 1999). Furthermore, men who attend evangelical Protestant churches do less household labor than other married men (Wilcox, 2004). Overall, then, the research to date suggests that men involved in sectarian religious communities focus more than other men on the relational but not necessarily practical work associated with family life. Accordingly, I propose the following two hypotheses:

> *Hypothesis 11*: Generic religiosity is associated with higher levels of male familial involvement in parenting and marriage but not necessarily housework.

> *Hypothesis 12*: Sectarian religiosity is associated with markedly high levels of male familial involvement in parenting and marriage but not housework.

CONCLUSIONS

Relying principally on research drawn from studies of religion and the family in the United States, this chapter delineates the range of interinstitutional dependencies linking religion and the family to one another. These mutual dependencies run so wide and deep as to suggest that, in most cases, religious vitality and family vitality will move in concert with one another; in other words, religious institutions will not typically be strong in societies and communities where the family is weak and the family will not usually be strong in societies or communities where religious institutions are weak. Because the American experience indicates that religious institutions depend in large part upon procreation, parenting, and successful marriages for their vitality, I argue that scholarly hopes that religious vitality may be found through a strategy of accommodating family modernization are not likely to be realized (cf. Marler, 1995; Roof & Gesch, 1995). I also argue that religious institutions in the United States continue to foster higher investments in parenting, marriage, and the domestication of men, contrary to the assertions of scholars who believe that family modernization has largely sidelined religious institutions when it comes to the family (cf. Coltrane, 2001). Finally, I argue that the basic dependencies that bind religious institutions and the family to one another vary along a church-sect continuum. Sects should be less dependent on the institution of the family for their vitality than churches. They also should foster higher levels of familial investments among their members, compared to churches.

Because this essay focuses largely on the American experience, and on Abrahamic religions, it remains to be seen if the propositions outlined in this chapter will be supported by future research focusing on other parts of the developed world. But demographic and religious trends in Europe and East Asia do appear to be moving in the expected directions. Specifically, declining fertility or marriage rates in European and Asian societies may well be linked to declining rates of religious practice in countries as different as Sweden and Taiwan (Lesthaege, 1995; Thornton, 2004). Of course, the religious and familial characteristics, not to mention the economic, political, and cultural characteristics, of East Asian societies are in many respects quite different from those of the United States. The dependencies between religion and the family found in the United States may be less central in these societies. Accordingly, future research will have to explore religion-family associations in cross-national perspective to see if they confirm the perspective articulated in this chapter.

But this analysis does cast additional light on an irony found in the literature on religion and the family in the United States: evangelical Protestantism champions the traditional family yet attracts a higher percentage of its members from nontraditional families than does mainline Protestantism, which champions nontraditional families but has comparatively few adults among its active membership who reside in nontraditional families (Roof, 1999; Edgell, 2003; Wilcox, 2002a). In Wade Clark Roof's (1999, p. 251) words, mainline churches "are open theologically to family diversity yet on the whole are bastions of familism." Likewise, evangelical churches may be theological proponents of the traditional family yet are more successful in attracting singles, stepfamilies, and single mothers to their congregations than are mainline Protestant churches (Wilcox, 2002a).

Part of what may be going on here is that mainline Protestantism is forced at the pastoral level to focus on married, two-parent families, regardless of its official rhetoric to the contrary, to maintain its religious vitality. After all, as a churchly tradition, mainline Protestantism depends largely on family-related factors for its vitality. By contrast, evangelical Protestantism is able to attract adults and children living in nontraditional families even though it valorizes the traditional family because it offers them a range of religious and social resources that can help them deal with the challenges of living in a nontraditional family. Specifically, the sectarian character of many evangelical congregations means that they can offer potential adherents a strong supernatural worldview and a sense of solidarity that is comforting to adults and children who find themselves unhinged by the family discontents of late modernity. So this chapter suggests, among other things, that the basic and fundamental dependencies between religion and the family chronicled herein may vary by the sectarian/churchly status of the religious institution under consideration.

ACKNOWLEDGMENT. This research was supported by the Lilly Endowment, grant #2002 2301–000. I am indebted to Young-Il Kim for research assistance and to David Dollahite and Penny Edgell for editorial suggestions and substantive advice. Portions of this chapter are adapted from Chapter 4, "Soft Patriarchs, New Fathers: Religion, Ideology, and Fatherhood" in my book, *Soft Patriarchs, New Men: How Christianity Shapes Fathers and Husbands* (Chicago, 2004).

REFERENCES

Abbasi-Shavazi, M. J. (2001, November). Fertility revolution in Iran. *Population & Société, INED, 373*, 1–4.

Alwin, D. F. (1986). Religion and parental child-rearing orientations: Evidence of a Catholic-Protestant convergence. *American Journal of Sociology, 92*, 412–40.

Amato, P. R., & Booth, A. (1997). *A generation at risk: Growing up in an era of family upheaval.* Cambridge: Harvard University Press.

Ammerman, N. T. (1997a). Golden rule Christianity: Lived religion in the American mainstream. In D. Hall (Ed.), *Lived religion in America: Toward a history of practice.* Princeton, NJ: Princeton University Press.

Ammerman, N. T. (1997b). *Congregation & community.* New Brunswick, NJ: Rutgers University Press.

Ammerman, N. T. & Roof, W. C. (1995). Introduction: Old patterns, new trends, fragile experiments. In N. Ammerman & W. C. Roof (Ed.), *Work, family, and religion in contemporary society.* New York: Routledge.

Argue, A., Johnson, D. R., & White, L. K. (1999). Age and religiosity: Evidence from a three-wave panel analysis. *Journal for the Scientific Study of Religion, 38*, 423–435.

Bartkowski, J. P. (2001). *Remaking the godly marriage: Gender negotiation in evangelical families.* New Brunswick, NJ: Rutgers University Press.

Bartkowski, J. P., & Wilcox, W. B. (2000). Conservative protestant child discipline: The case of parental yelling. *Social Forces, 79*, 265–290.

Bartkowski, J. P., & Xu, X. (2000). Distant patriarchs or expressive dads? The discourse and practice of fathering in conservative protestant families. *Sociological Quarterly, 41*, 465–485.

Baumrind, D. (1971). Current patterns of parental authority. *Development Psychology Monograph, 4*, 1–103.

Becker, P. E., & Hofmeister, H. (2001). Work, family, and religious involvement for men and women. *Journal for the Scientific Study of Religion, 40*, 707–722.

Berger, P. (1967). Religious institutions. In N. J. Smelser (Ed.), *Sociology: An introduction* (pp. 329–379). New York: John Wiley.

Booth, A., Johnson, D. R., Branaman, A., & Sica, A. (1995). Belief and behavior: Does religion matter in today's marriage? *Journal of Marriage and the Family, 57*, 661–671.

Bourdieu, P. (1990). *The logic of practice.* Stanford, CA: Stanford University Press.

Browning, D. S. (2003). *Marriage and modernization: How globalization threatens marriage and what to do about it.* Wm. B. Eerdmans.

Browning, D. S., Miller-McLemore, B. J., Couture, P. D., Lyon, K. B., & Franklin, R. M. (1997). *From culture wars to common ground: Religion and the American family debate.* Louisville, KY: John Knox Press.

Bumpass, L. L. (1990). What happening to the family? Interactions between demographic and institutional change. *Demography, 27*, 483–498.

Bumpass, L. L. (2001). Family-related attitudes, couple relationships, and union stability. In R. Lesthaeghe (Ed.), *Meaning and choice: Value orientations and life cycle decisions.* Hague, Netherlands: Netherlands Interdisciplinary Demographic Institute.

Bumpass, L. L., & Sweet, J. A. (1995). *Cohabitation, marriage, and union stability.* Madison, WI: Center for Demography and Ecology, University of Wisconsin-Madison.

Call, V. R. A., & Heaton, T. B. (1997). Religious influence on marital stability. *Journal for the Scientific Study of Religion, 36*, 382–392.

Cammack, M., Young, L. A., & Heaton, T. B. (1997). An empirical assessment of divorce law in Indonesia. *Indonesian Journal for Islamic Studies, 4*, 93–108.

Casanova, J. (1994). *Public religion in the modern world*. Chicago: University of Chicago Press.

Chaves, M. (1991). Family structure and protestant church attendance: The sociological basis of cohort and age effects. *Journal for the Scientific Study of Religion, 39*, 329–340.

Chaves, M. (1997). *Ordaining women: Culture and conflict in religious organizations*. Cambridge, MA: Harvard University Press.

Christiano, K. J. (2000). Religion and family in modern American culture. In S. K. Houseknecht & J. G. Pankhurst (Eds.), *Family, religion, and social change in diverse societies*. New York: Oxford University Press.

Clydesdale, T. (1997). Family behaviors among early U.S. baby boomers: Exploring the effects of religion and income change, 1965–1982. *Social Forces, 76*, 605–635.

Coltrane, S. (2001). Marketing the marriage "solution": Misplaced simplicity in the politics of fatherhood. *Sociological Perspectives, 44*, 387–418.

Coontz, S. (1992). *The way we never were: American families and the nostalgia trap*. New York: Basic Books.

Davidman, L. (1991). *Tradition in a rootless world*. Berkeley, CA: University of California Press.

Dollahite, D. C. (Ed.). (2000). *Strengthening our families: An in-depth look at the proclamation on the family*. Salt Lake City: Bookcraft.

Dollahite, D. C. (2003). Fathering for eternity: Generative spirituality in latter-day saint fathers of children with special needs. *Review of Religious Research, 44*, 339–351.

Dollahite, D. C., Marks, L. D., & Goodman, M. (2004). Families and religious beliefs, practices, and communities: Linkages in a diverse and dynamic cultural context. In M. J. Coleman & L. H. Ganong (Eds.), *The handbook of contemporary families: Considering the past, contemplating the future*. Thousand Oaks, CA: Sage.

Durkheim, E. (1951). *Suicide*. New York: Free Press. (Original work published 1897)

D'Antonio, W., & Aldous, J. (1983). *Families and religions: Conflict and change in modern society*. Bevery Hills: Sage.

Edgell, P. (2003). In rhetoric and practice: Defining "the good family" in local congregations. In M. Dillon (Ed.), *The handbook of the sociology of religion*. New York: Cambridge University Press.

Edgell, P. (2005). *Religion and family: Understanding the transformation of linked institutions*. Princeton: Princeton University Press.

Eggebeen, D., & Knoester, C. (2001). Does fatherhood matter for men? *Journal of Marriage and Family, 63*, 381–393.

Elder, G. H., Jr., & Conger, R. D. (2000). *Children of the land: Adversity and success in rural America*. Chicago: University of Chicago Press.

Ellison, C. G. (1991). Religious involvement and subjective well-being. *Journal of Health and Social Behavior, 32*, 80–99.

Ellison, C. G. (1994). Religion, the life stress paradigm, and the study of depression. In J. S. Levin (Ed.), *Religion in aging and health: Theoretical foundations and methodological frontiers*. Newbury Park, CA: Sage.

Ellison, C. G., & Bartkowski, J. P. (2002). Conservative protestantism and the division of household labor among married couples. *Journal of Family Issues, 23*, 950–985.

Ellison, C. G., Bartkowski, J. P., & Anderson, K. L. (1999). Are there religious variations in domestic violence? *Journal of Family Issues, 20*, 87–113.

Ellison, C. G., Bartkowski, J. P., & Segal, M. L. (1996). Conservative protestantism and the parental use of corporal punishment. *Social Forces, 74*, 1003–1029.

Ellison, C. G., & Sherkat, D. E. (1993a). Conservative protestantism and support for corporal punishment. *American Sociological Review, 58*, 131–44.

Ellison, C. G., & Sherkat, D. E. (1993b). Obedience and autonomy: Religion and parental values reconsidered. *Journal for the Scientific Study of Religion, 32*, 313–329.

Furstenberg, F. (1988). Good dads/bad dads: The two faces of fatherhood. In A. Cherlin (Ed.), *Changing American family and public policy*. Washington, DC: Urban Institute Press.

Gallagher, S. K. (2003). *Evangelical identity and gendered family life*. New Brunswick, NJ: Rutgers University Press.

Gesch, L. (1995). Responses to changing lifestyles: "Feminists" and "traditionalists" in mainstream religion. In N. T. Ammerman & W. C. Roof (Eds.), *Work, family, and religion in contemporary society*. New York: Routledge.

Goldscheider, F. K., & Waite, L. J. (1993). *New families, no families?: The transformation of the American home*. Berkeley, CA: University of California Press.

Goode, W. J. (1993). *World changes in divorce patterns*. New Haven, CT: Yale University Press.

Gottman, J. M. (1998). Toward a process model of men in marriages and families. In A. Booth & A. Crouter (Eds.), *Men in families: When do they get involved? What difference does it make?*. Mahway, NJ: Erlbaum.

Griffith, R. M. (1997). *God's daughters: Evangelical women and the power of submission.* Berkeley: University of California Press.

Heaton, T. B. (1984). Religious homogamy and marital satisfaction reconsidered. *Journal of Marriage and the Family, 46,* 729–733.

Heaton, T. B., & Pratt, E. L. (1990). The effects of religious homogamy on marital satisfaction and stability. *Journal of Family Issues, 11,* 191–207.

Hertel, B. R. (1995). Work, family and faith: Recent trends. In N. Ammerman & W. C. Roof (Eds.), *Work, family, and religion in contemporary society* (pp. 81–121). New York: Routledge.

Hofferth, S. 2003. Race/ethnic differences in father involvement in two-parent families: Culture, context, or economy. *Journal of Family Issues, 24,* 185–216.

Houseknecht, S. K., & Pankhurst, J. G. (2000). *Family, religion, and social change in diverse societies.* New York: Oxford University Press.

Hout, M., Greeley, A., & Wilde, M. J. (2001). The demographic imperative in religious change in the United States. *American Journal of Sociology, 107,* 468–500.

Kurtz, S. (1992). *All the mothers are one.* New York: Columbia University Press.

Laumann, E. O., Gagnon, J. H., Michael, R. T., & Michaels, S. (1994). *The social organization of sexuality: Sexual practices in the United States.* Chicago: University of Chicago Press.

Lawton, L., & Bures, R. (2001). Parental divorce and the "switching" of religious identity. *Journal for the Scientific Study of Religion, 40,* 99–111.

Lesthaeghe, R. (1995). The second demographic transition in western countries: An interpretation. In K. O. Mason & A.-M. Jensen (Eds.), *Gender and family change in industrialized countries.* Oxford, UK: Oxford University Press.

Mahoney, A., Pargament, K. I., Tarakeshwar, N., & Swank, A. B. (2001). Religion in the home in the 1980s and 1990s: A meta-analytic review and conceptual analysis of links between religion, marriage, and parenting. *Journal of Family Psychology, 15,* 559–596.

Marks, L. D., & Dollahite, D. C. (2001). Religion, relationships, and responsible fathering in latter-day saint families of children with special needs. *Journal of Social and Personal Relationships, 18,* 625–650.

Marler, P. L. (1995). Lost in the fifties: The changing family and the nostalgic church. In N. T. Ammerman and W. C. Roof (Eds.), *Work, family, and religion in contemporary society.* New York: Routledge.

Marquardt, E. (2004). *The spiritual lives of children of divorce.* New York: The Institute for American Values.

Marsiglio, W., & Pleck, J. (in press). Fatherhood and masculinities. In R. W. Connell, J. Hearn, & M. Kimmel (Eds.), *The handbook of studies on men and masculinities.* Thousand Oaks CA: Sage.

McLanahan, S., & Sandefur, G. (1994). *Growing up with a single parent: What hurts, what helps.* Cambridge: Harvard University Press.

Miller, A., & Stark, R. (2002). Gender and religiousness: Can socialization explanations be saved? *American Journal of Sociology, 107,* 1399–1423.

Myers, S. M. (1996). An interactive model of religiosity inheritance: The importance of family context. *American Sociological Review, 61,* 858–866.

Nason-Clark, N. (1997). *The battered wife: How Christians confront family violence.* Louisville, KY: Westminster/John Knox Press.

Niebuhr, H. R. (1929). *The social sources of denominationalism.* New York: Holt.

Nock, S. (1998). *Marriage in men's lives.* New York: Oxford University Press.

Palkovitz, R. (2002). *Involved fathering and men's adult development: Provisional balances.* Mahwah, NJ: Erlbaum.

Pankhurst, J. G., & Houseknecht, S. K. (2000). Introduction: The religion-family linkage and social change-A neglected area of study. In S. K. Houseknecht & J. G. Pankhurst (Eds.), *Family, religion, and social change in diverse societies.* New York: Oxford University Press.

Pargament, K. I. (1997). *The psychology of religion and coping: Theory, research, practice.* New York: Guilford Press.

Pearce, L. D., & Axinn, W. G. (1998). The impact of family religious life on the quality of mother-child relations. *American Sociological Review, 63,* 810–828.

Popenoe, D. (1988). *Disturbing the nest: Family change and decline in modern societies.* Hawthorne, NY: Aldine de Gruyter.

Popenoe, D. (1996). *Life without father.* Cambridge: Harvard University Press.

Riesebrodt, M. (1993). *Pious passion: The emergence of modern fundamentalism in the United States and Iran* (D. Reneau, Trans.). Berkeley: University of California Press.

Roof, W. C. (1993). A generation of seekers: The spiritual journeys of the baby boom generation. San Francisco: Harper.

Roof, W. C., & Gesch, L. (1995). Boomers and the culture of choice: Changing patterns of work, family, and religion. In N. Ammerman & W. C. Roof (Eds.), *Work, family, and religion in contemporary society*. New York: Routledge.

Sciolino, E. (2001). *Persian mirrors: The elusive face of Iran*. Free Press.

Shehan, C. L., Bock, E. W., & Lee, G. R. (1990). Religious heterogamy, religiosity, and marital happiness: The case of Catholics. *Journal of Marriage and the Family, 52*, 73–79.

Sherkat, D. E. (1991). *Religious socialization and the family: An examination of religious influence in the family over the life course*. Unpublished dissertation, Sociology Department, Duke University. Durham, NC.

Sherkat, D. E. (2003). Religious socialization: Sources of influence and influences of agency. In M. Dillon (Ed.), *The handbook of the sociology of religion*. New York: Cambridge University Press.

Sherkat, D. E., & Ellison, C. G. (1999). Recent developments and current controversies in the sociology of religion. *Annual Review of Sociology, 25*, 363–394.

Smith, C. (1998). *American evangelicalism: Embattled and thriving*. Chicago: University of Chicago Press.

Smith, C. (2000). *Christian America?: What evangelicals really want*. Berkeley, CA: University of California Press.

Smith, C., & Kim, P. Family religious involvement and the quality of family relationships for early adolescents. Chapel Hill, NC: National Study of Youth and Religion.

Smith, S. R. (2000). Land of the rising son? Domestic organization, ancestor worship, and economic change in Japan. In S. K. Houseknecht & J. G. Pankhurst (Eds.), *Family, religion, and social change in diverse societies*. New York: Oxford University Press.

Stark, R. (1996). *The rise of Christianity: A sociologist reconsiders history*. Princeton, NJ: Princeton University Press.

Stark, R., & Finke, R. (2000). *Acts of faith: Explaining the human side of religion*. Berkeley, CA: University of California Press.

Stolzenberg, R. M., Blair-Loy, M., & Waite, L. J. (1995). Religious participation in early adulthood: Age and family life cycle effects on church membership. *American Sociological Review, 60*, 84–103.

Straus, M. A. (1994). *Beating the devil out of them: Corporal punishment in American families*. San Francisco: Jossey-Bass.

Swidler, A. (1986). Culture in action: Symbols and strategies. *American Sociological Review, 51*, 273–286.

Thompson, L., & Walker, A. (1989). Gender in families: Women and men in marriage, work, and parenthood. *Journal of Marriage and the Family, 51*, 845–871.

Thornton, A. (1985). Reciprocal influences of family and religion in a changing world. *Journal of Marriage and the Family, 47*, 381–94.

Thornton, A. (2004). *Reading history sideways: The fallacy and enduring impact of the developmental paradigm on family life*. Chicago: University of Chicago Press.

Thornton, A., Axinn, W. G., & Hill, D. H. (1992). Reciprocal effects of religiosity, cohabitation, and marriage. *American Journal of Sociology, 98*, 628–651.

Thornton, A., & Lin, H.-S. (1994). *Social change and the family in Taiwan*. Chicago: University of Chicago Press.

Tilley, J. R. (2003). Secularization and aging in Britain: Does family formation cause greater religiosity? *Journal for the Scientific Study of Religion, 42*, 269–278.

Trost, J., & Palm, I. (2000). Family and religion in Sweden. In S. K. Houseknecht & J. G. Pankhurst (Eds.), *Family, religion, and social change in diverse societies*. New York: Oxford University Press.

Waite, L., & Gallagher, M. (2000). *The case for marriage*. New York: Doubleday.

Waite, L., & Lehrer, E. (2003). The benefits from marriage and religion in the United States: A comparative analysis. *Population and Development Review, 29*, 255–275.

Wallace, J. M., Forman, T. A., Caldwell, C. H., & Willis, D. S. (2003). Religion and U.S. secondary school students: Current patterns, recent trends, and sociodemographic. *Youth and Society, 35*, 98–125.

Warner, R. S. (1993). Work in progress toward a new paradigm for the sociological study of religion in the United States. *American Journal of Sociology, 98*, 1044–1093.

Wilcox, W. B. (1998). Conservative protestant childrearing: Authoritarian or authoritative? *American Sociological Review, 63*, 796–809.

Wilcox, W. B. (2002a). For the sake of the children?: Family-related discourse and practice in the mainline. In R. Wuthnow & J. H. Evans (Eds.), *The quiet hand of God: Faith-based activism and the public role of mainline protestantism* (pp. 287–316). Berkeley, CA: University of California Press.

Wilcox, W. B. (2002b). *Sacred vows, public purposes: Religion, the marriage movement, and public policy.* Washington, DC: Pew Forum on Religion and Public Life.

Wilcox, W. B. (2002c). Religion, convention, and paternal involvement. *Journal of Marriage and Family, 64,* 780–792.

Wilcox, W. B. (2002d, June 25). *Religion, parenting, and child well-being.* Commission on Children at Risk, Hanover, NH: Dartmouth Medical School.

Wilcox, W. B. (2003). Conservative protestants and the family: Resisting, engaging, or accommodating modernity? In M. Cromartie (Ed.), *A public faith: Varieties of evangelical civic engagement.* Lanham, MD: Rowman and Littlefield.

Wilcox, W. B. (2004). *Soft patriarchs, new men: How Christianity shapes fathers and husbands.* Chicago: University of Chicago Press.

Wilcox, W. B. (2005). Mainline protestantism and the family. In D. Browning & D. Clairmont (Eds.), *American religions and the family.* New York: Columbia University Press.

Wilcox, W. B., & Bartkowski, J. P. (2000). The conservative protestant family: Traditional rhetoric, progressive practice. In E. J. Dionne & J. J. DiIulio (Eds.), *What's God got to do with the American experiment? Essays on religion and politics.* Washington, DC: Brookings Institution Press.

Wuthnow, R. (1989). *Communities of discourse: Ideology and structure in the reformation, the enlightenment, and European socialism.* Cambridge, MA: Harvard University Press.

Wuthnow, R. (1998). *After heaven: Spirituality in America since the 1950s.* Berkeley: University of California Press.

CHAPTER 6

Adolescence

PETER L. BENSON, PH.D., AND PAMELA EBSTYNE KING[1]

Interest in adolescent religious and spiritual development has gained momentum in the last decade. This trend is likely because of a combination of scientific, political, and societal factors. The interdisciplinary field of positive youth development (Benson & Pittman, 2002) has recently identified religious engagement as a developmental resource that lessens risk behavior or enhances positive outcomes (Bridges & Moore, 2002; National Research Council, 2002; National Research Council, 2002; Scales & Leffert, 2004). This, in turn, has led to renewed interest in the study of religion in the fields of public health, social work, education, developmental psychology, and prevention. At the same time, new global conflicts have heightened interest in the role of religious ideology in creating or exacerbating intertribal and international animosity.

These two themes (religion as developmental resource and religion as generator of conflict) are contemporary reminders that religion can be a wellspring for the best of human life (e.g., generosity, unity, sacrifice, altruism) as well as for the darkest side of human life (e.g., genocide, terrorism, slavery). Exploration of these two sides of religious influence have a long scientific history (Benson, Roehlkepartain & Rude, 2003; Pargamet, 2002).

Additionally, interest in adolescence and religion has been triggered by significant changes in the American religious landscape. Among these are the emergence of new religious forms, the demographic shifts affecting mainline religious denominations, and the growth in opportunities to purse spiritual development outside traditional religious institutions.

This review focuses primarily on the theoretical and empirical literature emerging in the last decade. It complements published reviews of earlier literature, including Strommen (1971); Nelsen, Potvin, and Shields (1977); Benson, Donahue, and Erickson, 1988; and Donahue and Benson (1995). The review covers four major topics: the demography of religious engagement during adolescence, the role of religion in adolescent development, religious socialization, and the consequences of religious/spiritual engagement.

PETER L. BENSON, PH.D. • President, Search Institute, Minneapolis, Minnesota 55413
PAMELA EBSTYNE KING • Fuller Theological Seminary, Pasadena, California 91182

THE DEMOGRAPHY OF RELIGIOUS ENGAGEMENT

The American Context

Although it varies in form and level of intensity, a high level of religious/spiritual engagement has been documented across cultures and in different societies. A Gallup International Association (1999) poll of 50,000 adults in 60 countries found that, on average, 87% of respondents consider themselves part of a religion, 63% indicate that God is highly important in their lives (between 7 and 10 on a 10-point scale), and 75% believe in either a personal God or "some sort of spirit or life force." There is wide variability across cultures in specific beliefs about religious or spiritual matters and in whether people participate in religious activities (with significantly lower levels of religious involvement on some continents than religious affiliation or spiritual beliefs). Yet, the overall patterns reinforce that religion remains an important part of life around the globe, with some of the strongest commitments being evident in developing nations.

Self-reported engagement by North Americans is far above the international average. A 2001 Gallup Poll in the United States showed that 55% of adults said religion was "very important" in their lives, with another 30% reporting it as "fairly important" (Gallup Organization, 2000). Many have written about the high and persistent engagement percentages in the United States, particularly in comparison to Western Europe (Eck, 2001; Kerestes & Youniss, 2003; Wuthnow, 1994). This American pattern of engagement has remained fairly constant across the last several decades, in spite of sociological predictions that processes of modernization and secularization would lead to a significant withering of religious interest (Berger, 1999).

What has shifted, of course is the diversity of religious forms. Harvard professor Diana Eck captures this theme in the title of her recent book, *A New Religious America: How a "Christian Country" Has Become the World's Most Religiously Diverse Nation* (Eck, 2001). This is the story of the rapid rise of Muslim, Hindu, and Buddhist communities. A second transformation of religious engagement—not covered in Eck's work—is the rapid rise of Pentecostalism in the United States (and throughout Latin America and Africa). Finally, there is the growing number of American adults (and, one presumes, young people) who consider themselves "spiritual, but not religious" (Fuller, 2001) each of these changes provides additional challenge for monitoring the breadth and depth of religious/spiritual sentiment.

In a nation in which religious/spiritual engagement is so normative, it is confounding that the social sciences have, by and large, marginalized the inquiry of the development and consequences of the religious/spiritual impulse. Many scholars have documented the relative lack of research attention in mainstream psychology (Gorsuch, 1988; Paloutzian, 1996); in sociology (Smith, Denton, Faris, & Regnerus, 2002); within the study of adolescence (Benson, Donahue, & Erickson, 1989; Bridges & Moore, 2002); and in child development (Nye, 1999). Benson, Roehlkepartain, and Rude (2003) scrutinized the social science literature to determine the frequency with which keywords religion and spirituality are found in recent published literature. Three findings clearly show what appears to be a "sin of omission." First, a search of Social Science Abstracts for the years 1990–2002 shows that only 1.1% of all articles on children and adolescents address religion and/or spirituality. Second, less than 1% of 1990–2002 articles in the six leading developmental psychology journals (*Child Development, Developmental Psychology, International Journal of Behavioral Development, Journal of Adolescent Research, Journal of Early Adolescence, and Journal of Research on Adolescence*) include keywords for religion or spirituality.

Youth Religious Engagement

There are, nevertheless, a number of research studies published in a variety of fields (e.g., social psychology, social work, sociology, the psychology of religion, sociology of religion, medicine, religious studies, education, public heath) that constitute a body of knowledge— though incomplete—from which we can extract a portrait of religious engagement. Ongoing national studies such as Monitoring the Future and the National Longitudinal Study on Adolescent Health provide useful descriptive data. Another source of data is an aggregated sample of 217,277 students in grades 6–12 in public and alternative schools who completed the *Search Institute Profiles of Student Life: Attitudes and Behaviors* survey in the 1999–2000 school year (Benson, Scales, & Roehlkepartain, 1999). This self-selected sample— which includes urban, suburban, and rural schools—was then weighted to reflect the 1990 Census data for community size and race-ethnicity. New analyses of this data set were used to probe into greater detail on the predictive utility of religiosity among adolescents, with a particular eye to testing how well patterns of relationships hold across demographic subgroups. Greater details about this survey instrument and the concepts of developmental assets, thriving behavior, and risk behavior can be found in a series of publications (Benson et al., 1999; Leffert et al., 1998; Scales et al., 2000).

The ongoing Monitoring the Future study coordinated by the University of Michigan (Bachman et al., 2000) shows that the religious engagement of American adolescents is both stable and changing. In the senior high school class of 2000, 83.7% report affiliation with a religious denomination or tradition. Although affiliation is still dominated by Christian denominations, trend lines across 20 years (1976–1996) of Monitoring the Future studies show increases in the percentages of youth affiliating with non-Christian traditions (Smith et al., 2002).

Several reexaminations of Monitoring the Future annual surveys of high school students show fairly high stability in both affiliation and self-reported religious service attendance across time (Donahue & Benson, 1995; Smith et al., 2002). From 1976 to 1996, only small declines are observed in both indicators (Smith et al., 2002). However, the major point to be made here is that on general measures of engagement, the vast majority of American adolescents report affiliation and at least occasional service attendance.

Using the two most commonly used indicators of religious/spiritual engagement (importance or salience and attendance), a comparison of two large sample studies conducted in 1999–2000 suggests that more than half of high school seniors are engaged at a meaningfully high level. Comparing seniors in 2000 via Monitoring the Future and seniors in 1999–2000 via Search Institute's composite dataset across several hundred communities shows that: (1) both studies place frequent participation in a religious institution at about 50%; and (2) both find the self-report of religion/spirituality as quite or very important to be above 50%.

Variability by Major Demographic Variables

The Search Institute composite data set from 1999 to 2000 has recently been analyzed to estimate religious engagement by grade in school, gender, race/ethnicity, city size and maternal education (Benson, Scales, & Sesma, 2005). Five of these demographic analyses are reported here.

1. *Grade Trends*—As shown in Tables 6.1 and 6.2, both religious participation (hours per week attending programs or services at a religious institution) and importance of

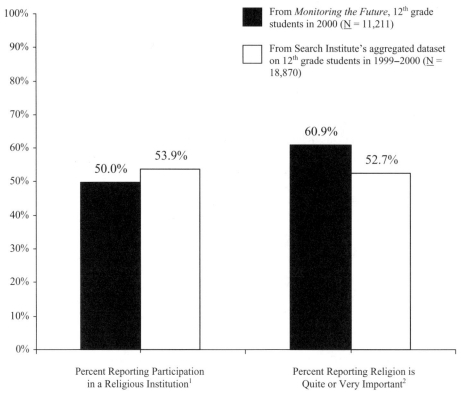

FIGURE 6.1. Religious Importance and Participation among High School Seniors (Class of 2000): Comparisons of Two Datasets.
[1]*Monitoring the Future* data are form items C13B ("how often do you attend worship services?"). Responses for "once or twice a month" and "about once a week or more" were combined; Search Institute data are from survey item #64 ("during an average week, how many hours do you spend going to groups, programs, or services at a church, synagogue, mosque, or other spiritual place?"). Responses of one hour or more per week were combined.
[2]The *Monitoring the Future* item reads "how important is religion to your life?" Reponses for *pretty important* (29.2%) and ***very important*** (31.7%) were combined. The Search Institute item reads "how important is each of the following in your life (being religious or spiritual)." Responses for ***quite important*** (25.9%) and ***very important*** (26.8%) were combined.

"being religious or spiritual" decline with grade. Summing across categories shows that 70% of 6th grade students report one hour or more per week of participation, falling to 54% in grade 12, with a fairly linear downward trend. However, the percentage reporting that religion or spirituality is "quite" or "very" important remains more stable across grades, as follows:

Grade 6:   55%
Grade 7:   57%
Grade 8:   55%
Grade 9:   54%
Grade 10:   53%
Grade 11:   56%
Grade 12:   53%

TABLE 6.1. Hours Per Week Attending Programs or Services at a Religious Institution: By Gender, Grade, Race/Ethnicity, Town Size, and Maternal Education (1999–2000)

Demographic Category		N	During an average week, how many hours do you spend going to groups, programs, or services at a church, synagogue, mosque, or other religious or spiritual place?					
			0 (%)	1 (%)	2 (%)	3–5 (%)	6–10 (%)	11 or more (%)
Total		216,382	37.4	20.4	17.7	15.9	4.4	4.2
Gender	Male	102,377	40.7	20.7	16.8	14.0	3.7	4.1
	Female	112,415	34.5	20.1	18.5	17.7	5.0	4.3
Grade	6	25,822	30.1	23.2	20.1	16.2	4.2	6.2
	7	27,395	31.3	21.7	19.6	17.3	4.6	5.5
	8	47,314	34.2	20.8	18.9	17.2	4.5	4.3
	9	30,109	39.0	19.5	17.2	15.9	4.5	3.9
	10	37,498	42.1	19.5	16.8	14.2	4.1	3.3
	11	28,999	41.6	18.1	16.3	16.3	4.7	2.9
	12	18,903	46.1	19.8	13.4	13.5	3.9	3.3
Race/Ethnicity	American Indian	2,085	46.6	19.3	13.4	11.4	3.6	5.8
	Asian or Pacific Islander	6,486	46.6	6.8	14.4	14.3	3.8	4.1
	African American	29,393	30.0	14.1	17.9	21.8	6.9	9.3
	Hispanic	22,716	41.0	23.2	16.6	11.1	3.3	4.8
	White	147,074	37.6	21.5	18.2	15.7	4.1	3.0
	Bi-racial	8,629	41.0	17.2	15.8	15.7	4.8	5.6
City Population	Under 2,500	21,956	38.8	21.8	17.7	14.7	3.4	3.5
	2,500–9,999	12,438	37.2	21.8	18.2	15.7	3.8	3.3
	10,000–44,999	13,803	35.7	21.3	18.1	16.9	4.4	3.6
	50,000–250,000	76,849	37.7	21.0	17.8	15.6	4.4	3.6
	Over 250,000	56,947	39.0	17.4	16.5	16.1	5.1	5.9
Maternal Education	Grade school or less	6,039	42.9	19.4	15.2	12.2	3.7	6.6
	Some high school	15,136	48.7	17.3	13.4	12.3	3.7	4.5
	High school	49,855	41.7	20.7	16.4	13.7	3.8	3.7
	Some college	34,686	36.5	19.6	17.6	17.2	4.9	4.1
	College graduate	57,225	31.8	21.2	20.1	18.5	4.8	3.6
	Graduate or professional school	31,931	31.3	21.0	19.8	18.1	5.2	4.6

Search Institute (2003). Unpublished tabulations.

Note however the slight increase in the percentage reporting that being religious or spiritual is "not important": this rises from 10% in grade 6 to 16% in grade 12.

2. *Gender Differences*—As shown in many studies (Benson, 1992; Bridges & Moore, 2002; Donahue & Benson, 1995), females report higher levels of engagement than males. As seen in Table 1, female reports of 1 hour or more per week of attendance stands at 65% and males are at 59%. As shown in Table 6.2, a small difference

TABLE 6.2. Importance of Religion and Spirituality, By Gender, Grade, Race/Ethnicity, Town Size, and Maternal Education (1999–2000)

Demographic Category		N	How important is each of the following to you in your life: Being religious or spiritual?				
			Not Important (%)	Somewhat Important (%)	Not Sure (%)	Quite Important (%)	Very Important (%)
Total		216,044	12.9	15.5	17.1	26.2	28.5
Gender	Male	102,205	15.6	15.8	17.0	25.7	25.8
	Female	112,251	10.4	15.1	17.1	26.6	30.9
Grade	6	25,771	10.0	12.7	22.6	25.0	29.7
	7	27,400	10.1	13.2	20.3	26.1	30.4
	8	47,165	12.1	14.7	18.1	26.2	28.9
	9	30,057	13.2	16.1	16.9	26.8	27.1
	10	37,419	15.1	17.3	14.9	26.1	26.6
	11	29,004	14.1	16.4	13.0	26.8	29.7
	12	18,870	15.9	18.2	13.2	25.9	26.8
Race/ Ethnicity	American Indian	2,089	17.2	15.8	23.0	22.7	21.2
	Asian or Pacific Islander	6,461	9.5	13.1	25.0	27.9	24.5
	African American	29,319	8.7	10.2	16.6	23.1	41.4
	Hispanic	22,680	10.5	13.3	22.1	30.1	24.0
	White	146,883	14.1	17.0	15.9	26.2	26.8
	Biracial	8,613	14.6	15.3	17.3	23.9	29.0
City Population	Under 2,500	21,918	14.1	16.5	17.0	25.8	26.5
	2,500–9,999	12,423	13.1	16.8	16.1	26.5	27.5
	10,000–49,999	13,792	12.3	15.7	15.4	26.7	27.7
	50,000– 250,000	76,704	12.6	16.4	16.8	26.7	27.7
	Over 250,000	56,865	13.2	13.4	18.9	25.0	29.5
Maternal Education	Grade school or less	6,031	12.3	13.2	22.1	26.7	25.7
	Some high school	15,100	16.0	14.9	22.3	23.7	23.1
	High school	49,787	13.6	16.7	17.5	26.3	25.8
	Some college	34,642	11.1	15.7	15.1	26.5	31.5
	College graduate	57,131	11.9	15.6	14.0	27.0	31.4
	Graduate of professional school	31,895	13.3	15.0	14.1	27.1	30.4

Search Institute (2003). Unpublished tabulations.

is also found with importance (58% of girls say religion/spirituality is "quite" or "very" important compared to 52% of boys).

3. *Race/Ethnicity*—The major finding here is that the highest rates for participation and importance are reported by African-American youth. This has been documented in a

number of other studies (Benson, Donahue, & Erickson, 1989; Benson & Donahue, 1989; Swanson et al., 2002).

4. *City Size*—As seen in Tables 6.1 and 6.2, there is little change in participation and importance rates across five categories of population size.

5. *Maternal Education*—This demographic item provides a glimpse at the relationship of religious engagement to socioeconomic status (SES) (given the assumption that maternal education is a proxy for family income). Among studies of adults, religious engagement and SES tend to be inversely related. In this composite dataset, however, we see some evidence for religious participation increasing with maternal education (Table 6.1).

Though attendance and importance (or salience) are commonly used indicators, we have identified only one publication that documents an attempt to see these two items combine (Benson, Scales, & Sesma, 2005). At a descriptive level, it is useful to discover how these items interrelate, beyond the fact that the correlation between them is .47 ($N = 216,383$) in the Search Institute composite dataset. Because one of the two items (attendance) has an institutional face, and the other (importance) more directly taps salience or commitment, it seems likely that there will be cases where adolescents are institutionally active but report low importance (a combination that could emerge where teenagers are compelled by parents to attend) and where the reverse is true (that is, high importance, low attendance). This category represents what some presume to be a growing form of spiritual expression in the United States (i.e., importance—and perhaps even an active life of practice—outside religious institutions or communal expressions of spirituality.)

To describe these categories of engagement, two binary variables (low/high on importance and low/high on attendance were created. For the religious/spiritual importance item, not important, somewhat, and not sure were coded as low; quite important and very important were coded as high. For the attendance item, 0 hours per week was coded as low; 1 hour or more per week was coded as high.

Results are shown in Table 6.3. For the total sample ($N = 216, 383$), 44.6% were high/high and 27.7% were low/low. As expected, particularly during adolescence, there is a sizeable percentage (18.0) that combine high attendance with low importance. There are multiple explanations for this phenomenon. As noted earlier, this could be the result of parental pressure. Equally probable, however, is that the social/friendship aspect of participation is the primary motivator for some young people's attendance in programs, activities, and services, not necessarily religious or spiritual importance. Finally, some youth spend time in religious institutions participating in youth programs that may or may not have an explicitly religious or spiritual theme. An after-school tutoring program, for example, may be based in a congregation's facility but be largely secular in its orientation.

About 1 in 10 of the young people in this sample (9.7%) attach high importance to religion/spirituality, yet report no attendance. As shown in Table 6.3, this percentage ranges from 8.5% in grade 6 to 11.5% in grade 12.

Benson, Scales, and Sesma (2005) also combined percentages for youth high on one or both items to yield a global indicator of religious/spiritual engagement. Overall, 72.3% of the total sample met this condition (high on one or both). This combination puts into perspective the normative nature religious/spiritual engagement in the United States. That is, nearly three of four adolescents in this 6th- to 12th-grade sample evidence either importance or attendance (or both). In addition, two thirds or more of youth in each race/ethnicity category reported "high" on one or both indicators. The percentages moved

TABLE 6.3. Percent Reporting Importance and/or Participation, by Gender, Grade, and Race/Ethnicity[1]

Religious/Spiritual Importance⟶		Low	Low	High	High	High on Importance and/
Participation in Religious Community▸		Low	High	Low	High	or Participation
Sample		N				
Total		216,383	27.7%	18.0%	9.7%	44.6%	72.3%
Gender	Male	102,377	30.7	18.1	10.0	41.2	69.3
	Female	112,406	24.9	17.9	9.6	47.6	75.1
Grade	6	25,822	21.6	24.1	8.5	45.8	79.4
	7	27,395	22.7	21.2	8.6	47.5	77.3
	8	47,314	25.3	19.9	8.8	45.9	74.7
	9	30,108	28.8	17.6	10.2	43.4	71.2
	10	37,497	31.7	15.8	10.4	42.1	68.3
	11	29,000	30.5	13.1	11.0	45.3	69.5
	12	18,903	34.6	12.9	11.5	41.1	65.4
Race/ Ethnicity	Native American	2,085	34.2	22.0	12.3	31.4	65.8
	Asian or Pacific Islander	6,485	30.4	17.5	16.3	35.9	69.6
	African American	29,395	17.1	18.9	12.8	51.1	82.9
	Hispanic	22,716	26.3	19.8	14.7	39.1	73.7
	White	147,073	29.6	17.5	8.0	44.9	70.4
	Biracial	8,628	29.8	17.8	11.3	41.2	70.2

Search Institute (2003). Unpublished tabulations.
[1] For the religious/spiritual importance item, not important, somewhat important and not sure are coded as low; quite important and very important are coded as high. For the attendance items, 0 hours of attendance at programs or services is codes as low; 1 hour or more per week is coded as high.

from a low of 65.8% of Native Americans to 82.9% of African Americans. And the type composed of high importance/low institutional attendance was more common for each category of minority youth (e.g., Hispanic, Black, Native American, Asian, biracial) that it was for whites.

One other effort to map the religious landscape of adolescents combines findings from three national and federally funded surveys of youth (Smith, Denton, Faris, & Regnerus, 2002). While replicating the age, gender and race findings described earlier, this synthesis provides four additional findings:

1. 47% of high school students reported their religious affiliation as Catholic (24%) or Baptist (23%). Thirteen percent claimed no religious affiliation.
2. Over a 20-year period (1926–1996), a majority of American youth reported a Christian affiliation for each year in this 20-year span. However, protestant affiliation declined 10%, with two categories increasing 5%—religions other that Catholic, Protestant, or Jewish—and those report no affiliation.
3. Regional differences mimic those found with adults (Smith, Sikkiuk, & Bailey, 1998). Adolescents reporting no religious affiliation ranged from 8% of Southern youth to 17% of youth residing in Western states.

RELIGION AND ADOLESCENT DEVELOPMENT

Developmental Patterns

Historically, nearly all research on religion and individual-level variables have been cross-sectional in design. Fortunately, four longitudinal studies have been published since 2002 (Benson, Scales, & Sesma, 2005; Gunnoe & Moore, 2002; Kerestes, Youniss, & Metz, 2004; Regnerus, Smith, & Smith, 2004). The Regnerus, Smith, and Smith (2002) study examined the role of social and religious contexts on religious formation. And the study by Gunnoe and Moore (2002) examined predictors of religiosity captured during the third of a three-wave study. The key findings of these two studies will be discussed in the section on religious socialization.

The two remaining longitudinal studies give us a rare glimpse at religious trajectories during adolescence. Both report percentages for each of four religious patterns. Kerestes, Youniss, and Metz (2004) devised their four types (low during sophomore year, low during senior year of high school; low-high; high-low; high-high) from distributions on a religious perspective scale. It was based on a six-item measure which identified a "positive and well-rounded religious perspective" (p. 41). A binary variable was created by placing the lowest third in the low category and the highest third in the high category (the middle third were excluded from the analysis). Although the reported analyses are useful for examining the relationship of the four types to behavior, the analytical process used here does not provide data useful for describing the frequency of various religious development trajectories. We will examine this study's findings in the section on the consequences of engagement.

Finally, we turn to the study reported in Benson, Scales, and Sesma (2005). This longitudinal study consisted of 370 students surveyed at three points in time (fall of 1997, when students were in grades 6, 7, or 8; the fall of 1998 (grades 7, 8, or 9) and the fall of 2001 (grades 10, 11, or 12). All are public school students in a fairly heterogeneous suburb of a major Midwestern city. On a self-reported religious importance item, low and high importance categories were created as follows: not important, somewhat important or not sure responses were coded as low; quite important or very important were coded as high.

For the total sample, ($N = 370$), 35.5% remain low on religious importance from 1997 to 2001; 31.1% stay high from 1997 to 2001. Another 20% changed from high to low across the 4 years, and 13% change from low to high. By this fairly global measure, the data suggest, overall, that about two thirds of youth stay constant in religious importance across 4 years, whereas one third experience a shift (from low to high or high to low). Patterns for boys and girls are similar.

Religion and Developmental Processes

One of the dominate lines of empirical and theoretical inquiry in research on adolescent religiousness has to do with the role of cognitive factors. It is axiomatic in the developmental literature that a qualitive change occurs during the adolescent years. Based on the work of Piaget (1965/1932), the change is usually defined as a gradual shift from concrete operations to formal operations (often expressed as abstract thinking).

Since 1970, several researchers have extended inquiry about this shift into the religious domain. Drawing heavily on Goldman's (1964) work, researchers have looked at three interrelated issues: whether a qualitive change occurs during adolescence in religious cognition, how this change is related to other cognitive processes, and how this change is tied to religious commitment.

One consistent finding is that religious thinking between ages 12 and 18 becomes less literal and more abstract (Elkind, 1971; Nelsen et al., 1977; Potvin et al., 1976). Goldman (1964) encouraged these investigations with his seminal work on the age-related sequencing of religious belief stages. Based on samples of British children, he postulated the occurrence of three stages: intuitive, concrete operational, and formal or abstract. The shift from concrete to abstract was placed in the 13 to 14.5 age span. Goldman concluded that the concrete-to-abstract shift in religious thinking requires that this shift had already occurred in general cognitive functioning; the shift to abstract religious thinking occurs more slowly than in other areas of cognitive functioning.

In a major contribution to the literature, Hoge and Petrillo (1978) sought to both replicate and extend this line of inquiry. This work documented three important findings:

1. Abstract religious thinking among adolescents tends to be negatively related to creedal asset and religious practice, suggesting that the advent of abstract thinking is one factor accounting for the decline in adolescent religiousness documented earlier.
2. Abstract religious thinking is correlated with the general cognitive ability to do abstract thinking.
3. Contrary to Goldman's (1964) hypothesis, the discrepancy between level of religious thinking and overall cognitive capacity does not promote rejection of doctrine and church. The level of abstract religious thinking predicts rejection better than does the discrepancy.

The Hoge and Petrillo (1978) conclusions, however, have been challenged by later research (Batson, Schoenrade, & Ventis, 1993). Although these two authors argued that Goldman had overestimated the role of cognitive factors in religious development and underestimated the role of religious training, there continues to be considerable disagreement about the intersection of religious and cognitive development (Spilka, Hood, Hunsberger, & Gorsuch, 2003).

A second line of theory and research examines the interplay of religious development and identity formation. Erickson, of course, moved identity formation to the forefront of adolescent development (1968, 1969). One of the dominant strands of research links measures of religiosity to Marcia's (1966) fourfold taxonomy of identity statuses. These four move, theoretically, from more immature statuses (foreclosed and diffused) to more mature ones (moratorium and achieved). The empirical literature investigating those intersections is difficult to summarize, since studies utilize widely disparate samples and measures of religion. Even when looking at a most obvious prediction—that more "mature" forms of religious thinking will be linked to achieved identity (the most mature of the four identity statuses), the literature is conflicted due conceivably to the fact that researchers define mature religion in different and sometimes incompatible ways (Spilka, Hood, Hunsberger, & Gorsuch, 2003).

Spencer and her colleagues (Spencer, 1995; Spencer, Dupree & Hartman, 1997; Swanson et al., 2002) provide an important step forward in this area of theory and research. This group of scholars has proposed some new ways to look at how social, cultural and historical contexts influence and interact with adolescent identity formation. The point of departure here is the process of identity creation and how it is informed by context, with particular focus on African-American youth. Key constructs in Spencer's phenomenological variant of ecological systems theory (PVEST) include net stress engagement level, reactive coping methods, and self-appraisal. These scholars have generated a body of theory and research that explains the import of the black church for circumnavigating societal barriers to positive identity formation as well as buttressing positive self-appraisals of one's competence.

Closely related to the process of identity formation is the development of meaning, a construct that has, of course, both psychological import (Haste, 1987) and is simultaneously tied to one of religion's major functions (George, Ellison, & Larson, 2002). This tie has been used to explain adult engagement in religion—and particularly the up tick in religious engagement after age 50 (Benson, 1991). The role of religion as meaning-making among youth has received sparse attention in the literature. Kerestes and Youniss (2002), however, provide a useful advance in this understudied topic. Grounded in Erikson's notion that identity formation during adolescent triggers interest in connecting to "the ideologies of enduring social institutions and structures" (p. 179), these authors suggest that religious traditions and institutions have meaning-making capacity for youth, particularly in periods of rapid social change.

Furrow, King, and White (2004) propose and test several hypotheses linking religion, identity and meaning. As predicted, religious identity among urban high school students was positively linked to both personal meaning and prosocial personality.

Recent theoretical explorations of the concept of spiritual development (in contrast to religious development) raise the possibility that the former is a universal developmental process having to do with "the process of growing the intrinsic human capacity for self-transcendence, in which the self is embedded in something greater than the self" (Benson, Roehlkepartain, & Rude, 2003, p. 205). The implication here is that religion is one of multiple pathways for exploring the intrinsic press for connectedness, meaning and purpose.

RELIGIOUS SOCIALIZATION

Multiple contextual and ecological factors inform the development of adolescent religiosity. Most research focuses on factors within a particular domain (e.g., family, peers, congregations). However, several recent studies have begun to examine the interplay among these factors.

FAMILY INFLUENCES.   Many studies have found that children and adolescents follow in their parents' religious footprints, adopting their denominational preference more often than switching to another denomination or becoming unaffiliated (Spilka et al., 1985). Argyle and Beit-Hallahmi (1975) found that affiliation among adolescents conformed to parental affiliation 40 to 90% of the time, with liberal Protestant denominations having lower rates of retention and Catholics and Jews have higher rates.

A number of family dynamics have been documented that appear to enhance the religious commitment of children and adolescents. These include the amount of religious activity in the home, the religious modeling done by both mothers and fathers, and the frequency of parent-child communication about religious matters (Benson, Williams, & Johnson, 1987; Hoge & Petrillo, 1978; Ozorak, 1989; Potvin & Sloane, 1985). Religious socialization tends to "take hold" best when families are characterized by closeness or harmony (Benson et al., 1986; Ozorak, 1989). Hoge and Petrillo (1978) suggest that positive religious socialization is enhanced when parents are consistent in providing religious messages.

Overall, the kinds of family dynamics tend to have more influence on religious development that other domains. Benson et al. (1986) estimated several multiple regression equations predicting faith commitment (personal religiousness) and church commitment (institutional religiousness) from their national survey data of Catholic high school seniors. The three key factors predicating church and faith commitment were the student's perception of the importance of religion for mother and father, a positive family life, and the amount of religious activities in the home. The zero-order correlations between the predictors and the criteria were in the .20 to .30 range.

A number of studies have sought to document which parent has the greatest influence on religious development. Although there is some ambiguity in the patterning of results, the most typical finding is that the religious sentiments and practices of the mother are more influential than those of the father (Acock & Bengston, 1987; Benson & Eklin, 1990; Dudley & Dudley, 1986; Hunsberger & Brown, 1984).

Several family factors appear to interfere with the transmission of religious values from parents to children. These include conflict between parent and child (Hunsberger & Brown, 1984), parental discord (Hoge & Petrillo, 1978), and mixed-religion marriages (Spilka et al., 1985).

CONGREGATIONAL INFLUENCES.   Surprisingly, relatively little research has been devoted to the question of how churches and synagogues influence religious development. This would seem to be an important line of inquiry, given the fact that the vast majority of children and adolescents are institutionally involved. Three studies have taken an in-depth look at religious education programs within religious denominations, with the goal of identifying the program dynamics that promote religious commitment (Benson & Donahue, 1990; Benson & Eklin, 1990; Kelly, Benson, & Donahue, 1986). Across these studies, involving multiple denominations (Catholic, Seventh-Day Adventist, Lutheran, Southern Baptist Convention, Methodist, Presbyterian, Christian Church [Disciples of Christ], United Church of Christ), it was found that programs marked by educationally effective practices have a profound influence on religious development. These practices include trained and committed teachers, learner-centered educational processes, positive climate, and a content emphasis on issues of importance to children and adolescents. These dynamics are similar to those found in recent public school research on "what works" in promoting academic achievement. When these effectiveness dynamics are in place in a religious education program, the impact on religious commitment is substantial, revealing the impact of families (Benson & Eklin, 1990). However, many of these dynamics are not found in congregational programs.

OTHER INFLUENCES.   The role of peers and peer groups in religious socialization has not been a strong focus in research. In the few studies that do exist, weak to modest relationships are reported (Hoge & Petrillo, 1978; King, Furrow, & Roth, 2002; Roberts, Koch, & Johnson, 2001). When peer influence is studied along with family and other contextual influences, peer influence appears to be less important than these other factors (Erickson, 1992; Hunsberger, 1983, Ozorak, 1989). In a rare longitudinal inquiry, Begnerus, Smith, and Smith (2004) found that parents and friends informed both religious service attendance and religious importance.

Much of the research on the effects of parochial education has occurred in Catholic schools. Generally, studies find that parochial education increase religious commitment. Greeley and his colleagues (Greeley, McCready, & Mccourt, 1976; Greeley & Rossi, 1966) used retrospective accounts by Catholic adults to establish that the number of years of Catholic schooling is positively related to a wide range of pro-religion beliefs and practices. A comparison of Catholic students attending Catholic schools found that Catholic school attendance enhanced both faith commitment and church involvement after statistical controls for family and socioeconomic differences were made (Guerra, Benson, & Donahue, 1989).

INTERPLAY AMONG RELIGIOUS INFLUENCES. Several analytically rich studies have begun to add new knowledge about multiple and interacting pathways to religious development. Erickson (1992) employed linear structural modeling techniques to investigate religious influences. His analyses suggest that parental influence is less direct than previously posited in the literature. Instead, he proposed that parents exercise religious influence primarily by directing their children to more salient influences, including peers and religious education.

Gunnoe and Moore (2002) investigated a series of eight potential predicators of youth religiosity, including childhood training, religious schooling, gender, parenting style and role models. Via secondary analysis of data from the National Survey of Children, predictors were measured at ages 7–11 and 11–16, with religious variables captured at ages 17–22. The strongest predictors were ethnicity and peers' church attendance during high school. Also important was an interaction variable comprised of mother's religiosity who were high on support.

Regnerus, Smith, and Smith (2004) also utilized a federally funded longitudinal study, the Longitudinal Study of Adolescent Health. In one of the more theoretically grounded studies of adolescent religious development, these authors concluded that: parents are the primary influence in shaping church attendance patterns; and church attendance rates also are informed by peer group and by rates of church engagement by youth in one's school. Like Erickson (1992), these authors suggest that religiously engaged parents also "channel" their children into peer groups and schools that share their religious worldview.

Benson (1992) explored the additive nature of three religious socialization contexts, hypothesizing that consistency in socialization messages is a factor in religious development. In a large national study of youth and their family, congregational, and school contexts, it was found that faith maturity and related measures of religious engagement rise exponentially when youth are embedded in three networks (family, school, church) each of which teaches and models a shared religious worldview.

PREDICTING DEVELOPMENTAL OUTCOMES

There is a growing body of literature that documents the role of religious factors among youth. Generally, this research establishes a dual role of religion: as a protective factor inhibiting risk-taking behavior and as a factor that promotes positive developmental outcomes, including prosocial behavior and academic achievement. The literature, however, is only beginning to explore more theoretically grounded approaches to these issues.

Several syntheses of this literature have been published (Benson, Donahue, & Erickson, 1989; Benson, Masters, & Larson, 1997; Bridges & Moore, 2002; Smith & Faris, 2002; Spilka, Hood, Hunsberger, & Gorsuch, 2003). An overall summary of these behavioral influences can be found in Benson, Roehlkepartain, and Rude (2003). In terms of positive behaviors and outcomes, religious involvement or religious importance are positively associated with:

1. Overall well-being (Donahue & Benson, 1995; Markstrom, 1999).
2. Positive life attitudes, satisfaction, and hope for the future (Smith & Faris, 2002).
3. Altruism and service (Hodgkinson & Weitzman, 1997; Smith & Faris, 2002; Youniss, McLellan, & Yates, 1999; Furrow, King, & White, 2004).
4. Access to internal and external developmental resources that contribute to risk reduction and well-being and thriving (Wagener, Leffert, Furrow, King, & Benson, 2003).
5. Resiliency and coping (Benson, Masters, & Larson, 1997).
6. School success (Regnerus, 2000).
7. Physical health (Jessor, Turbin, & Costa, 1998; Wallace & Forman, 1998).
8. Positive identity formation (Donelson, 1999; Youniss et al., 1999).

And religiosity among youth is consistently and negatively related to a wide range of health-compromising behaviors:

1. Alcohol and other drug use (Gorsuch, 1995; National Center on Addiction and Substance Abuse at Columbia University, 2001; Resnick et al., 1997).
2. Crime, violence, and delinquency (Johnson, Jan, Larson, & Li, 2001; Smith & Faris, 2002).
3. Depression (Wright, Frost, & Wisecarver, 1993).
4. Danger-seeking and risk-taking (Smith & Faris, 2002).
5. Early sexual activity (Holder et al., 2000; Whitehead, Wilcox, & Rostosky, 2001).

What accounts for this consistent and generalizable relationship between religious importance or attendance with both the suppression of risk behavior and the enhancement of thriving? A fairly recent line of inquiry supports the hypothesis that developmental assets (in particular, religious contexts that function as asset-building resources) mediate the influence of religion. (For a review of developmental assets—support, empowerment, boundaries and expectations, constructive use of time, commitment to learning, positive values, social competencies, and positive identity—see Benson, 1997; Benson et al., 1998; and, linked to the religious context, Roehlkepartain, 1998).

A recent analysis provides strong evidence that religious engagement does enhance the developmental asset landscape (Wagener et al., 2003). A related study, using a national sample of 614 adolescents (ages 12 to 17), provides strong evidence that frequency of attendance enhances positive engagement with adults outside of one's family (Scales, Benson, & Mannes, 2003). Such networks of adult relationships can be powerful influences as both risk behaviors and thriving (Scales & Leffert, 1999). Several recent publications build on this research and suggest strategies for enhancing the developmental impact of religious communities within many faith traditions (e.g., Roehlkepartain, 1998, 2003a, 2003b; Roehlkepartain & Scales, 1996).

Consistent with this reasoning, Kerestes, Youniss, and Metz (2004) suggest that religious engagement promotes social integration (into adult relationships and prosocial values). Tracking four religious development trajectories during the high school years, they found that stable or upward trajectories were associated with greater civic participation and less alcohol and other drug use in comparison to low or downward trajectories.

Regnerus and Elder (2003) offer an important extension to this line of thinking. They find that more public forms of religious expression—such as church attendance—are associated with educational progress, particularly in economically-stressed neighborhoods. With considerable caution and creativity these authors propose a theoretical frame for understanding these findings. It suggests that church attendance functions as a protective mechanism in high-risk neighborhoods, generating relationships, values and sanctions which build "a transferable skill set of commitments and routines" (p. 646) useful for promoting success.

CONCLUSIONS

There are some signs that the study of religions and spiritual development during adolescence is taking a renewed energy. Some of this is because of interest in applied arenas of social science research, including prevention, health promotion and positive youth development. As the range of research "tribes" interested in religious and spiritual development broadens, there emerges an opportunity (and a need) for interdisciplinary dialogues and conversations about this historically undervalued line of inquiry.

In thinking about the possibility that the field is ready for evolutionary advances, it is useful to call attention to several of the most pressing issues, many of which have been identified in a number of recent publications (Bridges & Moore, 2002; Pargament, 2002; Benson, 2004; Smith, 2003). These include the need for: (1) the definitional and conceptual advances in understanding the terrains of religion and spirituality; (2) longitudinal study of religious and spiritual development; (3) advances in measurement; and (4) a heightened focus on how religious and spiritual trajectories are informed by culture, race and ethnicity.

NOTE

1. Peter Benson is president of Search Institute, Minneapolis; Pamela Ebstyne King is assistant professor, Family Studies, Graduate School of Psychology, Fuller Theological Seminary, Pasadena, CA.

REFERENCES

Acock, A. C., & Bengston, V. L. (1987). On the relative influence of mothers and fathers: A covariance analysis of political and religious socialization. *Journal of Marriage and the Family, 40*, 519–530.

Argyle, M., & Beit-Hallahmi, B. (1975). *The social psychology of religion.* London: Routledge & Kegan Paul.

Bachman, J., Johnston, L. D., & O'Malley, P. M. (2000). *Monitoring the future.* Ann Arbor: University of Michigan Institute for Social Research.

Benson, P. L. (1991, August). *Religious development in adolescence and adulthood.* (August). Paper presented at the annual convention of the American Psychological Association, San Francisco, CA.

Benson, P. L. (1992). Patterns of religious development in adolescence and adulthood. *Psychologists Interested in Religious Issues Newsletter (APA Division 36), 17*(2), 2–9.

Benson, P. L. (2004). Emerging themes in research on adolescent spiritual and religious development. *Applied Developmental Science 8*(1), 47–50.

Benson, P. L., Leffert, N., Scales, P. C., & Blyth, D. A. (1998). Beyond the 'village' rhetoric: Creating healthy communities for children and adolescents. *Applied Developmental Science, 2*(3), 138–159.

Benson, P. L., & Donahue, M. J. (1989). Ten-year trends in at-risk behavior: A national study of Black adolescents. *Journal of Adolescent Research, 4*(2), 125–139.

Benson, P. L., & Donahue, M. J. (1990). *Valuegenesis.* Silver Spring, MD: North American Division Office of Education, Seventh-Day Adventist Church.

Benson, P. L., Donahue, M. J., & Erickson, J. A. (1989). Adolescence and religion: A review of the literature from 1970 to 1986. *Research in the Social Scientific Study of Religion, 1*, 153–181.

Benson, P. L., & Eklin, C. H. (1990). *Summary report: The national study of mainline Protestant denominations.* Minneapolis: Search Institute.

Benson, P. L., Masters, K. S., & Larson, D. B. (1997). Religious influences on child and adolescent development. In N. E. Alessi (Ed.) *Handbook of child and adolescent psychiatry, Vol. 4: Varieties of development* (206–219). New York: Wiley.

Benson, P. L., & Pittman, K. J. (2001). *Trends in youth development: Visions, realities and challenges.* Boston, Kluwer Academic.

Benson, P. L., Roehlkepartain, E. C., & Rude, S. P. (2003). Spiritual development in childhood and adolescence: Toward a field of inquiry. *Applied Developmental Science.*

Benson, P. L., Scales, P. C., Leffert, N., & Roehlkepartain, E. C. (1999). *A fragile foundation: The state of developmental assets among American youth.* Minneapolis, Minnesota: Search Institute.

Benson, P. L., Scales, P. C., & Sesma, A. (2005). Adolescent spirituality. In K. Moore & L. Lippman (Eds.), *What do children need to flourish? Conceptualizing and measuring indicators of positive development.* Boston: Kluwer Academic.

Benson, P. L., Williams, D., & Johnson, A. (1987). *The quicksilver years: The hopes and fears of early adolescence.* San Francisco: Harper & Row.

Benson, P. L., Yeager, R. J., Wood, P. K., Guerra, M. J., & Manno, B. V. (1986). *Catholic high schools: Their impact on low-income students.* Washington, DC: National Catholic Educational Association.

Berger, P. (1999). *The desecularization of the world: Resurgent religion and world politics.* Grand Rapids, MI: Eerdmans.

Bridges, L. J., & Moore, K. A. (2002). *Religion and spirituality in childhood and adolescence.* Washington, DC: Child Trends.

Donahue, M. J., & Benson P. L. (1995). Religion and the well-being of adolescents. *Journal of Social Issues, 51*(2), 145–160.

Donelson, E. (1999). Psychology of religion and adolescents in the United States: Past to present. *Journal of Adolescence, 22,* 187–204.

Dudley, R. L., & Dudley, M. G. (1986). Transmissions of religious values from parents to adolescents. *Review of Religious Research, 28,* 3–15.

Eck, D. L. (2001). *A new religious America: How a "Christian country" has become the world's most religiously diverse nation.* San Francisco: Harper.

Elkind, D. (1971). The development of religious understanding in children and adolescents, In Strommen, M. P. *Research on religious development: A comprehensive handbook.* New York: Hawthorne.

Erikson, E. (1968). *Identity: Youth and Crisis.*, London: Faber & Faber.

Erikson, E. (1969). *Gandhi's Truth: On the Origin of Militant Nonviolence*, New York: W. W. Norton.

Fuller, R. C. (2001). *Spiritual, but not religious: Understanding unchurched America.* New York: Oxford University Press.

Furrow, J. L., King, P. E., & White, K. (2004). Religion and positive youth development: Identity, meaning, and prosocial concerns. *Applied Developmental Science, 8*(1), 17–26.

Gallup International Association. (1999). *Gallup international millennium survey.* Retrieved September 9, 2002, from http://www.gallup-international.com/surveys1.htm.

George, L. K., Ellison, C. G., & Larson, D. B. (2002). Explaining the relationships between religious involvement and health. *Psychological Inquiry, 13*, 190–200.

Goldman, R. (1964). *Religious Thinking from Childhood to Adolescence.* London: Routledge and Kegan Paul.

Gorsuch, R. L. (1988). Psychology of religion. *Annual Review of Psychology, 39*, 201–221.

Gorsuch, R. L. (1995). Religious aspects of substance abuse and recovery. *Journal of Social Issues, 51*(2), 65–83.

Greeley, A. M., McCready, W., & McCourt, K. (1976). *Catholic schools in a declining church.* Kansas City, MO: Sheed & Ward.

Greely, A. M., & Rossi, P. H. (1966). *The education of American Catholics.* Chicago: Aldine.

Guerra, M., Benson, P. L., & Donahue, M. (1989). *The heart of the matter: Effects of Catholic high schools on student values, beliefs, and behaviors.* Washington, DC: Catholic Educational Association.

Gunnoe, M. L., & Moore, K. A. (2002). Predictors of religiosity among youth aged 17–22: A longitudinal study of the National Survey of Children. *Journal for the Scientific Study of Religion, 41*(4), 613–622.

Haste, H. (1987). Growing into rules. In J. Bruner and H. Haste (Eds.), *Making sense.* London: Methuen.

Hodgkinson, V. A., & Weitzman, M. S. (1977). *Volunteering and giving among American teenagers 14 to 17 years of age* (1966 ed.). Washington, DC: Independent Sector.

Hoge, D. R., & Petrillo, G. H. (1978). Determinants of church participation and attitudes among high school youth. *Journal for the Scientific Study of Religion, 17*, 359–379.

Holder, D. W., Durant, R. H., Harris, T. L., Daniel, J. H., Obeidallah, D., & Goodman, E. (2000). The association between adolescent spirituality and voluntary sexual activity. *Journal of Adolescent Health, 26*, 295–302.

Hunsberger, G., & Brown, L. B. (1984). Religious socialization, apostasy, and the impact of family background. *Journal for the Scientific Study of Religion, 23*, 239–251.

Jessor, R., Turbin, M. S., & Costa, F. M. (1998). Protective factors in adolescent health behavior. *Journal of Personality and Social Psychology, 75*, 788–800.

Johnson, B. R., Jan, S. J., Larson, D. B., & Li, S. D. (2001). Does adolescent religious commitment matter: A reexamination of the effects of religiosity on delinquency. *Journal of Research in Crime and Delinquency, 38*, 22–43.

Kelly, F. D., Benson, P. L., & Donahue, M. J. (1986). *Toward effective parish religious education for children and young people: A national study.* Washington, DC: National Catholic Educational Association.

Kerestes, M., & Youniss, J. E. (2003). Rediscovering the importance of religion in adolescent development. In R. M. Lerner, F. Jacobs, & D. Wertlieb (Eds.), *Handbook of applied developmental science. Vol. 1: Applying developmental science for youth and families.* Thousand Oaks, CA: Sage.

Kerestes, M., Youniss, J., & Metz, E. (2004). Longitudinal patterns of religious perspective and civic integration. *Applied Developmental Science, 8*(1), 39–46.

Leffert, N., Benson, P. L., Scales, P. C., Sharma, A. R., Drake, D. R., & Blyth, D. A. (1998). Developmental assets: Measurement and prediction of risk behaviors among adolescence. *Applied Developmental Science, 2*(4), 209–230.

Markstrom, C. A. (1999). Religious involvement and adolescent psychosocial development. *Journal of Adolescence, 22*, 205–221.

National Center on Addiction and Substance Abuse at Columbia University. (2001). *So help me God: Substance abuse, religion, and spirituality.* New York: Author.

National Research Council and Institute of Medicine. (2002). *Community programs to promote youth development.* Washington, DC: National Academy Press.

National Research Council and Institute of Medicine. (2000). *From neurons to neighborhoods: The science of early childhood development.* Washington, DC: National Academy Press.

Nelsen, H. M., Potvin, R. H., & Shields, J. (1976). *The religion of children.* Unpublished manuscript, Catholic University of America.

Nye, R. M. (1999). Relational consciousness and the spiritual lives of children: Convergence with children's theory of mind. In K. H. Reich, F. K. Oser, & W. G. Scarlett (Eds.), *Psychological studies on spiritual and religious development* (Vol. 2, pp. 57–82). Lengerich, Germany: Pabst.

Orozak, E. W. (1989). Social and cognitive influences on the development of religious beliefs and commitment in adolescence. *Journal for the Scientific Study of Religion, 28*, 448–463.

Paloutzian, R. F. (1996). *Invitation to the psychology of religion* (2nd ed.). Needham Heights, MA: Allyn and Bacon.

Pargament, K. I (2002). The bitter and the sweet: An evaluation of the costs and benefits of religiousness. *Psychological Inquiry, 13*, 168–181.

Potvin, R. H., Hoge, D. R., & Nelson, H. M. (1976). *Religion and American youth: With emphasis on Catholic adolescents and young adults.* Washington, DC: United States Catholic Conference.

Potvin, R. H., & Sloane, D. M. (1985). Parental control, age, and religious practice. *Review of Religious Research, 27*, 3–14.

Regnerus, M. D. (2000). Shaping school success: Religious socialization and educational outcomes in metropolitan public schools. *Journal for the Scientific Study of Religion, 39*, 363–370.

Regnerus, M. D., & Elder, G. H. (2003). Staying on track in school: Religious influences in high- and low-risk settings. *Journal for the Scientific Study of Religion 42*(4), 633–649.

Regnerus, M. D., Smith, C., & Smith, B. (2004). Social context in the development of adolescent religiosity. *Applied Developmental Science, 8*(1), 27–38.

Resnick, M. D., Bearman, P. S., Blum, R. W., Bauman, K. E., Harris, K. M., Jones, J., et al. (1997). Protecting adolescents from harm: Findings from the National Longitudinal Study on Adolescent Health. *Journal of the American Medical Association 278*(10), 823–831.

Roehlkepartain, E. C. (1998). *Building assets in congregations: A practical guide for helping youth grow up healthy.* Minneapolis, MN: Search Institute.

Roehlkepartain, E. C. (2003a). Building strengths, deepening faith: Understanding and enhancing youth development in Protestant congregations. In R. M. Lerner, F. Jacobs, & D. Wertlieb (Eds.), *Handbook of applied developmental science: Promoting positive child, adolescent, and family development through research, policies, and programs; volume 3 Promoting positive youth and family development: Community systems, citizenship, and civil society* (pp. 515–534). Newbury Park, CA: Sage Publications, Inc.

Roehlkepartain, E. C. (2003b). Making room at the table for everyone: Interfaith engagement in positive child and adolescent development. In D. Wertlieb, F. Jacobs, & R. M. Lerner (Eds.). *Handbook of applied developmental science: Promoting positive child, adolescent, and family development through research, policies, and programs; Volume 3, Promoting positive youth and family development: Community systems, citizenship, and civil society* (pp. 535–563). Thousand Oaks, CA: Sage Publications, Inc.

Scales, P. C., Benson, P. L., Leffert, N., & Blyth, D. A. (2000). Contribution of developmental assets to the prediction of thriving among adolescents. *Applied Developmental Science, 4*(1), 27–46.

Scales, P. C., Benson, P. L., & Mannes, M. (2003). *Grading grown-ups 2002: How do American kids and adults relate? A national study.* Minneapolis, MN: Search Institute.

Scales, P. C., & Leffert, N. (1999). Developmental assets: A synthesis of the scientific research on adolescent development. Minneapolis, MN: Search Institute.

Scales, P. C., & Leffert, N. (2004). Developmental assets: A synthesis of the scientific research on adolescent development (2nd ed.). Minneapolis, MN: Search Institute.

Smith, C. (2003). Theorizing religious effects among American adolescents. *Journal for the Scientific Study of Religion, 42*(1), 17–30.

Smith, C., Denton, M. L., Faris, R., & Regnerus, M. (2002). Mapping American adolescent religious participation. *Journal for the Scientific Study of Religion, 41*(4), 597–612.

Smith, C., & Faris, R. (2002). *Religion and American adolescent delinquency, risk behaviors, and constructive social activities.* Chapel Hill: National Study of Youth and Religion, University of North Carolina at Chapel Hill.

Smith, C., Sikkink, D., & Bailey, J. (1998). Devotion in Dixie and Beyond: A Test of the 'Shibley Thesis' on the Effects of Regional Origin and Migration on Individual Religiosity. *Journal for the Scientific Study of Religion, 37*(3), 494–506.

Spencer, M. B. (1995). Old issues and new theorizing about African American youth: A phenomenological variant of ecological systems theory. In R. L. Taylor (Ed.), *Black youth: Perspectives on their status in the United States* (pp. 37–69). Westport, CT: Praeger.

Spencer, M. B., Dupree, D., & Hartmann, T. (1997). A phenomenological variant of ecological systems theory (PVEST): A self-organization perspective in context. *Development and Psychopathology, 9*, 817–833.

Spilka, B., Hood, R. W., Hunsberger, B., & Gorsuch, R. (2003). *The psychology of religion: An empirical approach* (3rd ed.). New York: Guilford.

Spilka, B., Hood, R. W., & Gorsuch, R. L. (1985). *The psychology of religion: An empirical approach.* Englewood Cliffs, NJ: Prentice Hall.

Strommen, M. P. (Ed.). (1971). *Research on religious development: A comprehensive handbook.* New York: Hawthorn Books.

Swanson, D. P., Spencer, M. B., Dell'Angelo, T., Harpalani, V., & Spencer, T. R. (2002). Identity processes and the positive development of African Americans: An explanatory framework. *New Directions for Youth Development* (Fall), 73–100.

Swanson, D. P., Spencer, M. B., Dell'Angelo, T., Harpalani, V., & Spencer, T. (Fall 2002). Identity processes and the positive youth development of African Americans: An explanatory framework. In Noam, G. (Series Ed.) & C. S. Taylor, R. M. Lerner, & A. von Eye (Vol. Eds.), *New directions for youth development: Theory, practice and research: Pathways to positive youth development among gang and non-gang youth* (Vol. 95). San Francisco: Jossey-Bass.

Wagener, L. M., Leffert, N., Furrow, J. L., King, P. E., & Benson, P. L. (2003). Religious involvement and developmental resources in youth. *Review of Religious Research, 44*(3), 271–284.

Wallace, J. M. & Forman, T. A. (1998). Religion's role in promoting health and reducing risk among American youth. *Health Education and Behavior, 25*, 721–741.

Whitehead, B. D., Wilcox, B. L., & Rostosky, S. S. (2001). *Keeping the faith: The role of religion and faith communities in preventing teen pregnancy.* Washington, DC: National Campaign to Prevent Teen Pregnancy.

Wright, L. S., Frost, C. J., & Wisecarver, S. J. (1993). Church attendance, meaningfulness of religion, and depressive symptomatology among adolescents. *Journal of Youth and Adolescence, 22*, 559–568.

Wuthnow, R. (1994). *Producing the sacred: An essay on public religion.* Urbana: University of Illinois Press.

Youniss, J., McLellan, J. A., & Yates, M. (1999). Religion, community service, and identity in American youth. *Journal of Adolescence, 22*, 243–253.

CHAPTER 7

Aging

Neal Krause

INTRODUCTION

In the year 2000, there were approximately 35 million people age 65 and older in the United States. This figure is expected to double by the year 2030 (Morbidity and Mortality Weekly Review, 2003). The same trend is predicted worldwide (Morbidity and Mortality Weekly Review, 2003). Given the phenomenon of global aging, it is not surprising to find that sociologists are becoming increasingly interested in studying older people. Recently, a good deal of this interest has focused on religion and aging. Over the past several years, a number of volumes have been devoted to this topic (e.g., Kimble & McFadden, 2003; Koenig, 1994), and articles on religion and aging now routinely appear in gerontology journals (e.g., the *Journal of Gerontology: Social Sciences*), as well as mainstream journals in religion (e.g., the *Journal for the Scientific Study of Religion*).

The purpose of this chapter is to selectively review research on religion and aging with a special emphasis on the relationship between religiousness and health in late life. There are a number of topics that could be examined within the context of religion and aging, but as the discussion that follows will reveal, focusing on the interface between religion and health is important because this substantive domain is especially well developed in social gerontology (Levin, 2003). As a result, it provides one way of illustrating how work on religion and aging has matured, and how sophisticated models and theoretical insights are emerging at an accelerating pace.

The discussion that follows is divided into four main sections. This chapter begins by evaluating current levels of religious involvement among older people. In the process, an effort is made to see if patterns of religiousness change over the life course. The second section examines research on the social foundations of religion. One key facet of religion figures prominently in this respect—church-based social support. In the third section, a body of work that is especially well developed in the gerontological literature is reviewed. This research deals with race differences in the relationship between religion and health. Finally, this chapter closes with some general remarks about research on religion in late life. Recommendations for future studies are provided at this juncture as well.

Neal Krause • University of Michigan, Ann Arbor, Michigan 48109

RELIGIOUS INVOLVEMENT OF OLDER PEOPLE

If religion is associated with health in late life, then reviewing current levels of religious involvement among older people represents a good point of departure for examining this relationship. However, this task is more difficult than it seems because religion is a complex multidimensional phenomenon that comprises a number of different factors. For example, a panel of experts recently reported that there are at least 12 major dimensions of religion (Fetzer Institute/National Institute on Aging Working Group, 1999). Similarly, based on extensive qualitative research with older people, Krause (2002a) identified 14 dimensions of religion. Given the broad content domain of religion, it is important to know if older people are more deeply involved in some aspects of religion, or whether their involvement is more broad-based.

Religiousness in the Current Cohort of Older Adults

So far, no one has conducted a comprehensive examination of religiousness among older people across all the dimensions of religion that have been identified in the literature. Instead, most investigators focus on a few basic measures of religiousness, such as the frequency of church attendance and private prayer, as well as the importance of religion in the lives of older study participants. Nevertheless, the evidence that is available clearly indicates that older people are deeply immersed in religion. For example, Gallup and Lindsay (1999) report that 79% of people between the ages of 65 and 74 claim that religion is very important in their lives. Moreover, these investigators indicate that during the typical week, 52% of the people in this age range attend a church service. Finally research by Barna (2002) reveals that approximately 89% of older people pray during the typical week, and about 50% say they read the Bible during the same time period.

Religious Involvement over the Life Course

The high level of religious involvement in late life has led a number of investigators to search for plausible explanations for this phenomenon. Some evoke life course explanations and argue that high levels of religiousness are the culmination of a lifelong process whereby people become more religious as they grow older. For example, writing over a century ago, Starbuck argued that, ". . . the belief in God in some form is by far the most central conception, and it grows in importance as the years advance" (Starbuck, 1899, p. 320). This life course view is important because it makes a fundamental statement about the nature of human development that is typically overlooked in most developmental psychology books. Given the potential impact of this perspective on the field, it is important to carefully evaluate the validity of these claims. This can be done in two ways. The first involves examining empirical research on age differences in religion while the second has to do with theoretical frameworks that have been devised to explain age-related change in religion.

EMPIRICAL STUDIES OF RELIGION AND THE LIFE COURSE.   Researchers have taken one of three approaches in order to empirically assess whether older people become more religious as they age. The first involves probing for age differences in current religious involvement with cross-sectional data; the second focuses on following the same people over extended periods of time to chart change and stability in religiousness; and the third has to do with reconstructing lifelong patterns of religious involvement with retrospective interviews.

By far, the most common way to empirically assess whether people become more religious with age is to compare levels of religious involvement among those who are currently young and those who are currently old. Many investigators claim these cross-sectional studies reveal that older people are more religious than those who are young. In fact, some researchers argue that these age differences have appeared consistently in cross-sectional surveys over the past 50 years (Levin, 2003). Although this research appears to be convincing, there are two reasons why this issue is not as straightforward as it seems. First, it is not clear that the claim made by Levin is entirely accurate. Some time ago, Maves (1960) reported results of several large cross-sectional surveys that failed to find significant age differences in religiousness. Second, when looking at data that have been gathered at one point in time only, it is difficult to differentiate between age, period, and cohort effects. The importance of making these distinctions is highlighted in a recent study by Argue, Johnson, and White (1999).

Argue et al. (1999) performed a sophisticated set of analyses on data that had been gathered from the same respondents over a 12-year period. These investigators found that the importance of religion increases in a nonlinear fashion with age, and that the steepest increase occurs in the middle adult years. Argue et al. also report that this nonlinear relationship was stronger for Catholics than Protestants. This study is especially noteworthy because the authors controlled statistically for cohort and period effects. Unfortunately, the data for this study were not sufficient for fully evaluating life course change in religiousness. The age range of study participants was 18 to 55 at the first interview. This suggests that the oldest person was only about 67 at the end of the 12-year follow-up. This rules out the possibility of studying change in religion beyond age 67. As some of the theoretical perspectives discussed later will reveal, this may be an important issue.

Although some researchers have attempted to confront the problem of age, period, and cohort effects head-on, there is a more fundamental issue that remains to be addressed. More specifically, these investigators typically focus on a limited range of religion measures, such as the frequency of church attendance and private prayer. As a result, it is not clear if other dimensions of religion, such as church-based social ties, become more important with advancing years.

More convincing evidence that people may become more religious with age is provided by a small number of longitudinal studies that have followed the same individuals for extended periods of time. For example, Wink and Dillon (2001) used data from the well-known studies done in Berkeley and Oakland, California. Data on religion were available for the same subjects for a period of approximately 40 years. Wink and Dillon focused solely on a measure assessing the importance of religion. Their findings reveal that the importance of religion decreased between the early 30s and 40s but then increased in the 50s and early 60s. Although the reason for this pattern of nonlinear change is not clear, it may reflect the waning influence of early childhood socialization patterns coupled with an increase in the importance of career-related issues.

Another long-term follow-up study was conducted by Shand (2000). He analyzed data that have been gathered from 84 male graduates of Amherst College over a period of 50 years. The data focused solely on certainty in the belief that God exists. Shand found little change in the belief that God exists over the course of his study.

Although the findings from long-term studies on religion and aging are thought provoking, there are some shortcomings in this research. First, the samples were not selected at random (e.g., male Amherst College graduates), making it difficult to generalize the findings to the typical or average individual. Second, these studies rely on limited measures of religion. Third, the two studies reviewed above have opposite outcomes, making it hard to draw any firm conclusions. Nevertheless, the work that has been done so far appears to suggest that age-related changes in religion may not occur across the board, and may instead be manifest in some, but not all, dimensions of religion.

The last way of assessing age differences in religiousness involves asking older people to retrospectively report levels of religious involvement at specific times in their lives. So, for example, researchers might ask older people how important religion was to them at age 20, age 40, and age 60. It is important to point out that some studies taking this approach utilize qualitative research designs (e.g., Ingersoll-Dayton, Krause, & Morgan, 2002).

Researchers using this retrospective strategy provide some intriguing findings that have not emerged from studies using the other methodological approaches. More specifically, research by George, Hayes, Flint, and Meador (2003), as well as Ingersoll-Dayton et al. (2002), suggest there may not be a single trajectory of religious involvement over the life course: Instead, there may be multiple patterns of religiousness over time. This means, for example, that some people remain deeply religious all their lives, others are never involved in religion at any time, and yet others follow a nonlinear pattern of change with high levels of involvement in early years followed by a decline and subsequent resurgence of interest in religion in the later years. Unfortunately, the validity of these findings depends, in part, on the ability of the study participants to recall and accurately report their involvement in religion at specific points in the life course. There do not appear to be any studies that evaluate this issue empirically.

Even so, the fact that there may be multiple patterns of religious involvement raises a fundamental issue that speaks directly to how researchers frame empirical as well as theoretical discussions of age-related change in religion. So far, most investigators assume that all people follow the same pattern of religious involvement over the life course. This creates the impression that age differences in religion can be explained by a single developmental theory. Although devising a single theory is conceptually and empirically expedient, it may not map well onto social reality because it fails to do justice to the complex and rich variation in the way individual lives unfold. Instead of being one, there may be multiple trajectories of change over time as George et al. (2003) and Ingersoll-Dayton et al. (2002) suggest. This more complex view of the life course is consistent with the basic tenets of Nelson and Dannefer's (1992) aged heterogeneity hypothesis. These investigators argue that regardless of the conceptual domain under study, there is a general tendency toward greater differentiation among people with advancing age. Nelson and Dannefer tested their theory by investigating a wide range of well-known psychosocial constructs, including feelings of personal control, self-esteem, and social networks. Their analyses provide convincing support for the notion that people become more dissimilar as they grow older.

If there are multiple patterns of religious involvement over the life course, then a whole new vista of research opportunities opens up. With respect to empirical analyses, researchers may wish to pursue a three-step data analytic approach. First, growth curve analyses can be used to plot each individual's trajectory of change or stability in religiousness as he or she grows older (see Karney & Bradbury, 1995, for an introduction to this statistical procedure). This involves estimating a separate regression slope and intercept for each study participant. Following this, cluster analysis can be used to identify study participants with similar trajectories of religiousness. In essence, this would allow researchers to empirically derive typologies of change and stability in religion over time. Finally, multinomial logistic regression can be used to identify the factors that influence the specific trajectory of religiousness that an individual is likely to experience (see Liang, Shaw, Krause, Bennett, Blaum, Kobayashe, Fukaya, Sugihara, & Sugisawa, 2003, for an application of this approach in a different substantive area). Ultimately, this kind of empirical work may provide valuable insights for developing not one, but a range of conceptual frameworks to explain why levels of religious involvement may either change or remain stable over the life course.

Implementing the strategy outlined here is an enormous undertaking because a wide range of religion measures must be explored and multiple observations must be made of the same study participants over extended periods of time. Nevertheless, this work holds out the promise of providing rich new insights into the factors that influence religious involvement over the life course. In the process, this type of research will allow sociologists of religion to make fundamental statements about the nature of human development.

THEORETICAL PERSPECTIVES ON RELIGION AND THE LIFE COURSE.   It is hard to draw firm conclusions from current empirical work about life course change in religion. But there is another way to approach this issue that focuses primarily on theory. Embedded in empirical studies on life course change in religion is the assumption that there is something about growing older that causes change in religiousness. Social scientists have been arguing for some time about the criteria needed to establish causality (Lazarsfeld, 1955). The criteria they typically derive deal solely with statistical and methodological issues. However, a more comprehensive perspective has been offered by several investigators, including Bradley and Schaefer (1998). They argue that in order to determine whether one variable causes another, researchers must provide a convincing theoretical rationale for why the two constructs should be related. Cast within the context of the present discussion, this means that in addition to empirically evaluating the relationship between age and religiousness, researchers must also provide a convincing theoretical explanation for the findings they expect to observe.

Several sociologists have provided detailed theoretical explanations of life course related change in religious involvement. Most of this work focuses on what is known as the Family Life Cycle hypothesis (Bahr, 1970). Viewed broadly, this perspective suggests that marriage increases religious participation and that adults who have preadolescent, school-age children also are more likely to be involved in religion than those who do not have children in this age group. The Family Life Cycle perspective has been empirically evaluated and expanded conceptually by a number of investigators (e.g., Myers, 1996). For example, Stolzenberg, Blair-Joy, and Waite (1995) propose a framework that focuses on how the interplay between divorce, cohabitation, and the dissolution of cohabitational relationships influences church membership. Their work reveals that church membership is a complex function of the age of the child, the age of the parent, and cohabitation status factors.

Although research on the Family Life Cycle perspective has made a number of valuable contributions to the literature, it suffers from a significant shortcoming. In particular, investigators who work with theoretical framework rarely discuss life course issues beyond midlife (i.e., age 50 or so). There are, however, two notable exceptions to this tendency. First, some discussion of late life influences is provided by Bahr (1970), but he focuses primarily on disengagement theory (Cumming & Henry, 1961), which has largely fallen out of favor in social gerontology. Disengagement theory specifies that as people grow older, both they and the society in which they reside mutually agree on the gradual withdrawal of the elder from midlife social obligations, social ties, and social roles. Presumably, this mutually sanctioned disengagement involves a decline in formal religious involvement (e.g., church attendance). But this application of disengagement theory provides a passive view of older people. Moreover, it is at odds with the data reviewed earlier on religious participation among older people.

Tornstam (1997) provides the second sociological framework that looks specifically at late life issues in religious involvement. His theory of gerotranscendence specifies that as people enter late life, there is a fundamental shift in the way they view the world. Although he doesn't discuss religion explicitly, a number of religious and spiritual themes run throughout his work. For example, he maintains that some people begin to think about the "cosmic dimension," including issues involving immortality (Tornstam, 1997, p. 145). But the lack of explicit and detailed discussion of religion, per se, makes it more difficult to adapt Tornstam's work to the study of life course issues in religious involvement.

In comparison to sociologists, it appears that psychiatrists and psychologists have provided more well-developed theoretical explanations of life course change in religious involvement during the later years. The widely cited work of Erikson (1959) provides a good example of this work. Erikson argues that as people enter late life, they are confronted by the crisis of integrity versus despair. This is a time of deep introspection when people look back over their life and makes an effort to weave their experiences into a more coherent and meaningful whole. Part of this involves reconciling the inevitable gap between what they hoped to do and what they actually accomplished. If they are successful, they attain the highest stage of development—integrity. But if they are unable to resolve this conflict successfully, they slip into despair.

During the later years of his life, Erikson's perspective on the crisis of integrity versus despair changed significantly. In fact, as Hoare (2002) points out, he actually used the word "faith" instead of "integrity" to describe the last stage of development (see Hoare, 2002, p. 80). As this change reveals, his later writings took on an increasingly religious orientation. Furthermore, and more explicit, evidence of this may be found elsewhere in Erikson's later work where he argued that, "Awareness of the coming reality of personal death creeps closer to the surface of consciousness and leads adults to contemplate and work toward a spiritual home . . . . Spirituality now becomes unavoidable" (see Hoare, 2002, p. 75).

Regardless of the discipline in which it has emerged, there are two problems with the theoretical work on life course change in religion. First, it is considerably underdeveloped. An articulate and sophisticated sociological theory of age change in religion across the entire life course has yet to appear in the literature. Second, many scholars assume that a single theoretical explanation is sufficient to cover the experiences of everyone. This perspective, which is called essentialism, was long ago rejected by some developmental psychologists who believe there is no single universal pattern of development that is followed by all people (Goldhaber, 2000). This makes a good deal of sense given the multiple trajectories of change and stability identified by George et al. (2003) and Ingersoll-Dayton et al. (2002). Instead, it appears that a range of theoretical mechanisms are needed to explain the different ways in which religion may unfold over the life course. Although this is more challenging than developing a single grand theory, it holds out the promise of providing richer insights that are more firmly grounded in the diverse ways that religion is experienced in the lives of people as they grow older.

RELIGION AND HEALTH IN LATE LIFE

A rapidly growing body of research suggests that people who are more deeply involved in religion tend to enjoy better physical and mental health than individuals who are less religious (see Koenig, McCullough, & Larson, 2001, for a review of this research). As the discussion provided above reveals, the hypothesis that people may become more religious with age has yet to be confirmed. Even so, most researchers would agree that those who are presently older are more involved in religion than those who are currently young. It follows that if religion is associated with better health, then the effects should be especially evident among the current cohort of older people.

The idea that religion may be related to health and well-being in late life is hardly new. For example, the Old Testament in the Christian Bible repeatedly indicates that a long life is a blessing and a reward for righteousness (e.g., Deuteronomy 5:33). Although there are many ways in which religion may influence health, a central premise in this chapter is that some of the most fundamental processes are inherently social in nature.

The social underpinnings of religion are especially evident in the work of the early social theorists. For example, as the following quotation from the work of Simmel (1902/1997) reveals, the powerful emotions generated by religious activity are fundamentally social in nature: "The individual feels himself bound to a universal, to something higher, from which he came and into which he will return, from which he differs and to which he is nonetheless identical. All of these emotions, which meet as in the focal point of God, can be traced back to the relationship the individual maintains with the species... with his contemporaries who condition the manner and extent of his development" (pp. 115–116). Simply put, Simmel (1902/1997) argued that the essence of religion may be found in the nature of the relationships that are shared among people of a common faith. Similar views were expressed by Mead (1934). He discussed something called "universal attitudes," which are broad ways of approaching relationships with others. One such universal attitude was neighborliness. He argued that neighborliness, "... passes over into the principle of religious relationships, the attitude which made religion as such possible" (Mead, 1934, pp. 292–293).

Although the work of the grand social theorists is thought provoking, it is hard to integrate their classic insights into current empirical research. This problem arises because the grand masters didn't discuss how to explicitly measure key constructs in their theoretical work, nor were they typically concerned with the relationship between religion and health. Moreover, the classic social theorists had little to say about religion among older people. In the discussion that follows, an effort is made to show how focusing on one social facet of religion—church-based social support—provides a way of bridging the work of the grand masters with contemporary empirical research on religion and health in social gerontology.

There are many issues that could be explored when assessing social ties in the church, but it is not be possible to review them all here. Instead, five are examined below in an effort to flesh out the core issues in this newly emerging conceptual domain. The first involves efforts to define church-based social support and stake out the content domain of this important construct. Second, research is reviewed which attempts to show why church-based social ties may be especially important for older people. Third, the social foundations of church-based social support are examined with an eye toward highlighting how these key social relationships arise in the first place. Fourth, research suggesting that church-based support may be related to health in late life is briefly reviewed. Finally, the discussion of social ties in religious settings is brought to a close by examining the reasons why it may have health-enhancing and health-maintaining effects.

Defining Church-Based Social Support

No satisfactory definition of church-based social support exists. This problem is endemic in the secular literature on social support as well (Krause, 2001). For now, this construct will be defined in the following manner: church-based social support is the emotional, tangible, and spiritual assistance that is exchanged among people who worship in the same congregation.

Although verbal definitions of church-based social support are limited, turning to operational definitions of this construct provides another way to approach this issue. In essence, good substantive definitions of a construct are embedded in the measures used to assess them. A recent study by Krause (2002b) provides what is probably the most comprehensive set of church-based support measures in the literature. He devised 12 different dimensions of social ties in the church. A list of these different facets of church-based support is provided in Table 7.1. Although many are familiar, three require a brief explanation. Church embeddedness assesses whether older study participants maintain contact with people in the church. This construct is measured with items that gauge the attendance at church services, Bible study groups, prayer groups, and whether older adults perform volunteer work at church. Measures of church embeddedness are important because they are based on the notion that older people must first come into contact with people in the church before they can exchange social support with them. Anticipated support is the belief that help will be provided in the future should the need arise. Research in secular settings reveals that anticipated support may exert a more positive effect on well-being than the actual supportive acts provided by significant others (Krause, 1997). The third support-related construct that may be less familiar is spiritual support. This domain assesses whether fellow church members share religious experiences with a focal older person, whether they encourage them to lead a more religious life, and whether they help them find solutions to their problems in the Bible.

Although the measures provided in Table 7.1 are fairly comprehensive they may, nevertheless, fail to capture some of the more subtle ways of gauging social relationships in the church. Deeper reflection reveals that the boundaries of church-based social support may be more difficult to determine than one might initially believe. This dilemma may be illustrated by focusing on two seemingly unrelated facets of religion—one is prayer, whereas the other involves having a close relationship with God.

TABLE 7.1. Dimensions of Church-Based Social Support

1. Church Embeddedness
2. Emotional Support from Church Members
3. Tangible Support from Church Members
4. Spiritual Support from Church Members
5. Emotional Support Provided to Church Members
6. Tangible Support Provided to Church Members
7. Negative Interaction with Church Members
8. Anticipated Support from Church Members
9. Emotional Support from the Clergy
10. Tangible Support from the Clergy
11. Negative Interaction with the Clergy
12. Anticipated Support from the Clergy

Research by Gallup and Lindsay (1999) reveals that 98% of the people who pray indicate they pray for the well-being of others, especially family members. Moreover, these investigators report that 95% of the people who pray believe their prayers are answered. If people pray for others, and they believe their prayers are answered, then praying for others may be construed as a legitimate form of helping behavior. To the extent this is true, praying for others may be a more subtle type of church-based social support.

Research by Krause (2002c) suggests that a number of older people believe they have a close personal relationship with God. More specifically, they believe that God is right there with them in daily life, that He listens to their prayers, and that He provides direct answers to their prayers. Viewed in the context of church-based support, having this type of relationship with God might be considered a form of religious (i.e., divine) support.

Sociologists are beginning to make significant advances in their understanding of church-based social support. However, as the discussion provided here reveals, a good deal of basic research must be done on the measurement and conceptualization of this core facet of religion.

Church-Based Social Support in Late Life

Some gerontologists have described aging as a process of role loss, with the concomitant loss of social ties (Rosow, 1976). For example, as people grow older, they may retire, become widowed, and their children may reach adulthood and leave the home. Each transition challenges the ability of older adults to maintain social relationships. Perhaps social ties in the church help fill the void created by these role exits.

But social relationships in the church may do more than merely substitute for severed secular ties. Instead, social relationships in the church may take on a special meaning in late life. Although adequate data are not available, it appears that some older people have worshiped in the same congregation for a good part of their lives. For example, a recent nationwide survey of people of all ages by Krause and Wulff (2003) reveals that approximately 28% of the study participants indicate they have been worshipping in the same congregation for at least 20 years. Those who have long-term ties with the same church are likely to have shared a number of key life transitions with their fellow church members, including baptisms, confirmations, weddings, and funerals. Sharing these key life transitions may create bonds that are especially strong and meaningful, and they may insure continuity of high quality support that is rarely found outside the family.

In addition to this, there are two reasons why social ties in the church may take on a special meaning for older people. First, basic principles of Christianity and Judaism (e.g., the Ten Commandments) highlight the importance of respecting elders. These beliefs are often not endorsed in the wider secular world, as research on ageism reveals (Butler, 1975). Second, many religious organizations encourage older people to perform volunteer work and they often provide them with the opportunity to do so. There is convincing evidence that elderly people avail themselves of these opportunities. More specifically, a recent report by the Department of Labor (2002) provides data on the number of hours people spent performing volunteer work during a recent one-year period. These data suggest that people aged 65 and over spent more time performing volunteer work than individuals in any other age group. But it is especially important to point out that when older people volunteer, they are especially likely to do so through religious organizations. Fully 45.2% of all older volunteers aged 65 and over helped others through religious organizations. The second most frequent setting was social and community service organizations (17.6%), but the difference between this and religious institutions is striking. Engaging in volunteer work is important for two reasons. First, it provides older people with the opportunity to come into contact with like-minded others, thereby increasing the opportunity for new social relationships to develop with fellow volunteers. Second, being involved in volunteer work helps older people engage in productive activities, which many believe is critical for successful aging (Rowe & Kahn, 1998).

The Social Foundations of Church-Based Support

If church-based social support plays an important role in the lives of older people, then it is important to explore the factors that cause close ties to emerge in the church in the first place. Simply put, more research is needed that treats social support in the church as a dependent variable. Undoubtedly, a number of factors contribute to the emergence and maintenance of close relationships in the church. Two that appear especially promising are examined briefly below: Organizational characteristics of the church and the wider social atmosphere of the congregation. Although there is very little empirical research on the topic, it is likely that the basic structural and organizational characteristics of church may influence the amount of support that is exchanged by fellow church members. For example, the sheer size of the congregation may impact the nature of the social ties that emerge. Perhaps social ties in smaller congregations are more tightly knit than social relationships in larger and more impersonal churches. In addition, many congregations have formal programs, such as Bible study and prayer groups, that act as an important forum for the development of close social relationships (Wuthnow, 1994).

In addition to these organizational factors, social ties in the church may be influenced by more subjective, social psychological factors as well. According to the homophily principle, similarity in attitudes, beliefs, and values in a group leads to greater interpersonal attraction and higher levels of social interaction (McPherson, Smith-Lovin, & Cook, 2001). Research by Krause (2002c) shows why this may be an important factor in the church. He devised a construct called congregational cohesiveness. This construct is measured by asking study participants if the members of their church share the same values, whether they have similar ideas about where their church should be headed in the future, and whether fellow church members have the same outlook on life (see Pargament, Silverman, Johnson, Echemendia, & Snyder, 1983, for a similar discussion of the congregational climate). Krause (2002c) reports that older adults who were members of congregations with high levels of cohesiveness tend to receive more emotional and spiritual support from their fellow church members than older people who attend churches that are less cohesive.

Church-Based Social Support and Health

A substantial body of work in secular settings suggests that older people who are embedded in vibrant social networks tend to have better physical and mental health than older individuals who do not maintain close ties with others (Krause, 2001). Some of the most compelling studies in this literature examine the relationship between social support and mortality (Berkman & Glass, 2000). This research indicates that people with strong social support systems tend to live longer than people who are not closely connected with others.

If the social ties that develop in the church are particularly strong, then it follows that church-based social support should have an especially beneficial effect on health.

Although there is a good deal of theoretical discussion in the literature about the potential health-enhancing functions of church-based support (e.g., Chatters, 2000; Ellison & Levin, 1998), relatively few studies have examined the relationship between these constructs empirically. Moreover, among those that do, most investigators focus on adults of all ages, not older people specifically (e.g., Krause, Ellison, & Marcum, 2002; Nooney & Woodrum, 2002). One of the few studies to examine church-based support and health among older people was conducted by Krause (2002c). His work reveals that higher levels of support from fellow church members are associated with better self-rated health in late life.

In order to move this literature forward, those who study social ties in the church must address an important issue. More specifically, we need to know whether there is something unique about assistance that is exchanged in religious settings, or whether similar processes arise in secular organizations, like the Rotary Club. There are two ways to address this issue. The first involves searching for types of support that are unique to the church and that cannot be found in the secular world. The second has to do with identifying ways in which religion may increase the efficacy of certain types of support that may be found in both religious and secular settings alike.

The first approach was implemented by Krause (2002c). He compared and contrasted the effects of two specific types of church-based support on the self-rated health of older people. The first type is emotional support, which refers to the provision of empathy, caring, love, and trust. Clearly, emotional support may be found outside as well as inside the church. The second type of church-based support that was examined in this study is spiritual support. This type of assistance is unique to religious settings. The findings indicate that spiritual support, but not emotional support from church members, exerted a positive effect on health.[1] This study is important because it suggests that the salubrious effects of church-based support may be attributed to a type of assistance (i.e., spiritual support) that is found only in the church.

But, as discussed earlier, religion also may influence support that is found outside the church as well. A vast literature conducted in secular settings suggests that emotional support is an especially important determinant of psychological well-being in late life (Krause, 1986). Following the classic work of Cooley (1902) and Mead (1934), people are able to provide emotional support in an effective way because they can take the role of the other, or as Cooley (1902) put it, enter sympathetically into the mind of the other. However, not all researchers would agree with the views of Cooley and Mead. As the following quotation taken from the work of William James reveals, he doubted that individuals are capable of sympathetically entering into the mind of the other: "Each is bound to feel intensely the importance of his own duties and the significance of the situations that call these forth. But this feeling in each of us is a vital secret, for sympathy with which we vainly look to others. The others are too much absorbed in their own vital secrets to take an interest in ours" (James, 1899, p. 311). Similar views are expressed by Carl Jung: "The vast majority of people are quite incapable of putting themselves individually into the mind of another. . . . The most we can do, and the best, is to have at least some inkling of his otherness, to respect it, and to guard against the outrageous stupidity of wishing to interpret it" (Jung, 1953, p. 153).

Perhaps one of the greatest contributions of religion is that it encourages people to meet this issue head-on by helping them recognize the basic humanness in each other. This may happen because sacred texts make a number of fundamental statements about human nature, including the inherent goodness and worth of each individual. Moreover, religion provides a number of basic tenets that outline how people should relate to each other. For example, great emphasis is placed on helping those in need. In addition, the Bible encourages people to speak with and try to better understand others when interpersonal conflict arises. This is especially evident when it comes to issues involving forgiveness. As Rye and his colleagues point out, virtually every major religion in the world places a high value on forgiveness (Rye, Pargament, Ali, Beck, Dorff, Hallisey, Narayanan, & Williams, 2000). This is important because forgiving others helps shore up and restore relationships that were previously a source of support. If these observations are valid, then even common types of assistance found in the secular world may take on a different quality and meaning in religious settings that imbues them with greater health-protective effects. The empirical evaluation of these finer nuances of church-based emotional support is likely to be challenging, but doing so should be a high priority for the future.[2]

Explaining the Relationship between Church-Based Support and Health

There are a number of ways to explain how church-based social support may influence the health and well-being of older people, but it is impossible to explore them all here. Instead, four that appear especially promising will be examined later. Following this, a small cluster of studies are reviewed, which suggest that interaction with fellow church members may not always be positive, and that this unpleasant interaction may have an adverse effect on health and well-being in late life.

THE FUNCTIONS OF SPIRITUAL SUPPORT.   The first way that church-based support may influence health may be found by examining spiritual support more closely. As research by Krause (2002c) reveals, spiritual support from fellow church members may bolster the health of older people because it helps them develop and maintain a closer relationship with God. Having a close relationship with God may, in turn, influence health in at least two ways. To begin with, unpublished findings from a nationwide survey by Krause (2002a) suggest that people who have a close relationship with God tend to have higher levels of God control. God control refers to the belief that God intervenes directly in the lives of the faithful and that He exerts a positive influence on the course of the events they experience. This construct is important, because as a recent study by Krause (2003a) reveals, a strong sense of God control is associated with a range of well-being outcomes, including greater life satisfaction and an elevated sense of self-esteem. In addition, research by Krause (2002c) further indicates that a deep personal relationship with God tends to promote a greater sense of optimism. This is important because this study reveals that greater optimism is, in turn, associated with better health. Viewed more generally, the relationship between spiritual support and optimism is noteworthy because it shows one way in which key facets of religion may be linked with well-known secular correlates of health (Peterson & Bossio, 2001).

CHURCH-BASED SUPPORT AND RELIGIOUS COPING RESPONSES.   A number of investigators argue that one of the primary functions of religion is to help people deal more effectively with the deleterious effects of stressful life events (Pargament, 1997). More specifically, this literature suggests that the noxious effects of stress on health and well-being are reduced significantly for people who rely on positive religious coping responses. Coping responses refer to the specific cognitions and behaviors that individuals engage in when they encounter a stressful event. So, for example, some individuals may turn to God for strength and guidance when they are faced with a difficult situation. Although research on religious coping has provided many valuable insights, this work has been largely dominated by psychologists. Unfortunately, psychologists often overlook the possibility that social factors may influence the choice and implementation of religious coping responses.

As the classic work of Gerald Caplan (1981) convincingly illustrates, when people are confronted by a stressful event in secular settings, they turn to significant others to define the problem situation and to jointly work out a coping strategy. Cast within the context of the present discussion, this means that one of the functions of church-based social support is to shape and influence the selection and implementation of religious coping responses.

Krause and his colleagues explored this issue with data provided by a nationwide sample of Presbyterians (Krause, Ellison, Shaw, Marcum, & Boardman, 2001). More specifically, these investigators examined the relationship between three types of church-based social support and positive religious coping responses: emotional support from church members, emotional support from the clergy, and spiritual support from fellow church members. The findings suggest that spiritual support was strongly associated with the use of positive religious coping responses, while the other types of assistance had a substantially smaller impact. One drawback of this study arises from the fact that the sample was composed of adults of all ages, making it difficult to generalize the findings to older adults. Examining this issue should be a high priority in the future.

CHURCH-BASED SUPPORT AND A SENSE OF BELONGING.   Social support in the church does much more than help older people deal with crisis situations. It also provides health-related benefits that arise during the course of ongoing interaction with others. One such benefit has to do with promoting a sense of belonging in a congregation. A sense of belonging is an attitude, a social reality, which encompasses a set of positive emotions and cognitions that arise from playing a meaningful role in a group. Simply put, a sense of belonging makes people feel that they are a valued part of a larger social whole, and as a result, it is an important source of meaning and purpose in life (Baumeister, 1991). Given the many role losses that occur in late life, it may be especially important for older people to feel as though they belong in their congregation, and that they play a meaningful role in the institution.

So far, there appears to be only one study in the literature that looks at the relationship between a sense of belonging in a congregation and health (Krause & Wulff, 2003). This study, which focuses on adults of all ages, suggests that a strong sense of belonging in a congregation is associated with greater satisfaction with health. It is especially important to point out that the study by Krause and Wulff (2003) also reveals that emotional support from fellow church members is an important source of belonging. When significant others provide assistance, they are doing much more than providing practical aid. Instead, the very act of helping conveys subtle messages to the support recipient that lets them know they are loved and valued highly. In the process, this positive feedback is likely to make older church members feel as though they are welcomed in their congregation and that they are a meaningful part of the group. Simply put, support from fellow church members should make older people feel as though they belong in a congregation.

PROVIDING ASSISTANCE TO OTHERS IN CHURCH. Although receiving support from others at church appears to have health-enhancing effects, it is important not to overlook the possibility that giving support to fellow church members may be just as beneficial. All the major religions in the world extol the virtues of tending to the needs of others and helping those who are faced with difficulty. Although helping others obviously benefits those who are in need, findings from research in secular settings reveal that helping others may benefit support providers as well (Krause, 1986; Reisman, 1965). According to this perspective, helping others may enhance the health and well-being of the support provider in at least two ways. First, assisting others makes support providers feel as though they are doing something worthwhile for someone in need. Research conducted in secular settings suggests that this may bolster the self-esteem of older people (Krause, 1986). Second, assisting others helps support providers take their minds off their own problems for a while, thereby providing a temporary respite from their own troubles and concerns.

Beyond the benefits that arise from helping others in general, it appears that helping others may be especially beneficial for those who are religious because it allows them to comply with the basic tenets of their faith. This may, in turn, bolster feelings of self-worth and life satisfaction.

Research on helping others in the church is largely underdeveloped. However, some support for the argument presented above may be found in a recent study by Musick and Wilson (2003). Their study dealt with performing volunteer work, which is simply a more formal way of helping others. Two important findings emerge from this longitudinal study. First, Musick and Wilson report that performing volunteer work at the baseline interview was associated with fewer symptoms of depression at the follow-up interview, but these findings hold only for people aged 65 and over. Second, their results reveal that performing volunteer work in religious institutions exerts a more beneficial effect on depressive symptoms than performing volunteer work in secular organizations. Once again, this effect was evident only among individuals who were at least 65 years of age.

NEGATIVE INTERACTION IN THE CHURCH. The church is largely a human endeavor, and like all other human creations, it is flawed. Cast within the context of the present discussion, this suggests that interaction with fellow church members may not always be pleasant, and at times, older people may encounter criticism, excessive demands, gossip, and disagreements with other individuals in their congregation (Krause, Morgan, Chatters, & Meltzer, 2000). Negative interaction in the church is important because a vast literature conducted in secular settings reveals that unpleasant social encounters tend to erode the physical (Krause & Shaw, 2002) and mental health of older people (Rook, 1984). In fact, some investigators maintain that the impact of negative interaction on health and well-being is greater than the positive things that people do for each other (Rook, 1984).

Unfortunately, there are relatively few studies of negative interaction in the church. Moreover, the work that has been done does not typically focus on older people. Even so, there are two studies that show why this may be an important area of inquiry. The first study is based on a nationwide survey of Presbyterians of all ages (Krause, Ellison, & Wulff, 1998). The findings indicate that negative interaction in the church tends to increase feelings of psychological distress and diminish positive feelings of well-being. There is, however, an important qualification. The data indicate that negative interaction in the church exerts a greater impact on members of the clergy and church elders (i.e., lay church leaders) than on rank-and-file church members. This makes sense because pastors and elders tend to be more deeply committed to the church than rank-and-file members. This means that negative interaction may be more troubling when religion plays an especially salient role in a person's life.

The second study on negative interaction in the church was done by Krause (2003b). It is important to point out that this study focused solely on older people. The findings suggest that negative interaction with members of the clergy tends to lower feelings of self-worth among older church members. However, the data further reveal that the noxious effects of negative interaction with the pastor are diminished when older people rely on positive religious coping responses.

If negative interaction in the church has a deleterious effect on health and well-being, then it is important to reflect on how these noxious effects may arise. Negative interaction may have an especially pernicious effect when it arises in the church because it stands out in sharp contrast to the basic precepts of the faith. Religion encourages people to love and support each other. So if people expect to find especially close ties in the church, but encounter negative interaction instead, then the impact of unpleasant interaction may be especially pronounced. These observations are consistent with secular research on expectancy theory (Olson, Roese, & Zanna, 1996). Expectancies are beliefs about what will happen in the future. According to this perspective, disconfirmation of closely held expectancies may be a significant source of psychological distress.

In addition to expectancy theory, there is another reason why negative interaction in the church may be especially troubling for older people. As Carstensen (1992) points out in her theory of socioemotional selectivity, emotionally supportive relationships become more highly valued as people grow older. If emotionally close ties become increasingly important with age, then older people may be especially vulnerable to the pernicious effects of unpleasant encounters with their fellow church members. This may be especially true given the fact that many people in the current cohort of older adults feel that religion and their church are very important to them (Levin, Taylor, & Chatters, 1994).

Clearly, a good deal of work remains to be done on negative interaction in the church. This research is especially important because it provides a much needed sense of balance in a literature that is overwhelmingly concerned with the positive influence of religion on health and well-being.

RACE DIFFERENCES IN RELIGION DURING LATE LIFE

Research on race differences in the relationship between religion and health represents one of the most important contributions social gerontologists have made to the field. However, the wide majority of these studies contrast older African Americans with older whites. Two major findings have emerged from this rapidly growing literature: (1) older African Americans are much more deeply involved in religion than older whites; and (2) the beneficial effects of religion on health and well-being appear to be more evident among older black than older whites. The discussion that follows begins with a theoretical overview of why these race differences may have emerged. Following this, empirical evidence is briefly reviewed in an effort to highlight the nature and scope of the pervasive race differences that have been observed so far.

Theoretical Perspectives on Race and Religion

There are both historical and cultural reasons why older blacks are more involved in religion than older whites. With respect to history, a number of scholars maintain that the church became the center of the black community because of centuries of discrimination and prejudice. More specifically, these investigators argue that black people turned to the church for spiritual, social, and material sustenance because it was the only institution that was built, funded, and wholly controlled by blacks (Nelson & Nelson, 1975). Evidence of this may be found in the classic studies of the black church by Du Bois (2000). Writing in 1887, he concluded that, "The Negro church . . . provides social intercourse, it provides amusements of various kinds, it serves as a newspaper and intelligence bureau, it supplants the theater, it directs the picnic and excursion, it furnishes the music, it introduces the stranger to the community, it serves as a lyceum, library, and lecture bureau—it is, in fine, the central organ of organized life of the American Negro" (Du Bois, 1887/2000, p. 21). There is ample evidence that these observations still hold today (Mattis & Jagers, 2001).

With respect to culture, Baldwin and Hopkins (1990) have gone to great lengths to identify the key elements of the African-American worldview or culture. They persuasively argue that African-American culture is characterized by an emphasis on harmony, coopera-tion, collective responsibility, "groupness," and "sameness." Because institutions reflect the wider culture in which they are embedded, it follows that these key cultural characteristics should permeate the church in the black community as well. To the extent this is true, the collective or communal aspects of black culture should more tightly bind church members to their congregations. This is an important consideration given the emphasis placed in this chapter on church-based social support.

When thinking about race differences in religion, it is important to distinguish be-tween two key perspectives: differential involvement in religion and the differential impact of religion on health and well-being (Krause, 2002c). The differential involvement perspec-tive specifies that older black people may derive more health-related benefits than older whites from religion simply because older blacks are more involved in religion in the first place. So, for example, older blacks may receive more spiritual support from their fellow church members than older whites. Because spiritual support is, in turn, associated with better health, it is reasonable to conclude that religion is more beneficial to older blacks because they are more immersed in it. The differential involvement perspective may be evaluated by testing for mean race differences in key religious constructs, like spiritual support.

But there is another way that race differences may emerge in the data. Subsequent anal-ysis may reveal that the relationship between church-based support and health is stronger for older blacks than older whites. This effect may be captured by seeing if the regression coefficients for the relationship between church-based support and health differ across sub-groups comprised of older blacks and older whites, respectively. If the subgroup coefficients are larger for older blacks, then it is important to think carefully about what these findings mean. In this instance, the results would indicate that at the same level of church-based support, assistance from fellow church members exerts a greater impact on the health of older blacks. This differential impact perspective suggests there is something qualitatively different about the nature of church-based support in the two racial groups. This unmea-sured influence may involve a number of factors, including the historical and cultural factors discussed earlier. Making a distinction between differential involvement in religion and the differential impact of religion is important because it helps sharpen our understanding of the processes that shape race differences in religion and health in late life.

Empirical Research on Race and Religion

Research on differential involvement in religion among older whites and older blacks is extensive and consistent. In one of the more comprehensive studies, Levin et al. (1994) explore race differences in religion across four national surveys. Race comparisons were made on 21 indicators of religion across the four data bases. The findings reveal that older blacks were more deeply involved in religion than older whites in 19 of the 21 tests. This study revealed, for example, that compared to older whites, older blacks attend church more often, read religious literature more often, and feel that religion is more important in their lives.

The recent research program by Krause extends these findings by examining a range of religion measures that were not included in previous studies. More specifically, his research indicates that older blacks are more likely than older whites to feel their congregations are highly cohesive and they are more likely to believe they have a closer personal relationship with God (Krause, 2002c). In addition, older blacks report exchanging more social support with their fellow church members than older whites. In fact, these race differences emerged in 10 of the 12 dimensions of church-based support listed in Table 7.1 (Krause, 2002b). Similarly, research by Krause and Ellison (2003) suggests that older blacks are more likely than older whites to forgive others for the things they have done. Finally, older blacks are more likely to pray for others (Krause, 2003c), find meaning in religion (Krause, 2003d), and have fewer doubts about their faith than older whites (Krause, 2003e).

In contrast, findings from research on the differential impact of religion on health are not as striking as the results that have emerged from studies on the differential involvement perspective. However, whenever evidence of a differential impact has emerged, the findings consistently favor older blacks. For example, Krause (2003d) found that the impact of finding meaning in religion on well-being was greater for older blacks than older whites. Similarly, Krause (2003b) reports that receiving emotional support from the clergy has a more positive impact on the self-esteem of older blacks than older whites. Finally, Krause (2002c) found that more frequent church attendance was associated with fewer depressive symptoms among older blacks than among older whites.

So in balance, the evidence that has emerged so far suggests that older blacks appear to reap more health-related benefits from religion than older whites primarily because older blacks are more deeply involved in religion in the first place. But there may be more to it than this. The research that has been done so far focuses exclusively on facets of religion than may be experienced by older whites and older blacks alike (e.g., prayer, church attendance, and church-based social support). However, as Krause (2003f) points out, there may be certain aspects of religion that are unique to, and can only be experienced by, older African Americans. More specifically, research shows that older blacks take great pride in the fact that religion helped their ancestors deal with the horrors of slavery (Paris, 1995). Moreover, many older blacks feel as though their faith has helped them cope more effectively with racial discrimination and prejudice. Krause (2003f) reports that feelings of life satisfaction are higher among older blacks who feel religion has sustained them in these ways. This research is important because it highlights the advantages of exploring both unique as well as common aspects of religion when studying race differences in religion and health in late life.

CONCLUSIONS

As the literature reviewed in this chapter reveals, sociologists are beginning to make significant inroads in research on religion, aging, and health. This research is exciting because advances are being made in both the conceptualization and measurement of key facets of religion (e.g., church-based social support), and more sophisticated theoretical models have appeared which highlight the way these constructs may influence the health of our aging population. In fact, interest in religion and aging has become so widespread, that a journal is now devoted solely to this topic (the *Journal of Religious Gerontology*).

Within this burgeoning field, research on religious social support and health appears to be especially promising. There are at least three reasons why this may be so. First, it provides an arena where current empirical research can be merged with our intellectual history as exemplified by the grand social theorists (e.g., Simmel). Second, research on church-based support may ultimately be used to inform work in applied settings. More specifically, a vast literature suggests that interventions aimed at increasing secular social support may significantly improve health and well-being (see Hogan, Linden, & Najarian, 2002, for a recent review of this research) As the research and theory on church-based social support continues to evolve, it may eventually be used to develop support-based interventions in religious settings as well. Third, the work on church-based support is noteworthy because it boldly underscores the inherent social underpinnings of religion in late life.

Although great strides have been made in the field, an incredible amount of work remains to be done. Five areas where further research is needed are discussed briefly below.

First, we need to know more about the relationship between aging and religion. More specifically, research is needed to trace lifelong patterns of religious involvement. The work of Argue et al. (1999) takes an important step in this direction, but this research needs to be replicated with samples that contain a wider range of ages in the later years. Similarly, the research of George et al. (2003) is promising, but studies are needed to evaluate the validity of self-reports of religiousness over the life course.

Second, throughout this chapter it has been assumed that religion affects health and well-being, but this assumption rests primarily on theoretical grounds. Even so, one could just as easily reverse the causal ordering and argue, for example, that people with poor health are less likely to be involved in various aspects of religion, such as attending worship services. Although some research has been done to address this issue (e.g., Idler & Kasl, 1997), we need to know much more about the direction of causality between other facets of religion (e.g., church-based social support) and health.

Third, a good deal of work remains to be done on church-based social support. For example, older people have not one, but a number of different social networks. Some are secular (e.g., neighborhood ties) while others are religious (i.e., church-based social support). Research is needed to explore the interface between the two. For example, does the quality of social relationships in the church spill over and influence secular ties in the community? And if it does, which dimensions of church-based support are most likely to have this kind if effect—emotional support from fellow church members or spiritual support from church members?

Fourth, research on differences in religion and health between older blacks and older whites has provided some important insights. However, much more work is needed on older people in other racial and ethnic groups. This is especially true for older people in Asian cultures as well as Hispanics.

Finally, race and ethnicity represent only one of three major dimensions of social structure, the others being socioeconomic status (SES) and gender. Unfortunately, far less research has been done on SES, gender, aging, and health. Bringing these other factors into play provides an opportunity to explore a range of interesting issues. For example, race and gender do not exist in isolation in the real social world. Instead gender is nested within race. This simple fact points to the need for more work that, for example, compares and contrasts religiousness among black women, black men, white women, and white men (see Levin et al., 1994, for an example of this approach).

During his exemplary career, Erikson expressed a good deal of interest in Martin Luther's translation of the Bible (see Hoare, 2002). One passage in Erikson's research on Luther speaks directly to the social themes developed in this chapter. In a classic Bible story, Jesus is asked where the kingdom of God resides. The standard King James version of the Bible indicates that Jesus responded by saying that it is "within you." According to Erikson, Luther maintained that Jesus' response really was, "Behold, the kingdom of God is in the midst of you" (as quoted in Hoare, 2002, p. 109). This interpretation shifts the focus of attention from the psychological (i.e., the kingdom is within you) to the social (i.e., the kingdom is in the midst of you). Viewed broadly, the intent of this chapter has been to show the validity of the social orientation taken by Luther, thereby highlighting the vital role played by sociology in the study of religion in late life.

NOTES

1. The findings in the study by Krause (2002c) involving spiritual support and health are more complex than this discussion implies. More specifically, the data suggest that more spiritual support is associated with having a closer personal relationship with God, a close relationship with God was, in turn, associated with greater optimism, and greater optimism was related to better self-rated health. Simply put, the effects of spiritual support on health operate indirectly through having a personal relationship with God and optimism.

2. The theoretical argument developed here suggests that emotional support from church members may be related to better health. However, this hypothesis was not supported in the work of Krause (2002c). Even so, there are two reasons why the connection between church-based emotional support and health is worthy of further consideration. First, the study by Krause (2002c) was the first to test this relationship. Before firm conclusions can be drawn, this work needs to be replicated by other investigators. Second, even though the relationship between church-based emotional support and health did not hold for all the older people in the study by Krause (2002c), emotional support from fellow church members may still be an important factor for important subgroups of older people. Some evidence of this may be found in a study by Krause, Ellison, and Marcum (2002). This study, which focused on adults of all ages, found that emotional support from church members was associated with better health for men, but not women.

REFERENCES

Argue, A., Johnson, D. R., & White, L. K. (1999). Age and religiosity: Evidence from a three-wave panel analysis. *Journal for the Scientific Study of Religion, 38*, 423–435.

Bahr, H. M. (1970). Aging and religious disaffiliation. *Social Forces, 49*, 59–71.

Baldwin, J. A., & Hopkins, R. (1990). African-American and European American cultural differences as assessed by the worldviews paradigm: An empirical analysis. *Western Journal of Black Studies, 14*, 38–52.

Barna, G. (2002). *State of the church.* Ventura, CA: Issachar Resources.

Baumeister, R. F. (1991). *Meanings of life.* New York: Guilford.

Berkman, L. F., & Glass, T. (2000). Social integration, social networks, social support, and health. In L. F. Berkman & I. Kawachi (Eds.), *Social epidemiology* (pp. 137–173). New York: Oxford University Press.

Bradley, W. J., & Schaefer, K. C. (1998). *The uses and misuses of data and models.* Thousand Oaks, CA: Sage.

Butler, R. (1975). *Growing old in America: Why survive?* New York: Harper & Row.

Caplan, G. (1981). The mastery of stress: Psychosocial aspects. *American Journal of Psychiatry, 138*, 413–420.

Carstensen, L. L. (1992). Social and emotional patterns in adulthood: Support for socioemotional selectivity theory. *Psychology and Aging, 7*, 331–338.

Chatters, L. M. (2000). Religion and health: Public health research and practice. *Annual Review of Public Health, 21*, 335–367.

Cooley, C. H. (1902). *Human nature and the social order.* New York: Charles Scribner's Sons.

Cumming, E., & Henry, W. E. (1961). *Growing old.* New York: Basic Books.

Department of Labor. (2002). *Volunteering in the United States.* http://www.bls.gov/cps

Du Bois, W. E. B. (2000). In P. Zukerman (Ed.), *Du Bois on religion.* New York: Alta Mira.

Ellison, C. G., & Levin, J. S. (1998). The religion-health connection: Evidence, theory, and future directions. *Health Education & Behavior, 25*, 700–720.

Erikson, E. (1959). *Identity and the life cycle.* New York: International University Press. Fetzer Institute/National Institute on Aging Working Group. (1999). *Multidimensional measurement of religiousness/spirituality for use in health research.* Kalamazoo, MI: Fetzer Institute.

Gallup, G., & Lindsay, D. M. (1999). *Surveying the religious landscape: Trends in U.S. beliefs.* Harrisburg, PA: Morehouse.

George, L. K., Hayes, J. C., Flint, E. P., & Meador, K. G. (2004). Religion and health in life course perspective. In K. W. Schaie, N. Krause, & A. Booth (Eds.), *Religious influences on health and well-being in the elderly* (pp. 246–282). New York: Springer.

Goldhaber, D. E. (2000). *Theories of human development: Integrative perspectives.* Mountain View, CA: Mayfield.

Hoare, C. H. (2002). *Erikson on development in adulthood: New insights from unpublished papers.* New York: Guilford.

Hogan, B. E., Linden, W., & Najarian, B. (2002). Social support interventions—do they work? *Clinical Psychology Review, 22*, 381–440.

Idler, E. L., & Kasl, S. V. (1997). Religion among disabled and nondisabled persons II: Attendance at religious services as a predictor of the course of disability. *Journal of Gerontology: Social Sciences, 52B*, S306–S316.

Ingersoll-Dayton, B., Krause, N., & Morgan, D. L. (2002). Religious trajectories and transitions over the life course. *International Journal of Aging and Human Development, 55*, 51–70.

James, W. (1899). *Talks to teachers on psychology and to students on some of life's ideals.* New York: H. Holt.

Jung, C. G. (1953). *C. G. Jung: Psychological reflections.* Princeton, NJ: Princeton University Press.

Karney, B. R., & Bradbury, T. N. (1995). Assessing longitudinal change in marriage: An introduction to the analysis of growth curves. *Journal of Marriage and the Family, 57*, 1091–1108.

Kimble, M. A., & McFadden, S. H. (2003). *Aging, spirituality, and religion.* Minneapolis: Fortress Press.

Koenig, H. G. (1994). *Aging and God.* New York: Haworth Pastoral Press.

Koenig, H. G., McCullough, M. E., & Larson, D. B. (2001). *Handbook of religion and health.* New York: Oxford University Press.

Krause, N. (1986). Stress, social support, and well-being among older adults. *Journal of Gerontology, 41*, 512–519.

Krause, N. (1997). Anticipated support, received support, and economic stress among older adults. *Journal of Gerontology: Psychological Sciences, 542B*, P284–P293.

Krause, N. (2001). Social support. In R. H. Binstock & L. K. George (Eds.), *Handbook of aging and the social sciences* (272–294). New York: Academic Press.

Krause, N. (2002a). A comprehensive strategy for devising closed-ended survey items for use in studies of older adults. *Journal of Gerontology: Social Sciences, 57B*, S263–S274.

Krause, N. (2002b). Exploring race differences in a comprehensive battery of church-based social support measures. *Review of Religious Research, 44*, 126–149.

Krause, N. (2002c). Church-based social support and health: Exploring variations by race. *Journal of Gerontology: Social Sciences, 57B*, S332–S347.

Krause, N. (2003a). God-mediated control and psychological well-being in late life. Under review at *Research on Aging.*

Krause, N. (2003b). Exploring race differences in the relationship between social interaction with the clergy and psychological well-being in late life. *Sociology of Religion, 64*, 183–205.

Krause, N. (2003c). Praying for others, financial strain, and physical health status in late life. *Journal for the Scientific Study of Religion, 42*, 377–391.

Krause, N. (2003d). Religious meaning and subjective well-being in late life. *Journal of Gerontology: Social Sciences, 58B*, S160–S170.

Krause, N. (2003e). A preliminary assessment of race differences in the relationship between religious doubt and depressive symptoms. *Review of Religious Research, 45*, 93–115.

Krause, N. (2003f). Common facets of religion, unique facets of religion, and life satisfaction among older blacks. *Journal of Gerontology: Social Sciences, 59B*, S109–S117.

Krause, N., & Ellison, C. G. (2003). Forgiveness by God, forgiveness of others, and psychological well-being in late life. *Journal for the Scientific Study of Religion, 42*, 77–93.

Krause, N., & Shaw, B. A. (2002). Negative interaction and changes in functional disability during late life. *Journal of Social and Personal Relationships, 19*, 339–359.

Krause, N., & Wulff, K. M. (2003). Church-based social ties, a sense of belonging in a congregation and physical health status. *International Journal for the Psychology of Religion, 15*, 73–93.

Krause, N., Ellison, C. G., & Marcum, J. P. (2002). The effects of church-based emotional support on health: Do they vary by gender? *Sociology of Religion, 63*, 21–47.

Krause, N., Ellison, C. G., & Wulff, K. M. (1998). Church-based emotional support, negative interaction, and psychological well-being: Findings from a national sample of Presbyterians. *Journal for the Scientific Study of Religion, 37*, 725–741.

Krause, N., Morgan, D. L., Chatters, L. M., & Meltzer, T. (2000). Negative interaction in the church: Insights from focus groups. *Review of Religious Research, 41*, 522–545.

Krause, N., Ellison, C. G., Shaw, B. A., Marcum, J. P., & Boardman, J. (2001). Church-based social support and religious coping. *Journal for the Scientific Study of Religion, 40*, 637–656.

Lazarsfeld, P. F. (1955). Interpretations of statistical relations as a research operation. In P. F. Lazarsfeld & M. Rosenberg (Eds.), *The language of social research: A reader in the methodology of social research* (pp. 115–125). New York: Free Press.

Liang, J., Shaw, B. A., Krause, N., Bennett, J. M., Blaum, C., Kobayashe, E., Fukaya, T., Sugihara, Y., & Sugisawa, H. (2003). Changes in functional status among older adults in Japan. *Psychology and Aging, 18*, 684–695.

Levin, J. S. (2004). Prayer, love, and transcendence: An epidemiologic perspective. In K.W. Schaie, N. Krause, & A. Booth (Eds.), *Religious influences on health and well-being in the elderly* (69–95). New York: Springer.

Levin, J. S., Taylor, R. J., & Chatters, L. M. (1994). Race and gender differences in religiosity among older adults: Findings from four national surveys. *Journal of Gerontology: Social Sciences, 49*, S137–S145.

Mattis, J. S., & Jagers, R. J. (2001). A relational framework for the study of religiosity and spirituality in the lives of African Americans. *American Journal of Community Psychology, 29*, 519–539.

Maves, P. B. (1960). Aging, religion, and the church. In C. Tibbitts (Ed.), *Handbook of social gerontology* (pp. 698–749). Chicago: University of Chicago Press.

McPherson, M., Smith-Lovin, L., & Cook, J. M. (2001). Birds of a feather: Homophily in social networks. *Annual Review of Sociology, 27*, 415–444.

Mead, G. H. (1934). *Mind, self, and society.* Chicago: University of Chicago Press.

Morbidity and Mortality Weekly Review. (2003). Public health and aging: Trends in aging—United States and worldwide. *Morbidity and Mortality Weekly Review, 52*, 101–106.

Musick, M. A., & Wilson, J. (2003). Volunteering and depression: The role of psychological and social resources in different age groups. *Social Science and Medicine, 56*, 259–269.

Myers, S. M. (1996). Families and the inheritance of religiosity. *American Sociological Review, 61*, 858–866.

Nelson, E. A., & Dannefer, D. (1992). Aged heterogeneity: Fact or fiction? The fate and diversity in gerontological research. *The Gerontologist, 32*, 17–23.

Nelsen, H. M., & Nelsen, A. K. (1975). *Black church in the sixties.* Lexington: University of Kentucky Press.

Nooney, J., & Woodrum, E. (2002). Religious coping and church-based social support as predictors of mental health outcomes: Testing a conceptual model. *Journal for the Scientific Study of Religion, 41*, 359–368.

Olson, J. M., Roese, N. J., & Zanna, M. P. (1996). Expectancies. In E. T. Higgins & A. W. Kruglanski (Eds.), *Social psychology: Handbook of basic principles* (pp. 211–238). New York: Guilford.

Pargament, K. I. (1997). *The psychology of religion and coping: Theory, research, and practice.* New York: Guilford.

Pargament, K. I., Silverman, W., Johnson, S., Echemendia, R., & Snyder, S. (1983). The psychological climate of religious congregations. *American Journal of Community Psychology, 11*, 351–381.

Paris, P. J. (1995). *The spirituality of African Peoples: The search for a common moral discourse.* Minneapolis: Fortress Press.

Peterson, C., & Bossio, L. M. (2001). Optimism and physical health. In E.C. Chang (Ed.), *Optimism and pessimism: Implications for theory, research, and practice* (127–145). Washington, DC: American Psychological Association.

Reisman, F. (1965). The "helper" therapy principle. *Social Work, 10*, 23–37.

Rook, K. S. (1984). The negative side of social interaction: Impact on psychological well-being. *Journal of Personality and Social Psychology, 46*, 1097–1108.

Rosow, I. (1976). Status and role change through the life span. In R. H. Binstock & E. Shanas (Eds.), *Handbook of aging and the social sciences* (pp. 457–482). New York: Van Nostrand Reinhold.

Rowe, J. W., & Kahn, R. L. (1998). *Successful aging.* New York: Pantheon.

Rye, M. S., Pargament, K. I., Ali, M. A., Beck, G. L., Dorff, E. N., Hallisey, C., Narayanan, V., & Williams, J. (2000). Religious perspectives on forgiveness. In M. E. McCullough, K. I. Pargament, & C. E. Thoresen (Eds.), *Forgiveness: Theory, Research, and Practice* (pp. 17–40). New York: Guilford.

Shand, J. D. (2000). The effects of life experiences over a 50-year period on the certainty of belief and disbelief in God. *International Journal for the Psychology of Religion, 10*, 85–100.

Simmel, G. (1902/1997). *Essays on religion.* New Haven, CT: Yale University Press.

Starbuck, D. E. (1899). *The psychology of religion.* New York: Charles Scribner's Sons.

Stolzenberg, R. M., Blair-Joy, M., & Waite, L. J. (1995). Religious participation in early adulthood: Age and family life cycle effects on church membership. *American Sociological Review, 60*, 84–103.

Tornstam, L. (1997). Gerotranscendence: The contemplative dimension of aging. *Journal of Aging Studies, 11*, 143–154.

Wink, P., & Dillon, M. (2001). Religious involvement and health outcomes in late adulthood: Findings from a longitudinal study of women and men. In T. G. Plante & A. C. Sherman (Eds.), *Faith and health: Psychological perspectives* (pp. 75–106). New York: Guilford.

Wuthnow, R. (1994). *Sharing the journal: Support groups and America's new quest for community.* New York: Free Press.

PART III

RELIGION AND INEQUALITY

CHAPTER 8

Race/Ethnicity

JOHN P. BARTKOWSKI AND TODD L. MATTHEWS

INTRODUCTION

Nearly 100 years ago, W.E.B. Du Bois declared, "The problem of the twentieth century is the problem of the color line" (Du Bois, 1903, p. 283). Many observers of American race relations would charge that the color line persists as a problem in the 21st century as well. In what ways, if any, does religious belief and belonging affect the American color line? Does religion institutionalize racial difference and reinforce stratification? Or does it subvert racial hierarchies and destabilize white privilege?

This chapter sets out to examine these questions by reviewing much of the best research conducted on religion and race within the past 15 years. Where the pursuit of racial equity is concerned, we argue that religion is both a blessing and a bane. On the one hand, religion has shown itself to be a powerful tool for those wishing to challenge racial stratification. In this sense, religion figures prominently into visions of a more racially just and equitable society. Yet, on the other hand, religious communities are sometimes a site for the reinforcement of racial difference and stratification.

This essay understands religion to be a powerful institution in the contemporary world, and highlights the multifarious force of faith in the domain of race. How is religion used— often simultaneously—to subvert and reinforce the color line? Religion is best understood as a complex set of cultural tools capable of being enlisted to accomplish diverse social ends (Bartkowski, 2000, 2004; Bartkowski & Read, 2003; Bartkowski & Regis, 2003; Emerson & Smith 2000; Gallagher, 2003; Read & Bartkowski, 2000; Smith, 1998, 2000). A good deal of recent scholarship charts how religious tools have been employed to challenge racial boundaries and promote social justice. Although the classic example typically cited to support the racially egalitarian character of faith in America has been the role of black congregations in the Civil Rights movement, a careful review of more recent research highlights many contemporary cases in which the progressive influence of religion on race is evident as well. At the same time, an even-handed appraisal of American religion also reveals that it is a powerful tool wielded by those who wish to reinforce racial difference,

JOHN P. BARTKOWSKI • Mississippi State University, Mississippi State, Mississippi, 39762
TODD L. MATTHEWS • Mississippi State University, Mississippi State, Mississippi, 39762

sometimes with the explicit goal of preserving white privilege. Although often overlooked by those who cite the progressive influence of religion in the Civil Rights movement, resistance to this movement was also expressed by many Southern whites whose opposition to black civil rights drew force from their religious convictions and affiliations (Marsh, 1997).

In what follows, we review current scholarship with an eye toward explicating the paradoxical relationship between religion and race. Our essential argument is simply stated. The very same constellation of religious beliefs and practices that can be used to eradicate racial stratification also can be enlisted to reinforce it. Throughout this review, we are guided by the assumption now commonly shared among social scientists that race is a socially constructed category rather than a biological fact (see Ladson-Billings, 2000, for review). Thus, although we focus solely on race in America, we recognize that various societies across the world define race quite differently—through ancestry and lineage, skin color, and a host of other physical features that are imbued with cultural meaning. In the United States, skin color remains the principal means of defining race. Thus, a great deal of our review focuses literally on the color line in America and religion's relationship to it. Because so much of the research on this topic focuses on black-white differences, this motif runs throughout our review. In the conclusion of this chapter, we delineate the merits of moving beyond dichotomous thinking about race.

Our review of current research is structured as follows. We begin by sketching the general contours of religion and race in America. Here we explore racial differences in religious participation (namely, denominational affiliation and worship service attendance) and subjective religiosity (theological beliefs, prayer, and the like). Then, we move to explore the first side of the paradox outlined earlier—namely, how religion has been used to subvert the racial order in America. We argue that religion counters racial oppression in two primary ways—first by shoring up subcultural enclaves of social support among marginalized groups, and second by challenging inequality directly through antiracist protest or interracial affiliation. The flipside of the race-religion paradox, of course, is that religion sometimes reinforces racial stratification. In this section of our chapter, we discuss how religion can be used to preserve racial privilege. We note instances in which religious beliefs and practices can encourage people to embrace racial stereotypes, often by insulating adherents from racial "others." Quite frequently, the religious reinforcement of racial boundaries is accompanied by the renegotiation of the color line. Because religion commonly both supports and challenges the racial status quo, the portrait that emerges from much of the literature is a complicated one. We conclude by highlighting the complexity of the relationship between religion and race, and by delineating the most fruitful directions for future research on race and religion.

THE CONTOURS OF RELIGION AND RACE IN AMERICA

American religious participation is relatively strong when compared to other nations (Sherkat & Ellison, 1999; Verweij et al., 1997). General Social Survey (GSS) data indicate that 61% of Americans claim membership in a religious organization, 29% report weekly or more frequent worship service attendance, and 45% claim at least monthly attendance (Sherkat and Ellison 1999). Other data, however, suggest that actual attendance figures may be somewhat lower. There is some evidence that Americans overreport churchgoing behavior, with actual attendance in a given week approximating 22% (Sherkat & Ellison,

1999; Hadaway et al., 1993). Regardless, these figures indicate that American religious institutions enjoy robust support, particularly when compared with those of other nations (Stark & Finke, 2000).

In the overall population, religiosity is quite mixed (Sherkat & Ellison, 1999). Approximately one quarter of Americans identify with Catholicism. Nearly the same percentage is conservative Protestant, with Baptists enjoying the greatest presence among this group. Almost 30% of Americans are affiliated with liberal or moderate Protestant churches. The remainder of the United States is divided between the nonreligious (approximately 10%), Jewish adherents (2.5%), and other non-Christian faiths (roughly 2%).

These general contours provide a useful backdrop against which to examine racial differences in religiosity. African Americans are believed to be "among the most religious people in the entire world" (Sherkat, 2002, p. 485). At the very least, black Americans exhibit clearly higher levels of religious participation than whites (Taylor, Chatters, Jayakody, & Levin, 1996). However, recent research has uncovered some important nuances in the religious participation of black Americans. The gap between black and white religious participation varies geographically by region and rural-urban locale (Hunt & Hunt, 2001). Specifically, African-American religious involvement is higher in the urban South than in the urban North. Moreover, African-American church attendance is noticeably higher among monthly churchgoers, whereas the gap diminishes considerably among weekly or intermittent attendees (Hunt & Hunt, 2001).

Regardless, significant racial differences in religiosity exist on most measures (Ellison & Sherkat, 1990). More than half of all African Americans (54%) are affiliated with the Baptist faith. Not surprisingly, the percentage of African Americans who are Catholic (7%) is much lower than the percentage of white Catholics. Beyond these stark differences, there are similar black-white rates of affiliation where other conservative Protestant, liberal Protestant, and non-Christian groups are concerned (Ellison & Sherkat, 1990). However, several scholars have argued that African-American denominational loyalties have declined in importance over the past three decades (see Sherkat, 2002; Wuthnow, 1993; Roof, 1993), as specific organizational attachments are believed to be of less importance than the overall "Black Sacred Cosmos" that permeates African-American religious involvement (Lincoln & Mumiya, 1990).

In analyzing the social sources of American Christianity from 1972 to 1998, Park and Reimer (2002) distinguish African-American Protestantism from evangelical and mainline Protestantism, as well as from Roman Catholicism (see also Steensland et al., 2000). African-American Protestantism turns out to be quite distinct from the other traditions in that it is disproportionately female, while being characterized by lower marriage rates and higher birth rates (Park & Reimer, 2002). Furthermore, black Protestantism is seen as representing " 'the disinherited' in the United States insofar as (1) African Americans maintain their religious commitments with this tradition and (2) structural inequality follows racial lines where African Americans are comparatively poor and uneducated" (Park & Reimer, 2002, p. 743). Clearly, racialized religious participation provides differential opportunities and barriers for minority groups in the United States, especially for African Americans.

Hispanics are another minority group that has been long viewed as highly religious. In the United States, Hispanics have traditionally been among the strongest adherents to the Roman Catholic Church; however, several researchers have observed that Protestantism is a "growing force" in Hispanic communities within the United States and throughout the Western Hemisphere (Hunt, 1999, p. 1602; see also Deck, 1994; Greeley, 1994; Martin, 1990; Stoll, 1990; Sylvest, 1990).

Mirroring higher levels of religious attendance among African Americans, blacks are also more religious than their white counterparts on most measures of subjective religiosity (Taylor et al., 1996). National survey data reveal that blacks are more inclined to deem religious beliefs as very important (80% of blacks versus 52% of whites). Moreover, 44% of blacks report almost always seeking spiritual comfort through religion, as compared with only 32% of whites that do so. Differences in the importance of religion by race are evident not only among adults but also among youth. Among high school seniors, 45% of blacks report that religion is very important in their lives, whereas only 21% of their white peers view religion in this way.

Where the consumption of religious media is concerned, there are also significant black-white differences. About 38% of blacks report reading religious materials at least once per week. Only 23% of whites report doing the same. Similarly, 36% of African Americans view religious broadcasts at least once per week, whereas only 12% of whites do so. Where the devotional dimension of subjective religiosity is concerned, African Americans also are more prone to pray and to use prayer as a means of religious coping (see Ellison & Taylor, 1996, for review).

CONTENDING WITH OPPRESSION: RELIGION SUBVERTS THE RACIAL ORDER

One of our central arguments concerns the ability of marginalized groups to use religion as a cultural tool to ameliorate or challenge oppression. The vast majority of research on this score concerns African Americans, the group that consequently gets the lion's share of attention in the following section. One of the ways that religion shows itself to be a valuable cultural tool in offsetting the adverse effects of oppression is through the creation of subcultural enclaves and alternative social space. In this sense, religion functions as a pro-social institution that can provide marginalized racial and ethnic groups with alternative avenues of acquiring social status and support.

Religion as a Form of Institutional Access and Social Support

Social service delivery and community development initiatives undertaken by black churches have attracted considerable scholarly attention (e.g., Bartkowski & Regis, 2003; Chaves & Higgins, 1992; McRoberts, 2003; Tsitsos, 2003). Some observers have argued that African-American congregations, although quite active in community development initiatives, nevertheless fail to address the most serious problems facing black America, such as high unemployment (Lincoln & Mamiya, 1990, p. 332). However, empirical support for this assertion is limited.

African-American congregations tend to offer programs that are quite different in focus than those sponsored by white congregations. White churches conduct outreach that typically involves the sponsorship of youth camps, recreational activities, and right-to-life programs, whereas black congregations focus on meal delivery, civil rights and social justice organizing, and community development initiatives (Chaves & Higgins, 1992). More recent data collected as part of the National Congregations Study paints a similar picture. These data reveal that African-American congregations are especially likely to offer programs on tutoring/mentoring and nonreligious education (Tsitsos, 2003). These initiatives complement other programs that are particularly common in African-American churches, namely, clothing provision efforts and substance abuse treatment. Thus, African-American congregations seem to be sensitive to the array of disadvantages faced by black Americans, and exert considerable effort to ameliorate them.

Several ethnographic studies have examined how religious communities composed of racial minorities navigate the challenge between what has been identified as "social service work" (community development, poverty relief) and "spiritual work" (worship, evangelism) (McRoberts, 2003; see also Bartkowski & Regis, 2003; Pattillo-McCoy, 1998; Wood, 2002). Religious congregations and faith-based organizations often try to walk a razor's edge between these two imperatives. Where race and faith-based activism are concerned, material welfare and spiritual sustenance are sometimes perceived as mutually exclusive options but more often are woven together seamlessly as complementary objectives. Much of this ethnographic research richly recounts the influence of context-specific circumstances (e.g., historical forces, local or regional racial dynamics, pastoral leadership) on faith-based community development initiatives. Where race is concerned, such studies outline the complicated means by which marginalized groups use religious resources to make demands for racial justice, economic change, and social inclusion (see esp. McRoberts, 2003; Pattillo-McCoy, 1998; Wood, 2002). The effects of such efforts are often quite positive. As Pattillo-McCoy (1998) has persuasively argued, the cultural tools of African-American Christianity such as petition-oriented prayer and call-and-response interaction provide a "cultural blueprint" for a vibrant and cohesive civic life in black neighborhoods. Within this broader literature, there is a mix of focused investigations that concentrate on social activism principally among black churches (e.g., McRoberts, 2003; Pattillo-McCoy, 1998) and comparative approaches that examine the larger mosaic of racial and religious diversity (e.g., Bartkowski & Regis, 2003; Wood, 2002). Both approaches are necessary to arrive at a holistic understanding of the connections between religion, race, and community development strategies.

Nowhere are the broad and diverse forms of social support provided by African-American churches more evident than among blacks living in the rural South. African Americans in the rural South have long faced discrimination. However, rural Southern blacks often use religion as a key social institution for combating disadvantage (Ellison & Sherkat, 1995, 1999). As argued by Ellison and Sherkat:

> the rural southern Black church—by virtue of its multifunctionality and symbolic centrality, and the absence of secular sources of status, assistance, and leadership—has traditionally been a "semi-involuntary" institution. That is, the decisions of rural southern Blacks about participation in congregational activities have been shaped to a considerable degree by social norms and expectations.... In the rural South, the Black church has been the institutional and symbolic core of African American life. (Ellison & Sherkat, 1995, p. 1416–1417)

By contrast, urban areas that are situated outside of the South offer their black residents a wide array of secular lifestyles and social benefits. In such locales, nonreligious options available to urban blacks include membership in secular voluntary associations and social clubs as well as educational, occupational, and recreational opportunities not linked to local congregations. Thus, the centrality of the black church is diminished in urban locales, particularly outside of the South. It is not surprising then, that African Americans in the South tend to be among the most diligent church attendees in the United States and tend to be enmeshed in highly religious social networks.

More recent work on what has come to be known as "the semi-involuntary thesis" has shown that race and region intersect to influence private forms of religious consumption among blacks in the South—particularly those living in rural areas. Recent work by Sherkat and Cunningham (1998) reveals that personal religious preferences have less influence on prayer, reading religious literature, or consuming religious radio and television broadcasts among African Americans in the rural South. Sherkat surmises that there are greater social expectations to keep up on religious media issues, read religious tracts, and participate in group prayer in the rural South, thereby making faith more of a public good and less of a personal choice than is the case in the rest of the country. This is especially the case for African Americans. Thus, Sherkat and Cunningham (1998) contend that the view of a monolithic black church is suspect, arguing instead that researchers must be sensitive to regional and rural-urban differences in the public and private religious activities of African Americans.

The semi-involuntary thesis, however, has not gone unchallenged. Some scholars have questioned the veracity of claims concerning the distinctiveness of African American religion in the rural South. These critics have instead contended that religious activities reported by southern blacks are quite similar regardless of whether they reside in rural or urban areas (Hunt & Hunt, 1999). However, even these critics concede that other elements of the semi-involuntary thesis are supported in their research.

Race and the Personal Benefits of Religious Belonging

Religion also can offset the negative personal effects of racial oppression among individuals affiliated with a racial-ethnic minority. How do members of racial minority groups use religion to bolster their psychological well-being and physical health? One primary line of research in this literature is the use of prayer as a coping strategy among African Americans. Ellison and Taylor's (1996) study on the social and situational antecedents of religious coping among African Americans provides an exhaustive review of prior research while breaking new empirical ground. Using data from the National Survey of Black Americans, this study examined whether or not respondents used prayer as a coping strategy in the face of specific life crises. The influence of religiosity was compared with other social antecedents hypothesized to influence the use of prayer—namely, problem domain (i.e., bereavement, personal health, health of others), social and psychological resources (i.e., subjective family closeness, number of friends, and personal mastery), and social location (i.e., age, gender, and education). They found that African Americans widely employed prayer—either through initiating personal prayer or soliciting the prayers of others—as a means of coping with serious personal problems. Prayer is a particularly important coping mechanism for highly religious blacks and for those confronting bereavement and health-related problems. Gender turns out to be a factor with critical influence on this relationship, such that black women are far more likely than their male counterparts to turn to prayer when facing life crises.

These findings are broadly consistent with related research that has examined the distinctive character of social support provided by network embeddedness within African-American religious communities. Krause's (2002) work has underscored the robustness of support networks within African-American congregations both among laity and between clergy and laypersons. A more recent study revealed that receiving emotional support from the clergy bolsters the self-esteem of elderly churchgoing blacks (Krause, 2003). Such effects were not observed for elderly churchgoing whites. When considering possible explanations for these disparate findings among blacks and whites, Krause (2003, p. 201) surmised that the "years of discrimination and prejudice [faced by African Americans] have elevated the church to a central position in the lives of many black elders. Due to these social structural blockages, this institution has, therefore, become a primary source of self-esteem."

Qualitative studies have shed further light on the use of subjective religiosity, especially prayer, as a coping resource-among African Americans. Black's (1999) interviews with impoverished, elderly African-American women living alone demonstrate the manner in which prayer is utilized as a coping strategy among those who face multiple disadvantages. Her use of a case study methodology fills a crucial gap left by survey research by featuring moving testimonials from various women focused principally on how black women (1) use faith to cope with and find meaning for their hardship, and (2) speak to God and understand the nature of God in light of the lifelong social disadvantages they face. The African-American women in this study felt that they enjoyed a partnership with God, who they believed to have reciprocated their continued faithfulness with blessings of various sorts. Moreover, their sense of familiarity with God was evidenced by the quality of their prayers, which were often marked by a conversational and petitionary character.

Another qualitative study examined how older African Americans enlisted spiritual coping as they provided care to younger relatives with HIV (Poindexter, Linsk, and Warner 1999). Given the stigmatization of HIV in many faith communities, these individuals were reluctant to reveal their HIV-caregiver status in organized religious settings. However, in seeking to face the psychological challenges associated with providing such care, they turned to prayer as a means of cultivating a direct relationship with God. In this context, personal prayer (spirituality) rather than externally defined religious observance (organized religion) among older blacks was a key coping resource for confronting the terminal illness of loved ones.

Research also has examined the relationship between religiosity, race, and health, typically with an eye toward testing two competing hypotheses. On the one hand, the social support hypothesis asserts that integration within social networks bolsters health. These networks may or may not be religious, because "religion is simply one gateway to supportive relationships" (Ferraro & Koch, 1994, p. 364). However, the connection between religious forms of social support and race is anticipated to be different for black Americans, because of black churches' pivotal role in addressing the material and psychological needs of their members. On the other hand, the religious consolation hypothesis asserts that "religion is used by oppressed people to make sense of the world of adversity" (Ferraro and Koch 1994, p. 365). According to this logic, religion may be associated with poor health because the sick would seek comfort and supplication in faith.

Using data from the American's Changing Lives survey, Ferraro and Koch (1994) tested these competing hypotheses. They found that social support (including religious integration) has a beneficial effect on health. However, no race differences surfaced in association with these effects. Thus, although black respondents in this survey (as in most others) are more religious than whites, higher levels of religiosity did not translate into distinctly improved health outcomes for African Americans. Thus, the social support hypothesis is empirically supported in this study; however, the linkage between social support and health does not seem to be affected by race. At the same time, race differences did surface concerning the religious consolation hypothesis. When compared with their white counterparts, black adults were much more likely to turn to religion in confronting health problems. This is an especially noteworthy finding because blacks are more likely to experience health problems. Thus, as a group, African Americans will have greater opportunity to turn to religion as a means of coping with poor health. As the authors conclude: "Physical suffering and bodily dysfunction exact a toll, and black adults appear much more likely to use religion to help make sense of the health adversity" (Ferraro & Koch, 1994, p. 372).

In a more recent follow-up study, Drevenstedt (1998) used data from the GSS to analyze variations in self-reported health assessments by religion and race among whites, blacks, and Latinos. Using a multidimensional measure of religiosity, he explored the influence of worship service attendance and subjective commitment to religion on self-reported health. In initial analyses, Drevenstedt found a positive association between religious attendance and health. However, for younger cohorts of blacks, Latinos, and white women, this association is attenuated when subjective religiosity is taken into consideration. Thus this study underscores "the importance of commitment to faith if younger respondents are to reap measurable health benefits from attending church more frequently" (Drevenstedt, 1998, p. 258). This seems to be particularly the case for young blacks and Latinos. However, the extensive reliance on subjective global measures of physical health in such studies merits some caution when interpreting relationships between religion, race, and health. Objective measures of health would be far more desirable, though admittedly difficult to obtain.

Challenging the Color Line: Religion Undermines Racial Oppression

Although religion is often used as a compensatory resource to offset the effects of racial oppression, it also can be employed more directly to challenge racist power structures and subvert discrimination. In what follows, we discuss how religion acts as a catalyst for antiracist protest by fostering political mobilization and collective action. We then explore how multiracial religious congregations challenge the monochromatic character of faith communities and social spaces in contemporary American society.

One of the ways in which religious communities challenge the color line is through the political mobilization of their members. Religious communities are significantly engaged in politics, such that 41% of congregations report engaging in such political activities as the following: telling their members about opportunities for political activity, distributing voter guides, holding forums for political discussion, and registering voters, among others (Beyerlein & Chaves, 2003). Moreover, approximately two thirds of the churchgoing population claims that civic improvement is among the principal reasons for their religious activity (Burns, Schlozman, & Verba, 2001, p. 106).

At first blush, the absolute percentages of political participation in religious congregations do not appear particularly impressive. However, scholars of religion are quick to point out that congregations are far more politically engaged than are secular organizations (e.g., parent-teacher associations, social lodges) (Beyerlein & Chaves, 2003).

Race figures prominently into the relationship between religion and political action. Research reveals religious involvement to be a consistently positive predictor of African-American political participation (Walton, 1985; Wilcox, 1990; Wilcox & Gomez, 1990). This body of scholarship challenges research from several decades ago that charged African-American faith with being an opiate that impeded black political activism. Where black religion in concerned, the opiate thesis has now largely been discredited.

More recent inquiries have shed additional light on African-American religion as an impetus for political action. Data from the National Congregations Study (Beyerlein & Chaves, 2003) reveal that:

- the percentage of black Protestant congregations that have featured a political candidate as a guest speaker (16%) is more than five times that of mainline Protestant congregations (3%), while far eclipsing Catholic and conservative Protestant congregations (1% each) who have done so;
- 29% of black Protestant congregations report having registered people to vote (versus 2% mainline Protestant and 3% conservative Protestant congregations);
- 24% of black Protestant congregations have ever distributed voter guides, as compared with 11% mainline Protestant, 13% Catholic, and 19% conservative Protestant); and
- after controlling for other factors, black Protestant congregations are significantly more likely to offer political opportunities to their members to (1) provide forums for discussing political issues, (2) host candidates as church speakers, (3) hold voter registration drives, and (4) distribute voter guides (especially non-Christian Right voter guides).

Therefore, it is clear that religion strongly influences race, political engagement, and civic participation. Even scholars who do not principally focus on religion readily recognize the civic and political power of black religious institutions. In his widely influential book, *Bowling Alone,* Robert Putnam[1] states that:

> faith-based organizations are particularly central to social capital and civic engagement in the African American community. The church is the oldest and most resilient social institution in black America, not least because it was traditionally the only black-controlled institution of a historically oppressed people. African Americans in all social strata are more religiously observant than other Americans. The black religious tradition distinctively encourages mixing religion and community affairs and invigorates civic activism. Both during and after the civil rights struggle, church involvement among blacks has been strongly associated with civic engagement, in part because the church provides a unique opportunity for blacks to exercise civic skills. (Putnam, 2000, p. 68)

This is not to say, however, that there is a homogeneous "black church" or that "black religiosity" uniformly spurs political activism among all churchgoing African Americans. Several recent studies illustrate important nuances in the relationship between religion, race, and politics. High levels of organizational religiosity (e.g., church attendance, congregational committee participation) among blacks are linked to support for integrationist-oriented means of black empowerment that include voting and lending support to the electoral process; however, an otherworldly religious orientation that privileges salvation is connected to separatist-oriented strategies for racial empowerment (Calhoun-Brown, 1998). Thus, different dimensions of African American religiosity are linked with particular strategies of racial empowerment. In a follow-up study, Calhoun-Brown found that holding a black image of Jesus Christ (a core tenet of black liberation theology, embraced by about 30% of African Americans) is linked with a desire for racial autonomy but fails to promote voting behavior or support for church involvement in politics (Calhoun-Brown, 1999). Outside the realm of black Christianity, a growing body of scholarship has also begun to examine the increasing prominence of Islam among African Americans (Curtis, 2002; DeCaro, 1998; Smith, 1999, Ch. 4; Turner, 1997). Taken together, studies such as these underscore the need to consider the variegated character of religion among black Americans, and highlight the ways in which diverse cultural forces within African-American religious communities influence political viewpoints.

Related research has explored the political views of black religious leadership. McDaniel's (2003) study of African Methodist Episcopal (AME) and Church of God in Christ (COGIC) pastors reveals that clergy share political views that are right of center on moral issues (sex education, gay rights) and left of center on economic issues (social welfare support for the poor, government solutions to social problems). Yet, despite these sources of political cohesion, noteworthy differences in policy preferences and patterns of political action surfaced across denominational lines. Although AME pastors were more internally fractured concerning the question of abortion, COGIC pastors were likely to favor a constitutional ban against it. Moreover, AME religious leaders showed a greater willingness to take direct action against policies they opposed, were more inclined to use their position of religious leadership to mobilize followers, and reported higher actual levels of political engagement than their COGIC counterparts. Ethnographic studies have lent further insight into the influential roles that black religious leaders often play in their congregations and communities concerning political issues (Bartkowski & Regis, 2003; Lee, 2003), but more research needs to be conducted on how the exercise of pastoral power varies across denominational contexts.

A burgeoning body of scholarship has begun to problematize the assumption that American religious communities are monochromatic (that is, racially or ethnically homogenous). The monochromatic congregation thesis stems from the theoretical presupposition of "homophily"—the idea that "birds of a feather flock together." Research on this issue suggests that race and religion are two key sources of intragroup connection that, by extension, have led to the racial segregation of religious communities (McPherson, Smith-Lovin, & Cook, 2001). Despite some research supporting this thesis, religious homophily has declined in recent years even as racial homophily has remained rather robust (e.g., Kalmijn, 1998; see McPherson, Smith-Lovin, & Cook, 2001, for review). Given these developments, a handful of scholars have begun to reexamine racial-ethnic diversity in religious congregations, thereby taking issue with the longstanding assumption that "11:00 AM Sunday morning is the most segregated hour in America" (Dougherty, 2003, p. 65; see also Becker, 1998; Ecklund, 2005a, 2005b; Emerson & Kim, 2003; Jenkins, 2003).

Using data from the 1993 American Congregation Giving Study, Dougherty examines racial-ethnic diversity within 625 congregations from five Christian traditions (Presbyterian, Lutheran, Southern Baptist, Assembly of God, and Roman Catholic). Rather than conceptualizing race as a black-white dichotomy, Dougherty argues for a continuum of racial-ethnic diversity within congregations. On one end of this continuum is the entirely homogeneous congregation, with the other end represented by the highly diverse multiracial congregation and different gradations of racial diversity situated between these poles. Dougherty's findings are startling and complex. He finds that approximately 43% of congregations in the study were marked by complete racial homogeneity, with not a single member of the congregation belonging to another racial-ethnic group. However, when calculating "mean racial-ethnic diversity" by region, location size, faith tradition, and small groups, the findings are more complicated. Among the most interesting findings, Dougherty discovers that larger communities feature more racially diverse congregations. Thus, rural congregations are more racially homogenous than their urban counterparts. Where faith tradition is concerned, Catholic congregations are more racially diverse than are the Protestant traditions examined in this study. Among Protestant faiths, Assembly of God congregations are considerably more racially diverse than their Presbyterian, Lutheran, and Southern

Baptist counterparts. In addition, higher educational levels among the members of religious congregations are a strong predictor of greater racial-ethnic diversity.

Other work has examined the social antecedents and persistence of racial diversification among religious congregations. Emerson and Kim (2003) explore three different impetuses for racial diversification: (1) mission (theological, cultural, and symbolic orientation), (2) resource calculation (changes in a congregation's resource level including declines in membership, budget constraints, or perceived opportunities due to an influx of new resources), and (3) external authority structure (mandates from denominational leaders). They analyze data from the Multiracial Congregations Project, participant-observations and 170 in-depth interviews with members and clergy in 20 multiracial congregations. Beyond examining the impetus for racial diversification, congregations are also analyzed in terms of source of diversification (proximity, culture and purpose, and preexisting organizational package), and congregational types (neighborhood embracing, neighborhood charter, niche embracing, niche charter, survival embracing, survival merge, and mandated). Among their primary findings, Emerson and Kim (2003, p. 224) discover that:

> although all multiracial churches face forces that make them at risk for instability, our research suggests that the *mandated* multiracial church faces even more initial risk. This is due to the source of the change coming from outside the congregation, sometimes producing resistance within the congregation. (italics in original)

Additional research has explored the personal costs of membership in multiracial religious organizations for members of different racial groups. In their case study of a multiracial congregation in suburban Los Angeles County composed of Filipino, Anglo, Hispanic, African American, Chinese, and Kenyan members, Christerson and Emerson (2003) find that minority group members disproportionately bear the costs of affiliation with a multiracial faith community. This church is located in a predominantly Filipino area, and slightly more than half of the congregation is Filipino. Costs of membership experienced by non-Filipinos within this church include difficulty in forming friendships, the experience of feeling like an outsider, and a lack of close social ties when compared with the experiences of their Filipino counterparts. An Anglo-American female featured in this study described her experiences in a particularly poignant way:

> For a long time I didn't have friends at church. I felt really out of place. I tried to understand the Filipino mentality and relate, but I couldn't do it. I was trying to fit in. I even started to try to dress sort of like them and act like them, but I couldn't fit in. (quoted in Christerson & Emerson, 2003, p. 173)

More recently, the literature on multiracial religious fellowships and the costs thereof has been pushed forward by comparative ethnographic research. Jenkins's case study of an International Churches of Christ (ICOC) congregation lays bare the social and cultural processes behind the maintenance of interracial fellowships in this high-boundary religious movement. Jenkins traces the cultivation of what she calls "intimate diversity"— that is, the creation and maintenance of close and caring relationships among a racially diverse membership. The ICOC was able to use the practice of "discipling" through which new members were proselytized and, once having joined, mentored and monitored. Strangely, the combination of sectarianism (nonmainstream religion) and hierarchy (asymmetrical social relationships) fostered intimate diversity. Jenkins (2003, p. 397) concludes that in high-boundary sects such ICOC, "multiculturalism/racialism was framed through exclusivity: racism was portrayed as a social evil, a sin rampant outside the group, while in-group intimate diversity emerged as sacred, salvific, and powerful," adding that:

> ICOC leaders consistently stressed the exclusive nature of diversity in their church.... ICOC members frequently heard about and witnessed high-level interracial/ethnic discipling relationships, fueling the image of their church community as uniquely driven by intimate diversity from top to bottom. The ICOC's worship style contributed to its image of exceptional group diversity through "ritual inclusion," welcoming diversity in music, language, and ritual practice.

Jenkins is careful to identify, however, how intimate diversity was predicated on two contradictory ideals—the celebration of racial-ethnic diversity on the one hand, and the attempt to erase racial-ethnic differences on the other. Findings such as these suggest that there are often countervailing tendencies at work even where the color line is most boldly transgressed.

REINFORCING AND RENEGOTIATING THE COLOR LINE

Religion's role in subverting the color line or countering racial suppression is only one side of the story. A relatively understudied but still important theme that has emerged in the religion and race literature during the past decade is the power of religion to deepen racial difference and exacerbate racial stratification. This much is to be anticipated from the early work of W.E.B. Du Bois (see Zuckerman, 2000), who was quite critical of the formidable color line in American Christianity. In various writings quoted by Zuckerman (2000, p. 11–12), Du Bois argued that white Christianity is marked by "racial prejudice ... [that is] openly recognized ... [and] considered the natural and normal thing .... [This is a] terrible comment upon the failure of its white followers ... [The] church was the bulwark of American slavery; and ... today is the strongest seat of racial and color prejudice." Du Bois contended that Catholics failed to ordain black priests "because they think Negroes have neither brains nor morals enough to occupy positions freely open to Poles, Irishmen, and Italians" (Zuckerman, 2000, p. 12).

Empirical research does reveal that religion can be a force for deepening racial prejudice and preserving racial privilege. Yet, often the boundary-reinforcing character of religion is interlaced with boundary-crossing tendencies. This paradox is the focus of much of our attention in the remainder of the chapter.

Studies of American religious history reveal the enduring character of religious stratification from colonial America to the contemporary period (Bartkowski & Regis, 2003, Ch. 2; Pyle & Davidson, 2003). And it is important to recognize that religious stratification in America has long been linked with racial and ethnic stratification. To take but one example, the religious and ethnic impetuses for the scientific charity movement of the middle and latter nineteenth century reveal that Protestant social reformers " 'found the new Catholic immigrants to be lazy, indolent, prone to drink, and far too ready to accept public relief' (Cammisa, 1998, p. 34)—labels that would later be applied to African Americans and Hispanics" (Bartkowski & Regis, 2003, p. 41). Thus, the intersection of religious stratification and racial-ethnic inequality has endured throughout the long stretch of American history, even if the particular groups victimized by such prejudice have varied from one period to the next.

The link between religious and racial forms of division remain alive today, even if it is less robust than in times past and is marked by complex patterns of boundary renegotiation

(Bartkowski, 2004; Kalmijn, 1998; McPherson, Smith-Lovin, & Cook, 2001). Among Catholics, there is evidence of continued racial divisions that have given rise to a distinctively Catholic "black sacred cosmos" (Cavendish, Welch, & Leege, 1998; Davis, 1990). Recent research confirms that:

> significant black/white differences in styles of religiosity do exist within the Catholic Church. Black Catholics display higher levels of more private, or personal, styles of religious devotion and report a greater frequency of spiritual experiences than white Catholics. Furthermore, because white Catholics display a higher level of religiosity on only . . . obligatory devotionalism . . . , it seems that black Catholics may be more comprehensively religious than their white counterparts. (Cavendish, Welch, & Leege, 1998, p. 405)

In at least one documented case, these racial differences resulted in the secession of a black Catholic congregation from the Roman Catholic Church. In 1990, Reverend George Stallings Jr. broke with the pope and his local bishop to form the independent Imani Temple African American Catholic Congregation because, he charged, the spiritual and cultural needs of black American Catholics were being overlooked by the Roman Catholic hierarchy. For this reason, researchers have recently suggested that the Catholic liturgy must begin to affirm the "black sacred cosmos" while retaining the distinctive elements of Roman Catholicism or risk losing their black members to competing religious traditions (Cavendish, Welch, & Leege, 1998).

Ethnographic research lends further confirmation to significant racial divisions within the Catholic Church, and the complicated means by which these cleavages are sustained. In their comparative study of white and Hispanic congregations in Mississippi, Bartkowski and Regis (2003, Ch. 6) found a substantial amount of antipathy and mistrust surfacing between all-Hispanic Catholic congregations and their all-white counterparts. In this case, racial-ethnic divisions were interlaced with differences in social class and nationality. Thus, the migrant working poor Mexicans and middle-class Anglos each attended their respective congregations. And, despite their shared religious convictions, divisions of race, class, and nativity created "two catholicisms"—one for Mexican migrants and another for whites. Even when outreach occurred across racial lines among these congregations through an immigration sponsorship initiative rooted in the practice of Catholic adoptive godparenting, it was marked by the preservation of racial boundaries. The researchers write that:

> some Anglo congregants fetishize the immigration sponsorship initiative as a cultural exchange program. This cultural-exchange approach to sponsorship exaggerates social distance between white sponsors and the Hispanic beneficiaries of such sponsorship while subverting any opportunity for both parties to discover what the [local] priest calls their "common humanity." According to [the local priest,] Father Dejean, these types of Anglo congregants say, "Well, you know, we tolerate you [Hispanics]. We like the kids. We like to have them come in. But do we really believe that they belong to us? No, they're still outsiders."

Episcopalians have had a more ambivalent history where race relations are concerned, one that highlights the complicated interweaving of progressive and regressive forces (Shattuck, 2000). To be sure, the Episcopal Church has long been at the forefront of struggles for racial justice and equality. As the Civil Rights Movement first emerged, a group of white and black Episcopalians formed the Episcopal Society for Cultural and Racial Unity. Visionary in its goals, this group committed itself to the eradication of all distinctions roots in race, ethnicity, and social class. The group's motto, taken from Psalm 133, claimed what a "good and joyful thing it is for brethren to dwell together in unity." However, Shattuck's thoughtful historical analysis reveals that the Episcopal Church often promoted racial equality in public while failing to provide sufficient resources and positions of authority to black clergy and African-American laity within the denomination. Thus, even as the Episcopal Church pled for racial equality in American society, it faced charges from within of antiblack prejudice and white paternalism.

Similar complexities are manifested in the Church of Jesus Christ of Latter-day Saints (Mormons), a lay-priesthood-run faith tradition. For quite some time, the Latter-day Saints (LDS) church had been subject to criticism for prohibiting black males from holding the priesthood, thereby opening itself up to charges of institutionalized racism, ethnic chauvinism, and race-based authoritarianism (see Lincoln, 1999, for criticism). On June 9, 1978, the LDS church rescinded the ban on black males holding the priesthood. Oral history research has catalogued the challenges that black male Mormons faced in integrating their religious and racial identities given the cognitive dissonance the priesthood ban created for them (White & White, 1995; on related LDS racial issues, see also White & White, 2000). Those who embraced the traditional Mormon ideology of race reduce cognitive dissonance by privileging their religious identity while downplaying their racial identity. At the other end of this identity negotiation continuum, some black LDS men attributed the priesthood ban to white racism. In so doing, they subordinated their religious identity to their racial identity. These black men viewed the priesthood ban as part of a racist past that the Mormon Church must acknowledge and repudiate. Other centrist ideologies defended the ban as revelation while conceding its inexplicability or simply relegated the ban to the past without further commentary.

Recent research has shown a dramatic redefinition of racial identity within the LDS Church, which now adamantly rejects the "curse of Cain" argument for black subjugation and has jettisoned unflattering portrayals of Native American lineage as well (Mauss, 2003). The move away from a deterministic definition of racial identity within Mormonism has been accompanied by a great deal of LDS missionary outreach and public relations efforts in African American communities. Despite the long tenure of this racial ideology within Mormonism, survey evidence consistently demonstrates that Latter-day Saints are more supportive of guaranteeing civil liberty protections for African Americans than are their non-LDS counterparts (Mauss, 2003, p. 252–255). This seeming paradox is probably best explained by the cultural sensitivity for blacks generated through the history of persecution in Mormons' collective memory.

Turning to conservative Protestantism, recent research renders a similarly complicated portrait. A long-standing tradition of research has suggested that conservative Protestants (particularly, fundamentalists) are more racially prejudiced (Altemeyer & Hunsberger, 1992; Hunsberger, 1995, 1996; Wylie & Forest, 1992; see Laythe, Finkel, Bringle, & Kirkpatrick, 2002, for review). This conclusion receives confirmation not only from survey-based investigations, but from qualitative research as well. After analyzing in-depth interviews with white evangelicals across the United States, Emerson and Smith (2000, p. 170) conclude: "Despite devoting considerable time and energy to solving the problem of racial division, white evangelicalism likely does more to perpetuate the racialized society than to reduce it" (see also Emerson, Smith, & Sikkink, 1999). Various factors contribute to persistent racial prejudice and division among white evangelicals. As noted earlier, when discussing the monochromatic character of religious communities in America, congregations have been formed along racial lines. Thus, congregations often act as sites for the reinforcement of racial segregation, and this is especially so among evangelical faith communities. Also, the cultural tools within the evangelical universe lend themselves to a blame-the-victim approach to social problems in general, and race relations in particular. Emerson and Smith (2000, p. 170) contend that these cultural tools "tend to (1) minimize and individualize the race problem,

(2) assign blame to blacks themselves for racial inequality, (3) obscure inequality as part of racial division, and (4) suggest unidimensional solutions to racial division."

Other scholars have argued that there is a more complex relationship at play here. Recent research into the relationship between religious fundamentalism and prejudice has found that other factors need to be considered, including the role of right-wing authoritarianism, which involves authoritarian submission, authoritarian aggression, and conventionalism (Laythe, Finkel, Bringle & Kirkpatrick, 2002; Laythe, Finkel & Kirkpatrick, 2001; Altemeyer, 1981, 1988). Laythe and colleagues (2001) argue that right-wing authoritarianism is the driving force behind the relationship between religious fundamentalism and prejudice. Indeed, they find that fundamentalism is inversely related to certain types of prejudice (including racial prejudice). Thus, adherents of faiths defined as fundamentalist actually demonstrate less racial prejudice than others when right-wing authoritarianism is statistically controlled.

Here again, ethnographic research supports this rather messy portrait of prejudice among conservative Protestants. The Promise Keepers, an evangelical men's movement committed to racial reconciliation (among other objectives), were able to raise awareness about racial divisions in Christian denominations and challenged born-again men to develop friendships across racial lines (Bartkowski, 2000, 2002, 2004). In the best of circumstances, such mandates created large-scale interracial fellowships in which black and white congregations would spend successive Sundays worshipping at one church and then the other. And for its part, the Promise Keepers organization was careful to feature a racially diverse slate of evangelical leaders at their stadium conferences as speakers and on their board of directors. Indeed, their current president, Tom Fortson, is African American. At the same time, the Promise Keepers were true to their evangelical roots in constructing racism in America as a product of individual sin rather than a structural problem of disparate opportunities (Allen, 2001). Not big on "government solutions" to the American dilemma of racial inequality, Promise Keepers encouraged personal reconciliation rather than societal transformation. What's more, Promise Keepers viewed racism as a problem among all people (whites and nonwhites alike). This perspective fails to recognize the greater toll, on average, that discrimination exacts on persons of color in a society that continues to privilege whiteness (Bartkowski, 2004).

Where the relationship between the Religious Right (one wing of conservative Protestantism) and the Jewish faith is concerned, similarly complex findings have surfaced (Smith, 1999). There is little difference among the general population in terms of political and social acceptance of Jews. Despite this fact, those who are part of the Religious Right tend to exhibit higher levels of support for biblical interpretations of the special status of the Jews, as well as protection for the state of Israel. However, there are subtle and important differences that emerge among religious conservatives. When controlling for political ideology (conservative/nonconservative), anti-Jewish scores are significantly higher among evangelicals than nonevangelicals. And the Religious Right tends to be less supportive of Jews in terms of specific social and economic issues. Smith (1999, p. 255) concludes:

> Jews have an ambivalent place in the heart and mind of the Religious Right. On the one hand they are the Hebrews of the Old Testament, God's chosen people, and Jesus' forebearers. On the other hand they are seen as outsiders–late arrivals, non-Christians, either Orthodox practitioners following strange customs or secular humanists following strange values.

The complex character of the relationship between religion and race may be understandable enough in mainstream religious denominations. Large religious denominations in America represent diverse constituencies and must negotiate an array of relationships with their members, competing religious bodies, and American society at large. But what of the explicitly racist ideologies and practices situated far to the right of American religious and social life? Should we expect nuance and complexity in white supremacy movements or explicitly anti-Semitic groups? Research on such groups has produced findings that are at once disturbing and surprising. Barkun's (1994) stunning analysis of Christian Identity traces the sect's origins from British-Israelism, and its many ideological and programmatic permutations through successive generations of adherents. Christian Identity is made up of a loose affiliation of independent congregations and a mélange of movement publications, encompassing a diverse range of White supremacist groups such as the Aryan Nations and the Ku Klux Klan, militant and survivalist groups, and organizations and isolated individuals working for change through the political system. The central preoccupation of this movement revolves around fears of racial mixing and Jewish conspiracy, and these fears have remained largely unchanged over time.

Although the core beliefs of the Christian Identity movement have remained largely intact, there have been significant ideological changes over the years. For example, there is considerable debate within Christian Identity about the specifics of "Satanic theory." Original crafters of the "serpentine seedline" theory charged that Cain was the literal descendant of Satan and Eve, based on the assumption that the original sin was Satan's sexual seduction of Eve. This demonization of the Jewish people distinguishes Christian Identity from other forms of conservative Protestantism. Yet, more recent expositors of the "serpentine seedline" theory take issue with this charge, saying it is pure fabrication. Even more, some Identity followers utilize Satanic theory to anti-Semitic ends while others employ it to foster antiblack sentiment. To outsiders, these disputes might seem like minor quibbles among racist zealots. However, to those inside of the movement, these are hotly contested issues that have fractured its adherents into competing constituencies. What's more, an ideology that defines Jews or, alternatively, African Americans as Satan's children has real-world consequences in terms of the particular group that becomes the actual target of racial animus. Finally, religious disputes among white supremacy groups can lead to an outcome that might be celebrated by those who do not share such racist ideas—namely, extreme ideological fragmentation can stifle movement growth and potentially contribute to their ultimate demise (Dobratz 2001).

CONCLUSION

This chapter has examined the complex relationship between religion and race in the United States. This review principally drew insights from research conducted during the past 15 years. Using Du Bois's concept of the color line, we have argued that religion is a valuable resource that racial minority groups have used to contend with, and sometimes subvert, an oppressive social order. However, under some circumstances, religion has been used to foster racial oppression. In the end, we find that a complicated picture emerges. Religion is capable of subverting and reinforcing the color line in America, and often does so simultaneously or in terribly complex ways. Where American race relations are concerned, religion is both a bridge connecting racial groups and boundary dividing them (cf. Bartkowski & Regis, 2003; Warner, 1997; Wuthnow, 2002).

What research needs to be conducted on religion and race as we look toward the future? Two key directions seem particularly promising. First, given the increasing degree of racial and religious diversity in American society, research needs to be move beyond a binary black/white framework for studying race. An especially fruitful cross-fertilization can occur between scholars who study race and religion and those focused on the religious dimensions of American immigration (see the chapter on religion and immigration in this volume). Du Bois is careful to remind us that the color line is not a singular boundary separating two groups of people. Rather, he suggests that the contours of the color line and the very definition of race may change dramatically among populations in the process of becoming increasingly diverse. Scholars of religion should attempt to keep their finger on the pulse of racial diversification in America, carefully examining the role that faith plays in this societal transformation. The comparative and triangulated approach that sociologists of religion have utilized to study religion and immigration (Ebaugh & Chafetz, 2000; Warner & Wittner, 1998) provides an excellent model for studying racial diversity in American religion as well. To their credit, some sociologists who study race and religion have emerged as pioneers in this effort.[2] However, more research of this kind is needed.

Second, many social scientists who now study race examine its socially constructed character. Such scholarship asks how race is defined and is attuned to the variegated and fluid constructions of race across social contexts. A great deal of scholarship has explored the social underpinnings of "blackness," "whiteness," "Jewishness," and other racial identities. Scholars of religion would do well to incorporate this crucial insight into their study of race and religion. Religion is not only an institutional structure, but it is also a cultural tool (or better, a repertoire of resources) through which racial identity is defined, negotiated, and contested. In many cases, there are competing constructions of race that emerge around a particular religion. The case of voodoo in the United States is but one example. By its detractors, voodoo has been variously defined as "black magic" and a "satanic cult" (Bartkowski, 1998). However, its practitioners have used voodoo to redefine blackness by imbuing it with power and respectability (Brown, 1991). Contested definitions of race also may be evident in other religious contexts but only if scholars are willing to expand the way they conceptualize race and its relationship to religion.

NOTES

1. Although we cite Putnam, more in-depth treatments of the religious underpinnings of African American political activism and civic participation are legion. See, for example, Billingsley, 1999; Harris, 1999; Lincoln and Mamiya, 1990; McRoberts, 2003; Morris, 1984; McAdam, 1982; Marsh, 1997; and Pattillo-McCoy, 1998. Space limitations keep us from reviewing many of these studies in a more thorough fashion.
2. Michael Emerson's Multiracial Congregations Project comes immediately to mind as an exemplary effort to explore the intersection of religion and race through a comparative and triangulated methodology. The work of Fenggang Yang (1999), although more focused in scope, also bears mentioning for its triangulated method and its conceptualization of religion's role in the transformation of (Chinese) ethnic identities. The field would profit a great deal from more work of this nature.

REFERENCES

Allen, L. D., II. (2000). Promise Keepers and racism: Frame resonance as an indicator of organizational vitality. *Sociology of Religion,* 61, 55–72.

Altemeyer, B. (1981). *Right wing authoritarianism.* Winnipeg: University of Manitoba Press.

Altemeyer, B. (1988). *Enemies of freedom: Understanding right wing authoritarianism.* San Francisco, CA: Jossey-Bass.

Altemeyer, B., & Hunsburger, B. (1992). Authoritarianism, religious fundamentalism, quest, and prejudice. *International Journal for the Psychology of Religion, 2*, 113–133.

Barkun, M. (1994). *Religion and the racist right.* Chapel Hill: University of North Carolina Press.

Bartkowski, J. P. (1998). Claims-making and typifications of voodoo as a deviant religion: Hex, lies, and videotape. *Journal for the Scientific Study of Religion, 37*, 559–579.

Bartkowski, J. P. (2000). Breaking walls, raising fences: masculinity, intimacy, and accountability among the Promise Keepers. *Sociology of Religion, 61*, 33–53.

Bartkowski, J. P. (2002). Godly masculinities: Competing discourses of evangelical manhood among the Promise Keepers. *Journal of Social Thought and Research, 24*, 53–87.

Bartkowski, J. P. (2004). *The Promise Keepers: Servants, soldiers, and godly men.* New Brunswick, NJ: Rutgers University Press.

Bartkowski, J. P., & Read, J. G. (2003). Veiled submission: Gender negotiation among evangelical and U.S. Muslim women. *Qualitative Sociology, 26*, 71–92.

Bartkowski, J. P., & Regis, H. A. (2003). *Charitable choices: Religion, race, and poverty in the post-welfare era.* New York: New York University Press.

Beyerlein, K., & Chaves, M. (2003). The political activities of religious congregations in the United States. *Journal for the Scientific Study of Religion, 42*, 229–246.

Billingsley, A. (1999). *Mighty like a river: The Black church and social reform.* New York and Oxford: Oxford University Press.

Black, H. K. (1999). Poverty and prayer: Spiritual narratives of elderly African-American women. *Review of Religious Research, 40*, 359–374.

Brown, K. McC. (1991). *Mama Lola: A vodou priestess in Brooklyn.* Berkeley: University of California Press.

Burns, N., Schlozman, K. L., & Verba, S. (2001). *The private roots of public action: Gender, equality, and political participation.* Cambridge, MA, and London: Harvard University Press.

Calhoun-Brown, A. (1998). While marching to Zion: Otherworldliness and racial empowerment in the Black community. *Journal for the Scientific Study of Religion, 37*, 427–439.

Calhoun-Brown, A. (1999). "The image of God: Black theology and racial empowerment in the African American community." *Review of Religious Research, 40*, 197–212.

Cammisa, Anne Marie. 1998. *From rhetoric to reform? Welfare policy in American politics.* Boulder, CO: Westview Press.

Cavendish, J. C., Welch, M. R., & Leege, D. C. (1998). Social network theory and predictors of religiosity for Black and White Catholics: Evidence of a "Black sacred cosmos"? *Journal for the Scientific Study of Religion, 37*, 397–410.

Chaves, M., & Higgins, L. M. (1992). Comparing the community involvement of Black and White congregations. *Journal for the Scientific Study of Religion, 31*, 425–440.

Christerson, B., & Emerson, M. (2003). The costs of diversity in religious organizations: An in-depth case study. *Sociology of Religion, 64*, 163–181.

Curtis, E. E., IV. (2002). *Islam in Black America: Identity, liberation, and difference in African-American Islamic thought.* Albany: State University of New York Press.

Davis, C., O.S.B. (1990). *The history of Black Catholics in the United States.* New York: Crossroad.

DeCaro, L. A., Jr. (1998). *Malcolm and the cross: The Nation of Islam, Malcolm X, and Christianity.* New York and London: New York University Press.

Deck, A. F. (1994). The challenge of Evangelical/Pentecostal Christianity to Hispanic Catholicism. In J. P. Dolan & A. F. Deck (Eds.), *Hispanic Catholic Culture in the U.S.* (pp. 409–439). Notre Dame, IN: University of Notre Dame Press.

Dobratz, B. A. (2001). The role of religion in the collective identity of the White racialist movement. *Journal for the Scientific Study of Religion, 40*, 287–301.

Dougherty, K. D. (2003). How monochromatic is church membership? Racial-ethnic diversity in religious community. *Sociology of Religion, 64*, 65–85.

Du Bois, W.E.B. (1903). *The souls of Black folks.* Chicago: A.C. McClurg.

Drevenstedt, G. L. (1998). Race and ethnic differences in the effects of religious attendance on subjective health. *Review of Religious Research, 39*, 245–263.

Ebaugh, H. R., & Chafetz, J. S. (2000). *Religion and the new immigrants: Continuities and adaptations in immigrant congregations.* Walnut Creek, CA: AltaMira.

Ellison, C. G., & Taylor, R. J. (1996). Turning to prayer: Social and situational antecedents of religious coping among African Americans. *Review of Religious Research, 38*, 111–131.

Ellison, C. G., & Sherkat, D. E. (1990). Patterns of religious mobility among Black Americans. *Sociological Quarterly,* 31, 551–568.

Ellison, C. G., & Sherkat, D. E. (1995). "The 'semi-involuntary institution' revisited: Regional variations in church participation among Black Americans." *Social Forces* 73, 1415–37.

Ellison, C. G., & Sherkat, D. E. (1999). Identifying the semi-involuntary institution: A clarification. *Social Forces,* 78, 793–802.

Emerson, M. O., & Kim, K. C. (2003). Multiracial congregations: An analysis of their development and a typology. *Journal for the Scientific Study of Religion,* 42, 217–227.

Emerson, M. O., & Smith, C. (2000). *Divided by faith: Evangelical religion and the problem of race in America.* New York: Oxford University Press.

Emerson, M. O., Smith, C., & Sikkink, D. (1999). Equal in Christ, but not in the world: White conservative Protestants and explanations of Black-White inequality. *Social Problems,* 46, 398–417.

Ferraro, K. F., & Koch, J. R. (1994). Religion and health among Black and White adults: Examining social support and consolation. *Journal for the Scientific Study of Religion,* 33, 362–375.

Gallagher, S. K. (2003). *Evangelical identity and gendered family life.* New Brunswick, NJ: Rutgers University Press.

Greeley, A. M. (1994). The demography of American Catholics: 1965–1990. In *The Sociology of Andrew Greeley* (pp. 545–564). Atlanta: Scholars Press.

Hadaway, C. K., Marler, P. L., & Chaves, M. (1993). What the polls don't show: A closer look at U.S. church attendance. *American Sociological Review,* 58, 741–752.

Harris, F. C. (1999). *Something within: Religion in African-American political activism.* New York and Oxford: Oxford University Press.

Hunsburger, B. (1995). Religion and prejudice: The role of religious fundamentalism, quest and right wing authoritarianism. *Journal of Social Issues,* 51, 113–129.

Hunsburger, B. (1996). Religious fundamentalism, right wing authoritarianism, and hostility in non-Christian religious groups. *International Journal for the Psychology of Religion,* 6, 39–49.

Hunt, L. L. (1999). Hispanic Protestantism in the United States: Trends by decade and generation. *Social Forces,* 77, 1601–1623.

Hunt, L. L., & Hunt, M. O. (1999). Regional patterns of African American church attendance: Revisiting the semi-voluntary thesis. *Social Forces,* 78, 779–791.

Hunt, L. L., & Hunt, M. O. (2001). Race, region, and religious involvement: A comparative study of Whites and African Americans. *Social Forces,* 80, 605–631.

Jenkins, K. E. (2003). Intimate diversity: The Presentation of multiculturalism and multiracialism in a high-boundary religious movement. *Journal for the Scientific Study of Religion,* 42, 393–409.

Kalmijn, M. (1998). Intermarriage and homogamy: Causes, patterns, trends. *Annual Review of Sociology,* 24, 395–421.

Krause, N. (2002). Exploring race differences in a comprehensive battery of church-based social support measures. *Review of Religious Research,* 44, 126–149.

Krause, N. (2003). Exploring race differences in the relationship between social interaction with the clergy and feelings of self-worth in late life. *Sociology of Religion,* 64, 183–205.

Ladson-Billings, G. (2000). Racialized discourses and ethnic epistemologies. In N. K. Denzin & Y. S. Lincoln (Eds.), *Handbook of qualitative research* (2nd ed., pp. 257–277). Thousand Oaks, CA: Sage.

Laythe, B., Finkel, D., & Kirkpatrick, L. A. (2001). Predicting prejudice from religious fundamentalism and right-wing authoritarianism: A multiple-regression approach. *Journal for the Scientific Study of Religion,* 40, 1–10.

Laythe, B., Finkel, D. G., Bringle, R. G., & Kirkpatrick, L. A. (2002). Religious fundamentalism as a predictor of prejudice: A two-component model. *Journal for the Scientific Study of Religion,* 41, 623–635.

Lee, S. (2003). The church of faith and freedom: African-American Baptists and social action. *Journal for the Scientific Study of Religion,* 42, 31–41.

Lincoln, C. E. (1999). *Race, religion, and the continuing American dilemma.* New York: Hill and Wang.

Lincoln, C. E., & Mumiya, L. H. (1990). *The Black church in the African-American experience.* Durham, NC, and London: Duke University Press.

Marsh, C. (1997). *God's long summer: Stories of faith and civil rights.* Princeton, NJ: Princeton University Press.

Martin, D. (1990). *Tongues of fire: The explosion of Protestantism in Latin America.* Blackwell.

Mauss, A. L. (2003). *All Abraham's children: Changing Mormon conceptions of race and lineage.* Urbana and Chicago: University of Illinois Press.

McAdam, D. (1982). *Political process and the development of Black insurgency, 1930–1970.* Chicago: University of Chicago Press.

McDaniel, E. (2003). Black clergy in the 2000 election. *Journal for the Scientific Study of Religion,* 42, 533–546.

McPherson, M., Smith-Lovin, L., & Cook, J. M. (2001). Birds of a feather: Homophily in social networks. *Annual Review of Sociology,* 27, 415–444.

McRoberts, O. M. (2003). *Streets of glory: Church and community in a Black urban neighborhood.* Chicago: University of Chicago Press.

Morris, A. D. (1984). *The origins of the Civil Rights Movement: Black communities organizing for change.* New York: Free Press.

Park, J. Z., & Reimer, S. H. (2002). Revisiting the social sources of American Christianity 1972–1998. *Journal for the Scientific Study of Religion,* 41, 733–746.

Pattillo-McCoy, M. (1998). Church culture as a strategy of action in the Black community. *American Sociological Review,* 63, 767–784.

Poindexter, C. C., Linsk, N. L., & Warner, R. S. (1999). "He listens . . . and never gossips": Spiritual coping without church support among older, predominantly African-American caregivers of persons with HIV. *Review of Religious Research,* 40, 230–243.

Putnam, R. (2000). *Bowling alone: The collapse and revival of American community.* New York: Simon and Schuster.

Pyle, R. E., & Davidson, J. D. (2003). The origins of religious stratification in colonial America. *Journal for the Scientific Study of Religion,* 42, 57–75.

Read, J. G., & Bartkowski, J. P. (2000). To veil or not to veil? A case study of identity negotiation among Muslim women in Austin, Texas. *Gender & Society,* 14, 395–417.

Roof, W. C. (1993). *A generation of seekers: The spiritual journeys of the baby boom generation.* San Francisco, CA: Harper.

Shattuck, G. H., Jr. (2000). *Episcopalians and race: Civil war to civil rights.* Lexington: University Press of Kentucky.

Sherkat, D. E. (2002). African-American religious affiliation in the late 20th century: Cohort variations and patterns of switching, 1973–1998. *Journal for the Scientific Study of Religion,* 41, 485–493.

Sherkat, D. E., & Cunningham, S. A. (1998). Extending the semi-involuntary institution: Regional differences and social constraints on private religious consumption among African Americans. *Journal for the Scientific Study of Religion,* 37, 383–396.

Sherkat, D. E., & Ellison, C. G. (1999). Recent developments and current controversies in the sociology of religion. *Annual Review of Sociology,* 25, 363–394.

Smith, C., Gallagher, S., Emerson, M., Kennedy, P., & Sikkink, D. (1998). *American evangelicalism: Embattled and thriving.* Chicago: University of Chicago Press.

Smith, C. (2000). *Christian America? What evangelicals really want.* Berkeley: University of California Press.

Smith, J. I. (1999). *Islam in America.* New York: Columbia University Press.

Smith, T. W. (1999). The religious right and anti-Semitism. *Review of Religious Research,* 40, 244–258.

Stark, R., & Finke, R. (2000). *Acts of faith: Explaining the human side of religion.* Berkeley: University of California Press.

Steensland, B., Park, J. Z., Regnerus, M. D., Robinson, L. D., Wilcox, W. B., & Woodberry, R. D. (2000). The measure of American religion: Toward improving the state of the art. *Social Forces,* 79, 291–318.

Stoll, D. (1990). *Is Latin America turning Protestant?* University of California Press.

Sylvest, E. E., Jr. (1990). Hispanic American Protestantism in the United States. In M. Sandoval (Ed.), *On the move: A history of the Hispanic Church in the United States* (115–130). Orbis Books.

Taylor, R. J., Chatters, L. M., Jayakody, R., & Levin, J. S. (1996). Black and White differences in religious participation: A multisample comparison. *Journal for the Scientific Study of Religion,* 35, 403–410.

Tsitsos, W. (2003). Race differences in congregational social service activity. *Journal for the Scientific Study of Religion,* 42, 205–215.

Turner, R. B. (1997). *Islam in the African-American experience.* Bloomington and Indianapolis: University of Indiana Press.

Verweij, J., Ester, P., & Nauta, R. (1997). Secularization as an economic and cultural phenomenon: A cross-national analysis. *Journal for the Scientific Study of Religion,* 36, 309–324.

Walton, H. (1985). *Invisible politics: Black political power.* Albany: SUNY Press.

Warner, R. S. (1997). Religion, boundaries, and bridges. *Sociology of Religion,* 58, 217–238.

Warner, R. S., & Wittner, J. G. (1998). *Gatherings in diaspora: Religious communities and the new immigration.* Philadelphia: Temple University Press.

White, O. K., Jr., & White, D. (1995). Integrating religious and racial identities: An analysis of LDS African American explanations of the priesthood ban. *Review of Religious Research,* 36, 295–311.

White, O. K., Jr., & White, D. (2000). Negotiating cultural and social contradictions: Interracial dating and marriage among African American Mormons. *Virginia Social Science Journal,* 35, 85–98.

Wilcox, C. (1990). Religious sources of politicization among blacks in Washington, D.C. *Journal for the Scientific Study of Religion,* 29, 387–394.

Wilcox, C., & Gomez, L. (1990). Religion, group identification, and politics among American Blacks. *Sociological Analysis,* 51, 271–286.

Wood, R. L. (2002). *Faith in action: Religion, race, and democratic organizing in America.* Chicago: University of Chicago Press.

Wuthnow, R. (1993). *The future of Christianity.* Princeton, NJ: Princeton University Press.

Wuthnow, R. (2002). Religious involvement and Status-bridging social capital. *Journal for the Scientific Study of Religion,* 41, 669–684.

Wylie, L., & Forest, J. (1992). Religious fundamentalism, right wing authoritarianism and prejudice. *Psychological Reports,* 71, 1291–1298.

Yang, F. (1999). *Chinese Christians in America: Conversion, assimilation, and adhesive identities.* University Park: Pennsylvania State University Press.

Zuckerman, P. (2000). Introduction. In P. Zuckerman (Ed.), *Du Bois on Religion* (pp. 1–18). Walnut Creek, CA: AltaMira.

CHAPTER 9

Social Class

James D. Davidson and Ralph E. Pyle

This chapter examines the relationship between religion and the vertical ranking of persons and families in terms of their access to resources such as wealth, political power, and prestige. Part I contends that "fair shares" (or conflict) theory is better suited to the study of religion and stratification than either "fair play" (functionalist) theory or "religious economy" (rational choice) theory. Part II shows how fair shares theory illuminates our understanding of "religious stratification" in America (that is, the ranking of religious groups in terms of their members' access to power, privilege, and prestige). Part III shows how the fair shares approach also helps to explain religion's dual role of perpetuating social inequality at the same time that it promotes social equality.

PART I: THEORETICAL DEVELOPMENTS

Well into the 1950s, fair play theory dominated studies of religion and social stratification (Davis & Moore, 1945; Ryan, 1981). This approach viewed religion as a social institution that contributes to social order by providing answers to ultimate questions—questions about the meaning and purpose of life, questions that cannot be answered by science or other worldly means. One of these questions has to do with the reasons why some members of society have better jobs, more money, more political influence, and more prestige than others do. According to fair players, there are three explanations. First, some social tasks are more important and more demanding than others. Second, society must find a way to locate its most talented members and route them into these demanding and important positions. Third, as a reward for the sacrifices they must make in preparation for these awesome responsibilities, and as inspiration to do their very best after assuming them, society's most talented members deserve higher incomes, more political influence, and more respect than other people. These worldly advantages also are signs to the elect that they are in good standing with the Creator and will enjoy eternal salvation.

James D. Davidson • Purdue University, West Lafayette, Indiana 47907
Ralph E. Pyle • Michigan State University, East Lansing, Michigan 48824

Meanwhile, people with fewer talents gravitate toward less demanding positions that are more suited to their limited abilities and skills. Because these positions are less important and require less preparation, they do not offer as many social and economic benefits. The lack of worldly rewards, however, does not necessarily mean the people in these lower-status positions are destined to eternal damnation. If they believe in God and live righteous lives, they too can enjoy eternal life.

Thus, from a fair play perspective, religion assures the most talented that they are entitled to abundance in this life and that the advantages they enjoy in this life are indications of the rewards they will enjoy in the next. It also comforts and consoles those who find themselves in lower ranks, reassuring them that, by living according to God's plan, they, too, can gain salvation. By explaining social stratification in such terms, religion contributes to the well being of society and its members.

The Fair Shares Alternative

A few scholars dissented from this prevailing view (Tumin 1953; Mills 1956). Using a fair shares approach, they suggested that society is inherently unstable, mainly because of conflicts between groups with competing values and interests. They also insisted that religion is divisive in at least two ways. Some analysts suggested that religious groups are in conflict with one another. According to these researchers, the religious groups that achieved power and prosperity in the nation's colonial period have had an interest in preserving their worldly advantages. To protect their interests, they have seen to it that religious affiliation affects admission to elite colleges and universities, job placement and promotion, wages and benefits, and access to public office. Thus, the Protestant insiders—such as Episcopalians and Congregationalists—who were over-represented among the nation's elite in the colonial period were still dominant over Catholics, Jews, and other religious outsiders in the middle of the 20th century (Anderson, 1970; Konolige & Konolige, 1978; Korman, 1988). Other scholars argued that the rich and powerful intentionally have used religion as a means to justify their elevated status and subordinate the masses. According to these writers, economic and political elites have sought to control religious organizations so they can promote religious ideas and programs that serve their interests (Pope, 1942; Howe, 1981).

These fair shares interpretations flew in the face of the fair play perspective that dominated sociology in the 1950s. Although widely read and frequently acknowledged, they were seen as overemphasizing the extent of turmoil in society, cynically pitting religious groups against each other, and not appreciating religion's many contributions to society. As a result, they did not gain widespread acceptance.

However, in the 1960s, tensions rose between groups such as blacks and whites, men and women, antiwar protestors and the power elite, and the "counterculture" and the "establishment." As these tensions grew, fair play theory was called into question. Increasingly, it was criticized for overstating the orderliness of society, being unable to explain the social turmoil that appeared in the news nearly every day, and legitimating economic inequality and social injustice. As fair play theory lost traction, fair shares theory gained momentum in many areas of social research. Its emphasis on the disorderly nature of society and the conflicting interests of social groups now seemed to make more sense. Studies of conflict based on race, class, and gender increased dramatically.

Fair play theory prevailed for a longer period of time in the sociology of religion, due mainly to analyses touting the societal benefits of "civil religion" and the personal benefits of "official" (or, denominational) religion (Bellah, 1967; Ferraro & Kelley-Moore, 2000;

Hummer et al., 1999). But, even in this area of study, fair play theory lost some of its luster during the 1970s and 1980s. As it did, it gave way to religious economy theory, not fair shares theory, as had occurred in other areas of research.

Religious Economy Perspective

Religious economy theory focused attention on religious pluralism and religious groups' competition for members (Finke & Stark, 1992; Stark & Finke, 2000). In a free and open religious market, these scholars said, religious seekers can choose between religious groups ranging from churches to sects. Churches tend to affirm the world around them, make relatively few demands on their members, and provide few rewards. Sects, on the other hand, are in high tension with their environment, place many countercultural demands on their members, and provide many social as well as spiritual benefits.

These groups are inevitably linked to one another. Sectarian groups recruit members from the ranks of the unchurched but also lose some members who seek churches that make fewer demands and offer more accommodation to society. Churches tend to "grow their own" members but lose some members who yearn for more spiritual benefits and are willing to abide by sect demands to get them. Over time, sects tend to gain market share, whereas churches tend to lose. Religious economy theory has attracted a great deal of attention and has produced many new insights into high-tension sects, low-tension churches, and their competition for members. However, some of its key propositions have been challenged by recent research (Chaves & Gorski, 2001; Voas, Olson, & Crockett, 2001). Moreover, it has focused far more attention on horizontal distinctions between religious groups (such as liberal-conservative theologies) than it has on the vertical ranking of religious groups based on their access to power, privilege, and prestige. Also, it has paid far more attention to the personal choices of religious consumers in unregulated markets than it has to religion's relationship to social inequality.

Overview

Thus, fair play theory and religious economy theory have not proved to be very useful platforms from which to view the relationship between religion and inequality. As we have argued in previous publications, fair shares theory is a more suitable framework for exploring religion's role in social stratification (Davidson, 1985a, 1994; Davidson, Pyle, & Reyes, 1995; Pyle, 1993, 1996; Pyle & Davidson, 2003). Its suitability is grounded in several a priori assumptions. First, by its very nature, social inequality divides people into vertical rankings of power, privilege, and prestige. Second, these divisions contribute to social disorder and instability. Third, as sociologists try to explain these divisions and instabilities, religion cannot be exempted from consideration. Fourth, the sphere of religion is best understood not as an abstract social institution but as an arena in which there are hundreds, even thousands, of religious groups with different values and interests. Fifth, as religious groups act on these values and interests, religious affiliation itself becomes a basis of social stratification (with adherence to some groups increasing access to social rewards, and loyalty to others diminishing access to the very same benefits). We explore recent research on this topic in Part II. Sixth, religious groups have different consequences, with some groups perpetuating inequality, whereas others promote equality. This topic is addressed in Part III.

PART II: RELIGIOUS STRATIFICATION

Religious stratification refers to a vertical ranking of religious groups according to their members' access to three scarce resources: power (the ability to get one's way even in the face of opposition), privilege (wealth and income), and prestige (social honor). In other words, religious stratification exists to the extent that members of some religions have more access to these resources than others do (Pyle & Davidson, 2003). Many social conditions and considerations contribute to religious stratification, with religious affiliation being among the most important.

Origins

Under what conditions does religious stratification emerge? Religious diversity is a necessary but not sufficient condition. Three other conditions are also needed: religious prejudice, competition, and differential power (Noel, 1968; Pyle & Davidson, 2003).

Religious adherence does not require sharp divisions between religious groups. Religious groups are quite capable of viewing their differences with mutual respect, even admiration. However, when religious differences are accompanied by judgments about the superiority of some worldviews over others, strong ingroup-outgroup distinctions are likely to emerge, and religious prejudice tends to evolve. When that happens, religion serves as a potential battle line along which people divide. However, religious prejudice by itself is not enough to produce religious stratification.

Relations between religious groups can range from cooperation (based on shared goals and objectives) to competition (based on mutually exclusive goals and objectives). When cooperation prevails, religious stratification is not likely to evolve. The situation is very different when groups are in competition with one another. Religious competition may be over any number of scarce resources, such as land, political office, or members. The more valuable the resources are to the groups, the more intense the competition. The more intense the competition, the greater the likelihood that religious stratification will result. But, competition also is not enough. A third ingredient is needed.

That ingredient is power. If all of the religious groups in a given area are equal in size and equally well organized, it is unlikely that any one group will gain an advantage over others. However, if some groups are larger and better organized, they are likely to get the upper hand over smaller, less-well-organized groups. As they do, they try to shape the society according to their own values and interests. One way to do this is to write religious affiliation into the law as a criterion by which power, privilege, and prestige are to be distributed. Another way is to build religious adherence into the culture and customs of the society. Even without laws, more powerful religious groups can establish social norms that work to the advantage of their own members and the disadvantage of other religious groups. To the extent that such laws and social norms become engrained in the social fabric, they become taken-for-granted assumptions that are widely shared, and religious stratification is seen as a normal part of the social order.

COLONIAL AMERICA. This theory helps to explain the origins of religious stratification in colonial America. European settlers brought religious prejudices with them and cultivated even more interfaith hostilities after their arrival in the New World. For example, Anglicans in the South and Congregationalists in New England disliked Catholics and Jews, but evangelical Protestants groups also were objects of considerable scorn.

The competition between religious groups also was intense. In Virginia, Anglicans fought against Protestant sects, which were growing rapidly in the colony. Fearing that they might lose their advantages, Anglican insiders dissolved nonconforming vestries and attacked dissident Baptists. In the middle colonies such as Pennsylvania, there was stiff competition between Quakers and Anglicans, both of whom were opposed by Presbyterians and other groups of lesser stature. In New England, Congregationalists clearly had the upper hand but felt threatened by Anglicans who received considerable outside support from the Church of England.

But, over time, the Congregationalists in New England and the Anglicans in the South clearly established themselves as the dominant religious groups in the colonies. They were superior in membership size, had more congregations, relied on strong kinship ties and patronage arrangements to solidify their support, and had help from foreign governments (such as the English crown) and church allies (such as the Church of England).

These conditions led to a highly institutionalized pattern of religious stratification. Religious establishments prevailed in 9 of the 13 colonies. Even colonies that did not have established churches usually had antitoleration laws denying residence to groups such as Catholics and Jews and preventing them from voting and holding public office. With religious affiliation so embedded in colonial laws and customs, a clear ranking of religious groups emerged. Anglicans, Congregationalists, and, to a lesser extent, Presbyterians were so overrepresented among business, political, and educational elites that they became known as "the Protestant Establishment." Other elites of somewhat lower stature included the Unitarians and Quakers. Further down the social hierarchy were other Protestant groups such as Baptists, Methodists, Lutherans, and Dutch and German Reformed churches. At the bottom of the ladder were non-Protestant groups such as Catholics, Jews, and people with no religious preference.

Thus, in accordance with fair shares theory, religious stratification arose when there was considerable animosity between two or more religious groups, the groups were in competition for scarce resources, and some groups gained enough political advantage to institutionalize laws and customs that solidified their advantages over other groups.

Persistence and Change

But what happens once religious stratification develops? To what extent and under what conditions does it tend to persist? How much and when is it most likely to change?

Fair shares theory suggests that religious stratification persists to the extent that religious insiders are able to perpetuate laws and social customs restricting access to power, privilege, and prestige to their own members and excluding religious outsiders (Piven & Cloward, 1977; Ryan, 1981). What kinds of laws and customs do insiders try to promote? Among other things, they try to restrict immigration and citizenship to their kind, limit the choice of political candidates to people who share their values and interests, vote for such candidates, and appoint their own kind to political office. They also marry within their own group, limit membership in social clubs and business organizations to their own people, pass their businesses and wealth on to their children and other members of the in-group, go to school with and are taught by their own kind, and restrict leadership at the most elite schools to members of their own group.

Religious outsiders tend to oppose these efforts, seeking more inclusive laws and customs. They try to expand immigration and access to citizenship, run for political office, persuade people to vote for outsider candidates, and force political leaders to appoint outsiders to political office. They also seek to marry insiders' sons and daughters, become members of the same social clubs and business organizations insiders belong to, increase their access to corporate ownership and wealth, attend school with insiders, become members of the faculty at the school insiders attend, and gain access to administrative posts at these elite schools. Religious stratification changes to the extent that religious outsiders demand such changes and force insiders to accept them (Piven & Cloward, 1977; Ryan, 1981).

RELIGION AMONG AMERICA'S ELITES.   What evidence is there that the older religious hierarchies have persisted over the years, and what indications are there of change in the religious affiliation of American elites? A number of writers have claimed that America's Protestant Establishment is no longer an important force in the governance of the nation's political, economic, and cultural affairs (Schrag, 1970; Roof & McKinney, 1987; Christopher, 1989; Hutchison, 1989; Hammond, 1992; Schneiderman, 1994). According to these observers, Episcopalians, Presbyterians, and Congregationalists—who dominated America's cultural and political landscape in the colonial period—no longer have the prominence they once enjoyed, and Catholics, Jews, and other non-WASPs have gained in power, privilege, and prestige.

To assess the degree of change in the Protestant Establishment, we have conducted studies of the religious affiliations of Americans listed in *Who's Who in America* (Davidson, Pyle, & Reyes, 1995; Pyle, 1996; Pyle & Koch, 2001). *Who's Who* is a biographical directory that has been publishing information about American leaders for over 100 years, and it is generally regarded as the best single source of information about American elites (Baltzell, 1966; Lieberson & Carter, 1979; Priest, 1982; Williams & Rodeheaver, 1989; Pyle, 1996).

We gathered information on people listed in four editions of *Who's Who:* 1930–1931, 1950–1951, 1970–1971, and 1992–1993. We used Fry's (1933) tabulation of every person listed in the 1930–1931 edition. For the other three time periods, we selected 1-in-20 systematic samples of listees ($N = 2,217$ in 1950–1951; 3,224 in 1970–1971; and 4,018 in 1992–1993). The results are presented in Table 9.1.

Our analysis shows that religious groups associated with a Protestant Establishment have lost some ground since the 1930s. Episcopalians, Presbyterians, and Congregationalists/UCCs, who accounted for 53% of *Who's Who* listees reporting an affiliation in 1930–1931, represented 35% of listees in 1992–1993. Episcopalians were the most stable of the three Establishment groups, comprising 22% of all listees in 1930–1931 and 18% in 1992–1993. Presbyterians accounted for 20% of the listings in 1930–1931 and 14% in 1992–1993. Congregationalists/UCCs declined the most during the period, falling from 11% in 1930–1931 to just 3% in 1992–1993. Other historically elite groups (Unitarian-Universalists and Quakers) also declined at a relatively consistent rate, from 7% in 1930–1931 to 3% in 1992–1993.

Groups included in the Other Protestants stratum were 29% of elites in 1930–1931 and 21% in 1992–1993. Over the years Baptists, Disciples of Christ, Methodists, and the Reformed Church have all declined; only Lutherans have gained. At the same time, Catholics and Jews have made substantial gains. Catholics, who were just 4% of elites in 1930–1931, increased to 23% in 1992–1993. Jews, who were only 1% of elites in 1930–1931, were

TABLE 9.1. Reported Religious Affiliation of Individuals in *Who's Who* (percentages)

Religious Group[a]	1930–31	1950–51	1970–71	1992–93
Protestant Establishment				
Episcopalian	21.9	23.1	20.2	18.0
Presbyterian	20.3	18.4	19.6	13.9*
Congregationalist/UCC	11.3	8.8	5.9	3.2*
Other Elite				
Unitarian-Universalist	6.0	4.0	3.6	2.4*
Quaker	1.1	1.8	1.5	.7
Other Protestant				
Baptist	9.0	6.2	5.1	4.7*
Disciples	2.0	2.4	2.2	.4*
Lutheran	2.4	2.7	3.7	6.0*
Methodist	14.5	15.5	14.2	9.6*
Reformed	1.0	.4	.3	.4
Other				
Catholic	4.5	8.4	13.2	23.1*
Christian Science	.7	.7	.6	.2
Jew	1.3	2.5	6.9	12.3*
Mormon	.4	.3	1.1	1.5*
All Others	3.6	4.7	1.8	3.6
	100.0	100.0	100.0	100.0
No Affiliation Listed	43.9	48.5	69.0	65.6

[a]The 1930–31 figures are reported by Fry (1933).
*1930–1992 difference significant, $p < .001$.

12% in 1992–1993. Thus, we see that America's elite is more religiously pluralistic today than it was in the 1930s. Another way of viewing the data is to consider the extent to which religious groups are over- or underrepresented among elites relative to their numbers in the total population (exact proportional representation is defined as 1.00). Table 9.2 shows that all three Establishment groups have been overrepresented in *Who's Who* during the four periods. In 1930–1931, there were 6.3 times as many Episcopalians among elites as there were in the total population. By 1992–1993, the Episcopalian index of representation had increased to 7.0. The index for Presbyterians declined from 3.4 in 1930–1931 to 2.8 in 1992–1993. For Congregationalists/UCCs, the index was 5.7 in the 1930s and 2.6 in the 1990s. Unitarian-Universalists and Quakers continue to be overrepresented among *Who's Who* listees. Taken together, these two groups were overrepresented by a factor of 13.6 in 1930–1931. By 1992–1993, the index had dropped to 8.2.

Other Protestants were underrepresented among elites in the 1930s, and they remain underrepresented today. Of those in the "Other Protestants" stratum, Methodists had achieved parity in the 1990s. Lutherans had gained over the years, from .4 in the 1930s to .8 in the 1990s. Baptists have been the most underrepresented of all groups. Their index was .3 in the 1930s and .2 in the 1990s.

The index of representation for Jews increased dramatically over the years. During the 1930s and 1950s Jews were underrepresented in *Who's Who* relative to their numbers in the U.S. population, with an index of around .7. Their index jumped to 2.4 in 1970–1971 and 6.0 in 1992–1993, indicating that Jews are six times as likely to be represented in *Who's Who* as

TABLE 9.2. Denominational Representation in *Who's Who* in Proportion to U.S. Church Membership

Religious Group	1930–31	1950–51	1970–71	1992–93
Protestant Establishment				
Episcopalian	6.3	6.4	7.4	7.0
Presbyterian	3.4	3.2	3.9	2.8
Congregationalist/UCC	5.7	4.0	3.9	2.6
Other Elite				
Unitarian-Universalist	20.6	17.5	20.0	9.6
Quaker	4.8	12.5	9.4	6.5
Other Protestant				
Baptist	.3	.3	.2	.2
Disciples	.6	.9	1.6	.3
Lutheran	.4	.4	.4	.8
Methodist	.8	1.1	1.0	1.0
Reformed	.7	.9	.6	.9
Other				
Catholic	.1	.3	.5	.9
Christian Science	1.3	1.3	2.1	1.2
Jew	.7	.8	2.4	6.0
Mormon	.3	.2	.6	.7
All Others	.6	.5	.2	.2

one would expect based on their numbers in the general population. Catholic increases also have been impressive. The Catholic index increased from .1 in the 1930s to .9 in the 1990s.

The analysis shows that groups identified with a Protestant Establishment are not as prominent among the nation's elite as they used to be. At the same time, the three Establishment groups remain overrepresented at the highest levels of political, economic, and cultural influence. Although Presbyterians and Congregationalists/UCCs do not have as much stature as they used to, Episcopalians continue to be well positioned at the apex of society. Over the years Catholics and Jews have been successful in securing a foothold in the nation's power structure, but conservative Protestant groups are not well represented in a social index like *Who's Who*.

RELIGIOUS STRATIFICATION IN THE GENERAL POPULATION. What are the trends in the stratification of religious groups in the general population? Some researchers claim that socioeconomic status today is irrelevant in predicting one's religious affiliation. However, others suggest that denominations continue to be distinguished on the basis of the socioeconomic standing of their members. In this section, we look at socioeconomic distinctions between America's religious families, and we examine the degree to which these differences have diminished, expanded, or stabilized in recent years.

Since the publication of Niebuhr's (1929) classic analysis of the social sources of denominationalism, researchers have investigated the degree to which religious groups can be ordered along a status hierarchy based primarily on the socioeconomic standing of their members. From the 1940s through the 1970s, studies of denominational socioeconomic rankings concluded that Liberal Protestants (Episcopalians, Presbyterians, Congregationalists/UCCs) and Jews ranked highest in income, educational attainment, and occupational prestige (Cantril, 1943; Pope, 1948; Demerath, 1965; Glenn & Hyland, 1967; Goldstein, 1969; Davidson, 1977; Roof, 1979; Greeley, 1981). Ranked just below these groups were those with no religious affiliation ("nonaffiliates"). Catholics and Moderate Protestants (e.g., Lutherans, Methodists, Disciples of Christ) occupied the middle ranks of the socioeconomic hierarchy, with Black and Conservative Protestants (e.g., Southern Baptists, Nazarenes, Churches of God, Assemblies of God) positioned at the bottom (Roof & McKinney, 1987, p. 109–110).

However, starting in the 1980s, some analysts argued that socioeconomic factors were no longer as important as they once were in separating America's faith traditions (Wuthnow, 1988; Christopher, 1989; Park & Reimer, 2002; Stark, 2003.) Wuthnow (1988) suggested that the boundaries separating the major religious traditions have been recast since World War II. Rising levels of education have contributed to a decline in interdenominational status differences at the same time that we have experienced a pattern of convergence among the various denominations in terms of their demographic characteristics. The implication is that the status ordering of religious groups is not as clearly defined as it once was.

Park and Reimer (2002) have also suggested that denominational socioeconomic boundaries have blurred in recent decades. Park and Reimer believe that evangelical Protestantism today is not very distinct demographically, and they disagree with the status theories of Pope (1942) and Glock (1964), which focus on social or economic deprivation as a basis for sectarian affiliation. Park and Reimer claim that sectarian affiliation is not significantly influenced by class background: "At best, class has a weak effect on religious affiliation, since both the rich and poor are attracted to sects" (2002, p. 741–742). Their analysis suggests converging levels of income and education among the major faith traditions. Stark (2003) agrees that social class is an unreliable predictor of religious adherence. Arguing against deprivation theories of religiosity, Stark maintains that members of evangelical and fundamentalist Protestant groups "are as likely to have gone to college and to earn high incomes as are members of more liberal denominations as well as Roman Catholics" (2003, p. 6).

However, other research suggests that socioeconomic factors continue to be important in distinguishing America's religious traditions. Several studies have emphasized the persistence of socioeconomic distinctions between "mainline" and conservative Protestants. Darnell and Sherkat (1997), in a study of education and religious adherence, found a negative link between fundamentalism and educational attainment, which partly explains the persisting socioeconomic deficits for conservative Protestants. Coreno (2002) found significant differences between mainline and conservative Protestants in terms of their education, income, and occupational prestige, with mainliners having more education, greater incomes, and more prestigious occupations. Keister (2003), looking at religious affiliation and the accumulation of wealth, found that conservative Protestants have significantly less wealth than Jews, Catholics, and mainline Protestants. Sherkat (2001), in a study of religious switching, has argued that there has not been a breakdown in status differences between denominations, and he concludes that status theories of denominational affiliation cannot be disconfirmed.

Thus, in the context of conflicting claims about the degree to which we have witnessed the erosion of denominational socioeconomic differences in recent decades, there is a need to examine religious group socioeconomic rankings since the 1970s.

The 1972–2000 General Social Surveys (GSS) were used to analyze socioeconomic differences among the major faith traditions. Respondents were classified into 25 denominational categories, in accord with the classification method presented in Roof and McKinney (1987, pp. 253–256). Members of Protestant denominations were then assigned to four

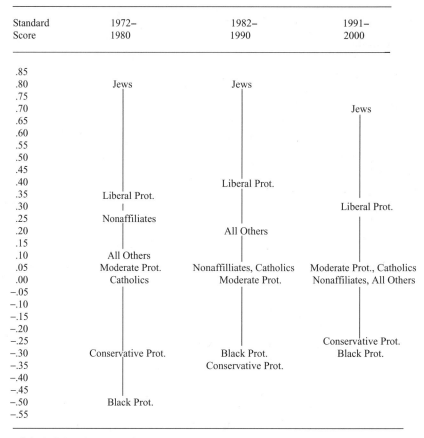

Standard Score	1972– 1980	1982– 1990	1991– 2000
.85			
.80	Jews	Jews	
.75			
.70			Jews
.65			
.60			
.55			
.50			
.45			
.40		Liberal Prot.	
.35	Liberal Prot.		
.30			Liberal Prot.
.25	Nonaffiliates		
.20		All Others	
.15			
.10	All Others		
.05	Moderate Prot.	Nonaffilliates, Catholics	Moderate Prot., Catholics
.00	Catholics	Moderate Prot.	Nonaffiliates, All Others
−.05			
−.10			
−.15			
−.20			
−.25			Conservative Prot.
−.30	Conservative Prot.	Black Prot.	Black Prot.
−.35		Conservative Prot.	
−.40			
−.45			
−.50	Black Prot.		
−.55			

FIGURE 9.1. Religious Group Rankings on Socioeconomic Index*.
*7-category index combining RINCOME, EDUC, and PRESTIGE (1972–1990). PRESTG80 was used for the 1991–2000 analysis.
The All Others category includes Mormons, Jehovah's Witnesses, Unitarians, Christian Scientists, and Others.

religious families (Liberal, Moderate, Conservative, and Black Protestants) following Roof and McKinney's classification scheme. Jehovah's Witnesses, Unitarians, Christian Scientists, Mormons, and Others were placed in an All Others category.

To facilitate a comparison of denominational socioeconomic differences over time, standard scores were computed for income, education, and occupational prestige during three time periods (1972–1980, 1982–1990, 1991–2000). To generate an overall socioeconomic index, an additive scale was constructed. RINCOME, EDUC, and PRESTIGE (1972–1990) or PRESTG80 (1991–2000) were rescaled (1–low, 2–medium, 3–high) and then combined to form a seven-category socioeconomic index: INDEXST was used for the 1972–1990 surveys (Cronbach's alpha = .64), and INDEXSV was used for the 1991–2000 surveys (Cronbach's alpha = .66). Standard scores indicate each group's score relative to the population mean on the various measures.

Figure 9.1 indicates the relative position of the religious families on the socioeconomic index during the three time periods. (The vertical scale indicates the number of standard deviation units above or below the national mean for each religious family on the socioeconomic index.) Figure 9.1 appears to lend some support to the claim that there has been a reduction of religious group socioeconomic differences since the 1970s. However, the narrowing of differences is primarily the result of improvement in the socioeconomic scores for Black Protestants and a slight decline in the scores for Jews. We also see some narrowing of differences between Liberal Protestants and Conservative Protestants over the period and a decline in the relative socioeconomic position of Nonaffiliates, who today score near the national mean on the socioeconomic index. Although Figure 9.1 indicates some reduction in socioeconomic differentials between the major religious families over the period, the rank ordering of the major Protestant families remains largely unchanged.

We also performed separate analyses of the income, educational, and occupational gains and losses for the various religious groups during the period. Although Jews had the highest income scores, there was a slight reduction in the income advantages for Jews during the period. Black Protestants increased their income scores but continued to be positioned at the bottom of the income hierarchy. In terms of educational attainment, we found that Jews and Liberal Protestants had the highest rankings during all three periods, whereas Black and Conservative Protestants had the lowest scores. Except for a decline in the educational attainment scores for Nonffiliates from the 1970s to the 1990s, we found little sign of a trend toward convergence in religious group educational differences. The analysis of occupational prestige was similar to that for education. Jews and Liberal Protestants maintained the highest occupational rankings, Catholics and Moderate Protestants scored near the national mean, and Conservative and Black Protestants had the lowest occupational scores. We found that the major faith traditions continue to be distinguished on the basis of the occupational standing of their members.

To summarize, despite some narrowing of differences among the religious families on socioeconomic indicators, religious groups continue to be differentiated based on their socioeconomic positioning, and the overall religious group status ranking has remained largely unchanged since mid-century. Consistent with the findings of earlier studies, Jews and Liberal Protestants have the highest socioeconomic rankings, Catholics and Moderate Protestants continue to occupy the middle ranks of the socioeconomic hierarchy, and Black and Conservative Protestants remain at the bottom. The deficits for Black Protestants have lessened during the period, indicating some advance in their relative socioeconomic positioning. Nevertheless, Black Protestants continue to rank near the bottom of the socioeconomic scale. One notable change is the decline in the relative socioeconomic standing of those with no religious preference, who have moved from an elevated socioeconomic position thirty years ago to dead center in the status hierarchy today. No longer can it be said that "those with no religious affiliation exceed the national average today on every status indicator" (Roof & McKinney, 1987, p. 114).

These findings are more consistent with a fair shares interpretation of religious change than with the fair play approach. Although there has been some narrowing of income differentials among the major religious groupings (and some of that is attributed to the scaling of the income variable), there is not much indication of converging scores on educational attainment and occupational prestige. Thus, we see the perpetuation of socioeconomic boundaries among the religious traditions. It is certainly an exaggeration to claim, as some fair play analysts have, that socioeconomic distinctions between religious families are of little consequence today. There is little in the findings of the *Who's Who* and General Social Survey analyses to challenge Weber and Niebuhr's assertion that different faith traditions cater to those of different social ranks.

PART III: PERPETUATING INEQUALITY AND
PROMOTING EQUALITY

Social inequality is a tenacious, even intensifying, fact of life in our society. It has persisted throughout the course of U.S. history. In our lifetimes alone, the economic gap between the rich and poor has grown, power has become more concentrated in the hands of a few, and the social distance between aristocrats and the masses has grown (Braun, 1997; Oliver & Shapiro, 1999; Davidson & Pyle, 1999; Keister, 2000). What is religion's role in this? Does it perpetuate inequality? Does it promote equality?

Even as a subordinate theme in the sociology of religion, fair shares theory has made an important contribution over the years: its claim that religion tends to perpetuate social inequality. This claim can be traced to Marx and Engels (1964) and Weber (1964). In one way or another, both writers suggested that people of high social standing gravitate toward churches that promote religious worldviews legitimating the abundance they have accumulated, whereas people in lower social stations are attracted to worldviews that take their minds off their suffering in this world and, instead, focus their attention on the Creator's promise of far greater rewards in the next life.

Unfortunately, this scholarly tradition has led some people to falsely conclude that religion's *only* consequence is to perpetuate social inequality. This one-dimensional understanding of religion is commonly found in the writings of Marxist and neo-Marxist sociologists, many of whom hope that religion will someday disappear from modern society. However, the same idea is found in most introductory sociology texts, textbooks in social stratification, and even texts in the sociology of religion. As a result, it is a widespread misconception of religion's role in society.

Fair shares theory and recent research offer two important refinements of previous research on this topic. For one thing, they identify the conditions under which religion is most likely to perpetuate inequality. They also point to conditions under which religion is most likely to have the opposite effect of promoting social equality.

One of these conditions has to do with the worldview—or "theodicy"—religious groups promote. A theodicy of good fortune (also called a theodicy of privilege) and a theodicy of disprivilege (also known as a theodicy of despair, fatalism, or escape) are analytically different but have essentially the same social implication: to perpetuate inequality. A theodicy of social justice (sometimes called a theodicy of liberation or black power), by contrast, has the effect of promoting equality (Tamney, Burton, & Johnson, 1988; Tamney & Johnson, 1990; Mock, Davidson, & Johnson, 1991; Davidson, Mock, & Johnson, 1997; Hall, 1997; Davidson & Pyle, 1999; Emerson, Smith, & Sikkink, 1999; Hunt, 2002).

These worldviews are affected by, but not strictly aligned with, social status (see Figure 9.2). As Weber argued, a theodicy of good fortune is most closely associated with the privileged classes, and a theodicy of disprivilege is more often linked to lower strata, but elements of both can be found in all social ranks. Likewise, a theodicy of social justice is most likely to take root in the lower ranks of society, but—as we will explain—it can be found at many points in the social hierarchy.

Interests have to do with religious groups' stake in the prevailing structure of social stratification. On the one hand, there are groups that are heavily dependent on existing social arrangements for their well being and, thus, have many reasons to defend the status quo. These groups tend to be prosperous or affluent churches, but also include a number of less fortunate groups. On the other hand, there are groups that are less dependent on the status quo and, thus, have the ability to challenge the system without as many negative repercussions.

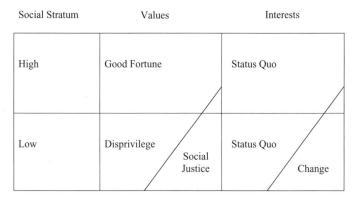

FIGURE 9.2. Values and Interests of Social Strata.

These groups are most likely to be on the lower rungs of the socioeconomic ladder, but—as we will explain shortly—some can be found on higher rungs (see Figure 9.2).

From a fair shares perspective, interests are more consequential than values, although values have effects of their own (Weber, 1964; Ryan, 1981). Moreover, although analytically separate, values and interests tend to be empirically correlated. Having a big stake in the system fosters theodicies of good fortune and—to a lesser extent—disprivilege. Together, these circumstances perpetuate social inequality. By contrast, having little stake in the system fosters theodicies of social justice and, when combined, these conditions lead religious groups to promote social equality.

Religious groups are found at virtually every point along a continuum ranging from the perpetuation of social inequality to the promotion of equality (Davidson & Koch, 1999; Davidson & Pyle, 1999). Very few, if any, have values and interests whose only effect is to perpetuate inequality, just as very few have values and interests whose only effect is to promote equality. Most groups have a mixture of values and interests and, as a result, have both effects, at least to some degree. However, starting at the center point of this continuum, it is possible to separate the groups which perpetuate inequality more than they promote equality from those which promote equality more than they perpetuate inequality. In the remainder of this chapter, we summarize the evidence relating to these two orientations.

Perpetuating Social Inequality

Business owners and managers, agricultural elites, and leaders of the Republican Party are among those most likely to believe that there should be no limits on how much money people can earn and no redistribution of wealth that would benefit people in low socioeconomic strata. They support policies, such as deregulation and tax cuts, that would maximize their wealth. They also oppose policies, such as government ownership of industries and limitations on inheritances, that would set limits on their wealth. Moreover, they oppose policies, such as collective bargaining and increases in the minimum wage, that would increase the economic resources of people of more modest means (Verba & Orren, 1985; Barton, 1985; Kluegel & Smith, 1986; Davidson, 1994).

These elites often volunteer for, or are invited into, leadership roles in religious groups (e.g., becoming members of the board of directors). In more informal and indirect ways (e.g., through financial contributions), they also have an influence on religious groups in which they do not personally participate. When these elites are in positions to do so, they promote policies and practices that are compatible with their values and interests. They are likely to recruit pastoral leaders who come from privileged social and educational backgrounds. They also are likely to provide the leaders with large salaries and generous benefit packages. These circumstances increase religious leaders' dependence on elites and their stake in the prevailing system of social inequality, both of which increase their interest in defending the status quo (Davidson & Pyle, 1999).

Leaders and members of these groups also are likely to embrace a theodicy of good fortune (Mock, Davidson, & Johnson, 1991; Davidson, Mock, & Johnson, 1997; Davidson & Pyle, 1999). This religious worldview assumes that human nature is intrinsically evil and that human beings' natural inclination to sin must be constrained through involvement in value-producing social institutions, especially families, churches, and schools. In these institutions, which are seen as essentially benign, people learn to love their neighbor and do good for others. They also learn that inequality is a natural social condition flowing from individual differences in intelligence and ambition. According to this worldview, the best and brightest rise to the top of society, performing the most important work for the good of the whole society. In return, they receive—and deserve—rewards such as lofty salaries, comprehensive benefit programs, stock options, and generous retirement packages. People of lesser intelligence and ambition occupy positions that are less important and, as a result, are not as highly rewarded. Thus, based on individual variations in talent and personality, a fair and reasonable system of social inequality emerges. That system is functional for both society (because the most important tasks are accomplished by the best people) and its individual members (who become involved in work that is suited to their talents and personalities and who are justly rewarded). Thus, problems such as poverty and homelessness are not systemic disorders. Instead, they can be traced to individuals with attitudes and lifestyles that deviate from prevailing standards of social responsibility. Such lifestyles include not holding a job, not belonging to a church, not being responsible for one's family.

Religious groups advancing this worldview believe it is their responsibility to get at the root cause of such behavior. To this end, they focus their energies on saving individual souls. They allocate sizeable portions of their annual budgets to self-help programs aimed at recruiting the unchurched, providing them with opportunities to build a strong personal relationship with their Creator, and helping them develop lives of righteousness and social respectability. The assumption is that, in due time, the converts will become responsible citizens and participate fully in society.

Even as these groups enhance individual well-being, they perpetuate social inequality in two ways. In some cases, they overtly affirm social policies and structural conditions that contribute to inequality (for example, by supporting tax cuts for the rich and opposing increases in the minimum wage). In other cases, they choose not to address these policies and conditions and, in effect, turn responsibility for such public policies over to business and political elites who favor policies that foster inequality. Second, despite improving the quality of individuals' lives, they also prepare people to participate in social arrangements that, left unchanged, are likely to produce other incidents of poverty, hunger, and homelessness.

RECENT RESEARCH.   This scenario is depicted in many studies of affluent religious groups. For example, in his study of churches in Gastonia, North Carolina, Pope (1942) found that mill owners belonged to and supported "uptown" churches. "For uptown people," Pope said, "religion—well, it's just religion—which is to say, it is a set of actionways and thoughtways associated with, and largely confined to, the church." To the extent that uptown churches played any public role, they were "to a considerable degree a sanction of prevailing economic arrangements" (1942, p. 92). For example, clergy in uptown churches publicly praised the generosity of mill owners and were reluctant to speak out against their business practices. A restudy of Gastonia churches in the 1970s revealed similar tendencies among uptown churches (Earle, Knudsen, & Shriver, 1976).

A more recent study of 31 affluent churches in Indiana showed that most congregations "do very little to alleviate the plight of the disadvantaged through charitable services or to promote the social change necessary for greater equality and justice.... Seldom do their programs confront root causes of social problems and seek long-term solutions" (Mock, Davidson, & Johnson, 1991). Affluent churches in which business leaders and Republicans were in key leadership positions were especially unlikely to sponsor social service and social action programs (Davidson, Mock, & Johnson, 1997). Other recent evidence also indicates that congregations with large percentages of "well-off constituents" do not provide as many social services as congregations with less fortunate members (Chaves & Tsitsos, 2001).

But people in lower social ranks also have a stake in the system. They cling to whatever jobs they can find for whatever wages they can earn, and they depend on government for assistance in times of special need. As Weber (1964, p. 108) said, "Their particular need is for release from suffering." Weber describes their religious worldview as follows:

> What [the disprivileged] cannot claim to *be*, they replace by the worth of that which they will one day *become*, to which they will be called in some future life here or hereafter; or replace ... by their sense of what they signify and achieve in the world as seen from the point of view of providence. Their hunger for a worthiness that has not fallen to their lot, they and the world being what it is, produces this conception from which is derived the rationalistic ideas of a providence, a significance in the eyes of some divine authority possessing a scale of values different from the one operating in the world of man. (Weber, 1964, p. 106)

Not surprisingly, then, the religious groups of the disprivileged classes are likely to stress religion's vertical, other-worldly, and personal aspects more than its horizontal, this-worldly, and social dimensions. Even though their members are generous in other ways (Regnerus, Smith, & Sikkink, 1998), these religious groups tend to perpetuate social inequality (Tamney & Johnson, 1990; Kanagy, 1992; Will & Cochran, 1995; Emerson, Smith, & Sikkink, 1999; Chaves, 1999; Smith, 2001; Chaves & Tsitsos, 2001; Chaves, Giesel, & Tsitsos, 2002).

Promoting Social Equality

Although a majority of elites are socially conservative, some are more accurately described as social liberals. These elites believe there should be limits on how much the wealthy can earn, and there should be a floor below which low-income households should not fall. Research shows that such elites are most likely to be involved in academic and intellectual life, represent labor unions and minority groups, and belong to the Democratic Party (Verba & Orren, 1985; Kluegel & Smith, 1986; Davidson, 1994).

When these elites occupy leadership roles in religious groups, they, too, promote policies and practices that are compatible with their values and interests. They are likely to search for leaders who have social and spiritual talents, but come from social backgrounds that increase their ability to identify and communicate with people who are average to below average in social status. They also are likely to provide leaders with incomes and benefit packages that are in line with those of the people they will be working with. They might even prefer leaders, such as priests and religious sisters, who are committed to lifestyles that include vows of poverty and celibacy—which would reduce leaders' stake in the system of social inequality and, thereby, increase their autonomy. With such autonomy, they would be able to speak and act prophetically without much repercussion.

Leaders and members of these groups are more likely to cultivate a theodicy of social justice (Davidson & Pyle, 1999; Davidson, Mock, & Johnson, 1997). This religious outlook assumes that human nature is intrinsically good, but that human beings are corrupted by what they learn through participation in social institutions such as business and politics. In these spheres, which are seen as evil, people learn to be selfish and greedy—looking out for one's self and not caring about the effects one's actions have on others. They also learn that inequality is an unnatural social condition flowing from the greed and selfishness of people who have climbed to the top of business and politics. These people use their positions and coercive power to create policies and practices that maximize their own well being. As a result, they unethically accumulate rewards they do not deserve, such as inordinately large salaries, lavish lifestyles involving luxurious mansions, travel to exotic lands, and servants waiting on them hand and foot. Others in society are left to cope with less satisfying lives marked by dull and repetitive work, limited wages and few—if any—benefits, broken families, and a sense of hopelessness. In short, an unequal, unfair, and unjust distribution of resources arises from corrupt policies and practices that are instituted by a handful of greedy people and imposed on the masses. This systemic injustice must be rooted out. Doing so requires social movements aimed at replacing corrupt leaders with ethical and moral ones, changing social laws and customs that benefit the rich and powerful, and bringing about a redistribution of wealth and power.

These religious groups believe their role is to participate in this revolution in whatever way they can. Thus, they emphasize sermons and publications that expose the social sins of the elite and provide visionary alternatives of a better society. They sponsor programs that foster closer ties between the rich and poor, mobilize volunteers to canvas neighborhoods and workplaces with plans to bring about a new social order, and organize assistance programs that will care for the needs of the poor and powerless until the system is changed. Considerable portions of their annual budgets are devoted to such efforts. In their attempts to build a more just and equal world, these religious groups believe they will demonstrate the Creator's love and lead people to faith.

RECENT RESEARCH.   This profile is supported by recent research on the prophetic role that national religious bodies (headed by relatively autonomous leaders of specific faith traditions) have played in matters of racial and economic equality (Wood, 1970, 1981; Tamney, Burton, & Johnson, 1988; D'Antonio et al., 1989; Kraus, 2003). Several studies also have documented the social activism of interfaith organizations led by relatively autonomous, social justice-oriented elites (Hadden & Longino, 1975; Takayama & Darnell, 1979; Davidson, 1985b; Hall, 1997; McRoberts, 1999; Wood, 2002). Other writers have shown that affluent congregations and parishes in which such elites have leadership roles have tendencies to be actively involved in social reform and social service (Wood, 1981; Roozen, McKinney, & Carroll, 1984; Dudley & Johnson, 1993; Davidson, Mock, &

Johnson, 1994; Regnerus, Smith, & Sikkink, 1998). Other research also indicates that mainline Protestant churches and Jewish organizations (which tend to be above average in social stature) are more likely than conservative Protestant congregations (which, on average, are lower in stature) to express an interest in, or actually be involved in, social welfare programs (Chaves, 1999; Chaves & Tsitsos, 2001; Wood, 2002; Wuthnow & Evans, 2002).

But some lower status groups also have a have a degree of autonomy from the system and cultivate a theodicy of social justice. Pope (1942) found that the congregations attended by the millhands in Gastonia aligned themselves with the workers in labor disputes with mill owners. Research also has shown that black churches often have provided African Americans with the autonomy and justice-oriented theology needed to challenge the prevailing structure of social and racial inequality (Nelsen & Nelson, 1975; Morris, 1984; Gilkes, 1990; Baer & Singer, 1992; Patillo-McCoy, 1998; Billingsley, 1998; McRoberts, 1999; Cavendish, 2000; Wood, 2002; Tsitsos, 2003).

Finally, Figure 9.2 suggests that the number of religious groups with values and interests perpetuating inequality exceeds the number of groups with a predisposition to promote equality. Recent research consistently supports this generalization (Davidson, 1985b; Davidson & Koch, 1998; Chaves & Tsitsos, 2001). Thus, even though religion has both effects at the same time, its tendency to perpetuate inequality predominates over its propensity to promote equality.

CONCLUSIONS

This chapter makes three claims. First, fair shares theory is a better theoretical platform than either fair play or religious economy theory for studying the relationship between religion and social stratification. Second, this claim is supported by recent research explaining the origins and persistence of religious stratification. Third, it also helps to account for recent analyses of religion's dual role in perpetuating social inequality at the same time it promotes equality.

These findings challenge sociologists of religion to give fair shares theory more credit than they have given it to date. It has proved to be a productive framework for colleagues in other areas of study and, with proper care, it also can be a fruitful line of inquiry in the study of religion. It certainly seems better suited to research on religion and stratification than the theoretical alternatives, as we believe the findings in this chapter indicate.

Our analysis also has implications for other sociologists as well, especially those who study social stratification. It challenges these colleagues to take religion seriously. Like race and gender, religion affects people's access to power, privilege, and prestige. Further research is needed before we know exactly how much of the variance religion accounts for, but recent studies suggest it might be considerable. More chapters and books should be dedicated to the study of religious stratification in the United States and elsewhere around the world.

Finally, social researchers of all stripes should beware of analyses that dwell on religion's tendency to perpetuate inequality, while leaving out its role in promoting equality. Religion has both effects at the same time and, certainly, it contributes to inequality more often than it fosters equality, but religion's prophetic voice is often decisive in public debates about policies related to social welfare and social reform (Hofrenning, 1995). For this reason alone, it should not be overlooked. Moreover, fair shares theory and recent research point to conditions under which religion is likely to have these countervailing effects. So far, it seems that affluent groups that are dominated by socially conservative business and agricultural leaders with Republican Party affiliations, and lower status groups that have a significant stake in the current system of stratification develop worldviews and programs that focus on personal reform more than societal reform and, in doing so, tend to perpetuate inequality. Conversely, prosperous groups headed by socially liberal intellectuals, women and minority leaders, and Democrats, and less affluent groups that are relatively autonomous from the prevailing structure of inequality tend to cultivate a theodicy of social justice and, in the end, promote equality. There is a need for additional research aimed at refining and extending these results.

REFERENCES

Anderson, C. (1970). *White Protestant Americans.* Englewood Cliffs, NJ: Prentice Hall.

Baer, H. A., & Singer, M. (1992). *African-American religion in the twentieth century: Varieties of protest and accommodation.* Knoxvillle: University of Tennessee Press.

Baltzell, E. D. (1966). "Who's Who in America" and "The Social Register": Elite and upper class indexes in metropolitan America. In R. Bendix & S. M. Lipset (Eds.), *Class, status, and power* (pp. 266–275). New York: Free Press.

Barton, A. H. (1985). Determinants of economic attitudes in the American business elite. *American Journal of Sociology, 91,* 54–87.

Bellah, R. (1967). Civil religion in America. *Daedalus, 9,* 1–21.

Billingsley, A. (1998). *Mighty like a river: The Black church and social reform.* New York: Oxford University Press.

Braun, D. (1997). *The rich get richer.* Chicago: Nelson Hall.

Burns, G. (1992). *The frontiers of Catholicism: The politics of ideology in a liberal world.* Berkeley: University of California Press.

Cantril, H. (1943). Educational and economic composition of religious groups. *American Journal of Sociology, 47,* 574–579.

Cavendish, J. C. (2000). Church-based community activism: A comparison of Black and White Catholic congregations. *Journal for the Scientific Study of Religion, 39,* 371–384.

Chaves, M. (1999). Religious congregations and welfare reform: Who will take advantage of "charitable choice"? *American Sociological Review, 64,* 836–846.

Chaves, M., & Gorski, P. S. (2001). Religious pluralism and religious participation. *Annual Review of Sociology, 27,* 261–281.

Chaves, M., & Tsitsos, W. (2001). Congregations and social services: What they do, how they do it, and with whom. *Nonprofit and Voluntary Sector Quarterly, 30,* 660–683.

Chaves, M., Giesel, H. M., & Tsitsos, W. (2002). Religious variations in public presence: Evidence from the national congregations study. In R. Wuthnow & J. H. Evans (Eds.), *The quiet hand of God* (pp. 108–128). Berkeley: University of California Press.

Christopher, R. (1989). *Crashing the gates.* New York: Simon and Schuster.

Christiano, K. J., Swatos, W. H., Jr., & Kivisto, P. (2002). *Sociology of religion.* Lanham, MD: AltaMira.

Coreno, T. (2002). Fundamentalism as a class culture. *Sociology of Religion, 63,* 335–360.

Darnell, A., & Sherkat, D. E. (1997). The impact of Protestant fundamentalism on educational attainment. *American Sociological Review, 62* (April), 306–315.

Davidson, J. D. (1977). Socio-economic status and ten dimensions of religious commitment. *Sociology and Social Research, 61,* 462–485.

Davidson, J. D. (1985a). Theories and measures of poverty: Toward a holistic approach. *Sociological Focus, 18,* 177–198.

Davidson, J. D. (1985b). *Mobilizing social movement organizations.* Storrs, CT: Society for the Scientific Study of Religion.

Davidson, J. D. (1994). Religion among America's elite: Persistence and change in the Protestant establishment. *Sociology of Religion, 55,* 419–440.

Davidson, J. D., Mock, A. K., & Johnson, C. L. (1997). Through the eye of a needle: Social ministry in affluent churches. *Review of Religious Research, 38,* 247–262.

Davidson, J. D., Pyle, R. E., & Reyes, D. V. (1995). Persistence and change in the Protestant establishment, 1930–1992. *Social Forces, 74,* 157–175.

Davidson, J. D., & Koch, J. R. (1998). Beyond mutual and public benefits: The inward and outward orientations of non-profit organizations, In N. J. Demerath et al. (Eds.), *Sacred companies* (pp. 292–306). New York: Oxford University Press.

Davidson, J. D., Koch, J. R., & Pyle, R. E. (1999). Public religion and economic inequality (pp. 101–114). In W. H. Swatos, Jr. & J. K. Wellman, Jr. (Eds.), *The power of religious publics.* Westport, CT: Praeger.

Davis, K., & Moore, W. E. (1945). Some principles of stratification. *American Sociological Review, 10,* 242–249.

Demerath, N. J. (1965). *Social class in American Protestantism.* Chicago: Rand McNally.

Dudley, C. S., & Johnson, S. A. (1993). *Engergizing the Congregation.* Louisville, KY: Westminster/John Knox Press.

Earle, J., Knudsen, D., & Shriver, D. (1976). *Spindles and spires.* Atlanta: John Knox Press.

Emerson, M. O., Smith, C., & Sikkink, D. (1999). Equal in Christ, but not in the world: White conservative protestants and explanations of Black-White inequality. *Social Problems, 46,* 398–317.

Ferraro, K. F., & Kelley-Moore, J. A. (2000). Religious consolation among men and women: Do health problems spur seeking? *Journal for the Scientific Study of Religion, 39,* 220–234.

Finke, R., & Stark, R. (1992). *The churching of America (1776–1990).* New Brunswick, NJ: Rutgers University Press.

Fry, L. C. (1933). The reported religious affiliations of American leaders. *Scientific Monthly, 36,* 241–249.

Gilkes, C. T. (1990). Until my change comes: Faith and Social Ministry in the African-American baptist tradition (pp. 179–202). In J. D. Davidson, C. L. Johnson, & A. K. Mock (Eds.), *Faith and Social Ministry.* Chicago: Loyola University Press.

Glenn, N. D., & Hyland, R. (1967). Religious preference and worldly success: Some evidence from national surveys. *American Sociological Review, 32,* 73–85.

Glock, C. Y. (1964). The role of deprivation in the origin and evolution of religious groups (pp. 24–36). In R. Lee & M. Marty (Eds.), *Religion and social conflict.* New York: Oxford University Press.

Goldstein, S. (1969). Socioeconomic differentials among religious groups in the United States. *American Journal of Sociology, 74,* 612–631.

Greeley, A. M. (1981). Catholics and the upper middle class. *Social Forces, 59,* 824–830.

Hadden, J. K., & Longino, C. (1974). *Gideon's gang.* Philadelphia: Pilgrim Press.

Hall, C. F. (1997). The Christian left: Who are they and how are they different from the Christian right? *Review of Religious Research, 39,* 27–45.

Hammond, P. E. (1992). *Religion and personal autonomy.* Columbia, SC: University of South Carolina Press.

Hofrenning, D. J. B. (1995). *In Washington but not of it: The prophetic politics of religious lobbies.* Philadelphia: Temple University Press.

Howe, G. N. (1981). The political economy of American religion (pp. 110–137). In S. McNall (Ed.), *Political economy.* Glenview, IL: Scott, Foresman.

Hummer, R. A., Rogers, R. G., Nam, C., & Ellison, C. G. (1999). Religious involvement and US adult mortality. *Demography, 36,* 273–285.

Hunt, M. O. (2002). Religion, race/ethnicity, and beliefs about inequality. *Social Science Quarterly, 83,* 810–831.

Hutchison, W. R. (1989). Protestantism as establishment (pp. 3–18). In W. R. Hutchison (Ed.), *Between the times.* Cambridge: Cambridge University Press.

Kanagy, C. L. (1992). Social action, evangelism, and ecumenism: The impact of community, theological, and church structural variables. *Review of Religious Research, 34,* 34–51.

Keister, L. A. (2000). *Wealth in America.* New York: Cambridge University Press.

Keister, L. A. (2003). Religion and wealth: The role of religious affiliation and participation in early adult asset accumulation. *Social Forces, 82,* 175–207.

Kluegel, J. R., & Smith, E. R. (1986). *Beliefs about inequality.* New York: Aldine de Gruyter.

Konolige, K., & Konolige, F. (1978). *The power of their glory.* New York: Wyden Books.

Korman, A. K. (1988). *The outsiders: Jews in corporate America.* Lexington, MA: Lexington Books.

Kraus, R. (2003). *Western faith traditions on Capitol hill: Social origins of Washington offices.* Paper presented at Annual Meeting of the Society for the Scientific Study of Religion, Norfolk, Virginia.

Lazerwitz, B. (1964). Religion and social structure of the United States. In L. Schneider (Ed.), *Religion, culture, and society* (pp. 426–439). New York: Wiley.

Lieberson, S., & Carter, D. K. (1979). Making it in America: Differences between eminent Blacks and White ethnic groups. *American Sociological Review, 44*, 347–366.

Marx, K., & Engels, F. (1964). *On religion*. New York: Schocken Books.

McRoberts, O. M. (1999). "Understanding the new" Black Pentecostal activism: Lessons from ecumenical urban ministries in Boston. *Sociology of Religion, 60*, 47–70.

Mock, A. K., Davidson, J. D., & Johnson, C. L. (1991). Threading the needle: Faith and works in affluent churches. In C. S. Dudley, J. W. Carroll, & J. P. Wind (Eds.), *Carriers of faith* (pp. 86–103). Louisville, KY: Westminster/John Knox Press.

Morris, A. D. (1984). *The origins of the civil rights movement: Black communities organizing for change*. New York: Free Press.

Nelsen, H. M., & Nelsen, A. K. (1975). *The Black church in the sixties*. Lexington, KY: University of Kentucky Press.

Niebuhr, H. R. (1929). *The social sources of denominationalism*. New York: Henry Holt.

Noel, D. L. (1968). A theory of the origins of ethnic stratification. *Social Problems, 16*, 157–172.

Oliver, M. L., & Shapiro, T. M. (1999). *Black wealth/white wealth*. New York: Routledge.

Park, J. Z., & Reimer, S. H. (2002). Revisiting the social sources of American Christianity 1972–1998. *Journal for the Scientific Study of Religion, 41*, 733–746.

Patillo-McCoy, M. (1998). Church culture as strategy of action in the Black community. *American Sociological Review, 63*, 767–784.

Piven, F. F., & Cloward, R. A. (1977). *Poor people's movements: Why they succeed, how they fail*. New York: Pantheon Books.

Pope, L. (1942). *Millhands and preachers*. New Haven, CT: Yale University Press.

Pope, L. (1948). Religion and the class structure. *Annals of the American Academy of Social and Political Science, 265*, 84–91.

Priest, T. B. (1982). A note on who's who in America as a biographic data source in studies of elites. *Sociological Methods and Research, 2* (August), 81–88.

Pyle, R. E. (1993). Faith and commitment to the poor: Theological orientation and support for government assistance measures. *Sociology of Religion, 54*, 385–401.

Pyle, R. E. (1996). *Persistence and change in the Protestant establishment*. Westport, CT: Praeger.

Pyle, R. E., & Koch, J. R. (2001). The religious affiliation of American elites, 1930s to 1990s: A note on the pace of disestablishment. *Sociological Focus, 34*, 125–137.

Pyle, R. E., & Davidson, J. D. (2003). The origins of religious stratification in Colonial America. *Journal for the Scientific Study of Religion, 42*, 57–75.

Regnerus, M., Smith, C., & Sikkink, D. (1998). Who gives to the poor? The influence of religious tradition and political location on the personal generosity of Americans toward the poor. *Journal for the Scientific Study of Religion, 37*, 481–493.

Roof, W. C. (1979). Socioeconomic differences among White socioreligious groups in the United States. *Social Forces, 58*, 280–289.

Roof, W. C., and McKinney, W. (1987). *American mainline religion*. New Brunswick, NJ: Rutgers University Press.

Roozen, D. A., McKinney, W., & Carroll, J. W. (1984). *Varieties of religious presence*. New York: Pilgrim Press.

Ryan, W. (1981). *Equality*. New York: Pantheon Books.

Schneiderman, H. G. (1994). Introduction: Thoughts out of season: E. Digby Baltzell and the Protestant establishment. In E. D. Baltzell (Ed.), *Judgment and sensibility* (pp. 1–23). New Brunswick, NJ: Transaction.

Schrag, P. (1970). *The decline of the wasp*. New York: Simon and Schuster.

Sherkat, D. E. (2001). Tracking the restructuring of American religion: Religious affiliation and patterns of religious mobility, 1973–1998. *Social Forces, 79*, 1459–1473.

Smith, R. D. (2001). Churches and the urban poor: Interaction and social distance. *Sociology of Religion, 62*, 301–313.

Stark, R. (2003). Upper class asceticism: Social origins of ascetic movements and medieval saints. *Review of Religious Research, 45*, 5–19.

Stark, R., & Finke, R. (2000). *Acts of faith*. Berkeley: University of California Press.

Takayama, K. P., & Darnell, S. B. (1979). The aggressive organization and the reluctant environment: The vulnerability of an inter-faith coordinating agency. *Review of Religious Research, 20*, 315–334.

Tamney, J., & Johnson, S. (1990). Religious diversity and ecumenical social action. *Review of Religious Research, 32*, 16–26.

Tamney, J., Burton, R., & Johnson, S. (1988). Christianity, social class, and the Catholic bishops' economic policy. *Sociological Analysis, 48*, 78S–95S.

Tsitos, W. (2003). Race differences in congregational social service activity. *Journal for the Scientific Study of Religion, 42*, 205–215.

Tumin, M. (1953). Some principles of stratification: A critical analysis. *American Sociological Review, 18*, 387–394.

Verba, S., & Orren, A. (1985). *Equality in America*. Cambridge, MA: Harvard University Press.

Voas, D., Olson, D. W. A., & Crockett, A. (2001). Religious pluralism and participation: Why previous research is wrong. *American Sociological Review, 67*, 212–230.

Weber, M. (1964). *The sociology of religion* (E. Fischoff, Trans). New York: Free Press of Glencoe.

Will, J. A., & Cochran, J. K. (1995). God help those who help themselves?: The effects of religious affiliation, religiosity, and deservedness on generosity toward the poor. *Sociology of Religion, 56*, 327–338.

Williams, J. L., & Rodeheaver, D. G. (1989). Changes in the social visibility of Black and White women from 1925–1988. *Sociology and Social Research, 73*, 107–113.

Wood, R. L. (2002). *Faith in action*. Chicago, IL: University of Chicago Press.

Wood, J. R. (1981). *Leadership in voluntary organizations*. New Brunswick, NJ: Rutgers University Press.

Wood, J. R. (1970). Authority and controversial policy: The churches and civil rights. *American Sociological Review, 35*, 1057–1069.

Wuthnow, R. (1988). *The restructuring of American religion*. Princeton, NJ: Princeton University Press.

Wuthnow, R., & Evans J. H. (Eds), (2002). *The quiet hand of God*. Berkeley: University of California Press.

Zweigenhaft, R. L., & Domhoff, G. W. (1998). *Diversity in the power elite*. New Haven, CT: Yale University Press.

CHAPTER 10

Gender

NANCY NASON-CLARK AND
BARBARA FISHER-TOWNSEND

Evidence of religious beliefs and religious practices seem to be obvious to just about everyone except those whose research and passion is linked to feminism or gender studies. We selected from our bookshelves five recent books discussing gender issues or women's lives.[1] Even though this was not a random experiment, it revealed a stark and rather troubling finding: in not one of these anthologies was there an article or a chapter devoted specifically to religion or spirituality. At first blush, you would think that religion does not matter to feminists or scholars studying women. Spirituality is apparently not on the gender radar screen; it is outside of feminist consciousness as it were.

Evidence of the advancement of the feminist agenda and the growing interest in gender studies seems to be obvious to just about everyone except those whose research and passion is linked to religious studies or the sociology of religion. Again, we selected five recent edited collections or readers in the sociology of religion.[2] Each has one or, at most, two chapters (or less than 10% of their print space) that either relate specifically to the lives of women or employ a gender lens to interpret the social world they are attempting to explain.[3] A small dose of woman has been added, but very little stirring. Apparently, gender and feminism seem to be close to the margins: blink and you might miss them altogether.

Perhaps this is too cruel or too rudimentary an analysis with which to begin a chapter that proposes to explore the scholarly interchange between religion and gender in contemporary research and writing in sociology. Perhaps not. No matter whether you celebrate or curse the growing interest in gender issues in contemporary culture, it is clear that the relationship between gender studies and religious studies is in need of some romance or repair.

These scholarly oversights notwithstanding, a quick look around our social world suggests that religion and gender are indeed closely intertwined. Gender studies has a lot to contribute to the social scientific study of religious phenomena, just as religious expression and the spiritual quest is central in the lives of many, if not most, women.

NANCY NASON-CLARK • University of New Brunswick, Fredericton, New Brunswick, Canada E3B 5A3
BARBARA FISHER-TOWNSEND • University of New Brunswick, Fredericton, New Brunswick, Canada E3B 5A3

Without a doubt, religion continues to be a powerful and empowering force in societies around the world. It helps to shape—and indeed is shaped by—the needs, dreams and ideals of men and women everywhere. As the early social thinkers knew only too well, key aspects of human experience, such as birth, death, inequality, and suffering, are linked inextricably to religion. Religion helps to define the boundaries between good and evil and in so doing plays a major role in the moral decision making of believers and "visions of the good society" (Williams, 1999). Moreover, it shapes the social interactions between men and women, children and adults, communities and even nations. Transglobal religious movements, such as Pentecostalism and charismatic Christianity, are transforming contemporary Christianity as they view the entire world as their parish (Martin, 2002; Beyer, 1994). And the growing presence of fundamentalism in all major world religions (Hawley, 1994) suggests that the interface between religion and gender may be intensifying. The gendered experience of believers has never been more important to understand. Gender is a central and unifying theme of many religious beliefs and practices, and to account for the power of the sacred without reference to its differential impact is misguided at best.

Because "women take a more active interest in nearly all forms of religious expression than do men" (Wuthnow, 2003, p. 23) and because men have assumed the primary role in religion's codified forms (cf. Ruether, 1974), it seems peculiar that a gender lens is so marginalized in the discourse of religious research and study. Clearly women as well as men seek and find everyday experiences of otherness, *moments of sacredness*, yet may differ in their interpretations of these experiences in part as a result of the constraints of gendered life opportunities (Neitz, 1995; Jacobs, 1989). When scholars move from talking about official religion[4] and discuss folk religion, mythology, or lived religion (see the edited collection by David Hall, 1997), the experiences of women feature more prominently as do the number of women authors.

Picture the diversity of the following images:

- During a Roman Catholic mass, a laywoman serves the host and wine that has been consecrated by a male priest earlier in the day in direct response to the shortage of available ordained men (cf. Wallace, 1992).
- An American Muslim woman wears her headscarf to work as she teaches university students biology on a secular campus in America (cf. Bartkowski & Reed, 2003).
- An evangelical woman says "I Am Not a Doormat," although the belief that she must submit to her husband is an important part of her religious ideology (cf. Beaman, 1999; Bartkowski, 2001; Manning, 1999; Griffith, 1997).
- In a 1982 mass wedding in New York City, 2,075 Moonie couples had their vows solemnized by Rev. and Mrs. Moon (Palmer, 1994; cf. Barker, 1984).
- A woman from a gospel church in one of the Southern states looks in the Christian Yellow Pages to find a hairstylist that shares her worldview (cf. Ammerman, 1987).
- A shy, retiring computer company executive attends a weekend Esalen workshop, discovers the warrior archetype within himself, and turns up at work dressed in leather jeans (Goldman, 2003).
- A group of young and middle-aged professional women participate in a mitzvah (cleansing bath after menstruation) and regard this Jewish ritual as empowering their sense of true identity—both feminist and Jewish (cf. Davidman, 1991; Kaufman, 1991).

- Diane, a stay-at-home mother of three, co-founded Families for Life after being startled by the childlike features of an aborted fetus in a library book (Wiedam, 1997).
- Canadian homeschoolers fear that the message taught to children in the public school system will threaten faith in God and undermine parental authority so mothers take on the role of teacher and fathers serve as school principal, *in absentia* (Ruff, Lautard, & Nason-Clark, 2004).
- Susan, a middle-aged mother of two, claims that the image of the Virgin Mary as a feminine icon is one that continues to bind her to the Roman Catholic Church and helps her cope with life's difficulties (Spencer-Arsenault, 2000; cf. Ranke-Heinemann, 1991; Warner, 1976).
- The Rajneesh hold a "Sexual Fantasies" party at the end of their "Tantra" therapy groups in Poona; one man arrived at the event dressed as a prostitute, another as Lolita and one woman came as a male "flasher" (Palmer, 2003).
- Martha, a retired widow and Episcopalian by tradition, believes that the church is primarily about providing leadership in the community, on issues such as AIDS and gay and lesbian rights (Becker, 1997).
- Before the big football game at many state universities, religious players bow their knees and raise their voices in prayer for a successful finish to the season. Promise Keepers vow to keep all promises to their wives as they stand in solidarity with other men in sports stadiums across the United States (cf. Special Issue, *Sociology of Religion,* 2000, 61[1]).
- At a Wiccan Dragonfest, the embodiment of gender and sexuality is illustrated most clearly in the appearance of women with horns (Neitz, 2000).

The images are as diverse as they are plentiful. Across campuses in North America, students wear religious jewelry, such as a cross or a star of David (cf. McDannell, 1995), carry prayer cards to the patron saint of hopeless causes, St. Jude (Orsi, 1996), wear below the knee jean skirts as a mediated settlement between the modern unisex denim and rules mandating skirts for United Pentecostal Church (UPC) women, or reveal tattoos marking their body with religious symbols (Atkinson, 2003, 2002). Others wear bracelets (wwjd—what would Jesus do), headscarves, skull caps, or t-shirts advertising *Catholics for Peace.* Some students bring Bibles to class and others pray before meals or exams. In a secular university classroom setting, religious talk is minimal, but even here it emerges when topics such as marriage, divorce, or gay rights are the subject of discussion. Interestingly, most of the undergraduate women in our classes still want a church wedding or a religious blessing on their future marriage even though they may be living with a partner now. Religious images—many of which are gendered—abound even on the most secular university campuses.

Outside of the ivory towers, there is ample evidence of the connection between religion and the lives of men and women. Some of these images evoke notions of traditionalism, but others are a product of modernity. Ever wonder if you could find Jesus in Disneyland? David Lyon (2000) says yes. According to this postmodern scholar, the religious *realm* is far from dormant in these days, it is simply that there may be different modes of expression. Krogh and Pillifant (2004) explore the experiences of believers in Kemetic Orthodoxy and discover that you can practice this ancient Egyptian religion through the medium of the computer. "... [t]hrough a password protected internet relay channel ... the ritual elements of physical co-presence . . . are translated from the temple into online temporal co-presence, coordinated text messages and the manipulation of ritual objects by individuals sitting in front of their computers" (Krogh & Pillifant, 2004, p. 173). William Stahl (1999) in *God and the Chip: Religion and the Culture of Technology* claims that the computer has become interpreted as the masculine machine. He argues that the "computing culture is decisively shaped by white, middle-class, able-bodied males" (Stahl, 1999, p. 53).

The link between religion and gender has many interesting and multi-faceted dimensions, involving both technology and access to power. Amish women mow their lawns with hand-powered mowers while men labour in the barns utilizing the latest technology (Kraybill, 1989). Baptist battles have been intensifying over the role of women, particularly issues of leadership and ordination (Ammerman, 1990). Membership in Christians for Biblical Equality can be hazardous to the health of your career (Gallagher, 2004). Amongst second career clergy in training, women seminarians outnumber the men (Charlton, 1997; Chaves, 1997). Growing numbers of Jewish women are turning to orthodoxy to provide them with a sense of meaning and stability in their lives (Davidman, 1991; Kaufman, 1991).

Some women choose religious occupations, honouring the call they believe has been placed on their lives. In some traditions, the path to ordination is still very steep and the obstacles many (Lummis & Nesbitt, 2000; Lehman, 1993; Zikmund, Lummis, & Chang, 1998). The stained glass ceiling continues to operate in other contexts in which ordination is no longer contested (Charlton, 2000; Sullins, 2000; Nesbitt, 1997). In the Roman Catholic Church many nuns exited their religious orders in the aftermath of Vatican II (Ebaugh, 1993; Wittberg, 1994), whereas other sisters saw their religious service and community life transformed. Gender relations in contemporary Christian organizations include not only issues of leadership but also the division of lay labor during the weekly routine of church life. Women polish the brass, clean the linens, and fill the pews; men, by contrast, have input into church policy decisions, count the money and fill the platform (cf. Nason-Clark, 1993). What would a church look like if it took the responsibilities of men and women as equal partners? For one thing, the gender breakdown of the local church board or governing council would not differ from the nursery roster. Working out one's salvation has never been straightforward, but it has almost always been gendered. Nowhere is this clearer than in the context of family life, where undoubtedly religion continues to exert strong influence.

Familistic ideologies in America continue to define the family as "precious" (Edgell, 2003), or "sacred" (Nason-Clark, 1998b), the building block for a strong nation under God. Organizations such as Concerned Women for America or Focus on the Family preach the message of family unity to an astounding number of listeners and readers (cf. Bartkowski, 2001; Nason-Clark, 1997). In fact, the celebration of family life and its associated *family values* has been embraced so fully by many sectors of the Christian Right that Hunter (1991) argues that religious values are among the most significant and central in the current cultural warfare over the rights, roles and responsibilities of men and women, particularly in the domestic context.

In a collection of essays entitled *Fundamentalism and Gender*, the reader is presented with a poignant look at four religious traditions—American fundamentalism, Indian Islam, Hinduism and Japanese New Religions—that clearly and unequivocally demonstrate a current obsession with family values (Hawley, 1994). It appears that there is sustained support amongst factions in all world religions for a form of gender inerrancy. The ideal of femininity embraced by preachers like Billy Sunday and Jerry Falwell and by laity as diverse as Marabel Morgan and Dr. James Dobson is rooted in a nostalgia for a bygone era, a romantic version of rural nineteenth century America (Balmer, 1994). An example from Hinduism is the satï, a mythical ideal that celebrates female heroism and the actual practice of immolating real women who *voluntarily* place their bodies on the pyre of their deceased husband (Hawley, 1994). Hawley argues that the defence of the satï has so much support because it concerns a woman's "right" to sacrifice herself in the service of man: a "right" that modern cultures interpret as exploitation. While the sacred texts of various world religions differ, the message given to women is often linked to their child-bearing or childrearing roles. The emotional intensity of the struggle for gender inerrancy suggests that the very survival of some religious groups has been equated with gender stratification.

INCORPORATING A FEMINIST OR GENDER ANALYSIS

Dorothy Smith, the well-known Canadian feminist sociologist, has argued that feminist theory must begin with an alternative epistemology—one centered on the notion that all knowledge is socially organized, but individually experienced, dependent on one's social location (Smith, 1987).[5] Feminist theorists do not employ a unitary lens, but rather embody multiple, complex voices, sometimes only dimly heard from the margins. And yet, feminism has changed, and the messages matured or diluted since its "second wave" days.

As many feminist scholars completed graduate school and began earning their bread and butter by teaching in a university setting, we asked, "Where are the women?" This was as true in departmental meetings as it was in the pages of refereed journals.[6] So we did what seemed to come naturally, we attempted to bring the women in—in to our examples in class, into our departments as professors, and into both our research agendas and the publications to follow. Disillusioned by slow progress, significant obstacles and apathy or resistance, some scholars began to argue that a significant restructuring of our categories and our analysis needed to occur. Indeed, how would starting our research from the location of women alter both our processes of information gathering and our conclusions? This epistemological shift in its many and varied derivations has created a sustained literature in feminist studies concerning method and theory. In the sociology of religion, a recent example of reflective pieces concerning researcher and researched is the edited collection *Personal Knowledge and Beyond: Reshaping the Ethnography of Religion* by Spickard, Landres, and McGuire (2002).

To echo the words of Mary Jo Neitz, one such response for the field of feminist inquiry in the sociology of religion is "... a radical rethinking of how we know what we know and for whom we undertake this project of knowledge production." (Neitz, 2003, p. 276). In R. Stephen Warner's much-cited article (1993) on the new paradigm in the sociology of religion, a paradigm that challenges the notion that secularization has been marching forward at the expense of all things religious, he credits religion as empowering marginalized groups in our culture, such as women. Evidence for such notions include Cheryl Townsend Gilkes's (1985) work in black sanctified churches where black women played an instrumental role in both the emergence and maintenance of women's departments in their congregations (cf. Moreau [1999] details Canadian black Baptist women's organizations). Two recent books document the intersection between gender and religion in the lives of immigrants to the United States (Warner & Wittner, 1998, and Ebaugh & Chafetz, 2000), whereas other researchers, such as Peña and Frehill (1998) have been engaged in exploring transborder connections between women on both sides of the divide between Mexico and the United States.

Or, consider some of our recent fieldwork experiences:

- A young woman living in Kingston, Jamaica, has her prayer group pray that her husband will be less violent toward her and then takes one of his shirts to the shaman to ask that his abusive ways be curtailed;
- A middle-aged Roman Catholic mother in Croatia says that the abuse in her personal life has increased after her soldier husband returned from the war. She prays that God would help her to be forgiving;
- The average evangelical woman in Atlantic Canada holds three volunteer jobs in her local church irrespective of whether she is a full-time home-maker or career woman and at some point has helped another woman who was afraid of her husband's anger;
- Bonnie, a shelter worker, from the Midwestern United States expresses great surprise that abused women of faith can turn to their church in times of crisis and find help;
- Four hundred women of all ages gather on a Thursday evening in Eugene, Oregon, to sing praises and worship in a local church, followed by a message that is feminist and biblical in orientation that speaks out about woman abuse.

Below, we offer two detailed examples of how weaving the knowledge gleaned from feminist studies of our culture with sociological studies of religion clarify, account for, and indeed help to explain the social world in which we live and the struggles which we face. They are offered as illustrations of what happens when there is a genuine attempt to merge the axioms and the insights of these two fields of study. We do not claim such a merger as unique, but a cursory glance at the current sociological literature will indicate that it is rare. Nor is the call for its incorporation new.

In the last 25 years, there has been a large-scale shift in various academic disciplines occasioned by the expanding scholarship by, and about, women.[7] As an example, within the American Sociological Association, the Sex and Gender Section is the largest of the various sections. However, religion has not featured prominently in the list of priority issues to be studied. Early feminist writing tried to account for the various causes of inequality; much of this work emphasized differences between men and women (Neitz, 1995). As a result, gender was introduced as a variable into research while the conceptual frame and research design remained unaltered. This approach obscured the great differences amongst women, including differences of power. Giving voice to women's experience reveals both the constraints under which women operate and their personal resistance to the structures that would oppress them. The concept of women's agency gave feminists a tool by which to discuss the transformation that women bring to the particular social context in which they find themselves, never forgetting that such is embodied in a particular space and time (cf. Beaman, 1999; McGuire, 1997).

Within the journals devoted to a social scientific study of religion, in 1987 *Sociology of Religion* published four articles under the heading, Recent Research on Feminism and Religion. In 1993, the first special issue on gender was published by that journal. With the noted exception of Ruth Wallace's 1975 presidential address for the Association for the Sociology of Religion and an article by Marie Augusta Neal in 1979, there were few examples of feminist work in the field of sociology of religion published in the journals before the 1980s (see Neitz, 1993). In two presidential addresses, 20 years apart, Ruth Wallace asked two important questions: Why have women been underrepresented in studies of religion? and How visible are women in religion?[8] These questions still haunt us. To reflect further on these issues, we have examined the articles and book reviews over the past 10 years published in three international journals, *Journal for the Scientific Study of Religion, Review of Religious Research*, and *Sociology of Religion: A Quarterly Review.*

Between 1994 and 2003, the percentage of gender-related articles in these three journals ranged from 12% to 21.5%. Our analysis uncovered a variety of themes, including gender and spirituality/religion in contemporary and historical contexts; gender in new religious movements; family issues; the body; experiences of gender and religion internationally; sexual orientation; clergy careers; violence and abuse; and religious icons. Men outnumbered women authors in articles related to sexual orientation, the body, violence and abuse, and overwhelmingly, in the category of family (which includes a number of articles related to the Promise Keepers). In the remaining categories, female authors outnumbered males. The picture is somewhat different for book reviews—5% to 12.4% of books reviewed explore explicitly women's or gender issues. So, to answer Ruth Wallace's enquiry *"Where are the women?,"* they are largely still marginalized, at least in these journals.

The three largest categories, religion and the body, religion and sexual orientation and clergy careers, account for most of the articles that were published in the 10-year time frame. Included in religion and the body category were many papers that addressed physical and mental health problems, suicide ideation, sexual initiation and attitudes toward abortion: most of these were authored by men. In the religion and sexual orientation group were many papers (mostly authored by men) that focussed on the dissonance experienced by lesbian/gay/transsexual/bi/questioning individuals who either wish to maintain their connection with a particular religious group or who are seeking an alternative setting for their spirituality. Not unrelated to these were other articles that examined sexual orientation and ordination to religious office. For many years now, there have been a significant number of articles related to gender and clergy careers, mostly authored by women. Issues discussed in these papers ranged from ministry styles and goals, to personality characteristics, differing career tracks, and levels of work satisfaction.

In their introduction to *Feminist Narratives in the Sociology of Religion*, Nason-Clark and Neitz (2001) argue that they were part of a particular cohort of women who became feminists and sociologists at the same point in their lives and saw these activities as being inextricably tied together. They write "Our desire to do sociological research that puts women, their lives and their experiences—as well as issues of gender—at the center of any sociological analysis was shaped by our participation in the women's movement." In part, this is a generational experience echoed by other feminist researchers of religion (Davidman, 2000; Jacobs, 2000) but not shared by those whose "encounter with postfeminism was less uniformly positive" (Becker, 2000).

However, for a variety of reasons, it is a path less well traveled than one might have expected. Perhaps it is not chosen because other alternatives are more appealing from a political or theoretical point of view. Perhaps it is deliberately avoided because it causes discomfort, with moral undertones that are difficult to silence. Perhaps it is related to the social location of the researcher, or the researched. Or maybe it has to do with the availability of data, or the possible publishing venues, or even the status of certain domains of our discipline. But, as social researchers, we have an opportunity (some might say obligation?) to look and listen to ordinary people as they make decisions about their lives and respond to social forces that can seem out of individual control. We also have the ability to consider the role of elites, those who make the decisions and others who try to enforce them. Sometimes we understand clearly what we see, because our own experience and training make sense of it easily. Sometimes we are troubled by what we see, because it defies the professional and personal categories on which we rely to make sense of our world. No one should underestimate the challenge. But neither should we avoid it.

ABUSE IN THE FAMILY CONTEXT

Until relatively recently, violence in the family context was absent from national research agendas, a problem that was kept hidden behind the closed bedroom doors of women around the globe. In *No Place for Abuse*, statistics from around the world are presented that reveal beyond any doubt that violence against women is a pervasive, global social problem (Kroeger & Nason-Clark, 2001).

The more we learn about family violence, from academic studies or community-based initiatives, the more it becomes apparent that abuse is complex and multifaceted (Stirling, Cameron, Miedema, & Nason-Clark, 2004; Timmins, 1995). No one profession or discipline can account for the prevalence and severity of the problem, nor can it in isolation respond fully to its victims. Family violence includes woman abuse, child abuse, sibling violence, and elder abuse: it incorporates all these violations and more (Miedema & Nason-Clark, 2004). Family violence is a gendered social problem, as most of its victims are female and most of the perpetrators are male. In many ways, the violations are not merely personal but reflect social inequalities and social constructions (Profitt, 2000; Duffy & Momirov, 1997). It impacts on the well-being of adults and children, producing fear and long-term consequences that impact on both the private and public spheres of life (DeKeseredy & MacLeod, 1997).

Understanding Religious Victims

Does religion augment or thwart the healing journey of a woman victim of abuse?[9] What is the role of personal choice versus deliberate, relentless outside pressure in how a victimized woman's options are presented to her?[10] Are religious women coerced into believing that they must stay in abusive marriages forever?[11] Is a secular battered women's shelter a safe place for a woman victim to disclose that she is religious?[12] These are some of the questions that have led to our growing interest in, and exploration of, the experiences of women who sought help from their faith communities in the aftermath of violence in their personal, intimate relationships. Faith communities worldwide have been slow to recognize and respond to the needs of victims of domestic violence (McDill & McDill, 1991; Adams, 1994). In part, this is a reaction to the high value placed on family values by Christian churches across the world, but most especially amongst evangelical congregations in the United States (Nason-Clark, 1999). The rhetoric of family unity and the sacredness surrounding intact families stands in stark contrast to the harsh reality of abuse and conflict experienced by many women, men and children. To be sure, there are religious and secular overtones to both the family problems that are endured as well as to the healing journey after abuse (Nason-Clark & Kroeger, 2004). The construction of the healing journey for a victim of domestic violence is sometimes coopted by care-givers, agencies, and professionals who claim that they know best what a battered woman needs (Timmins, 1995; Nason-Clark, 2003). Yet, there are some specific difficulties when secular agencies attempt to challenge misguided religious ideation (Whipple, 1987; Beaman-Hall & Nason-Clark, 1997). The road to recovery is augmented when faith communities and their leaders understand their unique opportunities and particular challenges in meeting the needs of victims and their families (cf. Miles, 2000; Fortune, 1991). Abused religious women want the violence to stop but they may not want to leave their abuser, temporarily or forever. As a result, religious women in particular, place a lot of trust in programs that purport to help men to stop the abuse and to alter their ways of coping with anger and frustration. Clergy may be especially prone to assist women and their partners who are still married and to use the language of reconciliation as motivation for the men to seek help.

Intervention Programs for Religious Batterers

Batterer treatment groups have been in existence since the 1970s when the once very private problem of spousal abuse began to be seen as a public issue (Russell, 1995). Since that time, the literature on this issue has been growing. Research techniques have varied, but a common focus has been identification of the context of abuse. There is now a wealth of data on men who batter and on secular programs that seek to change their behavior. Narratives of abused women have been examined (Boehm, Reinhild, Golec, Krahn, & Smyth, 1999; Ferraro, 1997; Wolf-Smith & LaRossa, 1992), and population surveys to ascertain the prevalence of abuse have been conducted (Straus & Gelles, 1986; Kantor & Strauss, 1990). Other researchers have examined the responses of the criminal justice system (Fagan, 1993; Websdale, 1995; Gondolf, 2002) or identified characteristics or typologies of abusive men (Dalton, 2001; Faulkner, Cogan, Nolder, & Shooter, 1991). Numerous variables that contribute to attrition or recidivism have been identified, including demographic characteristics, attitudinal and personal variables, and levels of motivation (Gondolf, 2000; deHart et al., 1999). Yet, prediction of program effectiveness, including completion rates and subsequent nonviolence, remains difficult (Scott & Wolfe, 2000; Hanson & Wallace-Capretta, 2000; Edleson, 1995).

Until our research, initiated several years ago, what had been missing from the agenda was a strategy that considered the impact that religion has on both the women victims as they seek hope and healing and on the male batterers as they journey toward accountability for their abusive behavior. Hopefully the victim's perspective increasingly will be recognized and understood as men in intervention programs are required to think about their behavior and to discuss it in circumstances in which trained therapists and other batterers can confront their beliefs and attitudes using the language of faith. Some would regard the worldview of men of faith as support for their rationalization of patriarchal authority, under which their wives are called to be "submissive." In two secular Texas batterer intervention programs, researchers found that religious men appealed to the Bible to justify their violence. "The most common word they used was submit: She will not submit, she did not submit, she should submit" (Shupe, Stacey, & Hazlewood, 1987, p. 93). A treatment context where this type of belief can be confronted is very important.

For men of faith, the availability of an intervention program where they can share experiences with men who have a common worldview, where their faith will not be attacked, and where, importantly, they will not be able to justify their actions using the language of their faith tradition, is essential. It is necessary that abusive men of faith have their behavior condemned both by the leaders of their faith community and in a therapeutic program that understands the language of faith and its sacred texts. One of our recent findings relates to the role of clergy in encouraging or "mandating" men who seek their spiritual help to attend a faith-based batterers' intervention program (Nason-Clark et al., 2003). It is clear that when a faith leader suggests and supports attendance at an intervention program, completion rates do increase—one indicator of changed behavior. In terms of offering hope to victims, certainly completion of the program by their abuser is the first step, as it demonstrates a commitment to change.

Women of faith who are victims of abuse look for hope that the violence will end but they may also look for hope that there can be reconciliation of their relationship within the context of their faith community. They live in family situations that are not peaceful and safe yet their faith tradition highlights family unity and celebrates the divinely ordained nature of family life. In interviews with women of faith experiencing abuse, Boehm et al. (1999) noted that many of these women spoke of their spiritual anguish in the midst of family violence. To offer hope to these women it is important that therapeutic staff are able to condemn the abuse they have suffered using the language of faith (Nason-Clark & Kroeger, 2004). Shupe et al. (1987, pp. 93–94) report that "the most ominous use of religion occurred when men freely admitted that they had been violent but that since they had been "saved" by Jesus Christ, all their sins and weaknesses, including explosive anger, were forgiven . . . these men simply wrote off their violence as an unimportant foible. Their faith, they said, excused them entirely." From our perspective, an essential feature of a faith-based intervention program is the ability of therapeutic staff, who are knowledgeable of sacred texts and various religious traditions, to counter such use of religion in this context. Men in a faith-based intervention program will not be able to justify their violent behavior using the language of their faith tradition. Here, the rationale of any abusive man that his faith encourages or even justifies the violence he has meted out on his victim will not be tolerated.

CONCLUDING COMMENTS

Adding the experiences of women to our fieldwork and our analytical frames has a "wonderful disruptive potential" (Neitz, 2003, p. 292), for feminist theory shatters some of our preconceived notions about the world in which we live and presents a plethora of riddles and dislocations that beg for further study. It has often been said that "adding women and stirring" is a necessary but only partial response to the marginalization of women in our theoretical formulations and within our studies of ordinary people and the institutions and elites vying for power to control them. Employing the metaphor of stirring, for a moment, one might be tempted to ask whether our disciplines are willing to change cooks, change recipes, or deconstruct the kitchen with all its varying utensils. Have we explained hunger, looked for new sources of food, or even participated in feeding the hungry? For surely, there is a direct link between who we are, what we study and what we do with the knowledge we have participated in accumulating. In the last 25 years, there have been a lot of changes in our disciplines. Like other feminist writers, I remember only too well attending my first sociology of religion professional meetings where you could almost fit all the women in attendance in one bathroom. Times have changed. But, much has not changed. In many ways, women's experiences and issues of gender continue to be marginalized. But they are not silenced. There are many questions and issues that surface, much left yet to be accomplished, but there is also much to celebrate.

Let the conversations continue:

- What is the intersection of personal biography of researcher and the personal experience of loss (or collective experiences of loss) that can enrich our ability as researchers to ask and hear of the emotional intensity and longer-term impact of issues particularly related to the family context? *Whereas Davidman (2000) discusses Motherloss, Jacobs (2002) explores contemporary Crypto-Jews and their attempt to reclaim a hidden heritage.*

- What is the interface between the rhetoric of increasing accountability of religious men for their behaviour at home, and beyond, and the actual reality of their personal and collective stories? *Bartkowski (2001) analyzes evangelical marriages, whereas a recent edited volume by Shupe, Stacey, and Darnell (2000) discusses clergy misconduct in modern America.*

- What are the intersections of race and class in the discussion of women and religion? *Cheryl Townsend Gilkes (2000) has recently asked us: If it wasn't for the women, what would happen to African-American religious organizations and communities? Milagros Peña has framed her answer in terms of Anglos and Latinas on both sides of the Mexican/US border (Peña & Frehill, 1998).*

- When gender and sexuality are central to our analytical frames and notions surrounding women and nonheterosexuality are no longer placed at the boundaries, what will we as sociologists of religion be empowered to see and what narratives will we be able to describe? *In her 1999 Paul Hanly Furfey Lecture at the Association for the Sociology of Religion, Mary Jo Neitz explores two central moments in her fieldwork study of contemporary witchcraft which prompt her to combine queer theory and feminism to analyze cultural change. Building upon notions of "sheilaism" in* Habits of the Heart,[13] *Melissa Wilcox (2002) asks what happens when Sheila's a lesbian?*

- How have innovations in technology impacted on the gendered nature of the religious lives of believers? *An edited collection by Lorne Dawson (2003) offers us some interesting clues for NRMs, as does Bill Stahl's book* God and the Chip *(1999).*

- What is the link between research and social action? Under what conditions does "partnering for change" work? *A recent edited collection by Stirling, Cameron, Nason-Clark, and Miedema (2004) explores the link between researcher, researched and social strategies for change by focusing on the issue of woman abuse; the role of religion is highlighted in several places. Several chapters in Spickard, Landres, and McGuire (2002) reflect on knowledge creation and social action among scholars of religion. From a different vantage point, Ammerman (1997) in* Congregations and Community *explores the role of congregations in initiating change in their community.*

- How do ordinary believers—men and women alike—respond to the multiple identities that converge to compose their life narrative and everyday experiences? *Nancy Ammerman (2003) argues that religious narratives extend well beyond religious boundaries, for stories are replete with sacred symbolism, collective mission and community solidarity. In* Defecting in Place: Women Claiming Responsibility for Their Own Spiritual Lives, *Winter, Lummis, and Stokes (1994) examine how feminist women make sense of their participation in a context that challenges one of their core identities. Dufour (2000) discusses this phenomenon as identity sifting with regard to Jewish feminists.*

NOTES

1. Crow, Barbara A. and Lise Gotell. 2000. *Open Boundaries: A Canadian Women's Studies Reader.* Toronto, ON: Prentice Hall Allyn and Bacon Canada.:
   Kimmel, Michael S. with Amy Aronson. (ed.) 2004. *The Gendered Society Reader.* 2nd ed. Oxford: Oxford University Press.
   Lips, Hilary M. 2000. *Sex and Gender: An Introduction.* 4th ed. Mountain View, CA: Mayfield Publishing Company.
   Spade, Joan Z. and Catherine G. Valentine. 2004. *The Kaleidoscope of Gender: Prisms, Patterns and Possibilities.* Belmont, CA: Wadsworth/Thomson Learning.
   Wood, Julia T. 2003. *Gendered Lives: Communication, Gender and Culture.* 5th ed. Belmont, CA: Wadsworth.
2. Aldridge, Alan. 2000. *Religion in the Contemporary World: A Sociological Introduction.* Cambridge, UK: Polity Press.
   Dawson, Lorne L. (ed.) 2003. *Cults and New Religious Movements: A Reader.* Oxford: Blackwell Publishing.
   Dillon, Michele (ed.) 2003. *Handbook of the Sociology of Religion.* Cambridge: Cambridge University Press.
   Hood, Ralph W. Jr. (ed.) 1995. *Handbook of Religious Experience.* Birmingham, Alabama: Religious Education Press.
   Swatos, William H., Jr., (ed.) 1998. *Encyclopedia of Religion and Society.* Walnut Creek, CA: AltaMira Press.
3. In the case of the *Encyclopedia of Religion and Society*, published in 1998, far less than 10% of the entries are indexed with reference to issues relating to gender or women in particular (e.g., abortion, marriage, sexism, feminism). Moreover, fewer than 5% of indexed name entries are female. By contrast, 15% of the contributors to the volume are female.
4. For an excellent discussion of official religion, see McGuire, 1997.
5. For a concise overview of Smith's work, see Neitz, 2003, pp. 286–288.
6. Ruth Wallace asked this publicly in her 1975 Association for the Sociology of Religion Presidential Address and repeated her call again in 1995 as president of the Society for the Scientific Study of Religion.
7. For one of the earliest accounts, see *Feminist Scholarship: Kindling in the Groves of Academia* by E. Dubois, G. P. Kelly, E. L. Kennedy, C. Korsmeyer, and L. Robinson. Urbana: University of Illinois Press, 1985; c.f., Stacey and Thorne, "The Missing Feminist Revolution in Sociology," *Social Problems* 32:301–16.
8. In an article published in 2000, entitled "Women and Religion: The Transformation of Leadership Roles," Wallace returned to the issue of women and religion in an exploration of women's leadership roles in the sociology of religion. Also in 2000, David O. Moberg asked "what most needs the attention of religion researchers in the twenty-first century?" The seven challenges he delineates make no mention of gender differentiation or gendered analysis. In fact, since 2000, there have been no further articles that address the underrepresentation of women in studies of religion, the visibility of women in religion and sociology or the need to ask new questions.
9. This is a question on which there has been some speculation but very little solid data or social science inquiry. For a critique of how religious institutions have responded in the past to the needs of abused women, see Brown and Bohn, 1989; Bussert, 1986; Kroeger and Nason-Clark, 2001; and Livezey, 1997.
10. See Nason-Clark, 1997.
11. See Dobash and Dobash, 1979; Horton and Williamson, 1988; and Thorne-Finch, 1992. For an alternative view, see Halsey, 1984; Fortune, 1991; Nason-Clark, 2000a; Nason-Clark and Kroeger, 2004.
12. See Nason-Clark, 2001.
13. Bellah, Robert N. Richard Madsen, William M. Sullivan, Ann Swidler, and Steven M. Tipton. 1985. *Habits of the Heart: Individualism and Commitment in American Life.* New York: Harper and Row.

REFERENCES

Adriance, M. C. (1995). *Promised land: Base Christian communities and the struggle for the Amazon.* Albany: State University of New York Press.

Aldridge, A. (2000). *Religion in the contemporary world: A sociological introduction.* Cambridge, UK: Polity Press.

Ammerman, N. T. (1987). *Bible believers: Fundamentalists in the modern world.* New Brunswick, NJ: Rutgers University Press.

Ammerman, N. T. (1990). *Baptist battles: Social change and religious conflict in the Southern Baptist Convention.* New Brunswick, NJ: Rutgers University Press.

Ammerman, N. T. (1997). *Congregations and community.* New Brunswick, NJ: Rutgers University Press.

Ammerman, N. T. and Roof, W. C. (Eds.). (1995). *Work, family and religion in contemporary society.* New York: Routledge.

Atkinson, M. (2002). Pretty in ink: Conformity, resistance, and negotiation in women's tattooing. *Sex Roles, 47*, 219–235.

Atkinson, M. (2003). *Tattooed: The sociogenesis of a body art.* Toronto: University of Toronto Press.

Balmer, R. (1994). American fundamentalism: The ideal of femininity. In J. S. Hawley (Ed.), *Fundamentalism and gender* (pp. 47–62). New York: Oxford University Press.

Barker, E. (1984). *The making of a Moonie: Choice or brainwashing?* Oxford: Blackwell.

Bartkowski, J. P. (2000). Breaking walls, raising fences: Masculinity, intimacy, and accountability among the Promise Keepers. *Sociology of Religion, 61*, 33–53.

Bartkowski, J. P. (2001). *Remaking the Godly marriage: Gender negotiation in evangelical families.* New Brunswick, NJ: Rutgers University press.

Bartkowski, J. P., & Read, J. G. (2003). Veiled submission: Gender negotiation among Evangelical and U.S. Muslim Women. *Qualitative Sociology, 26*(1), 71–92.

Beaman, L. (1999). *Shared beliefs, different lives: Women's identities in evangelical context.* St. Louis, MO: Chalice Press.

Beaman-Hall, L., & Nason-Clark, N. (1997). Partners or protagonists? The transition house movement and conservative churches. *Affilia: Journal of Women and Social Work, 12*(2), 176–96.

Becker, P. E. (1997). What is right? What is caring? Moral logics in local religious life. In P. E. Becker & N. L. Eiesland (Eds.), *Contemporary American religion: An ethnographic reader.* Walnut Creek, CA: AltaMira Press.

Becker, P. E. (2000). Boundaries and silences in a post-feminist sociology. *Sociology of Religion, 61*(4), 399–408.

Becker, P. E., & Eiesland, N. L. (Eds.). (1997). *Contemporary American religion: An ethnographic reader.* Walnut Creek, CA: AltaMira Press.

Bellah, R. N., Madsen, R., Sullivan, W. M., Swidler, A., & Tipton, S. M. (1985). *Habits of the heart: Individualism and commitment in American life.* New York, NY: Harper and Row.

Berger, H. (1998). *A community of witches: Contemporary neopaganism and witchcraft in the United States.* Columbia: University of South Carolina Press.

Beyer, P. (1994). *Religion and globalization.* Thousand Oaks, CA: Sage.

Boehm, R., Golec, J., Krahn, R., & Smyth, D. (Eds.). (1999). *Lifelines: Culture, spirituality and family violence, understanding the cultural and spiritual needs of women who have experienced abuse.* Edmonton: University of Alberta Press.

Brown, J., & Bohn, C. (1989). *Christianity, patriarchy and abuse: A feminist critique.* Cleveland, OH: Pilgrim Press.

Brown, K. M. (1991). *Mama Lola: A Voudou priestess in Brooklyn.* Berkeley: University of California Press.

Brown, K. M. (1994). Fundamentalism and the control of women. In J. S. Hawley (Ed.), *Fundamentalism and gender* (pp. 175–202). New York: Oxford University Press.

Bussert, J. (1986). *Battered women: From a theology of suffering to an ethic of empowerment.* New York: Lutheran Churches of American, Division for Mission in North America.

Chang, P.M.Y. (1997). Female clergy in the contemporary protestant church: A current assessment. *Journal for the Scientific Study of Religion, 36*, 565–573.

Charlton, J. (1997). Clergywomen of the pioneer generation: A longitudinal study. *Journal for the Scientific Study of Religion, 36*, 599–613.

Charlton, J. (2000). Women and clergywomen. *Sociology of Religion, 61*(4), 419–424.

Chaves, M. (1997). *Ordaining women: Culture and conflict in religious organizations.* Cambridge, MA: Harvard University Press.

Crow, B. A., & Gotell, L. (2000). *Open boundaries: A Canadian women's studies reader.* Toronto, ON: Prentice Hall Allyn and Bacon Canada.

Dalton, B. (2001). Batterer characteristics and treatment completion. *Journal of Interpersonal Violence, 16*(1), 971–91.

Davidman, L. (1991). *Tradition in a rootless world: Women turn to Orthodox Judaism.* Berkeley: University of California Press.

Davidman, L. (2000). *Motherloss.* Berkeley: University of California Press.

Dawson, L. L. (Ed.). (2003). *Cults and new religious movements: A reader.* Oxford: Blackwell.

deHart, D., Kennerly, R., Burke, L., & Follingstad, D. (1999). Predictors of attrition in a treatment program for battering men. *Journal of Family Violence, 14*(1), 19–34.

Dekeseredy, W., & MacLeod, L. (1997). *Woman abuse: A sociological story.* Toronto: Harcourt Brace.

Dillon, M. (Ed.). (2003). *Handbook of the sociology of religion. Cambridge*: Cambridge University Press.

Dobash, R. P., & Dobash, R. E. (1979). *Violence against wives: A case against the patriarchy.* New York: Free Press.

DuBois, E., Kelly, G. P., Kennedy, E. L., Korsmeyer, C., & Robinson, L. (1985). *Feminist scholarship: Kindling in the groves of academia.* Urbana, IL: University of Illinois Press.

Duffy, A., & Momirov, J. (1997). *Family violence: A Canadian introduction.* Toronto: James Lorimer.

Dufour, L. R. (2000). Sifting through tradition: The creation of Jewish feminist identities. *Journal for the Scientific Study of Religion, 39*, 90–107.

Ebaugh, H. R. (1993). *Women in the vanishing cloister: Organizational decline in Catholic religious orders in the United States.* New Brunswick, NJ: Rutgers University Press.

Ebaugh, H. R., & Saltzman, J. (2000). *Religion and the new immigrants: Continuities and adaptations in immigrant congregations.* Walnut Creek, CA: AltaMira.

Edleson, J. L. (1995). *Do batterers' programs work?* Accessed June 28, 2001, from http:// www.mincava.umn. edu/papers/battrx.htm

Edgell, P. (2003). In rhetoric and practice: Defining "The good family" in local congregations. In M. Dillon (Ed.), *Handbook of the sociology of religion* (pp. 164–178). Cambridge: Cambridge University Press.

Fagan, J. (1993). The social control of spouse assault. In F. Adler & W. Laufer (Eds.), *New Directions in criminological theory* (pp. 187–225). New Brunswick, NJ: Transaction.

Falk, N. Auer & Gross, R.M. (2001). *Unspoken worlds: Women's religious lives* (3rd ed.). Belmont, CA: Wadsworth/Thomson Learning.

Faulkner, K. K., Cogan, R., Nolder, M., & Shooter, G. (1991). Characteristics of men and women completing cognitive/behavioural spouse abuse treatment. *Journal of Family Violence, 6*(3), 243–254.

Ferraro, K. J. (1989). Policing woman battering. *Social Problems, 36*(1), 61–74.

Fortune, M. (1991). *Violence in the family: A workshop curriculum for clergy and other helpers.* Cleveland, OH: Pilgrim Press.

Gallagher, S. (2004). The marginalization of evangelical feminism. *Sociology of Religion, 65*(3), 215–238.

Gilkes, C. T. (1985). Together and in harness: Women's traditions in the sanctified church. *Signs, 10*, 678–99.

Gilkes, C. T. (2000). *If it wasn't for the women . . . Black women's experience and womanist culture in church and community.* Maryknoll, NY: Orbis Books.

Goldman, M. (2000). *Passionate journeys: Why successful women joined a cult.* Ann Arbor: University of Michigan Press.

Goldman, M. (2003, March). *Doctrine, diffusion, and the development of Esalen.* Paper presented at the On the Edge of the Future Conference, Esalen Institute.

Goldman, M. S., & Isaacson, L. (1999). Enduring affiliation and gender doctrine for Shiloh Sisters and Rajneesh Sannyasins. *Journal for the Scientific Study of Religion, 38*, 411–22.

Gondolf, E. W. (2000). A 30-month follow-up of court-referred batterers in four cities. *International Journal of Offender Therapy and Comparative Criminology, 44*(1), 111–128.

Gondolf, E. W. (2002). *Batterer intervention systems: Issues, outcomes and recommendations.* Thousand Oaks, CA: Sage.

Griffin, W. (Ed.). (2000). *Daughters of the goddess: Studies in healing, identity and empowerment.* Walnut Creek, CA: AltaMira.

Griffith, R. M. (1997). *God's daughters: Evangelical women and the power of submission.* Berkeley: University of California Press.

Hall, D. H. (Ed.). (1997). *Lived religion in American: Toward a history of practice.* Princeton, NJ.: Princeton University Press.

Halsey, P. (1984). *Abuse in the family: Breaking the church's silence.* Office of Ministries with Women in Crisis, General Board of Global Ministries, United Methodist Church.

Hanson, R .K., & Wallace-Capretta, S. (2002). *Predicting recidivism among male batterers 2000–06.* Ottawa: Public Works and Government Services Canada.

Hawley, J. (Ed.). (1994). *Fundamentalism and gender.* New York: Oxford.

Hood, R. W., Jr. (Ed.). (1995). *Handbook of religious experience.* Birmingham, Alabama: Religious Education Press.

Horton, A., & Williamson, J. (Eds.). (1988). *Abuse and religion: When praying isn't enough.* New York: D.C. Heath and Company.

Hunter, J. D. (1983). *American evangelicalism: Conservative religion and the quandry of modernity.* New Brunswick, NJ: Rutgers University Press.

Hunter, J. D. (1987). *Evangelicalism: The coming generation.* Chicago: University of Chicago Press.

Hunter, J. D. (1991). *Culture wars: The struggle to define America.* New York: Basic Books.

Ice, M. L. (1995). *Clergy worldviews: Now the men's voices.* Westport, CT: Praeger.

Jacobs, J. L. (1989). *Divine disenchantment: Deconverting from new religious movements.* Bloomington: Indiana University Press.

Jacobs, J. L. (1996). Women, ritual and secrecy: The creation of Crypto-Jewish culture. *Journal for the Scientific Study of Religion, 35,* 97–108.

Jacobs, J. L. (2000). Hidden truths and cultures of secrecy: Reflections on gender and ethnicity in the study of religion. *Sociology of Religion, 61*(4), 433–442.

Jacobs, J. L. (2002). *Hidden heritage: The legacy of the Crypto-Jews.* Berkeley: University of California Press.

Kaufman, D. R. (1991). *Rachel's daughters: Newly orthodox Jewish women.* New Brunswick, NJ: Rutgers University Press.

Kraybill, D. (1989). *The riddle of Amish culture.* Baltimore, MD: Johns Hopkins University Press.

Kantor, G. K., & Straus, M. A. (1990). The "drunken bum" theory of wife beating. In M. A. Straus & R. J. Gelles (Eds.), *Physical violence in American families: Risk factors and adaption to violence in 8,145 families* (pp. 203–224). New Brunswick, NJ: Transaction.

Kimmel, M. S., & Aronson, A. (Eds.). (2004). *The gendered society reader* (2nd ed.). Oxford: Oxford University Press.

Kroeger, C., & Nason-Clark, N. (2001). *No place for abuse: Biblical and practical resources to counteract domestic violence.* Downers Grove, IL: InterVarsity Press.

Lehman, E. C. (1993). *Gender and work: The case of the clergy.* Albany: State University of New York Press.

Lips, H. M. (2000). *Sex and gender: An introduction* (4th ed.). Mountain View, CA: Mayfield.

Livezey, L. W. (1997, November 5–7). *Challenging the theology of violence.* Paper presented at the Annual Meetings of the Religious Research Association, Dan Diego, CA.

Lummis, A. T., & Nesbitt, P. D. (2000). Women clergy research and the sociology of religion. *Sociology of Religion, 61*(4), 443–454.

Lyon, D. (2000). *Jesus in Disneyland: Religion in postmodern times.* Cambridge, UK: Polity Press.

Manning, C. (1999). *God gave us the right: Conservative Catholic, Evangelical Protestant, and Orthodox Jewish women grapple with feminism.* New Brunswick, NJ: Rutgers University Press.

Martin, D. (2002). *Pentecostalism: The world their parish.* Oxford: Blackwell.

McDannell, C. (1995). *Material Christianity: Religion and popular culture in America.* New Haven, CT: Yale University Press.

McGuire, M. B. (1997). *Religion: The social context* (4th ed.). Belmont, CA: Wadsworth.

Miedema, B., & Nason-Clark, N. (2004). Introduction. In M. L. Stirling, C. A. Cameron, N. Nason-Clark, & B. Miedema (Eds.), *Understanding abuse: Partnering for change* (pp. 3–19). Toronto: University of Toronto Press.

Moberg, D. O. (2000). What most needs the attention of religion researchers in the twenty-first century? *Research in the Social Scientific Study of Religion, 11,* 1–21. Stamford, CT: JAI Press Inc.

Moreau, B. (1999). The feminization of the Black Baptist church in Nova Scotia. In K. A. Blackford, M.-L. Garceau, & S. Kirby (Eds.), *Feminist success stories, Célébrons nos réussites féministes* (251–260). Ottawa: University of Ottawa Press.

Nason-Clark, N. (1993). Gender relations in contemporary Christianity. In T. Hewitt (Ed.), *The Sociology of Religion: A Canadian Focus* (pp. 215–234). Toronto: Butterworths.

Nason-Clark, N. (1997). *The battered wife: How Christians confront family violence.* Louisville, KY: Westminster/John Knox Press.

Nason-Clark, N. (1998a). Abuses of clergy trust: Exploring the impact on female congregants' faith and practice. In A. Shupe (Ed.), *Wolves among the fold* (pp. 85–100). New York: Rutgers University Press.

Nason-Clark, N. (1998b). The evangelical family is sacred . . . but is it safe?" In C. Clark Kroeger & J. R. Beck (Eds.), *Healing the hurting: Giving hope and help to abused women* (109–125). Grand Rapids, MI: Baker Book.

Nason-Clark, N. (1999). Shattered silence or holy hush: Emerging definitions of violence against women. *Journal of Family Ministry, 13*(1), 39–56.

Nason-Clark, N. (2000a). Making the sacred safe: Woman abuse and communities of faith, *Sociology of Religion, 61*(4), 349–68.

Nason-Clark, N. (2000b). Defining violence in religious contexts. In A. Shupe (Ed.), *Bad pastors: Clergy malfeasance in America* (69–89). Albany: New York University Press.

Nason-Clark, N. (2001). Woman abuse and faith communities: religion, violence and provision of social welfare. In P. Nesbitt (Ed.), *Religion and social policy* (pp. 128–145). Walnut Creek, CA: AltaMira.

Nason-Clark, N. (2003). The making of a survivor: Rhetoric and reality in the study of religion and abuse. In J. Beckford and J. Richardson (Eds.), *Challenging religion* (pp. 181–191). London: Routledge.

Nason-Clark, N., & Kroeger, C. Clark (2004). *Refuge from abuse: Hope and healing for abused Christian women.* Downers Grove, IL: InterVarsity Press; 2004.

Nason-Clark, N., & Neitz, M. J. (Eds.). (2001). *Feminist perspectives and narrative in the sociology of religion.* Walnut Creek, CA: AltaMira.

Nason-Clark, N., Murphy, N., Fisher-Townsend, B., & Ruff, L. (2003). An overview of the characteristics of the clients at a faith-based batterers' intervention program. *Journal of Religion and Abuse, 5*(4), 51–72.

Neitz, M. J. (1993). Inequality and difference: Feminist perspectives in the sociology of religion. In W. H. Swatos, Jr. (Ed.), *Future for religion: New paradigms for social analysis* (165–84). Newbury Park, CA: Sage.

Neitz, M. J. (1995). Feminist theory and religious experience. In R. W. Hood, Jr. (Ed.), *Handbook of religious experience* (520–34). Birmingham, AL: Religious Education Press.

Neitz, M. J. (2000). Queering the Dragonfest: Changing sexualities in a post-patriarchal religion. *Sociology of Religion, 61*, 369–391.

Neitz, M. J. (2003). Dis/Location: Engaging feminist inquiry in the sociology of religion. In M. Dillon (Ed.), *Handbook of the sociology of religion* (pp. 276–293). Cambridge: Cambridge University Press.

Neitz, M. J., & Nason-Clark, N. (2000). Introductory essay, special issue on gender and religion. *Sociology of Religion*, 393–397.

Nesbitt, P. (1997). *Feminization of the clergy in America.* New York: Oxford University Press.

Nesbitt, P. (Ed.). (2001). *Religion and social policy.* Walnut Creek, CA: AltaMira.

Orsi, R. (1996). *Thank you, St. Jude: Women's devotion to the patron saint of hopeless causes.* New Haven, CT: Yale University Press.

Palk, N. A., & Gross, R. M. (2001). *Unspoken worlds: Women's religious lives.* Belmont, CA: Wadsworth/Thomson Learning.

Palmer, S. (1994). *Moon sisters, Krishna mothers, Rajneesh lovers: Women's roles in new religions.* Syracuse, NY: Syracuse University Press.

Palmer, S. (2003). Women's "cocoon work." In L. L. Dawson (Ed.), *New religious movements: Sexual Experimentation and feminine rites of passage* (pp. 245–256). Malden, MA: Blackwell Publishing Ltd.

Peña, M., & Frehill, L.M. (1998). Latina religious practice: Analyzing cultural dimensions in measures of religiosity. *Journal for the Scientific Study of Religion, 37*, 620–635.

Profitt, N. J. (Ed.). (2000). *Women survivors, psychological trauma and the politics of resistance.* New York: Haworth Press.

Ranke-Heinemann, U. (1991). *Eunuchs for the kingdom of God: Women, sexuality and the Catholic church.* New York: Penguin USA.

Rose, S. (1987). Woman warriors: The negotiation of gender in a charismatic community. *Sociological Analysis, 48*, 245–58.

Ruether, R. R. (Ed.). (1974). *Religion and sexism: Images of woman in the Jewish and Christian traditions.* New York: Simon and Schuster.

Ruff, L., Lautard, H., & Nason-Clark, N. (2004). *Keeping God in the classroom: Homeschoolers take the lives of their children's education into their own hands.* Manuscript in preparation.

Russell, M. (1995). *Confronting abusive beliefs: Group treatment for abusive men.* Thousand Oaks, CA: Sage.

Scott, K., & Wolfe, D. (2000). Change among batterers: Examining men's success stories. *Journal of Interpersonal Violence, 15*(8), 827–842.

Shupe, A., Stacey, W. A., & Hazlewood, L. R. (1987). *Violent men, violent couples: The dynamics of domestic violence.* Lexington, MA: D.C. Heath and Company.

Smith, C. (1998). *American evangelicalism: Embattled and thriving.* Chicago: University of Chicago Press.

Smith, D. (1987). *The everyday world as problematic.* Boston, MA: Northeastern University Press.

Spade, J. Z., & Valentine, C. G. (2004). *The kaleidoscope of gender: Prisms, patterns and possibilities.* Belmont, CA: Wadsworth/Thomson Learning.

Spencer-Arsenault, M. (2000). Mother Mary: The (re)construction of a female icon. *Sociology of Religion, 61*(4), 479–483.

Spickard, J., Landres, V, Shawn, J., & McGuire, M. B. (Eds.). (2002). *Personal knowledge and beyond: Shaping the ethnography of religion.* New York: New York University Press.

Stacey, J., & Thorne, B. (1985). The missing feminist revolution in sociology. *Social Problems, 32*(4), 301–16.

Stirling, M. L., Cameron, C. A., Nason-Clark, N., & Miedema, B. (Eds.). (2004). *Understanding abuse: Partnering for change.* Toronto: University of Toronto Press.

Straus, M. A., & Gelles, R. J. (1986). Societal change and change in family violence from 1975 to 1985 as revealed by two national surveys. *Journal of Marriage and the Family, 8,* 465–479.

Sullins, P. (2000). The stained glass ceiling: Career attainment for women clergy. *Sociology of Religion, 61*(3), 243–266.

Swatos, W. H., Jr. (Ed.). (1998). *Encyclopedia of religion and society.* Walnut Creek, CA: AltaMira.

Thorne-Finch, R. (1992). *Ending the silence: The origins and treatment of male violence against women.* Toronto, ON: University of Toronto Press.

Timmins, L., ed. (1995). *Listening to the thunder: Advocates talk about the battered women's movement.* Vancouver: Women's Research Centre.

Wallace, R. A. (1975). Bringing women in: Marginality in the churches. *Sociological Analysis, 36*(4), 291–303.

Wallace, R. A. (1992). *They call her pastor: A new role for Catholic women.* Albany: State University of New York Press.

Wallace, R. A. (1997). The mosaic of research on women: Where are the women? *Journal for the Scientific Study of Religion, 36,* 1–12.

Wallace, R. A. (1997). The mosaic of research on religion: Where are the women? 1995 presidential address. *Journal for the Scientific Study of Religion, 36*(1), 1–13.

Wallace, R. A. (2000). Women and religion: The transformation of leadership roles. *Journal for the Scientific Study of Religion, 39*(4), 4.

Warner, M. (1985). *Alone of all her sex: The myth and the cult of the Virgin Mary.* London: Pan Books (Original work published 1976).

Warner, R. S. (1993). Work in progress toward a new paradigm for the sociological study of religion in the United States, *American Journal of Sociology, 98,* 1044–93.

Warner, R. S., &. Wittner, J.G. (Eds.). (1998). *Gatherings in diaspora: Religious communities and the new immigration.* Philadelphia, PA: Temple University Press.

Websdale, N. (1995). An ethnographic assessment of the policing of domestic violence in rural Eastern Kentucky. *Social Justice, 22*(1), 102–122.

Wessinger, C. (Ed.). (1996). *Religious institutions and women's leadership: New roles inside the mainstream.* Columbia: University of South Carolina Press.

Wiedam, E. (1997). Splitting interests or common causes: Styles of moral reasoning in opposing abortion. In P. E. Becker & N. Eiesland (Eds.), *Contemporary American religion: An ethnographic reader* (pp. 147–168). Newbury Park, CA: Alta Mira/Sage.

Wilcox, M. (2002). When Sheila's a lesbian: Religious individualism among lesbian, gay, bisexual and transgender Christians. *Sociology of Religion, 63*(4), 497–513.

Williams, R. H. (1999). Visions of the good society and the religious roots of American political culture. *Sociology of Religion, 60*(1), 1–34.

Winter, M. T., Lummis, A., & Stokes, A. (1994). *Defecting in place: Women claiming responsibility for their own spiritual lives.* New York: Crossroads.

Wittberg, P. (1994). *The rise and decline of Catholic religious orders: A social movement perspective.* Albany: State University of New York Press.

Wolf-Smith, J. H., & LaRossa, R. (1992). After he hits her. *Family Relations, 41*(3), 324–29.

Wood, J. T. (2003). *Gendered lives: Communication, gender and culture* (5th ed.). Belmont, CA: Wadsworth.

Wuthnow, R. (2003). Studying religion, making it sociological. In M. Dillon (Ed.), *Handbook of the Sociology of Religion* (pp. 16–30). Cambridge: Cambridge University Press.

Zikmund, B., Lummis, A., & Chang, P. (1998). *Clergy women: An uphill calling.* Louisville, KY: Westminster/John Knox Press.

PART IV

RELIGION AND SOCIAL CONTROL

CHAPTER 11

Law

JAMES T. RICHARDSON, J.D., PH.D.

INTRODUCTION

Social control can be exerted in many ways, from the raising of an eyebrow to the murder of someone in a self-help "moralistic killing" (Black, 1999) to right some perceived wrong that has been visited on a person, their family, or clan. Donald Black (1976, 1999), building on the earlier work of Durkheim and of Weber even as he criticizes them, offers four major types of social control (Black, 1999, pp. 6–9), including *penal, compensatory, therapeutic,* and *conciliatory,* with the end goal of each being, respectively, *punishment, restitution, treatment,* and *dispute resolution.* These types of social control, all of which may involve applications of formal law, will be referred to herein, to characterize various approaches to exerting social control over religion and religious groups.

In many modern societies, law has become a social control methodology of choice, often serving to undergird other efforts at social control, even if those other, less formal, methods of social control are more ubiquitous (Richardson, 2001). Those in positions of power can get laws passed that implement their negative evaluation of participants in groups defined as deviant, including religious groups. The process of passage of such specific and targeted laws is a process worth examining, using the dialectical theoretical approach of William Chambliss (Chambliss & Zatz, 1993). Laws already on the books can be applied in innovative ways toward unpopular groups. This process also is of interest to scholars and policy makers. There is much testing of boundaries as authorities seek to exert social control over religion and religious groups, including deviant ones such as New Religious Movements (NRMs). Such experimentation reveals what can and cannot be done, with the approval of those whose opinions matter within a given society or external to the society. Characterizing the various approaches to legal social control will assist in understanding major distinctions in how social control operates concerning religion.

JAMES T. RICHARDSON, J.D., PH.D. • University of Nevada, Reno, NV 89557

LEGAL SOCIAL CONTROL AND TRADITIONAL
RELIGIONS

Traditional religious groups must operate within the confines of the legal structure of a given society, abiding by the constitutional provisions and statutory laws enacted with a given society.[1] However, in many modern societies, it is clear that some religious groups enjoy a position of relative privilege, and that the usual legal structures dealing with religious groups may not be applied to dominant religious organizations in the same way they are used with less popular religions (see chapters in Richardson, 2004a). Indeed, in many European countries, including former communist ones, certain religions are accorded a privileged legal status in the constitution or laws of the country. The Catholic Church has such status in a number of European countries, and also in a number of Latin and South American countries. The Russian Orthodox Church has special legal status in Russia (reaffirmed in recent years since the fall of communism), as does the Greek Orthodox Church in Greece, and the Lutheran Church in Germany, where it shares special legal status with the Catholic Church. In the United Kingdom, the Church of England is defined as the dominant church by law, even to the extent of a legal requirement that the presiding king or queen must be a member (Beckford, 2002). Even in China, one of the last bastions of communism, certain religious groups are designated as officially acceptable, as long as they accede to the dominance of the Communist Party and the Chinese government (Edelman & Richardson, 2003).

The United States, which claims equality of all religious groups as part of its basic values, nonetheless grants special privileges to the Catholic Church as well, through, for instance, the operation of its tax laws. For example, the Catholic Church retains a blanket exemption from filing individual annual tax reporting documents for all its many convents, monasteries, and other communally oriented operations, whereas other religious groups, especially new ones, must prove their right to exempt status annually (Lawrence and Zelenak, 1985). In certain regions of the United States, other denominations occupy a relatively privileged status, including the Latter-Day Saints (Mormons) in Utah and Southern Baptists in the South. Within the confines of federal and state laws and constitution provisions, these religious groups operate as a part of the establishment, with attendant privileges, not as simply an ordinary religious organization subject to various laws.

This latter point invites a potentially fruitful application of concepts from Black's theories to the area of religion, something that has seldom been done (Black, 1976, 1999). Black makes much of the *status* of parties involved in legal actions. His predictions of the "behavior of law" is that law virtually always operates in favor of those of higher status, and is used more frequently by those of higher status, especially in their effort to exert social control over those of lower status. Indeed, he points out that those individuals and institutions of higher status in a society can engage in self-serving *construction of legal systems,* which they can then use to maintain their position of social dominance against pressures from those of lesser status. Chambliss's classic study of the derivation of vagrancy laws (Chambliss, 1964) seems an excellent example of the effects of political power and status, as he points out that labor shortages brought on by the Black Plague led to the first laws being passed forcing people to work, whether they needed to or not. The infamous "enticement statutes" passed in the South after the collapse of Reconstruction made it illegal to offer a job to a former slave at a higher wage, a legal stricture obviously designed to maintain former slaves as agricultural workers on plantations.

Important historical examples of the operation of status in constructing legal systems also can be found in the area of religion. The Russian Orthodox Church (ROC), although initially in favor of religious freedom while still under the yoke of communism, shifted its position rapidly after communism fell. The ROC took a leadership role in getting the liberal laws concerning religion that were established in the early 1990s over-turned in favor of laws that implicitly and explicitly gave a privileged status to the ROC. The ROC worked openly with conservative politicians to accomplish this end, and used relatively powerless minority faiths as pawns in the effort to assert itself as the dominant faith in Russia (Shterin & Richardson, 2000, 2002).

Another variable of import in Black's scheme is personal and cultural *intimacy,* which refer to the degree that people share each other's values and in each other's lives. If people share basic values, or if they know each other personally, then they are able to understand each other, and be able to assist each other in promoting shared values, even if unconsciously. This variable operates within legal systems when those in decision making positions are "intimate with" those about whom decisions are to be made. An example would be a judge who is a member of the dominant religion in a society, hearing a case involving that religious organization. Such occurred in a major legal case in Russia in 1996 when a functionary of the ROC was being sued for libel by members of several small and controversial newer religious groups. That case, fully described in Shterin and Richardson (2002), clearly showed a bias in favor of the ROC in how the case was handled, as well as in the outcome.

The intimacy variable as it operates within the legal system does not, of course, always guarantee that the dominant church will win in legal battles. But, it does mean that the decision maker, if he or she shares the values espoused by the dominant church, will at least understand what representatives of that church organization are saying. Chances are the decision maker may agree with much of what is said, and be sympathetic to the perspective being promoted by the dominant church's representatives. Thus, the odds of the traditionally dominant church being dealt with harshly are lower than would be the case if smaller, controversial, and unfamiliar religious groups were involved.

Another way to state this conclusion is that, in situations involving dominant traditional religious groups, because of the operation of status and intimacy variables, there will be a tendency for social control to operate in a less *penal* or punitive manner toward such groups, and instead there will be more efforts to resolve disputes with *conciliatory* and *therapeutic* processes. In cases in which major religious organizations have been involved in wrongdoing, or the organization sanctioned illegal activities, then the emphasis may well be on *restitution* as opposed to more punitive forms of punishment. It is informative to test this notion by examining the recent major problem with child sex abuse in the Catholic Church using the types of social control developed in Black's theorizing. This problematic area does seem to demonstrate attempts, at least early on, to deal with the scandal less punitively and more therapeutically. Only later, when the full extent of the problem became known, *and* considerable media attention was focused on the issue, was there any serious move toward more punitively oriented legal solutions to the problem, and toward significant restitution.

When a smaller and controversial group does successfully initiate a legal action, or succeed in defending itself against an action brought by parties attempting to ex-ert social control through the legal system, such episodes demand explanation. Such was the case in a major court battle that took place in Hungary in the early 1990s, when the Hare Krishna were successful in a libel action against a major figure in the dominant Protestant church there (Richardson, 1995a). Here again Black's theorizing is helpful, as the concept of *third-party partisanship* can be applied (Black & Baumgartner, 1999). This means that people in positions of power decide, for various reasons, to side with a lower status and "non-intimate" party in its legal battles. This situation will be developed more in the section that follows on minority religions and social control.

LEGAL SOCIAL CONTROL OF NEWER AND SMALLER RELIGIOUS GROUPS[2]

New religious movements (NRMs), pejoratively referred to as "cults" or "sects," have tested the boundaries social control in many societies since they came to public attention several decades ago in the United States. Other, not so new minority faiths also may operate on the margins of acceptable behavior in a society. While informal efforts at social control, especially of the "self-help" variety (Black, 1999), have been very frequent toward participants in such groups, legal and judicial solutions often have been sought, as well, and have sometimes been crucial in support of self-help remedies.

Such efforts at control have been promoted especially by participants in what sociologists call the Anti-Cult Movement (ACM), which started in the United States, and is made up mainly of disaffected former members, parents of participants, and leaders of a few traditional religious groups (Shupe & Bromley, 1980). More recent ACM groups have mimicked the activities of earlier groups critical of more traditional minority faiths such as the Mormons and Jehovah's Witnesses. The ACM has become international in scope, melding the recent American based ACM with older ACM groups, and has expanded to include campaigns against a large number of minority religions (Shupe & Bromley, 1994; Shterin & Richardson, 2000; Barker, 1989). Some political leaders have been quick to join the social control effort being led by ACM groups, even if for reasons of self-interest (see chapters in Richardson, 2004a). Key societal legitimators such as journalists and major news media also contributed, even as they simply were "doing their jobs" as media representatives (Beckford, 1994). Sometimes political, legal, and judicial officials at every level combine efforts, often supported by the media, to exert control over NRMs. See, for example, analysis of the situation in Oregon with social control efforts directed toward the Bhagwan Shree Rjaneesh's group in Richardson (2004b).

The law, therefore, can be a major instrument of social control toward newer and minority religious groups in many societies. The courts function *normatively,* promoting societal values that often are not sympathetic toward minority religions. Courts as well as other parts of institutional social control apparatus in societies can exercise considerable *discretion* as they deal with unpopular religious groups (Richardson, 2000). Such an approach often disadvantages minority faiths within the legal arena, as is well illustrated in places as far removed as the United States, Russia, Japan, and France (see chapters in Richardson, 2004b, and Richardson, 1995a). Legal sanctions against unpopular minority faiths tend to be more punitive in nature, and there is less opportunity to resolve differences through conciliation. Examples of this more *penal* approach include the tax evasion trial of Reverend Moon in the United States (Richardson, 1992; Sherwood, 1991; H. Richardson, 1984), the aforementioned situation with the Rajneesch group in Oregon (Carter, 1990), as well as criminal charges being brought against Christian Science parents who treated their children's illnesses unsuccessfully with Spiritual Healing

(Richardson & DeWitt, 1992). Restitution also is often sought against minority faiths, especially in the United States with its civil legal system designed to allow plaintiffs more access to the courts than is the case in many countries (Anthony & Robbins, 1992, 1995).

The manner in which preexisting laws have been used against NRMs and other minority religious groups in various societies is of interest, as are creative methods whereby legal procedures have been augmented during efforts to exert social control over such religious groups, and new laws are approved. Also notable are variations in the application of law to smaller religious groups in different countries and regions of the world. These major variations on the theme of law as an instrument of social control toward minority faiths will be examined, as will efforts by these groups to make use of the law to challenge their detractors (also see Richardson, 1998b).

EARLY EFFORTS TO CONTROL NRMs

NRMs first came to the attention of the general public and policy makers in the United States in the late 1960s and early 1970s, but they were not viewed initially as a social problem. However, it quickly became clear that some NRMs were "high demand" religions seeking to affect major changes in the lives of participants. Young relatively affluent members of society were dropping out of school to become missionaries, or were fund raising on the streets. Parents of recruits sometimes sought help from government officials, but then ran into the protections of First Amendment of the U.S. Constitution, which guarantees religious freedom. This situation sometimes led to self-help solutions, such as "deprogramming" and the use of the legal system to gain the physical control necessary for deprogramming to occur. Other countries without First Amendment protections adopted a more paternalistic approach toward NRM participants, leading to fewer "self-help" efforts toward NRMs. Instead, the state itself was prone to take official paternalistic actions designed to discourage participation.

Initially the legal system in the United States was used to seek temporary guardianships or "conservatorships," so that parents could gain physical control their children, with the assistance of law enforcement (Bromley, 1983; LeMoult, 1983). Such legal devices allowed attempts to "deprogram" NRM participants. Conservatorship laws have historically had as their main focus allowing adult children to assume legal responsibility for elderly parents no longer able to properly care for themselves. However, conservatorship laws were used successfully against participants in NRMs in the mid-1970s. Courts conveniently overlooked that the fact that the focus of such applications was on young people, usually of a legal age, who had joined a religious group of which their parents did not approve.

Conservatorship laws being used in NRM situations were dealt a severe blow in the United States in 1977 in *Katz v. Superior Court* (73 Cal. App. 3d 952). The California Supreme Court overruled a lower court decision that had allowed the parents of some Unification Church members the right to deprogram their children. This case became persuasive precedent in other legal actions around the country, causing the use of conservatorship laws for purposes of deprogramming to lessen considerably. Efforts were made in a number of U.S. states to expand conservatorship laws to incorporate young adults who had joined religious groups, but none succeeded, although some efforts came close to being fully approved (Flinn, 1987; Guttman, 1985).

"BRAINWASHING" CLAIMS AGAINST NRMs

Claims that participants in NRMs had been "brainwashed" surfaced early in the United States as a part of efforts to exert social control over NRMs (Richardson & Kilbourne, 1983; James, 1986; Barker, 1984). Such claims ultimately failed in conservatorship cases but were found to be effective for a time in civil actions against NRM groups by former members and their parents (Anthony, 1990; Richardson, 1991). Such cases were brought in civil courts, seeking damages for alleged harms that had been done by a religious group and its leaders. Such cases have been popular "self-help" remedies in the United States particularly, as the First Amendment to the U.S. Constitution precluded some overt and direct action by the government against religious groups that were not violating laws. These actions were promoted for a time by organizations in the Anti-Cult Movement, as a way to force NRMs to limit recruiting, or even stop operating if civil damages that might be awarded would bankrupt the groups.

"Brainwashing" claims in these civil actions were used to support several traditional tort claims such as intentional affliction of emotional distress, fraud, and deception. These traditional torts would be claimed in the court filings, but then the plaintiff's argument would discuss, if allowed, "brainwashing" and "mind control," conflating the popular pseudoscientific terms with ordinary tort claims (Ginsburg & Richardson, 1998; Anthony, 1999). Trial judges usually allowed such claims, and juries were prone to accept the claims as valid, as concerns about the groups were acted on by judges and juries, acting in a normative fashion (DeWitt, Richardson, & Warner, 1996; Pfeifer, 1999). Thus, juries often would find liability and award damages that were sometimes quite large (Richardson, 1991). The inherent discretion of the Court and the jurors usually was used in ways favoring those who would attack NRMs using the legal system. Eventually such brainwashed based legal claims also were disallowed, this time by decisions in federal courts (Anthony, 1990).

The major decision in this area was *Fishman v. United States* (1990, N.D. California), a criminal case involving a former Scientology member who was charged with mail fraud. Fishman claimed an insanity defense, saying that he was brainwashed by Scientology into committing criminal acts. This defense was not allowed on the grounds that such explanations were not generally accepted within relevant scientific disciplines. A federal civil case had also seen such theories disallowed two years earlier in a case involving a suit by a former member of Transcendental Meditation (*Kropinski v. World Plan Executive Council* (D.C. Circuit, 1988). Thus such brainwashing-based actions became less prevalent in the United States after these decisions disallowed the testimony of some key proponents of brainwashing theories.

Brainwashing based legal theories were more successful as a defense in cases where those who were kidnapped for purposes of deprogramming later sued their kidnappers and deprogrammers (and sometimes their parents who hired them) in a civil court action, using a false imprisonment claim. Also brainwashing factored into the defense in some of the relatively few times that public prosecutors actually brought criminal kidnapping charges against deprogrammers. The deprogrammers would use a "necessity "or "choice of evils" defense (Bromley & Robbins, 1993; Richardson, 2004a), claiming that, because the deprogramee had been brainwashed and was under mind control, the deprogrammer had done the lesser of two evils in kidnapping the convert and rescuing them from the clutches of the "evil cult." When such defenses were allowed, and they often were, this enabled the defendant an opportunity to discuss the beliefs and lifestyle of the NRM in question, something usually not acceptable under the U.S. Constitution's First Amendment. However, such cases against deprogrammers were rare, and are seldom seen today, in large part because of there being far fewer deprogrammings in the United States, where the furor over NRMs has died down in recent years.

The rarity of these cases against deprogrammers, and their often successful use of brainwashing based defenses, illustrates well the theories of Black (1976, 1999), who would predict that ways would be found to allow those of relatively higher status and who shared values with the decision makers to prevail in such legal actions, or to avoid legal action against themselves altogether. Black also would not be surprised to note the successful use of brainwashing based civil actions that occurred for a number of years. He would note that the parties winning such cases were usually of higher status and shared the values of those doing the decision making in such cases.

Mark Cooney, a student of Black, has written insightfully about the "partisanship of evidence" (Cooney, 1993), a concept with clear implications for the use of pseudoscientific brainwashing based testimony in civil actions against unpopular religious groups. Leaders in the legal system were so intent on finding ways to exert control over NRMs that they were willing to allow very questionable testimony against them. Thus, such evidence received, for a time, a positive sanction by the courts in cases involving the controversial groups. Only after the intervention of some powerful *third-party partisans,* who exerted what they thought were higher values that should be considered in the brainwashing based cases, did the minority faiths begin to occasionally prevail within the legal arena.

Two major groups of third party partisans emerged on behalf of the religions. One grouping included such organizations as the American Civil Liberties Union (ACLU) and the National Council of Churches, both of which took strong positions that kidnapping and deprogramming, as well as civil actions based on brainwashing ideas, were violative of basic civil and human rights of participants in the religious groups. The other major group that acted in ways served the partisan interests of NRMs being sued by former members and others for allegedly brainwashing participants included a number of social scientists whose research did not support brainwashing based claims. Several scholars and organizations became involved in effort to preclude such testimony, with some success, although doing so was not without controversy (Richardson, 1996b, 1998; Robbins, 1998).

Brainwashing based theories also have been promoted in other countries, the critique offered above notwithstanding, and have gained credence outside the United States where NRMs were and still are viewed by some as a major social problem (Richardson, 1996a). Brainwashing-based theories, which also have been applied to other minority faiths in some countries, have become an important cultural export from the United States, where such ideas first came to prominence. The ideology of brainwashing was developed during the decades-long battle against communism, but then were transformed for application against NRMs (Richardson & Kilbourne, 1983; James, 1986; Anthony, 1990, 1999). As a result, brainwashing based ideas diffused from the United States have lent support to claims made in legal cases and legislative efforts at control in a number of other countries (Richardson, 1996a; Anthony, 1999; also see many chapters in Richardson, 2004a). This includes Western ones as well as countries that were formerly affiliated with the former Soviet Union, and even in Catholic regions such as South and Latin America. Brainwashing-based theories continue at the time of this writing to justify hundreds of deprogrammings in Japan, where members of the Unification Church have undergone, and continue to experience, significant numbers of deprogrammings, often with Protestant ministers serving as the deprogrammer (Richardson & Edelman, 2004).

In some other countries, brainwashing-based claims have been used to undergird new legislation designed to make it harder for NRMs to enter the countries and function effectively. This is the case in France, where new legislation passed in 1990 made "mental manipulation," a term referring to "brainwashing," a crime (see chapters on France in Richardson, 2004a). Russia is another where the 1997 revision of a liberal new law concerning religions was approved to control NRMs coming into the country. Often such new laws have the backing of traditional churches, as was the case in Russia, because those traditional churches see such legislation as a way to stop the flood of NRMs from the West.

LEGAL CONCERNS DERIVING FROM PRESENCE
OF CHILDREN IN RELIGIOUS GROUPS

Another major arena of legal action designed to exert control over religious groups involves children. A number of older minority faiths have encountered difficulties in the legal arena over care of children, with the state trying, sometimes successfully, to exert control over children in a religious group, at the expense of parental rights (Wah, 2001). Christian Scientists have had a number of major cases against parents whose children died after being treated with Spiritual Healing methods. Such cases aroused considerable negative publicity for the religion, and has even led to efforts to change laws that were designed to offer some protections for parents who chose to use Spiritual Healing (Richardson & DeWitt, 1992). Jehovah's Witness parents also have encountered difficulties in court cases involving children. Custody battles have been particularly problematic, after one member of a couple withdraws from the family and the church but seeks custody of the children. There also have been battles over forced transfusions that have led to laws being passed giving medical authorities protections if they give a transfusion to a child in order to save its life (Coté & Richardson, 2001; Wah, 1995, 2003).

New Religious Movements have also become embroiled in legal controversies over children. As the NRMs matured, families were often formed, and children were born into the groups, a development that eventually led to two major and sometimes related types of legal problems. Custody battles erupted when one member of a couple in the group decided to divorce their partner or leave the group with their children. Such custody battles sometimes became quite heated, with accusations of all sorts being exchanged. A second problem that arose with the onset of children in the groups was that the State entered the picture to varying degrees, depending on the society, exerting control over how the children were cared for and schooled. Indeed, the state often was obligated to intervene if certain types of accusations were made, and sometimes graphic accusations of child abuse, including sexual abuse, were made in the heat of a custody battle or by ACM representatives intent on harming the group (see, for instance, Swantko, 2004).

Custody of children is always a major issue when couples divorce. The issue becomes even more salient when one member of a couple is of a different faith, and a member of a "high demand" religion that has strict expectations about how to rear children (Bradney, 1999). Courts in most modern societies are supposed to make custody decisions based on the criterion of "best interest of the child," which is a very flexible guideline allowing much discretion on the part of the judge or other authorities of the state (Homer, 1999). Often custody decisions are made that favor the party not a member of a minority religion or other controversial religious group, thus disadvantaging participating parents in such battles, a result in keeping with the predictions based on Black's theory. The court may exercise its judgment in a manner that illustrates the normative function of courts, as the basic values of a society, including the view of what is and is not an acceptable religion, are used to justify a custody decision.

When custody battles become rancorous, claims of various kinds of child abuse may surface, and be communicated via the media or directly to state authorities who may choose, or be obligated, to act on them. In many modern societies in recent decades a plethora of laws designed to protect children have been enacted. These laws have had the overall effect of redefining children as more the property of the state, as opposed to being the property of their parents. These new laws have made it easier to attack religious groups for not treating children as the society expects. Four major areas of law that come into play concerning some NRMs and other minority religions are schooling, corporal punishment, health care, and possible sex abuse of children (see Richardson, 1999, for a fuller discussion of these four areas, as well as Swantko, 2004).

Home schooling is legal in some countries if carried out with reasonable supervision of the state authorities to ensure that the child is being given at least a minimal education. But, in some societies, France and Germany, for instance, home schooling is not legal to the degree it is in the United States and other societies. Some religious groups also practice corporal punishment with children, spanking them for misbehavior. Spanking can, and has been, quickly translated by the media into "beating" the children, which is, of course, thought to be child abuse by most citizens and policy makers. Such claims have arisen in custody disputes involving NRMs in a number of countries. Health care needs of children in minority religions are also of concern for authorities of the state, and, as noted, this is also an issue that impacts older minority faiths. These concerns have been made more prominent in recent decades by controversies over the blood transfusion issue with the Jehovah's Witnesses and the "Spiritual Healing" practices of the Christian Scientists.

These concerns notwithstanding, the most significant accusation that can and has been raised against some NRMs is that of child sex abuse. Such accusations have become more prevalent in child custody disputes in divorce actions of ordinary people in society. Such claims change the entire dynamic of a divorce action, as has been demonstrated many times. When they are made in a situation involving a controversial NRM, then the impact is even greater, and can lead to immediate state intervention in a number of countries around the world. Large numbers of children of NRM members have been seized in raids by state authorities in Argentina, Australia, France, the United States, and there have been interventions involving smaller numbers of children in other countries (Palmer, 1999, Richardson, 1999; Swantko, 2004). In all of these instances, the children have eventually been returned to their parents, and the charges dropped. But, the damage done to accused groups has been immense, and represents an ultimate kind of social control.

OTHER LEGAL ISSUES RAISED AFFECTING MINORITY RELIGIOUS GROUPS

There are many other legal issues that have been raised around the world concerning minority religions (Emory and Zelenak, 1985). The outcomes of these other legal conflicts usually also are easily interpreted using Black's explanation of how the law operates. Communal NRMs have sometimes run afoul of zoning regulations that limit the number of unmarried adults who can live in a residence. Solicitation laws have been enforced in various countries in an attempt to stop NRMs from raising money. The Unification Church has won many such battles in the United States, but in other countries the legal precedents are not so helpful. In the United States, the Hare Krishna have found limits placed on their solicitation for funds in airports and other public settings. Laws requiring contribution to social security and health schemes have been applied to communal NRMs in some countries, as have minimum wage statutes, thereby undercutting some of the benefits of communal living. Immigration laws have been used to limit the ingress of members of some NRMs to various countries, including the United States, but also other countries such as those of the former Soviet Union, some of which have imposed severe restrictions on members of some NRMs and other minority religions coming into the country (Shterin & Richardson, 1998, 2000).

One of the most complicated legal situations involving an NRM may be that of the Bhagwan Rajneesh group that settled in Antelope, Oregon, in the 1980s (Carter, 1990; Richardson, 2004b). The Rajneesh group bought up the entire town and controlled all that occurred there. Only members or invited guests could be present in the town. This had many ramifications, as the group ran the local schools, the local police force, and was serving as the local government for the town. The state of Oregon, working closely with federal government agencies and the courts, managed to exert control over the situation after many legal battles, by claiming that to assist the town in any way (such as sending state revenues to fund operation of the schools and law enforcement) would violate the Anti-Establishment Clause of the U.S. and Oregon constitutions. This view prevailed, and led to the demise of the group in Oregon, although not before a violent backlash developed by some leaders of the group.

USE OF LAW BY MINORITY FAITHS

New and small religious groups have sometimes been able to use the legal system in their defense, especially in countries such as the United States, which has First Amendment protection for religious freedom. Many other Western-oriented countries have statutory or constitutional provisions that allow minority religions to take legal action against those who criticize them or refuse to allow privileges granted to other religious organizations.[3] Such legal actions might include suits against tax officials who have exercised their judgment in ways that preclude a minority religion from claiming tax exemptions available to other religious organizations. Scientology has had some success in legal battles with tax officials and other governmental agencies in a number of countries, and thus has succeeded in getting the organization granted legal privileges that otherwise would not have been obtained. Also, a number of NRMs and other minority religions are attempting to make use of the European Court of Human Rights (ECHR) in an effort to deter the exercise of legal social control over them in the more than 40 Council of Europe countries, which includes a growing number of former Soviet Union countries. So far this record is decidedly mixed, as the ECHU prefers a posture of deferring to member countries in matters having to do with religion (Richardson & Garay, 2004).

Scientology is perhaps the best-known NRM for using legal action as a way to deter detractors and promote its organization. Other NRMs also have developed legal prowess, even if only via the process of being forced to defend the organization or its leaders and members in court actions. Jehovah's Witnesses have also made heavy use of litigation, both defensively and offensively, winning some major battles in the United States and

Canada (Coté & Richardson, 2001), as well as before the European Court of Human Rights (Richardson & Garay, 2004). This tactic causes a major allocation of group resources toward legal action, as has been done with the Witnesses, Scientology, and the Unification Church, particularly. However, many other minority faiths also have had to expend resources in legal battles, something that may "deform" such groups, and detract from the group's overall goals. Such has occurred with "brainwashing" based cases for damages by former NRM members in civil actions. But, particularly with the advent of efforts by various governments to assume authority over children of group members, some groups such as The Family (formerly known as the Children of God), have invested heavily in developing an adequate legal defense. The Witnesses also have fought many legal battles over control of their children in terms of lifestyle and blood transfusions.

Some NRMs also have launched liable and defamation actions against their detractors, a tactic that is not usually successful but that has been on occasion. In Hungary, the Hare Krishna won a major victory against a prominent religious leader who had published a brochure defaming the group. However, in Russia, a major defamation action failed against a prominent representative of the Russian Orthodox Church who published extreme accusations against a number of NRMs and other minority faiths. This case was actually used by the ROC and political authorities in the successful effort to gain approval for restrictive legislation that would limit the activities of NRMs in Russia.

CONCLUSIONS

The law is a major instrument of social control over all religions, religious groups, and participants. However, the law is selective in how it operates toward religious entities, depending on major variables such as status and intimacy (Black, 1976, 1999). Also, the behavior of law toward religious groups is importantly affected by the actions of third party partisans (Black & Baumgartner, 1999), which may upset the usual pattern of treatment of religious groups under a given legal system.

Traditional religions, especially those that hold a dominant position in a society, generally fare well when dealing with the legal system. Indeed, such entities make use of the law to work their will as well as to defend the organization when attacked. Dominant religious groups can even assist in constructing legal systems in ways that protect the major religious group. This has been done in a number of societies, as dominant religious groups support passage of laws that limit the actions of potential competitors, from both inside and outside the society, as well as grant the dominant religion special privileges (Richardson, 2000).

Minority religious groups have, in some societies, legal weapons that can be used in battles for legitimacy. Such groups can and have sometimes successfully defended themselves against legal attacks, and have been able to launch their own legal battles that have sometimes had a positive outcome for the organization and its members. In other societies, particularly those dominated by one particular traditional religious organization, the exercise of legal rights for smaller faiths has been decidedly more difficult. Indeed, unsurprisingly, such groups usually lose in legal actions whatever the societal context, as the courts exercise their normative function and make decisions in line with the basic values of a given society. When minority religions win in court this is surprising, and demands explanation. But such situations are not frequent, and the conclusion must be drawn that overall the relatively lower status and unpopular religious groups do not usually fare very well in the legal arena, a finding that fits with the theorizing of Black, as has been noted.

NOTES

1. In an age of globalization certainly there are agencies of social control that transcend national boundaries. Those that are particularly germane to this analysis are transnational judicial bodies such as the European Court of Human Rights. Also, the mass media are transnational and play a key role in exerting control over groups defined as deviant.
2. This section is an enlarged version of a presentation in Richardson (2001).
3. Sometimes, minority religious groups may lack legal standing if they have not followed rules about legal registration of the group, which is another form of legal discrimination against such groups (Durham, 1999; Richardson, 2004a).

REFERENCES

Anthony, D. (1999). Pseudoscience and minority religions: An evaluation of the brainwashing theories of Jean-Marie Abgrall. *Social Justice Research, 12*, 421–456.

Anthony, D. (1990). Religious movements and brainwashing litigation: Evaluating key testimony. In T. Robbins & D. Anthony (Eds.), *In Gods we trust* (2nd ed., pp. 295–344). New Brunswick, NJ: Transaction Books.

Anthony, D., & Robbins, T. (1992). Law, social science, and the "brainwashing" exception to the First Amendment. *Behavioral Sciences and the Law, 10*, 5–30.

Anthony, D., & Robbins, T. (1995). Negligence, coercion, and the protection of religious belief. *Journal of Church and State, 37*, 509–537.

Barker, E. (1989). *New religious movements: A practical introduction.* London: HMSO.

Barker, E. (1984). *The making of a Moonie: Brainwashing or choice?* Oxford: Blackwell.

Beckford, J. A. (2002). Banal discrimination: Equality of respect for beliefs and worldviews in the UK. In D. Davis & G. Besier (Eds.), *International perspectives on freedom and equality of religious belief.* Waco, TX: Baylor University Press.

Black, D. (1999). *The social structure of right and wrong.* New York: Academic Press.

Black, D. (1976). *The behavior of law.* New York: Academic Press.

Black, D., & Baumgartner, M. P. (1999). Toward a theory of the third party. In D. Black (Ed.), *The structure of right and wrong* (pp. 95–124). New York: Academic Press.

Bradney, A. (1999). Children of a newer God: The English courts, custody disputes, and NRMs. In S. Palmer & C. Hardman (Eds.), *Children and new religions* (pp. 210–226). New Brunswick: NJ: Rutgers University Press.

Bromley, D. (1983). Conservatorships and deprogramming: Legal and political perspectives. In D. Bromley & J. T. Richardson (Eds.), *The brainwashing/deprogramming controversy* (pp. 267–293). New York: Edwin Mellen.

Bromley, D., & Robbins, T. (1993). The role of government in regulating new and unconventional religions. In J. Wood & D. Davis (Eds.), *The role of government in monitoring and regulating religion in public life* (pp. 205–240). Waco, TX: Baylor University.

Carter, L. (1990). *Charisma and control in Rajneeshpuram.* Cambridge: Cambridge University Press.

Chambliss, W. (1964). A sociological analysis of the law of vagrancy. *Social Problems, 12*, 45–67.

Chambliss, W., & Zatz, M. (1993). *Making Law.* Bloomington: Indiana University Press.

Cooney, M. (1993). Evidence as partisanship. *Law and Society Review, 28*, 833–858.

Coté, P., & Richardson, J. T. (2001). Disciplined litigation, vigilant litigation, and deformation: Dramatic organization change in Jehovah's Witnesses. *Journal for the Scientific Study of Religion, 40*, 11–26.

DeWitt, J., Richardson, J. T., & Warner, L. (1996). Novel scientific evidence in controversial cases: A social psychological analysis. *Law and Psychology Review, 21*, 1–26.

Edelman, B., & Richardson, J. T. (2003). Falon Gong and the law: Development of legal social control in China. *Nova Religio, 6*, 312–331.

Emory, M., & Zelenak, L. (1985). The tax exempt status of communitarian religious organizations: An unnecessary controversy? In T. Robbins, W. Shepherd, & J. McBride (Eds.), *Cults, Culture, and the Law* (pp. 177–204). Chico, CA: Scholars Press.

Flinn, F. (1987). Criminalizing conversion: The legislative assault on new religions. In J. M. Day & W. S. Laufer (Eds.), *Crime, values, and religion* (pp. 153–192). Norwood, NJ: Ablex.

Ginsburg, G., & Richardson, J. T. (1998). "Brainwashing" evidence in light of *Daubert*. In H. Reece (Ed.), *Law and science* (pp. 265–288). Oxford: Oxford University Press.

Guttman, J. (1985). The legislative assault on new religions. In T. Robbins, W. Shepherd, & J. McBride (Eds.), *Cults, culture, and the law* (pp. 101–110). Chico, CA: Scholars Press.

Homer, M. (1999). The precarious balance between freedom of religion and best interests of the child. In S. Palmer & C. Hardman (Eds.), *Children and new religions* (pp. 187–209). New Brunswick, NJ: Rutgers University Press.

James, G. (1986). Brainwashing: The myth and actuality. *Thought: A Review of Culture and Ideas, 61*, 241–257.

LeMoult, J. (1983). Deprogramming members of religious sects. In D. Bromley & J. T. Richardson (Eds.), *The brainwashing/deprogramming controversy* (pp. 234–257). New York: Edwin Mellen.

Palmer, S. (1999). Frontiers and families: The children of Island Pond. In S. Palmer & C. Hardman (Eds.), *Children in new religions* (pp. 153–171). New Brunswick, NJ: Rutgers University Press.

Palmer, S., & Hardman, C. (1999). *Children in new religions.* New Brunswick, NJ: Rutgers University Press.

Pheifer, J. (1999). Perceptual biases and mock juror decision-making: Minority religions in court. *Social Justice Research, 12,* 409–420.

Richardson, H. (1984). *Constitutional issues in the case of Rev. Moon.* New York: Edwin Mellen Press.

Richardson, J. T. (1991). Cult/brainwashing cases and the freedom of religion. *Journal of Church and State, 33,* 55–74.

Richardson, J. T. (1992). Public opinion and the tax evasion trial of Reverend Moon. *Behavioral Sciences & the Law, 10,* 53–64.

Richardson, J. T. (1995a). Legal status of minority religions in the United States. *Social Compass, 42,* 249–264.

Richardson, J. T. (1995b). Minority religions ("cults") and the law: Comparisons of the United States, Europe, and Australia. *University of Queensland Law Journal, 18,* 183–207.

Richardson, J. T. (1996a). "Brainwashing" claims and minority religions outside the United States: Cultural diffusion of a questionable legal concept in the legal arena. *Brigham Young University Law Review,* 873–904.

Richardson, J. T. (1996b). Sociology and the new religions: "Brainwashing," the courts, and religious freedom. In P. Jenkins & S. Kroll-Smith (Eds.), *Witnessing for sociology* (pp. 115–134). Westport, CT: Praeger.

Richardson, J. T. (1998a). Accidental expert. *Nova Religio, 2,* 31–43.

Richardson, J. T. (1998b). Law and minority religions: "Positive" and "negative" uses of the legal system. *Nova Religio, 2,* 93–107.

Richardson, J. T. (1999). Social control of new religions: From "brainwashing" claims to child sex abuse accusations. In S. Palmer & C. Hardman (Eds.), *Children in new religions* (pp. 172–186). New Brunswick, NJ: Rutgers University Press.

Richardson, J. T. (2000). Discretion and discrimination in legal cases involving controversial religious groups and allegations of ritual abuse. In R. Ahdar (Ed.), *Law and religion.* Aldershot, UK:Ashgate.

Richardson, J. T. (2001). Law, social control, and minority religions. In P. Cote (Ed.), *Chercheurs de dieux dans l'espace [Public–frontier religions in public space]* (pp. 139–198). Ottawa: University of Ottawa Press.

Richardson, J. T. (2004a). *Regulating religion: Case studies from around the globe.* New York: Kluwer.

Richardson, J. T. (2004b). State and federal cooperation in regulating new religions: Oregon versus the Bhagwan Rajneesh. In J. T. Richardson (Ed.), *Regulating religion* (pp. 477–490). New York: Kluwer.

Richardson, J. T., & DeWitt, J. (1992). Christian Science spiritual healing, the law, and public opinion. *Journal of Church and State, 34,* 549–562.

Richardson, J. T., & Edelman, B. (2004). Cult controversies and legal developments concerning new religions in Japan and China. In J. Richardson (Ed.), *Regulating religion* (pp. 359–380). New York: Kluwer.

Richardson, J. T., & Garay, A. (2004). *The European Court of Human Rights and Former Communist State.* In D. M. Jeroliniov, S. Zrinščak, & Irena Borowik (Eds.), *Religion and Patterns of Social Transformation* (pp. 223–234) Zagreb: Institute of Social Research.

Richardson, J. T., & Introvigne, M. (2001). "Brainwashing" theories in European parliamentary and administrative reports on "cults and sects." *Journal for the Scientific Study of Religion, 40,* 143–168.

Richardson, J. T., & Kilbourne, B. (1983). Classical and contemporary applications of brainwashing models: A comparison and critique. In D. Bromley & J. T. Richardson (Eds.), *The brainwashing/deprogramming controversy* (pp. 29–46). New York: Edwin Mellen Press.

Robbins, T. (1998). In B. Zablocki & T. Robbins (Eds.), *Misunderstanding Cults.* Toronto: University of Toronto Press.

Sherwood, C. (1991). *Inquisition: The persecution and prosecution of the Reverend Sun Myung Moon.* Washington, DC: Regnary Gateway.

Shterin, M., & Richardson, J. T. (2002). The *Yakunin v. Dworkin* trial and the emerging religious pluralism in Russia. *Religion in Eastern Europe, 22*, 1–38.

Shterin, M., & Richardson, J. T. (2000). Effects of the Western anti-cult movement on development of laws concerning religion in post-communist Russia. *Journal of Church and State, 42*, 247–272.

Shterin, M., & Richardson, J. T. (1998). Local laws on religion in Russia: Precursors of Russia's national law. *Journal of Church and State, 40*, 319–341.

Shupe, A., & Bromley, D. (1994). *Anti-cult movements in cross-cultural perspective.* New York: Garland.

Shupe, A., & Bromley, D. (1980). *The new vigilantes.* Beverly Hills, CA: Sage.

Swatko, J. (2004). The Twelve Tribes Messianic Communities, the anti-cult movement, and governmental response. In J. Richardson (Ed.), *Regulating religion* (pp. 179–200). New York: Kluwer.

Wah, C. (2003). Restrictions on religious training and exposure in child custody and visitation orders: Do they protect or harm the child? *Journal of Church and State, 45*, 765–786.

Wah, C. (2001). Jehovah's Witnesses and child custody cases in the United States 1996–1998. *Review of Religious Research, 42*, 372–386.

Wah, C. (1995). The custodial parent's right to control religious training: Absolute or limited? *American Journal of Family Law, 9*, 207–217.

CHAPTER 12

Crime/Deviance

John P. Hoffmann and Stephen J. Bahr

The relationship between religion and deviance has been explored for many years. In fact, some of the seminal works in the sociology of religion addressed deviant behavior such as crime and suicide. The most famous of these works were written by Emile Durkheim, but several other founders of the modern social sciences, such as Branislow Malinowski, André Michel Guerry, and Adolph Quetelet, also considered whether crime, suicide, or other forms of deviance were associated with religious affiliation, participation, or other aspects of society's spiritual life. It should come as no surprise that these early scholars studied religion and deviance. After all, they were highly concerned with factors that made society, or more precisely social cohesion, possible, and religion has long been seen as a key integrative institution for good, as many early functionalists contended, or for ill, as implied by Marx and Freud (Bainbridge, 1989). Deviance, in its many forms, is seen as disruptive to the social fabric, and thus as something that religion should, in some way, attenuate.

Although it has been 100 or more years since these fathers of the social sciences completed their seminal studies, there continues to be a search for the types of relationships that might exist between religion and deviance. The terms moral communities, social integration, and hellfire hypothesis have become commonplace in both the sociology of religion and the sociology of deviance, including its subdisciplines such as criminology, suicidology, and the sociology of mental health. However, it is now a good time to step back and assess in broad strokes the research that has addressed religion and deviance. Much of this research is published in major deviance and sociology of religion journals, but there is a surprising lack of cross-fertilization between the core disciplines. An unfortunate consequence of the growing compartmentalization of the social sciences in general and sociology in particular is the heavy inbreeding that frequently occurs. For instance, many criminologists who are interested in the effects of religion address their work primarily toward other criminologists. Although there are exceptions to this trend, we contend that additional cross-fertilization will lead to better and more comprehensive research about the relationships among religion and the various behaviors that fall under the general scope of deviance.

John P. Hoffmann • Brigham Young University, Provo, Utah, 84602
Stephen J. Bahr • Brigham Young University, Provo, Utah, 84602

This chapter provides an overview of theory and research on religion and deviance. Deviance may be conceptualized to include many different behaviors and other chapters in this volume are designed to cover some of these activities. Therefore, the focus of this chapter is limited to crime, drug use, suicide, family violence, sexual deviance, and a brief section on religion as deviance (a topic perhaps deserving of its own chapter-length treatment; see Stark & Bainbridge, 1997, Part 2). We then discuss some areas that we see as needing particular attention by researchers interested in religion and deviance.

Before beginning, however, it is important to mention that, true to the etymological origin of the term *deviance*, we attempt to stay away from making ethical judgments about the behaviors discussed. Although there are many thorny issues involved in how individuals or groups judge these behaviors, deviance, for us, implies primarily behaviors that diverge from normal standards of behavior. Of course, as long recognized by legal scholars, philosophers, and social scientists, what constitutes normal standards is socially and culturally constructed (Horne, 2001). Hence, there is no simple rule of thumb for deciding which activities are deviant and which are normative. In some societies behavior that is considered deviant is considered normative in others (e.g., tattooing among traditional Maori vs. Old World Amish). Behaviors are also bounded temporally, with changing attitudes leading to redefinitions of deviant acts as normative or vice versa (e.g., ritual suicide [*seppuku*] among Samurai). We have thus opted to follow the list of deviant behaviors found in most textbooks and journals that specialize in this area. We deviate from this list, however, as we do not include mental illness or delinquency, because other chapters in this volume address them.

CRIME AND RELIGION

There is no shortage of studies on crime and religion. One estimate puts the average number of studies of this topic at two per year since the late 1960s (Baier & Wright, 2001). However, because a majority of most forms of criminal activities involves offenders ages 20 and younger (Steffensmeier & Allen, 2000), and because surveying adolescents—who often provide a captive sample—is less expensive than surveying adults, the bulk of research on crime and religion concerns adolescent involvement in delinquency.[1] Likewise, many of the prominent theories of criminal behavior focus mainly on delinquency. Social control, social learning, and general strain theories of crime, for example, were developed to explain youthful offending. Studies of religion and crime have tended to follow this pattern, with research on the hellfire hypothesis (Hirschi & Stark, 1969; Stark 1996) and studies of moral communities (Benda 1995) addressing primarily delinquent conduct. Because Chapter 13 of this volume focuses on delinquency, this section addresses the more modest field of adult crime.

A fundamental supposition of research on religion and crime is that, since most religious traditions prohibit engagement in most forms of crime, especially those considered *mala in se* (e.g., robbery, burglary, rape, murder), membership in a religious tradition or a high concentration of religious adherents in an area should reduce involvement in criminal behavior. Research that addresses the macro-level version of this hypothesis finds the expected negative association (Kposowa et al., 1995; Stark & Bainbridge, 1997). In particular, Bainbridge (1989) demonstrates that church membership rates (including Jewish synagogue membership rates) in U.S. metropolitan areas are negatively associated with assault, robbery, burglary, and larceny, but not with murder or rape. These significant associations persist in the presence of controls for other socially integrative factors such as residential mobility, divorce rates, and poverty rates. One explanation for these crime-specific effects is that religious affiliations, and the attitudes they inculcate, are more likely to deter deliberative crimes than "crimes of passion" (Bainbridge, 1989).

The thread of research on macro-level religion and crime has been extended in two directions. First, international research supports the notion that religious affiliation and attendance are negatively associated chiefly with property crimes such as burglary and larceny rather than violent crimes such as murder and rape (Ellis & Peterson, 1996). However, a Swedish study suggests that church membership rates are negatively associated with violent crimes but not property crimes (Pettersson, 1991). Hence, there are some inconsistencies that may be nation-specific but that should be considered in macro-studies of crime and religion. Nonetheless, it seems clear at this point that any association between religion and crime rates is crime-specific; global indicators of crime conflate the issue.

Second, Lee and Bartkowski (2004a,b) have recently described an important process that may provide a more persuasive theoretical link between religion and crime rates than has previous research. Their community resource perspective argues that communities draw upon certain interpersonal resources to attenuate the likelihood of crime. Rather than viewing the lack of institutional control or access as providing opportunities for crime, as social disorganization theory predicts, they contend that the presence of civic participatory programs enhances social networks and trust among community members and increases guardianship of residences and supervision of residents. Civic engagement in communities involves both religious and secular organizations, but each may function as a community resource that attenuates crime. Their perspective dovetails well with Sampson's (2002) work on collective efficacy as a community resource that attenuates violent victimization. It is also consistent with recent research that suggests that volunteer work, including faith-based activities, diminishes involvement in criminal behavior and attenuates the risk of arrest (Hoffmann & Xu, 2002; Uggen & Janikula, 1999). In an analysis of U.S. counties, Lee and Bartkowski (2004a) find that religious civic participation is associated with lower adult and juvenile homicide rates, even after controlling for the influences of other social integrative factors (e.g., divorce rates, population turnover, unemployment rates).

Although macro-level research provides compelling evidence that religious factors are associated with lower crime rates, the bulk of the attention centers on whether those who attend religious services, practice religious observances, or hold religious beliefs are less likely to commit criminal acts. The hellfire hypothesis formulated by Hirschi and Stark (1969), based on Hirschi's social control theory, predicts that, because most religious traditions condemn criminal activities and provide justification for abstaining from them (e.g., risking exile in the fires of hell, *hutama*, or *gehenna*), religious adherents are less likely to commit crimes than are others. However, as discussed in Chapter 13, evidence for the hellfire hypothesis has been inconsistent. Hence, there have been several attempts to contextualize it by focusing on the surrounding community. As Stark and Bainbridge (1997) argue, whether religious factors attenuate involvement in crime depends on whether the community supports religious-based moral sanctions. This moral communities hypothesis contends that when the community has a high concentration of religious adherents it will see a significant negative association between individual-level religion and criminal involvement. Consistent with key sociological principles, a large proportion of religious adherents provides support and integration—through networks, shared norms, and similar beliefs—of basic behavioral proscriptions and prescriptions. Thus, religious norms are reinforced in moral communities.

The moral communities hypothesis has been examined routinely with individual-level data among adolescents (Baier & Wright, 2001), but rarely with adult samples. In one exception, Welch et al. (1991) use data from adult Catholics in the United States. Defining the local moral community as respondents' parishes, they examine three forms of deviance (using a question that asks respondents to report their *likelihood* of committing the act) and find that individual-level private religiosity and a parish-level aggregate measure of private religiosity are associated modestly with a lower likelihood of tax evasion, alcohol use, and pilfering from one's employer. The effects are modest, however, and tests for interactions between the two religiosity measures yield no significant results. Hence, their study casts doubt on a moral communities explanation of the relationship between religiosity and adult crime.

Other individual-level studies attempt to further contextualize the relationship between religion and criminal involvement by considering (1) crime-specific effects, (2) specific aspects of religious beliefs and behaviors, and (3) potential indirect effects of religion on criminal involvement. For example, the antiasceticism hypothesis suggests that the main attenuating effect of religion involves those behaviors for which secular moral prescriptions have diminished. When secular denunciation remains powerful, there should be a modest or negligible association between religiosity and crime (Grasmick et al., 1991a; Tittle & Welch, 1983). Note that this hypothesis may complement macro-level studies, as they suggest that religious affiliation is associated primarily with property crimes rather than crimes against persons; the latter being more widely condemned by secular norms. Research on the antiasceticism hypothesis, however, indicates that religious service attendance and religious salience are associated with a lower intention to cheat on taxes, but not on intentions to commit theft (Grasmick et al., 1991a, 1991b), so carefully differentiating between particular offenses remains important. A key finding, moreover, is that religious salience is more consequential than religious service attendance in predicting intentions to cheat on taxes.

Another thread of this research has attempted to pay even closer attention to how religion is measured. Evans et al. (1995), for example, utilize four measures of religion: Membership in a conservative denomination, religious activities (attendance at various religion-sponsored events), religious salience (importance of religion in one's life), and "hellfire" (fear of God's punishment for misdeeds). After adjusting for the effects of secular controls such as fear of legal sanctions and informal social constraints, they find that only religious activities significantly influence involvement in adult criminality. Perhaps the networks and moral messages that are instilled during these activities are particularly influential in deterring criminal behavior. It is also likely, however, that the effects of religious measures on criminal behavior are indirect and channeled through secular controls, social networks, and perceptions of likely sanctions.

For instance, Grasmick et al. (1991a) show that the effects of religious salience and attendance on intentions to cheat on taxes are channeled largely through the presumed shame (expected feelings of guilt) and embarrassment (loss of respect by people one values), especially the former, which such a deviant act would cause.

Addressing the potential indirect effects of religion on crime is a promising avenue. As shown in several chapters of this volume and in numerous studies (e.g., Benda, 2002; Evans et al., 1995; Petee et al., 1994; Smith, 2003; Smith et al., 1999), religion in its various guises is associated with several intra- and interpersonal characteristics that are negatively related to criminal behavior. Religious participation, beliefs, and other aspects of one's spiritual life have been linked to low aggressiveness, altruism, shame at the prospect of wrongdoing, low self-arousal, high self-control, happiness, positive coping strategies, volunteerism, high parental supervision and moral expectations, strong parent-child attachments, and low peer deviance. Several of these characteristics are key components of prominent criminological theories such as social bonding, self-control, deterrence, symbolic interaction, social learning, and general strain. For instance, high levels of religious participation and salience may expose individuals to conforming peers, enhance normative identities, provide coping resources, and heighten expectations of shame or punishment at the prospect of criminal involvement. These potentialities suggest that religion is indirectly linked to certain forms of criminal behavior. The task for future research is to explore these links in greater detail.

DRUG USE AND RELIGION

Most research indicates that there is a negative relationship between religious involvement and drug use. Religious affiliates tend to have lower rates of drug use than nonaffiliates. Regardless of denomination, people who attend religious services regularly are less likely to use drugs than those who do not attend regularly. Individuals who belong to religious groups that teach abstinence have lower rates of drug use than those in religious groups that do not proscribe the use of alcohol, tobacco, or other drugs (Bahr & Hawks, 1995; Benda & Corwyn, 1997; Benson, 1992; Clarke et al., 1990). Most studies have focused on alcohol and marijuana use, although similar results have been found for tobacco and other drugs (Benson, 1992).

The negative association between religion and drug use is relatively consistent regardless of the measure of religion (e.g., attendance, public vs. private religiosity, core beliefs) or the type of substance studied (Bahr et al., 1998; Benson, 1992; Litchfield et al., 1997). The evidence is fairly consistent across a variety of samples in different geographical regions and time periods. The findings are similar among males and females, adolescents and adults, and different minority groups (Benson, 1992; Clarke et al., 1990).

It appears that religion may have a stronger influence on drug use than on deviant behaviors such as property or violent crime. The antiasceticism hypothesis explains this general finding by focusing on the social context of religion and drug use. If religion is only one among a number of social control and learning mechanisms, then it may duplicate control and learning from secular organizations. For example, there are strong cultural norms against interpersonal violence. Thus, whether or not one belongs to a religious organization, there are numerous ways secular organizations teach against and control violence. Because religious organizations reproduce what secular organizations do to control violence, it is not surprising that religious involvement often has little association with violence, net the effects of other variables. By contrast, there is little consensus about the use of alcohol and other drugs. Efforts to limit alcohol and drug use do not appear to be as strong in secular organizations as they are in many religious organizations. Thus, religious organizations may add unique controls not provided in the broader community. The result is that the association between religiosity and drug use is stronger than the association between religiosity and violence.

Although researchers consistently report that religiosity is inversely associated with drug use, the size of the association tends to be modest. Benson's (1992) review finds that coefficients range from −.10 to −.30, with an average coefficient of about −.20 for alcohol, tobacco, and marijuana. Measures of private religiosity, such as prayer, appear to be stronger predictors of drug use than measures of public religiosity, such as religious service attendance (Benda & Corwyn, 1997; Litchfield et al., 1997). When compared to other predictors of drug use, religiosity tends to be stronger than personality constructs (self-esteem, internal locus of control) and social class but not as strong as peer associations or parental characteristics (Benson, 1992).

An understanding of how religiosity affects drug use has been hampered by a lack of theoretical development (Benda, 1995, 2002; Benda & Corwyn, 1997). One of the major theoretical orientations used to explain religion and drug use is social control theory. According to this perspective, individuals develop bonds to society that restrain them from using drugs. Bonds to religious organizations deter drug use in several ways. First, individuals become attached to a faith community and its members. Because of this attachment and the negative sanctions that may follow drug use, those who attend services are less likely to use drugs than those who do not. Second, involvement in religious activities allows less time for drug experimentation. Involvement also may provide a network of support that insulates people from opportunities to use drugs. Third, commitment to a religious organization and its goals provides existential meaning that makes drug use less attractive. Fourth, the belief system of most religious groups opposes drug use and their teachings may reinforce personal beliefs against use. In short, religious organizations tend to involve people in conventional activities and a social network that disapproves of illicit drug use.

Another theoretical perspective frequently used to explain the association between religious involvement and drug use is social learning theory (Akers, 1992). According to this view, religion plays an important role in shaping attitudes about drug use. Religious organizations often instruct participants to refrain from drug use. They also provide an interpersonal network in which drug use may be considered inappropriate, harmful, or evil. If through religious activities individuals develop a network of friends who do not use drugs and whose attitudes are not tolerant of drug use, participation may reinforce attitudes against drug use. Even those who have friends who use drugs might refrain from use if they receive high levels of counterbalancing definitions from religious teachings and activities.

Both of these theories provide insights into the process of how religion influences drug use. Social control theorists assume that bonds to a religious organization and to others who are involved in the organization deter drug use. Social learning theorists focus on the learning of antidrug definitions through direct teachings and networks of non-drug-using peers. Nonetheless, this does not exhaust the theoretical perspectives that have been employed to explain drug use. Theories of deterrence, genetics/biological mechanisms, symbolic interaction, strain/anomie, self-esteem/self-derogation, rational choice, and various combinations of these perspectives also have been used to describe the etiology of drug use and abuse (Akers, 1992; Chaloupka et al., 1999; Hesselbrock et al., 1999) but rarely have discussed religion.

An important debate is whether or not the relationship between religiosity and drug use is spurious. Some maintain that religiosity has no effect after other relevant variables, such as peers and family, are taken into account. However, most research shows that even after relevant controls are introduced, a significant relationship between religiosity and drug use remains (Bahr et al., 1998; Benda & Corwyn, 1997; Cochran, 1993; Cochran et al., 1994; Cretacci, 2002; Harris, 1999).

The level of disorganization in the community may affect the association between religion and drug use. Johnson et al. (2000b) find, for example, that among inner-city African-American youth, church attendance is negatively associated with both drug use and nondrug crimes. Using a different data set, Johnson et al. (2000a) show that church attendance is inversely associated with various types of crime even after controlling for non-religious social bonding and social learning variables. They speculate that in communities that are more stable and organized, religious involvement is not needed to help deflect youth from drug use. In disorganized communities, however, the church may be one of the only protective institutions that decreases the attraction to drug use and other illegal behavior (Jang & Johnson, 2001).

In a study of 600 young offenders in a boot camp, Benda (2002) and Benda and Toombs (2000) observe that religiosity is negatively associated with both drug use and violent crime. Because these studies were conducted among inner-city youth and young offenders, it is likely that the influence of religion is greater among persons from disadvantaged communities. Religious organizations provide learning and social control functions in disorganized communities that are performed by other institutions in more stable communities.

As with crime, another important issue is the extent to which religious influences are mediated by other variables. In most studies, researchers assume that religion variables are unimportant if their coefficients become insignificant after controlling for the effects of other relevant variables. However, one should not conclude that they are unimportant; rather, their effects may be mediated by other factors. Several studies confirm that religion variables and drug use are indirectly related: Their relationship is mediated by peer selection (Bahr et al., 1998; Burkett, 1993; Burkett & Warren, 1987), beliefs about deviance (Benda & Corwyn, 1997), maternal attachment (Harris, 1999), or parenting styles (Stewart & Bollard, 2002). Overall, it appears that the religious influences on the risk of drug are at least partially mediated by other variables. However, most studies indicate that there is a significant association between religion and drug use even after other relevant variables are considered.

Much of the literature on drug use does not differentiate between use and abuse. There is no widely accepted consensus as to when drug use becomes abuse. For adolescents, any degree of drug use is often viewed as abuse. The American Psychiatric Association defines drug abuse as a pathological pattern of use, impairment of functioning in work and social relationships, and duration of at least a month (Botvin, 1995). However, this may ignore binge drinking, or consuming large quantities of alcohol during weekends, which for many people constitutes impairment.

Nonetheless, findings from studies of drug abuse and religion are similar to those on drug use and religion. Individuals who are high on religiosity tend to have lower rates of abuse, even after controlling for the effects of other variables (Donahue & Benson, 1995; Hodge et al., 2001). Gorsuch (1995) maintains that religious people are less likely to abuse drugs because they hold antiabuse norms, are involved with peers who do not abuse drugs, and have ways to associate and meet their needs without abusing drugs.

There also is evidence that religiousness aids in the treatment of substance abuse. Brome et al.'s (2000) study of African-American women in treatment for substance abuse concludes that spirituality is beneficial. In a study of drug abuse treatment among Native Americans, Gurnee et al. (1990) suggest that a lack of involvement in Indian religion and culture is an impediment to successful treatment.

SUICIDE AND RELIGION

Given that several 19th-century researchers, including Durkheim, Guerry, Wagner, Masaryk, and Morselli, were interested in the association between religion and suicide, it is no surprise that numerous studies of this association have been conducted in the ensuing years. However, in contrast to studies of crime and drug use, most of this research has involved macro-level data. The obvious reason for this pattern is that, unlike criminals, it is impossible to interview those who complete suicide. Therefore, studies about religion and suicide tend to be macro-level or address suicide ideation or ideology (see reviews in Stack, 1992, 2000).

Three general perspectives are typically used to link religion and suicide. First, from a Durkheimian perspective, various religious traditions foster more or less social integration. Members of traditions that promote more integration should have a lower likelihood of suicide. Second, several religious traditions maintain core beliefs that oppose suicide or attenuate stress by emphasizing other-worldly rewards. Third, religious participation enhances social networks and thus provides more social support when depression or sadness turns to suicidal thoughts (Stack, 1992). Unfortunately, none of these perspectives specifies whether these processes are more germane for macro- or micro-level links between religion and suicide.

The results of studies that focus on membership rates—typically using church membership as the standard—and suicide rates have been inconsistent. Research in the United States suggests that the association between church membership and suicide rates is spurious: It diminishes once residential mobility and the divorce rate are considered (Bainbridge, 1989). However, cross-national research continues to find a negative association between various aspects of religious behavior and suicide rates, especially when assessing female suicide rates (Neeleman et al., 1997; Stack, 1983). Moreover, one recent study reports that African-American suicide rates in U.S. SMSAs are negatively associated with church membership rates (Burr et al., 1999).

Most macro-level studies of religion and suicide are the common legacy of Durkheim's influential study *Le Suicide* (1897). This foundational study of modern sociology is best known for ascribing differences in Catholic and Protestant suicide rates in late-19th-century Europe to varying levels of social integration found in these religious traditions. The "social fact" (as Robert Merton termed it) of higher suicide rates among Protestants spawned a virtual mass production of studies in the following 100 years. However, few definitive conclusions have resulted from these efforts.

Several observers argue that Durkheim either used his data selectively or misunderstood basic religious tenets, and therefore he mistakenly concluded that Protestant suicide rates were higher than Catholic suicide rates. Reanalysis of data from late-19th-century Europe indicates that Catholic and Protestant suicide rates were either quite similar (Bainbridge & Stark, 1981; Stark & Bainbridge, 1997; van Poppel & Day, 1996; see, however, Simpson, 1998) or that any differences may be attributable to misreporting among Catholics (Day, 1987). Historical and contemporary data from the United States, and some cross-national data, also suggest few differences between Catholic and Protestant suicide rates (Bainbridge & Stark, 1981; Stark & Bainbridge, 1997; Pope & Danigelis, 1981; Stack, 1981; Wasserman & Stack, 1993).

It is important to recognize, however, that combining all Protestant groups into a single entity is unwise, especially in pluralistic nations, because the variation of beliefs and practices of Protestant groups is substantial. Pescosolido (1990; Pescosolido & Georgianna, 1989), by disaggregating the proportion of Protestants in U.S. counties into constituent groups, finds that there are varying suicide rates among religious traditions: Counties with a high proportion of Catholics have lower suicide rates than counties with, say, a high proportion of Methodists; but higher suicide rates than counties with a high proportion of Nazarenes. The key group-level characteristics that attenuate the risk of suicide are the integrative and regulative aspects of network ties. In religious traditions that provide strong network ties, furnish emotional and social support, and offer a balance between religious and secular authority, there is a lower tendency to engage in self-destructive behaviors. Looking over the list of denominations that Pescosolido and Georgianna (1989) assume have the lowest suicide rates, it is clear that these denominations match well with Iannaccone's (1994) list of strict churches, ones that ask much of adherents and presumably supply much in return (Stack & Wasserman, 1992).

However, Pescosolido and Georgianna (1989) also determine that counties with a large proportion of Catholic and Jewish members have lower suicide rates than most other counties. What might explain this finding? First, perhaps these religious traditions have better mechanisms for strengthening social networks. Second, one must not forget the power of beliefs and tenets: Although religious proscriptions against suicide in these faith communities have waned over the years, they still maintain powerful messages about what happens to the suicide (Stark, 2001; Stark & Bainbridge, 1997). Third, Burr et al. (1994) demonstrate that percent Catholic negatively affects suicide rates in U.S. metropolitan areas, but that part of this effect is mediated by the divorce rate. In other words, there are both direct effects of percent Catholic and indirect effects, through the attenuation of divorce rates, on suicide rates.

Research on suicide among African Americans illustrates how culture and religion may influence suicide rates. In an illustrative study, Early (1992) sought to understand why the African-American suicide rate in the United States is about half as large as the white suicide rate. Given the social disorganization, anomie, and powerlessness suffered disproportionately by African Americans, one might conclude that their suicide rate should be higher than the rate in the general population. Early argues, however, that African-American churches provide a normative climate that helps keep the suicide rates low. He observes that the church helps define suicide as alien to the African-American experience. It promulgates ethics, traditions, and moral values and serves a unifying function. Early concludes that these churches stand as bastions in social struggles and help individuals develop resilience against suicide. Religious involvement gives African Americans hope, strengthens them, and bonds them together in a tradition of unity.

The search for lower suicide rates among particular religious traditions has also motivated studies of Islamic influences. Cross-national research indicates that countries with high proportions of Muslims tend to have lower suicide rates, even after controlling for the effects of economic and social conditions (Huang, 1996; Simpson & Conklin, 1989; see, however, Lester, 1996). Researchers offer two explanations for these results: (1) Muslim practice encourages daily ritual and an immersion of self that strongly attenuates the likelihood of suicide (i.e., a social network explanation); and (2) traditional Islamic beliefs that proscribe suicide and teach the severe penalties for such acts continue to hold sway over individual actions.

Although it has been tempting to preserve Durkheim's legacy by comparing distinct religious faiths, a promising alternative is to explore the effects of religious pluralism on suicide rates. Ellison et al. (1997) contend that religious homogeneity—the relative concentration of denominations in a given geographical area—is a more appropriate focus for macro-level suicide studies. They reason that religious homogeneity encourages social interaction, enhances social support processes, allows the shaping of local culture so that it fits better with particular beliefs and practices, and augments positive identity formation. These, in turn, increase the likelihood of help-seeking behavior and diminish mental health problems that may lead to suicide. Consistent with Pescosolido (1990), however, they recognize that, at least in the United States, there are also regional issues: Religious homogeneity may have its strongest effect when it intersects with more extensive regional or ethnic cultures, such as when Southern Baptists are the majority group in particular southern counties or when Mormons are in Utah. Their analysis of U.S. counties indicates that religious homo-geneity has a more powerful effect on suicide rates than percentage of Catholics or rates of church membership, and that it is particularly consequential for Catholic concentration in the Northeast and for Evangelical Christian concentration in the South.

As with crime and drug use, there have been several studies of individual-level religion and suicide. However, these have involved almost exclusively research on suicide ideation or attitudes. It is obviously quite difficult—but not impossible (one could interview family members)—to gather data on the religious practices of those who have completed suicide. In the few studies that have gathered information about those who have attempted or completed suicide, there appear to be influences of religion, but they are confounded with mental health status or the data are drawn from limited clinical samples. For example, a Finnish study using autopsy data finds that a disproportionate number of religious adherents experienced psychotic disorders and sought help prior to completing suicide (Sorri et al., 1996). Studies of suicide attempts indicate that importance of religion among U.S. adolescents and a "spiritual cultural orientation" (traditional tribal orientations about balance and harmony in one's life) among American Indians are associated with a lower likelihood of suicide attempts (Garroutte et al., 2003; Nonnemaker et al., 2003).

Most of the individual-level research has addressed suicidal ideation or ideology. A consistent finding is that measures of religion are negatively associated with suicidal thoughts or tolerance (Cook et al., 2002; Neeleman, 1998; Neeleman et al., 1997; Stack, 1998a, 1998b; Stack & Wasserman, 1992, 1995). It is important to note, though, that toler-ance for suicide is associated with a higher rate of suicides at the national level (Neeleman et al., 1997). Moreover, there are some demographic groups that appear to benefit more than others from involvement in religion. African Americans, who tend to have less tolerance than whites for suicide and also tend to be more involved in faith communities, experience a weaker negative association between religious beliefs or attendance and tolerance for suicide (Neeleman et al., 1998; Stack & Wasserman, 1996). Measures of religion tend to be among the strongest correlates of suicide ideology among whites but not among African Americans (Stack, 1998a; Stack & Wasserman, 1996). This may be because of the lower variability in religious behaviors and suicidal ideology among samples of African Americans relative to whites. Although there is a gender difference in attitudes toward suicide (males are more tolerant; Stack & Wasserman, 1992), religion variables (e.g., affiliation, attendance) are equally predictive of less tolerance for suicide among male and female adults in the United States (Hoffmann, 2003).

In addition to searching for group-specific effects, there are two directions taken by individual-level studies of religion and suicide. First, similar to research on the moral communities hypothesis, studies have begun to look at whether religion plays a larger role in certain geographic areas. For instance, recent studies suggest that religious practices are linked more strongly to suicide ideology in less religious areas of the Netherlands, but also in nations that are "highly religious" (Neeleman, 1998; Neeleman et al., 1997). Although this appears inconsistent, it points generally to the need for more research on the cross-national context of religion and suicide.

Second, similar to research on the indirect effects of religion on crime and drug use, studies suggest that religion affects suicide ideology and ideation indirectly through femi-nist orientations, help seeking behaviors, and social support (e.g., Greening & Stoppelbein, 2002; Stack et al., 1994). Hence more studies are needed that explore intra- and interper-sonal characteristics that might mediate the relationship between religion variables and suicide.

FAMILY VIOLENCE AND RELIGION

Violence is not an uncommon occurrence between intimate partners. Data from the National Crime Victimization Survey (NCVS) indicate that each year about one million violent crimes are committed against persons by their current or former spouses, boyfriends, or girlfriends (Rennison & Welchans, 2000). About 85% of intimate partner victimizations are against women. Intimate partner violence (IPV) comprises about 22% of violent crime against women but only 3% of violence against men. Almost one third of female murder victims are killed by intimate partners (Rennison & Welchans, 2000).

Although there have been many studies of the correlates of domestic violence, relatively few examine religion. Using nationally representative data, both Straus et al. (1980) and Sorenson et al. (1996) find that intimate partner violence is higher among religious affiliates than among nonaffiliates. However, using a Canadian sample, Brinkerhoff et al. (1992) report only a weak association between religious affiliation and intimate partner violence. Ellison et al. (1999) find no difference between conservative Protestants and members of other denominations in their experience with domestic violence.

The frequency of intimate partner violence tends to be lower among those who attend religious services regularly. Using two different national surveys, Ellison et al. (1999) and Cunradi et al. (2002) find an inverse association between religious service attendance and domestic violence (see also Fergusson et al., 1986). Kennedy and Drebing (2002) observe that those with a history of abuse are less active in conventional religious practices. However, in their Canadian sample, Brinkerhoff et al. (1992) find only a weak association between attendance and spousal violence.

Gelles (1974) reports that domestic violence is more common when spouses differ in their religious affiliations. However, using data from the National Survey of Households and Families, Ellison et al. (1999) find that domestic violence is not related to denominational heterogamy. However, other dimensions of spirituality may attenuate involvement in physical violence against family members (Freeman, 1996).

Some observers hypothesize that traditional beliefs about men's and women's roles influence domestic violence. They maintain that ideals of male dominance and patriarchy lead to more frequent violence against women (Dobash & Dobash, 1992; Haj-Yahia, 1998; Moore, 2003; Sakalh, 2001). In addition, some assert that there is more domestic violence in conservative Protestant religions because of their strict interpretation of the Bible. Recent empirical research in the United States is not consistent with these hypotheses, however. Ellison et al. (1999) and Moore (2003) find conservative Protestants no more likely to commit domestic violence than other persons. Moore (2003) also observes that interpersonal violence is not associated with beliefs about patriarchy or traditional gender roles.

Although a number of researchers discover a negative association between religiosity and domestic violence, there have been few attempts to understand why this relationship exists. Ellison et al. (2001) explore a number of different explanations of this relationship. First, they hypothesize that those who are involved religiously tend to be more socially integrated and receive greater social support. Nonetheless, they find that support and social integration are not related to domestic violence. Another explanation is that religious participation bolsters self-esteem. This hypothesis is also not supported: self-esteem is not associated with domestic violence. A third hypothesis is that religion helps decrease depression, which may be related to domestic violence. There is some support for this hypothesis: higher levels of depression are associated with higher levels of domestic violence. Finally, Ellison et al. (2001) examine whether alcohol and drug use explain the association between religious involvement and domestic violence. This explanation is consistent with their data, as drug and alcohol problems increase the risk of domestic violence. However, these variables mediate only a small portion of the association between religious involvement and domestic violence. Nonetheless, Cunradi et al. (2002) find that when the effects of alcohol problems are controlled, the relationship between religiosity and intimate partner violence is attenuated substantially. They conclude that alcohol use is a mediator: Religiosity tends to reduce alcohol problems and alcohol problems tend to increase the risk of intimate partner violence.

Ellison et al. (1999, 2001) conclude that more research is needed to identify the processes by which religious involvement influences domestic violence. They identify four promising avenues for future research. First, many religious organizations emphasize the importance of marriage and family. Such a commitment may help individuals develop tolerance and patience, which may deter or defuse potentially violent situations. Second, religious involvement encourages informal support networks that protect against domestic violence. Third, many religious organizations provide information and sponsor classes/workshops that teach skills that protect against domestic violence. Fourth, the development of individual spirituality may be important in deterring domestic violence. The latter hypothesis is consistent with the research cited above by Kennedy and Drebing (2002). Research is needed to evaluate these different explanations.

Dating violence is another aspect of intimate partner violence. The research findings on dating violence are similar to those on marital violence. Young females who report that religion is important in their lives are less likely to be victims of dating violence (Halpern et al., 2001). Howard et al. (2003), in an attempt to identify the major predictors of dating violence, determine that adolescents who attend church regularly and who experience high parental monitoring are less likely to be victims of dating violence. By contrast, having peers who drink alcohol increases the risk of dating violence. They conclude that parents, peers, and clergy all play a role in developing a social context that discourages risky behaviors associated with dating violence.

A common interest of family violence researchers involves the physical punishment of children. Ellison and Sherkat (1993), using data from the General Social Survey (GSS), find that conservative Protestants are significantly more likely than other groups to support corporal punishment. Ellison et al. (1996a, 1996b), using data from the National Survey of Families and Households, determine that conservative Protestant parents are also more likely than other parents to use physical punishment. This relationship holds even after controlling for the effects of other relevant variables (e.g., socioeconomic status, education).

Wilcox (1998) examines the distinctive approach toward child discipline among conservative Protestant parents and finds that, although parents with orthodox beliefs are more likely to use corporal punishment, they are also more likely than other parents to praise and hug their children. This parenting style has similarities to Baumrind's (1991) authoritative style because it is strict but also warm and expressive.

Finally, child sexual abuse is an important type of abuse that has attracted increasing attention from scholars, practitioners, and the general public. Although there has been much discussion about why abuse occurs, there is relatively little empirical research on the relationship between religion and sexual abuse. Stout-Miller et al. (1997), in a survey of 397 college freshmen, discovers that that those who were abused by a relative are more likely to be affiliated with a fundamentalist Protestant religion and to have been raised in an isolated family environment. Persons sexually abused by a nonrelative are more likely to say they are atheists, agnostics, or involved in liberal religious denominations. Stout-Miller et al. (1997)

conclude that the relationship between religiosity and sexual abuse is multidimensional. Religiosity may protect against abuse through religious activities and beliefs because they create a healthy atmosphere in the home and lower the risk of sexual abuse. By contrast, religious fundamentalists who isolate their families may include or attract those who seek to sexually abuse children.

Research shows that child sexual abuse tends to increase alienation and decrease religious involvement. People who were sexually abused as children are more alienated from God, report lower levels of spirituality, and participate less in religious activities (Pritt, 1998; Swanson, 1998). By contrast, religious involvement may help sexual abuse victims recover from their trauma. Religiosity helps victims attenuate the negative mental health outcomes associated with child sexual abuse (Doxey et al., 1997).

A problem that has earned more attention in recent years is the sexual abuse of children in religious communities. According to Parkinson (2002), available evidence does not indicate that sexual abuse of children is a greater problem in religious communities than in the general population. He notes that most religious organizations provide social support that should protect against child sexual abuse. By contrast, they often create a trusting environment in which a small minority of people may exploit children for the purpose of abusing them. There continues to be a need for solid, empirical research that examines factors associated with sexual abuse, identifies ways to prevent abuse, and provides ideas to help victims overcome the effects of abuse. How religion plays a role in each of these areas remains to be seen.

CORRECTIONS AND RELIGION

Approximately 6.7 million persons are currently under correctional supervision in the United States (Glaze, 2003; Harrison & Beck, 2003). Two million are incarcerated, whereas 4.7 million are on probation or parole. Each year about 600,000 inmates are released into the community (Petersilia, 2000). Within three years of release more than 60% of inmates are rearrested for a new crime. The correctional system is a large, complex, and costly system. There are many programs designed to help prisoners and parolees adjust to reentry and become reintegrated into their communities. Although there have been many religious programs in prisons, we know relatively little about religion in prison and whether it helps inmates adjust either within the institution or after they are released.

Nevertheless, there appears to be renewed interest in the involvement of religious organizations in prisons (Smarto, 1993; McRoberts, 2003). Recent research indicates that participation in religious programs is helpful to prisoners and to the criminal justice system. Religious involvement by prisoners helps them overcome depression, guilt, and self-contempt (Clear et al., 1992). In a recent study of 769 inmates in 20 prisons in 12 states, Clear and Sumter (2002) report that religiousness and prisoner adjustment are positively correlated. High levels of inmate religiousness are associated with better psychological adjustment to the prison environment and fewer disciplinary confinements.

In an analysis of inmates in a large medium/maximum security prison, O'Connor and Perreyclear (2002) discover that, because of the large amount of volunteer work, the annual cost of religious services in prisons is small: about $200 per inmate per year. After controlling for the effects of a number of demographic and criminal history risk factors, they find an inverse association between religious involvement and inmate infractions.

Young et al. (1995) investigate the long-term recidivism of a group of federal inmates trained as volunteer prison ministers. Inmates attended a 2-week seminar run by Prison Fellowship Ministries, a volunteer organization. The 180 seminar participants were compared with a matched control group of 185 inmates. After release, those who had attended the seminar had a significantly lower recidivism rate than the control group.

Finally, Johnson et al. (1997) examine the impact of religious programs on institutional adjustment and recidivism of two matched groups of inmates from four New York prisons. One group ($n = 201$) had participated in programs sponsored by Prison Fellowship (PF), a nonprofit prison ministry. The other group ($n = 201$) had no involvement in PF. While incarcerated, the two groups had similar scores on measures of institutional adjustment. Those who were most active in Bible studies were significantly less likely to be rearrested during follow-up. Two other long-term studies of recidivism show that religiosity plays a significant role in helping prisoners adjust and remain crime free after release (Benda et al., 2003; Jensen & Gibbons, 2002). Overall, the evidence indicates that religious programs help inmates adjust to both prison life and find greater success once they reenter the community. Because of the involvement of volunteers in many religious ministries, their cost is much lower than other types of rehabilitation programs.

SEXUAL DEVIANCE AND RELIGION

The term "sexual deviance" is perhaps the most sensitive of topics in this chapter. It is impossible not to notice the changing norms about sexuality that have occurred in the United States and across much of the developed world over the past three or four decades. These changing norms have redefined what it means to be sexually deviant, and, although many deviance textbooks still discuss issues such as homosexuality and fetishism, these types of lifestyles are only tenuously defined as deviant in contemporary discussion. Therefore, rather than attempt to delineate the boundaries of sexual deviance, this section merely gives a flavor of some recent studies on the effects of religion.

Perhaps the most widely studied sexual deviance topic that addresses religion involves nonmarital sexual behavior. However, as almost half of adolescents in the United States report engaging in premarital sexual intercourse before the age of 18 (CDC, 2003), there is the question of whether this can still be termed deviant behavior. Nonetheless, most research that has addressed this issue finds that variables such as religious service attendance and importance of religion are negatively associated with premarital sex (Donahue & Benson, 1995; Nonnemaker et al., 2003; Paul et al., 2000). This relationship may have changed temporally, however, with membership in Evangelical denominations having a stronger negative impact on premarital sexual behavior over time (Brewster et al., 1998). Belonging to a Muslim group also appears to minimize the likelihood of premarital sex (Addai, 2000).

Religion variables also have relatively consistent associations with attitudes toward nonmarital sexual behavior. Survey data regularly indicate that members of religious groups, especially members of more orthodox groups, tend to be less tolerant of premarital and extramarital sexual relationships (Greeley, 1989; Hoffmann & Miller 1998; Petersen & Donnenwerth, 1997; Scott, 1998). In fact, members of conservative religious traditions have sustained much of the opposition to premarital sexual relations in the United States and elsewhere in the world (Scott, 1998). Similar to explanations given earlier in this chapter, conservative religious groups tend to have stronger and more consistent beliefs about particular types of behavior and their networks are apt to be more cohesive, thus allowing more efficient transmission of messages about moral behaviors (Cochran & Beeghley, 1991; Pescosolido, 1990).

The greater tolerance for homosexual behavior in the United States and elsewhere in the developed world has led to an increasing number of studies on the impact of religion. Any myth about the irreligiousness of homosexuals has been dispelled by research on religion and spirituality among gays and lesbians. However, unlike general research on religiosity that indicates that females are more religious than males (Miller & Stark, 2002), Sherkat (2002) finds that gay men have higher rates of religious participation than lesbians, bisexuals, or heterosexual men. Other studies suggest that gays and lesbians are marginalized by many religious traditions, thus they have a lower likelihood of participation in faith-based activities. Although Sherkat's research dispels this notion for gay men, he does find that lesbians attend religious services less often and are more likely to report "no religious affiliation" than others. Many lesbians experience spirituality through alternative means, such as female-based religious groups (e.g., Wicca) and individualized forms of spirituality (Neitz, 2000; Wilcox, 2002).

Attitudes about homosexual relations became more tolerant over the past two decades, especially during the 1990s (Loftus, 2001). However, those who attend religious services and who hold traditional religious beliefs have lagged behind others in their level of tolerance (Hinrichs & Rosenberg, 2002). This is likely because of the mechanisms discussed earlier, especially among Evangelical groups who base their doctrine on particular biblical prohibitions against homosexual relations (Sherkat, 2002).

Although there are several other forms of sexual deviance that garner the interest of researchers, most have not considered religion or spiritual-based factors in their assessments. Exceptions to this include child sexual abuse, which is discussed in an earlier section of this chapter; polygamy, which is more appropriately considered under the topic *religion as deviance*, because it is typically based on religious teachings; and cohabitation, which is more suitably considered a family issue rather than a specific issue of sexuality. Studies also have addressed religious influences on the development of sexual identities (Levitt, 1995; Eliason, 1995) and on attitudes toward pornography (Sherkat & Ellison, 1997). Sherkat and Ellison's (1997) study of conservative Protestantism and opposition to pornography is instructive for studies of religion and deviance because they provide a model that helps explain oppositional attitudes. Briefly, they posit that commitment to biblical inerrancy supports moral absolutism and beliefs about societal contamination through immorality. These two mechanisms, in turn, heighten opposition to pornographic materials. The value of their model is that it describes specific indirect influences of religion on attitudes toward behaviors that have been identified as deviant. Therefore, it is consistent and, in some ways elaborates, research on how religion indirectly affects deviance through cognitively and socially based mediating processes.

RELIGION AS DEVIANCE

A topic that is too broad to consider in this chapter involves the deviance process, or how certain behaviors or lifestyles come to be labeled as deviant (Pfuhl & Henry, 1993). There are numerous examples of the way in which a majority group's religious doctrines have been used to justify the passage of laws targeting specific behaviors (e.g., witchcraft trials; Prohibition in the United States) or the labeling of faith-based groups as deviant (Christians in 1st-century Rome; Scientologists in Germany; the Children of God; the

Branch Davidians). Moreover, the role of the media and popular culture in defining certain behaviors as deviant has, at times, taken on a religious flavor or drawn from popular religion (Simpson, 1998). The role that the dominant group's religious beliefs have played in defining certain behaviors as deviant is a topic too extensive to be included in this chapter.

A slightly more circumscribed topic involves *religion as deviance*. There are numerous studies of historical and contemporary manifestations of religion as deviance in the United States and elsewhere. Most of these studies focus on new religious movements or schism groups, or on extreme forms of religious behavior that are defined as mental illness (Dawson, 1998; Stark & Bainbridge, 1997). Recent research on religion and mental illness has dismissed the notion that religious adherents are more likely to suffer from mental disorders, although some clinical psychology studies continue to discuss the exacerbating role that extreme religious beliefs play in depression and suicide attempts (Exline et al., 2000).

New religious movements or religious cults have been the topic of many studies. Since this literature is voluminous and would require an additional chapter to discuss, we do not address its studies in any detail. We only wish to point out that there are many examples of behaviors that are labeled as deviant mainly because they are promulgated by new religious movements. Examples of these behaviors include polygyny among Mormons in the 19th century and among fundamentalist Mormons in contemporary U.S. society; avoidance of certain medical procedures among Christian Scientists; the establishment of utopian communities—which normally are isolated from the broader society—by several new religious movements; animal sacrifice among Santeria; and sexual practices that are deemed non-normative by others in the surrounding community (e.g., sexual abstinence among adult Shakers). Finally, there is the issue of the control of deviance within religious groups: How do they develop and enforce sanctions to attenuate behavior that falls outside their normative boundaries? The general issue of social control within religious groups is a common motivation for conducting research on new religious movements, and has led to numerous studies of deviance within groups (e.g., Straus, 1986; Wright, 1986). As deviant behaviors become common in groups, there is, finally, the issue of how this affects group stability, schismatic behavior, or accommodation to the broader culture.

CONCLUSIONS

Interest in the relationship between religion and deviance has generated a large body of impressive studies. The presumed opposite social pulls of integration and fragmentation that concern much of the social sciences virtually mandates a concern with religion—usually seen as a force for integration—and deviance—by definition a force for fragmentation. Although there have been numerous studies of religion and deviance over the past 150 years or so, there continue to be large gaps in our understanding of how these two factors are related. Given our review, we discuss four areas that are in particular need of further consideration.

First, studies have accomplished much empirically to help us understand whether religion is associated with suicide, criminal behavior, drug use, sexuality, and family violence. However, we lack a comprehensive understanding of why these factors might be linked. Theories of criminal behavior and drug use, for instance, have done a poor job of incorporating religion variables into their models. At the individual-level, how might a religious upbringing affect the motivations or impediments for drug use or criminal behavior?

This should be a key concern for social learning, social bonding, strain, deterrence, and symbolic interaction theories of deviance. Furthermore, are there reciprocal relations between religion and deviance? Most studies include only one-way causal arrows, from religion to deviance, but participation in deviant behavior also may attenuate involvement in religious activities (Benda & Corwyn, 1997; Burkett & Warren, 1987).

At the group or macro-level, what role do religious institutions play in community social control, the development of community norms, or providing alternatives for youth who may otherwise find themselves on a path toward crime, gang membership, violence, or drug use? Johnson et al.'s (2000a) and Lee and Bartkowski's (2004b) recent research suggests that faith-based institutions affect the likelihood of youth involvement in crime, drug use, and violence. Both sets of researchers take a social capital approach to understanding these connections, but we should not preclude addressing other theoretical perspectives such as routine activities and rational choice as well. Moreover, we ought not to ignore potential macro-micro links between religion and deviance, both theoretically and empirically. What does it mean, for instance, to have a "moral community?" Will a critical mass of religious adherents in a neighborhood allow more control over deviant activities? Are there threshold effects? Is deviant behavior affected by interactions between the proportion of religious adherents in a neighborhood and individual-level characteristics such as self-control, criminal propensities, peer associations, and so forth? Theories of deviance are richer when they incorporate both macro- and micro-level factors into their models. Johnson et al. (2000a; see also Jang & Johnson, 2001) provide a promising multilevel model for understanding the role that religious institutions play in reducing youth crime and drug use in disadvantaged neighborhoods.

Second, there has been too little attention to the measurement of religion and deviance. Evans et al. (1995) show that how religious participation is measured affects whether there is a consistent association with criminal behavior. Ellison et al. (1997) find that religious homogeneity is a better predictor of suicide rates than is percent Catholic or Protestant. Note that these illustrative studies address limitations in how religion is measured. Yet, criminologists also have begun considering the measurement of crime and drug use in a more careful manner. Recent studies demonstrate that the predictors of criminal behavior differ depending on whether one measures *participation* in crime (a yes-no question) versus *frequency* of offending (counts of offending over a set time period). A question that comes to mind is whether religious behavior is a more consequential influence for whether individuals cross a threshold and participate in crime, drug use, or violence at all; or whether it affects frequency of offending. Is it more influential in affecting drug use or abuse? Initiation or escalation? In our view, it remains to be seen under what circumstances religion affects involvement in criminal or drug using behavior.

Third, the role that religion plays in rehabilitation, drug treatment, forgiveness, healing from the effects of abuse, desistance from crime or drug use, or correctional success has rarely been investigated. Many community and correctional programs designed to treat perpetrators and victims of crime or other forms of deviance are based on principles of spirituality, such as recognition of a higher power, the therapeutic effects of forgiveness, and other faith-based concerns. Recent research on spiritual-based correctional programs and on religious therapy indicates that there are positive effects such as less recidivism, better reentry adjustment, and improved mental health following abuse. Most of these studies, however, have been limited in scope and have not conducted sufficient follow-up of participants. Therefore, research on faith-based programs should be expanded to determine if the initial promise demonstrated in existing studies is generalizable. Do particular types of programs work better than others? Are the positive effects found thus far unique to certain types of programs, offenders, or victims?

Finally, there has been far too little attention to race, ethnicity, and gender in research on religion and deviance. Although some studies have addressed whether African Americans, Hispanics, or females benefit more from religious participation than whites or males, there are few conclusions available at this point. It has been observed repeatedly that African-Americans and females are more likely than Whites or males to participate in religious activities (religious service attendance, prayer, etc.). Whether this translates into less deviant behavior is unclear, however. Considering that African Americans are disproportionately represented in the U.S. correctional system, assessing the role of religion in their lives and how it affects involvement in criminal behavior should be a high priority. A similar observation applies to Hispanics in the United States. Moreover, if females are more involved in religion, yet less likely to engage in crime or complete suicides, perhaps there should be an emphasis on whether their spirituality attenuates involvement in deviant activities. Or are there traits distinctive to females that affect both religious involvement and less deviance?

The study of religion and deviance has left us with a rich set of results and a provocative set of ideas. There seem to be consistent and persistent effects of religion on several forms of deviance, including criminal behavior, drug use, family violence, and suicide. But are these effects simply a reflection of a common set of traits that influences religious behavior *and* deviant behavior, or is religious behavior part of a casual pathway that leads one away from deviant behavior? Are the effects of religion on deviant behavior stronger in certain groups or cultures? Developing more careful research on religion and deviance is clearly recommended, but it also promises to yield important guidance for understanding the myriad factors that integrate and fragment contemporary society.

NOTE

1. A recent meta-analysis of studies of religion and crime demonstrates the disproportionate number of studies that address delinquency. A comprehensive analysis of 60 studies conducted between 1969 and 1998 included only five that sampled from general populations of adults; the remaining studies used samples of high school or college students (Baier & Wright, 2001).

REFERENCES

Addai, I. (2000). Religious affiliation and sexual initiation among Ghanaian women. *Review of Religious Research, 41*, 328–343.
Akers, R. L. (1992). *Drugs, alcohol, and society.* Belmont, CA: Wadsworth.
Bahr, S. J., & Hawks, R. D. (1995). Religious organizations. In R. H. Coombs & D. M. Ziedonis (Eds.), *Handbook on drug abuse prevention* (pp. 159–179). Boston: Allyn and Bacon.
Bahr, S. J., Maughan, S. L., Marcos, A. C., & Li, B. (1998). Family, religiosity, and the risk of adolescent drug use. *Journal of Marriage and the Family, 60*, 979–992.
Baier, C. J., & Wright, B. R. E. (2001). If You Love Me, Keep My Commandments: A meta-analysis of the effect of religion on crime. *Journal of Research on Crime and Delinquency, 38*, 3–21.
Bainbridge, W. S. (1989). The religious ecology of deviance. *American Sociological Review, 54*, 288–295.
Bainbridge, W. S., & Stark, R. (1981). Suicide, homicide, and religion: Durkheim reassessed. *Annual Review of the Social Sciences of Religion, 5*, 33–56.
Baumrind, D. (1991). The influence of parenting styles on adolescent competence and substance use. *Journal of Early Adolescence, 11*, 56–95.

Benda, B. B. (1995). The effect of religion on adolescent delinquency revisited. *Journal of Research on Crime and Delinquency, 32*, 446–466.

Benda, B. B. (2002). Religion and violent offenders in Boot camp: A structural equation model. *Journal of Research in Crime and Delinquency, 39*, 91–121.

Benda, B. B., & Corwyn, R. F. (1997). A test of a model with reciprocal effects between religiosity and various forms of delinquency using 2-stage least squares regression. *Journal of Social Service Research, 22*, 27–52.

Benda, B. B., & Toombs, N. J. (2000). Religiosity and violence: Are they related after considering the strongest predictors? *Journal of Criminal Justice, 28*, 483–496.

Benda, B. B., Toombs, N. J., & Peacock, M. (2003). Discriminators of types of recidivism among Boot camp graduates in a five-year follow-up study. *Journal of Criminal Justice, 31*, 539–551.

Benson, P. L. (1992). Religion and substance use. In J. F. Schumaker (Ed.), *Religion and mental health* (211–220). New York: Oxford University Press.

Botvin, G. J. (1995). Principles of prevention. In R. H. Coombs & D. M. Ziedonis (Eds.), *Handbook on drug abuse prevention* (pp. 19–34). Boston: Allyn and Bacon.

Brewster, K. L., Cooksey, E. C., Guilkey, D. K., & Rindfuss, R. R. (1998). The changing impact of religion on sexual and contraceptive behavior in adolescent women in the United States. *Journal of Marriage and the Family, 60*, 493–504.

Brinkerhoff, M. B., Grandin, E., & Lupri, E. (1992). Religious involvement and spousal violence: The Canadian case. *Journal for the Scientific Study of Religion, 31*, 15–31.

Brome, D. R., Owens, M. D., Allen, K., & Vevaina, T. (2000). An examination of spirituality among African American women in recovery from substance abuse. *The Journal of Black Psychology, 26*, 470–486.

Burkett, S. R. (1993). Perceived parents' religiosity, friends' drinking, and hellfire: A panel study of adolescent drinking. *Review of Religious Research, 35*, 134–154.

Burkett, S. R., & Warren, B. O. (1987). Religiosity, peer associations, and adolescent marijuana use: A Panel study of underlying causal structures. *Criminology, 25*, 109–131.

Burnee, C. G., Vigil, D. E., Krill-Smith, S., & Crowley, T. J. (1990). Substance abuse among American Indians in an urban treatment program. *American Indian and Alaska Native Mental Health Research, 3*, 17–26.

Burr, J. A., Hartman, J. T., Matteson, D. W. (1999). Black suicide in U.S. metropolitan areas: An examination of the racial inequality and social integration-regulation hypotheses. *Social Forces, 77*, 1049–1081.

Burr, J. A., McCall, P. L., & Powell-Griner, E. (1994). Catholic religion and suicide: The mediating effects of divorce. *Social Science Quarterly, 75*, 300–318.

Centers for Disease Control and Prevention (CDC). (2003). *Results from the 2001 Youth Risk Behavior Surveillance System.* Atlanta, GA: Author.

Chaloupka, F. J., Grossman, M., Bickel, W. K., & Saffer, H. (Eds.). (1999). *The economic analysis of substance use and abuse.* Chicago: University of Chicago Press.

Clarke, L., Beeghley, L., & Cochran, J. K. (1990). Religiosity, social class, and alcohol use: An application of reference group theory. *Sociological Perspectives, 33*, 201–218.

Clear, T. R., Stout, B. D., & Dammer, H. R. (1992). Does involvement in religion help prisoners adjust to prison? *NCCD Focus* (November), 1–7.

Clear, T. R., & Sumter, M. T. (2002). Prisoners, prison, and religion: Religion and adjustment to prison. *Journal of Offender Rehabilitation, 35*, 127–159.

Cochran, J. K. (1993). The variable effects of religiosity and denomination an adolescent self-reported alcohol use by beverage type. *Journal of Drug Issues, 23*, 479–491.

Cochran, J. K., & Beeghley, L. (1991). The influence of religion on attitudes toward nonmarital sexuality: A preliminary assessment of reference group theory. *Journal for the Scientific Study of Religion, 30*, 45–62.

Cochran, J. K., Wood, P. B., & Arneklev, B. J. (1994). Is the religiosity-delinquency relationship spurious? A test of arousal and social control theories. *Journal of Research in Crime and Delinquency, 31*, 92–123.

Cook, J. M., Pearson, J. L., Thompson, R., Black, B. S., & Rabins, P. (2002). Suicidality in older African-Americans: Findings from the EPOCH study. *American Journal of Geriatric Psychiatry, 10*, 437–446.

Cretacci, M. A. (2002). *Religion and social control: An expansion of Hirschi's social bond.* Unpublished doctoral dissertation, Department of Sociology, State University of New York at Albany.

Cunradi, C. B., Caetano, R., & Schafer, J. (2002). Religious affiliation, denominational homogamy, and intimate partner violence among U.S. couples. *Journal for the Scientific Study of Religion, 41*, 139–151.

Dawson, L. L. (1998). *Comprehending cults: The sociology of new religious movements.* New York: Oxford University Press.

Day, L. H. (1987). Durkheim on religion and suicide: A demographic critique. *Sociology, 21*, 449–461.

Dobash, R. E., & Dobash, R. P. (1992). *Women, violence and social change.* London: Routledge.

Donahue, M. J., Benson, P. L. (1995). Religion and the well-being of adolescents. *Journal of Social Issues, 51,* 145–160.

Doxey, C., Jensen, L., & Jensen, J. (1997). The influence of religion on victims of childhood sexual abuse. *International Journal for the Psychology of Religion, 7,* 179–186.

Early, K. E. (1992). *Religion and suicide in the African-American community.* Westport, CT: Greenwood Press.

Eliason, M. J. (1995). Accounts of sexual identity formation in heterosexual students. *Sex Roles, 32,* 821–834.

Ellis, L., & Peterson, J. (1996). Crime and religion: An international comparison among thirteen nations. *Personality and Individual Differences, 20,* 761–768.

Ellison, C. G., & Anderson, K. L. (2001). Religious involvement and domestic violence among U.S. couples. *Journal for the Scientific Study of Religion, 40,* 269–286.

Ellison, C., Bartkowski, J. P., & Anderson, K. L. (1999). Are there religious variations in domestic violence? *Journal of Family Issues, 20,* 87–113.

Ellison, C. G., Bartkowski, J. R., & Segal, M. L. (1996a). Conservative protestantism and the parental use of corporal punishment. *Social Forces, 74,* 1003–1028.

Ellison, C. G., Bartkowski, J. R., & Segal, M. L. (1996b). Do conservative protestant parents spank more often? Further evidence from the national survey of families and households. *Social Science Quarterly, 77,* 663–673.

Ellison, C. G., Burr, J. A., & McCall, P. L. (1997). Religious homogeneity and metropolitan suicide rates. *Social Forces, 76,* 273–299.

Ellison, C. G., & Sherkat, D. E. (1993). Conservative protestantism and support for corporal punishment. *American Sociological Review, 58,* 131–144.

Evans, T. D., Cullen, F. T., Dunaway, R. G., & Burton, V. S. (1995). Religion and crime reexamined: The impact of religion, secular controls, and social ecology on adult criminality. *Criminology, 33,* 195–224.

Exline, J. J., Yali, A. M., & Sanderson, W. C. (2000). Guilt, discord, and alienation: The role of religious strain on depression and suicidality. *Journal of Clinical Psychology, 56,* 1481–1496.

Fergusson, D. M., Horwood, L. J., Kershaw, K. L., & Shannon, F. T. (1986). Factors associated with reports of wife assault in New Zealand. *Journal of Marriage and the Family, 48,* 407–412.

Freeman, D. R. (1996). *The relationship between spiritual wholeness and physical violence.* Unpublished doctoral dissertation, School of Social Services, Catholic University of America.

Freeman, R. B. (1986). Who escapes? The relation of churchgoing and other background factors to the socioeconomic performance of Black male youth from inner-city tracts. In R. B. Freeman & H. J. Holzer (Eds.), *The Black youth employment crisis.* Chicago: University of Chicago Press.

Garroutte, E. M., Goldberg, J., Beals, J., Herrell, R., Manson, S. M., & the AI-SUPERPFP Team. (2003). Spirituality and attempted suicide among American Indians. *Social Science & Medicine, 56,* 1571–1579.

Gelles, R. J. (1974). *The violent home.* Beverly Hills, CA: Sage.

Glaze, L. E. (2003). *Probation and parole in the United States, 2002.* Bureau of Justice Statistics Bulletin. Washington, DC: U.S. Department of Justice, Office of Justice Programs.

Gorsuch, R. L. (1995). Religious aspects of substance abuse and recovery. *Journal of Social Issues, 51,* 65–83.

Grasmick, H. G., Bursik, R. J., & Cochran, J. K. (1991a). Render unto caesar what is caesar's: Religiosity and taxpayers inclination to cheat. *Sociological Quarterly, 32,* 251–266.

Grasmick, H. G., Kinsey, K., & Cochran, J. K. (1991b). Denomination, religiosity, and compliance with the law: A study of adults. *Journal for the Scientific Study of Religion, 30,* 99–107.

Greeley, A. M. (1989). *Religious change in America.* Cambridge, MA: Harvard University Press.

Greening, L., & Stoppelbein, L. (2002). Religiosity, attributional style, and social support at psychosocial buffers for African-American and White adolescents' perceived risk for suicide. *Suicide and Life-Threatening Behavior, 32,* 404–417.

Haj-Yahia, M. M. (1998). A patriarchal perspective of beliefs about wife beating among Palestinian men from the west bank and the Gaza strip. *Journal of Family Issues, 5,* 595–621.

Halpern, C. T., Oslak, S. G., Young, M. L., Martin, S. L., & Kupper, L. (2001). Partner violence among adolescents in opposite-sex romantic relationships: Findings from the national longitudinal study of adolescent health. *American Journal of Public Health, 91,* 1679–1685.

Harris, M. A. (1999). *Neighborhood structure, religious involvement, and individual delinquency: Context and buffering hypotheses.* Unpublished doctoral dissertation, Department of Sociology, Ohio State University.

Harrison, P. M., & Beck, A. J. (2003). *Prisoners in 2002.* Bureau of Justice Statistics Bulletin. Washington, DC: U.S. Department of Justice, Office of Justice Programs.

Haskins, D. G., Piedmont, R. L., Greer, J.M.G. (2001). African American attitudes toward incest and child sexual abuse. *Journal of Religion and Abuse, 2*, 51–80.

Hesselbrock, M. N., Hesselbrock, V. M., & Epstein, E. E. (1999). Theories of etiology of alcohol and other drug use disorders. In B. S. McCrady & E. E. Epstein (Eds.), *Addictions: A comprehensive guidebook* (pp. 50–72). New York: Oxford University Press.

Hinrichs, D. W., & Rosenberg, P. J. (2002). Attitudes toward gay, lesbian, and bisexual persons among Heterosexual Liberal Arts College Students. *Journal of Homosexuality, 43*, 61–84.

Hirschi, T., & Stark, R. T. (1969). Hellfire and delinquency. *Social Problems, 17*, 202–213.

Hodge, D. R., Cardenas, P., & Montoya, H. (2001). Substance use: Spirituality and religious participation as protective factors among rural youths. *Social Work Research, 25*, 153–161.

Hoffmann, J. P. (2003). *Religion and tolerance of suicide: Are there gender-specific effects?* Working Paper No. 03–01, Department of Sociology, Brigham Young University.

Hoffmann, J. P., & Miller, A. S. (1998). Denominational influences on socially divisive issues: Polarization or continuity? *Journal for the Scientific Study of Religion, 37*, 528–546.

Hoffmann, J. P., & Xu, J. (2002). School activities, community service, and delinquency. *Crime & Delinquency, 48*, 568–591.

Horne, C. (2001). Sociological perspectives on the emergence of norms. In M. Hechter & K. D. Opp (Eds.), *Social norms* (pp. 3–34). New York: Russell Sage.

Howard, D., Qiu, Y., & Bockeloo, B. (2003). Personal and social contextual correlates of adolescent dating violence. *Journal of Adolescent Health, 33*, 9–17.

Huang, W. C. (1996). Religion, culture, economic and sociological correlates of suicide rates: A cross-national analysis. *Applied Economics Letters, 3*, 779–782.

Iannaccone, L. R. (1994). Why strict churches are strong. *American Journal of Sociology, 99*, 1180–1211.

Jang, S. J., & Johnson, B. R. (2001). Neighborhood disorder, individual religiosity, and adolescent use of illicit drugs: A test of multilevel hypotheses. *Criminology, 39*, 109–143.

Jensen, K. D., & Gibbons, S. G. (2002). Shame and religion as factors in the rehabilitation of serious offenders. *Journal of Offender Rehabilitation, 35*, 215–230.

Johnson, B. R., Jang, S. J., Li, S. D., & Larson, D. B. (2000a). The invisible institution and Black youth crime: The church as an agency of local social control. *Journal of Youth and Adolescence, 29*, 479–498.

Johnson, B. R., Jang, S. J., Li, S. D., & Larson, D. B. (2000b). Escaping from the crime of inner cities: Church attendance and religious salience among disadvantaged youth. *Justice Quarterly, 17*, 377–391.

Johnson, B. R., Larson, D. B., & Pitts, T. C. (1997). Religious programs, institutional adjustment, and recidivism among former inmates in prison fellowship programs. *Justice Quarterly, 14*, 145–166.

Kennedy, P., & Drebing, C. E. (2002). Abuse and religious experience: A study of religiously committed evangelical adults. *Mental Health, Religion & Culture, 5*, 225–237.

Kposowa, A. J., Breault, K. D., & Harrison, B. M. (1995). Reassessing the structural covariates of violent and property crimes in the USA: A county level analysis. *British Journal of Sociology, 46*, 79–105.

Lawson, R., Drebing, C., Berg, G., Vincellette, A., & Penk, W. (1998). The long term impact of child abuse on religious behavior and spirituality in men. *Child Abuse and Neglect, 22*, 369–380.

Lee, M. R., & Bartkowski, J. P. (2004a). Civic participation, regional subcultures, and violence: The differential effects of secular and religious participation on adult and juvenile homicide rates. *Homicide Studies, 8*, 5–39.

Lee, M. R., & Bartkowski, J. P. (2004b). Love thy neighbor? Moral communities, civic engagement, and juvenile homicide in rural areas. *Social Forces, 82*, 1001–1035.

Lester, D. (1996). Religion and suicide. *Psychological Reports, 78*, 1090.

Levitt, M. (1995). Sexual identity and religious socialization. *British Journal of Sociology, 46*, 529–536.

Litchfield, A. W., Thomas, D. L., & Li, B. D. (1997). Dimensions of religiosity as mediators between parenting and adolescent deviant behavior. *Journal of Adolescent Research, 12*, 199–226.

Loftus, J. (2001). America's liberalization in attitudes toward homosexuality, 1973 to 1998. *American Sociological Review, 66*, 762–782.

McRoberts, O. M. (2003). *Streets of glory: Church and community in a Black urban neighborhood.* Chicago: University of Chicago Press.

Miller A. S., & Stark, R. (2002). Gender and religiousness: Can socialization explanations be saved? *American Journal of Sociology, 107*, 1399–1423.

Moore, M. M. (2003, April). *Religion, patriarchal attitudes and domestic violence: Is there a link?* Paper presented at the Annual Meeting of the Southern Sociological Society, New Orleans, LA.

Neeleman, J. (1998). Regional suicide rates in the Netherlands: Does religion still play a role? *International Journal of Epidemiology, 27*, 466–472.

Neeleman, J., Halpern, D., Leon, D., & Lewis, G. (1997). Tolerance of suicide, religion, and suicide rates: An ecological and individual study in 19 western countries. *Psychological Medicine, 27*, 1165–1171.

Neeleman, J., Wessely, S., & Lewis, G. (1998). Suicide acceptability in African-and White Americans: The Role of religion. *Journal of Nervous and Mental Disease, 186*, 12–16.

Neitz, M. J. (2000). Queering the dragonfest: Changing sexualities in a post-patriarchal religion. *Sociology of Religion, 61*, 369–391.

Nonnemaker, J. M., McNeely, C. A., & Blum, R. W. (2003). Public and private domains of religiosity and adolescent health risk behaviors: Evidence from the national longitudinal study of adolescent health. *Social Science & Medicine, 57*, 2049–2057.

O'Conner, T. P., & Perreyclear, M. (2002). Prison religion in action and its influence on offender rehabilitation. *Journal of Offender Rehabilitation, 35*, 11–33.

Parkinson, P. N. (2002). What does the lord require of us? Child sexual abuse in the churches. *Journal of Religion and Abuse, 4*, 3–31.

Pescosolido, B. A. (1990). The social context of religious integration and suicide: Pursuing the network explanation. *Sociological Quarterly, 31*, 337–357.

Pescosolido, B. A., & Georgiana, S. (1989). Durkheim, suicide, and religion: Toward a network theory of suicide. *American Sociological Review, 54*, 33–48.

Petee, T. A., Milner, T. F., & Welch, M. R. (1994). Levels of social integration in group contexts and the effects of informal sanction threat on deviance. *Criminology, 32*, 85–106.

Petersilia, J. (2000). When prisoners return to the community: Political, economic, and social consequences. *Research in brief: Sentencing & corrections.* Washington, DC: Office of Justice Programs, U.S. Department of Justice.

Petersen, L. R., & Donnenwerth, G. V. (1997). Secularization and the influence of religion on beliefs about premarital sex. *Social Forces, 75*, 1071–1088.

Pettersson, T. (1991). Religion and criminality: Structural relationships between church involvement and crime rates in contemporary Sweden. *Journal for the Scientific Study of Religion, 30*, 279–291.

Pfuhl, E. H., & Henry, S. (1993). *The deviance process.* Hawthorne, NY: Aldine de Gruyter.

Pope, W., & Danigelis, N. (1981). Sociology's "One Law." *Social Forces, 60*, 495–516.

Pritt, A. F. (1998). Spiritual correlates of reported sexual abuse among Mormon women. *Journal for the Scientific Study of Religion, 37*, 273–285.

Rennison, C. M., & Welchans, S. (2002). *Intimate partner violence.* Bureau of Justice Statistics Special Report. Washington, DC: Office of Justice Programs, U.S. Department of Justice.

Sakalh, N. (2001). Beliefs about wife beating among Turkish college students: The effects of patriarchy, sexism, and sex differences. *Sex Roles, 44*, 599–610.

Sampson, R. J. (2002). Organized for what? Recasting theories of social (Dis)organization. In E. Waring & D. Weisburd (Eds.), *Crime and social Organization* (pp. 95–110). New Brunswick, NJ: Transaction.

Scott, J. (1998). Changing attitudes toward sexual morality: A cross-national comparison. *Sociology, 32*, 815–845.

Sherkat, D. E. (2002). Sexuality and religious commitment in the United States: An empirical examination. *Journal for the Scientific Study of Religion, 41*, 313–323.

Sherkat, D. E., & Ellison, C. G. (1997). The cognitive structure of a moral crusade: Conservative protestantism and opposition to pornography. *Social Forces, 75*, 957–982.

Simpson, J. H. (1998). Confessions, outings, and ordeals: Understanding media in the United States. In A. Shupe & B. Misztal (Eds.), *Religion, mobilization, and social action* (pp. 216–228). Westport, CT: Praeger.

Simpson, M. (1998). Suicide and religion: Did Durkheim commit the ecological fallacy or did Van Poppel and Day combine apples and oranges? *American Sociological Review, 63*, 895–896.

Simpson, M. E., & Conklin, G. H. (1989). Socioeconomic development, suicide and religion: A test of Durkheim's theory of religion and suicide. *Social Forces, 67*, 945–964.

Smarto, D. (Ed.). (1993). *Setting the captives free! Relevant ideas in criminal justice and prison ministry.* Grand Rapids, MI: Baker Book Press.

Smith, C. (2003). Religious participation and network closure among adolescents. *Journal for the Scientific Study of Religion, 42*, 259–267.

Smith, H. L., Fabricatore, A., & Peyrot, M. (1999). Religiosity and altruism among African American males: The Catholic experience. *Journal of Black Studies, 29*, 579–597.

Sorenson, S. B., Upchurch, D. M., & Shen, H. (1996). Violence and injury in marital arguments: Risk patterns and gender differences. *American Journal of Public Health, 86*, 35–40.

Sorri, H., Henriksson, M., & Lonnqvist, J. (1996). Religiosity and suicide: Findings from a nationwide psychological autopsy study. *Crisis, 17*, 123–127.

Stack, S. (1981). Suicide and religion: A comparative analysis. *Sociological Focus, 14*, 207–220.

Stack, S. (1983). The effect of religious commitment on suicide: A cross-national analysis. *Journal of Health and Social Behavior, 24*, 362–374.

Stack, S. (1992). Religiosity, depression, and suicide. In J. Schumaker (Ed.), *Religion and mental health.* New York: Oxford University Press.

Stack, S. (1998a). The relationship between culture and suicide: An analysis of African-Americans. *Transcultural Psychiatry, 35*, 253–269.

Stack, S. (1998b). Heavy metal, religiosity, and suicide acceptability. *Suicide and Life-Threatening Behavior, 28*, 388–394.

Stack, S. (2000). Suicide: A 15-year review of the sociological literature: Part II: Modernization and social integration perspectives. *Suicide and Life-Threatening Behavior, 30*, 163–176.

Stack, S., & Wasserman, I. (1992). The effects of religion on suicide ideology: An analysis of the networks perspective. *Journal for the Scientific Study of Religion, 31*, 457–466.

Stack, S., & Wasserman, I. (1995). The effect of marriage, family, and religious ties on African-American suicide ideology. *Journal of Marriage and the Family, 57*, 215–222.

Stack, S., Wasserman, I., & Kposowa, A. (1994). The effects of religion and feminism on suicide ideology: An analysis of national survey data. *Journal for the Scientific Study of Religion, 33*, 110–121.

Stark, R. (1996). Religion as context: Hellfire and delinquency one more time. *Sociology of Religion, 57*, 163–173.

Stark, R. (2001). Gods, rituals, and the moral order. *Journal for the Scientific Study of Religion, 40*, 619–636.

Stark, R., & Bainbridge, W. S. (1997). *Religion, deviance, and social control.* New York: Routledge.

Steffensmeier, D., & Allen, E. (2000). Looking for patterns: Gender, age, and crime. In J. F. Sheley (Ed.), *Criminology: A contemporary handbook* (pp. 85–127). Belmont, CA: Wadsworth.

Stewart, C., & Bolland, J. M. (2002). Parental style as a possible mediator of the relationship between religiosity and substance use in African-American adolescents. *Journal of Ethnicity in Substance Abuse, 1*, 63–81.

Stout-Miller, R., Miller, L. S., & Langenbrunner, M. R. (1997). Religiosity and child sexual abuse: A risk factor assessment. *Journal of Child Sexual Abuse, 6*, 15–35.

Straus, M. A., Geller, R. J., & Steinmetz, S. K. (1980). *Behind closed doors: Violence in the American family.* Garden City, NY: Anchor Books.

Straus, R. (1986). Scientology 'ethics': Deviance, identity and social control in a cult-like social world. *Symbolic Interaction, 9*, 67–82.

Tittle, C., & Welch, M. R. (1983). Religiosity and deviance: Toward a contingency theory of constraining effects. *Social Forces, 61*, 653–682.

Uggen, C., & Janikula, J. (1999). Volunteerism and arrest in the transition to adulthood. *Social Forces, 78*, 331–362.

Van Poppel, F., & Day, L. H. (1996). A test of Durkheim's theory of suicide—Without committing the ecological fallacy. *American Sociological Review, 61*, 500–507.

Wasserman, I., & Stack, S. (1993). The effect of religion on suicide: An analysis of cultural context. *Omega: Journal of Death and Dying, 27*, 295–305.

Welch, M. R., Tittle, C., & Petee, T. (1991). Religion and deviance among adult Catholics: A test of the 'moral communities' hypothesis. *Journal for the Scientific Study of Religion, 30*, 159–172.

Wilcox, M. M. (2002). When Sheila's a lesbian: Religious individualism among lesbian, gay, bisexual, and transgender Christians. *Sociology of Religion, 63*, 497–513.

Wilcox, W. B. (1998). Conservative protestant childrearing: Authoritarian or authoritative? *American Sociological Review, 63*, 796–809.

Wright, S. A. (1986). Dyadic intimacy and social control in three cult movements. *Sociological Analysis, 44*, 137–150.

Young, M. C., Gartner, J., O'Connor, T., Larson, D., & Wright, K. (1995). Long-term recidivism among federal inmates trained as volunteer prison ministers. *Journal of Offender Rehabilitation, 22*, 97–118.

CHAPTER 13

Adolescent Delinquency

MARK D. REGNERUS

> How exceeding beautiful, and how conducive to the adorning and happiness of the town, if the young people could be persuaded, when they meet together, to converse as Christians and as the children of God. This is what I have longed for, and it has been exceedingly grievous to me when I have heard of vice, vanity and disorder among our youth.
>
> —Jonathan Edwards, Theologian and Minister, 1750

INTRODUCTION

The social scientific study of religion on adolescent delinquency is not nearly as old as are popular linkages that have been made between the two, as the quote from Jonathan Edwards above suggests. For both heinous and harmless actions, many Americans—and perhaps many more worldwide—continue to draw connections, both real and imaginary, between diminished religiousness and heightened criminal activity. Intensive media coverage of occasional horrific crimes (such as the Columbine High School tragedy) might infer that the problem of adolescent crime and delinquency is increasing in scope or severity of effect. Although federal statistics do not appear to bear this out presently, fear of crime nevertheless ranks high among Americans' fears (Romer, Jamieson, & Aday, 2003). Safety inside and outside of schools remains a paramount parental concern (Schreck, Miller, & Gibson, 2003).

In response to real or perceived trends, organizations and movements have responded with all manner of competing and divergent ideas for the amelioration or attenuation of juvenile delinquency. Among these ideas are: increased spending on adolescent social services, a return to traditional forms of religion and childrearing, increasing family discipline, community policing, enhanced extracurricular involvement, a more efficient and equitable juvenile justice system, a return to "shame" or negative sanctions, earlier age limits for prosecuting adolescents as adults, federal restrictions on television and cinematic violence, popular boycotts of violent programming and its sponsors, and changes in parental childrearing practices away from acceptable violence in boys. That several of these measures infer a return to or renewed emphasis on a morally- or religiously inspired socialization

MARK D. REGNERUS • University of Texas, Austin, Texas 78712

of children and youth toward acceptable behavior indicates a popular perception (among many, although hardly all, Americans) of the ability of such solutions to affect juvenile delinquency.

The primary purpose of this chapter is to assess a relationship that many average people assume to be true—that religious belief and behavior keep youth out of trouble. The past 30 years of social science research has not always agreed with this assumption. Moreover, there is much that underlies the notion that religion curbs adolescent delinquency. Is religion a *key* concept in directly deterring deviance, or is it only indirectly related through its possible effects on such factors as adolescent self-control or family well-being? Moreover, what is meant by religion? Are religious beliefs and practices equally effective? And what types of delinquency are curbed? Fleeting, transitory actions like public rowdiness or more persistent and pernicious behaviors like drug abuse, or neither, or both?

This chapter will help clarify the connections we know about, note the ones we know less about, and point out possible future debates in this area. To be sure, writing a review of research is more art than science, and relies heavily on my own subjective evaluations of what fits, what does not, and where the boundaries between the two lay (Johnson et al., 2000). I have attempted to focus more on recent research (i.e., that published in the last 10 years), while trying not to neglect the seminal studies that have brought this field to the place where it currently stands. I attempt to glean from recent academic research on religious influences on adolescent delinquency, and to a lesser extent alcohol and drug use, and report findings from various studies. Findings about the religion-delinquency connection outside of North America are included here, but there are far fewer of these.

Why should religion matter for the behavior of adolescents? Indeed, religion can vary in the lives of teenagers from a compulsory hour-per-week period of intense boredom to a setting that sprouts a network of friends to an all-encompassing life-world of beliefs, behaviors, and ritual practices. There are a variety of theories about why or when religion does or does not affect adolescent delinquent behavior. I will not review them all here but, rather, draw attention to what are arguably the four most common frameworks within which religious effects on delinquency are understood: social control, social context, differential association, and victimless crimes.

RELIGION IN CRIMINOLOGICAL THEORY

Social Control

Religion has typically been considered an element of social control, in keeping with its assessment by Marx, Weber, and Durkheim. This theme continues to resonate in nearly all studies on the topic. For individuals and collectives, religion is commonly thought to provide practical order and a socially integrating influence (Durkheim, 1951 [1897]). In addition, social control theory does not ask why some people engage in crime. Rather, it takes delinquency for granted and seeks to understand what restrains most people from participating in it.

To draw on Gottfredson and Hirschi's (1990) vocabulary, religion constitutes a type of *involvement* in pursuits that affirm conventional forms of achievement when measured as attendance at traditional church services or youth group activities (Elder & Conger, 2000). Such involvement in religious communities is thought to encourage the formation of positive relationships and the routinization of practices, processes that work to reinforce conventional (rather than illegal) orientations toward success and are themselves conducive to achievement (Regnerus, 2000). Religion also can refer to *beliefs* that reinforce *commitments* to both the tenets of the religion as well as its typical proscriptions against illegal and immoral behaviors.

The social control approach is quite commensurate with how many religious people, especially those who are theologically conservative, understand human nature and behavior. Especially within conservative Protestant thought, human nature is understood to be inherently sinful (Curry, 1996). Although deviance from Scriptural commands or norms, cast as sin, may be understood as normal or at least acceptable outside the church, it is deemed unacceptable to its membership. Adherents are instructed that through their relationships to God and others within the church—internalized and externalized sources of social control—they have the ability to resist such behavior. The "hellfire" hypothesis, popularized by Hirschi and Stark (1969) is a variant of religion-as-social-control theory. This hypothesis, which is still tested today (e.g., Harris, 2003), predicts that religion deters individuals from committing crimes and engaging in delinquent behavior through the threat of supernatural sanctions (i.e., damnation, threat of eternal punishment in Hell). Those youth who take their (often conservative) religious beliefs seriously should, it was thought, restrain themselves from delinquency out of fear of future divine judgment and punishment.

Nevertheless, religious influences have been too frequently chalked up to social control without pursuing several important "why" questions. Why do some religious influences emerge in analyses of religion and delinquency and some fail to? Why might religious behaviors differ in their effect when compared with religious beliefs? Why does religion-as-social-control work well for some youth and not at all for others who are otherwise comparable (e.g., white, female, regular attender)?

"Strength in Numbers": Contextual Sources of Religious Influence

Connecting individual religious behavior or identity to the *contexts* in which these are given meaning, for the purpose of understanding human behaviors, remains unusual even within the sociology of religion. Those few studies that have done this (e.g., Ellison, Burr, & McCall, 1997; Pescosolido, 1990; Stark & Bainbridge, 1996) have uncovered new support for an old, Durkheimian idea—that participation in harmful behaviors is reduced in places where particular religions or religious rituals are widely practiced. The "moral communities" thesis that was prompted by Emile Durkheim and popularized by Rodney Stark is, in part, a reaction to the tendency of social scientists to focus only on individual religiosity. In its most general form, the thesis suggests that religion ought to be understood sociologically as a group property more than an individual one (Stark, 1996). When viewed this way, the deterrent effect of religion should be evident in places where religiousness is greatest. As an extension of this, such deterrence is also thought to exist where distinct religious homogeneity (e.g., densely Orthodox Jewish or evangelical Protestant) exists (Regnerus, 2003b).

Religious institutions comprise (among other things) relational networks that have the capacity to influence, if not outright control, the behaviors of youthful adherents, via sanctions, expectations, and demands placed on their time. Religious communities also increase the social support available to inhabitants (Ellison & George, 1994), and their central institutional resources (such as schools and churches) lend themselves to continuity in both the socialization as well as the social control of youth. Each of these are examples of what Putnam (2000) refers to as "bonding social capital," dense networks that enhance social and psychological support for community members. Moreover, community religious norms can actually operationalize social control. As simple examples, in select counties, towns, and suburbs throughout the United States, there is evidence of religiously inspired community norms, including those that promote marriage to legitimate sexual relationships and childbearing, and those that restrict alcohol sales, access to abortion, or prohibit Sunday athletic events (Raleigh, 2003).

The moral communities thesis not only suggests the existence of religious contextual influences on individuals' behavior—regardless of their own particular commitment to the religion—but also suggests that living with or near a considerable number of religious people will affect how any given religious individual will behave. I refer to this secondary effect as the "light switch" portion of the moral communities thesis. That is, only when a religious individual is in community with a critical mass of others (e.g., a friendship network, school, etc.) who share their beliefs and practices will that individual's religious beliefs significantly affect their behavior. As Stark (1996, p. 164) puts it—"what counts is not only whether a particular person is religious, but whether this religiousness is, or is not, ratified by the social environment." Communally ratified religiosity, in essence, "turns on" the light switch of an individual's own personal belief system. Without the support of a religious critical mass, the influence of religion on personal behavior—so the thesis argues—becomes ineffective. In statistical terms, the thesis proposes the presence of direct and indirect effects, as well as multilevel effects, of living in a devoutly religious context.

"Bad Friends": Religion and Differential Association

Although religion is most typically subsumed under social control approaches to delinquency and crime, it has received some recognition as well from researchers using a differential association approach. This is essentially an extension, or perhaps a variation, of the religion-as-context model, as its focus is on the social attachments of adolescents. It is those relationships to which an individual is "differentially associated" that are of most interest here. In other words, the individual's own beliefs or practices are thought to be less influential than are patterns of association—and their accompanying attitudes about delinquency—that adolescents exhibit. Understood this way, religion deters delinquency through both social selection and peer socialization. The focus is often on individuals' friends and peers, how they came to choose them and what influence such friends or peers have on one's behavior.

One variant of differential association theory is religious social bonding. Here religion is still about social control, no doubt, but concern shifts from friends and peers to the conventional attachments youth may have (e.g., parents, churches). Such attachments are psychological in nature, positive, and are also apt to take up time that could otherwise be spent engaged in delinquency. Simply put, spending time with one's family at church reduces time available for other activities, and in so doing reinforces conventional norms.

Such a focus on individuals to whom adolescents are attached—be they friends or family—is admittedly more difficult to model appropriately. Moreover, this theory moves the more important research question back in time, from how religious individuals act to first assessing who their associates are and to whom they are most strongly attached. This approach also lends itself to studies of reciprocal effects; that is, assumptions are typically made that religious youth select more conventional friends, whereas less religious youth are thought to identify with more delinquent friends. Thus, religion's true role in the differential association approach is difficult to pin down, and direct effects of religion on delinquency do little to mitigate suspicions about potential reverse causation. More complex modeling is required to test this theory, and ideal data with which to do so is difficult to come by, to say the least.

Nevertheless, even theories of differential association, which have made overtures to religion by considering it (and groups of religious friends) an important institution with which to be "differentially associated," have done so because of religion's ability to restrain behavior. Thus social control, no matter how one looks at it, is never far from studies of religious influence on adolescent delinquency.

Victimless Crimes

Finally, there has been research that suggests religion is most typically related to minor or victimless crimes, sometimes referred to as ascetic offenses, including behaviors that are illegal due to age (e.g., alcohol use, smoking). Building on Middleton and Putney's (1962) work, this theory suggests that the lack of relationship between religious behavior and offenses against persons and property is due to the masking influence of other social institutions—all of which, religious or otherwise, typically condemn such behavior (Burkett & White, 1974). Only religious institutions, by contrast, frown on victimless crimes. If society in general opposes certain behaviors, they argued, religious organizations will not stand out in their opposition. But for crimes like smoking or underage drinking, society is considered to be much more tolerant. It is then that researchers should be able to determine that religion curbs such behavior—when few or no other institutions suggest that it is a problem requiring attention. Thus, researchers should clearly be able to document religious influences on curbing minor forms of delinquency but should have little success in finding relationships between religion and more serious delinquency (since nearly all social institutions condemn the latter). Other studies have since narrowed the focus from religious institutions in general to particular religious theologies or traditions (most notably conservative Protestant ones) that appear more apt to treat all types of misbehavior seriously (Bartkowski & Ellison, 1995; Curry, 1996). Yet in nearly all such studies the measurement of institutional religion or theological traditions remains at the level of the individual religious believer or devotee, unlike in the moral communities or religious context research.

WHAT THE EVIDENCE SUGGESTS

Early Evidence

Contemporary research on juvenile delinquency began in 1969. It was in that year that Travis Hirschi and Rodney Stark published a provocative article entitled "Hellfire and Delinquency," spawning new life in a topic whose interest had waned (Hirschi & Stark, 1969). In sum, they suggested that religious practice and belief had *no* impact on delinquency. Sociologists took notice. Still today this article remains a benchmark against which much subsequent work on the topic has been written (e.g., Harris, 2003). "Hellfire and Delinquency" was based on a sample of junior and senior high school students in Western Contra Costa County, California. The authors concluded that students who believe in the Devil and the afterlife were no less likely to commit delinquent acts than those who did not hold such beliefs. Subsequent analyses soon emerged. Burkett and White (1974) replicated Hirschi and Stark's findings on high school students in the Pacific Northwest, but suggested narrowing the theory to crimes against persons and property. A clear relationship emerged, they suggested, between religion and "victimless" crimes such as underage drinking and drug use.

Little formal modeling of the relationship existed to this point. Elifson, Peterson, and Hadaway (1983, p. 521) began to correct this using a similar sample of Atlanta adolescents and standardized regression analysis to conclude that "the relationship of religiosity to delinquency is so closely tied to the family and other moral influences that it has little influence that is statistically independent of the other predictor variables." Their study reinforced the emerging disciplinary sentiment that religiosity and status (or victimless) offenses are related in a bivariate manner but largely disappear when examined in a more rigorous, multivariate setting. Later work by Perkins (1985) further reinforced this idea, showing that friendship environments are the strongest influences on drinking and drug use among college students, even while strong faith commitment to both Jewish and Christian traditions remained a moderating influence.

Meanwhile, Stark found a substantial negative relationship between religiosity and delinquency in secondary schools in which religious students are the majority (Stark, Kent, & Doyle, 1982). The relationship diminishes as the proportion of religious students shrinks and is not at all present in West Coast schools, where group religiosity is notably low. Indeed, there was no "hellfire effect" in Seattle but a strong one in Provo, prompting the adjustment in the direction of a more sociological, as compared to social psychological, direction. In keeping with this new conception, Higgins and Albrecht (1977), studying a sample of Atlanta teenagers, found consistently inverse relationships between religion and several forms of delinquency.

In his analysis of SMSA-level data (and perhaps the most direct test of religious context effects to date), Bainbridge (1989) found significant inverse relationships between church membership rates and rates of assault, burglary, and larceny independent of residential mobility, poverty rates, percentage African American, and percentage divorced. The church membership effects, however, appeared to be sensitive to the inclusion of percentage divorced, suggesting that the two may mediate one another.

Stark began to refine this "moral communities" theory, relocating the researcher's focus from the individual to the community. Interestingly, the particular nature of the religious beliefs or specific denominational affiliation is *not* important in the moral communities thesis. Articulated at length in his book with Bainbridge (Stark & Bainbridge, 1996), Stark suggests that religiosity is related to conformity only in distinctly religious contexts—places where the mean level of religiosity is high. This would explain the contrast in conclusions drawn from Pacific Coast and Southern U.S. samples. This position is largely where Stark remains today.

In contrast, Tittle and Welch (1983) quickly disputed Stark's approach, suggesting that only in contexts of moral ambiguity, low social integration, and low perceptions of peer conformity will religious individuals show significant differences with respect to delinquent behavior. Following an impressive review of previous work, in which they point out that only 11 of 65 previous studies controlled for *any* antecedent variables, they proposed an emergent "contingency" theory of religious effects on deviance. Building on Stark's contextual emphasis, they found that religiosity's inhibitory effects varied directly with the degree of normative ambiguity in a context, as measured by the mean standard deviation in responses to several morality "situations." Such ambiguity held greater effect where the community or reference group (context) is most distinct, as in small towns and among youth. In other words, where agreed-on moral guidelines are unavailable, the importance of religious proscriptions on delinquent behavior is enhanced because "secularized" social contexts lack the tools to produce conformity (Tittle & Welch, 1983, p. 672). This argument directly contradicts Stark's suggestion that intensely religious contexts reinforce prosocial behavior.

Although their results supported this hypothesis, their analysis was hampered by several measurement difficulties, including constructed "contexts" such as age groups or marital status categories rather than actual physical places or groups of linked individuals. Deviance was measured as the hypothetical likelihood to commit certain acts if the respondent "were in a situation where they had an extremely strong desire or need to," a unique approach that entails both merits and pitfalls (Tittle & Welch, 1983, p. 661). Their subsequent analysis of Roman Catholic parishes provides a more proximate test for the moral communities thesis (Welch, Tittle, & Petee, 1991). There they found significant negative effects of both individual and parish-level religiosity on adult deviance but no interaction between the two. Nevertheless, their study could not assess whether variation in religiosity between parishes shapes the influence of individual religiosity on deviance.

Relatively few studies to date, however, have been able to examine the *actual* effect of religious context on crime or delinquency, as Stark and others have theorized. The level of social control fostered by a community's religious fervor or homogeneity is typically overstated when compared directly with the influence of one's personal beliefs and practices. Empirical research continues to favor individual effects while not denying the helpfulness of supportive social contexts (Sampson & Groves, 1989; Simcha-Fagan & Schwartz, 1986). Finally, only recently have research methods (e.g., multilevel models) that can properly assess contextual effects become both available and more widely taught.

Moreover, certainly not all of the action in this area was concerned about moral communities or religious context. Peek, Curry, and Chalfant (1985) shifted the debate about religion and delinquency toward emphasizing longitudinal studies, assessing how religiosity affects delinquent behavior over the course of adolescence, and drawing attention to the concern that the two are reciprocally related. Curiously, what Peek and his associates were most interested in was the potential for heightened delinquency among youth whose religiosity has diminished over time—a sort of "making up for lost time" model that hypothesizes greater than average delinquency among such types. Their regression analyses mildly supported this hypothesis with respect to nonstatus offenses. Misgivings arise, however, about both their sample (with numerous missing cases and one third of the total N being unclassifiable on their preferred religious categories) and their "attitudes about religiosity" measures, as opposed to actual behavior. Among other suggestions was a neurological explanation for the spuriousness of the religion/deviance relationship, namely that the suboptimally aroused person is neurologically predisposed toward the intense stimulation of crime and away from the boredom of methodical church attendance (Ellis & Thompson, 1989).

Cochran and Akers, primarily criminologists attracted to the debate by accusations that researchers like themselves were neglecting religious factors, fired back at the primarily religious researchers by concluding that more parsimonious models of direct religious effects fare just as well as the more complex contextual analyses that were becoming popular. In a test of the "hellfire," antiasceticism, and moral community hypotheses, Cochran and Akers (1989) argued that the antiasceticism thesis was both the most straightforward argument and the one supported by the strongest evidence. They (1989, p. 221) concluded simply that "religiosity is inversely related to delinquent behavior."

Recent Research

Few debates within social science are ever settled, and this one was no different. Cochran and several associates (1994) picked up the subject in the mid-1990s, examining the relationship between religion and deviance with an eye to assessing exactly *how* it is spurious. They produced statistical evidence favoring both the aforementioned arousal theory and other more proximate measures of social control, such as peer and familial influences. The significance of religiosity and the salience of religious beliefs on all dependent variables except alcohol and drug use disappeared when arousal and social control variables were included in the same model.

More research began to concur with this conclusion. Benda and Corwyn (1997) found in their study of 1,093 public school adolescents that general social control measures displaced most religious effects on status offenses. They additionally found more evidence for the reciprocal relationship between religiosity and delinquency. Indeed, the former predicted less delinquency only for particular outcomes, but a variety of delinquent behaviors were consistently related to a decline in religiosity. Several studies indicated that religious social bonding is insignificant when peer delinquency or other "secular" social controls are accounted for (Cochran, Wood, & Arneklev, 1994). Yet this approach assumes (or at least infers) that religion does not matter for delinquency when, in fact, it may well matter—just indirectly. Placing religion in a head-to-head statistical competition against "secular" social controls for available variance in regression models seems unwise, because religion and social control variables are typically positively correlated with each other in a reciprocal causal fashion. Instead of attempting to model accordingly (or at least acknowledging this situation), researchers often include in their models along with religious variables such influences as family activities, friendship restrictions, formal legal deterrents, household rules, and quality of relationship with parents. Although well intentioned, this approach creates a statistical competition with religious social control measures such as church attendance or religious salience for the purpose of establishing the *direct* statistical importance of the variable for preventing delinquency. When religion appears insignificant as a direct effect, it may be thought to be altogether ineffective. This conclusion is prematurely drawn, however, as religious influence on "secular" social controls may (and arguably does) abound.

Using longitudinal data from the National Youth Survey, Johnson et al. (2001) tested a more appropriate and complex structural path model of religious influence on adolescent delinquency. In it, they evaluated a cross-lagged model, including pathways to/from both delinquent associations and behaviors as well as religiosity and religious beliefs. Their ambitious study of over 1,700 youth revealed that the influence of religiosity on delinquency is far from spurious, nor is it entirely indirect by means of religious influence on secular social controls. Religious involvement, they argued, increases adolescents' disapproval of delinquent acts as well as enhances the proportion of "conventional" friends within their peer networks. Little evidence was found that would suggest that religious *beliefs* are the primary vehicle for religious influence on delinquency; rather, religious commitment appears to be the key predictor variable. Finally, they note that the relationship between the two appears to be bidirectional; that is, engaging in delinquency appears to reduce subsequent levels of religious commitment. Indeed, this reciprocal effects approach has been reinforced in most well-designed recent studies.

Moreover, with this (and other studies) the evidence that religion is only related to non-victim offenses also began to crumble. Powell (1997) detected a protective religious factor in analyzing violent students in a sample of high-risk (for violence) schools in a Southeast city. Likewise, respondents' attitudes toward religion were significantly correlated with nonviolent behavior. She suggests churches intervene by promoting mentoring relationships with at-risk youth, especially during key developmental "windows of opportunity."

Finally, I turn to results from the most recent series of analyses concerning religion and delinquency—a set of studies not easily classifiable and quite wide-ranging in their scope. I begin with two studies employing data from the National Longitudinal Study of Adolescent Health. In the first, when both mothers and children reported high religiosity, the delinquency of the latter diminished (Pearce & Haynie, 2004). Yet when either a mother or child report dissimilar or unshared religiosity (e.g., mother more or less religious than child), the child's delinquency appeared to increase.

Using identical data, Regnerus (2003b) tested Stark's moral communities thesis using multilevel analysis. He found support for this perspective, in the form of interactions between contextual (county-level and school-level) religious variables and individual religiosity. Although individual religious effects remain strongest, conservative Protestant homogeneity in both counties and schools corresponds with lower theft and minor delinquency counts among individual students living in those counties and attending such schools. Additionally, such religious homogeneity interacts with individual-level measures of conservative Protestantism, further reducing incidence (especially of theft). In related work using structural equation modeling, Regnerus (2003a) documented the importance of parental religious factors in shaping adolescent delinquency; specifically, he found both direct and indirect effects of (a) parental religiosity and (b) parental conservative Protestantism on levels of adolescent delinquent behavior, even while controlling for the adolescent's own religiosity. For boys, higher parental religiosity proved to be a modestly aggravating effect on delinquency.

In a study of a sample of Mormon adolescents, Harris (2003) found that, along with religious social bonding, belief in "this-worldly" supernatural sanctions exhibited an independent effect on both perceived future ascetic deviance and perceived future delinquency. Harris appropriately notes the uniqueness of his sample. The application of a "perceived future behavior" measurement approach to a study of what is arguably the most well-behaved group of American youth (i.e., Mormons) may not tell us a great deal, elegant as its analyses are. Indeed, anticipated drinking and throwing things (e.g., rocks) were the *most frequently* cited behaviors (11% each) that such youth intended to ever undertake. Employing a very different sample, Ellis (2002) compared the self-reported behavior of more than 11,000 American and Canadian college students. Those that claimed to be atheist or agnostic displayed the highest illegal drug usage, and girls who identified as such were particularly prone to report property offenses. Respondents with no religious affiliation, however, did not appear either more or less delinquent than most other affiliations. No affiliation differences emerged among either gender on self-reported violent offenses.

Benda's (2002) unique analysis of Arkansas boot camp participants (i.e., incarcerated youth) revealed that religion (a latent variable that includes measures of religious expression and forgiveness) was inversely related to having carried a weapon, use of drugs, the sale of drugs, and violent offenses. Effects were direct, indirect, and reciprocal, whereas effect sizes were notable: the relationship between religion and violence was the fifth-strongest in the analyses, surpassed only by more proximate variables such as carrying a weapon and gang involvement. Again, little here suggests support for the thesis that religion only affects nonvictim crimes or minor offenses.

Despite these important studies, research on religion and delinquency appears to have slowed of late, at least in comparison to the 1970s and 1980s when the debate was a very lively one. Certainly it seems that the most visible studies are coming from fewer researchers than previously. However, there are at least two exemplary exceptions to this in the form of recent (and very helpful) meta-analyses of studies conducted on the very topic of religion and delinquency (Baier & Wright, 2001; Johnson et al., 2000). Meta-analyses seek to characterize similarities and differences between studies or sets of data analyses, providing helpful overviews about "study-level" variables that we otherwise could not see. They help us "see the forest," so to speak, instead of just staring at and comparing individual trees (i.e., studies).

In their meta-analysis of 40 studies of religion and delinquency, Johnson et al. (2000) found only one that suggested religiosity had a deleterious effect on delinquency. The remaining majority of studies noted a beneficial effect, while several were insignificant or inconclusive. Interestingly, they documented that those 13 studies that were rigorous enough to assess the reliability of their religious measures each found religion to have an inverse effect on delinquency.

In their analysis of 60 such studies, Baier and Wright (2001) documented that large datasets, secular samples, and nonviolent measures of delinquency were each conducive to finding larger effects (typically inverse) of religion on crime. Consequently, religious influences are less commonly found in studies that draw on smaller samples or that seek to explain its influence on more violent forms of behavior. About two thirds of the 60 studies they examined displayed religious effect sizes between–0.05 and–0.20. None of the effects, it should be noted, were positive. That is, religion was always found to deter crime and delinquency, not provoke it. Moreover, they found support for the idea that religion is more apt to affect nonvictim crimes. Studies of such crimes revealed effect sizes ranging between–0.15 and–0.24. Interestingly, more recent studies note larger effects, suggesting that (for whatever reason) the relationship is strengthening over time. Finally, studies using predominantly white samples found smaller religious effects than those employing more racially diverse samples.

International Studies of Religion and Delinquency

With a very few exceptions, there is not a great deal of recent international research on religion and delinquency. Most samples are American. Junger and Polder (1993) examined a sample of Moroccan, Surinamese, Turkish, and Dutch boys in the Netherlands. They found a modest inverse relationship between religiosity and delinquency among all groups except the Turks and the Hindustani (Surinamese). Having defined Moroccans and Turks as occupying a moral community and the Dutch as having a secular community, the authors nevertheless noted no support for the notion that moral communities exhibit lower crime rates nor that they augment the religiosity-delinquency relationship. To be sure, an ethnic identifier of a moral community is less in keeping with the original intent of the thesis (Stark et al., 1982). An analysis of approximately 1,000 German high school students revealed that over half did not attend religious services at all (Martin, Kirkcaldy, & Siefen 2003). Nevertheless, regular attenders tended to adopt healthier lifestyles, yet also displayed higher scores on a scale of social problems.

Brief Excursus on Alcohol, Tobacco, and Drug Use

Although this chapter is primarily concerned with delinquency, a few notes on religion's relationship with alcohol, tobacco, and drug use seem merited. How religion affects drinking and smoking is not unlike how it is thought to affect delinquency. Indeed, how religion affects alcohol and cigarette smoking—behaviors illegal only because the adolescent is underage—can be quite different from how it affects illegal drug use. Generally, religiosity shows modest protective effects, and is considered to be a less important factor than parent or peer drinking or age effects. Religious tradition is typically less important than is the extent to which adolescents have internalized or practice their religion (i.e., personal salience).

Perkins's (1987) study of college youth revealed a weak inverse relationship between drinking and personal religiosity. The influence of religion was found to be largely channeled through parents: whereas only 8% of Jewish fathers and 9% of Protestant fathers drank heavily, 31% of Catholic fathers did so; and when at least one parent drank heavily, the student was much more likely to report a similar problem with alcohol. Forthun et al. (1999) report less alcohol use and later initiation among religiously conservative students in a study conducted at a Southwestern state university. Cochran and Akers (1989), drawing on a survey of 3,065 adolescents in three Midwestern states, tested several existing theories about adolescent influence on alcohol and drug use. They found no evidence of an influence of "aggregate religiosity," or the average religiosity within each of the various school districts in the sample, in contrast to Stark's "moral communities" thesis. Likewise, no influence appeared from perceived denominational teachings concerning youthful drinking. Their findings supported the simpler thesis that primarily an individual's own religion matters, namely that religious youth are less likely to use either marijuana or alcohol when compared to their irreligious peers. A follow-up study by Cochran (1992) showed similar results: more devoutly religious youth displayed less proclivity toward using alcohol, marijuana, and several types of drugs. The authors again suggest a more parsimonious model of modest but stable inhibitory influence.

Burkett's (1993) study of Northwest U.S. high school students revealed interesting differences in the religion/alcohol use relationship by gender. For boys, parents' religiosity was not related to the adolescents' belief that drinking is a sin, the level of involvement with friends who drink, or the youth's own drinking behavior. Only indirect effects were found, however, with the types of friends with which the respondents were likely to associate. For girls, by contrast, stronger direct (protective) effects were noted between parents' religious involvement and both beliefs about drinking and actual behavior, in addition to the indirect effects through friendship choices.

A compelling and rigorous study of teenage twin girls (1,687 pairs) and their parents provided a unique opportunity to distinguish environmental from inherited/socialized influences on teenage smoking and alcohol use (Heath et al., 1999). The authors argue that the lower alcohol use patterns of African-American youth are in part the result of their greater religious involvement and stronger religious values. Interestingly, their measurable patterns of public religiosity were not remarkably higher than white and other ethnic youth, but the influence of religion was substantially stronger for them. In Cochran's (1993) study of types of alcohol use, he found religiosity more strongly related to avoiding liquor than beer or wine. Interestingly, he noted that the effect of personal religiosity on alcohol use is considerably stronger when the youth is affiliated with a denomination (e.g., Baptist, Pentecostal) that typically takes a stronger stand against alcohol.

In a novel longitudinal examination of religion and alcohol use among white and African-American adolescents, Brown et al. (2002) found that frequency of attendance and prayer curbed drinking among African-American youth, whereas religious fundamentalism and religious salience did so among whites. These results suggest that religious measures' effectiveness may differ across racial or ethnic identities. In a different study of middle adolescents, religious salience was associated with subsequent decisions to use alcohol, but here again (as with some analyses of delinquency) the association becomes insignificant when controlling for peer, family, and school influences (Mason & Windle, 2002). The same was not the case for religious attendance, which remained significant after these controls.

The relationship between adolescent religion and drug use generally differs from that between religion and alcohol or delinquency, due in part to its status as illegal regardless of age. As with studies of delinquent behavior, many studies of drug use conclude that peer influence is the key predictor. If one's friends are drug users, then the opportunities and pressures to use drugs obviously increases substantially. How religion shapes drug use is less clear. Nearly 25 years ago, Kandel (1980) reviewed existing research and concluded that involvement in religion was inversely associated with alcohol and marijuana use.

As measures for peer influence improve, however, data on drug use is beginning to display fewer direct relationships with religion. Bahr et al. (1993) studied 322 adolescents, applying a complex modeling approach to assessing religion's influence. They found that after accounting for peer drug use, parental cohesion and adolescent religiosity showed no relationship with either cocaine or marijuana use, as well as general substance abuse. Parental monitoring, however, remained important. Their model favored a social learning theory, wherein emphasis is placed on how youth come to model troubling behavior. However, a follow-up study by Bahr et al. (1998) showed different results. Controlling for peer drug use, respondents with more extensive religiosity displayed less marijuana and amphetamine or depressant use in a random sample of Utah youth. Compared to alcohol use, the relationship they found between religiosity and drug use was stronger. Outweighing each of these is the influence of religiosity on peer drug use—those adolescents who are involved in religion tend not to associate with peers who drink or do drugs. This again spells out the importance of accounting for the *indirect* (as well as direct) effects of religion on drug and alcohol use. One without the other is only half the story.

In a compelling evaluation of the influence of religiosity on black and white youths' drug use, Amey, Albrecht, and Miller (1996) found that religiosity was much more likely to predict abstention in whites than in blacks. Analyzing data from the Monitoring the Future study, the authors note that religious affiliation (or its absence) was not influential on the drug use of black students. Overall, however, black students were still much less likely to use all types of drugs than whites. Thus, although black youth exhibit higher religiosity than whites, it does not serve as a deterrent to drug use. Both here and in other studies (including Foshee & Hollinger, 1996) the aspect of parental or youth religiosity that was most influential in curbing drug and alcohol use was actual religious service attendance, rather than more private forms of religiosity or their particular religious affiliation.

Another study of twin pairs revealed strong correlations between religiosity and belief that drug use is sinful. Fundamentalist and Baptist youth were more apt than mainline Protestant and Catholic youth to believe that drug use was sinful. These beliefs, together with level of peer religiosity, mediated the relationship between the adolescent's own religiosity and their substance use. Notably, the inverse relationship between religiosity and drug, cigarette, marijuana, and alcohol use were considerably stronger among females than males.

A recent study of a wide range of outcomes documented that personal religious devotion and conservative religious affiliations predicted diminished use and dependence upon alcohol, marijuana, cocaine, and other illegal drugs (Miller, Davies, & Greenwald, 2000). Personal religious conservatism was only linked with lower levels of alcohol use. Corwyn and Benda's (2000) assessment of drug use documented that personal religiosity (i.e., salience or importance) appears to be more important than attendance in restraining individuals from using hard drugs. And quite strong—with each unit increase in personal religiosity, adolescents were found to be only half as likely to use drugs. This also suggests the antiascetic behavior thesis of religious influence is simply shortsighted; indeed, religiosity appears to curb both minor and serious illegal behaviors.

In a complex, contextual analysis, Jang and Johnson (2001) found that the influence of adolescent religiosity on drug use was strongest in disorganized communities. Their rigorous test of National Youth Study data using multilevel models found that religiosity influences drug use *independently* from social bonding and social learning variables, which partly mediated its effects. They also note in a rare examination of age-graded effects that religiosity's influence became stronger over the course of adolescence.

In a unique study controlling for the effects of the ALDH2 gene on heavy episodic drinking among Chinese-American and Korean-American college students, Luczak et al. (2003) found that religious service attendance significantly lowered drinking among Koreans, as well as among Chinese who practiced Western religions (e.g., Christianity). Moreover, attendance predicted less heavy drinking especially in individuals who were not already protected by genetic proclivities toward less drinking.

POTENTIAL POLICY IMPLICATIONS

As stated at the outset, religious or moral answers for juvenile delinquency are often cited by average Americans, if not social scientists, as effective and positive. However, at face value such solutions suffer from the pitfalls provided by current interpretations of the First Amendment to the U.S. Constitution. Court cases of late, wherein judges have sentenced delinquent youth to such practices as reading the Bible or writing the Ten Commandments, have been immediately called into question as unconstitutional. Yet given the recent penchant toward welfare reform and block grants given to states—which would be allowed to fund explicitly religious grantees—perhaps policies of adolescent rehabilitation linked to religious institutions are not far behind. Public-private initiatives, although certainly politically tenuous, are becoming increasingly common. The success experienced by one prominent example of this in Boston during the 1990s (between ministers and the police) has spurred similar ventures elsewhere (Winship & Berrien, 1999). Community-based policing is, in many ways, helping to construct a moral community (Adams, 1994). Such partnerships, however, are far from flawless. One does not have to look far to find programs wracked by political infighting or, worse yet, child abuse charges against employees of faith-based institutions ("Baltimore churches," 2001; "Staffer found guilty," 2001). Amidst the politicking, research on the efficacy of faith-based institutions in transforming troubled youth remains, unfortunately, sparse and expensive.

We do know some things, however. Gorsuch (1995) reports that a quasi-experimental study found that a religiously based drug program curriculum appeared to lower substance use rates among students better than health- and social studies–based programs. He argues from a review of research that religious social control based primarily on punishment does not appear to reduce the occurrence of substance abuse, and might even be related to its increase, as well as to antisocial behavior. Religiously based interventions can, however, help youth foster other use-reducing factors such as a positive peer group and family support. Studies comparing religious and secular treatment programs generally report comparable outcomes. Clergy and chaplains are reported to be valuable in assisting adolescents with alcohol or drug abuse problems, by listening, talking, and providing opportunities for shared experiences (e.g., prayer) during addiction struggles (Pullen et al., 1999). What is likely

beneficial is the immersion of at-risk youth in family-oriented religious worlds. The effectiveness of such from inner-city Philadelphia (Furstenberg et al., 1999) to rural Iowa
(Elder & Conger, 2000) is difficult to contest. Policy oriented toward the encouragement of
such—perhaps including such goals as funding after-school church programs for youth—
might prove beneficial. Were federal or state assistance earmarked along diverse religious
lines, it would be difficult to argue conclusively that such would constitute any establishment
(read preference) of religion.

LOOKING TOWARD THE FUTURE

Religion remains a large part of many persons' lives. Yet scholars who study religion's role
in curbing delinquency still struggle to gain acceptance of their research among critical
peers. Yet it is more apparent than ever before that religion is an often overlooked factor in
studies of crime and delinquency. Indeed, by excluding religious measures researchers are
risking misspecifying their models, in so doing creating statistical bias in the estimates of
the variables that they do include (Johnson et al., 2000).

Whereas the studies outlined here constitute a clear advancement on the topic of
religion and delinquency, each invariably suffers from limitations (some more than others).
Appropriate data and methods for empirical analyses of the relationship have often lagged
behind the ability to properly test theories. There has been too much reliance on cross-
sectional designs (Benda, 1997; Benda & Corwyn, 1997; Hirschi & Stark, 1969; Tittle &
Welch, 1983), dependence on exploratory factor analysis to establish relationships and
spur post-hoc theorizing, neglect of indirect relationships (Cochran et al., 1994; Cochran
and Akers, 1989; Elifson, Peterson, & Hadaway, 1983), and use of stepwise regression
methods (Dudley, 1993). Some limitations are endemic, others—including most of those
noted here—can be dealt with. I list below, and briefly expand on, five things that religion-
and-delinquency scholars do not know (or currently do not do), or at least not well enough.

First, the adolescence-only nature of much sociological research restricts us from
studying what perhaps is a key time and setting when religion affects the development
of youth: childhood. Developmental psychopathologists, as well as criminologists of many
theoretical commitments, argue that persistently antisocial youth are largely formed prior to
adolescence. Pursuing studies of antisocial behavior among younger children (ages 8–11),
their parents, and their collective religious practices and affiliations is certainly called for.

Second, we know less about *how* and *why* religious commitment reduces delinquency
than that it does (Johnson et al., 2001). The connections, if any, between religion and
shame/guilt, are even less well known, and have not been examined within the scope of
a study of religion and delinquency. Simply put, many of us have documented religious
influences, but few have done an adequate job of understanding the pathways of effect, and
fewer still articulate well *why* religion matters (or why, among some samples, it does not).

Third, advanced methods and optimal data are called for to properly test complex
theories (such as the moral communities thesis). Multilevel models applied to data that
includes characteristics about individuals' social environment (e.g., friends, schools, community) is required in order to accurately test those theories that explicitly concern such
concepts. Another methodological snafu that concerns very few researchers is selection
effects. Unlike gender or race, religion is not at all random but, rather, chosen. We need
to know more about whether those variables that predict religion (or religiosity, etc.) also
predict delinquency, and whether they can, in fact, account for most of the relationship

between religion and delinquency. One possible solution is the use of Heckman selection models, which have been used in studies of religion and sexual behavior (Meier, 2003). Like sex, the occurrence of delinquent events makes subsequent delinquency much more likely. Minimally, the use of prior delinquency or "delinquent propensity" variables ought to be included in regression models, even while we hope that studies will better ascertain religious influence (if any) on such propensities (Nagin & Paternoster, 1991). Longitudinal analyses must become central to this area; this will enhance scholars' ability to document robust, causal influences of religion. Finally, to address concern about public funding of religious organizational involvement in the lives of youth, more practical studies, including prison and recividism studies, are needed, paying attention to religion's indirect effects (e.g., such as on parolee/church partnerships, etc.).

Fourth, expanding the types of measures of religiosity is due. Johnson et al. (2000) appropriately noted that the vast majority of studies rely on one of two measures of religiosity—church attendance (85% of the studies) and religious salience (65%). Future examinations would do well to broaden their scope of analysis, especially in order to evaluate possible connections between spirituality and delinquency. National datasets now exist that include measures of spirituality. Among them are the National Study of Youth and Religion as well as the National Longitudinal Study of Adolescent Health.

Fifth, we should make progress toward a developmental approach to the study of religious influence. Religion should not be understood as a constant in practice or salience across the human life course, especially during adolescence. Religious beliefs, practices, affiliations, and commitments are not static phenomena. Although adolescence is only one stage of the life course, and a brief one at that, it is one of considerable change and a number of potential "turning points," such as the onset of puberty or menarche, transition from junior to senior high school, family relocations, legal driving age, high school graduation, and the commencement of higher education. It is also a period of a growing redefinition of self as separate from one's family of origin and more closely fashioned in response to peers and friends. Parent-child relationships are quite sensitive to religious differences during adolescence, and are themselves an important predictor of delinquent behavior (Regnerus & Burdette, 2003; Regnerus, 2002). An adequate account of adolescence, then, requires attention to intergenerational social bonds, changing family structures, valued practices and groups, community norms and proscriptions, and transactional relationships between parents, children, and peers, among other concerns. Just as the transmission of abusive and unstable family relations is an example of lives lived interdependently, so also prosocial behavior is learned from parents, peers, and other socializing agents in children's lives (Elder, Caspi, & Downey, 1986). Unfortunately, many scholars continue to evaluate religious influence as if it were a static phenomenon and as if the role of religion as experienced (possibly quite differently) within the family unit did not matter.

REFERENCES

Adams, C. F. (1994). Fighting crime by building moral communities. *The Christian Century, 111*, 894–896.

Amey, C. H., Albrecht, S. L., & Miller, M. K. (1996). Racial differences in adolescent drug use: The impact of religion. *Substance Use & Misuse, 31*, 1311–1332.

Bahr, S. J., Hawks, R. D., & Wang, G. (1993). Family and religious influences on adolescent substance abuse. *Youth & Society, 24*, 443–465.

Bahr, S. J., Maughan, S. L., Marcos, A. C., & Li, B. (1998). Family, religiosity, and the risk of adolescent drug use. *Journal of Marriage and the Family, 60*, 979–992.

Baier, C. J., & Wright, B.R.E. (2001). "If you love me, keep my commandments": A meta-analysis of the effect of religion on crime. *Journal of Research on Crime and Delinquency, 38,* 3–21.

Bainbridge, W. S. (1989). The religious ecology of deviance. *American Sociological Review, 54,* 288–295.

"Baltimore churches in slugfest over 'faith-based' program." (2001). *Church & State, 54,* 18–19.

Bartkowski, J. P., & Ellison, C. G. (1995). Divergent perspectives on childrearing in popular manuals: Conservative Protestants vs. the mainstream experts. *Sociology of Religion, 56,* 21–34.

Benda, B. B. (2002). Religion and violent offenders in boot camp: A structural equation model. *Journal of Research in Crime and Delinquency, 39,* 91–121.

Benda, B. B., & Corwyn, R. F. (2000). A test of the validity of delinquency syndrome construct in a homogeneous sample. *Journal of Adolescence, 23,* 497–511.

Benda, B. B., & Corwyn, R. F. (1997). A test of a model with reciprocal effects between religiosity and various forms of delinquency using 2-stage least squares regression. *Journal of Social Service Research, 22,* 27–52.

Benda, B. B., & Corwyn, R. F. (1997). Religion and delinquency: The relationship after considering family and peer influences. *Journal for the Scientific Study of Religion, 36,* 81–92.

Brown, T. L., Parks, G. S., Zimmerman, R. S., & Phillips, C. M. (2001). The role of religion in predicting adolescence alcohol use and problem drinking. *Journal of Studies on Alcohol, 62,* 96–705.

Burkett, S. R. (1980). Religiosity, beliefs, normative standards and adolescent drinking. *Journal of Studies on Alcohol, 41,* 662–671.

Burkett, S. R. (1993). Perceived parents' religiosity, friends' drinking, and hellfire: A panel study of adolescent drinking. *Review of Religious Research, 35,* 134–154.

Burkett, S. R., & White, M. (1974). Hellfire and delinquency: Another look. *Journal for the Scientific Study of Religion, 13,* 455–462.

Cochran, J. K. (1992). The effects of religiosity on adolescent self-reported frequency of drug and alcohol use. *Journal of Drug Issues, 22,* 91–104.

Cochran, J. K. (1993). The variable effects of religiosity and denomination on adolescent self-reported alcohol use by beverage type. *The Journal of Drug Issues, 23,* 479–491.

Cochran, J. K., & Akers, R. L. (1989). Beyond hellfire: An exploration of the variable effects of religiosity on adolescent marijuana and alcohol use. *Journal of Research in Crime and Delinquency, 26,* 198–225.

Cochran, J. K., Wood, P. B., & Arneklev, B. J. (1994). Is the religiosity-delinquency relationship spurious? A test of arousal and social control theories. *Journal of Research in Crime and Delinquency, 31,* 92–123.

Corwyn, R. F., & Benda, B. B. (2000). Religiosity and church attendance: The effects on use of "hard drugs" controlling for sociodemographic and theoretical factors. *The International Journal for the Psychology of Religion, 10,* 241–258.

Curry, T. R. (1996). Conservative Protestantism and the perceived wrongfulness of crimes. *Criminology, 34,* 453–464.

Dudley, R. L. (1999). Youth religious commitment over time: A longitudinal study of retention. *Review of Religious Research, 41,* 110–121.

Durkheim, E. (1951). *Suicide.* New York: Free Press. (Original work published 1897)

Elder, G.H., Jr., Caspi, A., & Downey, G. (1986). Problem behavior and family relationships: Life course and intergenerational themes. In A.B. Sorensen, F.E. Weinert, & L.R. Sherrod (Eds.), *Human development and the life course: Multidisciplinary perspectives* (pp. 293–340). Hillsdale, NJ: Erlbaum.

Elder, G. H., Jr., & Conger, R. D. (2000). *Children of the land: Adversity and success.* Chicago: University of Chicago Press.

Elifson, K. W., Peterson, D. M., & Hadaway, C. K. (1983). Religiosity and delinquency: A contextual analysis. *Criminology, 21,* 505–527.

Ellis, L. (2002). Denominational differences in self-reported delinquency. *Journal of Offender Rehabilitation, 35,* 187–200.

Ellis, L., & Thompson, R. (1989). Relating religion, crime, arousal and boredom. *Sociology and Social Research, 73,* 132–139.

Ellison, C. G., Burr, J. A., & McCall, P. L. (1997). Religious homogeneity and metropolitan suicide rates. *Social Forces, 76,* 273–299.

Ellison, C. G., & George, L. K. (1994). Religious involvement, social ties, and social support in a Southeastern community. *Journal for the Scientific Study of Religion, 33,* 46–61.

Ellison, C. G., & Sherkat, D. E. (1993). Obedience and autonomy: Religion and parental values reconsidered. *Journal for the Scientific Study of Religion, 32,* 313–329.

Foshee, V. A., & Hollinger, B. R. (1996). Maternal religiosity, adolescent social bonding, and adolescent alcohol use. *Journal of Early Adolescence, 16,* 451–468.

Furstenberg, F. F., Jr. , Cook, T. D., Eccles, J., Elder, G. H., Jr., & Samsroff, A. (1999). *Managing to make it: Urban families and adolescent Success.* Chicago: University of Chicago Press.

Forthun, L. F., Bell, N. J., Peek, C. W., & Sun, S. W. (1999). Religiosity, sensation-seeking, and alcohol/drug use in denominational and gender contexts. *Journal of Drug Issues, 29,* 75–90.

Foshee, V. A., & Hollinger, B. R. (1996). Maternal religiosity, adolescent social bonding, and adolescent alcohol use. *Journal of Early Adolescence, 16,* 451–468.

Gorsuch, R. L. (1995). Religious aspects of substance abuse and recovery. *Journal of Social Issues, 51,* 65–83.

Gottfredson, M. R., & Hirschi, T. (1990). *A general theory of crime.* Stanford, CA: Stanford University Press.

Harris, M. A. (2003). Religiosity and perceived future ascetic deviance and delinquency among Mormon adolescents: Testing the "this-worldly" supernatural sanctions thesis. *Sociological Inquiry, 73,* 28–51.

Heath, A., Madden, P., Grant, J. D., McLaughlin, T. L., Todorov, A. A., & Bucholz, K. K. (1999). Resiliency factors protecting against teenage alcohol use and smoking: influences of religion, religious involvement and values, and ethnicity in the Missouri adolescent female twin study. *Twin Research, 2,* 145–155.

Higgins, P. C., & Albrecht, G. L. (1977). Hellfire and delinquency revisited. *Social Forces, 55,* 952–958.

Hirschi, T., & Stark, R. (1969). Hellfire and delinquency. *Social Problems, 17,* 202–213.

Jang, S. J., & Johnson, B. R. (2001). Neighborhood disorder, individual religiosity, and adolescent use of illicit drugs: A test of multilevel hypotheses. *Criminology, 39,* 109–143.

Johnson, B. R., Jang, S. J., Larson, D. B., & Li, S. D. (2001). Does adolescent religious commitment matter? A reexamination of the effects of religiosity on delinquency. *Journal for Research in Crime and Delinquency, 38,* 22–43.

Johnson, B. R., Li, S. D., Larson, D. B., & McCullough, M. (2000). A systematic review of the religiosity and delinquency literature. *Journal of Contemporary Criminal Justice, 16,* 32–52.

Junger, M., & Polder, W. (1993). Religiosity, religious climate, and delinquency among ethnic groups in the Netherlands. *British Journal of Criminology, 33,* 416–435.

Kandel, D. B. (1980). Drug and drinking behavior among youth. *Annual Review of Sociology, 6,* 235–285.

Luczak, S. E., Corbett, K., Oh, C., Carr, L. G., & Wall, T. L. (2003). Religious influences on heavy episodic drinking in Chinese-American and Korean-American college students. *Journal of Studies on Alcohol, 64,* 467–471.

Martin, T., Kirkcaldy, B., & Siefen, G. (2003). Antecedents of adult wellbeing: Adolescent religiosity and health. *Journal of Managerial Psychology, 18,* 453–470.

Mason, W. A., & Windle, M. (2001). A longitudinal study of the effects of religiosity on adolescent alcohol use and alcohol-related problems. *Journal of Adolescent Research, 17,* 346–363.

Meier, A. M. (2003). Adolescents' transition to first intercourse, religiosity, and attitudes about sex. *Social Forces, 81,* 1031–1052.

Middleton, R., & Putney, S. (1962). Religion, normative standards and behavior. *Sociometry, 25,* 141–152.

Miller, L., Davies, M., & Greenwald, S. (2000). Religiosity and substance use and abuse among adolescents in the national comorbidity survey. *Journal for the American Academy of Child and Adolescent Psychiatry, 39,* 1190–1197.

Nagin, D. S., & Paternoster, R. (1991). On the relationship of past to future participation in delinquency. *Criminology, 29,* 163–189.

Pearce, L. D., & Haynie, D. L. (2004). Intergenerational religious dynamics and adolescent delinquency. *Social Forces, 82*(4), 1553–1572.

Peek, C. W., Curry, E. W., & Chalfant, H. P. (1985). Religiosity and delinquency over time: Deviance deterrence and deviance amplification. *Social Science Quarterly, 66,* 120–131.

Perkins, W. H. (1985). Religious traditions, parents, and peers as determinants of alcohol and drug use among college students. *Review of Religious Research, 27,* 15–31.

Perkins, W. H. (1987). Parental religion and alcohol use problems as intergenerational predictors of problem drinking among college youth. *Journal for the Scientific Study of Religion, 26,* 340–357.

Pescosolido, B. A. (1990). The social context of religious integration and suicide: Pursuing a network explanation. *Sociological Quarterly, 31,* 337–357.

Powell, K. B. (1997). Correlates of violent and nonviolent behavior among vulnerable inner city youths. *Family and Community Health, 20,* 38–47.

Pullen, L., Modrcin-Talbott, M. A., West, W. R., & Muenchen, R. (1999). Spiritual high vs. high on spirits: Is religiosity related to adolescent alcohol and drug abuse? *Journal of Psychiatric and Mental Health Nursing, 6,* 3–8.

Putnam, R. D. (2000). *Bowling alone: The collapse and revival of American community.* New York: Simon & Schuster.

Raleigh, K. (2003). Dry and devout or wet and wild? A regional geographic challenge of correlating religious presence with alcoholic laws. *Bulletin of the South Carolina Academy of Science, 112.*

Regnerus, M. D. (2003a). Linked lives, faith, and behavior: An intergenerational model of religious influence on adolescent delinquency. *Journal for the Scientific Study of Religion, 42*, 189–203.

Regnerus, M. D. (2003b). Moral communities and adolescent delinquency: Religious contexts and community social control. *Sociological Quarterly, 44*, 523–554.

Regnerus, M. D. (2003c). Religion and positive adolescent outcomes: A review of research and theory. *Review of Religious Research, 44*, 394–413.

Regnerus, M. D. (2002). Friends' influence on adolescent theft and minor delinquency: A developmental test of peer-reported effects. *Social Science Research, 31*, 681–705.

Regnerus, M. D. (2000). Shaping schooling success: A multi-level study of religious socialization and educational outcomes in urban public schools. *Journal for the Scientific Study of Religion, 39*, 363–370.

Regnerus, M. D., & Burdette, A. (2003, October). *Religion and adolescent family well-being.* Paper presented at the annual meeting of the Society for the Scientific Study of Religion, Norfolk.

Romer, D., Jamieson, K. H., & Aday, S. (2003). Television news and the cultivation of fear of crime. *Journal of Communication, 53*, 88–104.

Schreck, C. J., Miller, J. M., & Gibson, C. L. (2003). Trouble in the school yard: A study of the risk factors of victimization at school. *Crime & Delinquency, 49*, 460–484.

Sampson, R. J., & Groves, W. B. (1989). Community structure and crime: Testing social-disorganization theory. *American Journal of Sociology, 94*, 774–802.

Simcha-Fagan, O., & Schwartz, J. E. (1986). Neighborhood and delinquency: An assessment of contextual effects. *Criminology, 24*, 667–703.

"Staffer at 'faith-based' juvenile home in Texas found guilty of abuse." (2001). *Church & State, 54*, 18.

Stark, R. (1996). Religion as context: Hellfire and delinquency one more time. *Sociology of Religion, 57*, 163–173.

Stark, R., & Bainbridge, W. S. (1996). *Religion, deviance, and social control.* New York: Routledge.

Stark, R., Kent, L., & Doyle, D. P. (1982). Religion and delinquency: The ecology of a 'lost' relationship. *Journal of Research in Crime and Delinquency, 19*, 4–24.

Tittle, C. R., & Welch, M. R. (1983). Religiosity and deviance: Toward a contingency theory of constraining effects. *Social Forces, 61*, 653–682.

Welch, M. R., Tittle, C. R., & Petee, T. (1991). Religion and deviance among adult Catholics: A test of the "moral communities" hypothesis. *Journal for the Scientific Study of Religion, 30*, 159–172.

Winship, C., & Berrien, J. (1999). Boston cops and black churches. *The Public Interest, 136*, 52.

PART V

RELIGION AND CULTURE

CHAPTER 14

Sport

James A. Mathisen

"In our family, there was no clear line between religion and fly-fishing." So begins Norman Maclean's novel *A River Runs through It* (1976). That opening line, the book's plot, and the family portrayed therein collectively represent a twofold relationship between religion and sport in North America that was being comprehended more fully—perhaps for the first time—about a quarter century ago. On the one hand, fly-fishing is but one example of how sport or serious recreation might be religion, primarily for many males in modern America. On the other hand, the Presbyterian minister and his sons in the story lived out an increasingly likely interpersonal and institutional interaction of these two realities, with the father's peculiarly Reformed theological understanding of Christian faith informing all of life, including fly-fishing.

In reflecting further on the relationship between religion and sport, one is struck with a fundamental distinction between it and virtually every other topic addressed in this volume. Whereas the other chapters consist of institutional or cultural analyses of the relationship between religion and another aspect of modern life, no other chapter has the parallel obligation to include a discussion of its topic *as* religion. Because I am writing in the context of an impending Super Bowl championship game of American football, such an added cultural obligation is particularly salient. But juxtaposed with sport *as* religion is a growing awareness of how symbiotic and deeply seated the institutional relationship between sport *and* religion also has become. So the last half-century has witnessed a bewildering increase in the connections between these two American institutions.

That religion and sport might be related is in itself not a recent insight. Historians of sport have examined versions of that relationship among indigenous Americans of long ago or with the ancient Greeks and their recurring competitive festivals that were religious and sporting in nature. A considerable literature also exists on the muscular Christian movement in Britain in the second half of the 19th century that attached itself to the YMCA in North America, then taking a variety of forms. And biographers of religiously motivated athletes including Amos Alonzo Stagg, James Naismith, and Billy Sunday, have spread the word that lingering Puritanical constraints on mixing piety with athleticism were losing much of their sanctioning power in the early 20th century. Instead, what appears to be more recent,

---

James A. Mathisen • Wheaton College, Wheaton, Illinois 60187

probably now well into a second generation, is a gradual awareness on the parts of scholars, some journalists, and an increasing number of lay practitioners that the relationships between religion and sport are in fact complex and manifest themselves in various ways, many of which appear peculiarly American. But that growing awareness is also problematic, in large part because it is diffuse, scattered, and manifests little sense of any overall coherence or continuity (Price, 2001).

In terms of the goals of this essay, the current situation is ambiguous. Because the extant literature on religion and sport is modest and concentrated in the past 40 years, the task of assessing the "state-of-the-art" is within reach. But the literature also reflects the incoherent state of the larger field. Sports studies scholars, religionists, sociologists, and other academics who care about interpreting a religion-and-sport connection have had few opportunities to engage each other and so often practice their idiosyncratic crafts unaware whether any shared intellectual context exists. In sociology of religion specifically, little activity examining a role for sport has occurred in that 40-year period.

Such modest interest is not unique to sociologists who have overlooked a religion-and-sport relationship. Given the increased visibility and importance of both institutions in American life, however, thinking about their increased interaction would have seemed likely. Given the reality that several sociological giants of a century ago including Emile Durkheim (1912/1965), Max Weber (1904–1905/1958), and Thorstein Veblen (1899/1934) also noted variations of a religion-and-sport connection in their day, one might also have expected that this state-of-the-art would be more advanced by now. For example, one social systems assessment of "Sport and Religion" consisted of fewer than four pages (Loy, McPherson, & Kenyon, 1978). More recently and from a distinctly sociology of religion perspective, Gregory Baum and John Coleman lamented that "the meaning of sport has received little in the way of serious attention. . . . One looks almost in vain for any more serious spiritual and theological assessment of this important topic" (1989, p. 4).

Given these realities, plus the dual relationship between religion and sport, this essay has two goals. The first is a topical survey of the relevant literature, its themes, and emphases when observing both sport *as* religion and sport *and* religion. The second is an initial effort at synthesizing those emphases, with an interpretation of what that means specifically for the social scientific study of religion, as well as for some sense of what these emphases suggest for the coming generation of both scholars and practitioners.

SPORT AS RELIGION

For sociologists of religion interested in sport, one taken-for-granted context for thinking about sport as religion is the heritage of Emile Durkheim. Before attempting that in some detail, one must consider several definitional and conceptual issues.

Conceptual Concerns: Play, Magic, and An Analogy

From a sociology of religion perspective, one must begin thinking conceptually about sport with *play* and then the relationship between play and sport. The insights of the Dutch philosopher Johan Huizinga provide a starting point. In the 1930s, Huizinga delivered a series of lectures that became *Homo Ludens: A Study of the Play Element in Culture.* Huizinga contrasted the importance of humans playing with prior notions of *Homo Sapiens* and *Homo Faber,* humans reasoning and humans working. "Next to *Homo Faber,* and perhaps on the same level as *Homo Sapiens,* Homo Ludens, Man the Player, deserves a place in our nomenclature.... Civilization arises and unfolds in and as play" (1944/1955, p. i). Representative of Huizinga's thesis were these statements:

> We may well call play a "totality" in the modern sense of the word.... In all its higher forms [play] at any rate belongs to the sphere of festival and ritual—the sacred sphere .... The Platonic identification of play and holiness does not defile the latter by calling it play, rather it exalts the concept of play to the highest regions of the spirit .... In play we may move below the level of the serious, as the child does; but we can also move above it—in the realm of the beautiful and the sacred. (1944/1955, pp. 3, 9, 19)

Huizinga defined play as "a free activity standing quite consciously outside 'ordinary' life as being 'not serious,' but at the same time absorbing the player intensely and utterly. It is an activity connected with no material interest, and no profit can be gained by it. It proceeds within its own proper boundaries of time and space according to fixed rules and in an orderly manner. It promotes the formation of social groupings which tend to surround themselves with secrecy and to stress their difference from the common world by disguise or other means" (1944/1955, p. 13). So play is free; it exists outside the ordinary; it is bounded by its own rules; and perhaps most importantly, play is intrinsic. Play is not simply a means to an end; it is the end ... as well as the beginning.

Although a review of the literature that Huizinga stimulated is beyond the limits of this essay, several responses emerged, some reacting more directly to him than others. Hugo Rahner's *Man at Play,* which had appeared in German, argued that instead of *Homo ludens,* one must begin with *Deus ludens* and consider God the Creator whom humans understand "in the wonderful play of his works" (1949/1967, p. 24). Subsequent works by Robert Neale (1969), Harvey Cox (1969), David Miller (1970), and Jurgen Moltmann (1972) all interpreted the significance of play. When one looks for a parallel literature in sociology, it existed only by implication. George Herbert Mead (1934), Georg Simmel (1955), and Erving Goffman (1961) all used play as a device for theorizing about society and human interaction. In *The Precarious Vision,* Peter Berger expanded on Simmel and Mead, suggesting that the "possibility of 'playing society' would not exist at all unless society had in itself the character of a play" (1961, p. 71).

Berger later argued for play as one of five "signals of transcendence," phenomena from our everyday reality that point beyond (1969, pp. 52–75). "In joyful play it appears as if one were stepping not only from one chronology into another, but from time into eternity.... The experience of joyful play ... constitutes a signal of transcendence, because its intrinsic intention points beyond itself and beyond man's 'nature' to a 'supernatural' justification." Play is an experience constituting an "inductive faith [that] moves from human experience to statements about God" (1969, pp. 58, 60, 57).

Ironically, Berger's interpretation of play did not become a sociological basis for conceptualizing sport as religion. His "signals of transcendence" had appeared in the context of the secularization thesis and the "death of God," so an extrapolation from play as a signal of transcendence to interpreting sport as religion was too great a leap to make. Among sociologists of sport, a parallel gap existed between thinking theologically about play versus a more institutional sense of how sport qua play might act as religion.

One further question is whether the human penchant for play can be transformed into something resembling modern sport. At one level, Huizinga allowed for play to undergo development or transformation. Thus play "at once assumes fixed form as a cultural phenomenon. Once played, it endures as a new-found creation of the mind, a treasure to be retained by the memory. It is transmitted, it becomes tradition.... All play has its rules. They determine what 'holds' in the temporary world circumscribed by play. The rules of a game are absolutely binding and allow no doubt" (1944/1955, pp. 9–10, 11). So sport with its structure, rules, and competition may find its basis in play.

Paradoxically, although sport maintains vestiges of Huizinga's "playfulness," the qualities now defining sport often resemble their antitheses. If play is free, sport is highly structured; if play is outside the ordinary, sport has become worklike; and, importantly, if play is intrinsic, sport is extrinsic. Sport participation is a principal means to various ends—whether winning a college scholarship or earning a living or promulgating a political ideology. As play has been transformed to sport, any larger religious meaning such as Huizinga or Berger suggested has been disenchanted or desacralized. Play may still be the basis of culture, but one would not readily conclude that by observing modern sport.

Rather than invoking play as the starting point for analyzing sport *as* religion, two likely alternatives emerged, both becoming prominent in the 1970s. Sport scholars have either connected sport to magic, or they have argued analogically, that is, sport is like religion. In the case of sport and magic, although the sociology of religion has a long tradition of juxtaposing magic and religion, sport scholars typically have taken a more utilitarian approach, linking magic to sport by way of superstition and ritual performance.

This perspective is often based on Malinowski's interpretation that his Trobriand Islands' subjects in the 1920s made a clear-cut division between natural forces within their control and those beyond control. Given that distinction, magic was employed solely in the second "domain of the unaccountable and adverse influences, as well as the great unearned increment of fortunate coincidence. The first conditions are coped with by knowledge and work, the second by magic ... to master the elements of chance and luck" (1948, pp. 29, 31). Subsequently magic was projected onto sport, given sport's frequent "situations where circumstances are not fully under human control and [where magic] is used to reduce the anxiety that uncertainty creates" (Gmelch, 2001, p. 142).

Sport scholars still employ Malinowski's interpretation nearly exclusively to explain magic and superstition in sport. For example, the anthropologist (and former professional baseball player) George Gmelch has investigated magic in hitting, pitching, and fielding in baseball (1971). As he hypothesized, baseball players experienced far more uncertainty in hitting and pitching than in fielding where the players know empirically that they have a greater likelihood of success. As a result, magical practices occur less frequently there as means to reduce widespread chance and uncertainty than when performing the other two tasks. Thirty years later, Gmelch reaffirmed his thesis. "Obviously the rituals and superstitions of baseball do not make a pitch travel faster or a batted ball find gaps between the fielders.... What both do, however, is give their practitioners, at no cost, a sense of control and added confidence" (2001, p. 143).

Where similar interpretations have been limited is in their making a magic-as-coping-with-uncertainty explanation when alternative interpretations were as plausible. If an athlete crosses herself before shooting a free throw, it is unclear whether that signifies superstition, a magical performance, or an intrinsically religious act. Similarly, the presence of public prayer—by individuals or in groups—in competitive sport settings has increased recently. Reductionistic explanations of those acts as merely magic seem shortsighted, if not clearly incorrect. Where magic and sport performances find common ground is in their shared pragmatic approaches to utilizing "whatever works" as means to improving performances. In Felson and Gmelch's words, "Tribal man has faith that his magic works; modern man lacks faith but is not taking any chances" (1979, p. 589).

If relating sport to religion via play did not gain broad support, and if the role of magic in sport is invoked too broadly, a third explanation of the relationship between religion and sport from the 1970s was analogical—sport is like religion. In sociology of sport, this analogy has been examined from both critical and functional perspectives, with the critical view popularized by the sociologist of sport Harry Edwards. In the context of the Black Power movement of the late 1960s, Edwards argued that "if there is a universal popular religion in America, it is to be found within the institution of sport." He also outlined eleven common features "apparently characteristic of both traditional religions and the 'secular religion' of sport" (1973, pp. 90, 262). Edwards displayed his critical orientation most explicitly when contrasting black and white, noting a preference for whiteness that was common to both Christianity and American sport.

Recently, the sociologist Jay Coakley has promoted a more nuanced "combination of critical, critical feminist, and interactionist theories." He identified 12 similarities between "religious systems of meaning and modern sports," including their shared ability to "distract attention from important social, political, and economic issues and thereby become an 'opiate' of the masses" (2004, pp. 534, 532). Far more common than the critically analogical approaches, however, has been a Durkheimian-based and functional one, such as a thesis on "Sport as a Functional Equivalent of Religion" (Milton, 1972). Interpreting sport functionally as religion has dominated the field in North America since the 1970s, perhaps for two reasons. One is that both physical educators and a few sociologists interested in sport found common cause originally in presupposing cultural consensus and a conservative role for sport in American life. They continue to depict sport as a "mirror," reflecting back key emphases of the American way of life.

A second stimulus was the heritage of Talcott Parsons in sociology. Viewing sport as part of a larger social system and locating it within Parsons's AGIL model of functional prerequisites were major steps (Parsons, 1955; Luschen, 1969, pp. 60–62). Given that view, many sociologists of sport identified specifically integrative functions that sport fulfilled as part of a system, followed by an argument for "functional equivalence" when relating sport to religion. For many sport scholars, sport functions as "a civil religion or quasi-religious institution, which replaces sectarian religion for the purpose of fostering social integration" (Loy, McPherson, & Kenyon, 1978, p. 301). If both sport and religion contribute to group solidarity, if both are expressed in highly ritualistic ways, if both are powerful means of socialization into groups, and if both are capable of inducing high levels of group identity and enthusiasm, then one can conclude that they were related. Sport must be a new secular religion or perhaps a civil religion.

Unfortunately, scholars from religious studies or sociology of religion were less likely to have been party to those interpretations. Any corrective in the form of "Yes, but" from their perspectives rarely occurred. Instead, sport studies advocates were the usual spokespersons for a functionally analogical position. One helpful note came from the philosopher-theologian Michael Novak, who derived sport from play in *The Joy of Sports* (1976) despite its functional-analogical limitations. Novak argued that "for quite sophisticated and agnostic persons, the rituals of sport really work . . . [to] provide an experience of at least a pagan sense of godliness. Among the godward signs in contemporary life, sports may be the single most powerful manifestation" (1976, p. 20). In his book, Novak cited Huizinga directly only once, but as fellow Roman Catholics, they shared an appreciation of the inherent potential for play, for joy, and for freedom that sport still possesses. In the end, Novak was probably too analogical, too inclusive, and too idealistic in his paean to sport as natural religion. But he clearly made a strong case for sport like a religion and continues to be a voice to be reckoned with.

Religion and play, sport and magic, sport like a religion—these have been the primary means of interpreting the significance of sport as religion. In the end, each is seriously limited, so that applying a distinctly Durkheimian perspective provides a preferable alternative for best understanding this puzzling phenomenon.

Applying Durkheim: Sport as Folk Religion

When one peruses the attempts at interpreting sport as religion, the possibilities are nearly endless—sport can be a civil religion (Loy, McPherson, & Kenyon, 1978), a cultural religion (Albanese, 1981), a popular religion (Price, 2001), a quasi-religion (Dunning, 1986), a secular religion (Edwards, 1973), or a surrogate religion (Coles, 1975). If this were a quiz with those six possible answers, perhaps the best answer is that sport is a civil religion. The sociologist of religion Philip Hammond noted that competitive sports may be "crucial social structures for the transmission and maintenance of America's civil religion" (1968, p. 383). Religion and sport often interact within political contexts that promote local or national cohesiveness in ways that civil religions do.

Significant limitations of the sport-as-civil-religion position also exist. As Robert Bellah (1967, 1975), Martin Marty (1974), and others have suggested, civil religions are elitist, often episodic, and likely provide some sense of national self-understanding. Civil religions are at their best in times of trial, whereas sport as religion seems more constant and pervasive. Most important, sport often appears to do something other than, or perhaps does only one of several versions of, what civil religion does.

Following Durkheim (1912/1965), the profane becomes sacred through collective acts and shared redefinitions. Symbols once understood as ordinary take on new meaning and significance, perceived with shared awe and reverence. Beliefs that had no sacred importance are transformed, as the clan gathers regularly to rehearse their newly sacred understanding and belief. Given the orientation of this chapter, this is why the decades of the 1960s–1970s were crucial. Before then, sociologists and anthropologists had little reason to think about sport as religion. It was not sacred; it was merely profane.

But unexpectedly, with the collapse of an earlier cultural consensus including that contributed by American civil religion in the 1960s, sport functionally took on a new sense of the sacred. Robert Bellah's seminal essay, "Civil Religion in America" (1967), related any demise of civil religion to the Vietnam War that challenged an existing consensus, although Vietnam may have been an "effect," as well as a "cause." Later Bellah lamented, "Today the American civil religion is an empty and broken shell," and he wondered how a new vision and myth could emerge (1975, pp. 142, 151–163).

In a Durkheimian sense, that decline of a post–World War II consensus provoked a larger cultural anomie, with new needs for social integration. Unlike more elitist civil religions that provide integrative symbols and rituals, sport is not primarily a religion of elites; it is most widespread among the masses, the folk. Gradually during the 1960s–1970s, the values, beliefs, and rituals of sport were elevated from their prior profane meanings and took on newly sacred significance as a folk religion among the masses. Sociologists of sport then began writing about sport as religion, apparently for the first time, in the late 1960s and early 1970s, although largely unaware that only recently had sport begun meeting new integrative and regulatory needs for many Americans, particularly males. So, by the time Norman Maclean wrote *A River Runs through It*, fly-fishing, too, was religion.

The journalist Robert Lipsyte noted this shift, and he coined the term "SportsWorld" to convey "a dangerous and grotesque web of ethics and attitudes, an amorphous infrastructure that acts to contain our energies, divert our passions, and socialize us for work or war or depression.... [SportsWorld] has surpassed patriotism and piety as a currency of communication, while exploiting them both. By the end of the 1960s, SportsWorld wisdom had it that religion was a spectator sport while professional and college athletic contests were the only events Americans held sacred" (1974, pp. ix, xv).

Elsewhere I have identified the role played in the 1960s by public figures such as President John Kennedy and football coach Vince Lombardi as highly visible "priests" of the new folk religion of sport (Mathisen, 1992). Similarly, the British journalist James Lawton juxtaposed them in this way: "Kennedy was preaching to Americans about the value of self-sacrifice, directing them toward heroism," [while Lombardi] "expressed the mood on the football field. Win, said Lombardi. Win for your school, your college, your pro team, your country, yourself" (1984, p. 95). Fortuitously, network television and the popular, mass-circulation magazine *Sports Illustrated* were communicating effectively to the masses the new cultural meanings that sport represented. For the religionist John Wilson, writing in the 1970s, modern sport was "invented to fill a new pattern of cultural space and time created by the communications industry," which reflected a new "commitment to athletic performance [that] can be seen at one level as a fundamental dramatization of the basic values and goals of the society" (1979, p. 135).

Obviously, the last thing that the National Football League intended when originating the Super Bowl in 1967 (although not yet named as such) was that it was creating a highly visible, folk religious spectacle to celebrate annually this new role for sport in American life. But in 1984 Price asserted, "Like festivals in ancient societies, which made no distinctions regarding the religious, political and sporting character of certain events, the Super Bowl succeeds in reuniting these now disparate dimensions of social life.... As a cultural festival, it commands vast allegiance while dramatizing and reinforcing the religious myths of national innocence and apotheosis" (1984, pp. 190–191). Price got it right, and Durkheim would likely have nodded in assent.

To conclude, deciphering the sport-as-religion relationship is not simple. Sport retains some of its play-fulness, but deriving sport as religion from theological notions about play is not a normal extension and raises many counterexamples. To look to magic in sport as a basis for thinking about sport as religion may be more difficult, if for no other reason than the reductionistic tendencies usually occurring. Analogically, sport and religion do have some functions in common, but as with most analogies, this one eventually breaks down. If sport is merely like a religion, then what? So sport is also something like a civil religion, but not quite. Instead, it exists as a folk religion expressing the shared values, symbols, and aspirations of many Americans, especially men. To claim broadly that sport is a religion is not particularly helpful. To qualify that statement in light of the past 40 years, however, by asserting that many expressions of sport have been transformed from profane to sacred to become a folk religion for many Americans seems the best way of representing the sport *as* religion relationship.

SPORT AND RELIGION

Given the institutional orientation of the essays in this volume, thinking about sport and religion should be cast primarily in those terms. Chronologically, this implies that one would limit attention to the last 125 years, given that American sport as a social institution is a new phenomenon, evolving as such in the 1880s–1890s. Such a tactic would be shortsighted, however, in two ways. Conceptually, interaction between religion and sport is at least 3,000 years old, and some vestiges of that connection still exist. Prior notice must be paid to the contexts of the ancient Olympics and the Common Era. More importantly, further attention also must be given to the British antecedents of the religion-and-sport relationship, especially during the 19th century, given their continuing direct influence on American sport. These two contexts set the stage for interpreting the American scene of the last 60 years.

Ancient Sport: The Olympics

Understanding religion *and* sport in the 21st century begins by acknowledging the ancient Greek heritage and to a lesser degree the Romans who followed. Although the modern myth that "sport builds character" was derived in part from the 19th-century British ideal of *mens sana in corpore sano* (a sound mind in a sound body), the British did not originate that mythical goal. Instead, they borrowed it from the Roman satirist Juvenal, whose Tenth Satire from the early 2nd century included this advice: "You should pray for this: A sound mind in a sound body. Pray for courageous spirit that's not afraid of death and can say long life is the least of nature's gifts" (Juvenal, c. 150).

By the time of Juvenal, however, that long-standing Greek ideal was declining. The Greeks had created a circuit of festivals that included athletic events, perhaps beginning with the Olympic games in 776 B.C.E. Two hundred years later, three more festivals were in place—the Pythian games, the Isthmian games, and the Nemean games—and occurred on regular 2- or 4-year cycles. For the American political columnist and baseball afficionado George Will, "Greek philosophers considered sport a religious and civic—in a word, moral—undertaking. . . . It is an activity, a form of appreciating that is good for the individual's soul, and hence for society" (1991, p. 2).

Typically, the 5-day festival at Olympia was divided between religious rituals, processions, and prayers and times of spirited competitions in running, the pentathlon, equestrian events, and combat. Athletes took an oath in, and dedicated their winners' crowns to, the name of Zeus. The classicist Mark Golden observed that the "Greeks located the origin of the Olympic games squarely in the sphere of the divine; gods and heroes found and compete in them as well as simply receiving worship." Even though the "ties between religion and sport at Olympia are apparent," Golden cautioned about making too much of those ties. "Greek sport seems very religious in contrast with most of contemporary professional sport. Is it really exceptionally so in a society in which every part of life was pervaded by cult activity and invocation of the gods?" (1998, pp. 14, 17, 23). Although the Olympics lasted until 384 C.E., they also likely had been "secularized" somewhat by then, especially in the context of an increasing Roman influence.

So while it is not inaccurate for modern American religion-and-sport to claim some distant roots in the ancient Greek tradition, those roots have to be qualified considerably. The strongest basis for this claim is a persisting version of the ideal of *mens sana in corpore sano*. How that Greco-Roman ideal more recently has gotten "filtered" through distinctly American interpretations is a separate matter.

Ancient Sport: Christians and Jews in the Common Era

One of the more provocative recent books on religion and sport was sport historian William J. Baker's *If Christ Came to the Olympics* (2000). Baker projected a Jesus of Nazareth who had "heard about some Jewish boys of His day who shocked their elders by staging Greek-style athletic contests of their own" (2000, p. 25). Baker hinted not only that Jesus was familiar with, but also would have approved of, those contests although he did not say exactly that. Worth noting, however, is that Jesus frequently used many real-world examples in his teaching, including numerous agrarian metaphors and parables, but never is recorded as employing an athletic example or story.

What Baker also implied, however, was that the Jews of Jesus's day would have been divided (2000, pp. 24–25). Those who were more cosmopolitan and assimilated into Roman culture would readily have accepted the nudity, violence, and emperor worship that the festivals supported; those from more provincial and theologically conservative backgrounds would have been aghast. Apparently Herod the Great established a gymnasium in Jerusalem, and athletic contests were held there that Freyne depicted as "a departure from ancestral customs. Many aspects were operative—nudity, the religious associations of the games for the Greeks as well as the introduction of graven images.... These Jerusalem games occasioned violent Jewish reaction, despite the fact that other Jews appear to have actually participated in the events" (1989, pp. 95–96).

By comparison, it was the classically trained Paul of Tarsus who infused an abundance of athletic metaphors into his New Testament writings. Athletic figures of speech were common to philosophers of Paul's day, and he cited numerous areas of everyday life, including athletics, that his readers were aware of without necessarily making moral judgments of the activities. Of the Pauline athletic images, Victor Pfitzner has argued for the *agon,* or struggle, as the central motif (1967). Paul adapted it from its classical Greek origins to depict the Christian life as a contest or struggle of cosmic proportions, without endorsing or disparaging athletic activity per se.

Paul's most salient athletic allusion occurred in I Corinthians. Corinth was the site of the Isthmian games, and Paul had been there for 18 months, perhaps overlapping with the biennial games (Acts 18). His readers would have been aware of the games, and the lesser strict among them—especially male non-Jews—may have been spectators. The context of Paul's athletic allusion was a didactic one, capitalizing on their familiarity, although his purpose was to get his readers to exercise their religiously based freedom responsibly. To do so, he used seven different athletic terms in I Corinthians 9:24–27, that collectively emphasized the importance of exercising self-control (cf. v. 25). In the context of having to confront fellow believers with moral problems in their eating and sexual behavior (Chs. 7–10), Paul chose an analogy of athletes in training. Just as athletes practiced self-control in their preparation for the Isthmian games—including in their eating and sexual behavior—so his readers should be more controlled in their conduct.

What Oriard (1991) and others have demonstrated is that for the next 15 or 16 centuries, Christianity had recurring problems interpreting Paul's athletic imagery. On the one side was a minority who sought support from Paul for their pro-athletic and recreational interests. On the other side was a prevailing majority who read Paul through more dualistic eyes, emphasizing the spiritual over the physical. Although these Greek and Common Era influences have been significant for interpreting religion and sport, what mattered more for an American understanding were the recent British antecedents.

Essential British Antecedents

Although inferences from the Greek ideal of "a sound mind in a sound body" and the Pauline injunctions such as "run in such a way as to get the prize" (I Corinthians 9:24) still resonate with many Americans, arguably a more direct line for interpreting the religion-and-sport relationship today winds through our British ancestors. Four different British expressions have contributed to Americans' understanding of religion and sport.

ENGLISH RELIGION AND SPORT: THE PURITANS.   With the turn of the 17th century, the culture wars between the ruling Stuarts and the Puritan reformers in England existed on several fronts. James I and his supporters encouraged sporting activities that traditionalists and reformers found unacceptable. In 1618 James issued his *Declaration on Lawful Sports,* since known as *The King's Book of Sports.* Puritan suspicions about sports were clearly a target in James's proclamation: "After the end of divine service our good people be not disturbed . . . or discouraged from any lawful recreation such as . . . ". The specific activities that James named were symbolic of the persisting religiopolitical struggle. When Oliver Cromwell and the Puritans gained the upper hand, retribution was widespread, including the prohibition of sporting activities for reasons of conscience as well as of pragmatic politics. But in 1647, with the Puritans controlling Parliament, one Tuesday a month was set aside as a holiday with shops and warehouses closed, "for the recreation of workers" (Ryken, 1986, p. 190).

The nearly simultaneous arrival of Puritans in New England and non-Puritans in Virginia had guaranteed that early Americans replicated those opposing British positions, and so employed differing strategies. "The Jamestown settlers forbade play as a temporary, expedient measure, whereas Pilgrim leaders dumped a heavy bag of moralistic prohibitions on the heads of New England colonists" (Baker, 1988, p. 83). The Puritan scholar Leland Ryken asserted two generalizations that summarized the overall attitudes of Puritans toward sport and recreation, given the context of their "disapproval of all sports *on Sundays* and of *selected sports* at all times" (1986, pp. 189–191).

First, the Puritans held legalistic views that prohibited anything that distracted the accomplishing of God's purposes. If the Puritans made a "theoretic endorsement of recreation," the "legalism drastically dampened" that support; assuming associations of sport with gambling, cruelty, and illicit sexuality reinforced the legalistic ethos. Second, the Puritans objected to sport and recreation because of their inability to value "recreation for its own sake, or as celebration, or as an enlargement of one's human spirit." Clearly, the Puritans contributed to a "utilitarian play ethic [that] was a result of the Puritans' overemphasis on work" and that still persists (Ryken, 1986, pp. 190–191).

In the 21st century, nearly all of the first attitude—the legalism—has been lost, except for lingering questions about Sunday observance among some sectarian groups. Meanwhile, the second attitude—the utilitarianism—has been compounded by a highly rationalized approach to sport as a means to other ends. Sport historian Allen Guttmann offered a distinctly Weberian interpretation of this rationalized-plus-utilitarian connection between religion and sport. Because Protestants most likely championed "an empirical, experimental, mathematical *Weltanschauung,*" so the "form [sports] take is that dictated by modern society" (1978, pp. 85, 89). "The correlation between Protestantism and participation in sport" derived from a scientific worldview has led in turn to several of modern sports' defining characteristics, including their "specialization, rationalism, bureaucratic organization, and quantification" (1978, pp. 84–85, 80–81). For Overman, sport "became both a profession and a business. It was organized on the business model. . . . Sport as an activity took on the nuances of rational work" (1997, p. 349).

So the Puritans remain important in a variety of ways: they influenced much of the early Anglo-American ideas about sport; their legalistic notions about sport have not totally disappeared; and most importantly, their utilitarian emphases were transformed by a modern worldview and resulted in a highly rationalized approach to pursuing sport.

ENGLISH ORIGINS OF MUSCULAR CHRISTIANITY.   Another British contribution— "muscular Christianity"—significantly challenged many of the still-lingering Puritanical doubts about the compatibility of religion and sport. Muscular Christianity is traced back to Thomas Arnold, the headmaster at Rugby School in England in the 1830s–1840s. Although Arnold encouraged students to play team games, one of them, Thomas Hughes, collaborated with the novelist Charles Kingsley to formulate the grounds for much of the doctrine of muscular Christianity in the 1850s–1860s.

A reviewer of Kingsley's *Two Years Ago* (1856) coined the label "muscular Christian" to depict Kingsley's merging athletic participation with ideals of manliness, morality, and patriotism. In Hughes's 1856 novel *Tom Brown's School Days,* his hero, Tom Brown, incarnated these and other virtues as he strove for excellence in the athletic venues at Rugby. Although not everyone approved of these literary emphases, "among the staunchest advocates were Victorian educators, who liked [the] propagation of the muscular Christian values of fellowship, honor, and service" (Putney, 2001, p. 15).

In an 1861 sequel, Hughes celebrated muscular Christians: "The least of the muscular Christians has hold of the old chivalrous and Christian belief, that a man's body is given him to be trained and brought into subjection, and then used for the protection of the weak, the advancement of all righteous causes, and the subduing of the earth which God has given to the children of men" (1861, p. 83). Notions about muscular Christianity in the British schools expanded, resulting in "the belief that team sports were at once the training ground for the typically British values of fairness and leadership, and at the same time the vehicle through which these values could be demonstrated" (Miracle and Rees, 1994, p. 38).

Tom Brown's School Days was a sensation and quickly diffused to America—Tom Brown as boy-hero; Thomas Hughes as celebrity; and, most significantly, "muscular Christianity" as an ideal. This British notion that "helped to invent the tradition that sport builds character" then adapted to justify American sport, "build[ing] morale and esprit de corps in [high] schools all across America." So school sport was legitimized, in part because of its alleged role in fostering unity, "to socialize the children of immigrants into traditional American values" (Miracle & Rees, 1994, pp. 36–37, 59, 63). The *Atlantic Monthly* immediately made a case for another version of muscular Christianity that was consonant with a larger Protestant vision of America into which immigrants could readily be converted or assimilated (Higginson, 1858).

By the time Thomas Hughes visited America and lectured at Harvard in 1870 on "the proper limits" of muscular Christianity (Putney, 2001), it was clear that rather than simply embracing his British-originated vision, American variants were emerging, some of them religiously motivated and others less so. One distinctively Christian variant merged with American revivalism, with urban reform, and eventually with the YMCA.

THE YMCA AND THE CAMBRIDGE 7.   The YMCA fulfilled George Williams's dream in the 1840s of providing care for adolescent lads moving to London. Williams created the YMCA to provide Bible studies and prayer meetings while getting them off the streets. For Williams, however, there was little apparent connection between his vision and that of Thomas Arnold and Thomas Hughes at Rugby School, so recreation and sport were not on his original YMCA agenda.

The first YMCA in America was established in Boston in 1851. "Here Christian fellowship, intellectual stimulation, and wholesome physical exercise supplanted the loneliness of boarding houses and the evils of commercial amusements" (Gorn & Goldstein, 1993, p. 103). The YMCA spread quickly to 56 localities by 1856 (Putney, 2001, p. 65), moved onto college campuses in 1858, and "came into its own in the United States" with a boost from the so-called Businessmen's Revival of 1857–1858 in many American cities (Long, 1998, p. 61). Meanwhile, the YMCA also had begun adding gymnasiums, and the *New York Times* took note in 1869 when a new facility there included one. "This concession to the muscular Christianity of the time has been made, we are glad to hear, almost without dissent, nor can any one who appreciates the moral force of the *sana mens in sano corpore* find fault of the athletic character it is proposed to give the young Christians of New York" (A Christian Club, 1869, p. 5).

Dwight L. Moody became Chicago's YMCA's first full-time worker in 1861, which provided a platform for his foray into muscular Christianity. As president of and chief fund-raiser for the YMCA, Moody made five visits to England between 1867 and 1884. On one trip a wealthy tea planter, Edward Studd, heard Moody preach and converted to Christianity. Studd influenced his three sons, who were excellent cricket players, to follow his lead (Ladd & Mathisen, 1999, pp. 44–47). These connections among the YMCA, Moody, and the Studd family had two immediate results with implications for how many Americans still view the relationship between religion and sport.

First, the youngest Studd son, J.E.K. (Kynaston) visited the United States and Canada in 1885 at Moody's invitation. J.E.K. was a popular attraction at colleges throughout the Northeast. As one result, Moody initiated summer meetings for college students at his Northfield, Massachusetts, base. The "Northfield conferences" then became an informal training site for muscular Christian, campus leaders (Ladd & Mathisen, 1999). In 1887 Henry Drummond, the Scottish theologian-educator, asserted in a talk at Northfield that "the key to a boy's heart [was] athletics," and he hoped that athletics could be a way to "influence[d] those boys in the direction of muscular Christianity" (Shanks, 1887, pp. 235–236). Initially paralleling these summer conferences and eventually supplanting them was the development of Springfield College as a permanent YMCA training school that more systematically inculcated muscular Christian ideals into future directors.

Another implication of the YMCA-Moody-Studd connection was the keen British interest in the exploits of the Cambridge Seven. J.E.K. Studd's older brother C. T. was the best cricketeer of the three brothers. Following his conversion to Christianity, C. T. influenced six of his fellow Cambridge students to become missionaries to China (Putney, 2001). As a group, those seven muscular Christians originated a model of missionary proselytizing based on athletic notoriety that persists today. Using their reputations and celebrity, the young men caught the attention of many in the British religious and sporting worlds in ways that sports fans would still recognize.

What makes this combination of muscular Christianity and the institutionalization of religion and sport in the YMCA important for this essay is that it occurred during the decades of the 1880s–1890s, just as sport was institutionalizing in the United States. Although the YMCA had been a respected presence for a generation by then, once it fused a utilitarian approach to sport as a means to its religious ends with the muscular Christianized version of *mens sana in corpore sano,* many qualities of today's religion-and-sport scene were clearly identifiable. On college campuses and in many cities throughout America, the YMCA—symbolized by its inverted red triangle of "body, mind, spirit" (based on Deuteronomy 6:5)—incarnated organizationally a relationship of religion and sport.

THE MODERN OLYMPICS. A less-known connection between muscular Christianity and the modern Olympics occurred in 1886 when Pierre de Coubertin stood at Thomas Arnold's tomb at Rugby School. Coubertin had a powerful vision that confirmed his vocation to begin a " '21-year campaign' to bring to France what he took to be Arnold's legacy, . . . a 'proven method' for the production of 'Muscular Christianity' " (MacAloon, 1981, p. 51). As a 12-year-old, Coubertin had read *Tom Brown's School Days* years earlier, and he had internalized powerful images of the mythically heroic Tom Brown, as well as of an idealized Thomas Arnold, the headmaster at Rugby.

Coubertin then combined three religious elements—a "loose deism," "Hellenism" as a fascination with the ancient Greek ethos, and a Comte-like fixation with a "cult of humanity" (MacAloon, 1978, pp. 162–163)—as his focus shifted from the French schools to join an existing movement to revive the ancient Olympic games and craft a new "religion of Olympism." Kortzfleisch has summarized his religious vision in this way: "Coubertin wrote in his memoirs: 'For me, sport is religion with church, dogma, cult . . . but especially with religious feeling.' . . . Thus Coubertin set out to found a religious movement as well, but without publicly declaring it as a religion. He made a pilgrimage . . . to the sacred forest of Olympia in Greece, that is to his spiritual sources. . . . He thought that this way the *religio athletae* would be convincing in action. . . . Coubertin clearly had a religious understanding of Olympism" (1970, pp. 233–235). Similarly, Coubertin emphasized the "ritual symbols—solemn music, processions, flights of birds, sacred plants, flags, mythic and divine images, invocations, crownings, wreath laying, statue dedications—[that] populated the opening, victory, and awards ceremonies. . . . Ample evidence has been brought forward to suggest that, in Olympic rites, many individuals encountered sacred forces" (MacAloon, 1981, p. 270).

Both Coubertin's timing and motivation are significant here. During the 1880s–1890s, the Olympic movement had powerful support in America, leading up to the opening ceremony in Athens on Easter Sunday, 1896, concurrent with sport's institutionalization in the United States. As Americans had assumed a religious justification for the increasing role of competitive sport in American schools, so they attached themselves to the reinforcing vision of Olympism to celebrate the fusion of religion and sport internationally. Granted, not everyone who witnessed the Athens Games made an inherently religious association, but Coubertin's motivation to create Olympism as an international religion based on his idiosyncratic application of muscular Christian assumptions cannot be questioned.

With these powerful British images of the religious significance of sport in mind, it is fair to say that they played a significant, formative role in how many Americans perceived the rationale for and legitimacy of sport. The fact that the institutionalization of sport per se occurred simultaneously with new religious meanings being attributed to sport secured a gradual institutional symbiosis between religion and sport in America.

RELIGION AND SPORT IN MODERN AMERICA

Religion and sport in America in the first 40 years of the 20th century were an unpredictable and paradoxical combination of trends and cross-purposes. In one sense, American sport institutionally followed a course of secularization away from any earlier religious justification. This occurred for any number of reasons—key leaders such as D. L. Moody died or withdrew from the movement (e.g., Amos Alonzo Stagg and James Naismith); the YMCA redirected its vision and goals; the educational context became inimical to a religiously influenced sport; sport per se grew increasingly extrinsic and consumer-oriented; and other possibilities. For the cultural historian Mark Dyreson, a key issue for the post–World War I generation was that by then "sport had become a part of the landscape of given consciousness.... After 1920 sport no longer seemed such a powerful tool" (1998, pp. 202–203). Sport was on its own, with or without religion.

In another sense, however, the 19th-century Anglo-American vision of religion and sport did not disappear, although it lost salience, in part because of the variant forms it took. For example, in the 1920s when the Cathedral of St. John the Divine in New York considered including a stained glass window portraying athletes in its sports bay alcove, Bishop Manning simply asserted that sports "have just as important place in our lives as our prayers. It is my opinion that the beautiful game of polo, in its place, is as pleasing to God as a beautiful service in a beautiful cathedral" (Putney, 2001, p. 64).

Meanwhile, Roman Catholics and Jews were more ambivalent, caught between the Protestant-based, cultural attractiveness of sport and their desire to stress other, more culturally appropriate means of Americanization such as education. Given that situation, the University of Notre Dame took the lead in the 1920s by providing a "completely formed and self-contained world with an athletic culture that not only included the students but also lay faculty members, administrators, and priests" as a highly visible example of an evolving, proathletic ethos among Catholics (Sperber, 1993, p. 76). So the religious picture was mixed, but on balance, the relationship between religion and sport was no longer in ascendance as it had been two generations earlier.

In accounting then for a direct line from this ambiguous context of the interwar era to the 21st century, one must look instead to a most unlikely religious tradition, that of Protestant fundamentalism. In 1893, the baseball hero-turned-fundamentalist preacher, Billy Sunday, had warned against sport, specifically baseball, for several reasons including its being "a life which has an undesirable future"; "it is better to benefit mankind than to simply amuse them"; and "it is a life in which morality is not an essential to success" (1893, p. 1). Ironically, although Sunday often used flamboyant athletic imagery in his preaching— such as shadow boxing with the devil and sliding into the home plate of heaven—many conservative Protestants of the first third of the 20th century echoed Sunday's suspicions of sport. Those echoes would change dramatically.

In the early 1940s as marginalized fundamentalists sought to reenter the American cultural mainstream, sport became a primary means in their quest for legitimacy. This was accomplished initially through the efforts of youth organizations such as Youth for Christ (YFC) and energetic speakers including Billy Graham. In the post–World War II context of suspicions about communism and delinquency, YFC used radio and weekend "youth rallies" to offer religious solutions to the problems America's youth faced, especially to adolescent males (Ladd & Mathisen, 1999).

As part of its innovative programming geared toward youth, YFC also discovered the value of "the sports appeal" (Larson, 1948, pp. 69–70). In Graham's words, "We used every modern means to catch the attention of the unconverted—and then we punched them right between the eyes with the Gospel" (Frady, 1979, p. 160). YFC had discovered a new application of the old muscular Christian—YMCA—Cambridge Seven formula that athletic heroes could be effective in attracting a youthful crowd to hear a religious message.

So 65,000 kids came to a YFC rally on Memorial Day, 1945 at Soldier Field in Chicago to hear the American mile champion, Gil Dodds, tell his story (Mathisen, 1990). *Newsweek* covered the event and reported that Dodds "raced a mile around the field in a track suit. 'Running is only a hobby,' the bespectacled athlete-preacher said. 'My mission is teaching the gospel of Jesus Christ'" (Wanted, 1945, p. 84).

When Graham struck out on his own in 1947, he replicated the Chicago event, but with a twist. Not only could athletes attract adolescents males, but adults responded as well. Graham had Dodds join him at one of his early "crusades" in Charlotte, North Carolina (Frady, 1979). What YFC and Graham then routinized was their discovery that sport and its heroes could be highly pragmatic means to specifically religious ends. If an audience showed up and the press took note, the perception that their support relocated fundamentalists closer to the mainstream of American life was an additional benefit.

Over the next decades, three steps led to the institutionalizing of religion and sport that extended the fundamentalists' pragmatic vision. First, the YFC-Graham formula was exported to Europe and Asia, only to return in another variant form. When YFC sent a basketball team to Taiwan in 1952, it had experimented with using an athletic venue as a context for presenting a religious service to a captive audience. Team members sang and gave personal testimonials during halftimes and following the games, thereby adapting the sport setting for overtly religious purposes (Ladd & Mathisen, 1999). That strategy became a taken-for-granted over the next 20 years that continues to this day. Second, the YFC experiment in Taiwan evolved to become the first religious organization—renamed Sports Ambassadors in 1952—to use sport explicitly as a basis in its proselytizing and teaching efforts. Heretofore, religious groups used athletes and the symbols of sport to promote religious messages; beginning in 1952 an entirely new genre of religious organizational forms was created, with sport occupying an essential presence.

Third, within 20 more years, this Billy Graham-YFC-Sports Ambassadors model was institutionalized and pluralized into hundreds of large and small religious efforts via sport. Fellowship of Christian Athletes in 1954 and then Athletes in Action as part of the Campus Crusade for Christ organization in 1966 (in addition to Sports Ambassadors) composed a "Big 3" of Protestant sports ministry organizations. But complementing those highly organized and well-funded efforts, numerous more specific and specialized "mom-and-pop ministries" appeared as well (Ladd & Mathisen, 1999). By the early 1970s, Baseball Chapel and Pro Athletes Outreach added another target audience, that of professional and major university athletes. Soon nearly every professional and major university athletic team had a "chaplain," typically a former athlete and/or ex-minister, who perceived his or her "calling" as a ministry to, as well as among, elite athletes.

Given the similarities between the 20th- and 21st-century efforts and those of the late 19th century, one contrast stood out. In the 19th century, sport's allying with religion in both Britain and America was crucial to the religious and cultural legitimation of sport. The muscular Christian movement, especially the YMCA, reversed centuries of suspicion about sport, dating back to the Common Era and the Puritans. In the mid-20th century, that legitimation process was reversed, from sport to religion. Culturally marginalized Protestant fundamentalists capitalized on the popularity of sport and the prominence of athletic heroes as strategic means, both to achieving cultural legitimacy and to their overtly religious goals of proselytizing and conversion. Religion and sport institutionally have been symbiotic since then, although their interdependence has worked variously to the advantage of one or the other party, over time, and in different cultural settings.

Although much of the story of the past 60 years has been told here primarily from the perspective of conservative Protestants, that does not mean they were the only religious groups to ally with sport. Surely, Roman Catholics, Jews, and more recently Mormons, Muslims, and others have created their own connections with athletics and with athletes. But when one reads "John 3:16" on a poster at a televised athletic event, or hears an interview with a professional athlete who feels compelled to "Thank my savior, Jesus," one can assume that the Youth for Christ–Billy Graham discovery of the "sports appeal" is now well entrenched. The interaction of religion and sport today is not limited to their evangelical Protestant descendants, but it more likely occurs among them than among their religious cousins from other Christian or non-Christian traditions.

IN CONCLUSION

As America moves well into the 21st century, religion and sport are inextricably intertwined. The relationship exists as closely as it ever has and in two manifestations—at a more cultural level, sport functions as a folk religion; and at interpersonal and institutional levels, religion and sport exist in symbiotic interdependence. As occurs with social symbioses, the participants all benefit, although not equally and consistently so, and alongside the benefits are recurring costs or risks to each party.

Both of the present relationships occurred in the recent past, moreso in the case of sport as a folk religion. If sport was "sacralized" in a Durkheimian sense in the 1960s–1970s, the possibility of its subsequently risking "profanation" already exists. Although many of the values, symbols, and rituals of big-time, competitive sport continue to resonate folk religiously for many Americans, the past 10–20 years have also witnessed a simultaneous, paradoxical profaning of sport. Protests of the cultural status of sport come from many quarters—including those who decry its anti-academic place on university campuses, others who challenge futilely the near-impunity of athletes who openly use performance-enhancing drugs, and still others saddened by the crass consumerism that accompanies both its participants and its competitive settings. By neglect or default, the sacred always can be profaned, and in the case of American sport that process is well underway.

Meanwhile, the interpersonal and institutional statuses of religion and sport seem more secure. Because these relationships have existed for a over a century since the 1880s, they now appear as a "social fact," given their proliferation since the 1950s. At an interpersonal level, athletes who also profess a religious commitment retain near-celebrity status for many believers in religion-and-sport. Their numbers continue to grow, and despite apparently increasing criticism, both within the church and from the media, these modern "muscular Christians" continue to enjoy widespread credibility.

Institutionally, the picture is more complex. As the story was told earlier, it was largely a mainline Protestant vision of using sport as a means to build character, often through sport's visible role in the public schools, that initially achieved popular acceptance in 19th-century America. Roman Catholics and Jews were often caught between the demands to assimilate into American life, while also remaining distinct within it. To a large degree, assimilation won out. But this process stagnated in the post–World War I era, only to be discovered by fundamentalist Protestants a generation later.

Fundamentalists seized onto sport for two reasons—as a means to their own cultural acceptance, but primarily as a means to attract new converts, initially among adolescent males. Today, that dual attraction has been well routinized by a legion of conservative practitioners and organizations. Granted, other religious traditions have forged their own alliances with sport, but the conservative Protestants have the strongest ties to sport. Their churches are more likely to sponsor "sports ministries," often with professional leaders, and their colleges and seminaries now provide the requisite training and support (Mathisen, 1998). In the long term, this relationship could be severed, but the shorter-term prospects suggest otherwise, given their appearance as a social fact.

Religion and fly-fishing; *mens sana in corpore sano;* Pauline metaphors; Puritan suspicions; muscular Christianity; Olympism; the sports appeal; and other permutations of religion-and-sport relationships continue. Perhaps what these disparate examples most strongly suggest is that the past 60 years have revealed only a larger tip of the potential iceberg of cultural, interpersonal, and institutional relationships between religion and sport that many Americans—academics and lay observers alike—continue to discover. As sociologists of religion, we are still playing "catch-up," necessarily needing to interpret more carefully what these relationships will mean in the foreseeable future.

REFERENCES

A Christian club. (1869, July 18). *New York Times, 5.*

Albanese, C. (1981). *America: Religions and religion.* Belmont, CA: Wadsworth.

Baker, W. J. (1988). *Sports in the western world* (Rev. ed.). Urbana: University of Illinois.

Baker, W. J. (2000). *If Christ came to the Olympics.* Sydney, Australia: University of South Wales Press.

Baum, G., & Coleman, J. (1989). Editorial: Sport, society and religion. In G. Baum & J. Coleman (Eds.), *Sport* (Concilium 205), (pp. 3–8). Edinburgh: T & T Clark.

Bellah, R. N. (1967). Civil religion in America. *Daedalus, 96,* 1–21.

Bellah, R. N. (1975). *The broken covenant: American civil religion in time of trial.* New York: Seabury Press.

Berger, P. L. (1961). *The precarious vision.* Garden City, NY: Doubleday.

Berger, P. L. (1969). *A rumor of angels.* Garden City, NY: Doubleday.

Coakley, J. (2004). *Sports in society: Issues & controversies* (8th ed.). New York: McGraw-Hill.

Cox, H. (1969). *Feast of fools.* New York: Harper and Row.

Coles, R. (1975). Sport as a surrogate religion. In M. Hill (Ed.), *A sociological yearbook of religion in Britain* (Vol. 8, pp. 61–77). London: SCM Press.

Dunning, E. (1986). The dynamics of modern sport. In N. Elias & E. Dunning (Eds.), *Quest for excitement* (pp. 205–223). Oxford: Blackwell.

Durkheim, E. (1965). *The elementary forms of the religious life* (J. W. Swain, Trans.). Glencoe, IL: Free Press. (Original work published 1912)

Dyreson, M. (1998). *Making the American team: Sport, culture, and the Olympic experience.* Urbana: University of Illinois Press.

Edwards, H. (1973). *Sociology of sport.* Homewood, IL: Dorsey Press.

Felson, R. B., & Gmelch, G. (1979). Uncertainty and the use of magic. *Current anthropology, 20,* 587–589.

Frady, M. (1979). *Billy Graham: Parable of American righteousness.* Boston: Little, Brown.

Freyne, S. (1989). Early Christianity and the Greek athletic ideal. In G. Baum & J. Coleman (Eds.), *Sport* (Concilium 205, pp. 93–100). Edinburgh: T & T Clark.

Gmelch, G. (1971). Baseball magic. *Transaction, 8,* 39–41, 54.

Gmelch, G. (2001). *Inside pitch: Life in professional baseball.* Washington, DC: Smithsonian Institution.

Goffman. E. (1961). *Encounters: Two studies in the sociology of interaction.* Indianapolis: Bobbs-Merrill.

Golden, M. (1998). *Sport and society in ancient Greece.* Cambridge: Cambridge University Press.

Gorn, E. J., & Goldstein, W. (1993). *A brief history of American sports.* New York: Hill and Wang.

Guttmann, A. (1978). *From ritual to record: The nature of modern sports.* New York: Columbia University Press.

Hammond, P. (1968). Commentary. In D. R. Cutler (Ed.), *The religious situation: 1968* (pp. 381–388). Boston: Beacon.

Higginson, T. W. (1858). Saints and their bodies. *Atlantic Monthly, 1,* 582–595.

Hughes, T. (1856). *Tom Brown's school days.* London: Macmillan.

Hughes, T. (1861). *Tom Brown at Oxford.* London: W. Nicholson & Sons.

Huiginza, J. (1955). *Homo ludens: A study of the play element in culture.* Boston: Beacon. (Original work published 1944)

Juvenal. (c. 150/1963). *Satires* (H. Creekmore, Trans.). New York: New American Library.

Kingsley, C. (1856). *Two years ago.* London: Macmillan.

Kortzfleisch, S. (1970). Religious Olympism. *Social research, 37,* 231–236.

Ladd, T., & Mathisen, J. A. (1999). *Muscular Christianity: Evangelical Protestants and the development of American sport.* Grand Rapids, MI: Baker Books.

Larson, M. (1948). *Gil Dodds: The flying parson* (2nd ed.). Grand Rapids, MI: Zondervan.

Lawton, J. (1984). *The all American war game.* London: Blackwell.

Lipsyte, R. (1975). *SportsWorld: An American dreamland.* New York: Quadrangle.

Long, K. T. (1998). *The revival of 1857–58: Interpreting an American religious awakening.* New York: Oxford University Press.

Loy, J. W., McPherson, B. D., & Kenyon, G. (1978). *Sport and social systems.* Reading, MA: Addison-Wesley.

MacAloon, J. J. (1978). Religious themes and structures in the Olympic movement and the Olympic games. In F. Landry & W. A. R. Orban (Eds.), *Philosophy, theology, and history of sport* (pp. 161–171). Miami: Symposia Specialists.

MacAloon, J. J. (1981). *This great symbol: Pierre de Coubertin and the origins of the modern Olympic games.* Chicago: University of Chicago.

Maclean, N. (1976). *A river runs through it.* Chicago: University of Chicago.

Malinowski, B. (1948). *Magic, science and religion and other essays.* Glencoe, IL: The Free Press.

Marty, M. (1974). Two kinds of two kinds of civil religion. In R. E. Richey & D. G. Jones (Eds.), *American civil religion* (pp. 139–157). New York: Harper & Row.

Mathisen, J. A. (1990). Reviving "muscular Christianity": Gil Dodds and the institutionalization of sport evangelism. *Sociological focus, 23,* 233–249.

Mathisen, J. A. (1992). From civil religion to folk religion: The case of American sport. In S. Hoffman (Ed.), *Sport and religion* (pp. 17–33). Champaign, IL: Human Kinetics.

Mathisen, J. A. (1998, May/June). "I'm majoring in sport ministry": Religion and sport in Christian colleges. *Books and culture, 4,* 24–28.

Mead, G. H. (1934). *Mind, self, and society.* Chicago: University of Chicago.

Miller, D. L. (1970). *God and games: Toward a theology of play.* New York: Harper & Row.

Milton, B. (1972). *Sports as a functional equivalent of religion.* Unpublished master's thesis, University of Wisconsin, Madison.

Miracle, Jr., A. W., & Rees, C. R. (1994). *Lessons of the locker room: The myth of school sports.* Amherst, NY: Prometheus Books.

Moltmann, J. (1972). *Theology of play.* (R. Ulrich, Trans.). New York: Harper.

Neale, R. E. (1969). *In praise of play.* New York: Harper & Row.

Novak, M. (1976). *The joy of sports.* New York: Basic Books.

Oriard, M. (1991). *Sporting with the gods: The rhetoric of play and games in American culture.* Cambridge: Cambridge University.

Overman, S. J. (1997). *The influence of the Protestant ethic on sport and recreation.* Aldershot, UK: Avebury.

Parsons, T. (1951). *The social system.* New York: Free Press.

Pfitzner, V. C. (1967). *Paul and the agon motif: Traditional athletic imagery in the Pauline literature.* Leiden: E. J. Brill.

Price, J. L. (1984, February 22). The Super Bowl as religious festival. *Christian Century,* 190–191.

Price, J. L. (2001). From Sabbath proscriptions to super Sunday celebrations. In J. L. Price (Ed.), *From season to season: Sports as American religion* (pp. 15–38). Macon, GA: Mercer University.

Putney, C. (2003). *Muscular Christianity: Manhood and sports in Protestant America,* Cambridge, MA: Harvard University.

Rahner, H. (1967). *Man at play* (B. Battershaw, Trans.). New York: Herder & Herder. (Original work published 1949)

Ryken, L. (1986). *Worldly saints: The Puritans as they really were.* Grand Rapids, MI: Zondervan.

Shanks, T. J. (1887). *College of colleges: Led by D. L. Moody.* Chicago: Fleming H. Revell.

Simmel, G. (1955). *Conflict and the web of group affiliations.* (K. H. Wolff & R. Bendix, Trans.) New York: Free Press.

Sperber, M. (1993). *Shake down the thunder.* New York: Henry Holt & Company.

Sunday, B. (1893, July 27). Why I left professional baseball. *Young men's era,* 1.

Veblen, T. (1934). *Theory of the leisure class.* New York: Macmillan. (Original work published 1899)

Wanted: A miracle of good weather and the "Youth for Christ" rally got it. (1945, June 11). *Newsweek,* 84.

Weber, M. (1958). *The Protestant ethic and the spirit of capitalism* (T. Parsons, Trans.). New York: Charles Scribner. (Original work published 1904–1905)

Will, G. F. (1990). *Men at work: The craft of baseball.* New York: Macmillan.

CHAPTER 15

Media

Stewart M. Hoover, Ph.D.

To account for the place of media research within the broader field of sociology of religion requires some reflection on the history of the disciplines involved. In short, the social-scientific study of religion and media has had a checkered history. A scholarly record has gradually developed, but at the same time, the project has tended until recently to lack the kind of theoretical *gravitas* that propels a substantive body of work forward. Such momentum began to develop in the 1990s, driven by a growing recognition of its importance, and by a growing cadre of (typically younger) scholars committed to answering its burning questions.

INTRODUCTION

As a scholarly discipline, the field of mass communication studies has generally considered itself to be a social science, notwithstanding recent—and significant—cross-disciplinary developments. Many in the field trace its roots back to pragmatism and to the thought of Dewey in particular, who saw social understanding and the re-invigorating of social communication as a central project of the social sciences (Peters, 1986). To Dewey, the social sciences were to be about helping the emerging mass societies of the industrial age imagine themselves in new and creative ways through new patterns and means of communication. Throughout most of the last century, however, communication theory and research (along with much of the social sciences) found itself drawn toward more instrumental and pragmatic ends and projects (Rowland, 1983).

Paul Lazarsfeld, for example, one of the most prominent mid-century Sociologists, made his Bureau of Applied Social Research into a major venue for the study of mass communication with emphasis on specific content and its effects, rather than a more wholistic approach. Mass communication research became important and prominent, but, as one of its other significant founders, Wilbur Schramm (1980) describes the times, it was viewed rather casually and instrumentally by social scientists from other disciplines. Today we tend to see the early efforts of Lazarsfeld, Schramm, and others as leading

Stewart M. Hoover • University of Colorado at Boulder, Boulder, Colorado 80309

the developing scholarship of mass communication research to see itself primarily as an *applied* science, directed at *policy* (Carey, 2000; Delia, 1987; Rowland, 1983). Fundamental to this application is what we might call an "instrumental syllogism" that holds that autonomous and rational actors in the various media industries produce self-evident media messages that have known, knowable, and predictable affects on audiences, readers, and listeners.

Many other social sciences also see the media as significant primarily in terms of their instrumental relations to known structures, movements, and practices in the social universe. This has been typically put in terms of the "effects" of media "on" one or more of these other phenomena. Extensive efforts have been devoted to studying the way the media affect voting, sexual and violent behavior in children and adolescents, health-related behaviors, mental and emotional well-being, and other social and psychological problems by scholars in public opinion, sociology, psychology, and mass communication.

Religion and mediated communication have shared a long-standing relationship, particularly in the American context. Historians (e.g., Noord, 2004; Underwood, 2002) have demonstrated convincingly that religious motivations, frameworks, and markets were at the heart of American publishing and later electronic mass communication. Religion was a vibrant subgenre in the radio era (Hangen, 2002) and continues to be today (Mitchell, 1999). However, media and religion really first attracted the attention of sociologists in the television era, when a few programs rose to prominence in the 1950s (Parker, Barry, & Smythe, 1955), but more importantly, with the advent of the phenomenon of televangelism in the mid 1970s.

Whereas religious programming had long been a fixture of American broadcasting, it had been seen as marginal and of little significance until changes in federal regulation of satellite broadcasting made it possible for relatively small broadcasters to find their way onto stations and cable outlets nationwide. This development drew broad public attention, as well as the concern of religious leaders (who understandably felt threatened), and the interest of scholars. There was a virtual explosion of research and publication, with a range of studies focused on historical and institutional analysis (Hadden & Swann, 1981; Horsfield, 1984; Frankl, 1987; Bruce, 1990, and some contributions to Schultze, 1990), sociological studies of content and audiences (Hoover, 1988, Abelman & Hoover, 1990; Hoover, 1990), considerations of political implications and effects (e.g., Hadden & Shupe, 1988; Hadden, 1991), and critical cultural analyses (e.g., Schultze, 1987, Peck, 1993).

COMPONENTS OF ANALYZING MASS MEDIA

As reflected in this literature, sociologists, psychologists, and mass communication scholars have tended to share a particular way of dividing up the turf of mass communication and the instrumental syllogism into three distinct and studiable components or domains: (1) the institutions, structures, and professional cohorts responsible for producing media; (2) the content, "message systems," or "texts" they produce; and (3) the effects of those messages on various audiences. These questions are clearly rooted in some of the central concerns of sociology and social theory, including: structures, institutions, economies, and power relations; socialization, social identity, and solidarity; structural and role differentiation; relations between individuals and collectivities; and social change and social stability. Each of the three domains of the mass communication process has been the focus of attention within Sociology of Religion.

Producers of Media Content

In the area of media institutions, work in religion sociology has tended to focus on studies of media *people*: professional cohorts and their conventions of professional practice (for an early example, see Hynds, 1986). A significant discourse exists particularly around the question of whether journalists who cover religion are in some way professionally biased by their own religious commitments or lack thereof (see Silk, 1995; Hoover, 1999; and Underwood, 2002, for discussions of this issue). Significant differences of opinion exist among those who have studied this question. The Lichter, Rothman, and Lichter "media elite" studies (1986) have provided the most provocative analysis which demonstrates that for the "elite" national media, at least, the newsroom staff differ significantly from the American population as a whole in terms of their religiosity. They are less religious than the public at large, with the implication that their capacity to cover religion or to do so fairly, must be questioned. Contrasting survey data exist (e.g., Dart & Allen, 1993, Buddenbaum, 1988), and this issue remains far from settled.

The above debate, in fact, demonstrates a limitation of the instrumentalist or "effects" approach to mass communication. Underlying the Lichter et al. research, and similar arguments by its proponents, is the notion that journalists' private religiosity necessarily influences their approach to their work (for a recent argument to this effect, see Barnes, 2003). It remains arguable within journalism that it is possible—even necessary—to separate personal belief from pofessional practice (Underwood, 2003; Hoover, 1999). And, even though studies (see Lichter, Amundson, & Lichter, 1991) have demonstrated seeming bias against specific religions in media content, the link to attitudes and values of journalists and editors remains a complex one.

One of the most important reasons for this complexity is that the media are *cultural* as well as *social* entities. It is one of the tenets of contemporary media theory that the media function within a cultural context that acts along with other factors to frame and determine the constraints within which they (the media) find themselves. This cultural surround is expressed and felt, with reference to professional practice, through such things as received, consensual ways of understanding and describing the world that the journalist writes and reports about. Silk (1995) calls these received descriptions and stereotypes "*topoi*" and argues that they are the common substance of journalistic accounts of all topics, not least religion, and that they emerge not from the structural and ideological location of the journalist so much as from a wider set of consensual understandings that journalists share with their presumed audiences.

Media Content

In the second domain of traditional media research, studies of media content or media texts relevant to religion have tended to look at media *representations* of religion. Some content analyses have measured the relative presence or absence of religion in print (e.g., Buddenbaum, 1986) or broadcast news coverage (Buddenbaum, 1990). Others have shown systematic misrepresentations of religion in general (Medved, 1993) or specific religions (Lichter et al., 1991). Such approaches often assume the instrumentalist paradigm, focusing on the implication that media representations would necessarily affect audience beliefs and attitudes about religion.

Media content can be looked at in other ways, however, some more consistent with media scholarship's pragmatist roots. The media scholar Horace Newcomb has proposed the idea that media culture be looked at not as an influencer of culture, or as a reflector of it alone, but as a "cultural forum" (Newcomb & Hirsch, 1976), a place where important ideas and values are presented, discussed, and evaluated. From the perspective of Sociology of Religion, Robert Wuthnow (1987) pursued such a line of analysis in a study of the television mini-series *The Holocaust,* arguing that it became just such a cultural forum through which moral symbols and languages were negotiated.

Effects of Mass Media

There have been relatively few efforts focused on the third domain of research predicted by the instrumentalist syllogism—the *effects* of mass media with respect to religion. We might have expected some of the work discussed earlier that focused on the biases of the media with respect to religion to be followed by studies to demonstrate that those biases in fact influenced audiences to think or behave in certain ways. This has been the classic approach in instrumentalist mass communication studies, best represented by the long and evolving record of research on media "effects" in areas such as television violence and its influence on children (for the definitive account, see Liebert and Sprafkin, 1988; for a scholarly critique and appraisal, McGuire, 1986). Although a wide range of thought has speculated about specific "effects-like" religious implications of media consumption (e.g., Fore, 1990, Schultze, 2002; for application to religious marketing, see Engel & Norton, 1976), there has never been the energy or momentum behind research on religion-oriented media effects that has pursued questions in other areas of attitudes, beliefs, and social behaviors.

The exceptions have been studies conducted on the effects of religious broadcasting and televangelism. The earliest research, conducted by Parker, Barry, and Smythe in the 1950s (1955), focused on the emergence of religious figures in secular media, most prominently Fulton Sheen, and found that he was actually not very influential over non-Catholics, and that an important "effect" of his program was improved senses of social belonging and social participation by American Catholics. Other smaller and more limited studies followed, until an explosion of interest in televangelism in the 1970s brought about significant efforts at studying the effects of religious television on religious audiences (Gaddy & Pritchard, 1985). The major effort in this regard was a study funded by a coalition of religious groups and conducted by the University of Pennsylvania's Annenberg School and the Gallup organization (Gerbner et al., 1986). The study was subject to considerable commentary and critical review (cf., Hadden & Frankl, 1987; Schultze, 1985; a response, Gerbner et al., 1989). At the same time, some significant questions were answered by the study. Most significant at the time, little evidence was found that televangelism diverted membership or financial support from existing congregations. Instead, these ministries seemed to be preaching primarily to the choir (Hoover, 1987). A more complete analysis of the data from the study, elaborated by in-depth field research, amplified some of its findings (Hoover, 1988). Most significantly, the primary "effect" of these programs was a sense of identity and solidarity they built up in their audiences. Although Evangelicals and Pentecostals dominated in the audiences for televangelism, and others were unlikely to view or be influenced, the core audience found itself supported and reinforced in its beliefs by ministries that were present on the national stage of the mass media. Subsequent effects in such areas as political mobilization were possible (Hadden & Shupe, 1988), but further research was limited to studies of specific programs and denominational cohorts, and various demographic groups, for example, the studies in Abelman & Hoover, 1991).

Research on audience effects since the televangelism era has gone in two directions, studies focusing on specific kinds of media and their relation to intended or unintended audiences (Buddenbaum, 2001), and research on specific kinds of religious audiences, and their differential readings of religious content (i.e., studies in Stout & Buddenbaum, 2001, which focus on Mormons, Southern Baptists, and Nazarenes).

In the work devoted to audience effects, the record is mixed. There is little definitive evidence of major impacts of media exposure on religiosity, religious belief, or religious practice. What significant effects have been found are largely informational effects (something we will see is also an important dimension in the digital era) and the reinforcement effects demonstrated most convincingly in research on Televangelism. More important, though, is a stream of research that has focused on the information-seeking and selectivity of viewers and readers. Religiously identified and religiously motivated audiences do seem to exhibit practices that are uniquely tied to their religiosity (Buddenbaum, 1996; Hoover, 1998; Buddenbaum & Hoover, 1996). This is significant in that it predicts the kind of broadening of the definition of relations between religion and media that has come to dominate the field in recent years.

A SHIFTING PARADIGM

One way of looking at the scholarly record on media and religion is to see the history described as a subset of the overall field of mass communication research. As I noted earlier, many of the tools and paradigms that have typified research on media in religion have, in fact, been drawn from there. In that light, the research record on religion as a category of the larger "whole" of mass communication is rather thin, dispersed, and unremarkable. The instrumentalist syllogism has taken us only so far in accounting for what is, by all accounts, a growing and broadening set of phenomena at the intersection of media and religion. The fact that the most convincing implications of media for religion are in areas of information and reinforcement, and that religiously-motivated audiences are in some ways unique, is thin gruel indeed. It is coming to be accepted by many that part of the reason for this is that the basic paradigms and questions have themselves been too limited to account for the phenomena we have wished to study.

At the same time, the field of media and religion scholarship is growing, for a number of reasons. The major reason is that the phenomenon under study, the interaction between the domains of "media" and "religion," seems increasingly important. Media and religion came together in unprecedented ways in the events of 9/11 and its aftermath, although there were important precursors (Hoover, forthcoming). Press coverage of religion in the recent election cycles played an important role in the definition of the supposed "religion gap" underlying the so-called culture wars. Media tastes and behaviors have come to be important, even definitive markers of religiously modulated social meaning and social experience, particularly for cohorts such as teens, preteens, those interested in alternative and non-Western spiritualities, and those who are motivated to seek out information about an increasingly diverse religious landscape (Clark, 2003). The media are becoming the definitive—and in some cases the only—sources of the symbols and claims about that landscape. For individual readers, viewers, and listeners, the media provide both information about the various religious "others" that we increasingly encounter domestically and globally, and information about "our own" religious faiths and traditions, serving needs of definition and social solidarity.

Changes in the world of religion, in the media, and in the scholarship devoted to studying religion and media have all served to bring about shifting and evolving paradigms. Media and religion scholarship have experienced parallel developments in a turn toward the analysis and understanding of the social world through the lens of lived experience, with the result being a convergence of interest and approach in both spheres.

In mass communication research and media studies, this has been described as a turn toward *culture*, influenced by developments in the humanities and elsewhere in the social sciences. The field of Cultural Studies has exerted great influence in media and communication studies in both theoretical and methodological directions. In a definitive essay, Carey (1975) proposed a challenge to the dominant instrumentalist paradigm in media studies, calling instead for what he called a "ritual" approach to understanding media. Although his use of the term "ritual" was more metaphoric than stubstantive (Grimes, 2002), it articulated a growing sense that the media needed to be seen in terms of their grounding in and contribution to the making of social meaning rather than in terms of the intended consequences of messages intentionally produced and directed at audiences.

This paradigm shift bears much in common with the call by Jeffrey Alexander for a "strong program" in cultural sociology (Alexander & Smith, 2002), focused on a "hermaneutics" of culture, attention to the narratives and codes that make up social texts, and "... the power of the symbolic to shape interactions from within, as normative precepts or narratives that carry an internalized moral force" (p. 139). In its own terms, culturalist media studies conceives of the primary concerns of scholarship to revolve around the cultural texts and practices that constitute the context of social meaning (Turner, 1990; Hall, 1982; Grossberg et al., 1992). As a practical, methodological matter, this has led culturalist scholarship in the direction of qualitative, interpretive, and ethnographic methods (Silverstone, Hirsch, & Morley 1992; Morley, 1997, 1992; Gauntlett & Hill, 1999), again consistent with paradigmatic trends in cultural sociology. In the media studies version, culturalism is typified by this qualitative methodology, a focus on practices of reception and meaning-construction among individuals and groups, and the articulation of cultural meanings into the overall context of social life. In addition is the focus on problematization of the relationship between mediated cultural texts and consequences, functions, and meanings, and a continuing theoretical discourse focused on the question of whether practices of media audiences or the structuring logics of media institutions and messages are determinitve of the consequences of media practice.

In the field of religious studies, and specifically Sociology of Religion, a complementary shift in paradigms has been underway over nearly the same period. This change has been persuasively described by Warner (1993) as a change to a "new paradigm" that shifts the focus of religious scholarship in several important ways. First, there is a focus on practices and experiences of individuals in the making of religious and spiritual meaning rooted in fundamental characteristics of American religious culture, including its disestablishment, its pluralism, its adaptability, and its aspirations to individual empowerment. Second, there has been a fundamental shift in understanding of religion from religion "as ascribed" to religion "as achieved." A range of scholarly directions make up this new paradigm, including feminist, experiential, rational choice, performance, historical, and material culture studies.

The emergence of these new paradigms in religion and media scholarship has coincided with changes in the actually existing worlds of religion and media. Simply put, religion and media are converging in significant ways. Where once it was thought that a "bright line" could be drawn between the realm of religion and the realm of media, it is increasingly difficult to sustain this implicit dualism (Hoover and Venturelli, 1986). The reason is twofold.

First, sociologists of Religion have been noting for quite some time now the development of new approaches to religion and to "religions" (Albanese, 1981) that are rooted in what Hammond (1992) has called a rise in "personal autonomy" in matters of faith. Anthony Giddens (1991) has been one of the most prominent exponents of a description of late-modern social consciousness as verging more and more around the self and identity.

Hammond's personal autonomy is a consequence for religion of the focus on the self described by Giddens. New paradigm religion scholarship, in fact, differs from Giddens in terms of his own speculations about the future of religion in late modernity. Although Giddens projects a particular set of consequences for religion (1991, p. 207) it is really religious institutions that face the challenge over legitimacy or authority that he describes. Warner's "new paradigm," by contrast, recognizes the same consequences for religion as ascriptive institutions, but holds that, at the same time, important consequences and projects are achieved in religious terms, in individual and collective actions of meaning-making. Roof (1994, 1999) has described these developments persuasively in the case of the so-called baby boom. He argues that the "boomer" generation, in fact, constitutes an important marker or divide in the evolution of American religiosity and religious practice. Roof proposes that the practice of "seeking" or "questing" has become a fundamental mode of religious practice in the boom and postboom generations. Individuals today increasingly think of their religiosity as an ongoing project of constructing an ideal faith or spirituality suited to their own biography and their own needs. Similarly, in a culturalist theoretical turn, Wuthnow (1998) has suggested that a significant trend is movement away from a "dwelling" and toward this "seeking" form of religious practice. Combined with Hammond's notion that autonomy and the self are at the center, we see an emerging religiosity that necessarily embodies, and actually articulates, a critique of received institutions and structures, as well as clerical and doctrinal authority.

Although the so-called new age spirituality seems best to represent this particular approach to religion, it is a set of trends that transcends many religious contexts and religious traditions, as Giddens predicts. Roof, Wuthnow, and others have pointed out that, in spite of what appears to be a strong tendency for this individualized religiosity to express itself in anti-institutional ways, traditional religious institutions continue to exist, and traditionalist and conservative religiosity endure. Roof provides a persuasive explanation that combines acknowledgment of anti-institutionalism and of the endurance of institutions by suggesting that a major motivation is a desire to be "fluid, yet grounded." Autonomy is on the rise, as is an increasing suspicion of the authenticity claims and demands we attribute to conventional religion. At the same time, there is a sense that the traditional religions, as we have known them, still contain within them authentic and pure resources of religious enlightenment. Thus, what results is an ongoing conversation or negotiation through which individuals and groups systematically seek and appropriate resources, while attempting to do so with as little mediation by religious authority as possible (Lippy, 1994; Wuthnow, 1998; Roof, 1999).

These developments have accelerated trends that have been at the center of American religion for most of its history: a kind of "democratic" (Hatch, 1989; Warner, 1993) approach to religion, where individuals see themselves occupying (to a greater extent today than in the 19th century) a marketplace of religious choice; and the more or less easy acceptance of religious commodities of various kinds as valid mediators, sources, and transitional objects relevant to faith (Moore, 1994; McDannell, 1995; Morgan, 1998). Although such commodified and "materialistic" approaches to piety have traditionally been derogated in old line and orthodox Protestant traditions, they have been readily accepted and even encouraged within conservative Protestantism and Catholicism. A kind of cultural divide has existed within American religious culture between those who do and do not accept such commodification as normative, a divide that has always been, in part, about class tastes and interests (Promey, 1996).

These above arguments are essentially cultural as opposed to structural explanations for social behavior and it is the move to this cultural level that makes the so-called new paradigm in religion so amenable to culturalist and interpretive analysis, and leads to convergence with trends in the media and in media studies. In the world of the media, religion has always been problematic for a number of reasons (Hoover & Venturelli, 1996). Most significant to our considerations here has been the assumption on the part of both the broadcast and the print media that religion is an inherently unstable and controversial topic (Dart & Allen, 1993; Hoover & Wagner, 1998). For the print media, this has led to a reluctance to cover religion in the first place and a tendency to do so, when necessary, within rather constrained categories and conventions (Silk, 1995). For the electronic media, this led to policies intended to provide a context for religion, but at the same time keep it in a relatively safe place at the margins of the television or radio schedule (Rosenthal, 2003; Hangen, 2002).

This resistance to religion by the media has now begun to break down, at least in part because of the development of deeper and broader religious markets rooted in emerging autonomous, "seeking" religiosity. What has happened, in a sense, is that the media market-place has begun acting more and more *like* a marketplace when it comes to religion (Hoover, 2001). We should not forget, when analyzing the media, that they are unlike some other social institutions in that they are economic entities, and that a political economy explains a good deal of what they do. Structural and economic changes, including the increasing range of channels available through cable and satellite services, the boom in specialty publishing, and most importantly, perhaps, the integration of the Internet and the World Wide Web into the media marketplace have all played a role. The events of September 11, 2001, also have undoubtedly accelerated and modulated trends toward openness to religion, with more and more media producers, editors, and entrepreneurs realizing that a growing market exists for religiously relevant media materials. Phenomena such as the unprecedented success experienced by a self-consciously religious program, *Touched By an Angel*, through most of the 1990s, and the seeming boom in other television programs with religious and quasi-religious themes in recent years, also have served to reinforce the notion that religion is both acceptable and even logical as a genre in the mix of print, nonprint, and now digital media.

All of this serves to fit the argument I have been making, that the evolution of schol-arship on media and religion within the field of sociology of religion has undergone a paradigm shift in recent years. Earlier understandings of the appropriate questions stressed what I have called an "instrumentalist syllogism," which conceived of media in terms of their institutional structures, their messages, and their "effects," and saw a necessary connection between these three domains. Increasingly, media studies has been understanding media in more nuanced and less instrumental terms. Consistent with trends toward a new paradigm in the study of religion and the turn toward more interpretive or hermeneutic approaches to cultural sociology, media studies has begun to look seriously at the active practices of audiences and individuals and the ways that they achieve religious and spiritual meanings through the media they consume. In both fields—religion and media scholarship—this shift in approach has had both theoretical and methodological implications. In theory, there has been a rethinking of structure and function as key elements, turning instead toward *culture* as a domain that is also capable of generating socially significant processes and actions. In method, the tendency has been to move more toward qualitative and interpretive paradigms.

At the same time, there is an entirely separate argument that moves religion and media scholarship more in the direction of culturalism and qualitative/interpretive studies. The argument is that the traditional structuralist and functionalist assumptions have simply had a difficult time dealing persuasively with the phenomena under study. Religion is itself a subtle and complex dimension of social life. Sociology of Religion has found ways of measuring religion with some success, but has been less successful in developing theory at the level of prediction, at least until recently (Warner, 1993). As media scholarship has increasingly discovered, specific dimensions of media practice are, as well, exceedingly complex and subtle, and religion, spirituality, faith, and belief are doubly or triply so. Thus, culturalism in media/religion studies derives in important ways from necessity. In order to be able to study and account for important dimensions of the relationship between media and religion, it is necessary to do so in dense, layered, descriptive, and interpretive terms. That is where the action increasingly is in the field of media and religion scholarship.

Much of this work changes the focus from the instrumentalist syllogism in media studies and the older paradigm in religious studies toward looking in the social universe for evidence of the consequences of assumed structural or institutional determinants in media and religion at the level of whole cultures. Scholars today are assuming the subjective perspectives of religiously or spiritually motivated social actors, and from that perspective looking at the extent to which the media make sense as a context for the seeking and finding of religious meaning. In another iteration, they are asking further for whom, when, and where these things are happening. This is a fundamental shift in the understanding of the nature of religion, but is just as fundamental a shift in understanding the nature of the media. For some, it makes sense to think of the media as a kind of *marketplace of symbolic resources* out of which religious or spiritual meanings can be made. For others, the focus is on the *construction of meaning* that results from the interaction between the individual and the media. For still others, the important questions are how mediated resources, symbols, and experiences *come to be exchanged* and in other ways used in the development of social, spiritual, or cultural capital within and between demographic and social groups.

Studies that have focused on the complexity and subtlety of religious or spiritual impulses as they may be expressed or sought through mediated experience have found that just as the media sphere in some ways conditions the experience of religion, and the religious sphere conditions the experience of the media, a kind of reflexive engagement with each is rooted to a great extent in received or taken-for-granted ideas and expectations about what it means to be either a media consumer, a religious/spiritual practitioner, or an admixture of both. Hoover et al. (2004), for example, found through detailed in-depth ethnographic and observational studies in homes that the cultural meanings achieved through religiously modulated media experience are, in important ways, conditioned by social expectations of what it means to be a certain kind of media consumer, and that these are further deeply embedded in social values surrounding the meaning of parenting, domestic space, and family life.

There are also critical demographic dimensions that impact the above issues. A large and growing scholarship around teens and youth culture is increasingly understanding media and mediated experience in a variety of contexts as important in defining and conditioning the meaning of religion, spirituality, and religious experience (Clark, 2003; Smith, 2003). Other voices consider the extent to which "interpretive communities," rooted in part in religious and spiritual interests, form around specific media icons, programs, and genres

(McCloud, 2003). Examples can include everything from Elvis fans (Doss, 1999) to popular music (Sylvan, 2002; Hulsether, 2002; Ingersoll, 2000), to *Star Trek* (Porter & McLaren, 1999; Jindra, 2000), to film (Martin & Ostwalt, 1996).

This theoretical and methodological ferment continues to be built on a good deal of interdisciplinary contact and interchange. Mass-mediated and commodified experience is integrated into such things as the emerging rituals of alternative and new religious movements (Pike, 2001), and scholarship directed at those phenomena must necessarily therefore encounter and account for media. There are particularly deep disciplinary roots as well in cultural history. Scholars such as Moore (1994), Winston (1999), and Morgan (1995; 1998) have persuasively demonstrated that the interaction between religion and the media is nothing new, and is integrated into wider contexts of social experience. Other recent work has expanded our understanding of the social and cultural significance of taken-for-granted religious media (Hangen, 2002; Rosenthal, 2002; Mitchell, 1999; Dorgan, 1993).

THE DIGITAL AGE

The digital age has affected the development of the field of media and religion studies in two important ways. First, it has provided an important and compelling new set of phenomena to study. Second, it has come to embody, in one domain, some of the most important questions facing sociological study of media and religion. These include the extent to which such practices and phenomena can and should be seen as authentic and substantive in the way that more ascriptive categories of religious organization have traditionally thought to be. They exist, after all, at a level of social and cultural articulation that is on some level more removed from the structural and functional contexts to which we have been accustomed to attribute causation. At the same time, voices in cultural sociology (Alexander & Smith, 2002), cultural studies (Turner, 1990) and others point out that, as cultural artifacts, media materials must be given their due in relation to consciousness, social identity, and social action.

The Internet and World Wide Web have, in a way, made the theoretical point more precise and focused in that a range of observers, and then scholars (O'Leary, 1996; Zaleski, 1997; Brasher, 2001), have suggested that the internet may be forming the basis for whole new ways of seeing and doing religion and spirituality, and that a kind of restructuring of religion, rooted in these new media, may be underway. This would make the digital age the place where, at least, McLuhan's vision of a "global village" (or "villages") might actually become reality with regard to religion and media. A range of materials available on the Web, in fact, present such aspirations and prospects (Hoover & Park, 2002). There is a seeming concordance between the mode of "seeking" and a context that is interactive, unstructured, antistructural, and interactive (Campbell, 2002; contributions to Hadden & Cowan, 2000; Helland, 2004). In an important contribution, Helland (2000) has proposed an analytic distinction in the digital realm between what he terms *religion online*, or the self-conscious use of the Internet and Web by religious individuals and groups with manifestly "religious" intentions, and *online religion*, or religious behaviors and practices that are centered in the online environment.

It would be in this latter category, that of online religion, that new and emergent forms of mediated religious practice would be found. There is much in the digital environments that commends itself to such generative practices. A wide range of Websites, listsservs, and other resources present themselves as centering novel religious or spiritual construction, often with a specifically "new age" and certainly a "seeking" flavor. Research into the significance of both "religion online" and "online religion" is one of the cutting edges in the sociology of media and religion. Already, scholarship has begun to suggest that the issues here are complex and in some ways contradictory (Cowan, 2003; Dawson & Cowan, 2004). Although a certain generative momentum can be seen in sites and practices that present as *online religion*, actual participation there may be less significant than the numerically larger participation in various online contexts by individuals and groups that think of themselves in more conventionally religious ways (Hoover & Clark, 2004). Practices related to religion and spirituality that are becoming common in the digital realm include the seeking of information about religion and spirituality, as well as about the beliefs and practices of specific groups, the digital exchange of greetings and inspirational materials, and more mundane tasks related to the activities of local religious congregations and groups. Although these activities seem somewhat pedestrian in comparison with the possibility of new religious movements forming around internet practice, they nonetheless fit with the ongoing development of more individually and less institutionally focused religiosity. The longer-term implications remain to be seen and remain a rich field of analysis for Sociology of Religion.

CONCLUSIONS

I have painted a picture of the developing field of media and religion studies as it relates to sociology of religion in terms of movements to newer paradigms that are more interdisciplinary and more focused on cultural artifacts and cultural practices than was the case in the past. There is an inescapable reality at the center of this research—the fact of the media as a set of institutions and practices. The organizations, structures, artifacts, and practices that constitute what we oversimply call "the media" are unique and particular in their economic, cultural and social sources and location. They are centrally about cultural products and representations and the practices that surround them, and sociology of religion must necessarily focus in those directions.

The seeming narrowness of that focus belies, though, broader and farther-reaching historical and theoretical questions. The first among these is the question of whether the media support religion as a sollipsistic "language game" around its artifacts and practices, or whether something more substantive and significant may be happening. We can see mediated religion and religious practice as a strategy fitted to late-modern rationalization of a differentiated—but still fading in influence—religious project, or we can see these phenomena serving the construction of new forms of religion that reparticularize religion in the context of a new, global culture. The agenda is thus a large and ever-expanding one.

REFERENCES

Albanese, C. L. (1981). *America, religions and religion.* Belmont, CA: Wadsworth.
Abelman, R., & Hoover, S. (Eds.). (1991) *Religious television: Controversies and conclusions.* Norwood, NJ: Ablex.
Alexander, J., & Smith, P. J. (2002). The strong program in cultural theory. In J. H. Turner (Ed.), *Handbook of sociological theory* (pp. 135–150). Kluwer Academic/Plenum Publishers, New York.

Barnes, F. (2003, May 6). The media gets religion. *The Daily Standard Online.* http://www.weeklystandard.com

Brasher, B. (2001). *Give me that online religion.* San Francisco: Jossey-Bass.

Bruce, S. (1990). *Pray TV: Televangelism in America.* New York: Routledge.

Buddenbaum, J. M. (1988). The religion beat at daily newspapers. *Newspaper Research Journal, 9,* 57–69.

Buddenbaum, J. M. (1986). Analysis of religion news coverage in three major newspapers. *Journalism Quarterly 63,* 600–606.

Buddenbaum, J. M. (1990). Religion news coverage in commercial network newscasts. In R. Abelman & Stewart Hoover (Eds.), *Religious television: Controversies and conclusions.* Norwood, NJ: Ablex.

Buddenbaum, J. M. (1996). Mainline protestants and the media. In D. Stout & J. Buddenbaum (Eds.), *Religion and mass media: Audiences and adaptations.* Thousand Oaks, CA: Sage.

Buddenbaum, J. M. & Hoover, S. M. (1996). The role of religion in public attitudes toward religion news. In D. Stout & J. Buddenbaum (Eds.), *Religion and Mass Media: Audiences and Adaptations.* Thousand Oaks, CA: Sage.

Campbell, H. (2002). An investigation of the nature of the church through an analysis of selected email-based Christian online communities. Unpublished doctoral dissertation, University of Edinburgh.

Carey, J. (1975). Communication and Culture. *Communication Research, 2,* 173–91. (Repr., in J. Carey, *Communication as Culture: Essays on media and society.* Boston: Unwin-Hyman, 1989.)

Carey, J. (2000). Remarks to the Annual Meeting of the International Communication Association, Acapulco, June.

Clark, L. S. (2003). *From angels to aliens: Teenagers, the media, and the supernatural.* New York: Oxford.

Cowan, D. (2003. Remarks to a forum in honor of Jeffrey K. Hadden, Annual Meeting of the Society for the Scientific Study of Religion, Norfolk, November.

Dart, J., & Allen, J. (1993). *Bridging the gap: Religion and the news media.* Published report of the Freedom Forum First Amendment Center, Vanderbilt University.

Dawson, L., & Cowan, D. (Eds.). (2004). *Religion online/online religion: Finding faith on the Internet.* New York: Routledge.

Delia, J. (1987). Communication research: A history. In C. Berger & S. Chafee (Eds.), *Handbook of Communication Science.* Newbury Park, CA:Sage.

Doss, E. (1999). *Elvis culture: Fans, faith, and image.* Lawrence: University of Kansas Press.

Engel, J., & Norton, W. (1976). *What's gone wrong with the harvest?* Grand Rapids, MI: Zondervan.

Fore, W. F. (1990). *Mythmakers: Gospel, Culture, and the Media.* New York: Friendship Press.

Frankl, R. (1987). *Televangelism: The marketing of popular religion.* Carbondale: Southern Illinois University Press.

Gaddy, G., & Pritchard, D. (1985). When watching religious TV is like attending church. *Journal of Communication, 35*(1).

Gauntlett, D., & Hill, A. (1999). *TV living: Television, culture, and everyday life.* London: Routledge.

Gerbner, G., Gross, L., Hoover, S., Morgan, M., Signorielli, N., Wuthnow, R., & Cotugno, H. (1986). *Religion and television: The Annenberg-Gallup study of religious broadcasting.* Philadelphia: The Annenberg School of Communications.

Gerbner, G., Gross, L., Hoover, S., Morgan, M., & Signorielli, N. (1987). Response to "star wars of a different kind: Reflections on the politics of the religion and television research project." *Review of Religious Research, 31*(2), 94–98.

Giddens, A. (1991). *Modernity and self-identity: Self and society in the late modern age.* Stanford: Stanford University Press.

Grimes, R. L. (2002). Ritual and media. In S. M. Hoover & L. S. Clark (Eds.), *Practicing religion in the age of the media: Explorations in media, religion, and culture.* New York: Columbia University Press.

Grossberg, L., Nelson, C., & Treichler, P. A. (Eds.). (1992). *Cultural studies.* New York: Routledge.

Hadden, J. K., & Swann, C. (1981). *Prime-time preachers: The growing power of televangelism.* Reading, MA: Addison-Wesley.

Hadden, J. K., & Frankl, R. (1987). Star wars of a different kind: Reflections on the politics of the religion and television research project. *Review of Religious Research, 29*(2), 101–110.

Hadden, J. K., & Shupe, A. (1988). *Televangelism: Power and politics on God's frontier.* New York: Henry Holt and Co.

Hadden, J. K. (1991). The globalization of American televangelism. In R. Robertson & W. Garrett (Eds.), *Religion and Global Order.* New York: Paragon House.

Hadden, J. K., & Cowan, D. (Eds.). (2000). *Religion on the Internet: Research prospects and promises.* New York: JAI Press.

Hall, S. (1982). The rediscovery of "ideology": The return of the "repressed" in media studies. In M. Gurevitch, T. Bennett, J. Curran, & J. Woollacott (Eds.), *Culture, society, and the media.* London: Methuen.

Hammond, P. E. (1992). *Religion and personal autonomy: The third disestablishment in America.* Columbia: University of South Carolina Press.

Hangen, T. (2002). *Redeeming the dial: Radio, religion, and popular culture in America.* Chapel Hill: University of North Carolina Press.

Hatch, N. O. (1989). *The democratization of American Christianity.* New Haven, CT: Yale University Press.

Helland, C. (2000). Online-religion/religion-online and virtual communitas. In J. K. Hadden & D. E. Cowan (Eds.), *Religion on the Internet: Research prospects and promises* (pp. 205–223). New York: JAI Press.

Helland, C. (2004). Popular religion and the World Wide Web: A match made in [Cyber]heaven. In L. Dawson & D. Cowan (Eds.), *Religion online/online religion: Finding faith on the Internet.* New York: Routledge.

Hoover, S. M. (1987). The religious television audience: A question of significance or size? *Review of Religious Research, 29*(2), 135–151.

Hoover, S. M. (1988). *Mass media religion: The social sources of the electronic church.* Newbury Park, CA: Sage.

Hoover, S. M. (1990). Television, religion, and religious television: Purposes and cross purposes. In N. Signorelli & M. Morgan (Eds.), *Cultivation analysis: New directions in media effects research.* Newbury Park, CA: Sage.

Hoover, S. M., & Venturelli, S. (1996). The category of the religious: The blindspot of contemporary media theory? *Cultural Studies in Mass Communication, 13*, 251–265.

Hoover, S. M. (1998). *Religion in the news: Faith and journalism in American public discourse.* Newbury Park, CA: Sage.

Hoover, S. M. (2001). Religion, media, and the cultural center of gravity. In D. Stout & J. Buddenbaum (Eds.), *Religion and popular culture: Studies on the interaction of worldviews.* Ames: Iowa State University Press.

Hoover, S. M. & Park, J. K. (2002, September). *Religion and meaning in the digital age: Field research on Internet/Web religion.* Paper presented to AoIR 3.0, Maastricht, The Netherlands.

Hoover, S. M., Clark, L. S., & Alters, D. F., with Champ, J. G., & Hood, L. (2004). *Media, home, and family.* New York: Routledge.

Hoover, S. M., & Clark, L. S. (2004). *Personal religion online: A technical report of the Pew Internet in American life study.* Arlington, VA: Pew Internet in American Life Project.

Horsfield, P. (1984). *Religious television: The American experience.* New York: Longman Press.

Hulsether, M. (2002). Like a sermon: Popular religion in Madonna videos. In B. D. Forbes & J. H. Mahan (Eds.), *Religion and popular culture.* Berkeley: University of California Press.

Hynds, E. C. (1987). Large daily newspapers have improved coverage of religion. *Journalism Quarterly, 64*, 444–448.

Ingersoll, J. (2000). The thin line between Saturday night and Sunday morning: Meaning and community among Jimmy Buffett's parrotheads. In E. M. Mazur & K. McCarthy (Eds.), *God in the details.* New York: Routledge.

Jindra, M. (2000). It's about faith in our future: Star trek fandom as cultural religion. In B. D. Forbes & J. H. Mahan (Eds.), *Religion and popular culture.* Berkeley: University of California Press.

Lichter, S. R., Rothman, S., & Lichter, L. S. (1986). *The media elite.* New York: Adler & Adler.

Lichter, S. R., Amundson, D., & Lichter, L. S. (1991). *Media coverage of the Catholic church.* Washington, DC: Center for Media and Public Affairs.

Lichter, S. R., Lichter, L. S., & Rothman, S. (1994). *Prime time: How TV portrays American culture.* Washington, DC: Regnery.

Liebert, R. M., & Sprafkin, J. (1988). *The early window: Effects of television on children and youth* (3rd ed.). New York: Pergamon Press.

Lippy, C. (1994). *Being religious American style.* Westport, CT: Greewood Press.

Martin, J., & Ostwalt, C. (Eds.). (1996). *Screening the sacred: Religion, myth, and ideology in popular American film.* Boulder, CO: Westview Press.

McCloud, S. (2003). Popular culture fandoms, the boundaries of religious studies, and the project of the self. *Culture and Religion, 4*(2), 187–206.

McDannell, C. (1995). *Material Christianity: Religion and popular culture in America.* New Haven, CT: Yale.

McGuire, W. (1986). The myth of massive media impact: Savagings and salvagings. In G. Comstock (Ed.), *Public communication and behavior.* New York: Academic Press.

Medved, M. (1993). *Hollywood vs. America.* New York: Perennial.

Meyers, K. (1989). *All God's children and blue suede shoes: Christians and popular culture.* Grand Rapids, MI: Crossway.

Mitchell, J. (1999). *Visually speaking: Radio and the renaissance of preaching,* Edinburgh: T & T Clark.

Moore, L. (1994). *Selling god: American religion in the marketplace of culture.* New York: Oxford.

Morley, D. (1992). *Television, audiences and cultural studies.* London: Routledge.

Morley, D. (1997). Theoretical orthodoxies: Textualism, constructivism, and the "new ethnography" in cultural studies. In M. Ferguson & P. Golding (Eds.), *Cultural studies in question.* London: Sage.

Morgan, D. (1996). *Icons of American protestantism: The art of Warner Sallman.* New Haven, CT: Yale University Press.

Morgan, D. (1998). *Visual piety: A history and theory of popular religious images.* Berkeley: University of California Press.

Newcomb, H., & Hirsch, P. (1976). Television as a cultural forum. In H. Newcomb (Ed.), *Television: The critical view.* New York: Oxford.

Nord, D. P. (2004). *Faith in reading: Religious publishing and the birth of mass media in America, 1790–1860.* New York: Oxford University Press.

O'Leary, S. D. (1996). Cyberspace as sacred space: Communicating religion on computer networks. *Journal of the American Academy of Religion, 64*(4), 781–808.

Parker, E., Barry, D., & Smythe, D. (1955). *The television-radio audience and religion.* New York: Harper.

Peck, J. (1993). *The gods of televangelism.* Cresskill, NJ: Hampton Press.

Pike, S. (2001). *Earthly bodies, magical selves: Contemporary pagans and the search for community.* Berkeley: University of California Press.

Porter, J. E., & McLaren, D. (Eds.). (1999). *Star trek as sacred ground: Explorations of star trek, religion, and American culture.* Albany: SUNY Press.

Promey, S. (1996). Interchangeable art: Warner Sallman and the critics of mars culture. In D. Morgan (Ed.), *Icons of American protestantism: The art of Warner Sallman.* New Haven, CT: Yale University Press.

Rosenthal, M. (2002). Turn it off: TV criticism in Christian century magazine, 1946–1960. In S. M. Hoover & L. S. Clark (Eds.), *Practicing religion in the age of the media: Explorations in media, religion, and culture.* New York: Columbia University Press.

Rowland, W. D. (1983). *The politics of TV violence: Policy uses of communication research.* Beverly Hills, CA: Sage.

Schramm, W. (1980). The beginnings of communication research in the United States. In D. Nimmo (Ed.), *Communication Yearbook 4,* pp. 73–82. New Brunswick, NJ: Transaction.

Schultze, Q. (1987). The mythos of the electronic church. *Critical Studies in Mass Communication, 4*(3), 245–261.

Schultze, Q. (1985). Vindicating the electronic church? An assessment of the Annenberg-Gallup study. *Critical Studies in Mass Communication, 2*(3), 283–290.

Schultze, Q. (Ed.). (1990). *American evangelicals and the mass media.* Grand Rapids, MI: Academie Press.

Schultze, Q. (2002). *Habits of the high-tech heart: Living virtuously in the information age.* Grand Rapids, MI: Baker Books.

Silk, M. (1995). *Unsecular media: Marking news of religion in America.* Urbana: University of Illinois Press.

Silverstone, R., Hirsch, E., & Morley, D. (1992). Information and communication technologies and the moral economy of the household. In R. Silverstone & E. Hirsch (Eds.), *Consuming technologies: Media and information in domestic spaces.* London: Routledge.

Smith, C. (2003). Theorizing religious effects among American adolescents. *Journal for the Scientific Study of Religion, 42*(1), 17–30.

Stout, D., & Buddenbaum, J. (Eds.). (1996). *Religion and mass media: Audiences and adaptations.* Thousand Oaks, CA: Sage.

Stout, D., & Buddenbaum, J. (Eds.). (2001). *Religion and popular culture: Studies on the interaction of worldviews.* Ames: Iowa State University Press.

Tuner, G. (1990). *Cultural studies: An introduction.* Boston: Unwin Hyman.

Underwood, D. (2002). *From yahweh to yahoo! The religious roots of the secular press.* Urbana: University of Illinois Press.

Warner, R. S. (1993). Work in progress toward a new paradigm for the study of religion in the United States. *American Journal of Sociology, 98*(5), 1044–1093.

Winston, D. (1999). *Red-hot and righteous: The urban religion of the salvation army.* Cambridge, MA: Harvard University Press.

Wuthnow, R. (1987). *Meaning and moral order: Explorations in cultural analysis.* Berkeley: University of California Press.

Wuthnow, R. (1998). *After heaven: Spirituality in America since the 1950s.* Berkeley: University of California Press.

Zaleski, J. (1997). *The soul of cyberspace: How new technology is changing our spiritual lives.* New York: HarperCollins.

CHAPTER 16

Technology

WILLIAM A. STAHL

The last 10 years have been lively times for the discussion of science and religion. In 1994, Paul Gross and Norman Levitt published *Higher Superstition,* attacking environmentalism, feminism, and every form of the social study of science and touching off a bitter—at times vicious—debate that came to be known as the Science Wars. Also in 1994, the Sir John Templeton Foundation began offering substantial monetary awards for offering new classes in science and religion. The Science and Religion Course Program transformed what had been a small-scale, fragmented discussion over the relationship of religion and the natural sciences into a large international debate, which became known as the Science-Religion Dialogue. What was surprising about both debates was the absence of sociologists of religion.

Sociologists of religion went AWOL from the Science Wars. Sociologists of science were among the main combatants, but few of them showed much interest in religion. On the other side, Gross, Levitt, and other "science warriors" took it as an article of faith that science debunked religion and that good scientists were atheists (e.g., Levitt, 1999).

The Science-Religion Dialogue was entirely different in both form and content. Although those engaged in the Science Wars tended to argue that science and religion were incompatible, the participants in the Science-Religion Dialogue replied that conflict between science and religion was neither inevitable nor desirable. Two of the most prominent figures in the debate were Ian Barbour (1997, 2000) and John Pokinghorne (1996), both physicists who are cross-trained in theology (Pokinghorne also is an Anglican priest). Many biologists and philosophers defended evolution without dismissing religion (e.g., Gould, 1998; Miller, 1999; Ruse, 2001). Others talked about the spiritual dimension of science itself (e.g., Goodenough, 1998). Historians of science reinterpreted both archetypical conflicts—the trial of Galileo (e.g., Machamer, 1998; Wilson, 1999), the Scopes "Monkey Trial" of 1925 (Larson, 1997)—and the scientific revolution itself (e.g., Osler, 2000; Shapin, 1996). Others (e.g., Brooke, 1991) demonstrated the many complex ways science and religion have inter-related over the past four centuries. Unfortunately, this debate was also characterized by an almost complete absence of sociologists (see Stahl, Campbell, Petry, & Diver, 2002).

WILLIAM A. STAHL • University of Regina, Regina, Saskatchewan, Canada S4S 0A2

Both debates are now largely over. The Science Wars petered out by the end of the decade. The termination of the Science and Religion Course Program in 2002 signaled that much of the excitement of the dialogue was ending as its participants turned to institution- alizing their gains. Both discussions, however, raised important issues for the sociology of religion, even if they were not engaged at the time. This chapter will raise several questions crucial to the participation of sociology in debates over the natural sciences, technology, and religion. Using Thomas Gieryn's (1999) metaphor of "cultural cartography," we will examine some of the more important contributions that *were* made, and suggest several issues that might form an agenda for the sociological study of science and religion in the coming years.

CULTURAL MAPS AND AUTHORITY

Both the Science Wars and the Science-Religion Dialogue were debates about boundaries. As such, they were also debates about authority—who has the power to define the boundaries of science (and religion), who should be included within those boundaries, and who has the legitimate right to speak. Thomas Gieryn (1999) argues that a useful way to think about such disputes is as *cultural cartography,* that is, as debates over "maps" of culture. He contends that "As knowledge makers seek to present their claims or practices as legitimate (credible, trustworthy, reliable) by locating them within 'science,' they discursively construct for it an ever changing arrangement of boundaries and territories and landmarks, always contingent upon immediate circumstances" (1999, p. xi). Such conceptual maps delimit issues, establish agendas, and designate who are the legitimate interlocutors in any debate.

The participants in such discourse engage in *credibility contests,* in which they try to gain *epistemic authority,* which Gieryn (1999, p. 1) defines as "the legitimate power to define, describe, and explain bounded domains of reality." He sees three different kinds of credibility contests. The first, *expulsion* conflicts, occur when rival authorities each claim to be scientific. The fight over global warming is a good example. Each side claims that its own theories and models are exemplars of good science while their opponents propagate politically motivated junk science. (Of course, there is a long history of this in religion as well, with the loser in theological debates becoming heretic.) In fact, there is a whole genre of literature that serves to police the borders of science, maintaining the authority of the cultural map by denouncing pretenders as pseudoscience and fraud (e.g., Carey, 1994; Park, 2000). Second are *expansion* conflicts, in which the contending parties try to extend the boundaries of their jurisdiction. For example, some science popularizers, such as Richard Dawkins (1996, 1998, 2003), have debunked religion for years. In the United States, fundamentalists have waged a long, loud, and generally futile crusade against the theory of evolution (e.g., Morris, 1968, 1974). The Science Wars were largely this kind of conflict. The third form is *protection of autonomy.* Here contestants try to defend boundaries against attempts to redraw them. One of Gieryn's examples (1999, pp. 37–64) was the British scientist John Tyndall, who in the 19th century drew cultural maps demarcating science from religion, on the one hand, and "pure" science from technology, on the other. Attempts to maintain university autonomy against encroachment by government or corporations would be a current example (e.g., Dalton, 2003). Trying to establish the authority of a new discipline or program would be another. Some of the Science-Religion Dialogue would be an example of this last type.

Gieryn's cultural cartography provides a framework for tying together the disparate (and all too sparse) contributions sociologists have made to the study of science and religion.

We will examine four maps. First, the cultural cartography of the Science-Religion Dialogue has excluded social scientists from legitimate participation. We will consider why, and what alternatives sociologists might have. Second, we will discuss the secularization debate, as this is the issue that is most likely to engage sociologists in the discussion of science. Third, implicit religion is seen by some to be almost the opposite of secularization. From this perspective, we will review arguments that science is implicitly religious. Fourth, we will look at maps of religion and technology. We will conclude with a few reflections on reinterpreting maps.

CULTURAL CARTOGRAPHY IN THE
SCIENCE-RELIGION DIALOGUE

One of the possible reasons that sociologists participated so rarely in the Science-Religion Dialogue was that their involvement was not welcomed. The most influential maps of the relationship between science and religion, those of Ian Barbour and Stephen Jay Gould, left no room for sociology. Natural scientists, theologians, and philosophers all had a clearly visualized "place" in the debate while social scientists did not. If sociologists want to legitimately participate, they will have to redraw the cultural map.

Ian Barbour was a pioneer in the Science-Religion Dialogue. His map of the interaction between science and religion (Barbour, 1997, 2000) has clearly been dominant in the discussions over the past decade and has structured much of the debate that has taken place. It is widely copied in textbooks and was institutionalized in the John Templeton Foundation's approach to the dialogue. Other scholars have developed variations on Barbour (Haught, 1995; Southgate et al., 1999). Barbour probably has done more than anyone else to establish the credibility and legitimacy of dialogue between science and religion.

Barbour's approach is typological, mapping out four possible types of relationship between science and religion. The first type is *Conflict*, which sees science and religion as mutually exclusive and inherently incompatible. Proponents of this approach create strong and thick boundaries between science and religion, some claiming that science has a monopoly on truth, others making the same claim for religion. Barbour discusses scientific materialists such as Richard Dawkins, Stephen Weinberg, or Jacques Monod, who believe science is the only valid form of knowledge and that it can explain all of reality. Religion is, therefore, false. On the other side of the argument, biblical literalists argue that the first two chapters of Genesis give a full and accurate account of the formation of the universe. Scientific theories are therefore false.

The second type is *Independence*. Here science and religion are put in separate compartments that do not make claims on each other. For theologians and philosophers such as Karl Barth, Rudolf Bultmann, George Lindbeck, and the early Langdon Gilkey (interestingly, Barbour does not mention any practicing scientists), science and religion have contrasting methodologies, subject matter, and languages that simply do not compete. This approach has been institutionalized in the "mainstream" churches and is probably the most common and widespread position among the public.

Dialogue sees that the spheres of science and religion are separate but do indeed impinge upon each other, requiring dialogue between them. There are a wide variety of positions here. Typical kinds of questions are: what are the presuppositions and limits of science, are there methodological parallels between science and religion, and is there a nature-centered spirituality? Barbour mentions Wolfhardt Pannenberg, Karl Rahner, David Tracy, and Michael Polanyi as examples of people working from this position.

The final type is *Integration* which is "A more systematic and extensive kind of partnership between science and religion [which] occurs among those who seek a closer integration of the two disciplines" (Barbour, 2000, p. 3). This usually takes one of three forms, according to Barbour. Natural theology, as exemplified by the works of William Paley or Richard Swineborne, sees God's design revealed in scientific findings, or, as it is usually put, the Book of Nature reveals God as much as does the Book of Scripture. The theology of nature argues that specific scientific theories may affect the content of theology. This approach includes the works of Arthur Peacocke, Pierre Teilhard de Chardin, and Barbour himself. Finally, a systematic synthesis, as argued by process theologians such as John Cobb and Charles Hartshorne, tries to build an inclusive metaphysics uniting religion and science.

Barbour's map (together with its variants) has great value as a guide to the debate as it has occurred over the past decade. In Gieryn's (1999) terms, Barbour and his imitators were engaged in protecting the autonomy of the fledgling dialogue. But it was not the only map. Toward the end of the decade, Stephen Jay Gould (1998, 1999) articulated a map of the science-religion dialogue that was deliberately at variance with Barbour. Gould called his map NOMA, for Non-Overlapping Magisteria.

Gould defined a magisterium as "a domain where one form of teaching holds the appropriate tools for meaningful discourse and resolution" (1999, p. 3). Science and religion are each magisteria. Each holds sway over its own domain, science over the empirical realm of fact and theory and religion over the domain of ultimate meaning and moral value. The two domains do not overlap, but their boundaries are not permanently fixed either. "A magisterium," he said, "is a site for dialogue and debate, not a set of eternal and invariable rules" (Gould, 1999, p. 61). Although the two domains are separate, he argued, "the contact between magisteria could not be more intimate and pressing" (1999, p. 65). He explained: "The two magisteria bump right against each other, interdigitating in wondrously complex ways along their joint border. Many of our deepest questions call upon aspects of both magisteria for different parts of a full answer—the sorting of legitimate domains can become quite complex and difficult" (1998, p. 274). This means dialogue is essential between the two, because: "Any interesting problem, at any scale . . . must call upon the separate contributions of both magisteria for any adequate illumination" (1999, p. 65). On some questions theology has nothing to say, while others are beyond the scope of science. But for most of the important issues of the day—Gould uses the example of genetic engineering—debate is necessary to determine where the proper boundaries lie.

Gould consciously patterned his position after that of the 19th-century Darwinist Thomas Huxley, and for similar reasons, to protect the autonomy of evolutionary theory from outside attack. Gould savages Creationists for stepping over boundaries into the magisterium of science, and is just as harsh on those scientists who violate the domain of religion. The problem with Gould's map is that the philosophy behind it lies in the trifurcation of reason developed by Immanuel Kant during the Enlightenment. Science, for Gould as it was for Kant, is the domain of the cognitive-instrumental, religion that of the practical-moral. And although the aesthetic-expressive is not formally part of Gould's model, he recognizes its domain as well. Gould maintained that as magisteria, science and religion are different in their essence. However much they may need demarcation at the frontier, each is characterized at its core by unique, necessary, and invariant qualities that distinguish them from each other. So Gould is not presenting anything radically new—his separation of fact from value, of science from ethics, is part of the mainstream of modern thought.

Neither of these maps leaves much space for the social sciences to participate. Barbour presents a dialogue between academic theology and a rather surprisingly narrow range of scientific theories rather than between a full spectrum of science and religion. He discusses what the content of science means for theology, instead of seeing both as processes or practices. His map is very abstract, intellectual, and circumscribed and sharply separates theory and practice. It is also static and ahistorical. Positions are categorized without explanation of how those categories arose or of the dynamics of the debate within or between positions. Each position is defined by its essence, rather than being seen as the result of boundary work. Consequently, there is little room for the social sciences. In his expanded Gifford Lectures, for instance, the sociology of science is dismissed in less than two pages, while the sociology of religion is ignored altogether (1997, pp. 144–146).

Gould's map is not any more hospitable to the social sciences. In following Kant's division of reason, Gould partitions knowledge into two essentially different ways of knowing about the world, separating fact from value. It is not clear where the social sciences might fit into his scheme. But although separate magisteria may be clear so long as one remains in the realm of pure theory, it becomes problematic as soon as one becomes practical. Inevitably, when one becomes practical the empirical and moral are intermixed. For instance, Gould's model cannot give an adequate account of technology. Because technology is instrumental, both questions of *how* and *should* are inherent in its practice. Technology crosses the boundaries between the realms of facts and values, and defies separation into distinct domains.

Fortunately for the social sciences, neither Barbour's map (including its variants) nor Gould's are the only ones available for the science-religion dialogue. Ronald Cole-Turner (1998) suggested a more encompassing map, which we developed further in *Webs of Reality* (Stahl, Campbell, Petry, & Diver, 2002). Instead of a theoretical debate between scientific theory and academic theology, Cole-Turner envisions a more broadly based dialogue. He posits four elements—science, religion, technology, and ethics—each of which interacts with all of the others (see Figure 16.1). He begins by insisting on the communal and experiential dimensions of all four elements in his model. Religion is not reduced to theology nor science to theory. Both are the practices of communities and, as such, each is an interweaving of experiences, norms, values, symbols, and rituals as well as beliefs. This is equally true of technology and ethics. Theory is important but it is not given the privileged position it has on the other maps. Where the others are concerned with maintaining boundaries, Cole-Turner refuses to reify categories and recognizes that neat boundaries are rarely found in the lab or in the pew. Because they are concerned with practice, all four elements are inherently relationships or networks which means that far from being autonomous, each is a form of social action. In doing this he counteracts the tendency of the others to produce essentialist definitions. With more encompassing boundaries of what is legitimate to

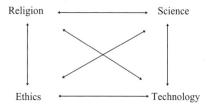

FIGURE 16.1. Ronald Cole-Turner's Map.

discuss, it is much harder to limit the dialogue to a few interlocutors. Cole-Turner's map is fully transdisciplinary, not only giving the social sciences a place in the Science-Religion Dialogue but also moving them into the very heart of the debate. What remains to be seen is whether or not sociologists will take advantage of his map.

SCIENCE AS SECULARIZATION

For most of the past two centuries, much of academic discourse has assumed that science and religion are incompatible. The more there is of the one, it is said, the less there will be of the other. This has been a central assumption in debates over secularization, the one place sociologists of religion regularly mention science.

After Newton, many Enlightenment thinkers believed that the only role for God was as Creator (Wertheim, 1995). The Enlightenment cultural map showed science and religion occupying the same territory. As science advanced its boundaries in the 18th and 19th centuries, the "space" for God kept retreating before continued scientific discoveries (often called the "God of the gaps" argument, in which theologians invoked the deity wherever science was unable to explain a phenomenon). The beginning of the social sciences in the 19th century opened a new, systematic attack on religion (Bellah, 1970). The founders of sociology were among the first to argue that science and religion were mutually exclusive.

In the 1830s, August Comte posited the "Law of Three Stages." Early humans, he argued, did not know the origin of natural events and so attributed everything to the gods. Later, as knowledge grew, religion began to be supplanted by philosophy, which replaced divine intervention with philosophical concepts (for example, phlogiston). But now, Comte claimed, we have achieved the stage of science in which positive facts will replace religious and philosophical speculation. The other founders of social science, such as Marx, Durkheim, Freud, and Weber, also believed that traditional religion would disappear, although their various arguments were more sophisticated than Comte's. But while the Law of Three Stages is rarely heard today, the idea that religion is only an inadequate explanation of nature and will be replaced by science is still popular among scientific atheists (e.g., Dawkins, 1996, 1998, 2003; Levitt, 1999).

Surprisingly, although a good deal is assumed about science among sociologists discussing secularization today, science itself is not a central issue. Science is *invoked* philosophically or ideologically in the secularization debate, but rarely is its relation to religion actually studied sociologically. In other words, science is treated as an abstraction, not as a practice (e.g., Buckser, 1996; Rioux & Barresi, 1997; Voyé, 1999; Lambert, 1999). When it is mentioned, it is usually either as *differentiation,* the separation of scientific from religious thought and institutions (e.g., Dobbelaere, 1999), or as *rationalization.* Rationalization may be understood in either a Weberian sense as disenchantment of the world or in a more Comtean sense as a change from a religious to a scientific worldview (Houtman & Mascini, 2002). In all these discussions, however, science is talked about as an abstract system of thought, but the theories and work of actual scientists are usually ignored.

When practicing scientists are questioned about their religious beliefs, the results are not what secularization theory predicts, as Edward J. Larson and Larry Witham (1998, 1999) discovered in their surveys of natural scientists. In 1914 and again in 1933 the psychologist James H. Leuba surveyed American physical and biological scientists, asking them two questions: did they believe in a God who could be influenced by worship and did they believe in an afterlife. Larson and Witham replicated Leuba's study. In both his surveys,

Leuba found that 40% of practicing scientists answered affirmatively to his question about God and 50% believed in an afterlife. Even given the Evangelical slant to the question, Larson and Witham found that 40% of American scientists today still believe in God as defined and 40% believe in an afterlife. Had they used a broader definition of God, they report, the number answering yes to the first question would have been higher. But Leuba also discovered that elite scientists were much more likely to reject both beliefs, with only 20% answering affirmatively. Larson and Witham found the same: "NAS [National Academy of Sciences] biologists are the most sceptical, with 95 percent of our respondents evincing atheism and agnosticism. Mathematicians in the NAS are more accepting: one in every six of them expressed belief in a personal God" (1999, p. 90). Why is there such a discrepancy between rank and file scientists and the elite? Larson and Witham point out that the NAS is a self-perpetuating body, in which current members elect new members. It may very well be that an *epistemic culture* (Knorr Cetina, 1999) encourages an orthodoxy of unbelief.

Interestingly, only Rodney Stark (1999) has seen the significance of Larson and Witham's work for the debate about secularization. If science in fact displaces religion from the cultural map, as Comte theorized, scientists should all be atheists. Yet, throughout history great scientists, not least among them Galileo, Kepler and Newton, were believers and significant numbers of practicing scientists remain so today. Conflicts there may be, but there is nothing inherent in either science or religion to compel them. Sociologists who wish to argue for secularization cannot continue to do so from the authority of science.

SCIENCE AS IMPLICIT RELIGION

If secularization theory argues that religion will disappear off the cultural map, the study of implicit religion finds it reemerging in all sorts of unlikely places. "Implicit religion" was coined by Edward Bailey (1998) but has a long pedigree in the sociology of religion. It can be defined as "those symbols and rituals directed to the numinous which are located outside formal religious organizations (e.g. churches) and which are often unrecognized, unacknowledged, or hidden" (Stahl, 1999, p. 3). To speak of science as implicitly religious is a bit of intellectual judo that turns conventional cultural maps inside out.

Some of the most significant studies of science as implicit religion have come from outside social science. Mary Midgley (1992) looked at science as a modern myth. Frederick Ferré (1993) saw scientism as an (inadequate) form of ultimate belief. Margaret Wertheim (1995) analyzed "God talk" and gender in theoretical physics. Mikael Stenmark's (2001) thorough analysis of scientism saw sociobiology as usurping religion. Several sociologists have contributed to this line of thought.

Dorothy Nelkin (1995, 2000, 2004) was sharply critical of current language in genetics, evolutionary psychology, and sociobiology. People such as Richard Dawkins and E. O. Wilson, for example, are among the fiercest critics of religion, yet their own work is itself implicitly religious. Nelkin (2000, pp. 20–27) explains: "Natural selection to evolutionary psychologists is a 'theory of everything,' an eternal principle that explains why we behave the way we do and what makes us what we are; it defines the very meaning of human existence." She continues: "Such beliefs are not theistic; they are not necessarily based on the existence of God or a spiritual entity. But they do follow a religious mindset that sees the world in terms of cosmic principles, ultimate purpose and design." Their language is full of religious rhetoric and Biblical imagery, they propagate their ideas with missionary fervour, and for them evolution is both a guide to moral behaviour and mandates a political agenda. Nelkin concludes: "More than a scientific theory, evolutionary psychology is a quasi-religious narrative, providing a simple and compelling answer to complex and enduring questions concerning the cause of good and evil, the basis of moral responsibility and age-old questions about the nature of human nature." Nelkin believes the boundaries between science and religion are best kept clear. The right-wing, anti-feminist political program of most evolutionary psychologists leads her to question the agenda of the whole Science-Religion Dialogue.

On Nelkin's cultural map, to see a science as implicitly religious is to deny it credibility. Steve Fuller (1997), Robert A. Campbell (2001), and the *Webs of Reality* team (Stahl et al., 2002) draw the map somewhat differently. Following Fuller's lead, these studies turn the "scientific study of religion" upside down, examining science through Weber's five characteristics of religion: soteriology, saintliness, magic, theodicy, and mystery. In every category, these studies find aspects of science which display the attributes traditionally assigned to religion.

The underlying issue in all these studies is authority. Fuller (1997, p. 43) says, "Faith in science marks a degree of deference to authority that is unprecedented in human history." Campbell (2001; see also Stahl et al., 2002) finds the basis of this in the sacred myth of science. He begins by noting the frequency with which prominent scientists engage in metaphysical speculations. "Many of the assumptions behind the so-called scientific worldview are implicitly religious," he argues, "As a sacred myth, science functions as soteriology, that is, it provides the salvation stories a religion provides for its adherents" (Stahl et al., 2002, pp. 26–35). The heart of that myth is the idea of progress. He concludes that "As long as scientific exploration is predicated on the notion that given enough time and resources, all of the questions that we can ask will be answered, the scientific worldview will remain a religion, blinded by faith in its own methods and accomplishments."

A map of science as implicitly religious is the reverse of seeing science as secularization. The clear boundaries of the latter disappear in the former. In both cases, the central question is authority.

TECHNOLOGY AND RELIGION

If science and religion have often been wary of each other, that is not the case with technology. The past decade has seen religious groups of every stripe enthusiastically embrace computer technology. The fantastic growth of the Internet has been accompanied by an enormous proliferation of religious databases and user groups. Nearly every church, sect, and cult has its own Web page. Computers have spread from the church office to the sanctuary, as projection technology was introduced to worship. There even are online churches.

Exuberant growth was accompanied by exuberant rhetoric. Both the media and the academy were full of talk of technology as a "brave new world." All of this was part and parcel of the hype surrounding the tech stock bubble of the 1990s. The bursting of the bubble in 2000 saw the beginning of a return to some long-overdue realism. Sociologists are just beginning to sort out what real changes are being mediated by computer technology and the Internet from what was merely wishful thinking. However overheated, the debate did raise some serious issues.

One line of questions asks if technology is enabling new kinds of religious community. Certainly the Internet is an important new communications medium. To the extent that it changes the social context for all religious groups, it will have some effect on religion.

But some have gone much further in claiming that the Internet is fostering a new kind of association—the virtual community—and that this will profoundly change religion in the future. (For the best summary and analysis of this debate, see Dawson, 2000, 2001, 2002.) It is too early to answer this question one way or the other, but Lorne Dawson (2002, p. 6) sets out some valuable criteria: "I would propose, in descending priority, that a group communication by computer warrants being considered a virtual community to the degree that it displays interactivity, stability of membership, stability of identity, and happens in a common public space, with a relatively large number of participants." Should a group display these characteristics, it might well have enough trust and shared experience to be considered a true community.

A second line of questions asks if technology itself is implicitly religious. Technological discourse is routinely utopian, but in the nineties rhetoric went beyond that to the magical and religious. Although some saw an imminent apocalypse (e.g., Joy 2000), others spoke of becoming like gods (e.g., Kurzweil, 1999). There were a number of analyses of technology as implicit religion (Noble, 1997; Stahl, 1995, 1999, 2002; Wertheim, 1999), which differed more in their evaluation of the phenomenon than in their analysis of its causes and development. Like Nelkin's dissection of science, David Noble (1997, p. 208) saw the religion of technology as overstepping boundaries and sought to delegitimate it: "The thousand-year convergence of technology and transcendence has thus outlived whatever historical usefulness it might once have had. Indeed, as our technological enterprise assumes ever more awesome proportions, it becomes all the more essential to decouple it from its religious foundation." By contrast, I (Stahl, 1999) argued that the only way to defeat a dangerous technological mysticism was to replace it with a redemptive technology.

As was the case with science, the debates over technology frequently resolved themselves into credibility contests between disputants trying to create or move boundaries in order to establish authority. So, for example, Kurzweil (1999) uses both his position as a leading computer scientist and "scientific" arguments based on technological determinism to give legitimacy to his fantastic visions. Wertheim (1999, p. 271) draws a different map in which such visions are only the most recent in a long line of technospiritual dreams and, further, that in comparison to more traditional spirituality these visions are seriously deficient. "The cyber-soul," she says, "has no moral context." It is an expression of the Ego without either a vision of the good or a sense of obligation to others.

The significance of such visions, as Wertheim points out, is that they express spirituality where none was possible before. If the Enlightenment map displaced spirituality from the domain of science, cyberspace has recreated some room for the spiritual at the heart of science and technology. However mythological, fantastic, or morally deficient any given vision might be, the fact that "respectable" scientists are getting them published is clear proof that cultural maps are changing.

CULTURAL MAP INTERPRETATION

An important branch of military science is called "map interpretation." It may be a useful metaphor for an agenda for the sociology of religion. The proliferation of cultural maps in recent years may very well make the ability to interpret such maps an important skill in the years ahead. What conclusions can we draw from the four sets of cultural maps we have uncovered?

First, we have to remember Gieryn's observation that maps are always the result of boundary work and the product of credibility contests. The fact that even this cursory overview found such a variety of maps is indicative that things are in a state of flux. Although it is perhaps not surprising that we should have quickly changing cultural maps in a time of rapid social and technological change, nevertheless the magnitude of the changes we have witnessed is still amazing.

It was not that long ago that the epistemic authority of science was virtually unquestioned in academia. Forty years ago, for those who bothered to study religion at all, the goal was to study it *scientifically* (see Gilbert, 1997). Even theologians were talking about the death of God and the secular city. Today, although that map is still strong in the academy—as witnessed by the secularization debate—it is no longer hegemonic. Some still believe that the "scientific worldview" is incompatible with religion, albeit the most vocal now are in the natural, rather than the social, sciences. But for many more the unquestioned authority of science is a thing of the past. Indeed, the Science Wars may well have happened because not a few natural scientists felt their power and authority slipping away. The emergence of studies defining science and technology as implicit religions is perhaps more a symptom than a cause of this trend.

All of this is why the maps of the Science-Religion Dialogue are important. Old maps and boundaries, some of which go back to the Enlightenment, are fading away. It is not yet clear what will take their place. Although the Science Wars may have been purely a reaction to social change, the Science-Religion Dialogue is more proactive, trying to fix new boundaries and chart new territory. Sociologists need to participate in that debate or risk having others fix the boundaries of the new cultural maps.

REFERENCES

Bailey, E. (1998). Implicit religion: What might that be? *Implicit Religion, 1,* 9–22.

Barbour, I. (2000). *When science meets religion.* New York: HarperCollins.

Barbour, I. (1997). *Religion and science.* New York: HarperCollins.

Bellah, R. (1970). *Beyond belief: Essays on religion in a post-traditional world.* New York: Harper & Row.

Brooke, J. H. (1991). *Science and religion: Some historical perspectives.* Cambridge: Cambridge University Press.

Buckser, A. (1996). Religion, science, and secularization theory on a Danish island. *Journal for the Scientific Study of Religion, 35*(4), 432–441.

Campbell, R. A. (2001). The truth will set you free: Toward a religious study of science. *Journal of Contemporary Religion, 16,* 29–43.

Carey, S. (1994). *A beginner's guide to scientific method.* Belmont, CA: Wadsworth Publishing Company.

Cole-Turner, R. (1998, July 19). *Theology's future with science.* Address to the John Templeton Foundation Toronto Workshop on the Design of Academic Courses in Science and Religion, Victoria College, University of Toronto.

Dalton, R. (2003, December 11). Berkeley accused of biotech bias as ecologist is denied tenure. *Nature, 426,* 591.

Dawkins, R. (2003). *Devil's chaplain: Selected essays.* (Ed. L. Menon). London: Weidenfeld & Nicolson.

Dawkins, R. (1998). *Unweaving the rainbow: Science, delusion and the appetite for wonder.* Boston: Houghton Mifflin.

Dawkins, R. (1996). *Climbing Mount Improbable.* (Original drawings by L. Ward). New York: Norton.

Dawson, L. (2004). *Religion and the quest for virtual community.* Paper presented to a joint session of the ASR/ASA, Chicago. *Religion Online: Finding Faith on the Internet,* edited by Lorne Dawson and Douglas Cowan, London: Routledge.

Dawson, L. (2001). Doing religion in cyberspace: The promise and the perils. *The Council of Societies for the Study of Religion Bulletin, 30*(1), 3–9.

Dawson, L. (2000). Researching religion in cyberspace: Issues and strategies. In J. Hadden & D. Cowan (Eds.), *Religion on the Internet* (Religion and the Social Order Vol. 8). New York: JAI Press.

Dobbelaere, K., (1999). Towards an integrated perspective of the processes related to the descriptive concept of secularization. *Sociology of Religion, 60*(3), 229–247.

Ferré , F. (1993). *Hellfire and lightning rods.* Maryknoll, NY: Orbis Books.

Fuller, S. (1997). *Science.* Minneapolis: University of Minnesota Press.

Geiryn, T. (1999). *Cultural boundaries of science.* Chicago: University of Chicago Press.

Gilbert, J. (1997). *Redeeming culture: American religion in an age of science.* Chicago: University of Chicago Press.

Goodenough, U. (1998). *The sacred depths of nature.* Oxford: Oxford University Press.

Gould, S. J. (1999). *Rocks of ages: Science and religion in the fullness of life.* New York: Ballentine.

Gould, S. J. (1998). *Leonardo's mountain of clams and the diet of worms.* New York: Harmony Books.

Gross, P. R., & Levitt, N. (1994). *Higher superstition: The academic left and its quarrel with science.* Baltimore, MD: Johns Hopkins University Press.

Haught, J. F. (1995). *Science and religion: From conflict to conversation.* New York: Paulist Press.

Houtman, D., & Mascini, P. (2002). Why do churches become empty, while new age religion grows? Secularization and religious change in the Netherlands. *Journal for the Scientific Study of Religion, 41*(3), 455–473.

Joy, B. (1999, April). Why the future doesn't need us. *Wired*, 238–262.

Knorr Cetina, K. (1999). *Epistemic culture: How the sciences make knowledge.* Cambridge, MA: Harvard University Press.

Kurzweil, R. (1999). *The age of spiritual machines.* New York: Penguin Books.

Lambert, Y. (1999). Religion in modernity as a new axial age: Secularization or new religious forms? *Sociology of Religion, 60*(3), 303–333.

Larson, E. J. (1997). *Summer for the gods.* New York: HarperCollins.

Larson, E. J., & Witham, L. (1999). Scientists and religion in America. *Scientific American, 281*(3), 88–93.

Larson, E. J., & Witham, L. (1998). Leading scientists still reject God. *Nature, 394*(32), 313.

Levitt, N. (1999). *Prometheus bedeviled,* New Brunswick, NJ: Rutgers University Press.

Machamer, P. (Ed.). (1998). *The Cambridge companion to Galileo.* Cambridge: Cambridge University Press.

Midgley, M. (1992). *Science as salvation: A modern myth and its meaning.* London: Routledge.

Miller, K. R. (1999). *Finding Darwin's God: A scientist's search for a common ground between God and evolution.* New York: HarperCollins.

Morris, H. M. (1974). *Scientific creationism.* San Diego, CA: Creation-Life.

Morris, H. M. (Ed.). (1968). *A symposium of creation.* Grand Rapids, MI: Baker Book House.

Noble, D. (1997). *The religion of technology.* New York: Penguin Books.

Nelkin, D. (2004). God talk: Confusion between science and religion. *Science, Technology & Human Values, 29*(2), 139–152.

Nelkin, D. (2000). Less selfish than sacred? Genes and the religious impulse in evolutionary psychology. In H. Rose & S. Rose (Eds.), *Alas, poor Darwin: Arguments against evolutionary psychology.* New York: Haromony Books.

Nelkin, D., & Lindee, M. S. (1995). *The DNA mystique: The gene as cultural icon.* New York: W. H. Freeman.

Osler, M. (Ed.). (2000). *Rethinking the scientific revolution.* Cambridge: Cambridge University Press.

Park, R. (2000). *Voodoo science: The road from foolishness to fraud.* Oxford: Oxford University Press.

Pokinghorne, J. (1996). *Beyond science.* Cambridge: Cambridge University Press.

Rioux, D., & Barresi, J. (1997). Experiencing science and religion alone and in conflict. *Journal for the Scientific Study of Religion, 36*(3), 411–428.

Ruse, M. (2001). *Can a Darwinian be a Christian?* Cambridge: Cambridge University Press.

Shapin, S. (1996). *The scientific revolution.* Chicago: University of Chicago Press.

Southgate, C., Deane-Drummond, C., Murray, P., Negus, M., Osborn, L., Poole, M., Steward, J., & Watts, F. (1999). *God, humanity, and the cosmos.* Edinburgh: T and T Clark.

Stahl, W. (2002). Technology and myth: Implicit religion in technological narratives. *Implicit Religion, 5*(2), 93–103.

Stahl, W. (1999). *God and the chip: Religion and the culture of technology.* Waterloo, ON: Wilfrid Laurier University Press.

Stahl, W. (1995). Venerating the black box: Magic in media discourse on technology. *Science Technology & Human Values, 20*(2), 234–258.

Stahl, W. A., Campbell, R. A., Petry, Y., & Diver, G. (2002). *Webs of reality: Social perspectives on science and religion.* New Brunswick, NJ: Rutgers University Press.

Stark, R. (1999). Secularization, R.I.P. *Sociology of Religion, 60*(3), 249–273.

Stenmark, M. (2001). *Scientism: Science, ethics and religion.* Aldershot, UK: Ashgate.

Voyé, L. (1999). Secularization in a context of advanced modernity. *Sociology of Religion, 60*(3), 275–288.

Wertheim, M. (1999). *The pearly gates of cyberspace.* New York: W. W. Norton and Company.

Wertheim, M/ (1995). *Pythagoras' trousers: God, physics and the gender wars.* New York: W. W. Norton and Company.

Wilson, D. (1999). Galileo's religion *versus* the church's science? Rethinking the history of science and religion. *Physics in Perspective, 1*, 65–84.

PART VI

RELIGION AS A SOCIAL INSTITUTION

CHAPTER 17

Church Membership in America: Trends and Explanations

ROGER FINKE

The received wisdom is that religion will recede as modernity arises (Wilson, 1982). Classic sociological theories argue that this religious recession will occur at all levels, from the behaviors and beliefs of individuals to the vitality of religious organizations. Indeed, to the extent that religious groups and their assertions about powerful supernatural forces do survive, the inherited model suggests that such groups will be restricted to small backwater groups protesting the advance of modernity (Berger, 1968, 1969). The remaining churches will gradually acquiesce to modernity and the once powerful supernatural forces will give way to more rational explanations and beliefs.

In America, however, modernity seemed to walk hand-in-hand with increasing levels of church involvement. As the United States became one of the most developed nations in the world, its people became some of the most actively involved in religion. Moreover, the religious organizations that displayed the rapid growth were not shy about god talk or making demands of their followers (Finke & Stark, 1992). The supernatural was alive and well. As these and many other anomalies have been noticed in America and throughout the world, a growing body of research has challenged the inherited model. With evidence mounting against the propositions of the traditional model and new explanations emerging, a new paradigm for the study of religion has emerged (Greeley, 1996; Stark & Finke, 2000; Warner, 1993; Young, 1997).

The purpose of this chapter is twofold. First, I document major trends in church membership over time. Here attention is restricted to church membership, because this is the only measure that can be garnered throughout the history of the nation. Second, I review recent research and explanations related to these major trends. Rather than focus narrowly on explanations of religious membership, I draw on a much larger literature that explains why religion is still plausible, why religious organizations rise and decline, and the effects of religious involvement.

ROGER FINKE • Pennsylvania State University, University Park, Pennsylvania 16802

The chapter is organized into five sections, with three of the sections reviewing specific historical time periods. Section I charts the rate of church adherence throughout the history of the United States and explains why religious involvement failed to follow the forecast of the inherited model. The second section documents the rise and decline of various religious organizations and reviews explanations for the rapid growth of upstart Protestant groups from 1776 to 1850. Section III documents the institutional role religion played for immigrants and freed slaves at the close of the 19th century, and how this contributed to high levels of religious involvement. Section IV briefly reviews recent trends of new upstart sects, mainline denominations, and the arrival of new immigrant faiths. The final section discusses the implications of this research for theory and how this growing body of research is related to work outside the United States.

I. CHURCHING AMERICA

When European scholars and church leaders visited early-19th-century America, they were quick to comment on the religious situation of the new nation. Reporting on his 1831–1832 visit, in the now famous *Democracy in America*, Alexis de Tocqueville (1969, p. 295) wrote that the "religious aspect of the country was the first thing that struck my attention." Tocqueville was not alone. Noted European scholars and clergy such as Francis Grund from Austria, Andrew Reed from England, Philip Schaff of Germany, and many others commented on the "voluntary principle" of religion, the peculiar "religious economy," and the religious "exceptionalism" of the new nation (Powell, 1967; Schaff, 1855). Accustomed to churches receiving generous support from the state, they marveled that church membership could be so attractive in a nation where it was so costly. Max Weber (1946, p. 302) explained that "church affiliation in the U.S.A. brings with it incomparably higher financial burdens, especially for the poor, than anywhere in Germany." He offered the example of a congregation located on Lake Erie where German immigrant lumberjacks voluntarily gave $80 of their $1,000 annual income to the local congregation. Weber noted that "[e]veryone knows that even a small fraction of this financial burden in Germany would lead to a mass exodus from the church."

Figure 17.1 charts the church adherence rate from 1776 to 2000.[1] Some, no doubt, will be surprised by the low rate of adherence in 1776. Powerful nostalgic memories of colonial religion supported by images of prayer at the first Thanksgiving or Pilgrims walking through the woods to church, suffuse our memories of religion in the new nation. What these images fail to illustrate, however, is that the colonies were open frontiers, oriented toward commercial profits, and were typically filled with a high percentage of recent male immigrants lacking social ties. Like other frontier areas throughout history, this resulted in high levels of social deviance (crime, prostitution, and alcohol abuse) and low levels of church involvement. Even the celebrated Puritan settlements in New England, with their high initial levels of involvement, were showing increasing signs of religious apathy and dissent by the mid-1600s. Neither the second generation nor the new immigrants shared the fervor of the founders.

Following the colonial period, however, adherence rates begin a long ascent. The rate more than doubles from 1776 to 1860 (17% to 37%), declines slightly following the immense dislocations of the Civil War, and continues on a steady increase from 1870 to 1926. Since 1926, the rate has hovered around 60%. If we were able to conduct a closer year-by-year inspection, the trend line might show a slight decline in the 1930s and late 1960s, and a small increase in the late 1950s. But the dominant trend since 1926 is that of

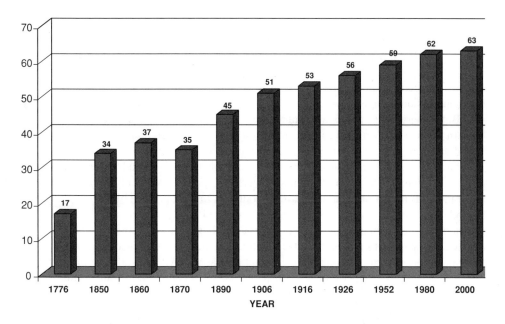

Sources: On calculation of rates, see Stark and Finke, 1988, for 1776; Finke and Stark, 1986
and 1992, for 1850–1926; Zelinsky, 1961, for 1952; Stark, 1987, for 1980, and Finke and Scheitle, 2005.
Note: Adherents include adult members and their children.

FIGURE 17.1. Church Adherence Rates, 1776–2000 (percentage of total population).

stability. Rather than declining, the proportion churched shows rapid growth from 1776 to 1890 and exceptional stability from 1926 to present (see Finke and Stark, 1992).[2]

These trends have generated a growing body of research attempting to explain the increase in church adherence and the more general topic of religious persistence? Why does religion continue to persist, despite modernity and even postmodernity? And, why did organized religion flourish in the United States?

The 19th-century European scholars and church leaders were the first to offer an explanation for the vitality of the churches. When Tocqueville (1969, p. 295) asked others to explain this atmosphere, he reported that "all agreed . . . the main reason for the quiet sway of religion over their country was the complete separation of church and state." Two of the earliest surveys of American religion, used the voluntary principle to explain the unique religious economy of America. Initially written for European audiences, *America*, by Philip Schaff (1855), and *Religion in the United States of America*, by Robert Baird (1844), invoked volunteerism as the cause of the unusually high level of religious activity and the growing number of sects in the United States. Swiss-born, German-educated Philip Schaff (1855, p. 11) quoted with favor an "impartial" Austrian editor: "The United States are by far the most religious and Christian country in the world . . . because religion is there most free."

Recent research in sociology and American religious history strongly supports these early insights and argues that deregulating American religion helped to spur the increasing rate of involvement (Finke and Stark, 1992). The argument is simple:

> Regulation restricts religious involvement by changing the incentives and opportunities for religious producers (churches, preachers, revivalists, etc.) and the viable options for religious consumers (church members) (Finke, 1990).

Like other new paradigm arguments, this argument stresses that changes in incentives and opportunities stimulate a new supply of churches from which people can choose (Finke & Iannaccone, 1993; Warner, 1993). As the regulation of religion declines, a new supply of religions arises seeking to mobilize the population to a higher level of commitment. Rather than placing attention on a changing demand for religion, this argument stresses how supply-side changes have fueled religious change.

But the larger question is why did religion persist at all? Why didn't the rationalism of modern science undermine arguments based on an unseen supernatural force or god? And, why didn't religious pluralism erode the plausibility of all beliefs?

First we should acknowledge the obvious: doubts about the gods have always been present. Even early prophets of the major world religions have openly expressed doubts about the gods they professed.[3] But are the doubts of today a product of something unique to modernity? When Christian Smith and colleagues (1998, p. 163) asked Americans who reported that they "often" doubted their religious faith why they did so. Few made mention of anything specific to modernity. Overwhelmingly they traced their doubts to the more traditional concerns of "personal tragedies and heartaches, evil and suffering in the world, human hypocrisy, the daily troubles of life ... human universals ... not problems that particularly afflict modern people." Similar results are found when using the 1988 General Social Survey (GSS). Respondents ranked personal suffering and evil in the world far above a concern over the conflict between faith and science (Stark & Finke, 2000, p. 77).

Finally, the concerns over modern religious pluralism, expressed so eloquently by Peter Berger (1969), failed to erode the plausibility of faith. Why? Mary Jo Neitz (1987, pp. 257–258) explains that for Charismatic Catholics an awareness of other religions "did not undermine their own beliefs. Rather they felt that they had 'tested' the belief system and had been convinced of its superiority." From her studies of women in Orthodox Judaism, Lynn Davidman (1991, p. 204) concludes that "pluralization and multiplicity of choices available in the contemporary United States can actually strengthen religious communities." She explains that "specialization of institutions and available options for 'being Jewish' brings vitality to modern Jewish life." After interviewing 178 evangelicals from 23 states, Christian Smith and colleagues (1998, p. 104) explain that "[f]or evangelicals, it is precisely by making a choice for Christ that one's faith becomes valid and secure."

Religion continues to answer questions about life, death, and ultimate meaning, provides guidance for day-to-day living, and promises rewards in the life hereafter. Modernity does little to increase or decrease these basic demands. The organizational growth witnessed in the 19th century United States was not fueled by a new demand but, rather, a new supply of religions aggressively competing for adherents.

But if the general trend during the 19th century was growth in religious involvement, not all religions benefited equally. Section II explains why.

II. UNLEASHING THE UPSTARTS, 1776–1850

By the middle of the 18th century, religious toleration was increasingly practiced throughout the colonies. The growing diversity of the settlers and their religions—combined with the vast amount of space, a desire for profitable colonies, and the religious apathy of most residents—resulted in eroding support for the establishments. As geographic size, economic interests, and increasing religious diversity pushed the colonies toward an increased acceptance of religious toleration, an unlikely alliance between the rationalists (such as Thomas

Jefferson) and the evangelical dissenting religions (such as Baptists) pulled the colonies toward religious freedom (Finke, 1990; Littel, 1962; Mead, 1963). Despite the disparity in the background and training of the rationalist and evangelical leaders, they agreed that religion was a concern for God and the individual, and that the state should not intervene. The rationalists often deplored the religious fervor of the new sects, and the evangelicals were clearly at odds with the beliefs of many rationalists, but the alliance proved effective as the rationalists provided legal justification for the emotional pleas of the evangelicals. In 1791 the First Amendment promised that "Congress shall make no law respecting an establishment of religion, or prohibiting the free exercise thereof." De facto establishments remained, and many states still refused to give religious liberties to Catholics, Jews, and those opposing Protestant Christianity, but the regulation of religion was declining rapidly. There would be no national church, and the groundwork was laid for a continuing separation of church and state.

The lifting of religious regulations not only offered new incentives and freedoms for existing religions, it opened the door for a new variety of religions. Religions that catered to the demands of the people not the state and reflected the diversity of the population they served. A host of new sects arose, each competing on equal footing for adherents. In short, religious deregulation unleashed the upstart sects and their preachers.

The traditional secularization model suggests that to the extent religious groups survive they will give less attention to the supernatural and place fewer demands on their members. Throughout American history, however, the groups with the steepest growth curves have been the less secularized faiths. A handful of marginal religious minorities and ethnic religious enclaves of one era become the powerful mainline denominations of the next. This trend of upstart growth and mainline decline began early (Finke & Stark, 1992).

The Congregationalists, Presbyterians, and Episcopalians (Anglicans) were the mainline religions of the colonies. Congregationalists dominated in New England, representing 63% of all New England churches in 1776. In the Middle Colonies the Presbyterians held 25% of all churches with the Episcopalians and Quakers holding 13% and 14%, respectively. Finally, the Episcopalians and Baptists each held 28% of the churches in the Southern Colonies, with the Presbyterians reporting 25%. Overall, the Congregationalists, Presbyterians, and Episcopalians claimed more than half of all colonial church adherents in 1776. Their dominance, however, was short-lived.

Figure 17.2 shows the collapse of the colonial mainline from 1776 to 1850. The Congregationalists, Presbyterians, and Episcopalians plummeted from 55% of all church adherents in 1776 to 19% in 1850—and now lay claim to the loyalties of a mere 4% of all adherents. Despite showing modest gains in membership, Congregationalists and Episcopalians plummeted from more than 36% of all adherents to less than 8%. The Presbyterians continued to grow at a pace roughly equal to the growth of the population, and they were able to support some growth in the new frontiers, but their share dropped because they could not keep pace with the surging upstart Baptists and Methodists and the emerging Catholics. The Methodists, in particular, showed a miraculous growth rate. Their efforts alone greatly expanded the percentage of the population involved in religion.

Part of the upstarts' growth came from their ability to adapt to the expanding frontiers, an area where the colonial mainline churches were slow to go. But they also showed sustained growth in areas where communities and congregations were well established. Table 17.1 shows that even in New England, the heart of the Congregational stronghold, the upstarts were rapidly dominating the religious landscape. In 1776 the Methodists and

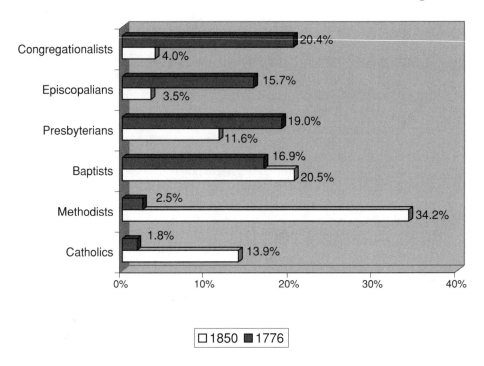

Sources and Notes: See Figure 1.

FIGURE 17.2. Church Adherents by Denomination, 1776 and 1850 (as a percentage of total adherents).

Baptists represented only a small minority of all religious adherents in New England. By 1850 their share of all adherents exceeds that of the once dominant Congregationalists.

The new religious freedoms gave the upstarts the opportunities to grow and gave the people the freedom to choose, but that alone does not explain the growth of Methodists and Baptists. Indeed, the majority of sects and other new religious movements show little promise for institutional growth. The Methodists and Baptists showed organizational growth for the same reasons churches grow today (Finke & Stark, 1992).

One reason was that their organizational structures allowed the local congregations to be highly responsive to the needs of the people without changing core beliefs.[4] Both the Methodists and Baptists were quick to adopt new forms of revivalism and music that proved so popular in the early 19th century (Hatch, 1989).[5] Although Presbyterian clergy helped to initiate the highly effective frontier revivals, it was the Baptists and Methodists that incorporated these strategies into their organizational routine. Francis Asbury, an early Methodist bishop, described the new revivals as "fishing with a large net" and encouraged clergy to convert their quarterly meetings into revival camp meetings (Asbury, 1958, p. 251). The clergy were instrumental in generating and adopting new innovations. Recruited from within local congregations, and largely trained there as well, the clergy were swayed more by local members than professional loyalties (Finke & Dougherty, 2002).

Local churches also were effective at forming distinctive religious communities without isolating their members from the larger culture. The upstarts placed higher demands on their members than the mainline denominations. These demands served to screen out potential free riders, generate higher levels of commitment and more resources for the local

TABLE 17.1. Percentages of All New England Adherents in Major Denominations, 1776 and 1850.

	1776	1850
NEW ENGLAND*		
Congregational Establishment	67%	28%
Baptist and Methodist	12%	41%
Roman Catholic	0%	11%
MAINE		
Congregational Establishment	61%	19%
Baptist and Methodist	8%	58%
Roman Catholics	0%	6%
NEW HAMPSHIRE		
Congregational Establishment	63%	30%
Baptist and Methodist	9%	46%
Roman Catholics	0%	3%
VERMONT		
Congregational Establishment	65%	29%
Baptist and Methodist	10%	44%
Roman Catholics	0%	6%
MASSACHUSETTS		
Congregational Establishment	72%	29%
Baptist and Methodist	15%	33%
Roman Catholics	0%	17%
CONNECTICUT		
Congregational Establishment	64%	37%
Baptist and Methodist	9%	39%
Roman Catholics	0%	11%

* New England totals exclude Rhode Island, which never supported an established church.
Sources and Notes: See Figure 1.

church, and provided boundaries for a distinctive religious community with close social ties (Dougherty, 2003; Finke, 2004; Iannaccone, 1994; Iannaccone, Stark, & Olson, 1995; Kelley, 1972; Stark & Finke, 2000). Relying heavily on clergy with full-time employment outside the church and stressing the autonomy of the local church, the small Baptist fellowships are well known for their democratic structure, high membership demands, and dense social networks. But it was the Methodists that sought this type of social density and accountability by design. Local Methodist congregations were divided into small, close-knit groups called classes. Each class met on a weekly basis and was composed of approximately a dozen or more members. Here is where the zeal of revivals was maintained, intimate fellowship was achieved, testimonials were offered, new converts were instructed, and the behavior of the faithful was monitored (Hardt, 2000). Known as the "sinews of Methodism," the class meetings were the primary source of spiritual and social support for members (Wigger, 1998, p. 81). By screening out free riders, generating more resources, and providing close social ties, the local congregations had much to offer the local member.

The upstarts also formed and maintained local congregations at relatively low costs. Whereas the colonial mainline relied on seminary clergy seeking full-time employment, the upstart clergy often served for little or no pay (Wigger, 2001). The result was that they could support new churches whenever and wherever new members (or potential members) arrived. For the Baptists, the local preacher was often a man of local origins whose "call" was ratified by the local congregation. Baptist preachers came with the people, because they were the people. Although Methodists did rely on the poorly paid itinerant preachers to coordinate religious activity in a given circuit, the local clergy, exhorters, and class leaders were all unpaid lay people. A Methodist congregation often began as a single class and gradually grew into a congregation with multiple classes or small groups. In contrast, the mainline denominations' requirements for seminary trained clergy resulted in a constant shortage of clergy and the clergy's requests for full-time employment hindered the mainline's ability to start churches in new settlements or maintain churches in sparsely populated areas. As a result, the Baptists and the Methodists were usually the only churches operating in these areas.

Finally, despite all of the changes and innovations the upstarts introduced, they guarded the core religious beliefs that motivated religious commitment and justified the demands they placed on the membership (Finke, 2004). The Baptist and Methodist clergy delivered a message of life changing conversion and dedication that justified the demands they placed on members and provided clear boundaries from secular behavior and beliefs. Moreover, they delivered the message in the vernacular, using imagery, metaphors, and stories that applied to the everyday life of their audience (Bilhartz, 1986). The carefully drafted and theologically rich sermons generated neither the emotion nor the urgency of their counterparts. If the goal was to arouse faith, the scholarly and often dry sermons of the learned clergy were no match for the emotional pleas of the uneducated preacher.

As the upstart Protestant sects continued to increase the rate of church adherence, the population of the new nation began to change. Annual immigration to the United States first exceeded 200,000 in 1847 and, with the exception of the Civil War era and a brief interval in the 1870s, immigration never dropped below 200,000 until 1931. The initial waves of immigrants were from Ireland, Germany and later Scandinavia. By the end of the century, however, the boats were filled with Central, Eastern, and Southern European immigrants. During an 80-year time span (1850–1930), more than 35 million immigrants arrived—immigrants who changed the religious landscape of America.

III. BUILDING RELIGIOUS ENCLAVES, 1850–1926

Just as the native-born Protestant sects took advantage of the religious freedoms of a deregulated religious economy, new immigrants and minorities with little power have found the church to be an institutional free space they could call their own (Dolan, 1985; Ebaugh & Chafetz, 2000; Evans & Boyte, 1986; Greeley, 1977; Yang & Ebaugh, 2001; Warner, 1993, 1994).

The religious freedoms of the new nation not only allowed the new religions to compete for members without fear of persecution or penalty; they also forced the local churches to become more responsive to the people. Local congregations became a safe haven where even oppressed minorities could build a church that was responsive to their needs. After the Civil War, the millions of new immigrants and freed slaves created churches that catered to their unique language, political, social, and religious needs. Despite holding limited resources, they effectively built institutions that carried their religious identity and culture.

The most dramatic shift in American religion was the rapid growth of Roman Catholics. As shown in Figure 17.3, Roman Catholicism was the largest denomination in the nation

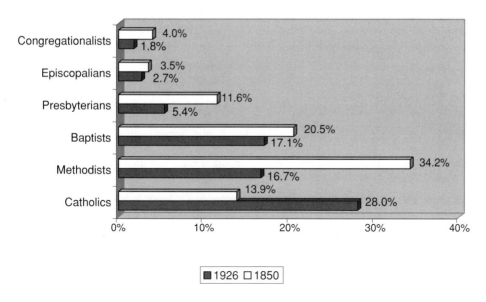

Sources and Notes: See Figure 1.

FIGURE 17.3. Church Adherents by Denomination, 1850 and 1926 (as a percentage of total adherents).

by the end of the nineteenth century. This might seem inevitable, with the heavy flow of immigrants from predominantly Catholic nations. In truth, however, most of the millions of immigrants from "Catholic" nations were at best potential American Catholic parishioners. To tap this potential, the Roman Catholic Church had to counteract the vigorous efforts of Protestant sects to recruit these immigrants and it had to activate them to entirely new levels of commitment and participation. The techniques they used were remarkably similar to their Protestant counterparts. At the center of this new evangelical surge was the Catholic revival campaign they called the parish mission. Using uniquely Catholic ritual, symbolism, and ceremony, the traveling evangelists would seek to stir the spirit and save the soul. Like the Protestants, Catholics aggressively recruited new members into the church (Dolan, 1978; Garraghan, 1984).

Once they were recruited, the Catholic parish offered new parishioners a distinctive Catholic society. From social groups to schools to literature, American Catholicism created a subculture that was parallel yet separate from the hostile dominant culture. Like Protestant sectarian movements, they stressed a distinctive lifestyle and placed high demands on their membership. But the Catholic subculture was strengthened by yet another dimension: ethnicity. Deviating from strict territorial parishes, they also founded national churches organized around a common language and nationality. As late as 1916 nearly half (49%) of all Catholic parishes held worship services in a language other than English. Considering that English was the native tongue for Irish-American parishes, this is a strong testimony to the ethnic identity of the local parish (Bureau of the Census, 1919).

The Protestant and Jewish immigrants would follow a similar pattern. The churches and synagogues quickly learned that they must appeal to the new immigrants or lose them to the aggressive sects. When Friedrich Wyneken (1982, p. 32) wrote his *Notruf* (Distress Call) to German religious and social leaders in 1843, he warned of the "dangerous" and large number of sects in America. He explained, "there is hardly a Lutheran or Reformed congregation which does not suffer from these swarming pests." Like the Catholics, the Protestant and Jewish immigrants developed institutions (often emphasizing educational institutions) that paralleled those in the dominant culture and offered a unique appeal to the new immigrants.

For the Lutheran and Reformed traditions, denominations were formed around nationality and the recency of their immigration. Composed of recent Dutch immigrants, the Christian Reformed Church (CRC) split from the Reformed Church of America (RCA) to form a more distinctive Dutch Christian church. Not surprisingly, 90% of the CRC congregations held services in a foreign language in 1906, compared to only 35% in the RCA (Bureau of the Census, 1910). The Lutherans were fractured into more than 20 different denominations based on nationality, recency of immigration, region of the country, and doctrine. The denominational nationalities included German, Norwegian, Swedish, Icelandic, Slovak, Danish, and Finnish. Once again, the more recent immigrants retained a more distinctive ethnic subculture and more frequently held services in their native tongue.

Finally, Jewish immigrants faced similar divisions. The immigrants arriving before 1880 tended to be German, middle-class, and were seeking to more fully assimilate. After 1880, a flood of poor, rural Eastern European immigrants developed a distinctively Jewish enclave. Yiddish became the vernacular and, in New York alone, the number of Jews increased from 80,000 in 1880 to more than 1 million by 1910.

Protestant, Catholic, and Jewish enclaves all served a dual role. Despite separating the new immigrants from a foreign world and supporting a distinctive religious and ethnic subculture, the enclaves also served to assimilate immigrants into the larger culture. Many of the institutions in the immigrant enclaves paralleled those in the dominant culture, providing immigrants with the skills, information, and training needed for success in the new land. Educational, recreational, and social service institutions are the most obvious examples, but the mutual benefit societies, professional associations, and social networks all served to integrate immigrants into the new nation.

The most impressive institution building of this era, however, was the development and growth of African American churches. Spurred on by the *conflicts* they faced with the dominant culture and by the *competition* they faced from other churches, the freed slaves of the late 19th century took greater advantage of the unregulated religious market than any group in American history (Finke & Stark, 2005; Finke & Schwadel, 2003). Like the immigrant faiths, religious freedoms allowed African Americans to use the churches as an institutional free space for supporting their members and their culture. E. Franklin Frazier (1974, p. 36) explained that "organized religious life became the chief means by which a structured or organized social life came into existence" for the freed slaves. Following the Civil War, the churches trained new leaders, mobilized political action, supported educational programs, provided supportive social networks, and developed mutual aid and fraternal associations (Lincoln & Mamiya, 1990; Nelson & Nelson, 1975; Nelson, Yokley, & Nelson, 1971). In Frazier's words, the "church provided a refuge in a hostile white world" (1974, p. 50). African-American churches became the key institution for uniting the former slaves, training new leaders, and building a new community.

The result was extremely high rates of religious involvement. Only 25 years after the close of the Civil War the 1890 Bureau of the Census (1894, Vol. IX) *Report on Statistics of Churches* found 19,448 churches in the nine Baptist and Methodist African-American denominations alone. When combined with the 4,322 churches in other denominations, African-American churches reported 2,673,977 members. With children included in the membership count, the total number of adherents rises to 4,626,561 representing over 59%

of all African Americans—an adherence rate that was fourteen percentage points higher than the church adherence rate of the total population (see Figure 17.1).

As African Americans and new immigrants were making bold changes to the religious landscape, other more subtle shifts were taking place. All of the major denominational families were increasing their membership totals but as a percentage of all Americans involved in religion their rates were falling (see Figure 17.3). The Episcopalians and Baptists showed a slight decline, the rates for Congregationalists, Presbyterians, and Methodists plummeted. A part of this change can be explained by the immigrants' attraction to churches supporting their language and ethnicity, with Catholic, Lutheran, Reformed, and Jewish congregations each holding a unique appeal to their cultural enclaves. But this doesn't explain the sudden changes for the Methodists. When they moved from a sect served by itinerant and untrained clergy promoting revivals to a mainstream denomination with settled and seminary-trained clergy, their growth rates began to resemble those of mainline churches. The divergent paths of the Methodists and Baptists is best illustrated by their changing fortunes in the South where there was little international immigration. From 1850 to 1926 the Methodists declined from 42 to 28% of all church adherents and the Baptists grew from 30 to 43% (Finke and Stark, 1992:147). As the Methodists drifted from their moorings of holiness teachings and revivalism at the turn of the century, they also spawned a series of holiness sects protesting these changes. Most would fade away, but a few served as catalysts for growing denominations in the 20th century.

IV. RECENT TRENDS AND DÉJÀ VU, 1925–2000

From 1925 to 1950, the religious landscape endured only modest changes. With the Immigration Act of 1924 taking effect in 1929 and with the onset of the Great Depression, the pace of change in American religion seemed to slow. Immigration dropped sharply from more than 4.3 million in the 1920s to less than 700,000 in the 1930s, and the existing immigrants were gradually assimilating into the American culture. Even the mainline denominations seemed to receive a short reprieve from their long declines. As shown in Table 17.2, the changes between 1925 and 1950 were modest for all of the major denominations, with the Episcopalians even showing a substantial increase. This proved to be the calm before the storm.

The latter half of the 20th century duplicated the changes of the 19th. The mainline denominations continued to lose market share; new sects were rapidly arising and a handful were showing rapid growth; and, immigrants from new lands were forming distinctive cultural and religious enclaves. Once again, new faiths were taking advantage of their religious freedoms to reshape the landscape of American religion.

From 1950 to 2000 the mainline Protestant religions not only continued to lose market share, their membership totals also showed significant declines. When measured as a percentage of the population, the 2000 rates for United Methodists, Presbyterian Church (USA), American Baptists, and the United Church of Christ (including the Congregationalists) were half or less of their 1950 rates. The older evangelical denominations, Southern Baptists and Lutheran Church–Missouri Synod, showed rapid growth until 1975 but have now started to plateau and even decline. Both have been embroiled in ongoing intradenominational conflicts. The Catholics have shown similar trends, increasing sharply from 1925 to 1975 and then leveling off for the remaining 25 years.

TABLE 17.2. **Church Adherence Rates for Major Denominations (Adherents Per 1000 Population)**

	1925	1950	1975	2000
Mainline Protestant Denominations				
The United Methodist Church	66	64	46	30
Presbyterian Church (USA)*	21	21	16	9
Evangelical Lutheran Church in America	15	26	25	18
United Church of Christ	14	13 (1949)	8	5
American Baptist Churches in the USA	13	10	7	6
Episcopal Church	10	17 (1949)	13	8
Evangelical Protestant Denominations				
Southern Baptist Convention	31	47	59	57
The Lutheran Church – Missouri Synod	5	11	13	9
Assemblies of God*	.4	2	4	5
Church of God (Cleveland, TN)	.2	1	2	3
Pentecostal Assemblies of the World, Inc.	.06 (1937)	.3	2 (1989)	5 (1998)
African-American Protestant Denominations				
Church of God in Christ	2 (1933)	N/A	14 (1973)	20 (1991)
National Baptist Convention, USA, Inc.	29 (1936)	29	32 (1958)	30 (1989)
National Baptist Convention of America	26	17	16 (1956)	12
African Methodist Episcopal Church	6	8	9 (1978)	9
African Methodist Episcopal Zion Church	4	4	5 (1973)	5
Other				
The Church of Jesus Christ of Latter-Day Saints	7	7	11	19
Jehovah's Witnesses*	N/A	1 (1955)	3	4
The Catholic Church (Roman Catholic)	139	189	227	229
Judaism	32 (1937)	33	28	24 (1990)

* "Inclusive membership" estimates are used for all denominations except the Assemblies of God, the Presbyterian Church (USA), and the Jehovah's Witnesses. Due to a lack of "inclusive" estimates for earlier years, their rates are based on the far smaller totals known as "full member" estimates.
Sources: All information is from the Yearbook of American and Canadian Churches, except for the most recent Jewish and National Baptist Convention, USA estimates and the 1973 estimate for the Church of God in Christ.
Other Notes: 1) Reported rates are rates of church adherence per 1000 members of the population, rather than the percentage of church adherents reported elsewhere. 2) All estimates before 2000 adjust for mergers and splits among denominations by including all denominations that comprise the denomination in question in 2000.

A small group of upstart sects, however, has continued to show rapid growth. The sudden surge of the various Pentecostal movements is seen most clearly. The Assemblies of God and Pentecostal Assemblies of the World, Inc., now outnumber the Congregationalists (United Church of Christ). Although the reliability of data for African American denominations is weak, a similar trend is clear for African American denominations (Sherkat, 2001). The rates for the pentecostal Church of God in Christ have increased 10-fold and now exceed all African American denominations except the reported rates for the National Baptist Convention, USA, Inc. Not shown in Table 17.2 are a host of other small groups that have shown rapid growth in the last few decades. For example, the Evangelical Free Church jumped from 649 churches and 71,134 adherents in 1980 to 1,365 churches and 285,699 adherents in 2000. Not starting their first church until 1974, the Vineyard reported 529 congregations and 155,170 adherents in 2000 (Jones et al., 2002; Miller, 1997). Finally, the Church of Jesus Christ of Latter-Day Saints (Mormons) and the Jehovah's Witnesses, which were minuscule religious outsiders in the 19th century, are showing consistent and rapid growth. Once largely confined to the state of Utah, the Mormons are now making a presence throughout the United States.

Once again, however, new immigrants are changing the religious landscape. By the late 1960s, new religious outsiders were arriving in increasing numbers. When the 1965 amendments to the Immigration and Nationality Act replaced country-of-origin quotas with a single quota for the Eastern and Western Hemisphere, immigration to the United States increased and the sources of immigration suddenly shifted. Immigration from India, for example, rose from 467 in 1965 to 2,293 the next year, and now runs around 30,000 a year. For Asia as a whole, immigration went from a modest 20,040 in 1965 to an average of nearly 150,000 per year in the 1970s and more than 250,000 in the 1980s. Immigration from Latin America, especially Mexico, was sizable before 1965, rose sharply throughout the 1970s, and remained the largest current of immigration in the 1980s and 1990s. In 1960 about 75% of all foreign-born residents were born in Europe. Forty years later (2000), 15% of the foreign-born were from Europe, 26% were from Asia, and 51% were from Latin America. This sudden shift in the nationality of immigrants has brought immediate changes to American religion.

One of the most potent effects of this new wave of immigrants is that world religions other than Christianity are being introduced to America. Buddhism and Hinduism are making a presence throughout the nation, with approximately 400 Hindu temples and more than 1,500 Buddhist temples rising. Estimates for Muslims are often erratic, but a series of major surveys projects their membership as falling between 1.6 to 2 million (Jones et al., 2002; Smith, 2002). These religions are also reaching beyond the confines of the immigrant enclaves. Although most were founded to serve the new immigrants, Buddhist temples have proven effective in appealing to middle-class whites, and the Islamic mosques are enrolling increasing numbers of African Americans. Although still small, these movements are having an impact on American religion.

Most immigrants, however, are reshaping the European foundations of American Christianity. The large flow of Latin Americans is redefining American Catholicism and is having a growing impact on American Protestantism, especially the pentecostal groups. More than 25% of all Americans identifying themselves as Catholic are now Hispanic (Gray & Gautier, 2003; Kosmin, Mayer, & Keysar, 2001). Even from nations where Christians are a minority, a disproportionate number of Christians emigrate and many convert to Christianity after they arrive. South Korea, for example, is 25% Christian, but an estimated 50% of Korean immigrants are Christian and half of the remainder join Christian churches after arriving in the United States (Chai, 1998; Hurh & Kim, 1990). China holds only a small minority of Christians, yet the number of Chinese Protestant churches in the United States jumped from 66 in 1952 to 697 by 1994 (Yang, 1999).

Often the immigrants bring distinctive versions of Catholicism and Protestantism. Many Chinese Christians find that the family-oriented and theologically conservative teachings of evangelical Protestantism are congruent with Confucian principles (Yang, 1998). Supporting more than 3,500 Spanish masses, Hispanics are giving new emphasis to the emotional or charismatic aspects of Catholicism. Immigrant churches that are members of the Protestant mainline (such as Presbyterian USA) often call for a return to more traditional teachings (Kim & Kim, 2001). In these and many other ways the new immigrant churches are remolding the foundation of American Christianity.

Yet for all of the changes immigrant religions (Christian and non-Christian) bring to America, the immigrant faiths are adapting in ways that closely resemble previous immigrants. Like the immigrant congregations before them, they seek to preserve the ethnic and

religious identity of the new immigrants as they adapt to a new world. Congregations teach
the younger generations to speak the native language as they teach the older generations
to speak English. They hold worship services in the native tongue and promote traditional
rituals as they assist members in getting citizenship, jobs, and training. They also know
that membership is voluntary and the religious alternatives are many, leading them to actively recruit new members and to seek higher levels of commitment from their members.
Finally, the congregations use community halls, recreational facilities, schools, and other organizations to promote tight social networks among their parishioners (Ebaugh & Chafetz,
2000).

Immigrant congregations emerging, new sects arising, and mainline denominations
declining: the most recent developments in American religion are but repeats of the past.

V. DISCUSSION AND CONCLUSIONS

The received wisdom from classic sociological theories is that religion will fall as modernity
arises. Forecasting only decline in the face of modernity, however, the inherited model is
ill-equipped to explain the dramatic increase in religious involvement throughout 19th- and
early-20th-century America—and the remarkable stability that followed. This chapter relied
on a religious economy model to explain the rise in religious involvement, but the model is
not confined to explaining increases. The model seeks to understand variation in religious
involvement and how these variations are related to the structure of the religious market.
Just as deregulating the American religious economy increased incentives and opportunities
for churches and their preachers, increasing regulation can reduce these incentives and
opportunities and reduce the viable options for religious consumers. Even very subtle shifts
have immediate effects. When the U.S. Supreme Court ruled in 1990 that the state was
no longer required to have "compelling interest" for denying religious freedoms, the door
was opened for regulations that allowed "formally neutral and generally applicable" laws
to hinder the forming and building of new churches and threatened the very survival of
small minority religions (Adamczyk, Wybraniec, & Finke, 2004; Richardson, 1995, 1998;
Robbins, 1985; Wybraniec & Finke, 2001).

Although not addressed in this chapter, the structure of the market will also change the
role of religion in the public arena. At the very time when the separation of church and state
increases the supply of religion, the role of religion in the public arena is often reduced.
Close ties between religious and political elites are inherent in religious monopolies, as
without such ties religious monopolies are impossible. As a result, when the state is supporting a monopoly religion the relationship between church and state might be described
as *sacralized* or one in which there is little differentiation between religious and secular
institutions and the primary aspects of life, from family to politics, will be suffused with
religious symbols, rhetoric and ritual (Stark & Finke, 2000, p. 199; Finke & Stark, 2003).
But when the state no longer ensures claims of exclusive legitimacy by the monopoly faith,
a *process of desacralization* must ensue. This process is accelerated when there is a plurality
of religious firms and no one of them is sufficiently potent to sustain a sacralization. This is
the same process that many have identified as structural or macro-secularization (Chaves,
1994; Collins, 1998; Dobbelaere, 1981; Smith, 2003). This may well be the reason that
sociologists have long regarded religious monopolies as the source of religious plausibility
and pluralism as inevitably eroding faith. By definition, the separation of church and state

will reduce the state's role in promoting religion and the church's role in wielding political authority.

This loss of state support for the established mainline religions, however, offers a boon for the religious groups lacking in power. As we saw in Section II, the Protestant upstart sects fueled an increasing rate of religious involvement by aggressively reaching out to segments of the population previously unserved. They responded quickly to new market conditions by starting new churches wherever new settlements emerged, forming distinctive social networks rich in social support, and offering a compelling religious message that was preached in the vernacular by common folk.

But Protestant sects were not the only groups to take advantage of the new religious freedoms. Section III revealed how the lack of state intervention allowed churches to become an institutional free space for freed slaves and the growing waves of new immigrants. Churches served to harbor their members from a hostile or foreign culture, as they helped to provide members with the personal resources and political privileges needed to succeed in the larger society. The result was extremely high levels of religious involvement by African-Americans and the new immigrants.

Section IV showed that similar trends continued throughout the 20th century. New upstart sects continued to emerge and several were growing at a torrid pace. With immigration increasing sharply in the 1960s, new immigrants formed religious enclaves to preserve their distinctive cultural and religious heritage. Unlike previous immigrants, however, the new immigration trends brought new world religions to America.

From early European visitors to advocates of the traditional secularization model, the religious situation in America has often been referred to as "American exceptionalism." But as religions openly compete for adherents around the world and religious revivalism is recorded throughout Africa, South and Central America, and many parts of Asia, America is no longer so exceptional. A rapidly mounting body of research has shown that religious economy arguments help to explain these global changes (Finke, 1997; Froese, 2001, 2004; Froese & Pfaff, 2001; Gill, 1998; Hamberg & Pettersson, 1994, 1997; Stark & Finke, 2000; Yang, n.d.). Just as religious deregulation stimulated a new supply of religions in the United States, the same has occurred in countries around the world (Iannaccone, Finke, & Stark, 1997). Regulations continue to control the incentives and opportunities that allow new religions to arise and the freedoms for people to choose.[6]

Given recent world changes, the United States is no longer the exceptional case or anomaly. All of this has led many to wonder about "European exceptionalism" (Martin, 2002).

NOTES

1. Church adherence is a measure of church membership that is inclusive of children. Since some denominations count children as members (e.g., Catholics) and others do not (e.g., Baptists), the church adherence measure provides a more standardized measure of church involvement across denominations. To estimate total adherents for denominations not counting children, the following equation is used: (Reported Members $*$ (Total Population/(Total Population $-$ Children 13 years and under). See Jones et al. (2002) for additional information.
2. Voluntary contributions and the value of church property have shown similar trends, with contributions to religious organizations still towering over other forms of voluntary charitable giving (Finke, 1992).
3. Even the most revered prophets (e.g., Moses and Muhammad) have expressed doubts as well as faith.

4. For a more detailed discussion on how churches balance the seemingly contradictory goals of generating innovations as they preserve core teachings, see Finke, 2004.
5. For examples of how contemporary sect movements introduce new innovations, see Miller, 1997.
6. The levels of religious involvement are explained by far more than the structure of the religious market (e.g., religious conflict often fuels commitment), but the structure of the religious market has proven to have far reaching effects on involvement around the globe.

REFERENCES

Adamczyk, A., Wybraniec, J., & Finke, R. (2004). Religious regulation and the courts: Documenting the effects of *Smith* and RFRA. *Journal of Church and State, 46*, 237–262.
Asbury, F. (1958). *The letters of Francis Asbury*. Nashville: Abingdon Press. (Original work published 1852)
Baird, R. (1969). *Religion in America; or, an account of the origin, progress, relation to the state, and present condition of the evangelical churches in the United States*. New York: Arno Press. (Original work published 1844)
Berger, P. (1968, April 25). A bleak outlook is seen for religion. *New York Times*, 3.
Berger, P. (1969). *The sacred canopy*. New York: Doubleday.
Bilhartz, T. D. (1986). *Urban religion and the second great awakening*. Rutherford: Associated University Presses.
Bureau of the Census (1894). *Eleventh census of the United States: 1890* (Vol. 9). Washington: Government Printing Office.
Bureau of the Census (1910). *Religious bodies: 1906* (Vol. 1). Washington: Government Printing Office.
Bureau of the Census (1919). *Religious bodies: 1916* (Vol. 1). Washington: Government Printing Office.
Chai, K. J. (1998). Competing for the second generation: English-language ministry at a Korean Protestant church. In R. S. Warner & J. G. Wittner (Eds.), *Gathering in diaspora: Religious communities and the new immigration*. Philadelphia: Temple University Press.
Chaves, M. (1994). Secularization as declining religious authority. *Social Forces, 72*, 749–775.
Collins, R. (1998). *The sociology of philosophies: A global theory of intellectual change*. Cambridge: Harvard University Press.
Davidman, L. (1991). *Tradition in a rootless world: Women turn to orthodox Judaism*. Berkeley: University of California Press.
Dobbelaere, K. (1981). Secularization. *Current Sociology, 29*, 3–213.
Dolan, J. P. (1978). *Catholic revivalism: The American experience (pp. 1830–1900)*. Notre Dame: University of Notre Dame Press.
Dolan, J. P. (1985). *The American Catholic experience: A history from colonial times to the present*. Garden City, NY: Image Books.
Dougherty, K. D. (2003). *Engaging and expanding: How boundaries and adaptability enhance congregational performance*. Dissertation, Purdue University.
Ebaugh, H. R., & Chafetz, J. S. (2000). *Religion and the new immigrants: Continuities and adaptations in immigrant congregations*. Walnut Creek, Calif.: AltaMira.
Evans, S. M., & Boyte, H. C. (1986). *Free spaces: The sources of democratic change in America*. New York: Harper and Row.
Finke, R. (1990). Religious deregulation: Origins and consequences. *Journal of church and state, 32*, 609–626.
Finke, R. (1992). An unsecular America. In S. Bruce (Ed.), *Religion and modernization: Sociologists and historians debate the secularization thesis*. Oxford: Clarendon Press.
Finke, R. (1997). The consequences of religious competition: Supply-side explanations for religious change. In L. A. Young (Ed.), *Assessing rational choice theories of religion*. New York: Routledge.
Finke, R. (2004). Innovative returns to tradition: Using core beliefs as the foundation for innovative accommodation. *Journal for the Scientific Study of Religion, 43*, 19–34.
Finke, R., & Dougherty, K. (2002). The effects of professional training: The social and religious capital acquired in seminaries. *Journal for the Scientific Study of Religion, 41*, 103–120.
Finke, R., & Iannaccone, L. R. (1993). Supply-side explanations for religious change in America. *The Annals, 527*, 27–39.
Finke, R., & Schwadel, C. (2005). Accounting for the uncounted: Computing correctives for the 2000 RCMS data. *Review of Religious Research, 47*(1).

Finke, R., & Schwadel, P. (2003). Religion and religious affiliation. *Dictionary of American history*. Charles Scribner's Sons.

Finke, R., & Stark, R. (1992). *The churching of America, 1776–1990: Winners and losers in our religious economy*. New Brunswick: Rutgers University Press.

Finke, R., & Stark, R. (2001). The new holy clubs: Testing church-to-sect propositions. *Sociology of Religion, 62*, 175–189.

Finke, R., & Stark, R. (2003). The dynamics of religious economies. In M. Dillon (Ed.), *Handbook of the sociology of religion*. New York: Cambridge University Press.

Finke, R., & Stark, R. (2005). *The churching of America, 1776–2005: Winners and losers in our religious economy*. New Brunswick: Rutgers University Press.

Frazier, E. F. (1974). *The negro church in America*. New York: Schocken Books. (Original work published 1963).

Froehle, B. T., & Gautier, M. L. (2000). *Catholicism USA: A portrait of the Catholic church in the United States*. Maryknoll, NY: Orbis Books.

Froese, P. (2001). Hungary for religion: A supply-side interpretation of the hungarian religious revival. *Journal for the Scientific Study of Religion, 40*, 251–268.

Froese, P. (2004). After atheism: An analysis of religious monopolies in the post-communist world. *Sociology of Religion, 65*, 57–75.

Froese, P., & Pfaff, S. (2001). Replete and desolate markets: Poland, East Germany, and the new religious paradigm. *Social Forces, 80*, 481–507.

Garraghan, G. J. (1984). *The jesuits of the middle United States*. Chicago: Loyola University Press.

Gill, A. J. (1998). *Rendering unto caesar: The Roman Catholic church and the state in Latin America*. Chicago: University of Chicago Press.

Gray, M. M., & Gautier, M. L. (2003). Latino Catholic leaders in the United States. A report for the Center for Applied Research in the Apostolate, Georgetown University, Washington, D.C.

Greeley, A. M. (1977). *The American Catholic: A social portrait*. New York: Basic Books.

Greeley, A. M. (1996). The new American paradigm: A modest critique. Paper read at the German Sociological Association Annual Meetings, Köln.

Hamberg, E. M., & Pettersson, T. (1994). The religious market: Denominational competition and religious participation in contemporary Sweden. *Journal for the Scientific Study of Religion, 33*, 205–216.

Hamberg, E. M., & Pettersson, T. (1997). Short-term changes in religious supply and church attendance in contemporary Sweden. *Research in the Social Scientific Study of Religion, 8*, 35–51.

Hardt, P. F. (2000). *The soul of methodism: The class meeting in early New York city methodism*. Lanham, Maryland: University Press of America.

Hatch, N. O. (1989). *The democratization of American Christianity*. New Haven: Yale University Press.

Hurh, W. M., & Kim, K. C. (1990). Religious participation of Korean immigrants in the United States. *Journal for the Scientific Study of Religion, 29*, 19–34.

Iannaccone, L. R. (1994). Why strict churches are strong. *American Journal of Sociology, 99*, 1180–1211.

Iannaccone, L. R., Olson, D., & Stark, R. (1995). Religious resources and church growth. *Social Forces, 74*, 705–731.

Iannaccone, L. R., Finke, R., & Stark, R. (1997). Deregulating religion: Supply-side stories of trends and change in the religious market place. *Economic Inquiry, 35*, 350–364.

Jones, D. E., Doty, S., Grammich, C., Horsch, J. E., Houseal, R., Lynn, M., Marcum, J. P., Sanchagrin, K. M., & Taylor, R. H. (2002). *Religious congregations and membership in the United States 2000: An enumeration by region, state and county based on data reported for 149 religious bodies*. Nashville, Tennesse: Glenmary Research Center. To review the 2000 results online or to download earlier collections, go to the American Religion Data Archive: www.TheARDA.com.

Kelley, D. M. (1972). *Why conservative churches are growing*. New York: Harper and Row.

Kim, K. C., & Kim, S. (2001). The ethnic roles of Korean immigrant churches in the United States. In H. Y. Kwon, K. C. Kim, & R. S. Warner (Eds.), *Korean American and their religions*. University Park, PA: Pennsylvania State University.

Kosmin, B. A., Mayer, E., & Keysar, A. (2001). *American religious identification survey, 2001*. The Graduate Center of the City University of New York.

Lincoln, C. E., & Mamiya, L. H. (1990). *The Black church in the African American experience*. Durham: Duke University Press.

Littell, F. (1962). *From state church to pluralism*. Chicago: Aldine.

Martin, D. (2002). *Pentecostalism: The world their parish*. Oxford: Blackwell.

Mead, S. E. (1963). *The lively experiment*. New York: Harper and Row. (1976 Reprint)

Miller, D. E. (1997). *Reinventing American protestantism*. Berkeley, CA: University of California Press.

Nelson, H. M., & Nelson, A. K. (1975). *Black church in the sixties*. Lexington: University of Kentucky Press.

Nelson, H. M., Yokley, R., & Nelson, A. K. (Eds.). (1971). *The Black church in America*. New York: Basic Books.

Neitz, M. Jo. (1987). *Charisma and community: A study of religious commitment within the charismatic renewal*. New Brunswick: Transaction.

Powell, M. B. (Ed.). (1967). *The voluntary church: Religious life, 1740–1860, seen through the eyes of European visitors*. New York: Macmillan.

Richardson, J. T. (1995). Legal status of minority religions in the United States. *Social Compass, 42*(2), 249–264.

Richardson, J. T. (1998). Law and minority religion: 'Positive' and 'negative' uses of the legal system. *Nova Religio, 2*, 93–107.

Robbins, T. (1985). Government regulatory powers and church autonomy: Deviant groups as test cases. *Journal for the Scientific Study of Religion, 24*, 237–252.

Schaff, P. (1961). *America: A sketch of its political, social, and religious character*. Cambridge, MA: The Belknap Press of Harvard University Press. (Original work published 1855)

Sherkat, D. E. 2001. Investigating the sect-church-sect cycle: Cohort-specific attendance differences across African-American denominations. *Journal for the Scientific Study of Religion, 40*, 221–234.

Smith, C. (2003). *The secular revolution: Power, interests, and conflict in the secularization of American public life*. Berkeley: University of California Press.

Smith, C., Emerson, M., Gallagher, S., Kennedy, P., & Sikkink, D. (1998). *American evangelism: Embattled and thriving*. Chicago: University of Chicago Press.

Smith, T. (2002). Religious diversity in America: The emergence of Muslims, Buddhists, Hindus, and others. *Journal for the Scientific Study of Religion, 41*, 577–585.

Stark, R., & Finke, R. (2000). *Acts of faith: Explaining the human side of religion*. Berkeley, CA: University of California Press.

Tocqueville, A. de. (1969). *Democracy in America*. Garden City, New York: Doubleday.

Warner, R. S. (1993). Work in progress towards a new paradigm for the sociological study of religion in the United States. *American Journal of Sociology, 98*, 1044–1093.

Warner, R. S. (1994). The place of the congregation in the contemporary American religious configuration. In J. P. Wind & J. W. Lewis (Eds.), *American congregations* (Vol. 2). Chicago: University of Chicago Press.

Weber, M. (1946). In H. H. Gerth & C. W. Mills (Eds.), *From Max Weber: Essays in sociology*. New York: Oxford University Press. (Original work published 1913)

Wigger, J. H. (1998). *Taking heaven by storm: Methodism and the rise of popular Christianity in America*. Urbana, Illinois: University of Illinois Press.

Wigger, J. H. (2001). Fighting bees: Methodist itinerants and the dynamics of methodist growth, 1770–1820. In N. O. Hatch & J. H. Wigger (Eds.), *Methodism and the shaping of American culture*. Nashville, TN: Kingswood Books.

Wilson, B. (1982). *Religion in sociological perspective*. Oxford: Oxford University Press.

Wybraniec, J., & Finke, R. (2001). Religious regulation and the courts: The judiciary's changing role in protecting minority religions from majoritarian rule. *Journal for the Scientific Study of Religion, 40*, 427–444.

Yang, F. (1998). Chinese conversion to evangelical Christianity. *Sociology of Religion, 59*, 237–258.

Yang, F. (1999). *Chinese Christians in America: Conversion, assimilation, and adhesive identities*. University Park, PA: Pennsylvania State University.

Yang, F. (n.d.). The open, black, and gray markets of religion in communist China.

Yang, F., & Ebaugh, H. R. (2001). Transformation in new immigrant religions and their global implications. *American Sociological Review, 66*, 269–288.

Young, L. A. (Ed.). (1997). *Rational choice theory and religion: Summary and assessment* (pp. 133–145). New York: Routledge.

CHAPTER 18

Denominationalism/ Congregationalism

Nancy T. Ammerman

Those who study organizational life have begun to discover that religious organizations offer both ample objects for observation and interesting challenges for theorizing. The intersection of organizational theory and the study of religion is a fruitful field of exploration that can yield insight into organizational dynamics, as well as insight into the many ways religion takes empirical social form. As Paul DiMaggio noted, "because much religious activity is institutionalized and carried out through formal organizations . . . students of religion may have something to learn from the experience of their colleagues in the organizations field" (DiMaggio, 1998). We will follow his lead in looking to the cultural and ecological turn in organizational studies for insight, drawing on research from diverse religious communities to sketch out an organizational view of religion.

Understanding religious organizations requires, however, that we avoid two common misconceptions. First, religious organizations are both "private" and "public" at the same time. Voluntary organizations have long had public aspirations and public consequences (Adams, 1986; Hall, 1998). As Alexis de Tocqueville observed in his 19th-century journeys to the United States, the religious voluntary sector had quickly filled a critical niche in American democratic life (Tocqueville, 1835). More recently, commentators have recognized congregations and other religious organizations as crucial generators of "social capital" (Putnam, 2000). Religious groups, in fact, facilitate a kind of boundary-spanning social interaction that deserves closer scrutiny.

The second misconception to be avoided is to assume that religious organizations have a unique institutional logic (Friedland & Alford, 1991). Religious organizations do have a moral and spiritual dimension that distinguishes them from other voluntary organizations, but this spiritual dimension is not reducible to doctrinal rigidity and otherworldliness that invariably dictates a uniquely "religious" institutional form. Taking African-American "storefront" churches as their subject, for instance, both Omar McRoberts (1999, 2003) and Timothy Nelson (1997) provide careful analysis of the variety of ways the organizational

Nancy T. Ammerman • Boston University, Boston, Massachusetts, 02215

cultures of congregations take the social fact of "the street" into account in shaping members' relationships and organizational goals. In a very different sector of American society, other congregational cultures reinforce an ethic of "Golden Rule Christianity" that helps members define who their neighbor is and how their congregations should organize to serve their communities (Ammerman, 1997b, 2004). The "social capital" being generated in congregations is substantial, but our understanding of its effects will remain partial so long as we assume that all religious organizations look alike and all religious messages have simply the logical consequences their words seem to imply. As in all organizations, stated goals and cultural patterns are not identical.

In addition, religious organizations must be understood in their specific cultural and historical context. Each nation has created different prescribed or possible organizational structures, with different relationships to the state, different sources of support, different degrees of competition among religious groups, and different responsibilities for key life-cycle rituals and certifications. All of those legal realities, along with each society's unique cultural history, mean that the study of religious organizations must always be context specific. We may be able to identify important factors that have an effect across cultural lines, but we should expect organizational fields to be fundamentally shaped by the specific state regulatory regime within which they operate.

In the United States, that regime has been shaped by the twin facts of religious pluralism and legal toleration. Religiously diverse almost from the beginning, by the time the Constitution was written in the eighteenth century, no one group in U.S. society was sufficiently strong to demand legal establishment (Butler, 1990). That one fact, Andrew Greeley asserts, is the key to understanding the religious history that has followed (Greeley, 1972). The Constitution refused the support of the state for any religious group, but also left each group free to pursue its own agenda. That voluntary character of American religious life is the key, Stephen Warner argues, to understanding the relative vitality of U.S. religion, when compared to the secularization European theorists had expected to prevail (Warner, 1993). Disestablishment created a space where all sorts of religious and social diversity could flourish, and that diversity has taken organizational form.

Religious organizations in the United States, then, must be understood in the context of their peculiar role as separate from, yet protected by, the state. With neither state requirements nor state support, voluntary groups of religious practitioners have been left free to create whatever organizations they desired; and the state, in turn, was prohibited from all but the most basic regulation of their activity. Today at least half the U.S. population has some connection to a religious organization, and at least a quarter participate in any given week (Hadaway, Marler, & Chaves, 1993). The result is an enormous proliferation of religious groups. No one knows for sure how many, precisely because the state is so insistent on leaving them to their own devices that there are no mandated registries or censuses. Our best estimates place the number of local congregations at about 350,000 (Chaves, Koneiczny, Beyerlein, & Barman, 1999; Hodgkinson & Weitzman, 1993). There are several hundred Christian denominations, and at least a thousand nationally organized religious special purpose groups (with the number of local and regional associations in the tens of thousands) (Wuthnow, 1988). Beyond those countable organizations are surely many more that have escaped the cataloguers notice.

In spite of diversity that spans everything from a local Fire-Baptized Holiness church to the Christian Booksellers Association and from the Conference of Catholic Bishops to the local church-sponsored homeless shelter, religious organizations in the United States fall into three broad organizational categories—congregations, denominations, and religious special purpose groups (sometimes called "parachurch" organizations). The first two of these clearly constitute organizational fields, as that term is commonly used by institutional theorists (Powell & DiMaggio, 1991). As we will explore later, both local religious gatherings (congregations) and national religious bodies (denominations) respond to isomorphic pressures from their organizational environment, resulting in similarities in structure and function that often transcend differences in theology and religious authority. Special purpose groups, on the other hand, often belong to the organizational field that corresponds to their particular activity—overseas relief and development or bookselling, for instance—as much as to any specifically religious organizational field. Nevertheless, we would be remiss in a discussion of religious organizations to overlook the distinctly religious sectors of these domains.

CONGREGATIONS

The study of congregations is much more common now than it was a generation ago. When the *Handbook for Congregational Studies* (Carroll, Dudley, & McKinney, 1986) was published in the mid-1980s, neither religious leaders nor sociologists were paying appreciable attention to local congregations. Since that time, both groups have shifted their focus so that a considerable body of literature is available for examining the organizational dynamics of congregations. Like the *Handbook* itself (and its successor, *Studying Congregations* [Ammerman, Carroll, Dudley, & McKinney, 1998]), much of that literature follows the lead of students of formal organizations in focusing attention on goals and strategies, structures and resources. The effort has been to understand the internal structures of formal and informal power and authority as they operate in congregations and other religious organizations (an approach perhaps best theorized by Mady Thung in *The Precarious Organisation* [1976]). As human institutions, human dynamics were expected to be at work.

Like all organizations, for instance, congregations are confronted with the challenge of accumulating sufficient resources to pursue organizational goals. The actual range of activities undertaken by a given congregation is strongly affected by simple organizational facts such as the number of active participants and the size of the budget (Ammerman, 2005; Pinto & Crow, 1982). Explaining why a given congregation fails to accomplish some ministry goal may be as straightforward as counting the number of people present on Sunday morning. In societies that support religious organizations through taxes or other means, this tie between attendance and organizational capacity is not present. In the United States, however, the voluntary nature of congregations makes them highly dependent on the willingness of participants to contribute their time, skill, and money to the collective work of the group (McKinney, 1998). Unlike businesses that are concerned with markets and profits and products, congregations produce less tangible things, like worship services, educational programs, social activities, and works of service—most of which flow directly from their own collective participation (Wuthnow, 1994). Unlike some other nonprofits, they are not primarily oriented toward a specific cause that can be supported by relative strangers. Both their organizational goals and the resources to pursue those goals are generated in the voluntary, face-to-face interaction of the group. They both produce social capital and depend on social capital as the basic resource that generates the monetary and human resources necessary for pursuing their goals.

The idea of looking at religious organizations as goal oriented and rationally organized was articulated a generation ago by Gibson Winter (1967). He asserted that religious

organizations, just like other organized agencies in modern society, had adopted bureaucratic structures and processes. There were rules and flow charts, short- and long-term goals
and quantifiable measures of success. This rationalized pattern has always been easier to
see at the level of national denominations than at the level of local congregations (a point
to which we will return below). Nevertheless, it was clear to Winter that religious organizations were not as "nonrational" and theologically driven as either they or their observers
often claimed. Many other students of organizations had ignored religious groups because
they presumed religious goals were too irrational, nonempirical and otherworldly to be
amenable to rationalized organization. Religious organizations provided writers in this tradition with convenient examples of what Weber would have called a "traditional" mode of
organization (1964), or perhaps one whose "normative" goals (Etzioni, 1961) or pursuit of
ultimate truths (Friedland & Alford, 1991) created distinct institutional demands. Winter
and his colleagues in that first generation of analysts pointed the way toward a recognition
that religious organizations were not isolated from the social and cultural world in which
they existed.

Today, most organizational theorists find it more plausible to believe that religious
organizations have this-worldly goals and structures than to believe that *any* organization
is finally "rational." Students of congregations, no less than students of other organizations
question the degree to which stated goals are widely shared and official structures actually
govern. Although no one has proposed a "garbage can model" (March, 1978) of congregational decision making, many observers have noted that unspoken values (honoring the
ancestors or maintaining social status, for instance) have often guided congregational action as surely as any theologically informed "mission statement." Dudley has also noted the
ways in which a congregation's informal modes of communication and decision making
often subvert (or facilitate) formal organizational procedures (Dudley, 1998). Like other
modern organizations, many congregations—especially those in the mainstream Protestant
traditions—have committees and councils, long-range plans and mission statements. But
also like those other organizations, congregations are just as likely to approach each new
challenge with their existing (sometimes outmoded) repertoire of strategic solutions and
just as likely to communicate via water coolers as via official newsletters. The intricate
negotiations by which systems of congregational power and status are maintained make for
lively reading in cases studies such as Heilman's (1973) description of a modern Orthodox
synagogue, Warner's (1988) description of a California Presbyterian church, and Williams's
(1974) description of an urban African-American Pentecostal church. Organizational researchers interested in these human dynamics of organizational life might do well to turn
additional attention to the combination of intimacy and task-orientation that characterizes
most congregations.

The very human dynamics of congregational life have been especially visible in the
variety of studies concerned with conflict. Both relationships and symbols take on a high
degree of salience in congregations, and strained relationships and disputed symbols can
easily result in schism. Zuckerman carefully traced those factors in the break-up of the
Oregon Jewish temple he observed (Zuckerman, 1998). He also noted the degree to which
differing external political and cultural alliances seeped into the congregation and exacer-
bated internal antagonisms. That link between external and internal is also noted by Shin
and Park (1988) in their study of schisms in Korean-American churches. Competition for
leadership and status (and limited external opportunities) sometimes made schism a logical
organizational alternative for innovative and ambitious lay and clergy leaders. Although it is
certainly true that congregations sometimes fight over ideas and theologies (the contentious

issue of homosexuality is but the most recent example, (e.g., Hartman, 1998)), they also divide when spaces for innovation are not sufficient, when members do not agree on modes of governance, and when members hold different understandings about basic institutional models of congregational life (Becker, 1999). Voluntary organizations of all sorts provide a fascinating arena for examining the nature of cohesion and conflict in an increasingly complex society.

Becker's (1999) examination of congregational conflict helped to articulate an understanding of congregations that drew on the "new institutionalism" in organizational studies (Powell & DiMaggio, 1991). She spoke of institutional models as bundles of expectations and practices that go together to shape what a congregation does and how it does it. Over the last decade, an increasing body of research has documented the degree to which "congregation" itself serves as an organizational template (an institution) that shapes the activities and relationships of religious groups we might not otherwise have expected to see in that form. Wind and Lewis provided the historical context for this insight in a set of case studies from diverse religious traditions (Wind & Lewis, 1994). Drawing on those examinations of local religious life, the historian Brooks Holifield (1994) identified a series of organizational patterns that have shaped congregational life in the United States. In each period, he noted, congregations across religious traditions tended to conform to basic organizational patterns. Reflecting on that same set of historical case studies, the sociologist Stephen Warner noted what he called "de facto congregationalism" as the typical pattern for local religious groups (Warner, 1994). No matter what their official theology proclaims about the purposes of local assemblies and their prescribed mode of governance, in this country, religion is "congregational." Religious groups assume that they can voluntarily form, that they should govern their own affairs, and that their own participation and leadership are necessary for carrying on the religious tradition (see also Jay Dolan's [1994] discussion of these effects on Catholic parishes). Following Parsons's theoretical lead, Warner describes the typical organizational pattern as functionally diffuse (almost any activity can be justified as legitimate), affectively significant for their participants, normatively particularistic (guided, that is, by particular, rather than universal criteria), and collectivity-oriented (concerned with the collective welfare of the group, but a group that is chosen rather than ascribed).

The pervasiveness of de facto congregationalism has been further documented as researchers have explored the many religious associations being formed by the "new immigrants" that have joined the American population since 1965 (Warner & Wittner, 1998). Many are being absorbed into existing religious institutions (most notably the Catholic church), but many others are forming religious societies that are looking increasingly like the Protestant congregations that have preceded them. Ebaugh and Chafetz (2000) carefully examined structural factors such as lay leadership, professional clergy, membership lists, and member financing and found that most of the immigrant groups they studied were significantly congregationalized. Most also had adopted various "community center" functions to provide social benefits to their members, in addition to facilitating religious obligation and transmission of tradition.

Such structural adaptation is best explained by the forces of institutional isomorphism (DiMaggio & Powell, 1983). Organizations come to resemble similar organizations in their "field" both through imitation and through compliance with regulation. Congregations, for instance, usually obtain tax-exempt status from the Internal Revenue Service (IRS) so that contributions can be reported by participants as charitable donations. Both that action and other basic organizational functions (from phone lines to building permits) push groups toward having boards of trustees and designated leaders. When they do get a phone, they will have to decide where they will be listed in the "Yellow Pages." And if they want to be represented on public religious occasions, they will need to designate someone as a "clergy equivalent." More subtly, if they want to be regarded as legitimate religious organizations, "just like" the Episcopalians and Baptists, they have to learn to play by American organizational and cultural rules. The advantage of doing so is both a claim to the benefits of tolerance and a structure that facilitates interaction with other congregations. Having a building, a phone, a leader, a board, a membership list, and a schedule of recognizably religious services and activities lends legitimacy and makes communication and cooperation more possible.

The presence of an organizational template is also discernable in the very range of religious services and activities a congregation is expected to provide. Most basically, congregations are expected to organize opportunities for worship, and when they do, they almost always include group singing and an inspirational talk (Chaves, 2004). What a congregation teaches is shaped by their own particular tradition, but that they have am organized weekly program of children's religious education is nearly universal, again shaped by that larger culturally determined organizational template. What they do when they socialize together may vary from bingo to quilting, but that they organize some sort of social activities is part of what the larger culture expects. And as soon as they have sufficient resources, the culture also expects a congregation to organize some sort of outreach into the community and the world. The culture provides an organizational blueprint, even if the materials are highly variable (Ammerman, 2005).

There are also institutional and cultural continuities within the variability. There are broad streams of religious tradition that shape the range and content of congregational activity (Ammerman, 2005). Mainline Protestants, Conservative Protestants, African American churches, Catholic and Orthodox churches, Jews, and others have each created organizational expectations that bring together their own theologies with their distinctive relationships with American culture. In African American churches, for instance, theology and social history combine to encourage congregations that are highly participatory, intensely spiritual, and deeply involved in community betterment (Lincoln & Mamiya, 1990).

Cross-cutting those traditions of religious practice are differing models of congregational life that provide predictable variations on the basic organizational template. Becker identified four models in her study of Oak Park congregations—the family (emphasizing close-knit relationships), the leader (emphasizing affecting the world beyond the congregation), the community (debating and expressing the diverse values of the members), and the house of worship (providing a sanctuary for individual encounters with the Divine) (Becker, 1999). Other models probably could be named, but the key insight is that congregational life is shaped by a combination of organizational forces—basic templates that identify it *as* a congregation, religious cultural templates that encourage particular ways of elaborating its design, and predictable bundles of variation on which of its functions get primary emphasis. Congregations provide, then, a fascinating location for observing interactions among macro-structures, cultural traditions, institutional constraint, and voluntary association and agency.

Among the primary organizational tasks of congregations is, in fact, the transmission and preservation of subcultural identities. People gather because there is something in their way of life that they want to celebrate. As Warner points out, the United States has made religion "presumptively legitimate," so that "religious difference is the most legitimate cultural difference" (Warner, 1999). That impulse to preserve and celebrate religious and cultural difference is especially evident in the work of immigrant congregations. They gather to worship, but they also eat together, teach each other (and their children) the songs of the homeland, provide spaces for wearing traditional clothing and doing traditional dances—and, of course, speaking the traditional language (Ebaugh & Chafetz, 1999; Kwon, Kim, & Warner, 2001; Warner & Wittner, 1998). A similar cultural role has long been played by African American churches. Robert Franklin (1994) vividly describes the distinctive multisensory experience of Black church worship, and Mary Patillo-McCoy (1998) notes how strategic elements of that church culture find their way into other sectors of community life, including politics. American Jews have also often found themselves on the outside of a pervasively Christian culture, and synagogue life has provided a similar safe space in which to reinforce and celebrate—and often rekindle and reinvent—a religious and cultural tradition (Prell, 2000). For still other reasons, Christian fundamentalists have found congregations equally essential in their fight to preserve the sort of Christian way of life they desire (Ammerman, 1987).

All of these groups have found congregations essential cultural spaces. All of them have found themselves on the outside of a white, mainstream-Christian, native-born American culture. Only recently, however, have sociologists turned their attention to the cultural traditions being preserved in the white mainline churches themselves. Their very position at the center of the culture, combined with liberal and ecumenical theologies of inclusiveness, conspired to emphasize the absence of boundaries and the illusion that theirs was merely ordinary culture (Hoge, Johnson, & Luidens, 1994). Perhaps not surprisingly, precisely in these decades of their decline, Presbyterians and Episcopalians have attracted the attention of students of congregational culture, alongside the more "exotic" groups that had been the object of study before. James Wellman (1999), for instance, has chronicled the history of Chicago's Fourth Presbyterian Church, whereas Joanna Gillespie (1995) has provided portraits of Episcopal parishes as seen through the eyes of the women who keep them going. Daniel Sack (2000) has highlighted the role of food in the culture of these "whitebread Protestants," as he calls them; and Margaret Bendroth (2002) places family at the center of her focus, describing how assumptions about family life have shaped the rhetoric and practices of white Protestant congregations (see also Marler, 1995).

Voluntary organizations—from choirs to PTAs to ethnic heritage societies to congregations—are the places in modern societies where relationships of trust are formed, where a sense of identity is nurtured, in short where social capital is generated (Smidt, 2003). Studying congregations in changing communities in the 1990s, I concluded that in otherwise strained environments, congregations were providing critical social anchors (Ammerman, 1997a). They facilitated bonds of trust and communication, and they provided basic well-being to their participants (see also Ellison & George, 1994). As attention has turned to the nature and functions of social capital, congregations have been a logical place to look. We have seen that congregations are especially critical as "subaltern counterpublics," where relatively disempowered people have a voice and learn to lead (Fraser, 1990). Among the many things accomplished within such subaltern counterpublics—as in all voluntary organizations—is the creation and enhancement of civic skills. Civic skills are the arts of communication, planning and decision-making that make collective life possible. Verba, Schlozman, and Brady note that such civic skills are often learned in school and on the job, but they are also learned through participation in voluntary organizations (Brady, Verba, & Schlozman, 1995). Every club that plans a special event, every society that needs officers, and every congregation that asks its members to teach classes and chair committees provides opportunities for the development and exercise of civic skills.

In his study of Latin American pentecostalism, David Martin argued that such processes also work in societies not yet fully democratic. The pentecostal emphasis on the "gift of tongues" means that everyone is given a voice, anyone can participate. Even the custom of testifying, Martin speculated, provided a kind of school for democracy. By establishing "lay and unmediated channels of communication," evangelical congregations provide a sheltered space where each person can "give 'tongue' to [both] frustrations and aspirations" (Martin, 1990). The practices established in such communities then lay down a cultural pattern that can gradually "leak" out into the rest of society. Martin's hunches are, in fact, confirmed by Verba, Schlozman, and Brady's (1995) research. Civic skills are not specific to the organizations in which they are developed and used. Over and above background characteristics like income and education—civic skills learned in one place do leak out into the political process, especially to activities beyond voting. And because people of all economic and educational levels belong nearly equally to congregations (whereas other voluntary organizations are disproportionately middle and upper class), congregations are the single most widespread and egalitarian providers of civic opportunity in the United States. Students of politics, no less than students of organizations may do well to pay attention to the everyday work of congregational life.

The study of congregations has, then, taught us a good deal about the basic organizational practices and structures that constitute this particular form of voluntary organization. We have learned a good deal about the internal dynamics of cultural reproduction, as well as the internal politics of these local religious gatherings. We also have begun to take account of the way congregations are situated in a larger organizational and cultural ecology. Taking a cue from others interested in the ecological pressures on organizations, several recent studies have given attention to places, networks, competition, and adaptation. Wedam (2003), for instance, describes the particular organizational effects produced by being located in an elite corridor at the social and geographical center of Indianapolis culture, whereas Farnsley (2000) analyzes the very different community relationships typical of congregations in other neighborhoods of that same city. McRoberts (2003) shows how factors ranging from the availability of empty storefronts to the history of housing discrimination have combined to concentrate a high density of small congregations in one Boston neighborhood. Religious traditions themselves play a role, as well. Gamm (1999) documents the very different approaches to territory exhibited by Roman Catholic and Jewish traditions, resulting in equally different responses to racial change in city neighborhoods (see also McGreevy, 1996). Different kinds of neighborhoods, different kinds of property, and different demographic realities create organizational constraints on congregational mission, resources, and activities.

Another of the concerns of ecological theorists is the process by which environmental change creates organizational response. In a study of congregations in nine U.S. communities, we were able to examine both the differential effects of different kinds of environmental change and typical forms of adaptation and their prevalence (Ammerman, 1997a). For instance, congregations that were geared to middle-class home-owning families found a population shift to transient singles and immigrant newcomers especially difficult. Changes in the economy of a community, however, had little direct effect on congregations, except as those changes resulted in actual losses to the available population of members. Although congregations do die, they actually take much longer to go out of existence than would a similarly-stressed business or civic group, and meanwhile nearly 20% of all the congregations we located in these communities were less than 10 years old, meaning that the overall population of congregations was at least stable, if not growing.

Further attention to shifting relationships between populations of persons and populations of congregations has come from Eiesland's study of an exurban community outside Atlanta (Eiesland, 2000). She shows, for instance, how the presence of a single megachurch in that community forced all the other congregations to redefine their mission and strategy—some more successfully than others. Ebaugh and her colleagues carefully mapped the immigrant congregations in Houston and assessed the residential dispersion of their members. They propose that "parish" and "niche" are two ends of a continuum of ecological types that must take both spatial dispersion and the number of competing congregations into account (Ebaugh, O'Brien, & Chafetz, 2000). The study of congregations, then, has begun to draw significantly on insights about density and competition, inertia and adaptation. That study, in turn, has contributed insight to our understanding of processes of innovation and decline in organizations of all kinds.

All of this attention to the external context of congregations stands in a long line of research that has been especially inspired by the Mainline Protestant theological concern for civic engagement. In the early 20th century, H. Paul Douglass pioneered sociological research on the relationship between congregational strategy and context (Douglass, 1927). That legacy was continued in studies such as *Varieties of Religious Presence* (Roozen, McKinney, & Carroll, 1984) that documented typical congregational "mission orientations"; and the work of Lowell Livesey's team in documenting the changing public role of congregations in Chicago further expanded this tradition (Livezey, 2000). Each has sought to understand how changing social conditions affect the ability of congregations to carry out their service to the community.

Changing external conditions also were a concern of religious leaders who sought to understand the precipitous decline of those same Mainline Protestant congregations. McKinney and Hoge (1983) documented the degree to which that decline was linked to local contextual factors such as declining neighborhoods, as well as to what congregations or denominations may or may not have done wrong. Other research showed, for instance, that Presbyterian churches, which tend to occupy a religious niche characterized by high levels of education, tend to have higher growth rates when located in high-education communities than when located in low-education communities (Thompson, Carroll, & Hoge, 1993). Like other organizations, congregations do best in situations in which a likely clientele can easily access what they have to offer and less well when separated from those likely participants.

As with other studies of the organizational ecology of congregations, these studies of growth and decline have clarified the rather complicated set of factors (both internal and external) that lead to congregational health. Far from producing a picture of inevitability and inertia, they have often revealed both the entrepreneurial energy at work in this organizational field and the adaptive energy at work as congregations go to the trouble of finding more suitable locations and moving or invest their human and material resources in remaking themselves. Again, as voluntary organizations with high interpersonal salience and strong cultural and symbolic weight, they add important variables to our picture of how organizational ecologies change.

DENOMINATIONS

Organizing denominations is a relatively new religious phenomenon in the long view of human history. Denominations stand in contrast to any culture in which religion is a taken-for-granted part of the whole society. They also lack the comprehensive state-sponsored legitimacy enjoyed by the Catholic Church in Italy or the Lutheran Church in Scandinavia. Still denominations are an organized cultural reality that allows us to see the regularities in and cooperation among local religious communities. H. Richard Niebuhr, following theologian Ernst Troeltsch, described "denominations" as somewhere between what Troeltsch had identified as "Church" and "Sect" (Niebuhr, 1929; Troeltsch, 1931). Like the sect, denominations depend on voluntary adherence for their membership, but like the church, they combine religious and social allegiances, often wrapping social divisions in a religious mantle. Sociologists and historians would not disagree with Niebuhr about the ways in which denominations enshrine a combination of religious and social differences. They would, however, be less likely to call it a sin.

In fact, the notion of a social system that forces each religious group to recognize the legitimacy of other religious groups is often seen as part of the genius of the American political system. Indeed many have argued that it is also to be credited for the relative vitality of American religion (Chaves & Cann, 1992; Iannaccone, 1991; Warner, 1993). By allowing religious groups to organize—as narrowly or as comprehensively as they might choose—the U.S. Constitution created a space for this distinctive form of national religious organization (Greeley, 1972; Martin, 1962; Mathews, 1969). And like congregations, voluntarily organized denominations are subject to the same cycles of birth, death, and merger (Chaves & Sutton, 2004; Liebman, Sutton, & Wuthnow, 1988).

Although the term "denomination" is often used to denote particular theological traditions or the clusters of practices and people who identify with those traditions, our concern here is with the organizations those people create (Ammerman, 1994). A denomination in this sense is a translocal cluster of mutually identified religious organizations that are relatively comprehensive in their scope of functions. They are chosen and developed by their members and exist alongside other, similarly constructed, more-or-less-distinct religious clusters.

Identifying which organizations properly belong to a given denominational cluster is made difficult, however, by the fact that denominations vary in the type of authority they exercise. Unlike a business franchise that can ensure standardization of products and control the use of key identifying symbols, denominations vary widely in the degree to which they control local programming, own local property, train and place local clergy, and the like (Cantrell, Krile, & Donohue, 1983). Even those with the most seemingly hierarchical religious authority may not centralize their functional agencies into a tightly linked system. The Roman Catholic Church, for instance, has no equivalent of a national "denominational headquarters" and has dozens of officially Catholic agencies (from publishers to charities) that have no functional links among themselves. At the opposite end of the spectrum, Southern Baptists have a theology that enshrines the "local autonomy" of each church; but a single system of state and national agencies is held together by a single system of finances that originates with gifts from those churches.

Polity (the theologically sanctioned mode of decision making) does still make a difference, just not a straightforward one. McMullen showed that hierarchical polities tend to channel policy communication through church structures and participation, whereas in looser congregationalist polities individual interests shape what members know about (McMullen, 1994). Hierarchies also can enforce unpopular policies, as Methodists did when southern churches resisted civil rights (Wood, 1970); and they can compel high rates of financial contribution from their member congregations (Ammerman, 2005). Religious authority structures are not irrelevant to the form these organizations take.

That national denominational practice does not conform perfectly to theological norms, however, was noted a generation ago by Paul Harrison in his study of the pragmatic authority assumed by American Baptist agencies in spite of norms of local autonomy (Harrison, 1959). The discrepancy between the religious authority structure and the agency or functional authority system was helpfully theorized by Mark Chaves (1993a). Although I would not agree with Chaves about the degree to which denominational agency structures have been "secularized" (Chaves, 1993b), there is no denying that most major denominations have adopted a bureaucratized and professionalized organizational form. Historian Ben Primer (1978) documented the early-20th-century adoption of these rationalized structures by denominations of very different theological orientations toward church authority (see also Richey, 1994; Weeks, 1992). Even so "nonmodern" a group as the Amish has created a "steering committee" that can perform for them many of the functions performed by the executives and specialists found in the headquarters of other groups (Olshan, 1990). Within each denomination, the norms and values prescribed by the religious tradition are often in tension with the professionalized codes modern organizations expect.

As we have seen with congregations, denominations are, in fact, subject to the pressures of institutional isomorphism. The typical organizational template includes a headquarters building with multiple specialized staffs to administer functions such as missionary work, educational programs, and the like. It also typically includes a publishing house and a pension board to serve its constituent congregations and clergy, respectively. Even the training and credentialing of clergy has been professionalized and standardized, across denominational traditions (Finke, 1994; Perl & Chang, 2000).

Not only do we see mimetic isomorphism, but there is regulatory pressure, as well. The credentialing of chaplains, for instance, requires that a religious endorsing body register with the Pentagon and be recognized there as a legitimate "denomination." No matter how much dissident Southern Baptists might have wanted to proclaim that they had not really left their denomination, for instance, when the Cooperative Baptist Fellowship registered with the Pentagon, it had to show that it was a separate and distinct religious body. Combined with the many other collective functions the Fellowship had already taken on, this action signaled that a new denomination had effectively been born (Ammerman, 2002). We have too often assumed that religious organizations are immune from the effects of various forms of regulation. Once that assumption is put aside, there is ample room for more detailed studies of the ways regulatory regimes shape national religious organizations.

We should not, however, take the bureaucratized rationality of these organizations any more seriously than we take the rationality of other formal complex organizations. The overt tension between religious norms and bureaucratic professionalism provides a very particular version of the way organizational culture and organizational goals are often in tension. Nor should we overlook the many sectors of the denominational field that have not opted for the standard organizational template. One of those sectors comprises the historic African American denominations. Black Baptists sponsor only minimalist national collective enterprises and have virtually no national professional staff. Even the National Baptists' headquarters building in Nashville is more a meeting house than an office building. The Black Methodist and Church of God in Christ denominations have created a somewhat more elaborate structure of professional offices and services, but what holds all these groups together is a sense of camaraderie and fellowship, fostered especially by large annual gatherings to which disproportionately large church delegations are likely to go (Ammerman, 2005). The dominant metaphor in the National Baptist Convention is "family" more than corporation, and what the family does is have an annual reunion. The rules that exist operate within a family-like system of patrimony (the limits of which were visible in the financial scandals surrounding the presidency of Henry Lyons) (Morris & Lee, 2004). Not all national religious organizations have taken predictable corporate form.

That predictable form is most likely to be found among moderate and liberal Protestant denominations, where virtually all have adopted centralized and rationalized methods of organizing. Perhaps as many as one third of Conservative (white) Protestant groups, however, have resisted creating a full-blown denominational bureaucracy, and there are many emerging new networks that are filling some denomination-like functions, but eschewing others (Ammerman, 1993). Even when demographic and other factors are controlled, these networked conservative groups are ironically distinctive for their ability to maintain a strong sense of identity and especially strong levels of congregational support for common enterprises. Without centrally funded pension boards, official publishing houses, and other denominational agencies, these groups nevertheless can often name a consistent set of ministries they (generously) support (Ammerman, 2005).

The Churches of Christ are perhaps the paradigmatic example of these long-standing conservative networks, but there are more recent models, as well. The Willow Creek Association, for instance, is a dues-based membership association that provides a variety of educational materials and training events for its members, but does not ask them to leave their primary denominational home. A second model brings together an informal network of churches that shares a loose sense of identity, fellowship, and accountability—a model adopted by World Ministry Fellowship, the Victory Outreach network, the Potters House Fellowship, and many others. These networks, like the Cooperative Baptist Fellowship, may eventually take on more denomination-like characteristics, but that is not a necessary trajectory. Still another model is being forged by "nondenominational" churches. Many see denominational labels as distracting in their quest to appeal to "seekers" (Sargeant, 2000), but most are nevertheless identifiable both by their evangelical or pentecostal cultural style and by the particular range of independent schools, publishers, and mission agencies with which they work (Thumma, 1999). Ironically, being nondenominational may begin to function as a "denominational" identity, a particular cultural and organizational model. All of these networked churches are creating cultural identities, while attempting to hold the organizational structures to a minimum.

The many ways in which the denominational field is being diversified were signaled by Robert Wuthnow in his analysis of the "restructuring" of American religion (Wuthnow, 1988). As we have seen, not all of American religion had been part of the older institutional model, but now even the professionalized Mainline Protestants are experiencing a weakening of their national organizations. In part, this is precipitated by declines in funding and consequent cutbacks in the projects and services denominations can undertake (Zech, 1997). In part, it is also a result of conflicts and a loss of legitimacy (Dykstra & Hudnut-Beumler, 1992; Roozen, Carroll, & Roof, 1995). Many of these groups have instituted a variety of efforts to reconnect local parishioners to the work of the denomination, including especially organizing opportunities for volunteer teams to work alongside overseas missionaries and other service personnel. Most have also attempted to reorganize so as to give local congregations more voice in national decisions. That process was seen most dramatically in the United Church of Christ, where a financially independent national agency gave up its independence in an effort to enhance the strength and legitimacy of the entire national denominational structure (Barman & Chaves, 2004). Once again, the mix of religious values (Congregationalist participatory decision-making, in this case) and rational calculation (which surely would have argued for a different agency strategy) makes national denominations a fascinating organizational study.

RELIGIOUS SPECIAL PURPOSE GROUPS

Even before there were recognizable national denominational organizations, there were religious special purpose groups. Mission societies were raising money and appointing missionaries (Hutchison, 1987; Robert, 1997). Publishers, such as the American Tract Society and the American Bible Society were producing religious books and literature. Temperance and abolition societies followed, almost always with religious motives and networks at their core (Scott, 1993; Young, 2002). From Hadassah to the Knights of Columbus, religious and ethnic pride flowered into hundreds of voluntary organizations—this in addition to the thousands of schools, hospitals, and orphanages being founded by associations of religious people. As denominations consolidated and centralized in the early 20th century, many specialized organizations were brought under their umbrella, but the impulse to begin an organization to pursue religious goals has never subsided. Each new religious or cultural crisis brings a new wave of religious voluntary organizations. The fundamentalist-modernist controversies, for instance, produced an explosion of new evangelical schools, mission agencies, broadcast ministries, and more (Carpenter, 1980); and the devolution of social service provision since the 1980s has meant hundreds of new religious service agencies.

Evangelicals have remained the most vigorous founders and supporters of special purpose groups. Michael Hamilton (2000) estimates that in 1992, nondenominational mission agencies raised over $1 billion in support of overseas work. He estimates that there are over one thousand evangelical organizations aimed at outreach within the United States, among the most familiar being Campus Crusade for Christ and Promise Keepers. Over 1,300 U.S. radio stations (one in eight) have an all-evangelical broadcast format. There are approximately 4,000 religious bookstores in the United States, three quarters of them evangelical, with annual sales exceeding $2 billion. There are over 15,000 evangelical elementary and secondary schools, and 91 evangelical colleges belong to the Council for Christian Colleges and Universities. One of the nation's largest relief and development agencies, World Vision, is a para-church organization. And on Capitol Hill, legislators hear from religious lobbyists that range from Christian Coalition on the right to SANE-Freeze on the left.

Each of these organizations is shaped in part by the particular religious constituencies it seeks to represent and serve. But they are also shaped by the organizational field they otherwise occupy. Christian Booksellers look like other booksellers, and World Vision largely conforms to institutional expectations about relief and development work (Lindenberg & Bryant, 2001). It is in this sector of religious organizing that we see most acutely the dilemmas posed by government regulation. All of these organizations have to conform to publicly-recognized fund-raising and accounting guidelines. When they fail, public scandal and even jail time may result (Jim Bakker, Henry Lyons, and Episcopal Church treasurer Ellen Cooke are among the more visible recent examples). How much further the state can intrude is, however, very much in flux. For over a century, various governmental organizations have been channeling money to religious agencies to care for widows and orphans, train the jobless, and tend to the downtrodden. A succession of challenges and clarifications resulted in the status quo that existed before the 1990s. When religious organizations accepted state funds, separate programming and accountability kept their service work distinct from other, non-state-funded, activities that were "pervasively sectarian" (Monsma, 1996). Charitable Choice legislation passed in 1996, and the "faith-based initiative" pushed by the second Bush administration significantly destabilized the field of state-funded religious social service delivery. Some new organizations are entering the field, although not always the ones the Bush administration had in mind (Chaves, 1999b; Sherman, 2000). But, more important, a new round of court challenges is raising anew questions about hiring (can a funded religious organization discriminate on the basis of religion?), about who is served (will only believers be served?), and about what services they get (must a Catholic hospital provide abortions?). The ability of the state to regulate is being negotiated alongside an equally momentous negotiation within the organizations themselves about whether and how their faith actually shapes what they do (Thiemann, 2004). As Jeavons (1998) has noted, the very public character of the work such organizations do has long posed challenges of both definition and leadership—just what makes a religious special purpose group religious? Those questions have now taken on renewed legal salience, as well.

The attention to Charitable Choice has, however, helped to encourage a spate of new research on religious charities. Cnaan and others have documented the contributions of congregations to the delivery of social services in local communities (Ammerman, 2001; Chaves, 1999a; Cnaan, 1999). Farnsley's research in Indianapolis has provided a careful analysis of the ways those contributions are, however, limited (Farnsley, 2003). Wineberg, in turn, points to the necessity of understanding religious organizations in the larger organizational (and political) ecology of a community (Wineburg, 2001). And still others have focused on more activist organizations aimed at political and economic changes more than immediate relief. The rise of faith-based community organizing, modeled explicitly on and often linked with Alinsky-style organizing, provides an additional opportunity to analyze the intersection of religious ideas and practices with the organizational dynamics of a social movement (Warren, 2001; Wood, 2002).

As this brief sketch suggests, religious special purpose groups are both more numerous and more important than the available research might suggest. There is simply much more to be done. Within many of the organizational sectors they occupy—from publishing to relief and development—what we know comes almost exclusively from the secular portion of the sector. As with all of the other religious organizational forms we have examined, important questions surround the intersection of cultures and practices shaped by religious life with cultures and practices shaped by organizational and regulatory demands. Each of those factors has its own institutional logic and its own potential for shaping the others.

CONCLUSION

Our understanding of all types of religious organizations will be enhanced as we recognize that intricate interplay of cultural logics, an interplay characteristic of all organizations, but perhaps most interestingly visible in the organizations we define as religious. Religious organizations are simply too numerous to be ignored, but they offer intriguing possibilities for addressing a variety of questions. How do regulatory logics pervade organizations to which they do not legally apply? How is the balance between rational/functional imperatives and ideological/cultural imperatives negotiated? How does one organizational field expand or contract in response to changes in other organizational fields? Why are the ecological dynamics of birth and death apparently so different in the population of religious voluntary organizations, as compared to businesses? The intersection of organizational studies and the study of religion will continue to be a very productive one.

REFERENCES

Adams, J. L. (1986). The voluntary principle in the forming of American religion. In J. R. Engel (Ed.), *Voluntary associations: Socio-cultural analyses and theological interpretation* (pp. 171–200). Chicago: Exploration Press.

Ammerman, N. T. (1987). *Bible believers: Fundamentalists in the modern world.* New Brunswick: Rutgers University Press.

Ammerman, N. T. (1993). SBC moderates and the making of a post-modern denomination. *Christian Century, 110*(26), 896–899.

Ammerman, N. T. (1994). Denominations: Who and what are we studying? In R. B. Mullin & R. E. Richey (Eds.), *Re-imagining denominationalism.* New York: Oxford University Press.

Ammerman, N. T. (1997a). *Congregation and community.* New Brunswick, NJ: Rutgers University Press.

Ammerman, N. T. (1997b). Golden rule Christianity: Lived religion in the American mainstream. In D. Hall (Ed.), *Lived religion in America: Toward a history of practice* (pp. 196–216). Princeton, NJ: Princeton University Press.

Ammerman, N. T. (2001). *Doing good in American communities: Congregations and service organizations working together.* Retrieved November 20, 2001, from http://hirr.hartsem.edu/about/about_orw_cong-report.html

Ammerman, N. T. (2002). Cooperative baptist fellowship. In J. G. Melton & M. Baumann (Eds.), *Religions of the world: A comprehensive encyclopedia of beliefs and practices* (pp. 363–364). Santa Barbara, CA: ABC-Clio.

Ammerman, N. T. (2004). Porous boundaries and busy intersections: Religious narratives, community service, and everyday public life. In M. J. Bane, B. Coffin, & M. Moore (Eds.), *Taking faith seriously: Valuing and evaluating religion in American democracy.* Cambridge, MA: Harvard University Press.

Ammerman, N. T. (2005). *Pillars of faith: American congregations and their partners.* Berkeley: University of California Press.

Ammerman, N. T., Carroll, J. W., Dudley, C. S., & McKinney, W. (Eds.). (1998). *Studying congregations: A new handbook.* Nashville: Abingdon.

Barman, E., & Chaves, M. (2004). Strategy and restructure in the United Church of Christ. In D. Roozen & J. Nieman (Eds.), *Adaptive change in national denominational structures: Practiced theology.* Grand Rapids, MI: Eerdmans.

Becker, P. E. (1999). *Congregations in conflict: Cultural models of local religious life.* Cambridge: Cambridge University Press.

Bendroth, M. (2002). *Growing up protestant: Parents, children, and mainline churches.* Piscataway, NJ: Rutgers University Press.

Brady, H. E., Verba, S., & Schlozman, K. L. (1995). Beyond SES: A resource model of political participation. *American Political Science Review, 89*(2), 271–294.

Butler, J. (1990). *Awash in a sea of faith.* Cambridge, MA: Harvard University Press.

Cantrell, R. L., Krile, J. F., & Donohue, G. A. (1983). Parish autonomy: Measuring denominational differences. *Journal for the Scientific Study of Religion, 22,* 276–287.

Carpenter, J. (1980). Fundamentalism institutions and the rise of evangelical protestantism, 1929–1940. *Church History, 49,* 62–75.

Carroll, J. W., Dudley, C. S., & McKinney, W. (1986). *Handbook for congregational studies.* Nashville: Abingdon Press.

Chaves, M. (1993a). Denominations as dual structures: An organizational analysis. *Sociology of Religion, 54*(2), 147–169.

Chaves, M. (1993b). Intraorganizational power and internal secularization in protestant denominations. *American Journal of Sociology, 99*(1), 1–48.

Chaves, M. (1999a). *Congregations' social service activities.* Washington, DC: Urban Institute.

Chaves, M. (1999b). Religious congregations and welfare reform: Who will take advantage of 'charitable choice'? *American Sociological Review, 64,* 836–846.

Chaves, M. (2004). *Congregations in America.* Cambridge, MA: Harvard University Press.

Chaves, M., & Cann, D. E. (1992). Regulation, pluralism, and religious market structure: Explaining religion's vitality. *Rationality and Society, 4*(3), 272–290.

Chaves, M., Koneiczny, M. E., Beyerlein, K., & Barman, E. (1999). The national congregational study; background, methods, and selected results. *Journal for the Scientific Study of Religion, 38*(4), 458–476.

Chaves, M., & Sutton, J. R. (2004). Organizational consolidation in American protestant denominations, 1890–1990. *Journal for the Scientific Study of Religion, 43*(1), 51–66.

Cnaan, R. A. (1999). *The newer deal: Social work and religion in partnership.* New York: Columbia University Press.

DiMaggio, P. J. (1998). The relevance of organization theory to the study of religion. In N. J. Demerath, P. D. Hall, T. Schmitt, & R. Williams (Eds.), *Sacred companies* (pp. 7–23). New York: Oxford University Press.

DiMaggio, P. J., & Powell, W. W. (1983). The iron cage revisited: Institutional isomorphism and collective rationality in organizational fields. *American Sociological Review, 48,* 147–160.

Dolan, J. P. (1994). Patterns of leadership in the congregation. In J. P. Wind & J. W. Lewis (Eds.), *American congregations* (pp. 225–256). Chicago: University of Chicago Press.

Douglass, H. P. (1927). *The church in the changing city.* New York: Doran.

Dudley, C. S. (1998). Process: Dynamics of congregational life. In N. Ammerman, J. W. Carroll, C. S. Dudley, & W. McKinney (Eds.), *Studying congregations: A new handbook.* Nashville: Abingdon.

Dykstra, C., & Hudnut-Beumler, J. (1992). The national organizational structures of protestant denominations: An invitation to a conversation. In M. J. Coalter, J. M. Mulder, & L. B. Weeks (Eds.), *The organizational revolution: Presbyterians and American denominationalism* (pp. 307–331). Louisville: Westminster/John Knox.

Ebaugh, H. R., & Chafetz, J. S. (1999). Agents for cultural reproduction and structural change: The ironic role of women in immigrant religious institutions. *Social Forces, 78*(2), 585–613.

Ebaugh, H. R., & Chafetz, J. S. (2000). Structural adaptations in immigrant congregations. *Sociology of Religion, 61*(2), 135–153.

Ebaugh, H. R., O'Brien, J., & Chafetz, J. S. (2000). The social ecology of residential patterns and membership in immigrant churches. *Journal for the Scientific Study of Religion, 39*(1), 107–116.

Eiesland, N. (2000). *A particular place: Urban restructuring and religious ecology.* New Brunswick, NJ: Rutgers University Press.

Ellison, C. G., & George, L. K. (1994). Religious involvement, social ties and social support in a southeastern community. *Journal for the Scientific Study of Religion, 33*(1), 46–61.

Etzioni, A. (1961). *A comparative analysis of complex organizations.* New York: Free Press.

Farnsley II, A. E. (2000). Congregations, local knowledge, and devolution. *Review of Religious Research, 42*(1), 96–110.

Farnsley II, A. E. (2003). *Rising expectations: Urban congregations, welfare reform, and civic life.* Bloomington: Indiana University Press.

Finke, R. (1994). The quiet transformation: Changes in size and leadership of southern baptist churches. *Review of Religious Research, 36*(1), 3–22.

Franklin, R. M. (1994). The safest place on earth: The culture of Black congregations. In J. P. Wind & J. W. Lewis (Eds.), *American congregations* (Vol. 2, pp. 257–284). Chicago: University of Chicago Press.

Fraser, N. (1990). Rethinking the public sphere: A contribution to the critique of actually existing democracy. *social text, 25*(26), 56–80.

Friedland, R., & Alford, R. R. (1991). Bringing society back in: Symbols, practices, and institutional contradictions. In W. Powell & P. DiMaggio (Eds.), *The new institutionalism in organizational analysis* (pp. 232–263). Chicago: University of Chicago Press.

Gamm, G. (1999). *Urban exodus: Why the Jews left Boston and the Catholics stayed.* Cambridge, MA: Harvard University Press.

Gillespie, J. B. (1995). *Women speak: Of God, congregations and change.* Valley Forge, PA: Trinity Press International.

Greeley, A. M. (1972). *The denominational society.* Glenview, IL: Scott-Forsman.

Hadaway, C. K., Marler, P. L., & Chaves, M. (1993). What the polls don't show: A closer look at U. S. church attendance. *American Sociological Review, 58*(6), 741–752.

Hall, P. D. (1998). Religion and the organizational revolution in the United States. In N. J. Demerath III, P. D. Hall, T. Schmitt, & R. Williams (Eds.), *Sacred companies* (pp. 99–115). New York: Oxford University Press.

Hamilton, M. S. (2000). More money, more ministry: The financing of American evangelicalism since 1945. In L. Eskridge & M. Noll (Eds.), *More money, More ministry: Money and evangelicals in recent North American history* (pp. 104–138). Grand Rapids, MI: Eerdmans.

Harrison, P. M. (1959). *Authority and power in the Free Church tradition.* Princeton, NJ: Princeton University Press.

Hartman, K. (1998). *Congregations in conflict: The battle over homosexuality.* New Brunswick, NJ: Rutgers University Press.

Heilman, S. (1973). *Synagogue life.* Chicago: University of Chicago Press.

Hodgkinson, V. A., & Weitzman, M. S. (1993). *From belief to commitment: The community service activities and finances of religious congregations in the United States: 1993 Edition.* Washington, DC: Independent Sector.

Hoge, D. R., Johnson, B., & Luidens, D. A. (1994). *Vanishing boundaries: The religion of mainline Protestant baby boomers.* Louisville: Westminster/John Knox.

Holifield, E. B. (1994). Toward a history of American congregations. In J. P. Wind & J. W. Lewis (Eds.), *American congregations: New perspectives in the study of congregations* (pp. 23–53). Chicago: University of Chicago Press.

Hutchison, W. R. (1987). *Errand to the world: American Protestant thought and foreign missions.* Chicago: University of Chicago Press.

Iannaccone, L. R. (1991). The consequences of religious market structure: Adam Smith and the economics of religion. *Rationality and Society, 3*(2), 156–177.

Jeavons, T. H. (1998). Identifying characteristics of 'religious' organizations: An exploratory proposal. In N. J. Demerath, , III, P. D. Hall, T. Schmitt, & R. H. Williams (Eds.), *Sacred companies: Organizational aspects of religion and religious aspects of organizations* (pp. 79–96). New York: Oxford University Press.

Kwon, H. Y., Kim, K. C., & Warner, R. S. (Eds.). (2001). *Korean Americans and their religions: Pilgrims and missionaries from a different shore.* University Park: Pennsylvania State University Press.

Liebman, R. C., Sutton, J. R., & Wuthnow, R. (1988). Exploring the social sources of denominationalism: Schisms in American denominations, 1890–1980. *American Sociological Review, 53,* 343–352.

Lincoln, C. E., & Mamiya, L. H. (1990). *The Black church in the African American experience.* Durham, NC: Duke University Press.

Lindenberg, M., & Bryant, C. (2001). *Going global: Transforming relief and development NGOs.* Bloomfield, CT: Kumarian Press.

Livezey, L. W. (2000). *Public religion and urban transformation: Faith in the city.* New York: New York University Press.

March, J. (1978). Bounded rationality, ambiguity, and the engineering of choice. *Bell Journal of Economics, 9,* 587–608.

Marler, P. L. (1995). Lost in the fifties: The changing family and the nostalgic church. In N. T. Ammerman & W. C. Roof (Eds.), *Work, family, and religion in contemporary society* (pp. 23–60). New York: Routledge.

Martin, D. (1962). The denomination. *British Journal of Sociology, 13,* 1–14.

Martin, D. (1990). *Tongues of fire: The explosion of Protestantism in Latin America.* Oxford: Blackwell.

Mathews, D. G. (1969). The second great awakening as an organizing process, 1780–1830. *American Quarterly, 21,* 23–43.

McGreevy, J. T. (1996). *Parish boundaries: The Catholic encounter with race in the twentieth-century urban north.* Chicago: University of Chicago Press.

McKinney, W. (1998). Resources. In N. T. Ammerman, J. W. Carroll, C. S. Dudley, & W. McKinney (Eds.), *Studying congregations: A new handbook* (pp. 132–166). Nashville: Abingdon.

McKinney, W. J., & Hoge, D. R. (1983). Community and congregational factors in the growth and decline of Protestant churches. *Journal for the Scientific Study of Religion, 22,* 51–66.

McMullen, M. (1994). Religious polities as institutions. *Social Forces, 73*(2), 709–728.

McRoberts, O. M. (1999). Understanding the "new" Black pentecostal activism: Lessons from ecumenical urban ministries in Boston. *Sociology of Religion, 60*(1), 47–70.

McRoberts, O. M. (2003). *Streets of glory: Church and community in a Black urban neighborhood.* Chicago: University of Chicago Press.

Monsma, S. V. (1996). *When sacred & secular mix: Religious nonprofit organizations and public money.* Lanham, MA: Rowman & Littlefield.

Morris, A. D., & Lee, S. (2004). The national baptist convention: Traditions and contemporary challenges. In D. Roozen & J. Nieman (Eds.), *Adaptive change in national denominational structures: Practiced theology.* Grand Rapids, MI: Eerdmans.

Nelson, T. J. (1997). The church and the street: Race, class, and congregation. In P. E. Becker & N. L. Eiesland (Eds.), *Contemporary American religion* (pp. 169–190). Walnut Creek, CA: AltaMira.

Niebuhr, H. R. (1929). *The social sources of denominationalism.* New York: World Publishing.

Olshan, M. A. (1990). The old order amish steering committee: A case study in organizational evolution. *Social Forces, 69*(2), 603–616.

Pattillo-McCoy, M. (1998). Church culture as a strategy of action in the Black community. *American Sociological Review, 63,* 767–784.

Perl, P., & Chang, P. M. Y. (2000). Credentialism across creeds: Clergy education and stratification in Protestant denominations. *Journal for the Scientific Study of Religion, 39*(2), 171–188.

Pinto, L. J., & Crow, K. E. (1982). The effects of size on other structural attributes of congregations within the same denomination. *Journal for the Scientific Study of Religion, 21,* 304–316.

Powell, W. W., & DiMaggio, P. J. (Eds.). (1991). *The new institutionalism in organizational analysis.* Chicago: University of Chicago Press.

Prell, R. E. (2000). Communities of choice and memory: Conservative synagogues in the late twentieth century. In J. Wertheimer (Ed.), *Jews in the center: Conservative synagogues and their members* (pp. 269–358). New Brunswick, NJ: Rutgers University Press.

Primer, B. (1978). *Protestants and American business methods.* Ann Arbor: UMI Research Press.

Putnam, R. D. (2000). *Bowling alone: The collapse and revival of American community.* New York: Simon & Schuster.

Richey, R. E. (1994). Denominations and denominationalism: An American morphology. In R. B. Mullin & R. E. Richey (Eds.), *Re-imagining denominationalism* (pp. 74–98). New York: Oxford University Press.

Robert, D. L. (1997). *Women in mission: A social history of their thought and practice.* Macon, GA: Mercer University Press.

Roozen, D. A., Carroll, J. W., & Roof, W. C. (1995). Fifty years of religious change in the United States. In W. Roof, Clark, J. W. Carroll, & D. A. Roozen (Eds.), *The post-war generation and establishment religion* (pp. 59–85). Boulder, CO: Westview.

Roozen, D. A., McKinney, W., & Carroll, J. W. (1984). *Varieties of religious presence.* New York: Pilgrim Press.

Sack, D. (2000). *Whitebread Protestants: Food and religion in American culture.* New York: St. Martin's Press.

Sargeant, K. H. (2000). *Seeker churches: Promoting traditional religion in a nontraditional way.* New Brunswick, NJ: Rutgers University Press.

Scott, A. F. (1993). *Natural allies: Women's associations in American history.* Urbana: University of Illinois Press.

Sherman, A. (2000). Churches as government partners: Navigating "charitable choice." *Christian Century, 117*(20), 716–721.

Shin, E. H., & Park, H. (1988). An analysis of causes of schisms in ethnic Churches: The case of Korean-American churches. *Sociological Analysis, 49,* 234–248.

Smidt, C. (Ed.). (2003). *Religion as social capital: Producing the common good.* Waco, TX: Baylor University Press.

Thiemann, R. F. (2004). What's faith got to do with it? Lutheran social ministry in transition. In M. J. Bane, B. Coffin, & M. Moore (Eds.), *Taking faith seriously: Valuing and evaluating religion in American democracy.* Cambridge, MA: Harvard University Press.

Thompson, W. L., Carroll, J. W., & Hoge, D. (1993). Growth or decline in presbyterian congregations. In D. Roozen & C. K. Hadaway (Eds.), *Church and denominational growth* (pp. 188–207). Nashville: Abingdon.

Thumma, S. (1999). *What God makes free is free indeed: Nondenominational church identity and its networks of support.* Retrieved January 4, 2002, from http://www.hirr.hartsem.edu/bookshelf/thumma_article5.html

Thung, M. (1976). *The precarious organisation: Sociological explorations of the church's mission and structure.* Hague: Mouton.

Tocqueville, A. D. (1835). *Democracy in America* (G. Lawrence, Trans.). Garden City, NY: Doubleday.

Troeltsch, E. (1931). *The social teaching of the Christian churches.* London: George Allen.

Verba, S., Schlozman, K. L., & Brady, H. E. (1995). *Voice and equality: Civic voluntarism in American politics.* Cambridge, MA: Harvard University Press.

Warner, R. S. (1988). *New wine in old wineskins.* Berkeley: University of California Press.

Warner, R. S. (1993). Work in progress toward a new paradigm for the sociological study of religion in the United States. *American Journal of Sociology, 98*(5), 1044–1093.

Warner, R. S. (1994). The place of the congregation in the contemporary American religious configuration. In J. Wind & J. Lewis (Eds.), *American congregations: New perspectives in the study of congregations* (pp. 54–99). Chicago: University of Chicago Press.

Warner, R. S. (1999). Changes in the civic role of religion. In N. J. Smelser & J. C. Alexander (Eds.), *Diversity and its discontents: Cultural conflict and common ground in contermporary American society* (pp. 229–243). Princeton, NJ: Princeton University Press.

Warner, R. S., & Wittner, J. G. (1998). *Gatherings in diaspora: Religious communities and the new immigration.* Philadelphia: Temple University Press.

Warren, M. R. (2001). *Dry bones rattling: Community building to revitalize American democracy.* Princeton, NJ: Princeton University Press.

Weber, M. (1964). *The theory of social and economic organization.* New York: Free Press.

Wedam, E. (2003). The 'religious district' of elite congregations: Reproducing spatial centrality and redefining mission. *Sociology of Religion, 64*(1), 47–64.

Weeks, L. B. (1992). The incorporation of the presbyterians. In M. J. Coalter, J. M. Mulder, & L. B. Weeks (Eds.), *The organizational revolution: Presbyterians and American denominationalism.* Louisville: Westminster/John Knox.

Wellman Jr, J. K. (1999). *The gold coast church and the ghetto: Christ and culture in mainline Protestantism.* Champagne: University of Illinois Press.

Williams, M. D. (1974). *Community in a Black pentecostal church.* Pittsburgh: University of Pittsburgh Press.

Wind, J. P., & Lewis, J. W. (Eds.). (1994). *American congregations: Portraits of 12 religious communities* (Vol. 1). Chicago: University of Chicago Press.

Wineburg, B. (2001). *A limited partnership: The politics of religion, welfare, and social service.* New York: Columbia University Press.

Winter, G. (1967). Religious organizations. In W. L. Warner (Ed.), *The emergent American society* (pp. 408–491). New Haven, CT: Yale University Press.

Wood, J. R. (1970). Authority and controversial policy: The church and civil rights. *American Sociological Review, 35,* 1057–1069.

Wood, R. L. (2002). *Faith in action: Religion, race, and democratic organizing in America.* Chicago: University of Chicago Press.

Wuthnow, R. (1988). *The restructuring of American religion.* Princeton, NJ: Princeton University Press.

Wuthnow, R. (1994). *Producing the sacred.* Urbana: University of Illinois Press.

Young, M. P. (2002). Confessional protest: The religious birth of U.S. national social movements. *American Sociological Review, 67*(5), 660–688.

Zech, C. E. (1997). Determinants of the mission funding crisis. In D. Campbell & R. Richey (Eds.), *Connectionalism: Ecclesiology, mission, and identity.* Nashville: Abingdon.

Zuckerman, P. (1998). *Strife in the sanctuary.* Walnut Creek, CA: AltaMira.

CHAPTER 19

Religious Leadership/Clergy

DEAN R. HOGE

OVERVIEW

Sociological research on clergy and religious leaders has been motivated mainly by institutional concerns. This field is filled with studies sponsored by religious denominations and church-supporting foundations to help solve practical problems. The main research topics are recruitment, training, morale, coping with stress, clarifying roles, and tracking changes. The clearest way to convey this research is denomination by denomination. Thus I will first review the research under the three headings of Protestant, Catholic, and other religions, then I will interpret the research from the viewpoint of sociological questions.

Historically, this subdiscipline began with Protestant studies in the 1930s. Catholic research began slowly in the 1950s and picked up speed in the 1970s. Studies of Eastern Orthodox priests, Jewish rabbis, and Muslim imams have been sparse. For historical overviews of Protestant studies, see Menges and Dittes (1965), Schreuder (1970), Pryor (1982), and Blizzard and Blizzard (1985); of Catholic studies, see Fichter (1961) and Hoge (2002). Francis and Jones (1996) edited a book of psychological and social psychological studies of clergy.

RESEARCH ON PROTESTANT MINISTERS

The Roles of a Minister

Whereas research on the roles of Protestant ministers began in the 1930s, the major advances came with the studies by Samuel Blizzard in the 1950s (published much later in a 1985 posthumous book). Blizzard identified three levels of ministerial roles: the master role—either theological or functional; integrative roles—identifying the groups and organizations with whom the minister works; and practitioner roles—the six specific tasks of ministry. The practitioner roles are preacher, pastor, teacher, priest, administrator, and organizer. They turned out to be very central to clergy's self-understanding. Blizzard's most influential

DEAN R. HOGE • Catholic University of America, Washington, DC, 20064 publication, entitled "The Minister's Dilemma" (1956), showed how ministers preferred to devote themselves to being a pastor, preacher, and teacher, but found themselves forced to spend their time and energy being administrator, pastor, and organizer. The greater the disjunction between roles preferred and roles actually performed, the lower was the minister's satisfaction. Later researchers (e.g., Hoge, Dyble, & Polk, 1981; Nauss, 1994) confirmed that ministerial morale was related to each person's enjoyment of the six specific roles, with enjoyment of the role of priest and preacher most associated with commitment to ministry.

A large cross-denominational study of role expections by laity and ministers was done by Schuller, Strommen, and Brekke (1980). It compared 47 denominations, including Catholics and Orthodox, in the priorities they gave to specific roles. Through factor analysis, the researchers identified four main models, "Spiritual Emphasis," "Sacramental-Liturgical Emphasis," "Social Action Emphasis," and "Combined Emphases." This study is the most thorough comparative study of the clergy role ever done.

Another approach to roles looked at conflicts between a clergyperson's ministerial roles and family roles. Ministry is commonly seen as a total way of life, and ministers are not expected (or expect themselves) to have another life in family or leisure time which is distinct from their church work. Carroll et al. (1981) defined this as "role hegemony," indicating that the Protestant ministerial role is widely defined as taking precedence over all else in a minister's life, so that he or she is on duty 24 hours a day, 7 days a week (also see Benda & DiBlasio, 1992). All research has found that ministers have complained about the inability to take time off and to escape their ministerial roles.

Brunnette-Hill and Finke (1999) carried out a partial replication of Blizzard's 1955 survey of Protestant ministers. They found that clergy in 1994 worked fewer hours per week than those in 1955; in 1955 the average work week for mainline Protestant pastors was 69 hours (excluding time leading worship services); in 1994 it was 48. Possibly some of this apparent decline was because of questionnaire wording, but even so, the average work week probably declined by several hours at least. The main drop was in the number of hours the 1994 clergy devoted to social interaction with members and potential members, visiting the sick, administration, and involvement with civic leaders. "Mainline Protestant clergy are now spending less time with church members, potential members, and religious and civic leaders than they did in the past" (Brunnette-Hill & Finke, 1999, p. 55). The 1994 researchers found that conservative Protestant ministers and Catholic priests had a longer workweek than mainline ministers.

Stress and Satisfaction

A practical problem that has stimulated research since the 1970s is occupational stress and satisfaction. A seminal study by Mills and Koval (1971) found that most ministers experience stress in their vocation, and that it decreases with age. Older ministers felt much less stress than younger ones. The most commonly reported source of stress was conflict with the congregation, particularly conflict with congregational leaders brought on by personal and ideological differences.

Later researchers (Blanton, 1992; Blanton & Morris, 1999) found that the long hours of work in ministry for comparatively low pay is a difficulty felt by many ministers. In addition, their families feel stress because they live a fishbowl existence in which they are expected to demonstrate exemplary family life. A study of stress in the Netherlands had similar findings (Schilderman, 1998).

A study by Lee (1999), which focused on the frequency and importance of stressors on ministers, found that ministers suffer frequent criticism by members and by lay leaders, and these experiences have a big impact on them. A second source of stress, with almost as much impact, is the assumption by lay members that a minister is available any time and can be called upon for help or ministry at short notice. In addition, there is a problem of setting boundaries between ministry and family life, so that ministerial demands intrude too much on family life, including on vacations and family decision making. Clergy families feel ambiguity about family boundaries, because the ministry is often seen as including the family life of the pastor. That is, the pastor's family is held up as an exemplary Christian family, with support for the pastor's ministry expected on the part of his or her spouse and children. It is assumed that the family should accept intrusions into family time whenever ministerial demands arose. These problems of family life and marriage are major sources of stress (see Morris & Blanton, 1994; Bender & DiBlasio, 1996).

Women Ministers

A major theme in Protestant research has been the increase in women ministers. The first Protestant women ministers were ordained in the late 19th century during the women's suffrage movement, yet their numbers were low until about 1970 (Lehman, 2002). The 1970s, 1980s, and 1990s were decades of rapid growth. By the 1990s, about one third of the students in major seminaries in curricula leading to ordination were women. Today in some of the most prestigious schools, such as Union Seminary in New York and Chicago Divinity School, women students outnumber men (Wheeler, 2001).

The suddenness of denominational acceptance of women ministers in the 1960s and 1970s was studied by Chaves (1997). Why so many? Why at this time? Chaves found that the changed cultural climate after passage of the 1964 Civil Rights Act put moral pressure on the denominational leaders, as all American institutions were moving toward gender equality. The feminist movement was an additional push. Protestant denominations, which have commonly espoused religious principles of equality and justice, felt the need to declare gender equality in ordination, and many did so even though the majority of the members did not want it. In many cases, the traditional gender roles that associated the job of senior pastor with maleness and the job of religious educator with femaleness militated against opening ordination to women, even as denominational leadership pressured for accepting women's ordination as a matter of justice. Most denominational leaders prevailed, but tensions have remained in these denominations ever since the 1970s.

Major research on women ministers began in the 1980s. Carroll and his associates (1981) carried out a survey of the experiences of men and women ministers in nine denominations. They discovered that women found it more difficult to get ministerial positions because of resistance from many laity and denominational officers, yet when women served in local ministry for several years they became well respected and well received. Older laity were especially resistant to having women ministers.

Three research efforts in the 1980s and 1990s greatly clarified the forces affecting women ministers. Edward Lehman carried out three surveys in the United States and England (Lehman, 1985, 1993, 2002). Nesbitt (1997) made a study of Episcopalians and Unitarians. Zikmund and her associates (1998) carried out a comprehensive study of men and women ministers, among other things replicating the 1981 Carroll study. The findings from these studies are consistent enough that we can summarize them here as a group.

Women entering ministry after 1970 tended to be older than men. Among them were more "second-career" persons, who were older and more experienced in church life. They possessed relatively more intellectual and spiritual maturity, and their life goals were clearer. The percentage of women who had been divorced was much higher than among men. They came from more educated families than did men, and in seminary they performed academically better.

Ministry has been more difficult for women than for men, especially in finding employment. Evangelical and Pentecostal denominations have offered very few positions, even though in principle most affirm women's ordination. In conservative groups, important influence has come from arguments based on biblical inerrancy, which cite New Testament teachings that women must always be submissive to men, especially in the family and in the church. From another theological angle, arguments about sacraments have been influential in the Eastern Orthodox churches, the Episcopal Church, and some Lutheran churches—holding that the human agent presenting the Gospel and the elements of communion represents none other than Christ and thus must be male (Lehman, 2002, p. 11). Thus, these two types of denominations have been very slow in affirming women ministers.

Women have found first placement after ordination more difficult than men. Women's placement takes longer, and their wages are lower. More women have found placements as associate pastors or ministers of education rather than as senior pastors. Also, in their second or third placements, fewer women find placements as senior pastors in high-prestige, high-paying churches. These barriers have seemed to recede over time. In a study of trends in placement, Chang (1997) found that the situation improved for women from the 1970s to the 1990s, so that the male advantage gradually diminished. This appears to be a result of more formalized hiring practices at the denominational level, which increases fairness in the system and minimizes the effects of the former "good old boy" networks.

Women ministers' salaries are lower than men's. In the Zikmund et al. study of 1993, women earned about 91% as much as men, when all other factors such as age, type of position, and size of congregation were held constant. Yet in studies of job satisfaction, women in the 1990s did not express greater dissatisfaction with their salaries. Why not? Carroll et al. (1981) speculated that women entered the ministry with lowered expectations and thus were happier with their placements regardless of the salary. Also, a majority of women ministers were married to husbands with good earning capacity in secular jobs.

In the Unitarian and Episcopalian denominations, Nesbitt (1997) found a gradual trend toward equality of placements for men and women after the 1960s, but the trend stopped in the 1980s. She found that in secular occupations, when 30% or more of the members are women, it triggers organizational responses that block further advances by women. This seems to have also happened in these denominations. She also found that for both men and women, entry-level jobs have long-lasting influence on subsequent placements. Ministers with better entry level jobs tended to get even more desirable placements for the second and subsequent jobs, while those whose entry-level placements were relatively low tended to advance less. Thus, differences between men and women in job status and in financial support in first placement expand in their second and third placements. Even when other factors are held constant—including age, family problems, and freedom for mobility, gender differences remain, and they increase in effect during the course of a typical career (Lehman, 2002).

Women, more than men, have found themselves in remote communities with small congregations. These situations are not what beginning ministers hope for. Men tend to see them as temporary stepping stones toward more attractive placements later, and this is often the case. Women, by contrast, find it difficult to move on, and therefore a next step for them entails either getting more education, going into a specialized nonparish ministry, or leaving the ministry altogether (Lehman, 1985).

Several researchers have investigated the situations in which resistance to women ministers softens (see Lehman, 2002). They developed a "contact hypothesis," which has been sustained, holding that prejudices against unknown persons tend to fall away after personal contact with that person, provided the contact is nonhierarchical in nature, that is, based on equal status, not superordinate-subordinate. Experience with women pastors reduces the wariness or resistance of laypersons about women leaders, provided the contact is continuous over a period of time.

The New Seminarians

Protestant seminarians have changed in two ways since the 1970s. Most important, the percent female has risen, so that about 35% of recent seminary graduates in curricula leading to ordination have been women (Wheeler, 2001; Carroll, Wheeler, Aleshire, & Marler, 1997). The second finding is that seminary students today are older; the average age of incoming students in a 1999 study was 35 years, compared with an average of 26 or 28 in the 1970s (Wheeler, 2001). What have been the causes and effects of these changes? Already we have reviewed studies of women. How about studies of older seminarians?

Most of the debate about older seminarians has been about their alleged ability as ministers. It is widely believed among seminary leaders today that the current crop of seminarians is less intellectually capable than was true 20 or 40 years ago, and this is bolstered by research on professional preferences of Phi Beta Kappa members (Wheeler, 1993, p. 95). Measured by academic criteria, the standards have dropped, and seminary admissions today are not as competitive as earlier. Wheeler surveyed seminary students in 1999 to see if men and women were different and if older students were different from younger ones just out of college. She found that the women performed as well as men in seminary studies. Older students, in general, came to seminary with lower academic credentials. Fewer had been honor students as undergraduates, and fewer had come from high-prestige colleges. The earlier flows of young men from such leading schools as Haverford, Vanderbilt, Davidson, or Oberlin have subsided. More of today's seminarians have had practical experience after college, but they have had less intellectual preparation. Fewer come from families in which the parents had graduated from college.

CATHOLIC RESEARCH ON PRIESTS AND LAY MINISTERS

The Priest Shortage

The main concern motivating research on the Catholic priesthood has been the decline in numbers. After the close of the Second Vatican Council in 1965 a large number of priests resigned, causing alarm in Catholic leadership. About 15 to 17% of priests resigned between 1966 and 1975 (Hoge, 1987, p. 10). In 1969 the American Catholic bishops commissioned three large studies of the priesthood, studies that constituted the best research done to date.

One book was sociological (Greeley, 1972), one was psychological (Kennedy & Heckler, 1972), and the third was a collection of historical essays. They covered topics such as how men were attracted to the priesthood, their morale and satisfactions, their spiritual lives, and their thoughts about resigning.

During the 1980s and 1990s, Schoenherr and Young produced definitive studies of the coming priest shortage. Their main work, *Full Pews, Empty Altars* (Schoenherr & Young, 1993) is the best study of trends of numbers of priests in the United States. They predicted a 40% decline from 1966 to 2005, a prediction that has been borne out. A few years later Young (1998) updated the projections to 2015, predicting further declines. By the end of the 1990s, American Catholic seminaries were producing ordinations at between 30 and 40% of replacement level (that is, the number needed to replace older priests who retired, resigned, or died).

Together with their associate Vilarino, Schoenherr and Young found the same pattern in Spain (Schoenherr, Young, & Vilarino, 1988; Vilarino & Tizon, 1998). On the situation in Italy, see Garelli (2003) and in Germany, Zulehner (2002).

Why are so few men going to seminary, and why are some of the priests resigning? Hoge (1987) surveyed Catholic college students nationwide to determine the main deterrents keeping men from becoming priests. He found that the celibacy requirement was the most important single deterrent, and if celibacy were made optional, the number of seminarians would increase by about four times. He also asked the college students if they would be interested in the priesthood if there were a tour of duty (not a lifetime commitment) of 10 or 15 years, and found that many would be interested. Finally, he asked how many would be interested in serving the Church as lay ministers. Many were. The pool of Catholic college students interested in lay ministry is about 50 times as large as the pool interested in becoming priests, brothers, or sisters.

Rodney Stark carried out two studies of determinants of priestly vocations in the United States. In the first (1998) he found in the 171 dioceses and also in the 50 states that the lower the percent Catholics in the population, the more men were ordained priests. In the second, Stark and Finke (2000) found that the more theologically conservative the diocese (measured by expert ratings), the more men were ordained priests. Also the more a religious community of priests and nuns offers an intense level of community life and a sharp separation from secular life, as measured by members' descriptions, the more members they recruit. The analysis of costs and rewards in recruiting men to the priesthood continues to be an urgent topic under debate, both at the institutional and at the theoretical level (see King, 1994; Schuth, 1999).

Harper and Schulte-Murray (1998) compared two dioceses in the American Midwest, one of which had a tightly controlled, traditional, bureaucratic organizational culture and the other which had a loosely coupled, nontraditional, collegial organizational culture. In the latter, priests had more autonomy and were given more voice in decision making at all levels. The former (controlled, hierarchical, bureaucratic) recruited more seminarians than the latter. This finding is counterintuitive from the viewpoint of research on professionals, which commonly finds an association between personal autonomy, morale, and the number of persons wishing to join. The authors had no explanation for the anomaly and suggested that the Roman Catholic priesthood is unique among American professions.

The Catholic priest shortage has no counterpart in Protestant denominations. No Protestant denomination has experienced a large decline in ordinations in recent decades. In overall terms, the supply exceeds the demand in all major denominations except the Lutheran Church-Missouri Synod (which does not ordain women). The Protestant problem, rather, is one of placement. Seminary graduates often refuse job offers from small rural churches, thus leaving them without ministers or at least without fully trained ministers. Most U.S. Protestant churches are small, with fewer than 100 regular participants, and thus they cannot afford (or can barely afford) a full-time pastor. There is a Protestant minister shortage, but only in small and marginal churches. Many clergy complain that there are no good jobs, while at the same time the majority of small churches cannot find pastors. The problem is worse in the mainline Protestant denominations than in evangelical denominations (Chang, 2004).

Satisfactions and Morale

The 1972 Greeley study devoted much of its attention to priestly satisfaction, priestly identity, and the causes of priestly resignations. Using these data, Schoenherr and Greeley (1974) tested a model for predicting which priests will remain in ministry and which will resign. The decision to continue was predicted best by inverse relationships with the desire to marry, loneliness, and modern theological values (the more desire to marry, the more lonely, and the more modern, the less probability of continuing), and by positive relationships with age and work satisfaction (the older and more satisfied, the more probability of continuing). Later, Verdieck, Shields, and Hoge (1988) replicated the model with data from a 1985 survey of American priests. The level of morale rose and the probability of resigning fell from 1970 and 1985. The predictive model was similar, even though the priests in 1985 were older and reported less desire to marry. The reduced desire to marry was not explained solely by the older age of priests in 1985, and the authors speculated that the level of homosexuality had probably risen. Using the same data, Hoge, Shields, and Verdieck (1988) documented a shift toward a more conservative theology of the church among young priests, reversing the trend toward a more modern ecclesiology in the 1960s.

In a 1993 survey, Hoge, Shields, and Griffin (1995) again tested the determinants of morale and of thoughts of resigning. Morale was higher in 1993 than in 1970 and 1985, and the percentage of priests pondering resigning was lower; the main increase was among younger priests. Later Hoge and Wenger (2003) reported that a 2001 survey found a further increase in priestly morale among young priests. In earlier surveys the morale of young priests was lower than the morale of older priests, but in recent years the gap has disappeared, probably because priests are in great demand today and new ordinands need wait only a few years to become pastors.

Numerous surveys have asked priests from where they derive their greatest satisfaction in the priesthood. The surveys have had the same outcome: satisfaction comes most of all from sacramental and liturgical aspects of ministry, and second, from opportunities to be a part of people's lives. Other priestly roles, including social witness, administration, and leadership of the community, are less important sources of satisfaction (Hoge & Wenger, 2003).

From 1970 to 2001, surveys of American priests have found a shift in the self-identity of priests, from the "servant leader" model current right after the Second Vatican Council to the "cultic" model in the 1990s (Hoge & Wenger, 2003). The cultic model, which was dominant in the 1940s and 1950s, sees the liturgical, sacramental, and teaching tasks as the central role of the priesthood, with emphasis on the holiness and separateness of priests. The servant leader model, by contrast, stresses spiritual leadership of the community, service, and collaboration of priests with laypersons. It was dominant among American priests from

Vatican II until the early 1980s, whereafter the cultic model was again the choice of young priests, a shift which produced a young-versus-old tension among priests today. In England and Wales, Louden and Francis (2003) surveyed parish priests with similar results—that the oldest and youngest priests are more traditional in ecclesiology and in their definition of priesthood than the priests ordained in the 1970s and 1980s.

Several studies have sought to find the determinants of priestly resignations. The largest effort was in 1970, as part of the Greeley study. Greeley gathered a sample of resignees from 1966 through 1969 and found that the two main reasons they left were a feeling that they could no longer live within the authority structure of the Church and a desire to marry (Greeley, 1972, p. 283). In 2000, Hoge (2002) interviewed a sample of priests ordained within the past eight years who had already resigned. He found that two conditions are necessary to produce a resignation: (1) The priest must feel lonely or unappreciated; and (2) he either falls in love, or rejects celibate living, or has a disillusioning experience, or (if he is homosexual) wants a homosexual partner. Unlike the resignees in 1970, almost nobody in 2000 mentioned the difficulty of ministering within the authority structure of the Church. Also unlike 1970, the desire for homosexual partners was openly discussed in 2000.

Sexuality and Homosexuality

Interest in the sexuality of priests arises from the vows of celibacy for the Roman Catholic priesthood, yet the common knowledge in many nations that a portion of the priests were not observing the vow. This situation was not researched in any systematic way until recently. The first description of the sexual practices of American priests was by Sipe (1990; 2003) based on his decades of practice as a psychoanalyst helping priests and women involved with priests. He estimated that about 20% of priests at any time are involved in heterosexual relations, and about 25 to 50% have a homosexual orientation (some of whom are active). His conclusions were widely attacked as being based on nonrandom samples, yet other Catholic leaders in positions to know the facts did not disagree with him. In the 1980s several researchers tried to estimate the percentage of American priests who have a homosexual orientation (Wolf, 1989) and came up with estimates ranging between 25 and 55%.

A scandal of priestly abuse of children and youth erupted in the 1980s and 1990s. The scandal to the Catholic community was more in the way the pedophiles and ephebophiles were defended and managed by bishops than in the acts of these miscreants themselves. Research on this topic has been scant due to the limitations of confidentiality. Two reviews of existing research were published by Shupe (1998) and Plante (1999). Research by John Jay College of Criminal Justice, sponsored by the Catholic bishops, found that 4% of priests active in the last five decades had accusations of sexual abuse of minors (USCCB, 2004).

Research on Lay Ministers

Because of the priest shortage, increasing numbers of professional lay ministers have been appointed to Catholic parishes in the United States. Two surveys of lay ministers were done in 1992 and 1997 (Murnion, 1992; Murnion & DeLambo, 1999), which described the lay ministers and the increase in their numbers. By 1997 there were more professional lay ministers working in American parishes than priests (29,000 compared with 27,000), of which 82% were female and 42% had a Master's degree or more. Their numbers increased

35% from 1992 to 1997. This raises issues of how well priests will collaborate with lay ministers.

Can lay ministers carry out effective leadership in Catholic parishes? Wallace (1992; 2003) visited priestless parishes to see how the lay administrators were faring. In this type of parish, which in 2002 comprised 16% of all American parishes, the lay leaders were being well received by laity, yet awkward problems remained concerning status and recognition by priests. Are lay ministers too expensive? A study by Hoge, Carroll, and Scheets (1988) inquired into the total financial cost of priests compared with the cost of lay ministers and Protestant clergy. Priests are more expensive to the institution than are lay ministers, but they are less expensive than Protestant ministers by about 20 to 30%. Are lay ministers satisfied? Wittberg (1993) surveyed lay ministers, members of religious orders, and priests to assess their job satisfaction, and found the lay ministers to be less satisfied than the others. Davidson, Walters, Cisco, Meyer, and Zech (2003) surveyed lay ministers to learn of their personal spiritual practices and found them to be committed and satisfied.

RESEARCH ON OTHER CLERGY

Sociological research on other religious leaders is scarce. There is only one published sociological study of Eastern Orthodox priests, done by Schuller, Strommen, and Brekke (1980) as part of a multidimensional study of expected ministerial roles. Orthodox clergy and laity agree that the sacramental-liturgical function is central to the priesthood. The priest is set apart in the office of priest, and the particular human who takes this office is of secondary importance. Community leadership roles and social activism are of no great concern. Most important is that the priest carries out the sacramental duties unerringly, teaches the tradition, and lives an exemplary holy life. This model of priesthood is similar to the cultic model of pre-Vatican Catholicism, as discussed earlier. But Orthodox secular clergy (not monks) may marry, and the vast majority are married (see Allen, 2001).

Sociological research on Jewish rabbis is scant; only a few studies have been published. Jewish rabbis are, in organizational terms, similar to free-church Protestant clergy in that they are directly responsible to the board of trustees of the congregation they serve; there is no higher branch (denominational) authority. The main topics of research involving rabbis have been their views of interfaith marriage, Jewish outreach, and Jewish identity. Mayer conducted a 1997 survey of American rabbis on interfaith marriages. Thirty-six percent of the rabbis said they would officiate at an interfaith wedding, but the numbers ranged widely, from zero among the Orthodox and Conservative rabbis to 62% of the Reconstructionist rabbis (Mayer, 1997).

Cohen, Kress, and Davidson (2003) surveyed 465 conservative rabbis and 560 lay leaders in synagogues, investigating rabbis' roles and satisfactions. They asked the rabbis and lay leaders to rate the importance of different roles a rabbi must play; both saw the roles of Jewish educator and pastor as being foremost. By contrast, both the rabbis and lay leaders rated managerial and administrative roles as least important. The rabbis reported that they wished they could spend more time in study and in-service training, and less time attending meetings and doing management tasks.

As with Protestant denominations, Jewish branches in America have varied in the degree to which they welcome women rabbis. At present the Orthodox branch has none, the Conservative branch has about 12%, the Reform branch about 22%, and the Reconstructionist branch, about 47% (Berkofsky, n.d.). Women rabbis find placement more difficult than men, a situation that one woman rabbi referred to as the "matzoh ceiling" (Firestone, 2003).

Literature on Muslim imams is mainly theological and historical. I know of only two sociological studies which include information on imams. The first is a survey of mosques in America (Bagby, Perl, & Froehle, 2001). It found that, compared with Christian churches, mosques have fewer staff; 55% have no paid full-time staff, and only 10% have more than two paid staff. Eighty-one percent have an imam, and the rest are led by learned laypersons willing to volunteer. Of all the imams, roughly 50% are paid and full time. This is the situation even though mosques are large; the average number of persons associated in any way with a mosque was 1625, and average attendance at Friday prayers was 292. An estimated 36% of imams have formal Islamic education.

Structurally, the majority of mosques resemble nonhierarchical Protestant churches in that final decision making rests not with the clergyperson but with a lay board of directors. But in 28% of the mosques, the imam has final decision-making power. There is no Muslim analog to denominational authority. Most mosques in the United States were established recently, since sizeable Muslim immigration took place only after 1970 (see Nimer, 2002).

INTERPRETATIONS OF THE ROLE OF CLERGY

Trends in clergy and religious leadership can best be understood when research findings are interpreted in terms of broader social change. I will point to four topics in which wider interpretation is crucial.

Egalitarianism and Loss of Authority

Over the centuries, societies have defined clergy in various ways. In ancient Judaism, priests were a separate tribe (Levites) which had legitimation for its teachings and its status. In Hindu culture a separate caste (brahmans) developed with similar legitimation. In medieval Catholicism, clergy were required to be celibate to avoid development of any dynasties or tribes, and they were given special privileges by the secular rulers in return for the support they gave to existing monarchs. During the Protestant Reformation, the special theological status of priests was attacked by the Lutheran doctrine of the "priesthood of all believers," which removed Holy Orders from the list of sacraments and demoted clergy from their exalted theological status. In the French Revolution, political and legal privileges of Catholic priests and bishops were removed. A strong anticlericalism spread across Europe after the French Revolution and strongly influenced the Founding Fathers of the United States. In sum, the definition of clergy has changed over time and will continue to change.

An attack on clerical authority has continued to this day. In American Protestantism it has proceeded very far, so that Protestant ministers today are perceived to possess limited authority solely by virtue of ordination. Instead, Protestant ministers need to win personal authority from their flocks through their own personal actions. The American Catholic culture is proceeding in the same direction decade by decade, with less and less authority being accorded by Catholic laity to priests and bishops. Surveys of Catholics show a gradual shift toward egalitarianism and withdrawal of ecclesial authority by the laity (D'Antonio, Davidson, Hoge, & Meyer, 2001).

If laity accord less and authority to clergy, how does this change ministry? How does it change the role of clergy? Is there still a role for a clergy if it has little authority? Probably, with a more educated and autonomous laity in the future, demands and expectations put on clergy will be higher than in the past, and clergy will be less able to fall back on institutionalized status for influence ("Do not forget, I am an ordained minister"). Possibly new forms of religious leadership will arise, which are less tied to traditional denominations than in the past.

Clergy as Professionals

Most sociological studies of clergy have been practical investigations aimed at solving problems. A major contribution they have made is that they have produced comparative information. Denominational leaders commonly lack information about other religions and other institutions, making comparative research very helpful.

From the vantage of broader social science, the clergy is a profession, yet a profession with some special characteristics. Like other professionals, clergy are a defined group of trained persons who possess knowledge and skills not accessible to the general public, persons who are relatively autonomous in that they are entitled to make judgments based on their expertise, and who are largely self-governing as a group. Like other professionals, clergy claim to have authority in their own domain, and this gives them status and influence. But unlike most other professionals, clergy are presumed to be in their positions out of religious motivation, not out of hope for monetary gain, and their role as ministers is presumed to be primary in their lives. In some religious groups such as Roman Catholics, clergy are presumed to live an ascetic life apart from the rest of the population. In Protestantism, married clergy are expected to have spouses who are helpmates in ministry or at least willing to subordinate family concerns to the demands of ministry. Also unlike most other professionals, Protestant clergy are employed by their constituents, and they need to maintain support from their members if they are to succeed. No other profession is subject to approval by a lay constituency in this way—which makes clergypersons resemble local politicians. Clergy are professionals, but different from most other professionals.

Should they see themselves as professionals? It has been argued that the perception of clergy as professionals would add to their influence in the general public and to their occupational satisfaction. By contrast, many ministers and priests asked, "Why be a professional? Was Jesus Christ a professional? Won't this remove us from close identification with our flock?" In Catholic circles, there is debate as to whether the priesthood is a profession or a religious *vocation* defined theologically (Hoge, Shields, & Griffin, 1995). More comparative study of professionals, including clergy, is needed to help everyone clarify questions of identity and role.

The Arrival of Women Ministers

Since the 1970s, the number of women ministers has risen dramatically in many denominations, but not all. Women clergy are still not accepted in the Roman Catholic Church, the Lutheran Church–Missouri Synod, and a few smaller evangelical bodies. The clergy has been slower to accept women than have other comparable professions and occupations, including law, medicine, social work, and academic work. The greater acceptance of women in other learned occupations has put pressure on the remaining denominations which don't accept women—especially the Roman Catholic Church. Broad social trends toward empowerment of women will put pressure on all religious traditions.

In this regard, we need to mention the issue of openly homosexual clergy. Should they be accepted, or not? Is open homosexuality something permitted by the teaching of the New Testament? Is their lifestyle an impediment to ministry, or not? Are there special forms of ministry for which they are suited, even uniquely suited, or not? An emotional and fractious debate has arisen in recent decades in all Christian denominations, and it promises to be a topic of both practical and theoretical interest in the future. Christian denominations, both Protestant and Catholic, are of mixed minds on the acceptance of openly homosexual clergy. Meanwhile, nationwide polls in the United States show increased acceptance of the homosexual lifestyle (Hoge & Wenger, 2003, p. 107). Broader social trends will be a source of pressures on churches.

Ecumenism

A final angle for viewing clergy is that of globalization and vanishing boundaries. Today's world has fewer barriers and boundaries than ever. Flows of international information are unprecedented. International travel is at an all-time high. Contact of Christians with devotees of other world religions is more frequent than ever, disallowing old-style demonizing or stereotyping of other religions. Other religions can less easily be dismissed as pagan or primitive. In a situation of prolonged cross-religious contact, the theological issues of universalism or particularism rise higher than ever. No longer can a minister preach that those who do not accept Jesus Christ will be sent to hell, because it will occur to everyone listening that millions of people born in other nations, who never heard of Jesus Christ in their lives, are thus too facilely consigned to eternal flames.

The problems of ecumenism will loom larger than ever in our new globalized society, affecting clergy and laity alike. Denominations will continue to legitimate clergy through their rules and rituals of ordination, but the specific authority of individual denominations probably cannot be maintained intact, and, hence, the definitions of who is clergy and who is a legitimate religious leader will change.

The sociology of clergy has been narrow and practical in the past, but today it needs to broaden its scope. It needs to learn from diverse scholarly communities working on organizations, professions, gender, and globalization. In turn, the sociology of clergy can enrich other sociological specialties to the benefit of all.

REFERENCES

Allen, J. J. (Ed.). (2001). *Vested in grace: Priesthood and marriage in the Christian East.* Brookline, MA: Holy Cross Orthodox Press.

Bagby, I., Perl, P. M., & Froehle, B. T. (2001). *The mosque in America: A national portrait.* Report. Washington, DC: Council on American-Islamic Relations.

Benda, B. B., & DiBlasio, F. A. (1996). Clergy marriages: A multivariate model of marital adjustment. In L. J. Francis & S. H. Jones (Eds.), *Psychological perspectives on Christian* ministry (pp. 323–334). Leominster, Wales: Gracewing.

Berkofsky, J. (n.d.) For female rabbis, finding a pulpit is easy, but getting equal pay is another matter. *JTA News,* Sept. 17. www.jta.org.

Blanton, P. W. (1992). Stress in clergy families: Managing work and family demands. *Family Perspectives, 26,* 315–330.

Blanton, P. W., & Morris. M. L. (1999). Work-related predictors of physical symptomatology and emotional well-being among clergy and spouses. *Review of Religious Research, 40,* 331–348.

Blizzard, S. W. (1956, April 25). The minister's dilemma. *Christian Century, 73,* 508–510.

Blizzard, S. W., & Blizzard, H. B. (1985). *The Protestant parish minister: A behavioral science interpretation.* Storrs, CT: Society for the Scientific Study of Religion.

Brunnette-Hill, S., & Finke, R. (1999). A time for every purpose under heaven: Updating and extending Blizzard's survey on clergy time allocation. *Review of Religious Research, 41,* 48–64.

Carroll, J. W., Hargrove, B., & Lummis, A. T. (1981). *Women of the cloth: A new opportunity for the churches.* New York: Harper & Row.

Carroll, J. W., Wheeler, B., Aleshire, D. O., & Marler, P. L. (1997). *Being there: Culture formation in two theological schools.* New York: Oxford University Press.

Chang, P. M. Y. (1997). In search of a pulpit: Sex differences in the transition from seminary training to the first parish. *Journal for the Scientific Study of Religion, 36,* 614–627.

Chang, P. M. Y. (2004). *Assessing the clergy supply in the 21st century.* Durham, NC: Duke Divinity School, Pulpit and Pew Report.

Chaves, M. (1997). *Ordaining women: Culture and conflict in religious organizations.* Cambridge, MA: Harvard University Press.

Cohen, S. M., Kress, J. S., & Davidson, A. (2003). Rating rabbinic roles: A survey of conservative congregational rabbis and lay leaders. *Conservative Judaism, 56,* 71–89.

D'Antonio, W. V., Davidson, J. D., Hoge, D. R., & Meyer, K. (2001). *American Catholics: Gender, generation, and commitment.* New York: AltaMira.

Davidson, J. D., Walters, T. P., Cisco, B., Meyer, K., and Zech, C. E. (2003). *Lay ministers and their spiritual practices.* Huntington, IN: Our Sunday Visitor.

Fichter, J. H. (1968). *America's forgotten priests: What they are saying.* New York: Harper & Row.

Fichter, J. H. (1961). *Religion as an occupation.* Notre Dame, IN: University of Notre Dame Press.

Firestone, T. (2003). *The receiving.* San Francisco: HarperSan Francisco Press.

Francis, L. J. & Rodger, R. (1996). The influence of personality on clergy role prioritisation, role influences, conflict, and dissatisfaction with ministry. In L. J. Francis & S. H. Jones (Eds.), *Psychological perspectives on Christian ministry* (pp. 65–81). Leominster, Wales: Gracewing.

Francis, L. J. & Jones. S. H. (Ed.) (1996). *Psychological perspectives on Christian ministry.* Leominster, Wales: Gracewing.

Garelli, F. (Ed.) (2003). *Sfide per la Chiesa del nuovo secolo: Indagine sul clero in Italia.* Bologna, Italy: Societa Editrice il Mulino.

Greeley, A. M. (1972). *The Catholic priest in the United States: Sociological investigations.* Washington, DC: United States Catholic Conference.

Harper, C. L., & Schulte-Murray, R. K. (1998). Religion and the sociology of culture: Exploring the organizational cultures of two midwestern Roman Catholic dioceses. *Review of Religious Research, 40,* 101–119.

Hoge, D. R. (1987). *The future of Catholic leadership: Responses to the priest shortage.* Kansas City, MO: Sheed & Ward.

Hoge, D. R. (2002). *The first five years of the priesthood: A study of newly ordained Catholic priests.* Collegeville, MN: Liturgical Press.

Hoge, D. R., Carroll, J. W., & Scheets, F. K. (1998). *Patterns of parish leadership: Cost and effectiveness in four denominations.* Kansas City, MO: Sheed and Ward.

Hoge, D. R., Dyble, J. E., & Polk, D. T. (1981). Influence of role preference and role clarity on vocational commitment of Protestant ministers. *Sociological Analysis, 42,* 1–16.

Hoge, D. R., Shields, J. J., & Griffin, D. L. (1995). Changes in satisfaction and institutional attitudes of Catholic priests. *Sociology of Religion, 56,* 195–213.

Hoge, D. R., Shields, J. J., & Verdieck, M. J. (1988). Changing age distribution and theological attitudes of Catholic priests, 1970–1985. *Sociological Analysis, 49,* 264–280.

Hoge, D. R., & Wenger, J. E. (2003). *Evolving visions of the priesthood: Changes from Vatican II to the turn of the new century.* Collegeville, MN: Liturgical Press.

Kennedy, E. C. & Heckler, V. J. (1972). *The Catholic priest in the United States: Psychological investigations.* Washington, DC: United States Catholic Conference.

King, E. (1994). Introduction and statistical overview. *CARA formation directory for men and women religious, 1994–1995.* Washington, DC: CARA, Georgetown University.

Lee, C. (1999). Specifying intrusive demands and their outcomes in congregational ministry: A report on the ministry demands inventory. *Journal for the Scientific Study of Religion, 38,* 477–489.

Lehman, E. C. (1985). *Women clergy: Breaking through gender barriers.* New Brunswick, NJ: Transaction.

Lehman, E. C. (1993). *Gender and work: The case of the clergy.* Albany: State University of New York Press.

Lehman, E. C. (2002). *Women's path into ministry: Six major studies.* Durham, NC: Duke University Pulpit and Pew Project.

Louden, S. H., & Francis, L. J. (2003). *The naked parish priest: What priests really think they're doing.* London: Continuum.

Lummis, A. T. (2003). What do lay people want in pastors? Answers from lay search committee chairs and regional judicatory leaders. *Pulpit and Pew: Research on Pastoral Leadership, 3,* 1–49.

Mayer, E. (1997). *What do rabbis think and do about intermarriage? Highlights of a new survey of the American rabbinate.* New York: Jewish Outreach Institute.

Mills, E. W., & Koval, J. P. (1971). *Stress in the ministry.* Washington, DC: Ministry Studies Board.

Menges, R. J. and Dittes, J. E. (1965). *Psychological studies of clergymen: Abstracts of research.* New York: Thomas Nelson and Sons.

Monahan, S. C. (1999). Role ambiguity among Protestant clergy: Consequence of the activated laity. *Review of Religious Research, 41,* 80–95.

Morris, M. L., & Blanton, P. W. (1994). The influence of work-related stressors on clergy husbands and their wives. *Family Relations, 43,* 189–195.

Murnion, P. J. (1992). *New parish ministers: Laity and religious on parish staffs.* New York: National Pastoral Life Center.

Murnion, P. J., & DeLambo, D. (1999). *Parishes and parish ministers: A study of parish lay ministry.* New York: National Pastoral Life Center.

Nauss, A. (1994). Ministerial effectiveness in ten functions. *Review of Religious Research, 36,* 58–69.

Nesbitt, P. D. (1995). Marriage, parenthood, and the ministry: Differential effects of marriage and family on male and female clergy careers. *Sociology of Religion, 56,* 397–416.

Nesbitt, P. D. (1997). *Feminization of the clergy in America: Occupational and organizational perspectives.* New York: Oxford University Press.

Nimer, M. (2002). *The North American Muslim resource guide.* New York: Routledge.

Perl, P. (2002). Gender and mainline Protestant pastors' allocation of time to work tasks. *Journal for the Scientific Study of Religion, 41,* 169–178.

Pino, C. J. (1980). Interpersonal needs, counselor style, and personality change among seminarians during the 1970s. *Review of Religious Research, 21,* 351–367.

Plante, T. G. (Ed.) (1999). *Bless me father for I have sinned: Perspectives on sexual abuse committed by Roman Catholic priests.* Westport, CT: Praeger.

Pryor, R. J. (1982). *High calling, high stress—the vocational needs of ministers: An overview and bibliography.* Bedford Park, Australia: Australian Association for the Study of Religions.

Schilderman, H. (1998). *Pastorale professionalisering. (Pastoral professionalization.)* Kampen, Netherlands: Kok.

Schoenherr, R. A. (2002). *Goodbye father: The celibate male priesthood and the future of the Catholic church.* New York: Oxford University Press.

Schoenherr, R. A., & Greeley, A. M. (1974). Role commitment processes and the American Catholic priesthood. *American Sociological Review, 39,* 407–25.

Schoenherr, R. A., & Young, L. A. (1993). *Full pews and empty altars: Demographics of the priest shortage in United States Catholic dioceses.* Madison: The University of Wisconsin Press.

Schoenherr, R. A., Young, L. A., & Vilarino, J. P. (1988). Demographic transitions in religious organizations: A comparative study of priest decline in Roman Catholic dioceses. *Journal for the Scientific Study of Religion, 27,* 499–523.

Schreuder, O. (1970). A review of ministry studies. *Social Compass, 17,* 579–588.

Schuller, D. S., Strommen, M. P., & Brekke, M. L. (Eds.). (1980). *Ministry in America.* San Francisco: Harper and Row.

Schuth, K. (1999). *Seminaries, theologates, and the future of church ministry: An analysis of trends and transitions.* Collegeville, MN: Liturgical Press.

Shupe, A. (Ed.) (1998). *Wolves within the fold: Religious leadership and abuses of power.* New Brunswick, NJ: Rutgers University Press.

Sipe, A. W. R. (1990). *A secret world: Sexuality and the search for celibacy.* New York: Brunner/Mazel.

Sipe, A. W. R. (2003). *Celibacy in crisis: A secret world revisited.* New York: Brunner-Routledge.

Stark, R. (1998). Catholic contexts: Competition, commitment, and innovation. *Review of Religious Research, 39,* 197–208.

Stark, R., & Finke, R. (2000). Catholic religious vocations: Decline and revival. *Review of Religious Research, 42,* 125–145.

USCCB. (2004, May 2nd). *The nature and scope of the problem of sexual abuse of minors by Catholic priests and deacons in the United States.* Report. Washington, DC: United States Conference of Catholic Bishops. www.nccbuscc.org/nrb/

Verdieck, M. J., Shields, J. J., & Hoge, D. R. (1988). Role commitment processes revisited: American Catholic priests 1970 and 1985. *Journal for the Scientific Study of Religion, 27,* 524–535.

Vilarino, J. P., & Tizon, J. S. (1998). The demographic transition of the Catholic priesthood and the end of clericalism in Spain. *Sociology of Religion, 59,* 25–35.

Wallace, R. A. (1992). *They call her pastor: A new role for Catholic women.* Albany: State University of New York Press.

Wallace, R. A. (2003). *They call him pastor: Married men in charge of Catholic parishes.* New York: Paulist Press.

Wheeler, B. G. (2001, April 11). Fit for ministry: A new profile of seminarians. *Christian Century,* 16–23.

Wittberg, P. (1993). Job satisfaction among lay, clergy and religious order workers for the Catholic church: A preliminary investigation. *Review of Religious Research, 35,* 19–33.

Wolf, J. G. (Ed.) (1989). *Gay priests.* New York: Harper & Row.

Young, L. A. (1998). Assessing and updating the Schoenherr-Young projections of clergy decline in the United States Roman Catholic church. *Sociology of Religion, 59,* 7–23.

Zikmund, B. B., Lummis, A. T., & Chang, P. M. Y. (1998). *Clergy women: An uphill calling.* Louisville, KY: Westminster/John Knox Press.

Zulehner, P. M. (2002) *Priester in modernisierungsstress.* Ostfildern, Germany: Schwabenverlag.

PART VII

RELIGION AND SOCIAL INSTITUTIONS IN A GLOBAL/TRANSNATIONAL PERSPECTIVE

CHAPTER 20

Immigration

Peggy Levitt

Sainthood is an unlikely title for a soldier accused of rape and murder and later executed for his alleged misdeeds. But Juan Castillo Morales, affectionately known as Juan Soldado, has become the unofficial patron saint of poor Mexicans trying to cross the U.S. border. Because, as the legend goes, Castillo Morales was unjustly blamed for a crime committed by his superiors, he has become a symbol of those who are treated unfairly and let down by the justice system. "He is very miraculous," said Luis Jiménez, a 60-year-old Mexican now living in Tijuana. When trying to cross the border from Mexico into California, Jiménez fell into a ditch and broke his ankle. He believed that he would perish in the parched desert all alone. Instead, a pickup truck appearing out of nowhere, drove by and found him. The California family not only rescued him but delivered him back across the border to a hospital in Mexico. "I believe that Juan Soldado sent them to find me," said Jimenez (Watson 2001, p. 1). Ever since, he visits the soldier's tomb to thank him every year.

This story suggests that religion introduces a unique set of questions about the American immigrant experience, guided by different ontological and epistemological assumptions, and requiring different kinds of data in response. Religion provides followers with symbols, rituals, and narratives with which to create alternative landscapes that fit within, transcend, or supersede national boundaries. These can facilitate host-country assimilation, encourage enduring homeland ties, or render such orientations meaningless because what really matters to the individual is belonging to a religious space.

As a result, religion reorients debates about immigration by expanding the boundaries of questions about incorporation and membership. It is not enough to focus only on the religious experience in the United States or on religion's role in incorporating newcomers and their offspring. Rather, we must ask how individuals use religion to become part of the countries that receive them, to stay connected to their countries of origin, or to imagine themselves in some other kind of spatial and temporal geography that overlaps with or takes precedence over political boundaries. Scholarship on religion and immigration should explore how these different kinds of memberships advance or impede each other. How does religion allow individuals to extricate themselves from some communities, reinsert themselves in others, or to imagine alternative social groups? To what extent are access and

PEGGY LEVITT • Wellesley College, Wellesley, Massachusetts 02481

power redistributed in the process and what kinds of alliances and conflicts arise in response (Cadena, 1998; Macguire, 1997)?

WHAT IS RELIGION?

National surveys reveal that the majority of American adults have a religious affiliation (59%), believe in God (95%) and the afterlife (80%), pray (90%), read the Bible (69%), and that a substantial number (40%) report regular attendance at a place of worship. In addition, 87% say that religion is important in their lives (Dillon, 2003). The United States is clearly a religious country.

But what does this actually mean? Debates over how to define religion generally revolve around two themes. Some scholars favor functional definitions while others adopt more substantive approaches. There are also those who define religion restrictively and those who advocate for a more expansive view (Hervieu-Léger, 2000). More often than not, substantive definitions, which focus on what religion is, tend to be restrictive and functional, whereas those which center on what religion does, tend to be more expansive (Beyer, 2001).

Those in the restrictive camp want to limit the study of religion to beliefs, institutions, and practices (Griel & Bromley, 2003). For them, the defining characteristic of religion is the reference to the "supernatural" or the "superempirical." "Inclusivists" argue for a definition of religion that embraces activities, ideologies, and structures that seem to share common features with religion although they are not always labeled as such. The essential feature, from this perspective, is not the reference to the supernatural but the ability to provide an overarching structure of meaning or grounding for the self. To bridge this divide, Griel and Bromley (2003) define religion as a category of social interaction and discourse whose meaning and implications are constantly negotiated. The core of the religious does not lie in doctrine but in the subjective experience and system of discourse of the practitioners. The everyday lived experience of religion matters just as much as theology or institutional practice (Hall, 1997).

According to Orsi (2003, p. 172):

> The study of lived religion situates all religious creativity within culture and approaches all religion as lived experience, theology no less than lighting a candle for a troubled loved one, spirituality as well as other, less culturally sanctioned forms of religious expression. Rethinking religion as a form of cultural work, the study of lived religion directs attention to institutions and persons, texts and rituals, practice and theology, things and ideas–as media of making and unmaking worlds. The key questions concern what people do with religious idioms, how they use them, what they make of themselves and their worlds with them, and how, in turn, men, women and children are shaped by the worlds they are making as they make these worlds.

From this perspective, the expectation that one identity be associated with one place is abandoned. Instead, the religious experience produces both hybrid individual and collective identities because it lies at the intersection of multiple life worlds and the ongoing interplay of "delocalization and relocalization" (Orsi, 1999). Global religious practices and ideologies interact with lived religion—specific religious practices, discourses, and institutions that are the stuff of daily religious experience.

Religious experience not only transforms notions of belonging and space but also those of time. Vásquez and Marquardt (2003) argue that to understand Latino religious life in the context of globalization, a hemispheric approach is required. In a globalized world, religion reorders time and social boundaries rendering discussions of bounded national religious practices off the mark. Individuals use religion to create new spatio-temporal arrangements and invent new mental maps with which to locate themselves within terrains that are constantly changed by globalization.

Scholars of the Latino religious experience have suggested several terms that capture the syncretism and synthesis that characterizes religious traditions in general. Elizondo (2000) proposes the idea of a *segundo mestizaje* to capture the mixing of two elements into a third. Understanding Mexican American religious traditions demands taking into account the two conquests that Mexican Americans have endured—the Spanish conquest of the indigenous peoples in the territories that became new Spain (and later Mexico) and the U.S. conquest of what is now the Southwest. Clearly distinguishing between "traditional" Mexican immigrants and their culture and more "assimilated" Mexican Americans creates a false dichotomy that misses the varied ways in which Mexican-descent residents respond to the U.S. milieu. Because Mexican immigrants, and some Mexican Americans, travel so frequently across the border, assessing the ways in which they collectively identify, and relegating individuals into distinct groups that have either lost or retained their language and culture is extremely problematic.

Others suggest the term, *nepantla,* or middle place, to characterize Latino religious practice (Espinosa, Elizondo, & Miranda, 2003). These individuals live in between, moving back and forth in a world that is not meant to be coherent but that tolerates and builds upon these differences. It is a borderlands world in which meanings, perspectives, and cosmologies, either in part or in their entirety, collide. The primary characteristic of this new worldview is found precisely in the colliding. Because this system of meaning is elastic and constantly evolving, it can bridge modern dichotomies such as individual and the community, the material and the spiritual, the public and private, or life and death (Goizueta, 2002).

In many traditions, then, syncretism, in-betweeness, and hybridity are the rule rather than the exception. Furthermore, looking only at officially sanctioned religious expressions within institutional contexts obscures critical parts of the story. Home-based, folk practices that combine official rituals with other traditions are at the heart of many religious experiences. What people do and say in the privacy of their own homes or in small, lay-led groups, and how they understand and interpret their activities, is often at the core of religious experience.

RELIGION AND THE "OLD AND NEW IMMIGRANTS"

How does this conceptualization of religion, and the assumptions embedded in it, dovetail with the study of immigrant religion in the United States?

Most of the newcomers arriving during the first great wave of immigration to the United States (1850–1924) came from Europe. They transformed the national religious fabric from one that was overwhelmingly Protestant to one which gradually incorporated Catholics and Jews. Following 40 years of restricted entry, the Hart-Cellar Act of 1965 radically altered U.S. immigration policy and dramatically changed the ethnic and religious origins of subsequent newcomers. Not only did the principal sending regions shift from Europe to Latin America and Asia but, as a result, Buddhism, Hinduism, and Islam also assumed their place among U.S. religious communities.

Studying the national origins of immigrants is much easier than studying their religious affiliations. The U.S. Census, the Immigration and Naturalization Service, and other government agencies are prohibited from collecting data on religious affiliations. Until recently, scholars of migration largely ignored the role of religion in the immigrant experience and scholars of religion paid little attention to immigrants. Whereas the General Social Survey (GSS) has studied the religious composition of the native-born population, it has not been possible to systematically study how immigrants shape the composition of religion or the spiritual life of the United States. No data on religious affiliation or religiosity based on a probability sample drawn from a well-defined population have been available (Jasso, Massey, Rosenzweig, & Smith, 2002). It is particularly difficult to make comparisons across immigrant groups.

The vast majority of Americans (over four fifths) identify as Christians. According to the 2002 General Social Survey, nearly two thirds (61%) are Protestant. The second largest group is Catholic (25%), whereas those claiming no religion make up 14% of the surveyed population. Jews and "Christians" make up 1.7% and 2.4%, respectively. In 2000, the Glenmary Research Center estimated membership in the Latter-Day Saints at 2.4 million, Conservative Christian and Churches of Christ at 1.4 million, Assemblies of God at 2.5 million, Roman Catholic Church at 62 million, Southern Baptists at 20 million, Jewish congregations at 6.1 million and Muslims at 1.5 million (Jones et al., 2002).

The profile of Hispanic Americans, the largest racial/ethnic group in the country, is somewhat different. The majority are Catholic (70%), whereas 23% claim to belong to a Protestant faith (Espinosa et al., 2003). Eighty-eight percent of Latino Protestants identity as Evangelical or "born-again" and 64% are members of Pentecostal or charismatic denominations (Espinosa et al., 2003).

Religiosity differs among native and foreign-born Americans. Among Protestants, only 4% are foreign-born compared to 12.5% of Catholics. This figure rises slightly among the second generation with 5% of the children of immigrants identifying as Protestant compared to 22% among Catholics. The foreign-born are the majority among Buddhists, Hindus, and Muslims, ranging from 50 to 75%. Roughly two thirds of both foreign and native-born report that they believe strongly in God. The native-born, however, are slightly more likely to agree with the statement, "I know God really exists but have doubts" (17% compared to 12% of the foreign-born). Most Americans report that they pray regularly, regardless of their birthplace. Although 62% of native-born Americans say they are church members, only 42% of the foreign-born make this claim. Both groups claim to attend church regularly (GSSDIRS 1972–2000).

The New Immigrant Survey, a large-scale sample of new legal immigrants will provide high-quality, public-use data on the religious life of immigrants and their children for the first time. A pilot study done in 1996 to prepare for this larger effort offers a first look at the religious lives of authorized immigrants soon after their arrival into the United States. The study revealed that two thirds of the new immigrants were Christian, substantially below the 82% of the native-born surveyed in the 1996 General Social Survey. The countries that sent the most Protestants were Mexico (12%), Jamaica (12%), and the former Soviet Union (6%). The proportion of Catholics among the new immigrants was 42%, almost twice as large as among the native-born (22%). The countries contributing the most new Catholics were Mexico (28%) and the Philippines (13%). The proportion of respondents that classified themselves as non Judeo-Christians was more than four times larger among recent immigrants than among the native-born (17 vs. 4%). Eight percent of respondents said they were Muslim, four percent claimed to be Buddhist, and three percent identified as Hindu. New Jewish and Hindu immigrants came overwhelming from the former Soviet Union (70%) and India (60%) respectively. In contrast, Buddhists and Muslims came from a variety of countries including Pakistan (18%) and Bangladesh (11%) for Muslims and Taiwan (21%), Thailand (20%), and Vietnam (17%) for Buddhists. Finally, 15% of the new immigrants reported no religious affiliation as opposed to 12% among the native-born (Jasso et al., 2002).

CONCEPTUAL AND METHODOLOGICAL IMPERATIVES FOR STUDYING THE RELIGIOUS LIVES OF "NEW" IMMIGRANTS

The New Immigrant Survey is one of several efforts undertaken in the last decade to rectify the lack of attention paid to religion in the immigrant experience. Much of this research takes Herberg's *Protestant, Catholic, Jew* as its point of departure. From its inception, American society was understood to include diverse and equal religious communities. As a result, collective religious identities have been one of the primary ways of structuring internal societal pluralism (Casanova, 2003). According to Herberg, immigrants were expected to retain their religion but to abandon their cultural and linguistic characteristics (Herberg, 1955). To be American was to be religious; moreover asserting a religious identity was an acceptable way to be American but to be different at the same time. In fact, Herberg predicted that ethnicity would ultimately wash out of the equation and that Irish, Italian, or Polish Catholics would eventually identify with one prong of the triple melting pot—Protestant, Catholic or Jew.

Clearly, Herberg underestimated the enduring salience of ethnicity in the United States. And, as Casanova (2003) points out, he also largely ignored race, the second key principle around which collective identities are organized. Race and religion work together but each according to its own logic. Racial differentiation is hierarchical, unequal, and discriminatory. Religious denominationalism, at least as defined by the Constitution, is egalitarian and positively promoted. It also involves a package of invisible, protected, voluntary resources that strongly affect the assimilation process.

Herberg also mistakenly focused on religion solely as a means of channeling host country incorporation. Clearly, national boundaries do not necessarily confine the religious lives of individuals nor are religious identities always predicated on a single membership. Increasing numbers of contemporary migrants belong to strong, enduring transnational social networks linking those who migrate with those who stay behind (Levitt, 2001b; Portes et al., 1999). They maintain regular, powerful contacts in their homelands and continue to organize some aspects of their lives across borders. As I will argue below, religious ideas and rituals, in particular, enable and are enabled by transnational membership.[1]

An enhanced set of methodological and conceptual tools is needed to capture the changing nature of contemporary migration and religious life. The first ontological shift is to locate the study of migrants and their religious practices more firmly within the social fields in which they are embedded. Social fields are the multiple interlocking networks of social relationships through which ideas, practices, and resources are unequally exchanged, organized, and transformed. Social fields are multidimensional, encompassing interactions of differing forms, depth, and breadth, such as organizations, institutions, and movements.

National boundaries are not necessarily contiguous with the boundaries of social fields. National social fields are those that stay within national boundaries, whereas transnational social fields connect actors, through direct and indirect relations across borders (Levitt & Glick Schiller, 2004).

Using a transnational optic is both a perspective and a variable. In each study, the researcher specifies the parameters of the social field of inquiry and empirically ascertains the scope, strength, and impact of its transnational elements. This is not to argue that all aspects of immigrants' religious lives are influenced by transnational factors. Rather, it is to argue for the need to begin the inquiry with a broad set of questions that take the interaction between homeland, host-country, and other kinds of cross-border factors into consideration.

Locating migrants within social fields is important for several reasons. First, it moves the analysis beyond the direct experience of migration to include those who do not actually move themselves but who maintain social relations across borders. Actual movement is not a prerequisite for engaging in transnational practices. Networks within the field connect people with no direct transborder connections to those without such connections (Levitt & Glick Schiller, 2004). Particular aspects of the religious lives of those who stay behind, and the religious institutions they belong to, may assume transnational properties in response to continuing ties between migrants and nonmigrants.

A social field perspective also brings to the fore the multiple layers and multiple settings that influence social experience. Migrants may carry out religious practices linking their sending community with a localized receiving context. But these localized ties often emerge within a multi-layered social field where cross-border connections develop between regional and national actors and institutions in the sending and receiving countries. Global values and institutions such as democracy, the free market, and the rule of law, that are promulgated by transnational institutions, the academy, NGOs, and the media also influence the transnational social field in which religious life is enacted.

Finally, locating migrants within transnational social fields makes clear that incorporation in a new state and enduring transnational attachments are not binary opposites. Instead, it is more useful to think of the migrant experience as a kind of gauge, which, although anchored, pivots between new land and a transnational incorporation. Movement and attachment is not linear or sequential but capable of rotating back and forth and changing direction over time. The median point on this gauge is not full incorporation but, rather, simultaneity of connection. Persons change and swing one way or the other depending on the context, thus moving our expectation away from either full assimilation or transnational connection but some combination of both (Levitt & Glick Schiller, 2004; Morawska, 2003).

RELIGION AND IMMIGRATION FROM A TRANSNATIONAL PERSPECTIVE

To date, only a very small body of research looks explicitly at religion from a transnational perspective. It is not my goal to comprehensively summarize this work or the work on immigration and religion.[2] Rather, it is to selectively review and synthesize research in these two arenas in an attempt to bring them in closer conversation with one another and to model directions for future research.

Not all religious cross-border connections are linked to migration. Many religions were organized across territories long before the emergence of the contemporary nation-state system. Merchant-traders, militias and missionaries have always carried religious visions, texts, and ideas across the seas and over the boundaries of nation, empire, and city-state (Mayaram, 2004). Many studies chart the course of Christian, Hindu, and Muslim beliefs and institutions that cross national-borders and that link various populations (Beyer, 2001; Robertson, 1991; Vertovec & Peach, 1997). These global religious institutions shape the transnational migration experience, whereas migrants push world religions to reinvent themselves through constantly renegotiated settlements between the global and the local (Levitt, 2003a).

Religion as a Tool for Producing, Reproducing, and Inventing Identity

A common set of themes concerns research on transnational migration and religion and on the immigrant religious experience. One is the role of religion in incorporation, whether it be into the host-country, the homeland, an imagined religious space, or some combination of the three. Until now, however, these three orientations have been treated as if they opposed one another, rather than as if they occurred simultaneously.

Religion provides symbols, rituals, and scripts used by individuals and religious organizations to affirm, pass on, or reinvent who they are. For example, the overlap between the Catholic religion and Latino or Latin American immigrant culture in the United States is often so strong that when families participate in baptisms, first communions, or marriages they are reasserting their religious and cultural identities at the same time. Frequently, Hindus from India, Muslims from Pakistan, and Catholics from Ireland are hard-pressed to distinguish what is "national" or "ethnic" about themselves and what is "religious" (Levitt 2003b). When migrants act out these identities, either privately and informally or collectively and institutionally, they express important parts of who they are and pass these formulations along to their children (Cook, 2000; Ebaugh, 2003; Hervieu-Léger, 2000).

Religion also satisfies human spiritual needs and provides solace. Religious institutions are familiar settings in what can be an unfamiliar, unfriendly world. Some religious communities function like extended families, their members filling in for distant relatives who cannot be present during an illness or a death because they live so far away. For instance, Menjívar's study of Salvadorans in three U.S. cities revealed that the church was "an effective antidote to forces that may undermine these immigrants' emotional, spiritual, material strength and resilience" despite differing urban contexts (2003, p. 15). In some cases, churchgoing strengthens families by changing behavior and providing a moral compass (Adams, 2002; Brusco, 1995).

Churchgoing also integrates members into ethnic and nonethnic social networks that provide information about jobs, housing, or social services. Because many first-generation immigrants worship in ethnically and linguistically segregated congregations, they meet others who are going through similar experiences or have already done so. Membership heightens access to social and cultural capital (Foley, McCarthy & Chaves, 2001; Greeley, 1997). Co-worshippers know about schools, doctors, and summer programs. They may know someone who can help find an apartment or a placement in an employment-training program.

Many religious communities, particularly Catholic and mainline Protestant denominations, provide social services, such as food pantries, emergency financial assistance, job hotlines, immigration status assistance, English-as-a-Second Language courses (ESL), citizenship advice, help for the undocumented, and Graduate Equivalency Diploma classes

(GED) (Ebaugh & Pipes, 2001; Guest, 2003). Ebaugh and Pipes (2001), however, found considerable variation in service provision across groups. Because many post-1965 immigrants come to the United States with advanced degrees and working English, they may not need the same kinds of services as low-skilled, non-English speakers or they may look to nonreligious organizations for support. Some faiths do not have strong traditions of combining social assistance with prayer.

Religious institutions have not always doubled as sites where groups could celebrate and teach the second generation about their traditions. The shifting orientations of the Catholic Church are a case in point. In the early 1900s, the Catholic Church established ethnic or national parishes, meant only as stopgap measures, where immigrants could pray in their own language and in their own style but were eventually expected to adopt Anglo-Catholic practices and English. The Second Vatican Council of the 1960s expanded the space for ethnic diversity within the Catholic Church as a whole. The Council wrested control from the clergy and returned it to lay members. It modernized the Church, democratized rituals so they were more accessible to followers, and mandated that variations in cultural expressions of faith be tolerated if not encouraged. As a result, Catholicism was no longer viewed as a European religion exported to other parts of the globe. The Church was "not bound exclusively and indissolubly to any race or nation, nor to any particular way of life or any customary patterns of living, ancient or recent" (Dolan, 2002, p. 219).

These reforms, which coincided with the Civil Rights and Black Power Movements in the United States, all drew attention to immigrant causes. The Liberation Theology movement, which reaffirmed the Church's commitment to fight for social justice and poverty alleviation by articulating a theology unique to the Spanish-speaking, was also gaining strength in Latin America. National Hispanic Pastoral Encounters were organized in 1972, 1979, and 1985 to respond to the Latino community, the Church's largest ethnic constituency. In a 1983 pastoral letter, entitled, "The Hispanic Presence: Challenge and Commitment," the Church finally laid to rest the notion of the melting pot and endorsed cultural pluralism as the guiding spirit of Hispanic ministry. The Hispanic community was now called a "blessing from God" which brought special gifts to the church (Dolan, 2002; Lampe, 1994).[3] These developments have led to certain irreversible changes in religion in the United States (Diaz-Stevens & Stevens-Arroyo, 1997:181).

As a result, Latino Catholic religious practice is no longer considered inferior to the Euro-American tradition. Permanent institutional spaces have been created for the maintenance of diverse language and cultural expressions. The Latino community has grown more confident and assertive about its unique approach to faith. In fact, during his 1996 visit to the United States, Pope John Paul II urged Latino youth to hold fast to their culture,

> The Pope also loves the sons and daughters of the church who speak Spanish. Many of you have been born here or have lived here for a long time. Others are more recent arrivals. But you all bear the mark of your cultural heritage, deeply rooted in the Catholic tradition. Keep alive that faith and culture. (cited in Díaz-Stevens & Stevens-Arroyo, 1997, p. 191)

Accepting and encouraging long-term ethnic and cultural diversity is not confined to the Catholic Church. A recent review of out-reach material to Latino immigrants published by nearly 30 Protestant Churches, ranging from the very liberal to the very conservative, found that each stressed reaching out to newcomers and welcoming them on their own terms. Leaders proposed a number of strategies to achieve this including advocacy around immigration policy and worker's rights to aggressive church planting (Levitt, 2004a).

Participation in religious rituals and institutions not only fosters host-country incorporation but furthers simultaneous, enduring homeland attachments as well. Some migrants use religion as a site for asserting transnational belonging through their continued membership in the religious organizations they belonged to prior to migration. They make major financial contributions to these groups, raise funds to support their activities, host visiting religious leaders, seek long-distance spiritual and practical guidance from them, participate in worship and cultural events during return visits, and are the subject of nonmigrants' prayers in their absence. Other migrants participate in religious pilgrimages, worship particular saints or deities, or engage in informal, popular religious practices that affirm their continued attachments to a particular sending-country group or place (Levitt, 2004b).

Participating in what some scholars call "transnational rituals" also reinforces family and household membership across borders. Gardner and Grillo's (2002) work on the rituals performed by Bangladeshis living in London revealed the different ways in which individuals came to conceptualize space and the ways in which the emotional costs of transnationalism differed by gender and generation. Fog Olwig (2002) examined weddings that brought together large, globally dispersed family networks from the Caribbean island of Nevis. She showed the complex social, economic, emotional, and cultural relations used to construct and negotiate notions of "home." Salih (2002) analyzed the rituals performed by Moroccans returning home for the summer after working in Europe and concluded these were sites in which these individuals reinvented themselves with respect to those who stayed behind.

Transnational Membership

Individual transnational religious practices are reinforced by the organizational contexts in which they take place. Some migrants belong to host-country religious institutions with formal ties to home-country "sister congregations." They may belong to a group that operates like a franchise or chapter of a sending-country group and that receives regular supervision and financial support from homeland religious leaders. Or migrant religious groups may be part of worldwide religious institutions that treats them as members wherever they are. Religious movements, such as the Charismatic Catholic movement or the Vishnu Hindu Parishad serve a similar function by providing migrants with arenas for participation regardless of their address.

Some religious institutions are more conducive to transnational membership than others. Wellmeier (1998) found that the independent storefront ministries the Guatemalan Mayans she studied belonged to were so cohesive that they had resources and energy to spare to devote to their hometowns. Similarly, because so many of the Protestants Menjívar (1999) studied came from similar regions in El Salvador, and they were not constrained by the requirements of membership in the Catholic Church, they participated in hometown oriented activities with little conflict. In contrast, Catholic Church leaders impeded transnational activism because they feared that homeland-oriented activities would re-kindle schisms within the community. Baia (1999) compared two Peruvian *hermandades* (religious brotherhoods) in New Jersey. She found that, in one case, transnational linkages reproduced Peruvian national identity, whereas, in the second, the multicultural context of the host society gave rise to a pan-Latino ethnicity. Belonging to Catholic Charismatic, Neucatecumenal, or Cursillo movements resulted in similar diverse identity clusters. Although Levitt (2001a) found that membership in Charismatic Catholic groups offered the Dominican migrants she studied "a membership card that worked everywhere," Peterson and Vásquez (2001) found that Charismatic Catholic activities encouraged individualized transnational religious engagement but few collective activities.

Migrants also use religion to create alternative geographies of belonging that either fit within, transcend but coexist with, or take precedence over national borders. Some individuals are as much or even more concerned about their location in a religious landscape as they are about home and host-country incorporation. For example, Haitian migrants in New York simply added Harlem to the roster of places where their spiritual work is enacted. By doing so, they extended the boundaries of their rituals and superinscribed them onto the actual physical landscape where they settled (McAlister, 2002). By building and conducting rituals at a shrine to their national patron saint, Cuban exiles in Miami created what Tweed (1999) calls transtemporal and translocative space. The rituals enacted within it enable migrants to recover a past when they lived in Cuba and to imagine a future when they would return. Haitian migrants from Ri Rivyé who settled in Palm Beach County, Florida not only use religion to locate themselves within an alternative sacred landscape but to extricate themselves from it as well (Richman, 2002). Although most of the members of this community are Catholic, many also believe in *Iwas* or "saints" who can afflict and protect members of the descent groups to which they belong. Although some Haitians see their success in Miami as proof of the *Iwa's* intervention on their behalf, others feel that too many of their remittances are wasted on the *Iwa's* care and have converted to Protestantism to extricate themselves from this system of kinship and ritual obligation.

These dynamics drive and are driven by other linkages emerging at other levels of the transnational social field. An increasing number of countries allow dual nationality or citizenship. Other countries recognize dual membership selectively, with specific signatories. By granting migrants permission to belong to two polities, states legitimize other kinds of dual membership, locating these squarely within the range of identity choices available to the individual. They also provide individuals with the cognitive categories and vocabulary to describe these multiple states of being.

Furthermore, global norms and institutions are also shaped and help shape transnational social fields. The high visibility of issues such as women's rights, and the cadre of institutions that has emerged to promote and protect them, generates a set of global values, narratives about them, and strategies for organization and mobilization that other actors and institutions can appropriate. Religious institutions encounter this global culture and either selectively incorporate its elements or push back against them. For example, in response to global norms about women's rights, some religious groups permit women to perform functions unheard of in the past, whereas others firmly reassert gender differences.

Emergent Institutional Forms

Several kinds of changes in the organization of religious life occur in response to migration. First, existing congregations transform themselves, to varying degrees, to accommodate newcomers. They may add foreign-language services, incorporate different musical styles into their worship, or add a new set of symbols and rituals to their roster. Supply and demand factors condition these changes. The Catholic Church's heightened responsiveness to Latinos is partially explained by leaders' predictions that Latinos will comprise the majority of its members by 2010 (USCCB, 1999). It is also a response to the perception that large numbers are leaving the Church for Protestant congregations and that the Church's traditional white-ethnic base is on the decline. (Levitt, 2004a). Similarly, the American Baptist Church in New England has been particularly responsive to Brazilian immigrants despite major differences in theology and worship style. This is, in part, because church leaders saw immigrants' commitment and active participation as a way to revitalize their aging congregations (Levitt, 2003a).

When immigrants establish new religious groups in the United States they tend to become more "congregational" than they were at home, following the model of the Christian majority (Warner, 1998). Congregations have official members, are primarily supported through membership contributions, elect a lay governing body and appoint lay committees to oversee day-to-day operations, and select their own clergy (Ebaugh, 2003). Even traditions like Hinduism and Buddhism, not characterized by a core, systematic set of beliefs and practices in the homeland, take on elements of congregationalism in the United States. They are responding to the U.S. legal and tax system, which is predicated on a particular set of expectations about the form and function of religious institutions. In order to rent or buy buildings, offer government-funded social services, or be granted tax-exempt status, religious institutions need congregational administrative and governance structures.

At the same time, migrants' religious activities aimed at their homeland also produce transnational organizational forms. Ebaugh and Chafetz (2002) examined the relationship between religious network ties between individuals, local-level corporate bodies, and international religious bodies, and found that ties at various levels frequently crossed between various types of nodes. At one end of the spectrum, ties between a Mexican Catholic Church in Houston and its sending community of Monterrey were almost completely interpersonal, even though they emerged within the context of the universal Catholic Church. At the other extreme, Vietnamese Catholics and Buddhists in Houston formed transnational connections to their homelands based solely on institutional, as opposed to interpersonal connections. Socioeconomic status, legality, distance from the homeland, the geographic dispersion of the immigrant community, and English language fluency influenced network types.

Yang (2002) also used a network strategy to analyze transnational Chinese Christian communities. He found three-layered, trans-Pacific networks connecting individuals, single churches, and para-church organizations in Taiwan, Hong Kong, and Mainland China to their counterparts in the United States and Canada. Political and economic instability in Asia propelled these individuals and institutions to forge transnational ties. Networks also formed because the weak denominational infrastructure in China encouraged loose associations between local congregations to emerge.

Werbner (2002) writes of diasporic religious groups that are chaordic or that have the capacity to expand across boundaries while remaining local and even parochial. Ultimately, she argues, there is no guiding hand or command structure organizing the politics, the protests, the philanthropic drives, the commemoration ceremonies or the aesthetics of these groups. The discourses and practices perpetuated by the transnational Sufi cults she studied, their way of living and seeing things as they moved across space, and the resulting material exchanges, provide models for combining transnational loyalty and local national citizenship.

Levitt (2003a) identified three types of transnational religious organizational patterns. The first, exemplified by the Catholic Church, is an *extended* transnational religious organization. When transnational migrants circulate in and out of parishes or religious movement groups in the United States, Ireland, the Dominican Republic, or Brazil, they extend and tailor the already global Catholic Church system into a site where simultaneous belonging in both sending and receiving nation can be expressed. Protestant churches with affiliates in the United States and in Latin America typify a second type of *negotiated* transnational religious organization. These groups also extend and deepen global organizational ties already in place but in the context of less hierarchical, decentralized institutional structures. Instead, flexible, evolving partnerships are worked out in response to a particular context. The experiences of Gujarati Hindus from the Baroda district in India suggest a third type of *recreated* transnational religious organization. Migrants established their own religious groups when they first came to the United States because the Hindu community was so small. Most now function like franchises or chapters of their "mother" organizations in India. Franchises are run almost entirely by migrants, who receive periodic support, resources and guidance from sending-country leadership, whereas chapters receive regular support and supervision from sending-country leadership.

Religious organizations are not the only arenas for the expression of religious transnationalism (Rivera-Sanchez, 2002). The Tepeyac Association, a Mexican immigrant organization in New York, reinforced homeland attachments by serving as a channel for the circulation of symbolic goods and a site of religious festivities, celebrations, rituals, and patron saint festivals. A weekly radio program and newspaper available in Puebla and New York also employed symbols of struggle, faith, and devotion in ways that speak to users' past in Mexico and the reality of their current situation in New York.

Both religious activities aimed at migrants' experience in the hostland as well as those that are homeland focused are enacted, to varying degrees, within the multiple layers of the transnational social field. The Catholic Church is the archetypal multi-sited and multi-layered transnational religious organization. Homeland and local receiving parish connections may reinforce and be reinforced by ties between sending and receiving country ties between dioceses, archdioceses, national Bishop's conferences, and the global governance system of the Catholic Church as a whole. The partnership between the New England and the Brazilian Baptists also formed within the context of hierarchical national denominations, whose various levels of governance communicate across borders with one another. The New England Baptists, who oversee the establishment of local Brazilian immigrant congregations according to directives from the national American Baptist Convention, also work with their regional and state-level equivalents in Brazil. Furthermore, these activities emerge against the backdrop of the missionary activities that these denominations have historically engaged in and within the context of a growing evangelical Christian presence worldwide.

Religion and Politics

Despite the clear purported separation of church and state in the United States, religious institutions strongly influence politics. Religious institutions fulfill three separate but complementary roles in politics: (1) as incubators for civic skills, (2) as agents for mobilization, and (3) as information providers (Lee, Pachon, & Barreto, 2002). Church leaders take stands on political issues, they endorse candidates, and they allow their churches to be sites where debate and mobilization occur. Members acquire skills through the fund-raising, leadership, and organizing that goes on at church they can apply to other civic arenas, even when such religious activities are not accompanied by an explicit political agenda.

The relationship between religiosity and political participation, both with respect to the homeland and the hostland, has been the subject of much debate. For instance, many assume that Pentecostals are apolitical, with respect to both transnational as well as national concerns. But despite the a- or anti-political nature of their message, some argue that these churches influence the secular settings in which they are located (Menjívar, 1999; Peterson, Williams, & Vasquez, 2001). The boundaries that Pentecostal communities attempt to erect between the safe, sanctified world of faith and its dangerous, secular counterpart are only partially successful. Because members fulfill multiple roles and participate in multiple settings, they influence the secular world and it continues to affect them.

Religious leaders also influence politics. Networks and quasi-official organizations of priests, ministers, members of religious orders, and laypersons working with religious groups have made significant contributions to the causes of immigration reform, worker's rights, and education. Faith-based organizing efforts have also made significant contributions to community development. The Industrial Areas Foundation in Texas, PICO in California, and the Greater Boston Interfaith Organization all have strong connections to religious roots (Wood, 2002).

Religious communities envision the relationship between religion and politics in a variety of ways. Menjívar (2003) found that the Catholic Church's communitarian orientation advanced panethnic models and encouraged members to seek collective solutions to problems, thereby encouraging their long-term integration into the United States. In contrast, evangelicals forged strong ties among coreligionists and their leaders, creating a vibrant, ethnically homogeneous group, which was united under the umbrella of its shared Christianity, but isolated from the wider community.

Chen's (2002) research revealed a seeming paradox between the "other-worldly" orientation of a Taiwanese immigrant Buddhist temple that is more publicly engaged than an "inner-worldly" Taiwanese immigrant Christian Church. She argued that differences in religious ideals, outreach strategies, and the ways in which each group represents racial and religious distinctions influence these congregations' respective public engagement. The temples' inner-worldly orientation of Buddhist practice leads it to public interaction through charity, whereas the church's evangelical ideal of exclusive salvation leads it to engagement through personal evangelism. Buddhist charitable outreach strategies turn out to be more culturally transferable to the wider society than evangelical Christian strategies because of the linguistic and cultural barriers that immigrants face when they try to evangelize to those outside their community. Furthermore, because Buddhists are construed as religious foreigners, they are under pressure to demonstrate their "American-ness" and to broadly reach out.

High rates of church attendance are said to promote mobilization, influence the practice of citizenship, and help to even out the political playing field (Verba, Scholzman, & Brady, 1995). But this is truer among some groups than others.[4] Verba and his colleagues (1995) found that although involvement in churches enhanced the resource base of the African American community, it did not have the same compensatory function for Latinos. Although Latinos went to church less often then African Americans, and more often than Anglos, they were the least likely to take part in other kinds of activities at church. Only 23% of their Latino sample said they participated in secular church-based activities compared to 35% and 27% among the African-American and Anglo groups, respectively. Latinos also engaged in fewer skill-building type activities than their non-Latino counterparts.

Verba and his colleagues (1995) proposed that membership in Protestant and Catholic congregations resulted in different kinds of "civic" education and concluded that Latino political participation rates were low because so many Latinos were Catholic. Jones-Correa and Leal (2001) agree that religion influences political activism but disputed particular denominational cleavages. They found no association between Catholicism and lower levels of electoral and non-electoral participation for Latinos or Anglos. Rather, it was church attendance, not denominational affiliation, which explained differences in political participation. Members of any kind of religious group learn how to participate in associational life and these skills are then transferable to other organizational arenas. Lee, Pachon, and Barreto (2002) disagree. They argue that it is not enough to simply attend church or to be exposed to political information during a religious service. Church leaders, regardless of their denomination, must also encourage mobilization and participation. Without that, church attendance alone is not enough to increase mobilization.

Here again, understanding the relationship between religion and politics requires going beyond the U.S. context and taking potential transnational influences into account. For some individuals, religion promotes long-term participation in homeland and host-country politics and it does so at multiple levels. The experiences of recent migrants to Boston from the Irish peninsula of Inishowen are a case in point. Inishoweners get an informal civics lesson each time they attend mass. The priests serving this community are, by and large, native-born and well informed about local politics. Unlike their non-English-speaking counterparts, Inishoweners participate directly in parish governance instead of in ethnic parish councils. As a result, Levitt (2003a) found that "signing petitions in favor of school vouchers" or "attending a candidate's night" were some of the new political experiences her respondents reported they acquired at church. The support groups for young families organized by the Irish Pastoral Center became clearinghouses for information about jobs, housing, and schools.

This local-level advocacy and social service provision has a national level equivalent in the form of the Irish Apostolate U.S. Irish clergy working around the country created this umbrella group in 1997. The group's founder had to get permission from the U.S. National Council of Catholic Bishops (NCCB) and from the Council of Bishops in Dublin. He did so, in part, by convincing the Irish Church and the Irish government that they were still partially responsible for the welfare of emigrants abroad. The Irish government makes a $300,000 grant each year to support these activities and expects a yearly accounting in return. The Irish Apostolate also serves as the Irish governments' point of contact with the migrant community in the United States (Levitt, 2004b).

The Irish experience stands in contrast to that of Hindus from Gujarat State in India living in the Boston area. For this group, religious and cultural activities are the principal sites where they construct boundaries between themselves and the wider community. Although many Gujaratis live and work among native-born Americans, they purposefully remain socially apart. Their religious lives tie them inextricably to India. When *Sadhus* or religious teachers accompany Gujaratis to the United States, they depend on their followers to orient them to their new surroundings rather than the other way around. Because the *Sadhus* tend to remain inside the Temple, and speak little or no English, they can offer little guidance about social and political incorporation.

Like struggles over incorporation, how religious communities balance their involvement in home and receiving-country activities is often a source of friction. The Greek Orthodox community in New York struggled over the proper role of religion. Whereas the "Americanizers" wanted to leave Greek politics and ethnicity out, others saw the Church as an appropriate platform for political activism (Karpathakis, 2001). Cadge's (2004) study of Theravada Buddhist congregations in the United States also uncovered struggles between native-born and immigrant practitioners about proper and legitimate Buddhist practice.

National and Transnational Religious Cultures

Immigrants' religious practice with respect to their new land and their homeland is also strongly shaped by the ideological and institutional climate in which it takes place. Both scholars and the public-at-large share the belief that immigrants become more religious in the United States than they were in their home countries (Williams, 1996). Much of this scholarship assumes that the disorientation and stress caused by adjusting to a new context is a theologizing experience. But the same immigrant group can display different levels of religiosity in different settings. The Italian peasants who migrated to Argentina in the early 1900s turned to socialism and labor activism while their compatriots who came to the United States became avid churchgoers.

It is the American context, not the experience of immigration that is responsible for this effect (Casanova, 2003). The American self-concept is as much about religiosity as it is about being a nation of immigrants. Robert Bellah (1967) argued that the United States was characterized by a civil religion or the widely shared view that the foundation of U.S. society and the historical events that mark its progress are part of a larger, divine scheme of things. The political structure and the political acts that flow out of that structure have a transcendental dimension. This civil religious umbrella, constructed from a generic, shared belief in one higher power is broad and inclusive enough to allow most Americans, regardless of their faith, to fit under its folds. One becomes American, in part, by subscribing to this monotheistic patriotism.

However, transnational migrants respond to two contexts, governed by two different narratives and sets of institutional arrangements. For Turkish migrants in Germany, for example, religious life results from home and host-country imperatives. Immigrants are encouraged to organize as Muslims both because the Turkish government provides them with resources to do so and because the German government extends tax benefits and support to officially recognized religious groups. Similarly, migrants from homelands in which national and religious identities are inextricably linked, and where race is a less salient social marker, may conform more easily to the expectation of religiosity in the hostland, using it to overcome the racialization they experience.

RETHINKING THE AMERICAN DREAM

Using a transnational approach to understand migration and religion brings to light important questions about the changing nature of democracy, citizenship, and socioeconomic development that both sending and receiving countries need to grapple with. Some transnational problems require transnational answers but how home and host country religious, education, and health organizations need to change, if at all, is not clear.

For example, when individuals belong, either formally or informally, to two countries, they are protected by at least two sets of rights and subject to at least two sets of responsibilities. Which states are ultimately responsible for which aspects of their lives and what should migrants be expected to contribute in return? What kinds of rights and responsibilities do transnational religious groups give to their followers and how do these compensate for or complement dual political belonging? The Paraguayan government recently tried to intercede on behalf of a dual national sentenced to death, arguing that although capital punishment was legal in the United States, it was illegal in Paraguay. The Mexican government began issuing a *matricula consular,* or consular ID card, to Mexican emigrants, including those living illegally in the United States. More than 100 cities, 900 police departments, 100 financial institutions, and 13 states, including Indiana, New Mexico, and Utah, accept the cards as proof of identity for obtaining a drivers' license or opening a bank account. These examples illustrate the ways in which sending countries still assume partial responsibility for emigrants and act on their behalf on problems that host countries do not address. What is the appropriate role for transnational religious institutions in representing and protecting migrants across borders?

Transnational migration also raises questions about how to define and address poverty. For one thing, some of those who live across borders earn their living and measure their success in two different socioeconomic contexts. How should class be defined when migrants receive government assistance toward their housing costs in the United States at the same time that they are building homes in their sending communities? What about those who have trouble paying their rent because they continue to support family members in their homelands? In cases like these, both remaining poor and getting ahead are influenced by home and host-country factors. Therefore, shouldn't secular and religious programs aimed at alleviating poverty, therefore, take both contexts into account?

These questions are part and parcel of a larger set of concerns about the relationship between assimilation and transnational practices. Some people worry, for example, when they see both home country and U.S. flags at a political rally. They fear that remaining involved in homeland politics automatically means that immigrants will be less politically active in and loyal to the United States. But assimilation and transnational engagement do not have to work against each other. And multiple belonging through religious channels may reinforce loyalties or redirect them. These are not easy questions; some of the answers we take for granted no longer work. As belonging to two cultures and societies becomes increasingly common, we need new approaches to social issues that not only recognize, but also take advantage of, these transnational connections.

EXPANDING THE CONVERSATION

Clearly, migration and religion are not the only social processes that transcend national boundaries. Numerous social movements, businesses, media, epistemic communities, and forms of governance cross borders. Persons living in transnational social fields engage in multiple transnational processes at the same time. The transnational identities and institutions that emerge in response to these other dynamics are not well understood. Although they are the focus of a growing body of scholarship, more often than not, this research treats transnational economic, political, and social processes as if they were not connected to each other. We must explore how transnational practices and processes in different domains relate to and inform one another to understand how these developments are redefining the boundaries of social life. Migration and religion scholars can begin this conversation by systematically examining the forms and consequences of different kinds of transnational activities and collectivities, analyzing how they relate to one another, and exploring how they define and redefine our world. How do migrant cross-border activities compare to those engaged in by indigenous rights proponents and religious group members? How do organizing strategies, diffusion of ideas, and cultural negotiations compare in transnational religious organizations to those undertaken by transnational professional groups or production networks? In what ways do these different kinds of transnational memberships complement or subvert one another?

New methodological and conceptual tools are needed to understand these transnational processes. Because the social sciences originated in the 19th and 20th centuries as part of the project of creating modern nation-states, terms such as "government," "organization," and "citizenship," carry with them embedded nationalist assumptions that impair our capacity to see and understand transnational processes (Wimmer & Glick Schiller, 2003). Our conceptual categories implicitly take as given that the nation-state is the natural default category of social organization. The best that social science generally does is to compare corporations across national contexts rather than focusing on firms and markets as parts of transnational *fields* of investment, production, distribution, and exchange. We need new analytical lenses that can bring to light social processes that cross boundaries. We need new conceptual categories that no longer blind us to these emergent social forms nor prevent us from reconceptualizing the boundaries of social life.

NOTES

1. This section of this paper draws heavily on an article by Levitt and Glick Schiller forthcoming (2004) in *International Migration Review,* entitled "Conceptualizing Simultaneity: A Transnational Social Field Perspective on Society."
2. For an excellent review of this literature, see Ebaugh, 2003.
3. Despite these shifts, the pastoral plans are still the subject of harsh criticism. López (2002, p. 5), for example, writes that the 1987 plan "reads like a missionary plan to evangelize some exotic tribe, not the largest and oldest ethnic group in the American Catholic Church."
4. These studies of political participation and religion are based almost entirely on data on Judeo-Christian groups.

REFERENCES

Adams, A. (2002). Perception matters: Pentecostal Latinas in Allentown, Pennsylvania. In M. P. Aquino, D. L. Machado, & J. Rodriguez (Eds.), *A reader in Latina feminist theology* (pp. 98–113). Austin: University of Texas Press.

Baia, L. R. (1999). Rethinking transnationalism: Reconstructing national identities among Peruvian Catholics in N. J. *Journal of Interamerican Studies and World Affairs. 41*(4), 93–109.

Bellah, R. (1967). Civil religion in America. *Daedalus 96,* 1–21.

Beyer, P. (2001). *Religion in the process of globalization.* Würzburg: Ergon.

Brusco, E. (1995). *The reformation of machismo.* Austin: Univeristy of Texas Press.

Cadena, G. (1998). Latinos and Latinas in the Catholic church. In M. Cousineau (Ed.), *Religion in a changing world* (pp. 109–119). Westport, CT, and London: Praeger.

Cadge, W. (2004). *Heartwood: The first generation of Theravada Buddhism in America.* Chicago and London: University of Chicago Press.

Casanova, J. (2003, October 31–November 2). Does religion matter in immigrant incorporation? *Transcending borders: Migration, ethnicity, and incorporation in an age of globalism.* Paper presented at International Conference of the Immigration and Ethnic History Association, New York University.

Chen, C. (2002). The religious varieties of ethnic presence: A comparison between a Taiwanese immigrant Buddhist temple and an evangelical Christian church. *Sociology of Religion, 63,* 215–239.

Cook, K. (2000). Iglesia Cristiana evangélica: Arriving in the pipeline. In H. R. Ebaugh & J. S. Chaftez (Eds.), *Religion and the new immigrants* (pp. 171–192). Walnut Creek, CA: AltaMira.

Diaz-Stevens, A. & Stevens-Arroyo, A. M. (1997). *Recognizing the Latino resurgence in U.S. religion: The Emmaus paradigm.* Boulder, CO: Westview Press.

Dillon, M. (2003). *Handbook for the sociology of religion.* New York: Cambridge University Press.

Dolan, J. (2002). *In search of an American Catholicism.* New York: Oxford University Press.

Ebaugh, H. R. (2003). Religion and the new immigrants. In M. Dillon (Ed.), *Handbook for the sociology of religion* (pp. 225–240). New York: Cambridge University Press.

Ebaugh, H. R., & Chafetz, J. S. (Eds.). (2002). *Religion across borders: Transnational immigrant networks.* Walnut Creek, CA: AltaMira.

Ebaugh, H. R., & Pipes, P. (2001). Immigrant congregations as social service providers: Are they safety nets for welfare reform? In P. Nesbitt (Ed.), *Religion and social policy for the 21st century* (pp. 95–110). Walnut Creek, CA: AltaMira.

Elizondo, V. (2000). *The future is mestizo: Life where cultures meet.* Boulder: University of Colorado.

Espinosa, G., Elizondo, V., & Miranda, J. (2003). *Hispanic churches in American public life: Summary of findings* (2nd ed., Vol. 2003.2). Notre Dame, IN: University of Notre Dame Institute for Latino Studies.

Fog Olwig, K. (2002). A wedding in the family: Home making in a global kin network. *Global Networks, 2,* 205–218.

Foley, M., McCarthy, J., & Chaves, M. (2001). Social capital, religious institutions, and poor communities. In S. Saegert, J. Thompson, & M. Warren (Eds.), *Social capital and poor communities* (pp. 215–245). New York: Sage.

Gardner, K. (1993). Mullahs, miracles, and migration. *Contributions to Indian sociology NS, 27,* 213–235.

Gardner, K., & Grillo, R. (2002). Transnational households and ritual: An overview. *Global Networks, 2,* 179–190.

General Social Survey (GSSDIRS) (1972–2000). Cumulative codebook. Retrieved from the Inter-Univeristy Consortium for Political and Social Research website: *http://www.icpsr.umich.edu:8080/GSS/,* May 2003.

Goizueta, R. (2002). The symbolic world of Mexican American religion. In T. Matovina & G. Riebe-Estrella (Eds.), *Horizons of the sacred* (pp. 119–139). Ithaca, NY, and London: Cornell University Press.

Greeley, A. M. (1997). *The Catholic myth: Behavior and beliefs of American Catholics.* New York: Simon & Schuster.

Griel, A. L., & Bromley, D. R. (Eds.). (2003). *Defining religion: Investigating the boundaries between the sacred and the secular.* Amsterdam and Boston: JAI Press.

Guest, K. (2003). *God in Chinatown: Religion and survival in New York's evolving immigrant community.* New York: New York University Press.

Hall, D. (Ed.). (1997). *Lived religion in America.* Princeton, NJ: Princeton University Press.

Herberg, W. (1955). *Protestant, Catholic, Jew: An essay in American religious sociology.* Garden City, NY: Doubleday.

Hervieu-Léger, D. (2000). *Religion as a chain of memory.* New Brunswick, NJ: Rutgers Univeristy Press.

Karpathakis, A. (2001). The Greek orthodox church and identity politics. In Carnes, Tony, & A. Karpathakis (Eds.), *New York glory: Religions in the city.* New York: New York University Press.

Jasso, G., Massey, D. S., Rosenzweig, M.R., & Smith, J. P. (2003). Exploring the religious preferences of recent immigrants to the United States: Evidence from the new immigrant survey pilot. In Y. Y. Haddad, J. I. Smith, & J. L. Espositio (Eds.), *Religion and immigration: Christian, Jewish and Muslim experiences in the United States.* Walnut Creek, CA: Rowman & Littlefield.

Jones, D. E., Doty, S., Grammich, C., Horsch, J. E., Houseal, R., Lynn, M., Marcum, J. P., Sanchagrin, K. M., & Taylor, R. H. (2002). *Religious congregations and membership in the United States 2000: An Enumeration by region, state and county based on data reported by 149 religious bodies.* Retrieved from http://ext.nazarene.org/rcms/groupnumbersandchange.html

Jones-Correa, M., & Leal, D. (2001). Political participation: Does religion matter? *Political Research Quarterly 54,* 751–770.

Lampe, P. (Ed.). (1994). *Hispanics in the church: Up from the cellar.* San Francisco: International Scholars.

Lee, J., Pachon, H. P., & Barreto, M. (2002, August) *Guiding the flock: Church as vehicle of Latino political participation.* Paper presented at the Annual Meeting of the American Political Science Association, Boston, MA.

Levitt, P. (2001a). *The transnational villagers.* Berkeley and Los Angeles: University of California Press.

Levitt, P. (2001b). Transnational migration: Taking stock and future directions. *Global Networks, 1,* 195–216

Levitt, P. (2003a). You know, Abraham really was the first immigrant: Religion and transnational migration. *International Migration Review, 37,* 847–873.

Levitt, P. (2003b, October 31–November 2). Religious, ethnic and racial boundaries. *Transcending borders: Migration, ethnicity, and incorporation in an age of globalism.* Paper presented at International Conference of the Immigration and Ethnic History Association, New York University.

Levitt, P. (2004a, January). I feel I am a citizen of the world and of a church without borders: The Latino religious experience. *Latinos: Past influence, future power.* Paper presented at Conference of the Tomas Rivera Policy Institute, Newport Beach, CA.

Levitt, P. (2004b) Redefining the boundaries of belonging: The institutional character of transnational religious life. *Sociology of Religion, 65*(1), 1–18.

Levitt, P. & Glick Schiller, N. (2004). Transnational perspectives on migration: Conceptualizing simultaneity. *International Migration Review, 38*(145), 595–629.

López, D. (2002). Whither the flock? The Catholic church and the success of Mexicans in America. Prepared for the Pew/SSRC Working Group on Religion, Immigration, and Civic Life. Seattle, WA.

Mayaram, S. (2004). Hindu and Islamic transnational religious movements. *Economic and Political Weekly, 39*(1), 10–15.

McAlister, E. A. (2002). *Rara! Vodou, power, and performance in Haiti and its diaspora.* Berkeley: University of California Press.

McGuire, M. B. (1997). *Religion: The social context.* Belmont, CA: Wardsworth.

Menjívar, C. (2003). Religion and immigration in comparative perspective: Catholic and Evangelical Salvadorans in San Francisco, Washington, D.C., and Phoenix. *Sociology of Religion, 64,* 1–25.

Menjívar, C. (1999). Religious institutions and transnationalism: A case study of Catholic and Evangelical salvadoran immigrants. *International Journal of Politics, Culture, and Society, 12,* 589–611.

Morawska, E. (2003). Immigrant transnationalism and assimilation: A variety of combinations and the analytic strategy it suggests. In C. Joppke & E. Morawska (Eds.), *Toward assimilation and citizenship: Immigrants in liberal nation-states* (pp. 133–176). Hampshire, UK: Macmillan.

Orsi, R. (2003). Is the study of lived religion irrelevant to the world we live in? Special Presidential plenary address, Society for the Scientific Study of Religion, Salt Lake City, November 2, 2002. *Journal for the Scientific Study of Religion, 42,* 169–174.

Orsi, R. (Ed.). (1999). *Gods of the city: Religion and the American urban landscape.* Bloomington: Indiana University Press.

Peterson, A., & Vásquez, M. (2001). Upwards: Never down: The Catholic charismatic renewal in transnational perspective. In A. Peterson, P. Williams, & M. Vásquez (Eds.), *Christianity, social change, and globalization in the Americas.* New Brunswick, NJ: Rutgers University Press.

Peterson, A., Williams, P., & Vásquez, M. (Eds.). (2001). *Christianity, social change, and globalization in the Americas.* New Brunswick, NJ: Rutgers University Press.

Portes, A., Guarnizo, L., & Landolt, P. (1999). Introduction: Pitfalls and promise of an emergent research field. *Ethnic and Racial Studies, 22,* 463–478.

Richman, K. (2002). *Anchored in Haiti and docked in Florida.* Paper prepared for the Pew/SSRC Working Group on Religion, Immigration and Civic Life, Meeting in Seattle, WA.

Rivera-Sanchez, L. (2002, May). *Searching expressions of identity: Belonging and spaces, Mexican immigrants in New York.* Paper presented at the Conference on Religion and Immigrant Incorporation, New York.

Robertson, R. (1991). The globalization paradigm: Thinking globally. In D. G. Bromley (Ed.), *New developments in theory and research: Religion and the social order* (Vol. I, pp. 204–224). Greenwich, CT: JAI, Press.

Russo, N. J. (1969). Three generations of Italians in New York: Their religious acculturation. *International Migration Review, 3*(2), 3–17.

Salih, R. (2002). Reformulating tradition and modernity: Moroccan migrant women and the transnational division of ritual space. *Global Networks, 2,* 219–232.

Tweed, T. (1999). *Our lady of exile.* New York: Oxford University Press.

United States Conference of Catholic Bishops (USCCB). (1999). *Hispanic ministry at the turn of the new millennium: A report of the Bishops' committee on Hispanic affairs.* Retrieved December 23, 2003, from http://www.usccb.org/hispanicaffairs/study.htm#C

Vásquez, M. A., & Marquardt, M. F. (2003). *Globalizing the sacred: Religion across the Americas.* New Brunswick, NJ: Rutgers University Press.

Verba, S., Scholzman, K., & Brady, H. (1995). *Voice and equality.* Cambridge, MA: Harvard University Press.

Vertovec, S., & Peach, C. (1997). *Islam in Europe: The politics of religion and community.* London: Macmillan.

Warner, R. S. (1998). Introduction. In R. S. Warner & J. Wittner (Eds.), *Gatherings in diaspora: Religious communities and the new immigration* (pp. 3–37). Philadelphia: Temple University Press.

Watson, J. (2001, December 16). Folk saint for Mexicans who cross border. *San Francisco Chronicle.*

Wellmeier, N. J. (1998). Santa Eulalia's people in exile: Maya religion, culture, and identity in Los Angeles. In R. S. Warner & J. Wittner (Eds.), *Gatherings in diaspora: Religious communities and the new immigration.* (pp. 97–123). Philadelphia: Temple University Press.

Werbner, P. (2002). The place which is diaspora: Citizenship, religion and gender in the making of chaordic transnationalism. *Journal of Ethnic and Migration Studies, 28,* 119–136.

Williams, R. B. (1998). Training religious specialists for a transnational Hinduism: A Swaminarayan Sadhu training center. *Journal of American Academy of Religion, 66,* 841–862.

Williams, R. B. (1996). *Christian pluralism in the United States: The Indian immigrant experience.* New York: Cambridge University Press.

Wimmer, A., & Glick Schiller, N. (2003). Methodological nationalism, the social sciences and the study of migration: An essay in historical epistemology. *International Migration Review, 37,* 576–610.

Wood, R. (2002). *Faith in action.* Chicago: University of Chicago Press.

Yang, F. (2002). Chinese Christian transnationalism: Diverse networks of a Houston church. In H. R. Ebaugh & J. Chafetz (Eds.), *Religions across borders: Transnational religious networks* (pp. 175–204). Maryland: AltaMira.

CHAPTER 21

Globalization

PETER BEYER

INTRODUCTION

Looking at religion from a global perspective requires that we first of all be clear about what that implies. What, sociologically, can we mean by "global"? A simple answer would be to say that we would be looking at the entire globe as our unit of analysis and not only some part of it, but that elaboration does not go far enough. To it must be added the understanding that social relations and therefore also social institutions have to be thought of in terms of their global reach. The exercise is not one exhausted by the idea of comparison, say, between geographically and socially distinct societies whose principal connection is in the comparative eye of the observer. Sociality itself has to be seen as seamlessly global. A global perspective implies the logical and empirical existence of a global society as the social unit that makes such a view possible. From that point of departure, looking at religion as a social institution in global perspective means asking about the nature of religion as a global institution. Moreover, and just as critical, such an examination has to incorporate the subglobal dimensions of religion. It has to be global and local at the same time (cf. Robertson, 1995), if only because sociality, as far as our methods allow us to discern, depends ultimately on human bodies, and these are always in some place at some time. The global always has to "come down" somewhere concretely.

A great many specific issues could inform a global perspective on religion. This chapter limits itself to three: the historical emergence of religion as a globalized category, along with its subcategories of particular religions; the multilocal institutionalization of these socially (re)constructed realities; and, because institutions are always selective in what they include, the relative exclusion of significant "religiousness" from this globalized institutional domain of religion. These three subjects are very much interconnected. A distinct and socially consequential category of religion points to institutional expressions of that category; those institutions will perforce vary in form, content and emphasis; and, since the meaning of a social category and its institutional manifestations will not be coterminous, much that may look like religion will fall outside the institutional expressions: it will look like religion in some respects but not be treated as religion, by its carriers, by outside observers, or by both.

PETER BEYER • University of Ottawa, Ottawa, Ontario K1N 6N5

There now exists in a way that was not the case only 200 years ago a relatively consistent and virtually worldwide idea of "religion." This shared notion is, to be sure, not the only understanding of the word that people have. Far from it. There are numerous other meanings used by different people, including sociologists. Yet these are not globally institutionalized as religion. The shared idea is also a highly contested category subject to a range of particular understandings and used as a basis for making different sorts of claims. Nonetheless, all major languages have a specific term for it, whether that word be "religion" itself in most European languages, "*din*" in Arabic, "*dharma*" in South Asian languages, "*zongjiao*" in Chinese, "*shukyo*" in Japanese, "*agama*" in Indonesian, or various others. Some of these are relatively recent neologisms (for example, *shukyo*), others are words that refer both to this more recent idea but overlayed onto older meanings as well (for example, *din* or *dharma*) (see Beyer, 2003c, with further references). In all cases, however, the reference is to a distinct domain of human endeavour and life, one that invariably concerns itself with a variously styled transcendent realm, reality, or dimension, and includes the possibility of communicative access to that dimension or realm. Moreover, the notion is inherently plural. There is religion, *agama, shukyo, din*, and so forth. Yet, the main manifestations of this idea are in fact a plurality of "religions," usually a limited list of them which most often includes, but is rarely limited to, what I will call the "R5," namely Christianity, Buddhism, Hinduism, Islam, and Judaism (Beyer, 1998b; Beyer, 2001). This common conception by no means excludes contestation, conflict, and a large amount of variation; rather, it specifically includes these. Most of us in the world understand religion as a plural and often controversial domain. It is not the only such domain, but it is definitely one of them.

Among the many lines of contestation associated with this modern notion of religion, two are of particular relevance in the present context. First, many observers, including a not insignificant number of scholars (e.g., Chidester, 1996; Fitzgerald, 1997; McCutcheon, 1997; Paper, 1995; Smith, 1988; Smith, 1991b), contest its reality and its globality, arguing that the whole idea is at best a useful analytic fiction and at worst an instrument of Western imperial projection and imposition on the rest of the world. Second, and of course connected with the first, even when religion is accepted as real, the boundaries of the concept are frequently problematic. Not only are there numerous arguments about what does and does not belong in the category, but the root notion of religion's "separateness" is a matter of almost constant debate. To what degree is religion a separate or even separable domain? In the social world that we all inhabit there is no agreement on this question whatsoever. Some, such as the current French government, maintain that religion is not only separable, but should be restricted to a "private" domain, inside people's heads and in designated buildings, where no one other than the participants need even be aware of it. Others, such as the current Iranian government, deem religion to be inseparable from social order as such, necessarily an organizing dimension of all aspects of human life. Both positions, and virtually anything on a continuum between them, are shared by numerous others around the world.

The contestation surrounding this globalized notion of religion points to the somewhat peculiar ways that it has been institutionalized in global society. Religion is in certain ways a quite "normal" institutional domain in the sense that its structures bear comparison with those of other globalized institutional domains, for instance, with the domain of political states or with the global capitalist economy. At the same time, however, religion is and is considered to be also different from any of these other spheres, and one might even say that it is structured in opposition to them, an idea captured in the notion that religion is somehow about matters "transcendent" or "spiritual," as opposed to "immanent" or "material." It is to the further elaboration of this central idea of a peculiarly normal institutional sphere or system for religion that the bulk of this chapter is dedicated.

THE HISTORICAL EMERGENCE OF MODERN RELIGION AND RELIGIONS

For the sake of brevity, our story begins in Western Europe of the Middle Ages, not because the modern notion of religion is somehow inherently European but, rather, because certain highly consequential institutional and ideational transformations began there (cf. Beyer, 1998a; Beyer, 2001). Two aspects stand out: a highly organized, reasonably centralized, and fairly powerful religious institution in the form of the Roman Catholic church; and a concept of religion that was both singular and understood more as a quality of life-conduct than as a separate or separable domain. *Religio* was more like intelligence or virtue; you could have it in degrees or not at all, it could manifest itself in many different (including better or worse) ways, but it was not understood as one domain of social life beside others, nor could one "belong to" or "have" different ones. During that period, however, began a complex set of transformations that included the rise of plural territorial political powers, burgeoning intellectual and artistic activity, cities that became somewhat independent economic hubs, along with the continued strengthening and elaboration of the church as the single institution overarching the entire territory. This context of centrifugal but also strongly interdependent institutional growth unfolded into a number of far-reaching developments, among them the European voyages of "discovery" that set off centuries of imperial, colonial, economic, and religious expansion; and the highly conflictual Protestant Reformation which lead both to an intensification of religious activity and the destruction of the old institutionally expressed assumption of Christian unity. One upshot of the expansion and the religious rupture was a gradual conversion in the understanding of religion. From the 16th to the 19th centuries, the singular and nondifferentiated notion gave way to one that saw religion as a distinct domain of social life, as well as something that inherently expressed itself in different religions, to any of which a given person could adhere or not. In the earlier phases of this semantic shift, European elites tended to think of roughly only four such religions: the Christian religion (oddly, still understood as a single religion), the Jewish religion, the Mohammedan religion, and Paganism/Heathenism. To this list was usually added the continued attempt to find the unity behind them all, for instance in the concept of a "natural religion" that all humans implicitly shared (see Byrne, 1989; Harrison, 1990; Pailin, 1984). Such attempts, however, consistently foundered on the social fact that such a foundational religion had no evident institutional expression, whether in an organization like the church, a recognized religious or social elite, or even in a consistent theology. The religious institutions all expressed particular religions. Moreover, in the context of their eventually worldwide expansion, the Europeans did not rediscover the old unity either. Instead, now armed with this new conception of what religion was, they found more of them in different parts of the world: Confucianism, Buddhism, and Hinduism in various regions of Asia; and a variable list of others, including "tribal religions" in the Americas, Africa, and elsewhere (see Chidester, 1996; Despland, 1979; Harrison, 1990; Smith, 1991b).

Corresponding to the semantic shift in the meaning of religion and religions, the concrete institutional realities changed as well. The organizational expressions of Western European Christianity multiplied. The Roman Catholic Church continued its elaboration, now to include worldwide missionary efforts from the Americas to East Asia. Yet it ceased to be the single, overarching European institution that it once claimed to be. Various Protestant churches arose, often as adjuncts of different rising states, sometimes as dissenting movements and organizations. From the later 18th century, these also engaged in global missions, but they expanded beyond Europe well before that, constituting, for instance, an important institutional dimension of New World colonization efforts. Moreover, beginning especially in the 19th century, almost all the Christian churches shifted to a more or less voluntaristic basis, meaning that they saw themselves as consisting of "adherents" who voluntarily "belonged" or identified with them. This was the case even in those several countries where vestiges of "establishment" remained. Increasingly, therefore, the most important institutional expressions of European Christianity became more clearly differentiated in their role, function, and extent from other institutions, notably the political, but also over the course of this long period from others such as the scientific, artistic, educational, economic, and health institutions. No aspect of this development of course excluded the possibility and often the reality of significant involvement across institutional boundaries. Differentiation meant clearer distinction and different "autologics," not isolation and irrelevance of one domain with respect to all the others.

What happened among Europeans is not the only important part of the story. The imperial expansion of European power introduced both the idea of religion and its corresponding institutional structures to various other parts of the world, but this was not sufficient for the effective global spread of either. How the people in these regions responded to this ingress, how they appropriated or rejected this attempted imposition or projection, is just as important and in fact varied a great deal. In the areas of New World colonization, this implanting was fairly straightforward, as it was carried by European migrants and their descendants, the indigenous people having been—at least until very recently—effectively eliminated or shunted aside. In sub-Saharan Africa, the idea has been very successfully appropriated in the form of the dominance of two of the "world religions," Islam and Christianity. In this case, the appropriation by Africans, and not just the imposition by Europeans has to be stressed (see Hastings, 1996, 437ff). In the various civilizational regions of Asia, however, the question was far less straightforward, both because the people there had greater power to resist or deflect the European imperial presence and because they possessed a complex institutional and ideational base that already approximated or parallelled the European's religion. They could thus move in the direction of adapting their structures and traditions in consonance with that notion, or expressly resist and seek an alternate path. Thus, the elites of South Asia ended up collaborating more or less in the reconstructing of their diverse religiocultural traditions as religions, especially Hinduism (Dalmia, 1995b; Sontheimer, 1989), but also Sikhism and Jainism (Oberoi, 1994). The corresponding East Asians pursued a complex combination of acceptance and resistance, refusing to reimagine what Westerners called Confucianism as one of the religions, but approximately accepting it for Buddhism and, more ambiguously, for Daoism and Shinto (Chan, 1985; Hardacre, 1989; Jensen, 1997). In West-South Asia and North Africa, well-developed Islamic institutional realities combined with a long-standing tradition of Muslim religious self-conception ensured that the process of reforming Islam as one of the religions would be no less straightforward (and disputed) than it had been among Western Christians and Jews (see Beyer forthcoming).

Irrespective of which area of the world is our focus, the institutional expressions of this complex historical construction of a distinctly religious domain have thus far shown a dominant pattern: an increase in the number and effective presence of religious organizations ranging from local churches, mosques, and temples to pilgrimage centers and transnational organizations; a constant emergence and proliferation of distinctly religious social movements with a similar range of diversity; and the frequent incorporation or thematization of religion in other institutional domains, notably the political, legal, mass media, and the educational, but not just these. The latter are not so much directly religious forms as they contribute to forming religion. They condition our understandings of religion, including our taken-for-granted understandings, whether positive or negative. Taken together, these institutional forms do not, of course, contain or control all conceivably religious activity, nor are they encompassing in the sense that all people necessarily participate in them. Far from it. What they do is to give religion its prevailing social shapes, its recognizable character in terms of which any social activity can be understood to be more or less "religious." Thus, much noninstitutional religiosity can and does occur, but it gains its recognition and frequently orients itself in comparison with the differentiated religious institutions. Should the question of its religiousness or nonreligiousness become an issue—and this will happen only in certain circumstances—the religious institutions will, directly or indirectly, largely determine the answer (cf. Beaman, 2003).

RELIGIOUS INSTITUTIONS IN GLOBAL CONTEXT

The further consideration of religion as an institutional domain can start with the following question: How and under what circumstances do people around the world perform something called "religion" in a way that constitutes this activity as recognizable and distinct? This is the fundamental question of religion's institutional differentiation. The answer to this question has two dimensions, namely how does religion institutionalize itself positively as religion; and how do other institutional domains constitute themselves as nonreligious, thus helping to profile that which operates as religion? Here I restrict myself to the former, although the latter is in the final analysis just as important and hovers in the background of what follows: a condition of religion's institutional distinctiveness is that there be a social environment of similarly differentiated, secular institutions.

Continuing from the previous section on the historical development of a modern and globalized idea of religion, one notes that this idea includes at least three defining aspects. First, there is the peculiar sort of activity that makes up religion, in particular religious ritual and other forms of religious practice like meditation, preaching, or the reading of sacred texts. Second, what lends this activity its quality as "doing religion" is that it refers to a specific kind of religious reality, often designated by terms such as transcendent, ultimate, absolute, infinite, sacred, divine, supra-empirical, or extraordinary—in short, a reality somehow other or supplementary to the immanent, the conditioned, the contingent, the finite, the profane, the human, the empirical, and the ordinary. That fundamental religious distinction is not necessarily important or even all that clear in societal contexts that do not feature differentiated religious institutions; but it is or happens to have become a defining feature of the contemporary globalized religious system. It expresses itself through self-referential, internally justified programs of belief and practice. Third, this activity is understood as communal. It includes a meaningful sense of belonging to a larger social whole, pointing not only to the importance of bodily co-presence in much religious ritual and practice, but also to the fact that interaction or communication among adherents *about* religion is as constitutive of it as the ritual and practice. Taken together, these three aspects allow religion to operate recursively and in this sense as a system: the actions or communications that constitute religion gain their meaning primarily with reference to one another. Like other spheres, such as science, the purposes and justifications of religious activity are again religious: attainment of nirvana or the *visio dei* are their own purposes.[1] Correspondingly, critical for all three aspects is that they are not just analytic abstractions of a particular observer, say myself or a religious thinker of some sort. Rather, this way of recognizing the religious is shared by most people involved in it and by a great many outside observers as well. Together these aspects reflect a social reality in which this religion is understood and performed as something distinct and self-referential. There is nothing essential about this arrangement; it is contingent on peculiar historical developments. Nonetheless, it is an operative and largely globalized reality today.

The modern idea of religion by itself is of course not enough actually to bring about the social differentiation of religion as a distinct domain. Two other dimensions are just as essential. First, as important as the understanding of religion are the institutional arrangements which represent it, which concentrate its performance and variation, in which it is played out. The clearest of these in the contemporary world are religious organizations ranging from local churches and temples to transnational organizations, but to these must be added the more fluid forms of religious social movements (mostly identified with particular religious movement organizations) and the more loosely structured religious social networks. The latter also range from very local groupings to those that span large regions and even the globe. Second, however, the picture is only complete when the twin factors of self-representation and other-recognition are added. The institutions have to represent themselves as religious; they must adopt and communicate that self-identity. And others, ranging from the general public outside the institutions to state authorities, have to treat them in one way or another precisely as religious institutions. This latter aspect especially points both to the interdependence of religion with other (global) institutions and to the many possibilities for challenge and ambiguity with respect to this differentiation.

Institutional differentiation implies no more than that specific and recognized social structures specialize in the reproduction of what people understand as religion. As in the cases of the non-religious institutional domains like education, science, health, or economy, it does not also mean that everything conceivably religious becomes the domain of these institutions, let alone the exclusive domain. The religious institutions are by their very specificity selective. Symptomatic of this characteristic is that the carriers of religion, especially religious authorities, are constantly faced with the problem of guarding that selectivity, for instance by combating heresy, engaging in dialogue or apologetics vis-à-vis other religions, decrying superstition, and generally seeking to define and maintain some sort of orthodoxy or orthopraxy. Accordingly, in spite of differentiation and perhaps because of it, much non- or quasi-institutionalized religiosity occurs in addition to the institutionalized sort simply because the religious institutions do not have the means to prevent it. This feature has two important consequences: the possibility of new religions forming or attempting to form all the time (along with the disappearance of old ones), and the persistent presence of social activity that in many respects looks like religion but does not (or not quite) count as such. Institutionalization is in this sense inherently contingent and subject to challenge. The religious institutions exist and remain vital only so long as they are actively defended and reproduced, not out of some inherent functional necessity or human need.

In the light of these abstract considerations, we can now move to a more concrete description of how these differentiated religious institutions actually operate in various regions of global society. That shift of attention, however, immediately brings us back to another critical general feature of this system, its multilocality. Religion, like the other institutional domains, does not operate globally on a center-periphery model but, rather, on one in which the unity of the system, such as it is, is more an emergent quality of multiple localizations or particularizations than it is the product of centralized authority (Beyer, 2003b). Even the Roman Catholic Church, perhaps the most obvious exception to this rule, operates substantially on a local level, the variations in emphasis and style being in some ways as significant as global differences in how newspapers are put together or state development policies are enacted. In other divisions of Christianity as well as in other religions, unity or singularity is much more visibly the product of local adaptations of globalized models than of effective structures of centripetal authority. A few selected illustrations can serve to make this point clearer.

Christian Pentecostalism

The highly organized and significantly centralized Roman Catholic Church is symptomatic of the degree to which contemporary Christianity, as a global religion, relies heavily on organization to lend itself distinct and differentiated social form. Whether in its various Protestant, Catholic, or Orthodox branches, the Christian religion has in more recent centuries favoured a strategy by which individual Christians "belong voluntarily" to particular organizations, almost always exclusively. Christians identify with and participate in specific organized churches, both locally in the form of congregations or parishes and more broadly through what are often called denominations or confessions. Although there has always been a certain amount of "switching" among these organized groups, and in spite of more recent evidence that this structure may be less important than it once was, by and large Christianity still structures itself internally by assigning individual Christians to these denominations or churches (Davie, 2000; Hoge, 1994; Roof, 1987). This denominational organization permits different degrees of centralized religious authority, but it also allows controlled multilocalization in virtually all parts of the world. The majority of Christian churches have "branches" in different countries and regions. These will be similar to one another, for instance in ritual practice, ecclesiastical (authority) structure, and theology. But they also can be significantly different in style and emphasis, thereby responding to different cultural settings and local religious understandings. This sort of multilocal modeling is fairly obvious among the more tightly organized denominations, for example in the Roman Catholic, Greek Orthodox, or Anglican churches. That it is not dependent on a high degree of centralization is perhaps most evident in Christian Pentecostalism.

There is a strong sense in which Pentecostalism refers simply to a style of Christianity, one which places great emphasis on certain biblically warranted possession or trance rituals and thereby on individual religious experience. As such, it has a long if also at times highly controverted history in Christian tradition. Toward the end of the 19th and beginning of the 20th centuries, however, a rapidly worldwide and significantly self-identified Pentecostal movement developed (Hollenweger, 1972). To a large extent, its adherents also adopted the congregational/church strategy—as exemplified, for instance, in the American-based Assemblies of God—forming denominations and above all local congregations with voluntary members and regular participants. That has only been a part of the picture, however. Throughout the 20th century, both the structure of Pentecostalism as well as its self-conception maintained the form of a social movement rather than stressing what Thomas O'Dea called organizational elaboration (O'Dea, 1966). Unlike roughly parallel Christian movements, such as the Jehovah's Witnesses or the Latter Day Saints, Pentecostalism has not spread around the world through organizationally initiated and controlled missionary efforts, but rather more spontaneously through individuals taking the "flame" to their countries and regions or simply starting up a new group in their own locality (Cox, 1995). Like social movements more generally, what identifies Pentecostalism is far less a defined organizational structure and much more a particular narrative and particular ritual practices in terms of which those participating in the movement identify. This feature lends a tremendous variety to different manifestations of Pentecostalism around the world and in any specific country or region; but it does not undermine the overall unity of the movement. Pentecostals, although recognizing no single or even a limited number of central authorities, nonetheless share a sense of belonging to the same thing, a sense that manifests itself and is reinforced by the significant amount of communication that occurs among Pentecostals, whether through traveling charismatic leaders, conferences, publications, or various other means (Dempster, 1999). That interconnectedness even extends to segments of the movement that have established themselves in other, more centrally organized Christian churches, ones that, to reflect this different location, often call themselves charismatic rather than Pentecostal (Poewe, 1994). What all the manifestations demonstrate, however, is how a religion can in the contemporary globalized world maintain its self- and other-recognized unity without centralized authority structures such as are exemplified in the Roman Catholic church. Pentecostals around the world establish and express their singularity by adopting and adapting a common religious model. Pentecostalism in such diverse countries as Canada, Korea, Sweden, Brazil, Ghana, Ethiopia, or India is thereby quite different; it is truly multilocal. Yet all these variations take a good part of their identity from the common model, which itself is controlled by no one. Multilocalization is expressive of systemic singularity at the same time as systemic singularity is the efflorescence of multilocalization.

Islamic Singularity and Diversity

Using Christian Pentecostalism as the first illustration of how religion operates as a global institutional domain that is nonetheless highly localized is important because it opens the way for understanding the global singularity of other religions that are not nearly as highly organized as Christianity. Few other religions, in fact, have adopted the typically Christian congregational form of incorporating or "churching" members. Among those that have not is Islam. Even in regions such as North America, Australia, or Europe, where what one might call the contextual pressure of Christian organizational patterns leads Muslims (and adherents of other religions) to form congregation-like structures centered on mosques, neither the typically Catholic parish nor the typically Protestant congregation-with-defined-members model has been adopted (Buijs, 2003; Deen, 1995; Haddad, 2002; Leonard, 2003). Mosques in these regions are rather more like local religious service centers with both a regular and an irregular clientele. Muslims go to a mosque, participate and perhaps are even very highly involved in mosque activities and services; but they do not usually belong to that mosque in the way that many of their Christian neighbors might belong to the local Catholic parish or Anglican Church. In this respect, these mosques are similar to many Christian Pentecostal churches. Elsewhere, especially in those regions from North Africa to central Asia that have historically been overwhelmingly Muslim, mosques operate even more like service providers open to the general public than they do as discrete organizations created by or for members. That difference does not, however, mean that Islam is thereby less institutionally differentiated, although it may be indicative of a different relation among institutional domains.

Although mosques in what one might call the Muslim heartlands are indeed distinct institutions that help to profile Islam as a religion, they are not alone in this regard. To the mosques also can be added other discrete and in many cases organized Islamic institutions, such as madrassas, universities, Sufi brotherhoods, and various Islamic social movements ranging from the highly politicized like Egypt's Muslim Brotherhood to the more religiously specialized like Pakistan's Tablighi Jamaat (Esposito, 1999; Levtzion, 1987; Voll, 1982). All of these help to lend Islam a positive, differentiated institutional face. Like corresponding institutions in other religions, their reach also varies from highly local to being more or less worldwide. Moreover, although Islam does not have nearly the complexity of clear internal confessional or denominational differences that is typical of modern Christianity (and in a different way, modern Judaism), these various institutions do carry a similar range of distinct versions or particularizations of Islam. Here again, the difference between the Christian and Muslim examples is the higher degree and different style of Christian organization, not the institutional distinctiveness of either. Differences expressed in labels such as Shia (Ismaili, Alevi, Ithna Ashari), Sunni, Wahhabi, Ahmadi, Naqshbandi, or Salafi, are just as socially consequential (or, at times, irrelevant) as those between Christian denominations. What varies are the precise forms of the institutions that express them. As in the case of Christian Pentecostalism (and Christianity more generally), what actually unites these variations into a singular religion is the common programmatic model that they all share and that they all self-descriptively claim to express. It is in terms of the interrelated "texts" or "traditions" of Quran, Hadith, prayer, pilgrimage, and so forth, that the different versions identify themselves and relate to one another, not through some sort of centralized authority. That includes the identification of Islam as a whole with respect to other religions, notably Christianity and Judaism. All this, they accomplish largely through the institutions.

In one important respect, contemporary Islam may seem to differ from most other religions in the way that it is institutionalized. This concerns the degree to which it informs the political system, or states, and legal systems (Esposito, 1987; Kepel, 2002). This question of the relation of religion to other institutional spheres is the subject of the concluding section. Here, however, it may be said that this difference is less significant than it might appear. Modern movements that have sought to imbue states and their laws with religion are to be found in all the more broadly recognized "world religions" (Marty, 1991–1995). Indeed, being thematized in other nonreligious institutions is integral to the recognition and identification of religion and religions more generally (Beyer, 2003a). It is not a feature of a particular religion. That said, currently Islam does feature many movements which explicitly seek the dedifferentiation of religious and political, legal, economic, and other institutional spheres. Some of these, such as the early revolutionary movement in Iran of the 1980s (Arjomand, 1988; Beyer, 1994) or the Afghan Taliban in the 1990s (Rashid, 2000) have at least temporarily succeeded with respect to the political and legal systems. These, however, are the exceptions even in Islam. In most regions where this religion has a significant presence, what may seem on first glance to be dedifferentiation really amounts to no more than religious influence in other institutional spheres. Such influence does not by itself already constitute dedifferentiation; no more so than business or scientific influence on government policy amounts to the dedifferentiation of economy or science and state.

Buddhist Globalization

A somewhat different picture emerges in the case of worldwide Buddhism. Institutionally, it also manifests itself through organizations like temples, monasteries, and defined movements such as Fo Guang Shan (Buddha Light International) or Soka Gakkai. Historically and today, monastic institutions have played a particularly important role in this regard, more so than perhaps in any other religion. Today, lay-based movements and organizations are gaining a larger profile. In addition, Buddhist organization is comparatively clearer in Western countries, again likely because of the contextual pressure of the highly organized and still dominant Christianity in these regions (Prebish, 1998; Prebish, 2002). Two features, however, make Buddhism at least seem to be significantly less institutionally singular than especially the Abrahamic religions of Judaism, Christianity, and Islam. One of these is programmatic, having to do with the content of Buddhist practice and belief. The other is historical.

Programmatically, Buddhism presents a far less exclusivist face. Above all, except perhaps in its core monastic institutions, it has rarely adopted the strategy of defining Buddhism in terms of who is or is not a Buddhist. One can follow a Buddhist path without doing so exclusively. An example of the fluidity that this introduces can be found in contemporary Japan, where Buddhism is quite strong. Here the majority of the population actually belongs as defined members to an array of Buddhist organizations, even though in a great many cases, that membership is not much more than nominal. Correspondingly, these members can and often do belong to other non-Buddhist religious organizations, and with respect to practice and belief do not consider themselves or act as exclusively Buddhist (Murakami, 1980; Reader, 1991). This nonexclusivity also manifests itself in Japanese Buddhist institutions, where, strictly speaking, non-Buddhist beliefs and practices at times meld with more programmatically Buddhist ones. Thus, especially if one insists on Abrahamic standards, Buddhism in Japan clearly expresses itself in defined and differentiated religious institutions, but appears less clearly bounded or differentiated because so many of its adherents or practitioners do not identify themselves as Buddhists and nothing else.

Reinforcing this programmatic feature of contemporary Buddhism is a historical peculiarity that specifically concerns China. Like most of East Asian Buddhism, the Chinese variety has historically exhibited both clearly defined institutions like monasteries as well as the typically Buddhist institutional and programmatic fluidity or nonexclusivity (Yang, 1967). In addition, however, modernist, nationalist, and especially communist movements in 20th-century China created an atmosphere little conducive to the solid construction of new Buddhist institutions and the revitalization of old ones, whether lay or monastic (Grieder, 1981; Jensen, 1997; Luo, 1991). In this respect, the largely failed efforts of a reforming monk like Tai Hsu in the mid-20th century are perhaps illustrative: a clear vision of a singular but internally varied Buddhism modeled on similar reconstructive efforts in other religions and in other Buddhist regions (for example, in Sri Lanka), but the inability to successfully build up viable institutions on that basis (Welch, 1968). If one considers that China demographically represents by far the largest even nominally Buddhist population in the world, the fate of this religion in that region cannot but have a significant effect of the face of worldwide Buddhism, all the more so as diaspora populations and missionary movements have been so critical to the global spread of other religions. The Chinese diaspora is the most significant East Asian one in the world; it may only be beginning to institutionalize its historically and culturally typical religious expressions. Symptomatically, the most important diasporic

Chinese religious institutions outside China are in fact Christian, not Buddhist, Daoist, or anything else (see, e.g., Guest, 2003; Yang, 1999).

That said, it also may be that Buddhism is becoming the single most successful non-Christian religion among Westerners in regions such as North America and Europe, albeit still in quite minority fashion (Baumann, 2000; Prebish, 2002). This trend is bringing about an accelerated Buddhist institution construction in these areas, paradoxically perhaps giving Buddhism some of its clearest institutional manifestations through a relatively small number of people in populations and regions not historically Buddhist. The overall result is that Buddhism has become a fairly evident worldwide and multilocalized religion, but the lack of clear dominance of a core programmatic vision as in the case of Islam, or of an elaborate and clearly delineated organizational structure as in the case of Christianity gives Buddhism the appearance of a less clearly differentiated and somewhat underinstitutionalized religion when compared to the others. In this respect, the high profile in many parts of the world of a symbolic presence such as that of the Dalai Lama gains that much more in importance: for so many, he represents Buddhism as such, even though in actual fact he represents only a small subvariant of it.

Hindu Construction

Where the other religions thus far considered actually have a long history of self-identification, at least as distinct traditions if not as modern, differentiated religions, even that has been a product of more recent invention in the case of Hinduism. Only after the beginning of British colonial dominance in the late 18th century does the idea of a singular religion called Hinduism coalesce (Frykenberg, 1989), first in the minds of British officials, then, throughout the 19th and 20th centuries in an ever larger segment of the Indian national elite and especially urban middle classes (Dalmia, 1995b). A combination of elaborate institutionalization in the form of organizations, movements, and social networks and a low level of clear programmatic singularity is symptomatic of this recent construction. The institutionalized and multilocal subvariants of this religion are only too evident, ranging from temple and pilgrimage organizations like the Vishnu temple in Tirupati or the Kumbh Mela organization in Allahabad to well-defined and often long-standing religious movements and their attendant organizations ranging from the Pushti Marga to the Ramakrishna Math and Mission (Dalmia, 1995a; Radice, 1998). Hinduism in no sense lacks a whole array of clearly delineated social institutions, which in one fashion or another identify themselves as Hindu and sometimes even claim to represent Hinduism as such. On the programmatic side, however, there appears to be as yet no clearly dominant vision of what constitutes and counts as Hinduism, although there are certainly various suggestions, perhaps the most influential of which is the neo-Vedantic vision represented by someone like Radhakrishnan (Radhakrishnan, 1980 [1927]). In recent decades, a highly politicized and currently quite powerful Hindu nationalist movement has attempted to address this situation at least organizationally with the founding and elaboration of the Vishwa Hindu Parishad or World Hindu Organization and its various subsidiaries in India and in the Hindu diaspora (Jaffrelot, 2001; Van der Veer, 1994). Although the representatives of this movement and this organization are certainly making themselves heard in India and abroad, they have not actually succeeded in presenting a convincing and broadly shared vision of what essentially constitutes Hindu religion beyond the long-standing vague references to the Vedas and the multiplicity of deities and paths. Nonetheless, the very existence of this contemporary development can be taken as symptomatic of the global contextual pressure to elaborate models of religion that can then, in multilocal fashion, be particularized throughout the world wherever Hindus find themselves.

NONINSTITUTIONAL RELIGIOUSNESS
IN GLOBAL CONTEXT

No more than the other institutional spheres such as those for politics or economy, that for religion is also far from including all social manifestations that might conceivably count as religion. In the case of religion, there is in fact a great deal that escapes solid incorporation into this system, and this along two related dimensions: there are those clearly institutionalized arrangements that for one reason or another do not count as religion, whether because they are not differentiated as such or are differentiated through another, nonreligious system. Then, there are those social phenomena that seem to be religious but are too fluid and irregular to constitute actual institutions. In the first case, we are dealing primarily with a combination of a lack of structuring as religion, including self-presentation and other-recognition as religion. In the second case, the issue is one of a lack of sufficient sociostructural regularity for there to be an institution, whether we consider it religious or not. The two types are best described further on the basis of some selected examples. For the first sort of nonreligious religiosity, Falun Gong and village religion in India will serve; for the second, the ideas of worldview and sacredness. In both instances, it should be stressed that these are only examples. The variety of manifestations that could come under consideration here is considerably larger than these examples suggest.

A socially consequential—and not just analytical—question with respect to Falun Gong is whether or not it is religion, and connected therewith, which religion it is or what it is if it is not religion. It is certainly an organized social movement, complete with central authority, self-identified adherents, a characteristic set of activities, and an elaborated ideology (see http://www.falundafa.org for the movement's official self-presentation). The activities look like religious practices, especially Daoist ones; the ideology reads like religious discourse, notably but by no means exclusively Buddhist (Penny, 2004). Yet Falun Dafists very often deny that what they do is religion; they rather claim the title of cultural practice or psychological and physical discipline. The reasons for this denial are complex, but they include a typically Chinese discomfort with the modern idea of religion in combination with the view shared by many outsiders, notably the current Chinese government, that Falun Gong is an antireligion or "cult" (xiejiao = "evil teaching"). What we have, then, is an organized movement that in its actual characteristics operates like other, clearly recognized religious institutions (Tong, 2002). Missing—or at least inconsistently present—are the twin factors of self-identification and other-recognition as religion. Falun Gong could be a religion, say, a new religion or a variant of Daoism, Buddhism, or both. At the moment, however, it is not quite there yet, although one suspects that, like other controversial new religious movements, it will eventually get there, assuming it lasts. Be that as it may, in the present context, Falun Gong demonstrates one of the ways that the margins of the religious institutional system operate, one of the gray areas of inclusion or exclusion, as it were.

What one might call local religious culture in many areas of the world presents a rather different kind of liminal religious manifestation, but one in which again self-description and other-recognition is more at issue than the presence or absence of otherwise typically religious activity and communication. The religious cultures of village India can serve as an example, but so too could the local, popular traditions of a great many regions of the world, ranging from Papua-New Guinea and China to Africa and Latin America. What is not missing in these cases is regular ritual and other practices with reference to transcendent or supra-empirical realities that take a communal form (Babb, 1975; Marriott, 1967). People in village India perform their *pujas*, conduct their cyclical ceremonies, perform their daily rituals with reference to a wide variety of spiritual beings, communally and individually, episodically and on a regular basis. Their understanding of these performances and the mythic explanations that surround them may be quite clear and even systematic. What they often will not do, however, is make an operative distinction between this sort of activity and other aspects of their lives, say the economic and political aspects, which is to say how they support themselves materially and how they arrange their public affairs. Nor will there be specialized institutions like temple and other organizations or distinctly religious movements to give religion a concrete and separate face. In other words, what is missing is the significant differentiation of this religious activity and correspondingly local people do not call it by a distinct name, whether religion or one of the religions, for instance Hinduism. They may use words like *dharma*, the standard word for religion in the larger or, perhaps more accurately, elite South Asian society. But what they mean will be closer to the older meanings of duty or rule rather than the newer meaning of religion. To be sure, such village situations can change quickly if the outside world impinges sufficiently, for example, if Hindu nationalist militants come and convince people that what they have been doing all along is both religion and Hinduism. The understandings of local elites may also be more in a differentiated direction. Overall, then, what renders such Indian religious activity marginal to the larger global and more local institutional religious system is a lack of self-identification as religion, whether in the form of specific institutions that concentrate the activity or in the from of explicit self-descriptions on the part of the people who carry it. All this, of course, does not prevent outsiders—for example, academic observers, law and government officials, or mass media reporters—from recognizing these local traditions as both religion and as a manifestation of one of the religions. That too can contribute to the ambiguity.

Another area of ambiguity concerns more or less exactly the opposite of individual cases such as Falun Gong or localized circumstances such as obtain in rural India. If these are examples of social phenomena that "look like" religion but for one reason or another escape being described or recognized as such, then in other instances we find the description and recognition, but without the clear manifestations of institutionalized activity with reference to a transcendent dimension. Two examples of this inverse situation are the idea of worldviews and the notion of sacredness. In both cases, what we have is a kind of metaphoric understanding of something as religion where the substantively institutional features are in fact missing. The attitude of scholars such as Ninian Smart (1983) and Thomas Luckmann (1967), that anything that provides human beings with fundamental and systematically meaningful orientation in their lives should be considered as religion is one shared by quite a number of people outside the academic fold. From such a functional perspective—religion is what religion does, in this case providing fundamental meaningful orientation—allows one to observe diverse phenomena like nationalism, secular humanism, Marxism, and atheism as religion. In some of these cases, it is indeed possible to find consistent systems of thought and ritual action embodied in differentiated institutions, notably the state. Perhaps the most notable example of this possibility is Robert Bellah's well-known analysis of American civil religion (Bellah, 1970). Suggestive as such cases are, however, and valuable for understanding key dimensions of contemporary social realities, the institutions in question do not specialize in this sort of "religious" activity, do not self-describe themselves as religious, and the status of transcendent references to things like "a nation under God" or "historical materialism" are weak at best and certainly not critical to the operation of the institutions the way God or Buddha are to respectively Abrahamic and Buddhist ones. That said, the very fact that people in various parts of the world can "do what religion does" through means and institutions that are not explicitly religious points to another way in which the institutional system of religion does not include within itself everything defensibly religious, and this, again, no more than the other institutional spheres.

A very similar analysis can be applied to the use of other terms, like sacredness. Adopting Durkheim's (1965) notion that the sacred is marked out in the way that things are treated—set apart and forbidden—there are indeed quite a number of seemingly non-religious "things" in today's world that are nonetheless treated sacredly. One thinks in this regard, for instance, of technology (sometimes as ultimate demon!), human rights, notions of democracy and equality, the natural environment ("Mother Earth," "Gaia"), heritage sites, or human life itself. Notable in this context is that many of the recognized and institutional-ized religions, through their representatives, have found it necessary or appropriate to take up such themes explicitly and formally incorporate them into their theologies and even rit-ual practice. The affinity of such "things" with the concerns of institutionalized religions is indeed not to be dismissed or underestimated. Neither is their "specialness" and importance in the operation of today's global society. Moreover, as with the idea of worldviews, there exist various institutions—organizations, social movements, social networks—in which such sacralized objects and ideas are main preoccupations. It is, however, clear that such sacralization largely escapes institutionalized religion: these matters are at most thematized there, interpreted in terms of religious meaning systems; they do not themselves constitute religion or religions as a specialized institution. Again, as with the other examples, impor-tant structures and processes that in some respects "look" like religion, escape institutional religion. They do not have the characteristic features of explicit and elaborated transcendent reference, they are not embodied in systematic programmes of belief and practice, and they have little communal manifestation. That said, what must also be emphasized is that they *could* provide the nodal points for the formation of new religions and for the transformation or variation of those that are already institutionalized as such (see, for instance, Roof, 1999). The "sacralized" can eventuate in the "religionized," but the formal affinity between the two does not by itself already establish their identity. That must be left to contingent, historical developments: it will happen or it will not, neither being necessary.

CONCLUSION: THE RELATION OF RELIGIOUS AND NONRELIGIOUS INSTITUTIONAL SYSTEMS IN GLOBAL SOCIETY

Having looked a bit more closely at religion as a global institutional system, we can conclude with a brief consideration of its relations to other, nonreligious institutional spheres. Two questions that arise immediately in this regard concern interdependence and interference. To what degree does each of these institutional domains assume the operation of the others; and to what degree do they condition the operation of the others?

It would be going too far to say that any of these institutional systems is necessary for society and thus for the other institutional spheres, because that would be to confuse the functions of these systems, what they happen to do, with the way that they do it. The most basic point of considering those manifestations that escape the control of each system yet seemingly fall under its functional purview is to underscore the selectivity of these systems. Not everything political is incorporated in the sovereign state system, not everything economic in the capitalist economic system, not all knowledge is produced in the institutions dedicated to empirical science; and, of course, not everything conceivably religious is thereby already institutionalized religion. This observation may be fairly obvious, but it needs to be emphasized if society as such is not to be confused with its most powerful institutions and if analytic distinctions are to be kept separate from those in terms of which people actually conduct their social lives. Accordingly, we can say that each of the institutional systems under discussion certainly assumes the operation of the others in its environment. The result is a fair degree of practical interdependence among most of them: capitalist economy would not work without the state and legal systems in its environment. All three of these have come to depend on the educational system for the formation of its professionals and experts. And all of them avail themselves rather consistently of the mass media system for everything from marketing of products and conducting election campaigns to vulgarizing scientific knowledge and proselytizing religions. That said, however, some institutional systems clearly have more global and local power than others, and therefore some appear to be more necessary than others; or at least the world would change very drastically if they lost their power or ceased to function the way that they do. That has certainly proven to be the case for the political and economic systems: crises in these domains typically result in a great deal of disruption, even social chaos. In this regard, religion is just as clearly one of the less powerful institutional domains: its weakness or strength in different parts of the world does not seem to have serious general repercussions. Europe and China can be said to have weak religious systems, whereas the United States and sub-Saharan Africa can be said to have strong ones. Those variations do not correlate with strong or weak operation of other institutional domains nor with degree of social order. Therefore, although it may be argued that society and humanity cannot get along without what religion typically provides, it does not seem to be that critical whether these functions are fulfilled by institutionalized and differentiated religion or not.

A further and just as important aspect of interdependence concerns the degree to which these institutional domains structure and define themselves in terms of each other. In this case, focus on the religious system will serve to illustrate the point nicely. Religion differentiates itself positively through more or less clearly identified religious programmes (systems of beliefs and practices) and structures (such as organizations, movements, networks) that identify themselves as religion and are so recognized by other institutions and by people not involved in them. A critical reason why this distinguishing is effective is that other institutional systems, such as education, science, state, economy, and so forth do likewise for their domains, thereby creating parallel social structures that are, by contrast, not religion. To put this another way, the institutional differentiation of religion depends on the "secularized" construction of other non-religious institutional systems. The rough similarity of these systems is a condition for distinguishing them practically; and it permits all of them to be more or less determinative for their domains without thereby actually having to include everything and anything that might fall within their domains: they can be specialized, selective, and distinct.

The existence of these institutional systems, of course, also raises the question of interference. None of these systems operates in autarchic and splendid isolation, as their interdependence indicates. Quite the contrary. Nonetheless, they do all operate on the basis of their own social logic, not on that of one of the other systems. They operate on a principle of, if not autarchy, then certainly autonomy. Correspondingly, they tend to define their limits, the limits of what is economically, political, religiously, and so on relevant, by their own criteria; and that can and does lead to attempts to influence, even control the processes of the other systems. Business corporations want to influence government regulatory policies, politicians want to control what is taught in schools, and, of course, religious leaders want to judge the actions of all these institutions by their own religious criteria, perhaps even to the point of determining who shall be elected, what wages shall be paid, what scientific research is proper, and what art shall be produced. Interference, therefore, will and does happen; but there is a difference between such mutual influencing and the blending or dedifferentiation of these institutional domains. For that to happen, there would have to be more than mere influence. The participants in one domain would have to start using the programmatic resources of others in their own operations. Politicians would, for instance, determine policy by how profitable it is or how aesthetically pleasing it was; business people would set the price of their products on the basis of how well they cured diseases; mass media personalities would determine what went on the air or into print on the basis of mystical or ecstatic visions; and religious leaders would grant absolution according to which of their charges could kick a football farthest or slam-dunk a basketball with the greatest ease. These sorts of things, of course, can happen; but they do not happen consistently, and if they happen too much the institutions in questions would lose their efficacy as economic, political, or religious institutions.

Seen in such a global perspective and in comparison with other institutional domains, therefore, modern religion appears as highly peculiar, historically unusual, and anything but encompassing or timeless. It has arisen historically and quite accidentally; it is therefore highly contested and subject to change. In a nutshell, what global and institutional comparison of religion does is demonstrate the utter contingency of institutional religion. Its typical perspective and meanings may require a great stress on matters eternal, absolute, and unconditioned; but as a contemporary social institution, it is anything but. From this angle, religion and religious institutions are a normal aspect of the global and modern social landscapes. They are an expression of that context, and certainly not something anomalous or obsolete that belongs more properly in other times.

NOTE

1. This way of conceiving the religious system owes much to the theoretical work of Niklas Luhmann (see Luhmann, 2000). For further elaboration, see Beyer forthcoming.

REFERENCES

Arjomand, S. A. (1988). *The turban for the crown: The Islamic revolution in Iran.* New York: Oxford University Press.

Babb, L. A. (1975). *The divine hierarchy: Popular Hinduism in central India.* New York: Columbia University Press.

Baumann, M. (2000). *Migration—religion—integration: Buddhistische Vietnamesen und hinduistische Tamilen in Deutschland.* Marburg: Diagonal Verlag.

Beaman, L. (2003). The myth of plurality, diversity and vigour: Constitutional privilege of Protestantism in the United States and Canada. *Journal for the Scientific Study of Religion, 42,* 311–328.

Bellah, R. N. (1970). Civil religion in America. *Beyond belief: Essays on religion in a post-traditional world.* New York: Harper & Row.

Beyer, P. (1994). *Religion and globalization.* London: Sage.

Beyer, P. (1998a). The modern emergence of religions and a global social system for religion. *International Sociology, 13,* 151–172.

Beyer, P. (1998b). The religious system of global society: A sociological analysis of an emerging reality. *Numen, 45,* 1–29.

Beyer, P. (2001). What counts as religion in global society? From practice to theory. In P. Beyer (Ed.), *Religion in the process of globalization/Religion im prozeß der globalisierung* (pp. 125–150). Würzburg: Ergon Verlag.

Beyer, P. (2003a). Constitutional privilege and constituting pluralism: Religious freedom in national, global, and legal context. *Journal for the Scientific Study of Religion, 42,* 333–339.

Beyer, P. (2003b). De-centring religious singularity; the globalization of Christianity as a case in point. *Numen, 50,* 357–386.

Beyer, P. (2003c). Defining religion in cross-national perspective: Identity and difference in official conceptions. In A. L. Greil & D. Bromley (Eds.), *Defining religion: Investigating the boundaries between sacred and secular* (pp. 163–188). London: Elsevier Scientific.

Beyer, P. (forthcoming). *The religious system of global society.*

Buijs, F. J., & Rath, J. (2003). *Muslims in Europe: The state of research.* Amsterdam: University of Amsterdam, Department of Political Science/IMES.

Byrne, P. (1989). *Natural religion and the nature of religion: The legacy of deism.* London: Routledge.

Chan, S. (1985). *Buddhism in late Ch'ing political thought.* Hong Kong and Boulder, CO: Chinese University Press and Westview.

Chidester, D. (1996). *Savage systems: Colonialism and comparative religion in Southern Africa.* Charlottesville: University Press of Virginia.

Cox, H. (1995). *Fire from heaven: The rise of Pentecostal spirituality and the reshaping of religion in the twenty-first century.* Reading, MA: Perseus Books.

Dalmia, V. (1995a). The only real religion of the Hindus: Vaisnava self-representation in the late nineteenth century. In V. Dalmia & H. von Stietencrom (Eds.), *Representing Hinduism* (pp. 176–210). New Delhi: Sage.

Dalmia, V., & Stietencron, H. von. (Eds). (1995b). *Representing Hinduism: The construction of religious traditions and national identity.* New Delhi: Sage.

Davie, G. (2000). *Religion in modern Europe: A memory mutates.* Oxford: Oxford University Press.

Deen, H. (1995). *Caravanserai: Journey among Australian Muslims.* St. Leonards, NSW: Allen & Unwin.

Dempster, M. W., Klaus, B. D., & Petersen, D. (Ed.). (1999). *The globalization of Pentecostalism: A religion made to travel.* Oxford: Regnum Books International.

Despland, M. (1979). *La religion en occident: Evolution des idées ed du vécu.* Montreal: Fides.

Durkheim, É. (1965). *The elementary forms of the religious life.* New York: Free Press.

Esposito, J. L. (1987). *Islam and politics.* Syracuse, NY: Syracuse University Press.

Esposito, J. L. (Ed.). (1999). *The Oxford history of Islam.* Oxford: Oxford University Press.

Fitzgerald, T. (1997). A critique of "religion" as a cross-cultural category. *Method & Theory in the Study of Religion, 9,* 91–110.

Frykenberg, R. E. (1989). The emergence of modern "Hinduism" as a concept and as an institution: A reappraisal with special reference to South India. In G. D. Sontheimer & H. Kulke (Eds.), *Hinduism reconsidered* (pp. 29–49). Delhi: Manohar.

Grieder, J. (1981). *Intellectuals and the state in modern China: A narrative history.* New York: Free Press.

Guest, K. J. (2003). *God in Chinatown: Religion and survival in New York's evolving immigrant community.* New York: New York University Press.

Haddad, Y. Y., & Smith, J. I. (Eds.). (2002). *Muslim minorities in the West: Visible and invisible.* Walnut Creek, CA: AltaMira.

Hardacre, H.. (1989). *Shinto and the state, 1868–1988.* Princeton, NJ: Princeton University Press.

Harrison, P. (1990). *"Religion" and the religions in the English enlightenment.* Cambridge: Cambridge University Press.

Hastings, A. (1996). *The church in Africa: 1450–1950.* Oxford and New York: Clarendon Press and Oxford University Press.

Hoge, D. R., Johnson, B., & Luidens, D. A. (1994). *Vanishing boundaries: The religion of mainline Protestant babyboomers.* Louisville, KY: Westminster/John Knox Press.

Hollenweger, W. J. (1972). *The Pentecostals.* London: SCM Press.

Jaffrelot, C. (2001). The Vishva Hindu Parishad: A nationalist but mimetic attempt at federating the Hindu sects. In V. Dalmia, A. Molinar, & M. Christoff (Eds.), *Charisma and canon: Essays on the religious history of the Indian subcontinent* (pp. 388–411). New Delhi: Oxford University Press.

Jensen, L. M. (1997). *Manufacturing Confucianism: Chinese traditions and universal civilization.* Durham, NC: Duke University Press.

Kepel, G. (2002). *Jihad: The trail of political Islam.* Cambridge, MA: Belknap Press.

Leonard, K.. 2003. *Muslims in the United States: The state of research.* New York: Sage.

Levtzion, N., & Voll, J. O. (Eds.). (1987). *Eighteenth-century renewal and reform in Islam.* Sycracuse, NY: Syracuse University Press.

Luckmann, T. (1967). *The invisible religion: The problem of religion in modern societies.* New York: Macmillan.

Luhmann, N. (2000). *Die religion der gesellschaft.* Franfkurt/M: Suhrkamp.

Luo, Z. (Ed.). (1991). *Religion under socialism in China* (D. E. MacInnis & Z. Xi'an, Trans.). Armonk, NY, and London: M.E. Sharpe.

Marriott, M. (Ed.). (1967). *Village India: Studies in the little community.* Chicago: University of Chicago Press.

Marty, M. E., & Appleby, R. S. (Eds.). (1991–1995). *The fundamentalism project* (Vol. 5). Chicago: University of Chicago Press.

McCutcheon, R. T. (1997). *Manufacturing religion: The discourse on sui generis religion and the politics of nostalgia.* Oxford: Oxford Univeristy Press.

Murakami, S. (1980). *Japanese religion in the modern century.* Tokyo: University of Tokyo Press.

Oberoi, H. (1994). *The construction of religious boundaries: Culture, identity, and diversity in the Sikh tradition.* Chicago: University of Chicago Press.

O'Dea, T. (1966). *The sociology of religion.* Englewood Cliffs, NJ: Prentice Hall.

Pailin, D A. (1984). *Attitudes to other religions: Comparative religion in seventeenth- and eighteenth-century Britain.* Manchester: Manchester University Press.

Paper, J. (1995). *The spirits are drunk: Comparative approaches to Chinese religion.* Albany: State University of New York Press.

Penny, B. (2004). *The body of Master Li.* Humanities Research Centre and Centre for Cross-Cultural Research, Australian National University. Retrieved May 2, 2004, from http://users.senet.com.au/~nhabel/lectures/penny.pdf.

Poewe, K. (Ed.). (1994). *Charismatic Christianity as a global culture.* Columbia: University of South Carolina Press.

Prebish, C. S., & Tanaka, K. K. (Eds.). (1998). *The faces of Buddhism in America.* Berkeley: University of California Press.

Prebish, C. S., & Baumann, M. (Eds.). (2002). *Westward dharma: Buddhism beyond Asia.* Berkeley: University of California Press.

Radhakrishnan, S. (1980). *The Hindu view of life.* London: Unwin Paperbacks. (Original work published 1927)

Radice, W. (Ed.). (1998). *Swami Vivekananda and the modernization of Hinduism.* Delhi: Oxford University Press.

Rashid, A. (2000). *Taliban: Militant Islam, oil and fundamentalism in Central Asia.* New Haven, CT: Yale University Press.

Reader, I. (1991). *Religion in contemporary Japan.* Honolulu: University of Hawaii Press.

Robertson, R. (1995). Glocalization: Time-space and homogeneity-heterogeneity. In S. Lash, M. Featherstone, & R. Robertson (Eds.), *Global modernities* (pp. 25–44). London: Sage.

Roof, W. C. (1999). *Spiritual marketplace: Baby boomers and the remaking of American religion.* Princeton, NJ: Princeton University Press.

Roof, W. C., & McKinney, W. (1987). *American mainline religion: Its changing shape and future.* New Brunswick, NJ: Rutgers University Press.

Smart, N. (1983). *Worldviews: Crosscultural explorations of human beliefs.* New York: Scribner's.

Smith, J. Z. (1988). "Religion" and "religious studies": No difference at all. *Soundings, 71,* 231–244.

Smith, W. C. (1991b). *The meaning and end of religion.* Minneapolis, MN: Fortress Press.

Sontheimer, G. D., & Kulke, H. (Eds.). (1989). *Hinduism reconsidered.* New Delhi: Manohar.

Tong, J. (2002). An organizational analysis of the Falun Gong: Structure, communications, financing. *China Quarterly, 171,* 636–660.

Van der Veer, P. (1994). Hindu nationalism and the discourse of modernity: The Vishva Hindu Parishad. In M.E. Marty & R. S. Appleby (Eds.), *Accounting for fundamentalisms: The dynamic character of movements* (pp. 653–668). Chicago: University of Chicago Press.

Voll, J. O. (1982). *Islam: Continuity and change in the modern world.* Boulder, CO: Westview Press.

Welch, H. (1968). *The Buddhism revival in China.* Cambridge, MA: Harvard University Press.

Yang, C. K. (1967). *Religion in Chinese society.* Berkeley: University of California Press.

Yang, F. (1999). *Chinese Christians in America: Conversion, assimilation, and adhesive identities.* University Park: University of Pennsylvania Press.

Index